EUROPEAN
SOCIAL
POLICY

EUROPEAN SOCIAL POLICY

Between Fragmentation and Integration

Stephan Leibfried
Paul Pierson
Editors

THE BROOKINGS INSTITUTION
Washington, D.C.

About Brookings

The Brookings Institution is a private nonprofit organization de-
voted to research, education, and publication on important issues of
domestic and foreign policy. Its principal purpose is to bring knowledge
to bear on current and emerging policy problems. The Institution was
founded on December 8, 1927, to merge the activities of the Institute
for Government Research, founded in 1916, the Institute of Economics,
founded in 1922, and the Robert Brookings Graduate School of Eco-
nomics, founded in 1924.

The Institution maintains a position of neutrality on issues of public
policy. Interpretations or conclusions in Brookings publications should
be understood to be solely those of the authors.

Copyright © 1995
THE BROOKINGS INSTITUTION
1775 Massachusetts Avenue, N.W., Washington, D.C. 20036

Library of Congress Cataloging-in-Publication data:

European social policy : between fragmentation and integration /
Stephan Leibfried and Paul Pierson, editors.
    p. cm.
    Includes bibliographical references and index.
    ISBN 0-8157-5248-2. — ISBN 0-8157-5247-4 (pbk.)
    1. European Union countries—Social policy. I. Leibfried,
Stephan, 1944– . II. Pierson, Paul.
HN373.5.E83   1995
361.6'1'094—dc20   95-32447
                                                                 CIP

9 8 7 6 5 4 3 2 1

The paper used in this publication meets the minimum requirements of the American
National Standard for Information Sciences—Permanence of Paper for Printed Library
Materials. ANSI Z39.48-1984

Set in Sabon

Composition by Harlowe Typography, Inc.
Cottage City, Maryland

Printed by R. R. Donnelley and Sons Co.
Harrisonburg, Virginia

Editors' Preface

THIS collaborative project grew out of conversations among researchers interested in the development of public policies in European countries. These discussions revealed a growing sentiment that the remarkable process of European integration was making it increasingly difficult to comprehend the dynamics of public policy without considering actions taken at both the national and the supranational levels. The traditional frameworks of comparative public policy seemed ill equipped for this investigation. So, too, did most discussions among international relations scholars, which cast European integration as a process of carefully constrained diplomatic bargains among essentially sovereign nation-states. Such a perspective had difficulty accounting for the major transformations in policymaking that are occurring in areas somewhat removed from the European Community's central goal of creating a common market.

Drawing on insights from research on federalism, but remaining attuned to the quite distinctive historical process that has led to European integration, our research stresses the extent to which member states now find themselves embedded in a new kind of polity. We emphasize the distinctive dynamics of integrating social policy in a multitiered system. Individual member states share policymaking responsibilities with central authorities, although these central authorities are generally too weak to launch major initiatives on their own. European social policy, emerging in conjunction with the construction of the common market, is the result of a pluralistic process in which member states, social actors, and European institutions such as the Commission and the European Court of Justice all vie for influence. The result is that European social policy has a highly fragmented structure. Policymaking is increasingly prone to gridlock or lowest-common-denominator agreement; initiatives originate from multiple sites of public authority and are poorly coordinated. In the new European polity, policy develops without being under the firm control of any particular group of political actors.

The completion of this project, involving researchers from four countries on two continents, has required a great deal of institutional support. First and foremost, we thank the Program for the Study of Germany and Europe at the Harvard Center for European Studies for generous financial and administrative help. Abby Collins was instrumental in both planning and carrying out this complicated collaborative effort. With Anna Kent, she organized the initial project workshop at CES. Stephan Leibfried is grateful to the Volkswagen Stiftung for helping to fund both research and editing for the project and also to the Center for Social Policy Research at Bremen University for institutional support. Paul Pierson would like to thank the Russell Sage Foundation for financial and logistical support during the final editing process. Melissa Grogan at RSF provided much-needed administrative assistance. The Brookings Institution Publications Program adhered to its usual high standards in producing the book. We are especially grateful to Nancy Davidson for her hard work throughout the project and to Donna Verdier for her skill in handling a herculean task of copy editing. We also wish to thank Deborah Styles, Beth Benevides, and Susan Woollen; Laura Amin and David Bearce, who verified the manuscript; and Julia Petrakis, who prepared the index.

A number of individuals generously provided the editors with comments on all or part of the manuscript at various stages. David Cameron and R. Kent Weaver provided extremely detailed and helpful comments after the workshop. We also thank Miguel Glatzer, Peter A. Hall, Robert O. Keohane, Gary Marks, Wayne Sandholtz, Alberta M. Sbragia, Fritz Scharpf, Bernd Schulte, and Alec Stone. While these readers saved us from many mistakes, any remaining errors are our own.

Stephan Leibfried
Paul Pierson

Contents

Tables

Figures

CHAPTER ONE

Multitiered Institutions and the Making of Social Policy

Paul Pierson and Stephan Leibfried

D URING THE PAST four decades, Europe has undergone a remarkable political transformation. Since signing the Treaty of Rome in 1957, the six original members of the European Community, together with the six members who had joined by 1986, have developed an extensive and highly institutionalized response to shared problems. Progress toward the promised "ever-closer union" has been sporadic, but the Single European Act (SEA) of 1986, with its goal of creating a single market within the Community by 1992, greatly accelerated the process of European integration. Despite a tumultuous ratification process, the approval of the Treaty of Maastricht in 1993 and the accession of three new members in January 1995 further consolidated and extended this new political structure, now renamed the European Union.[1]

Where this process of integration is leading is uncertain, but the EU is already far more than a free-trade zone. The European Union is no longer simply a multilateral instrument, limited in scope and firmly under the control of individual member states. Instead, the EU possesses characteristics of a supranational entity, including extensive bureaucratic competencies, unified judicial control, and significant capacities to develop or modify policies (see figure 1-1). Within Europe, a wide range of policies

For extensive comments on previous incarnations of this essay, we are grateful to David Cameron, John Myles, Elmar Rieger, Fritz W. Scharpf, R. Kent Weaver, and three reviewers for Brookings. Discussions with participants in the Workshop on European Integration and Domestic Politics, organized by Wayne Sandholtz and Alec Stone, were very helpful for the final drafting of the chapter.

1. In November 1993 the European Community was rechristened the European Union. Both terms, and their abbreviations (EC and EU) and short forms (Community and Union), are used throughout this book.

Figure 1-1. *Institutions of the European Union*

European Parliament

The popularly elected European Parliament provides a public forum for debate on European issues. Members sit in political groupings, with Socialists and Christian Democrats as major factions, rather than as representatives of member states. The Parliament has the right to question the commission and the council of ministers, force the commission to resign as a body, and amend or reject the EU annual budget. The Parliament also has rights of consultation on EU legislation.

European Commission

The commission consists of twenty members, two from each of the larger member states (France, Germany, Italy, Spain, and the United Kingdom) and one from each of the smaller ones. Commissioners are appointed by their respective national governments but are mandated not to represent or take orders from them. Except in the realm of foreign and security policy, the commission has a monopoly on proposing policies and legislation, supervises the administration of such policy in the EU, and oversees policy implementation. The commission may challenge member states in the European Court of Justice (ECJ) for noncompliance.

European Council

The council, which meets at least twice a year, comprises the heads of state or government of the fifteen member states and the president of the commission. Founded in 1974, the council did not become part of the treaty framework until the Single European Act of 1987.

Council of Ministers

The council of ministers represents the national governments in ministerial meetings organized by functional area and debates and votes on various commission proposals. Some decisions require unanimous vote, while others can be made by qualified majority. The council is the primary legislator of the EU.

European Court of Justice

The court interprets and applies EU treaties and other EU legislation. It comprises thirteen judges. Since the Single European Act, the ECJ has been supplemented by a court of first instance. Judges are appointed for six years by all members states under rules of unanimous consent. Court decisions are made by simple majority vote.

classically considered domestic cannot now be comprehended without acknowledging the role of the European Union within an increasingly integrated but still fragmented polity. The Union is more than an international organization. We will argue, in fact, that it is the central level— albeit a weak one—of an emergent multitiered system of governance.

This is a controversial claim, especially with respect to the social policy issues that are the central concern of this volume. For many observers, the absence of social policy initiatives at the EU level has been one of the clearest signs of its limited role. After all, the development of social policy was a key element in the history of European state building, and the welfare state is a central component of all advanced industrial nations. Yet by most accounts the social dimension of the EU remains rudimentary. Indeed, the recent acceleration of European integration was predicated on a tacit agreement that EU policy initiatives would generally aim to reinforce the market.[2]

Nevertheless, the Union has gradually assumed considerable authority in policy domains beyond those directly tied to the creation of a common market. If one accepts T. H. Marshall's definition of social policy as the use of "political power to supersede, supplement or modify operations of the economic system in order to achieve results which the economic system would not achieve on its own," then "Social Europe" already exists.[3] The EU is actively engaged in policies of redistribution among both sectors (through the Common Agricultural Policy, or CAP) and regions (through the structural funds). On certain issues, such as gender equality, the Union has established important social regulations—including protections and benefits for women workers that are sometimes far more extensive than those offered in the United States. Uniform regulations for workplace health and safety have been set at a very high standard. The EU is also expanding the scope of its authority, although haltingly, in areas such as industrial relations and immigration. Finally, and with less fanfare, the Union is becoming a formidable actor in the field of social policy by introducing "market compatibility requirements," which restrict certain social policy options of member states that conflict with the construction of the single market.

2. "In the 1992 compromise, the project of European integration became finally and formally bound up with a deregulation project." Wolfgang Streeck and Philippe C. Schmitter, "From National Corporatism to Transnational Pluralism: Organized Interests in the Single European Market," *Politics and Society,* vol. 19 (June 1991), pp. 133–64, 149. See also Streeck's contribution in chapter 12.

3. T. H. Marshall, *Social Policy* (London: Hutchinson, 1975), p. 15.

What is emerging in Europe is a system of shared political authority over social policy, though one that is far more decentralized than the arrangements of traditional federal states. The institutional, political, cultural, and technical barriers to extending EU social policy competence are high. As the process of economic (and, increasingly, political) integration unfolds, however, the EU's presence in social policy continues to expand. This book investigates the dynamics of this extraordinary process of social policy integration by carefully examining, and comparing, the evolution of EU social policy in several areas.

This investigation serves a number of purposes. The most straightforward is to determine the scope and dynamics of European social policy development, broadly defined. Our central concern is to understand why Europe's social dimension has taken the form it has so far, and to find out what these past developments and comparative analyses suggest about medium-term prospects for EU social policy. Social Europe is often dismissed as a pipe dream, or as an afterthought to the EU's main project of economic integration. Social policy has in fact taken a backseat to the single-market project; hopes (or fears) of some pan-European welfare state can be put to rest.[4] In its various guises, though, actual and potential European social policy is of considerable significance. As the empirical chapters of this volume make clear, scholars who analyze national social policy in Europe will have to pay attention to the EU.[5]

Yet this book is not solely about the European Union. We are interested more generally in the dynamics of social policy integration in multitiered political systems. We start from the assumption that the EU should not be studied in isolation, despite its considerable peculiarities. The European Union possesses characteristics loosely resembling those of other political systems, and these systems can usefully be compared. The implications of multitiered decisionmaking for social policy have not often been a subject of comparative research, but, as this introduction and the chapters that follow seek to establish, such systems are likely to create quite distinctive pressures and constraints on social policy development. Given the prevalence of federal systems, the growing tendencies within unitary states to experiment with more decentralized social policy

4. See Stephan Leibfried and Paul Pierson, "Prospects for Social Europe," *Politics and Society,* vol. 20 (September 1992), pp. 333–66, and the essays in part 3 of this volume.

5. Social policy thus constitutes a crucial case for students of the European Union. If the proposition that social policy is becoming increasingly integrated can be sustained, it is all the more likely to be true in policy arenas that are not seen as among the last bastions of member-state autonomy.

structures, and the development of various supranational regimes that raise social policy issues (the North American Free Trade Agreement, for example), the topic assumes importance even for those with limited interest in the European Union.

The book is organized in three parts. Part 1 focuses on the history and current status of the social components of European integration, exploring the processes that have produced the present mix of EU interventions and noninterventions. Part 2 introduces comparative evidence on the politics of social policy integration in multitiered systems, drawn from the experiences of the United States and Canada. Part 3 offers three essays that try to give a clearer sense of where Social Europe may be headed.

In the remainder of this introduction we set the stage for the chapters that follow. We first outline the main institutional features of the European Union, arguing that the EU can best be conceptualized as part of a multitiered system of governance rather than as an international organization; we then briefly contrast the main institutional characteristics of the EU to those of some existing federal systems. In the next section, we present a general analysis of how multitiered institutions influence social policy development. We suggest that multitiered systems exhibit distinctive features, such as a prominent role for their constituent political units, predictable dilemmas resulting from shared policymaking authority, and major transformations in the strategies and influence of social actors. We address the nature of the EU's social dimension in the final section by suggesting how the general features of multitiered systems might operate in the context of the European Union.

The European Union as an Emerging Multitiered System

The past few years have witnessed a resurgence of scholarly interest in political institutions.[6] The "rules of the game" have tremendous consequences for political life, influencing both the manner in which political actors are likely to organize and the goals that they choose to pursue as

6. For an introduction, see James G. March and Johan P. Olsen, *Rediscovering Institutions: The Organizational Basis of Politics* (New York: Free Press, 1989); Douglass C. North, *Institutions, Institutional Change, and Economic Performance* (Cambridge University Press, 1990); Sven Steinmo, Kathleen Thelen, and Frank Longstreth, eds., *Structuring Politics: Historical Institutionalism in Comparative Analysis* (Cambridge University Press, 1992); and R. Kent Weaver and Bert A. Rockman, eds., *Do Institutions Matter? Government Capabilities in the United States and Abroad* (Brookings, 1993).

well as the extent of their influence over political outcomes. While institutions alone may not determine policy, their contribution to policy development is often a central one.

This is especially likely to be true for the European Union, which is the result of an extraordinarily deliberate process of institution building. Over a period of four decades, a group of European nation-states have joined together to create a new system of governance. In a context of growing interdependence, the option of a collective response has increasing appeal; policy activity at the European level has therefore proliferated. EU law has become a crucial, if not dominant, influence in policy areas as diverse as agriculture, environmental protection, and industrial policy.

This transformation has created a unique structure of multitiered governance. Although the member states of the European Union retain a very powerful and often determinative role in policy development, the Union bears a growing institutional resemblance to the established multitiered systems of traditional federal states. This view of the European Unon contrasts with the usual depiction among American political scientists of the EU as essentially an international organization, albeit an unusually important one.[7] The disagreement is more than semantic. At its core, it concerns the extent to which member states exercise authority within the EU and the manner in which their authority is exercised. We agree that the member states remain extremely powerful, but their influence is increasingly circumscribed and embedded in a dense, complex institutional environment that cannot easily be described in the language of interstate bargaining. We begin by examining the foundations of member-state power within the Union and then turn to the limits on that influence.

7. For forceful statements of this perspective, see Andrew Moravcsik, "Preferences and Power in the European Community: A Liberal Intergovernmentalist Approach," *Journal of Common Market Studies*, vol. 31 (December 1993), pp. 473–524; and Andrew Moravcsik, "Why the European Community Strengthens the State: Domestic Politics and International Cooperation," paper presented at the Conference of Europeanists, Chicago, May 1994. As Sbragia has pointed out, European observers are far more willing to regard EU institutions as part of domestic policymaking and, thus, as quasi-federal. Alberta Sbragia, "The European Community in English: A Preliminary Sketch," University of Pittsburgh, November 1993. See also Christian Welz and Christian Engel, "Traditionbestände politikwissenschaftlicher Integrationstheorien: Die Europäische Gemeinschaft im Spannungsfeld von Integration und Kooperation," in Armin von Bogdandy, ed., *Die Europäische Option* (Baden-Baden: Nomos, 1993), pp. 129–69.

The Power of Constituent Members in the European Union

For "intergovernmentalists" who regard the Union as basically an international agreement, the central fact is the autonomy of EU members, which remain sovereign nation-states. The enormous influence wielded by the member states within the EU is impossible to ignore.[8] What most clearly distinguishes the European Union from traditional federal systems, of course, is precisely the predominant position of the member states. And yet the power of the member states is not merely pooled by the EU; it is increasingly constrained.

The structure of the EU itself, as outlined in the Treaty of Rome and in subsequent revisions, reserves wide areas of decisionmaking authority for member states and gives them most implementation power even in those domains where EU decisions govern. More generally, if ambiguously, the principle of subsidiarity encourages the allocation of authority to the member states for all actions not requiring centralized attention. Although the Single European Act and the Maastricht treaty revisions have chipped away at important elements of national sovereignty, by any comparative standard the decentralized orientation of the Union's design is striking.

In principle, however, few matters are outside the reach of EU intervention. The EU has been granted sweeping authority to intervene when it is necessary to further the development of the single market. As Fritz Scharpf concludes, "There will be hardly any field of public policy for which it will not be possible to demonstrate a plausible connection to the guarantee of free movement of goods, persons, services, and capital— and thus to the core objectives of the European Union."[9] Subsidiarity, which is notoriously open to interpretation, is intended to rein in the EU; it actually leaves the Union wide latitude. The crucial statement on subsidiarity, article 3b of the Maastricht treaty, holds that the EU may act

8. The following draws particularly on Fritz W. Scharpf, "The Joint-Decision Trap: Lessons from German Federalism and European Integration," *Public Administration*, vol. 66, no. 3 (1988), pp. 239–78; Alberta M. Sbragia, "Thinking About the European Future: The Uses of Comparison," in Alberta M. Sbragia, ed., *Euro-Politics: Institutions and Policymaking in the "New" European Community* (Brookings, 1992), pp. 257–91; and Alberta M. Sbragia, "The European Community: A Balancing Act," *Publius*, vol. 23 (Summer 1993), pp. 23–38.

9. Fritz W. Scharpf, "Community and Autonomy: Multilevel Policy-Making in the European Union," Working Paper RSC 94/1 (Florence: European University Institute, May 1994), p. 6.

in the broad areas in which it has competence only when "the objectives of the proposed action cannot be sufficiently achieved by the member states." Yet the Union is so diverse, and the administrative capacities of some member states so limited, that such a claim will almost always be plausible when complex issues are at stake.[10]

Union intervention generally has not been so much prohibited as profoundly hindered by decision rules that make European-level policymaking extremely difficult. Member states are well represented in the decisionmaking institutions of the Union. Grounded in procedural guarantees of member-state control over key decisions, the centrality of member states to institutional governance is evident.[11] Carefully designed by member states that have no desire to commit institutional suicide, the decisionmaking bodies of the European Union are structured to inhibit bold initiatives and to give member states considerable say over whatever initiatives are taken. As we discuss below, the extensions of power to the European Commission, the European Court of Justice, and even the European Parliament have been notable. Nonetheless, the European Council, made up of the fifteen representatives of the member states, remains the central decisionmaking arena.

Furthermore, decisionmaking is difficult even within the Council. The EU still possesses what Wolfgang Streeck and Philippe Schmitter have termed a "centripetal center."[12] Opponents of reform occupy the institutional high ground; initiating policies is far more difficult than sustaining nondecisions. It is crucial to recognize not just the strong role of member states in forging collective policies but also the considerable protections for individual member states. Where policies unacceptable to even one member can be blocked—under the unanimity rules that still apply for many policy issues—the EU may be restricted to "lowest-common-denominator" strategies in which the interests of the member state are necessarily safeguarded.

As we argue in the next chapter, this has often been the case for social policy. Until the mid-1980s, *all* decisions had to have the unanimous

10. Scharpf, "Community and Autonomy"; and Renaud Dehousse, "Community Competences: Are There Limits to Growth?" in Renaud Dehousse, ed., *Europe after Maastricht: An Ever Closer Union?* (Munich: Beck, 1994), pp. 103–25.

11. See the discussion in Robert O. Keohane and Stanley Hoffmann, "Institutional Change in Europe in the 1980s," in Robert O. Keohane and Stanley Hoffmann, eds., *The New European Community: Decisionmaking and Institutional Change* (Boulder, Colo.: Westview Press, 1991), pp. 1–39.

12. Streeck and Schmitter, "From National Corporatism to Transnational Pluralism," p. 142.

consent of member states. The qualified majority voting authorized in the Single European Act of 1986 streamlined decisionmaking on issues concerning the single market, but most social policy issues still require unanimity.[13] The SEA and its introduction of qualified majority voting, however, have made the institutional framework governing social policy the focus of sharp conflict. Advocates and opponents of the "social dimension" vie to determine the range of issues that can be addressed by majority vote under either article 100a, covering distortions of competition, or the SEA exception for proposals concerning the health and safety of workers.[14] The ratification of the Maastricht treaty creates even more uncertainty by generating a separate institutional track for social policy. Under a complex, last-minute compromise, all member states agreed to a separate protocol, allowing the members other than Britain to go forward on social policy issues under new rules expanding the scope of majority voting. Britain will not participate in such decisionmaking, nor will it be governed by any policies made within this framework.[15]

In several areas, then, single member states will no longer be able to block social policy initiatives. However, the large territorial component in Union decisionmaking—that is, the self-representation of the member states in the main aspects of common governance—remains intact despite these recent modifications. The structure of the European Union reveals roots in a treaty signed by sovereign nation-states: the Union is both decentralized and, more important, marked by strong representation of constituent-unit interests in central decisionmaking. The interests of member states are certain to be key to policy outcomes at the EU level.

13. Following the recent enlargement, France, Italy, Germany and the United Kingdom have ten votes each; Spain, eight; Belgium, Greece, the Netherlands, and Portugal, five; Austria and Sweden, four; Denmark, Finland, and Ireland, three; and Luxembourg, two. Sixty-two votes constitute a qualified majority, and twenty-five a blocking coalition. Thus two large countries with some small-state support can block reforms, as can a coalition of all the small states. As Sbragia has noted, this weighted voting system, with its mixed emphasis on territory and population, is characteristic of federal institutions rather than international organizations. Sbragia, "European Community."

14. Peter Lange, "The Politics of the Social Dimension," in Sbragia, ed., *Euro-Politics*, pp. 225–56.

15. For a contrasting account of the social protocol's origins, see George Ross, *Jacques Delors and European Integration* (Oxford: Polity Press, 1994); and Peter Lange, "Maastricht and the Social Protocol: Why Did They Do It?" *Politics and Society*, vol. 21 (March 1993), pp. 5–36. On the protocol's implications, see Martin Rhodes, "The Social Dimension after Maastricht: Setting a New Agenda for the Labour Market," *International Journal of Comparative Labour Law and Industrial Relations*, vol. 9 (Winter 1993), pp. 297–325; and John T. Addison and W. Stanley Siebert, "The E.C. Social Charter: The Nature of the Beast," *National Westminster Bank Quarterly Review* (February 1993), pp. 13–28.

The Limits of Constituent-Unit Control

If this were the whole story, an intergovernmentalist framework—in which the EU was treated as merely an international forum for bargaining among autonomous, sovereign nation-states—might be fitting. This, however, is far from being the whole story. As the essays in part 1 of this volume show, a wide range of policymaking activity in the European Union cannot be reduced to simple bargaining among autonomous member states. That this proves true for social issues—an area in which the role of the EU is thought to be modest—offers compelling evidence of the Union's changing status.

Four characteristics of the European Union suggest a distinct center that is not under the firm control of member states: (1) the autonomous activity of EU organizations; (2) the impact of previous policy commitments at the EU level, which lock member states into initiatives that they otherwise might not choose; (3) the growing scope and overlap of issues (or "issue density") in the European Union, which produces spillover to new initiatives and widespread unanticipated consequences; and (4) the activity of nonstate actors, operating independently rather than exclusively through member states.

The first limit on member-state power stems from the fact that the central institutions of the European Union represent autonomous sites of political authority. While all the organs of the Union possess a notable territorial component, that feature is balanced by other characteristics that make the institutions much more than simple delegates of territorial (member-state) interests.[16] As the chapters that follow indicate, the power of EU organizations—especially the Commission and the European Court of Justice (ECJ)—is considerable.

The Commission is made up of twenty appointed members and chaired by an appointed president. The institutional foundation of the Commission's power is its control over initiatives to be considered by the European Council. The Council can consider only those proposals that the Commission chooses to present. As George Ross argues in his contribution to this volume, this agenda-setting power gives the Commission a great deal of influence, especially where the application of qualified majority voting makes various coalitions conceivable. As the administrative organ of the EU, moreover, the Commission operates as "process manager" in the complex, fragmented development of new policies. Es-

16. For a lucid treatment of this, see Sbragia, "European Community," pp. 29–36.

pecially in the labyrinth of regulatory policymaking, this role may give the Commission substantial power.[17]

The role of the European Court of Justice is at least as significant. If the United States in the nineteenth century had a "state of courts and parties," the EU sometimes looks like a "state of courts and technocrats."[18] In the process of European integration, the ECJ has taken an active, even forcing, stance, gradually building a remarkable base of authority and effectively "constitutionalizing" the emerging European polity. The Court has more extensive powers of judicial review than do most of its national counterparts, and fewer impediments to action than other EU decisionmaking bodies. There is much about the European Court that points toward policy activism, only moderately constrained by the territorially grounded perspectives of the member states. If the Council is prone to gridlock, the necessity of deciding cases inclines the ECJ to action. This inclination is enhanced by rules allowing decisions by simple majority and by a secrecy (neither actual votes nor dissenting views are made public) that shelters judges from member-state and popular pressures. ECJ judges also have in common a professional background, a legal culture (at least on the continent), and a sense of mission that seems to effectively limit the influence of territory in judicial decisionmaking.

As several of the following chapters indicate, the Court has often taken an expansive view of its own role and that of the EU in social policy. European integration is to a large extent about "unification through law."[19] Legal instruments, rather than spending or taxing powers, are

17. For excellent discussions, see Giandomenico Majone, "Regulatory Federalism in the European Community," *Environment and Planning C,* vol. 10, no. 3 (1992), pp. 299–316; and Volker Eichener, "Social Dumping or Innovative Regulation? Processes and Outcomes of European Decision-Making in the Sector of Health and Safety at Work Harmonization," Working Paper 92-28 (Florence: European University Institute, 1992).

18. The description of the United States is from Stephen Skowronek, *Building a New American State: The Expansion of National Administrative Capacities, 1877–1920* (Cambridge University Press, 1982); the description of the EU is from Stephan Leibfried, "Towards a European Welfare State? On Integrating Poverty Regimes into the European Community," in Zsuzsa Ferge and Jon Eivind Kolberg, eds., *Social Policy in a Changing Europe* (Boulder, Colo.: Westview Press, 1992), p. 249.

19. See Mauro Cappelletti, Monica Secombe, and Joseph H. H. Weiler, eds., *Integration through Law: Europe and the American Federal Experience,* 8 vols. (New York: de Gruyter, 1986); Joseph H. H. Weiler, "The Transformation of Europe," *Yale Law Journal,* vol. 100, no. 1 (1991), pp. 2403–83; Anne-Marie Burley and Walter Mattli, "Europe before the Court: A Political Theory of Legal Integration," *International Organization,* vol. 47 (Winter 1993), pp. 41–76; and Alec Stone, "Constructing a Supranational Constitution: The Re-

dominant at the EU level. As we argue in the next chapter, a lot of integration has occurred through the complex, low-profile accumulation of legal decisions. Intergovernmentalist students of the high politics of treaty negotiations have therefore missed the extent to which EU member states find themselves subject to policies not of their choosing.

A second limitation on member-state control stems from the cumulative implications of past policy decisions and treaty commitments taken at the European level.[20] Once policies or institutional reforms are introduced, the decision rules governing further change—which require unanimity or near unanimity—make revisions extremely difficult. Equally important, adopted policies are likely to generate "sunk costs" as social actors adapt to new arrangements, greatly hampering future attempts to withdraw.[21] These sunk costs are enormously increased because the *acquis communautaire* (the body of existing EU law) represents a cohesive whole that member states cannot, with rare exceptions, reject in part. The price of any attempt to exit from previously agreed but presently undesired aspects of the Union simply is prohibitive. Thus as the policy preferences of member states change over time—as a result of either a change in government or altered domestic circumstances—national governments are likely to find themselves locked into options that they would not currently choose to adopt. Just as in traditional systems of domestic politics, the institutional framework and past policy decisions of the EU work to constrain member-state autonomy.[22]

The third factor constraining member states is the impact of issue density within the European Union. In sharp contrast to any existing international organization, the range of decisions made at the European level runs almost the full gamut of issues traditionally considered by sovereign states, from the setting of agricultural prices to the regulation of auto emissions and fuel content to the negotiation of international

---

ception and Enforcement of European Community Law by National Courts," unpublished manuscript, University of California at Irvine, 1994.

20. Stephen A. Krasner, "Sovereignty: An Institutional Perspective," in James A. Caporaso, ed., *The Elusive State: International and Comparative Perspectives* (Newbury Park, Calif.: Sage Publications, 1989), pp. 69–96; and North, *Institutions*.

21. On this dynamic of "policy lock-in" see Paul Pierson, "When Effect Becomes Cause: Policy Feedback and Political Change," *World Politics*, vol. 45 (July 1993), pp. 595–628.

22. This is essentially the argument developed in Wayne Sandholtz, "Choosing Union: Monetary Politics and Maastricht," *International Organization*, vol. 47 (Winter 1993), pp. 1–39. Sandholtz argues that the existence of the European Union changes the preferences of member states, although what he shows is that the Union's activities change the strategic options (or policy preferences) available.

trade agreements (such as the General Agreement on Tariffs and Trade). The sheer scope of this decisionmaking limits the ability of member states to firmly control the development of policy. This is in part because of spillover, that is, the tendency of tasks adopted to affect realms outside those originally intended, or to empower actors who generate new demands for extended intervention.[23] Chapter 2, which addresses the European Union and national welfare states, and chapter 6, by Elmar Rieger, on the development of the Common Agricultural Policy, give many examples of these processes.

At the same time, issue density tends to create governmental overload, as decisionmakers from member states must cope with time constraints and limited information in a complex, rapidly shifting environment. This overload makes it difficult for national governments to scrutinize every activity to determine whether member-state autonomy is adequately protected.[24] Of course, such scrutiny is likely to be extensive in the formation of the grand interstate bargains that are the favorite subject of intergovernmentalists, such as the Treaty of Rome, the Single European Act, and the Treaty of Maastricht. In the intervals between these agreements, however, when flesh is added to the skeletal frameworks and policy actually evolves, the ability of member states to control the process is generally weaker than at the conception of the accords. This is especially true when member states must contend with organizations such as the Commission and the ECJ, which are eager to take advantage of any opportunity to extend their authority. As complex regulatory judgments are rendered and requirements of previous decisions are legally determined, essential policymaking authority is often in the hands of bodies of experts, where the Commission plays a crucial role, or in the hands of the ECJ.

A final restriction on member-state control stems from the activities of nongovernmental actors at the European level. For scholars who see the EU as an extension of foreign policy, social groups act only through their respective member states. National governments are the gatekeepers, the only actors who sit at the table for both the domestic and international parts of a "two-level game."[25] In fact, social actors increasingly

---

23. The *locus classicus* for an analysis of spillover is Ernst B. Haas, *The Uniting of Europe: Political, Social and Economic Forces, 1950–1957* (Stanford University Press, 1958). We discuss the role of spillover in social policy in chapter 2 and in the conclusion to this volume.

24. See the discussion in Eichener, "Social Dumping or Innovative Regulation?"

25. For this view of the "domestic-international nexus" see Robert D. Putnam, "Di-

feel compelled to organize transnationally and to bring their lobbying efforts directly to Brussels.[26] This is, again, especially true in the detailed formulation of European regulations. To act effectively in Brussels, actors also organize cross-nationally, seeking to build effective Europewide coalitions. Networks of activity and influence are becoming more diverse.[27] Since organization itself often profoundly affects how groups perceive their own interests, these organizational changes will probably have important consequences. Although interest groups continue to act through their national governments when this proves efficacious, these actors now use various paths of influence. If member states continue to guard the gateways to Europe, gaps in the surrounding walls provide actors with alternative points of entry.

For now, these arguments about the restrictions on member-state autonomy in the EU are offered as assertions. Evidence for them is provided in the following chapters, and we return to the issues raised here in the conclusion to the book. In combination, these limitations on the member states provide a plausible rationale for treating the EU as the discernible center of a multitiered polity. Yet while we wish to suggest that the traditional international relations framework no longer describes the European reality, one must not go to the other extreme. Member-state autonomy may be restricted, but the European Union remains a polity that is notable for the formidable strength of its constituent units. This becomes more evident when we contrast the structure of the EU with the multitiered frameworks of traditional federal states.

---

plomacy and Domestic Politics: The Logic of Two-Level Games," *International Organization*, vol. 42 (Summer 1988), pp. 427–60; Peter B. Evans, Harold K. Jacobson, and Robert D. Putnam, eds., *Double-Edged Diplomacy: International Bargaining and Domestic Politics* (University of California Press, 1993); and Moravcsik, "Why the European Community Strengthens the State."

26. For a good illustration that focuses on the role of transnational business in the development of the Single European Act, see Maria Green, "Setting the Agenda for a New Europe: The Politics of Big Business in EC 1992," paper prepared for the study group on European integration and domestic policymaking, Center for European Studies, Harvard University, 1993.

27. Consider the not atypical German case. Welfare associations, local governments (which deal with social service and social assistance issues), and all the main social security organizations (except unemployment insurance) are now represented in Brussels. They actively seek coalitions, often shifting from issue to issue, with similar organizations in other member states. For a more general discussion, see Gary Marks, "Structural Policy and Multilevel Governance in the European Community," in Alan W. Cafruny and Glenda G. Rosenthal, eds., *The State of the European Community* (Boulder, Colo.: Lynne Rienner Publishers, 1993), pp. 391–410.

EU Institutions in Comparative Perspective

Introducing the concept of multitiered political systems to provide an analytical link between federalist systems and the European Union may strike many Americans as an excessive conceptual reach. For European observers, however, the federal conception is now quite common—"an obvious reference point for the European Community," in the words of one prominent analyst.[28] The point of reference has been clear for some time to those who study European law, a field with a long tradition of comparing the EU and federal systems.[29]

Although the economic, social, and political context of European integration differs radically from that of the formative periods of traditional federal systems, the Union has nonetheless become the locus of considerable policymaking authority. Part 1 of this volume demonstrates that in many areas of social policy, broadly defined, the EU now constitutes the center—though a weak one—of a multitiered system. We concur with Alberta Sbragia's judgment that while "the Community is unique, analysis is more likely to suffer from studying it in isolation from other systems than from using the comparative method in less than ideal circumstances." This is especially true if comparative evidence is used not to "offer a map of where the Community is going" but to identify "guideposts to the tensions the Community is most likely to experience even if it does not actually develop into a 'federal-type organization.'"[30]

It is this spirit that guided the development of the comparative contributions presented in part 2 of this volume. The federal systems of North America are not treated as direct parallels to the European Union. Instead, these chapters highlight some of the tendencies to which multitiered systems are prone, in line with the framework presented in the next section of this introduction. At the same time, by identifying specific factors on which policy outcomes turn in other multitiered systems, these comparative chapters may suggest where the Union's distinctive features

---

28. Dehousse, "Community Competences," p. 103.

29. Eric Stein, "Lawyers, Judges, and the Making of a Transnational Constitution," *American Journal of International Law*, vol. 75 (January 1981), pp. 1–27; Eric Stein, "On Divided Power Systems: Adventures in Comparative Law," *Legal Issues of European Integration*, vol. 1 (1983), pp. 27–39; Cappelletti, Secombe, and Weiler, eds., *Integration through Law*; and Terrance Sandalow and Eric Stein, eds., *Courts and Free Markets: Perspectives from the United States and Europe*, 2 vols. (Oxford: Clarendon Press, 1982).

30. Sbragia, "Thinking about the European Future," pp. 268, 267.

are most consequential for social policy. The comparative chapters thus emphasize both similarities to and differences from the European Union.

Federalism is an elastic concept, which, as Daniel Elazar notes, "provides many options for the organization of political authority and power."[31] Thus to our argument that multitiered decisionmaking introduces new features into the dynamics of social policy development, we append this caveat: much depends on the nature of the multitiered system in question. Three characteristics are particularly significant: the reservation of particular powers to constituent units; the structures for sharing policymaking authority across tiers; and the representation at the center of the interests of various tiers.

An important aspect of multitier design is the extent to which particular policy areas, or particular responsibilities within policy processes (implementation, for example), are reserved for constituent members rather than allocated to the center. The literature on federalism is full of culinary metaphors—marble, layer, and fruit cakes—designed in part to capture this variety. Such institutional arrangements are bound to have weighty implications for the dynamics of policy development.

A framework that delegates power to the constituent members may ultimately restrict central action. Such a system encourages what we term *policy preemption* on the part of constituent units. The program initiatives of member states cut off, or at least complicate, the pursuit of initiatives from the center. Because jurisdictional responsibilities can be contested, such arrangements are also susceptible to struggles over policy authority between tiers. Canada provides a good example of such a system. The British North America Act of 1867 allocated exclusive constitutional responsibility for health care, social services, education, and property and civil rights to the provinces, ensuring that initial policy reforms in these areas would occur at the provincial level and that prospects for federal intervention would be circumscribed.[32]

---

31. Daniel Elazar, *Exploring Federalism* (University of Alabama Press, 1987), p. 12.

32. Ironically, the framers' intent was to create a relatively centralized system. However, "many responsibilities that seemed relatively insignificant (or within the purview of private or religious organizations) when they were assigned to the exclusive jurisdiction of the provinces . . . have, with the growth of an industrial, urban, and secular society and of more interventionist governments, become among the most important." Ronald L. Watts, "The American Constitution in Comparative Perspective: A Comparison of Federalism in the United States and Canada," *Journal of American History*, vol. 71, no. 3 (1987), pp. 769–91. This story should perhaps be noted by "intergovernmentalist" students of the EU who remain sanguine about the possibility that institutional designs may yield unintended consequences.

Unless such reservation of powers is firmly institutionalized, however, the intrusion of central authorities is to be expected. Fritz Scharpf notes that efforts to "reserve" particular powers to constituent units in federal systems have often fallen by the wayside as interdependence and policy complexity grew. He points to the interstate commerce clause in the United States as a good example of how "fire walls" protecting state authority from national encroachment are gradually circumvented. Protected areas become so intertwined with other policy issues that it becomes difficult to block central government action.[33]

Partly for this reason, policymaking in multitiered systems is likely to be based on shared decisionmaking. Shared jurisdiction between tiers in a particular policy domain (marble-cake federalism) may make systems particularly vulnerable to *joint-decision traps*. This is the pattern in Germany, for example, where the federal government enacts most major policies and the *Länder* (states) usually have almost exclusive responsibility for policy implementation.[34] The United States, too, has evolved from a system of dual (or layer-cake) federalism, with different tiers responsible for different policy issues, to one in which policy responsibility in many domains is shared.

A final dimension of variation in multitiered systems concerns the nature of constituent-member representation at the center. In some cases, direct representation is extremely limited. In the United States, for example, decisionmaking at the center has a fair amount of territorial content (House and Senate members are elected from geographic districts, and the distribution of votes in the Senate is by territorial unit rather than by population), yet these representatives are directly accountable to groups of voters, not to the federation's constituent territorial units.[35] In Germany, by contrast, the *Bundesrat* provides *Länder* representation in national governance.

Other federal systems fall somewhere in between. The Canadian federal system has a parliamentary arrangement in which voters select their national representatives, but many issues are subject to intergovernmental negotiations, with provincial governments representing themselves.

33. Scharpf, "Community and Autonomy," pp. 5–11.
34. Scharpf, "Joint-Decision Trap."
35. Of course, senators were not directly elected until the seventeenth amendment was enacted in 1911. Before that time senators were appointed by state legislatures, which sought—not always successfully—to make them directly accountable to state government. See William H. Riker, "The Senate and American Federalism," *American Political Science Review*, vol. 49 (June 1955), pp. 452–69.

Indeed, some suggest that the relative weakness of territorial representation within the federal government has allowed provincial premiers to obtain a near-monopoly on the political expression of territorial interests. As Ronald Watts puts it, "To the question 'Who is to speak for Canada?' with which Prime Minister Trudeau was wont to challenge the [provincial] premiers, the commonly understood answer is 'The eleven heads of government: the prime minister and the premiers.' "[36]

The nature of territorial representation is consequential particularly when the interests of constituent members clash with those of central authorities. The stronger and more direct this representation is, the more likely it is that the interests of constituent members will be respected. In general, one might expect federal officials to be more responsive to the political interests of constituent units in Germany, for example, than in the United States. The effective veto power held by a majority coalition of *Länder* in the *Bundesrat* guarantees constituent units a strong say in the design of central policies.

The ability of a minority of territorially based constituent members to block action is also important. As Paul Pierson notes in chapter 9, while representation of constituent members is in some respects less secure in the United States than in other federal systems, aspects of institutional design may enable well-placed territorial representatives to protect the interests of even a few constituent members. Students of American social policy development have noted that this was often the case for the South. From the 1930s through the 1960s, control over key congressional committees in the fragmented, veto-ridden political system of the United States allowed southern interests to block reforms that a majority of states probably would have favored. Institutional design gave southern politicians power quite out of proportion to the population or economic strength of their states.[37]

Although multitiered institutions are likely to produce some broadly similar features of social policy development, there is also substantial variation within the universe of multitiered political systems. The extent of reserved powers, the nature of shared arrangements for decisionmaking, and the forms in which constituent units are represented at the center

---

36. Watts, "American Constitution," p. 784.

37. On congressional institutions as a transmission belt for territorial pressures in the United States, see Richard Franklin Bensel, *Sectionalism and American Political Development: 1880–1980* (University of Wisconsin Press, 1984). For the impact on social policy in particular, see Margaret Weir, Ann Shola Orloff, and Theda Skocpol, eds., *The Politics of Social Policy in the United States* (Princeton University Press, 1988).

have important consequences. The European Union is distinctive in all these respects. It has made considerable (though not always successful) efforts to place competence over many issues in the hands of the Union's constituent units; it provides extensive scope for shared competence in virtually every area in which the European Union is active; and it gives the constituent units tremendous influence within the institutional machinery of policymaking at the central level. This constitutes a particular but recognizable instance of multitiered governance. The EU represents a novel arrangement for creating fragmented responsibility over a wide range of policy arenas familiar to students of domestic politics.

Social Policy Integration in Multitiered Systems

Having outlined the reasons for conceptualizing the EU as a particular form of multitiered governance, we now consider the dynamics of social policy integration in such systems. What are the distinctive characteristics of social policy evolution when decisionmaking is shared by multiple tiers? The evolution of social policy in multitiered systems exhibits a pronounced territorial dimension. Social policy integration is a process that involves the interplay of policymakers and policies at the central level with the political actors and policies of a polity's constituent units. In federal systems the relevant territorial units are subnational (for example, provinces, regions, *Länder*, states); in the European Union the fifteen member states are the constituent units.

Comparative exploration is long overdue. Comparative analyses have usually subordinated institutional and territorial aspects of social policy development to issues of class conflict and compromise, because the former have been less pressing in the centralized political systems that provided the prototypical models of policy evolution (Sweden and Great Britain, for example).[38] Even where multitiered social policy structures existed, as in Bismarck's Germany, researchers treated the country in

38. See, for example, Hugh Heclo, *Modern Social Politics in Britain and Sweden: From Relief to Income Maintenance* (Yale University Press, 1974); Peter Flora and Arnold J. Heidenheimer, eds., *The Development of Welfare States in Europe and America* (New Brunswick, N.J.: Transaction Books, 1981); Gøsta Esping-Andersen, *Politics against Markets: The Social Democratic Road to Power* (Princeton University Press, 1985); and Peter Baldwin, *The Politics of Social Solidarity: Class Bases of the European Welfare State, 1875–1975* (Cambridge University Press, 1990).

stylized fashion as highly centralized.[39] Yet there are good reasons to think that if policy designs and systems of decisionmaking are multi-tiered, this institutional fact and its territorial dimension will be important.[40] The purpose of part 2 of this volume, which concentrates on the evolution of social policy in the multitiered political systems of Canada and the United States, is to highlight the ways in which territorially based institutional fragmentation transforms disputes over social policy.

Authorities at the central level in multitiered systems coexist with a multiplicity of actors in distinct territorial units. Because public officials at both levels are part of the same system yet partly autonomous, their social policy initiatives are interdependent but often only modestly co-ordinated. They may compete with each other, pursue independent projects that work at cross-purposes, or cooperate to achieve ends that they could not obtain alone. Their interdependence may allow them to draw on each other for ideas, or it may entangle them in institutional and policy structures of Byzantine complexity and rigidity. The implications of multiple jurisdictions are equally important for social actors, for whom a more complex and territorially fragmented institutional environment creates both difficulties and opportunities. Three broad consequences of multitiered governance have particular relevance to social policy development: the introduction of constituent members as autonomous policymakers and political actors, the prevalence of dilemmas associated with shared decisionmaking, and the modification of strategies and resources available to social groups.

Constituent Units as Autonomous Actors

In the analysis of multitiered systems, the interests and activities of constituent units assume central importance. The constituent units are autonomous political actors with the capacity to pursue (at least some of) their own policy options. They may also influence the possibilities for the pursuit of social policies at the center. The extent to which constituent

39. This misleading stylization, and the historical reasons behind it, are highlighted by E. Peter Hennock, *British Social Reform and German Precedents: The Case of Social Insurance 1880–1914* (Oxford: Clarendon Press, 1987). See also George Steinmetz, *Regulating the Social: The Welfare State and Local Politics in Imperial Germany* (Princeton University Press, 1993).

40. See especially Keith G. Banting, *The Welfare State and Canadian Federalism*, 2d ed. (Kingston, Ontario: McGill-Queen's University Press, 1987); and chapter 8 in this volume. Territorial factors have also received attention in discussions of the United States. See Weir, Orloff, and Skocpol, eds., *Politics of Social Policy.*

units play a role depends on the design and history of the multitiered system—and, as already pointed out, the importance of constituent units is nowhere more evident than in the European Union.

Because of the strong links between public social provision and political legitimacy, social policy development in multitiered systems is prone to a dynamic termed *competitive state-building* by Keith Banting. As he observes in chapter 8, social policy historically has been not only an object of class struggle but an "instrument of statecraft." Welfare states expanded in all the industrial democracies in part because politicians saw social programs as valuable sources of mass legitimacy.[41] The building of direct links with the electorate, through which government authorities could claim credit for assuring a degree of economic security, has had nearly universal political appeal.

In a multitiered system, the political attractiveness of providing social benefits is a source of potential conflict among competing centers of authority. All three of the comparative essays in part 2 argue that discussions of social policy in federal systems frequently become as much, or more, a struggle over the locus of policy control as over policy content. The two matters are not easy to separate. Many social actors care about the *site* of policy control precisely because it is likely to influence the *content* of social policy. By contrast, government authorities often care about policy control independent of policy content. They want the political benefits obtainable by claiming credit for social provision.[42] A classic example of such competitive state-building efforts is the struggle between the Canadian province of Quebec and the federal government in Ottawa. As Banting emphasizes, each authority has identified social policy as a critical instrument for constructing political legitimacy and has fought tenaciously over jurisdictional boundaries.[43]

Closely tied to the idea of competitive state-building is the concept of

41. Peter Flora, "Introduction," in Peter Flora, ed., *Growth to Limits: The Western European Welfare States Since World War II*, vol. I, *Sweden, Norway, Finland, and Denmark* (Berlin: de Gruyter, 1986), pp. vii-xxxvi; Flora and Heidenheimer, eds., *Development of Welfare States*.

42. Though in a time of austerity one must quickly add that they will also seek to shift blame for unpopular initiatives. Multitiered systems may create significant opportunities for blame avoidance—a point that is pursued below in this chapter and elsewhere in this volume. See R. Kent Weaver, "The Politics of Blame Avoidance," *Journal of Public Policy*, vol. 6 (October-December 1986), pp. 371–98; and Paul Pierson, *Dismantling the Welfare State? Reagan, Thatcher, and the Politics of Retrenchment* (Cambridge University Press, 1994).

43. See chapter 8 of this volume. See also Kenneth McRoberts, *Quebec: Social Change and Political Crisis*, 3d ed. (Toronto: McClelland and Stewart, 1988).

preempted policy space. For a multitiered system, the enactment of policies at a decentralized level may constrain the options available to authorities in the central tier. Once adopted, policies go through a gradual process of institutionalization. Established programs generate sunk costs and networks of political interests that diminish the prospects for radical reform.[44] The possibility of policy preemption suggests that an important source of variation among multitiered systems arises from the timing of social policy interventions by constituent members and central authorities. In this respect, as in many others, the EU represents one end of the continuum. The member states of the EU occupied vast stretches of the available social policy space before the Community was even established. And where constituent members act first, the dynamics of preemption are likely to have consequential effects on social policy development.

The relations between different governmental tiers are not exclusively ones of competition and preemption, however. Constituent members may also play a significant role as petitioners, seeking central government responses to collective action problems. The inability of local authorities to cope with particular social problems may lead them to view central authorities as potential allies as well as rivals. Economic integration may raise the prospect of "competitive deregulation," with constituent units eager for competitive advantage caught in a vicious cycle of benefit cuts. These pressures may give territorial subunits reason to turn to central authorities to create a more level playing field.[45] This is a crucial point: the interaction of governmental tiers involves more than zero-sum conflict; multitiered systems are also marked by "positive-sum" efforts to sort out responsibilities across tiers to best meet the needs of many parties.

An immediate complication for such attempts at collective action arises from the competition among constituent units. Constituent units may sharply disagree about the desirability of central intervention. Those possessing extensive social protections (or facing strong internal pressures to enact them) seem most likely to seek central intervention, while those without such protections may dismiss concerns about competitive dereg-

44. See the discussion in chapters 8 and 9.
45. On this issue in the United States, see, for example, Francis Fox Piven and Richard A. Cloward, *Regulating the Poor: The Functions of Public Welfare* (New York: Pantheon, 1971), chap. 2; David Brian Robertson, "The Bias of American Federalism: The Limits of Welfare-State Development in the Progressive Era," *Journal of Policy History*, vol. 1, no. 3 (1989), pp. 261–91; and Colin Gordon, "New Deal, Old Deck: Business and the Origins of Social Security, 1920–1935," *Politics and Society*, vol. 19 (June 1991), pp. 165–207.

ulation or "social dumping" as simply unpleasant names for attracting investment. This has often been the dynamic in the United States, where the South has resisted social policy integration. There is some evidence that similar territorial divisions exist in the EU.[46]

A final result of multiplying the number of jurisdictions with authority over social policy may be a climate in which policy experimentation and program diffusion flourish. While the fragmentation of policy control creates conditions for competitive deregulation that may inhibit policy development, it may also open up avenues of policy innovation and emulation. Individual jurisdictions with favorable political, social, or economic conditions may implement reforms; success can facilitate diffusion throughout the system, or it can provide central authorities with a rationale for universalizing the policy change. State governments, it has been argued in the United States, are the "laboratories of democracy."[47]

Much will depend, however, on the capacity and willingness of constituent units to act autonomously. As Harvey Feigenbaum, Richard Samuels, and Kent Weaver contend, the type of issue involved affects the prospects for innovation:

> Whether federalism inhibits or promotes policy innovation depends on the distribution of costs and benefits of innovation as well as on the nature of relations between national and subnational governments. Federalism is most likely to stimulate innovation when subnational units can act autonomously and there are economic or political benefits that can be captured by acting early. . . . But if innovation involves imposing losses (for example, imposing higher energy consumption taxes), there are strong incentives to be laggards, especially if those suffering losses can vote with their wheels (for example, by buying gasoline in another state or moving a business out of state).[48]

The argument that businesses and individuals "vote with their wheels"

---

46. Banting's observation about the eagerness of Canada's poor Atlantic provinces for social policy integration is therefore of great theoretical interest.

47. David Osborne, *Laboratories of Democracy* (Boston: Harvard Business School Press, 1988). See also Jack L. Walker, "The Diffusion of Innovations among the American States," *American Political Science Review*, vol. 63 (September 1969), pp. 880–99.

48. Harvey Feigenbaum, Richard Samuels, and R. Kent Weaver, "Innovation, Coordination, and Implementation in Energy Policy," in Weaver and Rockman, eds., *Do Institutions Matter?* pp. 103–04.

is applicable to social policy: constituent units may be reluctant to attempt innovations that would generate significant redistribution because businesses and wealthy individuals seeking lower tax rates might leave those constituent units that adopted redistributive policies.

Whatever the limits on constituent-unit innovation and autonomy, it is glaringly obvious that these units—which can enact their own policies and influence the characteristics of central-level actions—are important to any analysis of social policymaking in multitiered settings. Yet the preferences and impact of these actors have received very little examination. There has, in fact, been *no* systematic, comparative study of social policy development that considers the influence of constituent members in multitiered systems.

Dilemmas of Shared Social Policymaking

The expansion of policymaking circles to include multiple political authorities with distinctive interests and capacities for independent action is bound to complicate the formulation, implementation, and modification of social policies. To note that these institutional arrangements create problems is simply to recognize, as Sbragia puts it, that "any variant of federalism is likely to be more concerned with balancing claims of representation than with issues of efficiency and rationality in policymaking. Managing diversity typically requires 'side payments' in order to reach consensus, and such payments may run counter to the rational allocation of resources."[49]

For a study of social policy integration, however, the point is less to identify and deplore inefficiencies than to recognize how joint decisionmaking influences policy development. Multitiered systems with shared responsibility for individual social policies often generate complex policy designs to incorporate the concerns of each tier, as well as complex decision rules for policy reform to ensure that these interests continue to be met. As Scharpf has argued, this pattern of policymaking is prone to joint-decision traps in which efficiency and flexibility are subordinated to political accommodation and procedural guarantees.[50]

The comparative chapters in this volume are suggestive. They empha-

49. Sbragia, "Thinking about the European Future," p. 289n.
50. Scharpf, "Joint-Decision Trap." The following section is based partly on Scharpf's analysis, although we use the concept of joint decisions more broadly, referring to those situations in which each of two levels of government has a veto, or at least a substantial capacity for obstruction.

size three results of institutional arrangements that rely on joint decision-making: (1) policies that engender lowest-common-denominator approaches or complex logrolling arrangements; (2) policies that incorporate institutional protections, which produce inefficiencies and policy rigidity; and (3) intense searches for "escape routes"—alternative policy options or institutional reforms that mitigate the need for joint decisionmaking, even if these alternatives have substantive limitations.

LOWEST-COMMON-DENOMINATOR AND "PACKAGED" POLICIES. Where institutional actors cannot easily or effectively act alone, pressures to achieve mutually acceptable compromises will intensify. The stronger the obstacles to collective agreement, the greater the pressure to compromise. Under these circumstances, two options become increasingly probable. On the one hand, policymakers may pursue lowest-common-denominator policies, reflecting the views of the least ambitious participants in a minimum winning coalition.[51] On the other hand, they may resort to elaborate logrolling arrangements in which side payments are offered to buy off potential sources of opposition. The latter solution greatly increases the complexity of policymaking and holds new initiatives hostage to otherwise unrelated issues that can be used as bargaining chips.

INCORPORATION OF INSTITUTIONAL PROTECTIONS. For policymakers, multitiered systems superimpose the question, Who should do it? over the traditional question, What is to be done? The institutional actors involved in joint policymaking seek to protect both their substantive policy goals and their institutional positions; policy designs must accommodate the latter concern. The point is not that such an emphasis is good or bad, but simply that it has consequences for how policies are designed and operate. A policy with two goals (substantive outcomes and protection of various institutional actors) is less likely than a single-purpose policy to be fully effective. Margaret Weir points to several cases where the need to meet the institutional interests of constituent units considerably weakened the capacity of American social policies to achieve substantive results. Elmar Rieger, Jeffrey Anderson, and Patrick Ireland

---

51. Minimum winning coalitions in centralized parliamentary systems are often simple majorities. Because multitiered systems create institutional protections for constituent units, they generally require broader coalitions. Protection for constituent units may be de facto rather than de jure. For example, constituent units in some systems may have considerable power over proposed reforms by virtue of their authority over implementation.

make similar observations about the development of agricultural, regional, and immigration policies in the EU.

The desire to ensure that institutional interests are protected also fosters rigid policy designs. Keith Banting's account in chapter 8 of the Canadian contributory pension system offers a particularly dramatic example. The need to guarantee provincial interests led officials to adopt decision rules that make policy reform nearly impossible. Neither federal nor provincial officials have any real capacity to adapt the Canada Pension Plan to new circumstances.

THE SEARCH FOR ESCAPE ROUTES. Joint-decision traps can lead to complex and frequently unsatisfying policy arrangements. The ensuing frustration may motivate key actors to seek alternatives that avoid such traps. The difficulty of reforming Canada's earnings-related pension system, Banting notes, has fostered both a turn to private pensions (the response of private citizens to inadequate public benefits) and more federal reliance on means-tested alternatives (which officials in Ottawa can enact without provincial approval). Weir argues that joint-decision traps in the United States helped to push national initiatives for social reform in a rights-based, court-led direction, with disappointing results. As the next chapter suggests, the relatively activist role of the European Court of Justice in social policy stems in part from a similar desire of European federalists to avoid the daunting problems associated with joint decisionmaking through the European Council. The common thread in these cases is the channeling of reform efforts in directions less subject to the blockage and shortcomings typical of shared decisionmaking arrangements. Of course, these escape routes often generate problems of their own.

Needing to balance policy goals with institutional protections for constituent units, multitiered systems generally produce far more complex decisionmaking arrangements than do centralized systems. When the likely sources of conflict among institutional actors—over both policy substance and the locus of policy control—are added to the equation, the result is a set of predictable dilemmas for policymakers. Major theories of social policy development have largely ignored these distinctive dynamics of social policy reform in such an institutional context.

Societal Interests and Fragmented Institutional Authority

Multitiered systems of governance, as mentioned above, necessarily link the questions of what to regulate and at what level to regulate.

Because the answer to the latter question has implications for the former, societal actors with an interest in social policy are unlikely to remain aloof from the issue of who will have authority. As Renaud Dehousse notes, in multitiered systems the issues of what to do and who should do it "cannot be debated separately. On the American scene, for instance, the advocates of high standards of protection tend to favour federal intervention because it is more effective; conversely the States' Rights issue is often used as a fig leaf by those who oppose regulatory intervention."[52]

The presence of multiple, potentially competing jurisdictions creates both strategic opportunities and problems for social groups. It may offer considerable advantages for those opposed to extensive, highly redistributive social policies. As we have already said, the prospect of competitive deregulation introduces an important dynamic in multitiered systems that combine economic integration with territorially dispersed authority over social policy. *Competitive deregulation* refers to the possibility that firms in areas with low social wages may be able to undercut the prices of competitors, causing firms in areas with high social wages to either go out of business, relocate, or pressure local public officials and workers to reduce social-wage costs. In extreme scenarios, these actions could fuel a downward spiral in social provision, eventually producing rudimentary, lowest-common-denominator social policies.[53]

This possibility exists because local social policies in multitiered systems are situated within a larger environment marked by the mobility of labor and, especially, capital. Indeed, a principal reason for emphasizing the territorial aspect of multitiered systems is that many of the most interesting consequences of such arrangements have a prominent spatial component. The jurisdictions that constitute the system must deal with the movement of businesses and workers across their physical borders. The free movement of workers and investment constrains redistributive policies, which could produce an exodus of businesses and the affluent and thereby undermine public finances and the local economy. Generous policies might attract potential program beneficiaries and thereby generate prohibitive costs. Local jurisdictions in an integrated economy may

52. Renaud Dehousse, "Integration v. Regulation? On the Dynamics of Regulation in the European Community," *Journal of Common Market Studies*, vol. 30 (December 1992), pp. 383–402, quote at p. 398.

53. For a classic treatment of this dynamic, see William L. Cary, "Federalism and Corporate Law: Reflections upon Delaware," *Yale Law Journal*, vol. 83 (March 1974), pp. 663–705.

also be constrained in their ability to fashion forward-looking, preventive social measures. Because of the mobility of citizens across local borders, investment in human capital represents a kind of public good, with the investing jurisdiction often unable to capture a commensurate return.[54]

These kinds of pressures have in fact restricted social expenditures in the United States, where labor (and capital) mobility is far greater than it is in the EU.[55] There is also evidence that business interests (with the acquiescence, if not encouragement, of national governments) are using the strategic advantages of a multitiered system to push the European political economy in a more liberal, less interventionist direction. The prospect (and sometimes reality) of interjurisdictional competition changes not only the strategies of actors but their power as well. In particular, the strengthening of the exit option for business enhances its ability to exercise "voice."[56]

If multitiered systems create mobility options that increase the power and strategic options of business, they also increase the chances that economic interests will fragment along territorial lines. In particular, the interests of firms and workers in high social-wage areas are likely to diverge from those in low social-wage areas. The former may seek to establish a floor under competition, while the latter may be eager to exploit a potential competitive advantage. Political territory may be transformed into the foundation for interest-group organization. Alongside the familiar cleavage between capital and labor may emerge a less common, territorially grounded one between high and low social-wage areas—which may also encourage territorially grounded conflict among constituent units. Such territorially based coalitions have often been prominent in social policy debates in the United States (see chapter 9).

For many societal actors (and for some government officials), preferences for integration or decentralization are tightly linked to their attitudes toward free markets. Of course, the extent to which particular groups will desire and be able to impose a preference for a decentralized solution is an empirical question, one that is considered in several of the

54. The issue of competitive deregulation represents a variant of the broader question of whether welfare states can survive in the new global economy. See Alfred Pfaller, Ian Gough, and Göran Therborn, *Can the Welfare State Compete? A Comparative Study of Five Advanced Capitalist Countries* (Macmillan, 1991).

55. See also Paul E. Peterson and Mark C. Rom, *Welfare Magnets: A New Case for a National Standard* (Brookings, 1990).

56. Albert O. Hirschman, *Exit, Voice and Loyalty: Responses to Decline in Firms, Organizations, and States* (Harvard University Press, 1970).

chapters of this volume. Under certain conditions, for example, business interests may accept or even press for more centralized policy solutions.[57] The basic point is simply that the functioning of multitiered systems, and particularly the impracticality of certain policy options at the constituent-unit level, affects both the political power of economic groups and their likely attitudes toward policy activity undertaken by each tier.

Finally, multitiered structures may also affect the position of other social actors. The uneven distribution of distinctive ethnic and racial groups across the constituent units of a multitiered system can mean that struggles for increased political and economic power become intertwined with questions of jurisdictional control over social policy. For instance, the concentration of French Canadians in a single province has encouraged an enduring competition over control of social policy between Quebec and the federal government in Ottawa.[58] In the United States issues of race have long been central to political fights over social policy jurisdiction, with African-Americans generally pushing for expanded federal control while local white elites often fight equally hard for decentralization. Ronald Watts summarizes the sharply contrasting impact of federalism on the political identities and strategies of minorities:

> The result of the differing patterns of territorial diffusion [of minorities] has been a differing dynamic in the processes for the protection and maintenance of minority rights. In the United States blacks have looked to the federal government, particularly its courts and executive agencies, to support their rights, often against hostile and indifferent state governments, and to specially targeted federal financial support to provide the economic and social assistance that most states were unable or unwilling to provide. By contrast, in Canada, the concentration of francophones in Quebec has enabled them to look more to the provincial government in Quebec City than to the federal government in Ottawa to maintain and promote their interests.[59]

Territorial divisions may be relevant also for the providers of social

57. In the United States, for example, some businesses in high-wage areas have pushed for national social policy standards to level the playing field. In environmental policy, business has sometimes favored uniform standards over the complexity and unpredictability of confrontations with fifty regulatory authorities. On the first dynamic, see Colin Gordon, "New Deal, Old Deck." On the second, see Majone, "Regulatory Federalism."

58. See chapter 8 in this volume; and Watts, "American Constitution."

59. Watts, "American Constitution," p. 778.

benefits, whose political importance increases as welfare states mature. Centralized polities often centralize the organization of benefits provision as well. In multitiered systems like Germany or the United States, however, policy fragmentation appears to go hand in hand with a proliferation of social actors. Many of the "parapublic" organizations that are involved in German social insurance and welfare programs, for example, are structured along territorial lines.

Institutional settings clearly have important consequences for the political positions of social actors. The resources and strategies of social actors are not simply givens. They are heavily dependent on institutional contexts, which modify the options available to social actors and consequently the power that these actors are able to exert in competition with other groups. The activities and influence of social groups in multitiered political systems therefore seem likely to differ from that observed in unitary ones.

Conclusion

Multitiered institutional settings introduce important new political actors, create a number of distinct dilemmas for policymakers, and modify the strategies and influence of social groups. Some of the consequences of such an institutional arrangement are summarized in figure 1-2. The process of social policy integration in multitiered systems is not totally dissimilar to that of social policy development in more centralized polities; class-based conflicts over the degree and character of government intervention, for example, are likely to be evident in each. But a multitiered context both alters the terrain for these conflicts, potentially transforming the interests, strategies, and even organizational forms of traditional actors, and introduces new actors and issues. Investigations of the politics of social policy must be adjusted accordingly.

Studying Social Policy Integration in the European Union

The principal goal of parts 1 and 3 of this volume is to examine how Europe's emerging multitiered polity—in particular, its strong territorial dimension—affects the process of social policy integration in the European Union. The effects of the EU's peculiar structure and specific environment on several of the characteristics of multitiered systems are dis-

Figure 1-2. *Effects of Multitiered Institutions on Social Policy Development*

Impact on societal interests

"Exit" option strengthens capital and allows new strategies

Cross-class producer (capital/labor) alliances in rich areas are likely to oppose producer alliance in poor areas

Ethnic/racial minorities seek transfers of policy authority to more favorable institutional arenas

The emergence of constituent units as policy actors

Policymaking becomes in part a process of competitive state-building

Preemption of policy space by one tier limits prospects for action by other tiers

Constituent units may appeal for central government assistance to confront collective action problems

Constituent units with competing interests may conflict over appropriate central government role

Opportunities for policy innovation and diffusion increase

Dilemmas of shared social policymaking

Produces proclivities toward lowest-common-denominator and "packaged" policies

Policy designs are modified to incorporate institutional protections

Central and constituent-unit governments engage in searches for escape mechanisms from joint-decision traps

---

cussed below, as are some of the major questions to be explored in the chapters that follow.

The Autonomous Capacities of Constituent Members

We have argued that the autonomous policymaking capability of constituent units is an important feature of multitiered systems, and that this characteristic is far more prominent in the EU than in the federal system of any nation-state. It follows that the autonomous capacities of the member states will have a significant impact on the process of social policy integration in the European Union. Two aspects of this autonomy are particularly consequential: the scope of preempted social policy space and the prospects for competitive state-building. Each merits attention.

EU policy is made in the context of an extensive, diverse array of preexisting, territorially based social policies. Each constituent unit of the EU has its own welfare state; its patterns of intervention in the lives of its citizens are already well established. Although national welfare states will face many challenges during the current process of EU integration (see chapter 2), they will undoubtedly be an enduring part of the European landscape.

Preexisting policy structures pose barriers to an expanded social policy competence at the EU level. First, the sheer diversity of national regimes makes any simple process of harmonization unthinkable. In 1991 expenditures on social protection ranged from 19.4 percent of gross domestic product in Portugal to 32.4 percent in the Netherlands; Dutch spending per capita was more than five times the Portuguese level. These aggregate statistics, while striking, only hint at the true diversity of national social policy regimes. Even similar expenditures on particular programs may mask major differences in how money is spent. Member states vary widely in their emphasis on income transfers or publicly provided services and in their orientation toward means-tested, social insurance, or universal "citizenship" benefits. In the 1988–89 period, Greece allocated only about 10 percent of its expenditures to in-kind programs, compared with Denmark's 35 percent. In 1989, 1.4 percent of Greek social spending went to family policies, compared with 10.7 percent in Ireland.[60]

The differences among national policy structures make any attempt at social policy integration exceptionally difficult. The Single European Act facilitated the creation of an integrated market for goods and services by introducing the principle of mutual recognition. This success, however, was predicated on lowest-common-denominator, deregulatory policies— precisely the agenda most feared by advocates of a European social dimension. No simplifying rule similar to mutual recognition is likely to prove politically acceptable for social policy integration.

Exacerbating the barriers that structural diversity poses to European social policy integration is the sheer magnitude of national initiatives. In contrast to those pushing for the development of national welfare states in the nineteenth and early twentieth centuries, EU actors find that a great deal of the "space" for social policy is already occupied. Welfare state development was often a central component of national state-

---

60. Figures are from Eurostat, *Basic Statistics of the Community: Comparison with the Principal Partners of the Community,* 30th ed. (Luxembourg: Statistical Office of the European Communities, 1993) pp. 163, 166, 172–73. This diversity is reflected in the recent proliferation of efforts to develop typologies of European welfare states. Even these attempts to describe three or four types of welfare states are quickly met with the challenge that distinctive national characteristics or some basic variations are being ignored (for example, in the tendency to group together the quite diverse French, German, and Dutch regimes as "Christian Democratic" welfare states). Gøsta Esping-Andersen, *The Three Worlds of Welfare Capitalism* (Princeton University Press, 1990).

building processes on the continent, promoting both political legitimacy and centralized control over economic resources.

Because of member-state preemptions, developments in the European Union have not mirrored this process. The central components of national welfare states—provision of education, health care, and retirement security—are likely to remain largely under national control. EU initiatives are most evident around the edges of these national cores, in policy domains that are unoccupied or that the integration process renders particularly fragile. Alternatively, redistributive programs may operate quietly, under the cover of policy initiatives somewhat remote from traditional social policy; important examples are the Common Agricultural Policy (discussed by Elmar Rieger in chapter 6) and regional policy (discussed by Jeffrey Anderson in chapter 4). Either way, these initiatives will probably not have the tremendous legitimating potential typical of national welfare state-building processes.

The EU's limited resources will further circumscribe initiatives. National programs preempt not only policy space but administrative and fiscal space. The EU lacks the administrative capacity to implement ambitious policies without turning to national bureaucracies. Any system of extensive service provision or individualized transfers would have to rely on existing structures of national administration. The EU is similarly constrained fiscally. EU expenditures represent a little more than 1 percent of Community gross national product and less than 4 percent of the central government spending of member states. Furthermore, the CAP and the structural funds preempt roughly 80 percent of EU expenditures. The preexisting structures of national welfare states leave EU policymakers with a weak administrative and fiscal base and with limited access to core welfare state functions.

A crucial issue for this volume therefore is how this distinctive and weak fiscal and administrative base affects the development of social policy. As Giandomenico Majone has argued, policy preemption and the EU's limited fiscal capacity encourage an emphasis on regulatory approaches to social policy.[61] This is not the course that national welfare

---

61. Giandomenico Majone, "The European Community between Social Policy and Social Regulation," *Journal of Common Market Studies*, vol. 31 (June 1993), pp. 153–70; see also Leibfried and Pierson, "Prospects for Social Europe," pp. 354–56. Majone's interesting article overstates the extent to which reliance on regulation implies a shift in the goals of social policy. Traditional, redistributive social policies can easily be carried out through regulatory mandates on lower tiers of government or private actors (employers,

states have generally followed, but it may have some significant advantages.[62] Precisely because they do not require spending, regulatory policies have the political advantage of heightening the visibility of the benefits bestowed while obscuring the costs involved. A regulatory approach may help the EU overcome the difficulties of its heterogeneity: the Union can establish basic guidelines and leave taxing, spending, and administrative powers at the national level.

The scope of member-state activity in social policy not only limits the room for EU action; it also signals the considerable value that member states place on continued control over policy. Competitive state-building is sure to be a prominent aspect of European social integration. Member states are likely to resist a large transfer of fiscal capacity to the EU and to be quite protective of their social policy authority. Economic and geopolitical changes since World War II have gradually diminished the scope of national sovereignty in many domains. In vital areas such as macroeconomic policy, national autonomy has essentially disappeared. At the moment, the welfare state is one of the few key realms of policy competence where national governments still reign, and, given the popularity of most social programs, national administrators are reluctant to lose authority over social policy. What makes constituent units favor or at least accede to the transfer of social policy authority to the center is a critical topic for studies of multitiered systems. This question is addressed in many of the chap'ers in this volume.

An equally important concern is the extent of member-state control over the making of EU social policy. Although the strength of the EU's constituent units assures them a central role in policymaking, it is far from clear that the member states dictate policy outcomes at the European level. As we suggested earlier, developments such as the growing authority of EU organizations, the impact of previous policy commitments, the growing issue density of EU activity, and the expanding activity of nonstate actors all serve to constrain the influence of member states. All of these factors are explored in the chapters that follow in an effort

---

for example) without significant spending by the central tier. EU labor market mandates are criticized for doing precisely this in John T. Addison and W. Stanley Siebert, "The Social Charter: Whatever Next?" *British Journal of Industrial Relations*, vol. 30 (December 1992), pp. 495–513.

62. In fact, heightened fiscal constraints may be leading national welfare states down a similar path. In the United States, large budget deficits have forced the federal government to act through mandates, requiring state-level initiatives, while leaving to local politicians the unpleasant task of coming up with the money.

to gauge both the scope and limits of member-state influence in the Union's decisionmaking processes.

Dilemmas of Shared Social Policy Authority

Multitiered systems promote joint policy interventions or shared authority over policy areas. We have argued that such arrangements generate particular policymaking dilemmas that encourage the resort to lowest-common-denominator and packaged policies, encourage the use of institutional protections within policy designs, and prompt efforts to find escape mechanisms. How might these dynamics operate in the development of EU social policy?

The fragmentation of decisionmaking and the strong bargaining position of individual member states make the EU's multitiered system especially prone to lowest-common-denominator agreements and reliance on policy packages. Before the adoption of the Maastricht Protocol, almost all social policy decisionmaking within the European Council took place in the shadow of the British veto, sharply circumscribing the range of possible initiatives. Even the more relaxed rules of qualified majority voting put minority coalitions in a strong position. The widespread expectation is that policies, if they are enacted at all, will take the form of standards set at or near those of the least generous members of the Union.

This has not always been the case, however. Peter Lange has pointed to the puzzle of poor member states agreeing to a social protocol that will allow them to be outvoted, and Volker Eichener has documented the very high level of regulation for many aspects of workplace safety.[63] The next chapter discusses cases of standards that raise requirements for some members of the Union, while prohibiting any lowering of already high standards for others. Thus another important question concerns the circumstances that might make EU social policy diverge from lowest-common-denominator approaches.

The need for a super-majority to carry out policy also encourages resort to package deals, in which side payments induce support from members who would otherwise oppose a given initiative. Several impor-

---

63. Lange, "Maastricht and the Social Protocol"; and Eichener, "Social Dumping or Innovative Regulation?" Majone and Vogel have made similar observations about environmental policy. Majone, "Regulatory Federalism"; and David Vogel, "Environmental Protection and the Creation of a Single European Market," paper prepared for the 1992 annual meeting of the American Political Science Association.

tant consequences flow from the use of policy packaging. First, when progress toward integration requires "linkage" to other initiatives, the evolution of policy becomes less predictable and more dependent on events unrelated to social policy, such as the negotiation of a new treaty or an enlargement of the Union. Second, and related to the first consequence, the need to formulate complicated packages involving a range of issues may make the Union particularly susceptible to a "stop-go" or "big-bang" approach to policymaking, in which long periods of incremental adjustments within established frameworks are followed by brief bursts of major policy innovation.[64] The following chapters suggest that this stop-go dynamic has been typical of EC policymaking in a variety of fields. Finally, the need for packaging deals may encourage reliance on policy tools that make the size of benefits to individual member states especially transparent. As Jeffrey Anderson points out in chapter 4, the transparency of the Union's regional policies has made them a useful mechanism for facilitating linkage.

The scope of national welfare states within the EU assures that competitive state-building will remain an important dynamic. Discussions of social policy therefore will tend to involve the issue of institutional protections for constituent members. As George Ross emphasizes in chapter 11, the Commission has pursued a "Russian doll" strategy in which policy initiatives are designed to have a cascade effect, leading inexorably to new initiatives that expand the Union's—and the Commission's—authority. Member states have sought to prevent such a dynamic. To date in social policy, the constituent units have been cautious in their grants of authority. Institutional reforms have been circumscribed to prevent accretions of EU power, and programs have been designed to make the Union heavily dependent on member states for implementation.

As in other multitiered systems, the dilemmas of shared decisionmaking in the EU lead to strategies of circumvention. In many of the chapters that follow, the efforts of actors to escape the gridlock in social policymaking is a central theme. For advocates of social integration, institutional constraints within the Union have made court-led policy development an important path of social reform. As several chapters (those by Leibfried and Pierson, Ostner and Lewis, and Ireland) indicate, the ECJ

---

64. The argument that fragmented institutions encourage a pattern of social policy development based on "big bangs" is applied to the United States in Christopher Leman, "Patterns of Policy Development: Social Security in the United States and Canada," *Public Policy*, vol. 25 (Spring 1977), pp. 261–91.

has been willing to take an expansive view of its own role and that of the EU in social policy. Legal strategies have had the advantage of leaving taxing, spending, and administrative powers at the national level. In addition, at least on the continent, Court activities could rely on a shared Roman law tradition of codification, which often encompasses social welfare.[65]

The adoption of legal strategies may entail considerable costs, however. As Margaret Weir's discussion of efforts to use the courts to achieve social integration in the United States reveals (chapter 10), legal systems have their own internal standards for judging the appropriateness of policy designs. Reforms built around a judicial logic may have less capacity to achieve substantive goals. Furthermore, courts may have less need to consider political constraints in prescribing solutions. Thus in the United States, Thomas Byrne Edsall and Mary D. Edsall have argued, an expansion of social policy aimed at individual rights in general and the rights of minorities in particular exacerbated political cleavages based on race. This outcome made court initiatives difficult to sustain and may have encouraged a backlash against other social policy interventions.[66] Thus a possible danger of this particular escape route is that court initiatives may exceed the tolerance of important political actors within the system. After all, multitiered systems make centralized policymaking difficult for a reason—to protect local interests—and circumvention of these protections is likely to generate resentment. This is, of course, one aspect of the current disquiet over the Union's "democratic deficit." Both chapter 2 and chapter 5 (by Ilona Ostner and Jane Lewis) reveal considerable member-state grumbling over the ECJ's social policy decisions. The negotiations leading up to the Treaty of Maastricht—and the structure of the treaty itself—indicate that the member states view the ECJ's expanding power with great concern.[67]

The social protocol enacted along with the Treaty of Maastricht provides a second prominent example of an escape route taken by the EU.

---

65. England, with its common law tradition, is the major outlier in that respect, much more beholden to a tradition of largesse and of restrained court involvement. See also Anthony Ogus, "The Federal Republic of Germany as Sozialstaat: A British Perspective," Working Paper 3 (Manchester: University of Manchester, Faculty of Law, 1990). On the general background for this argument, see Kenneth H. F. Dyson, *The State Tradition in Western Europe: A Study of an Idea and Institution* (Oxford University Press, 1980).

66. Thomas Byrne Edsall and Mary D. Edsall, *Chain Reaction: The Impact of Race, Rights, and Taxes on American Politics* (W. W. Norton, 1991). Margaret Weir questions this claim in chapter 10 of this volume.

67. Dehousse, "Community Competences."

Eager to circumvent Britain's blockade on European policymaking, the other member states negotiated an agreement authorizing an alternative mechanism that was supposed to facilitate decisionmaking. The new rules, however, have further complicated an already complex system. How this procedure will play out remains uncertain, although a long-controversial directive on European works councils has now been passed and two further initiatives are being pursued.[68] What is clear is that the new arrangement, grafting an additional element of fragmentation and uncertainty onto an already complex institutional arrangement, offers no easy escape from joint-decision traps.

As the preceding discussion suggests and as the chapters that follow show in detail, social policy integration in the European Union reveals all the dilemmas of shared decisionmaking—often in extreme forms. Lowest-common-denominator policies and complex logrolling arrangements predominate; an emphasis on protecting the interests of multiple institutional actors fosters the development of rigid programs, often of doubtful efficacy; and central authorities frequently resort to problematic escape routes in an effort to circumvent these effects. This points to one of the volume's central themes. The picture that emerges from these characteristics is one of highly fragmented, poorly coordinated policy-making in which jurisdictional disputes and the restricted capacities of particular sets of decisionmakers place severe limits on the design of social programs.

Societal Actors and the Politics of EU Social Policy

Social policy development requires the construction of strong political coalitions. As in the development of social policies at the national level, the role of societal actors is likely to be of central importance in the European Union. The chapters that follow focus on two distinct aspects of this topic: the degree of influence of various actors and the development of their policy preferences.

Studies of the development of national welfare states have often stressed the "power resources" of left-of-center parties and strong union confederations.[69] These groups have traditionally been considered the

---

68. There is some disagreement among this volume's authors about the implications of the protocol. For differing views, see the chapters by Rhodes, Ross, Streeck, and Pierson and Leibfried.

69. Michael Shalev, "The Social Democratic Model and Beyond," *Comparative Social*

most likely supporters of social policy initiatives. Yet in the European Union the representatives of social democracy are quite weak, especially in the European Council. Part of this weakness stems from a gradual erosion of the position of labor and social democrats in the national polities of Western Europe. The Union's multitiered structure, however, may well enhance their political opponents' ability to block social policy initiatives. How much does this new, fragmented institutional setting for social policy shift the balance of power between business and organized labor? We have already suggested that institutional fragmentation generally increases the influence of business, but how have the specific features of the European Union affected the nature of that influence? This is a topic that is explored in more detail in the chapters by Wolfgang Streeck and Martin Rhodes.

In assessing the influence of economic actors, one must also consider whether other organized actors are gaining importance at the European level. Social policy debates are often thought to involve only business and unions. With the expansion of social services and income transfer programs, a very wide range of actors—including many nonprofit or quasi-public organizations, groups representing welfare-state employees or clienteles, producers of services, and local or regional governments—develops large stakes in the course of policy development.[70] Are these actors effectively organizing at the European level, and, if so, to what effect?

Investigations of social actors need to consider not only who has influence but to what ends that influence is wielded. Is business, as some argue, relentlessly hostile to social initiatives, or might it acquiesce to or even favor EU policies in some circumstances? Do the cleavages within the business community lead to divergent policy preferences?[71] The social policy preferences of business have received only sporadic attention from students of comparative politics, but the question is extremely important in a political context where firms and business associations are certain to wield enormous clout.

One important aspect of this issue concerns the territorial dimension that is so pronounced in multitiered institutional settings. To what extent does the EU's growing significance encourage territorial fragmentation

---

Research, vol. 6 (1983), pp. 315–51; and Esping-Andersen, *Three Worlds of Welfare Capitalism*.

70. See Pierson, *Dismantling the Welfare State?*

71. See Cathie Jo Martin, "Basic Instincts? Sources of Firm Preference for National Health Reform," *American Political Science Review*, vol. 89 (forthcoming, 1995).

of economic interests? There are good reasons to think that multitiered systems encourage the formation of regional blocs of economic actors, with the interests of those in poor regions diverging from those of more affluent regions. Whether such geographically based, cross-class coalitions become prominent will no doubt have considerable consequences for the evolution of social policy within the European Union.

Viewing the European Union as a specific case of social policy integration within a multitiered institutional environment highlights a set of crucial questions. It provides a framework not only for identifying some of the main characteristics of social policy development within the Union but also for reconsidering the processes through which particular social policy interventions come into being and are modified or replaced. There has been extensive and sophisticated research on the evolution of national welfare states in the advanced industrial democracies, yet much of this research has focused on the unitary political structures prevalent in northern Europe and Scandinavia. The role of institutions, and particularly the implications of multitiered decisionmaking for the evolution of social policy, has been inadequately appreciated.

A multitiered political setting has weighty consequences: significant new institutional actors emerge, various new policy dilemmas arise for those charged with the design of social programs, and the influence and strategies of societal actors change. Thinking clearly about how multitiered institutional structures influence the development of social policy can help us understand not only the remarkable process of social integration occurring in the European Union but also the processes of policy development in many national welfare states.

Part 1

The Development of Social Europe

CHAPTER TWO

Semisovereign Welfare States: Social Policy in a Multitiered Europe

Stephan Leibfried and Paul Pierson

T HIS VOLUME EMPLOYS a broad definition of social policy. Social policies modify market outcomes to facilitate transactions, to correct market failures, and to carry out regional, interclass, or intergenerational redistribution. These efforts are produced through a range of mechanisms, including industrial relations policies, education and vocational training, and family policies, in addition to traditional social security. As the other chapters in this book demonstrate, the broader the definition of social policy, the more we see the European Union actively involved, be it through coping with immigration, regional inequalities, or declining sectors, such as agriculture. Yet if the focus is exclusively on traditional components of the welfare state—confronting the risks of sickness, old age, invalidity, unemployment, and poverty—does the EU play a significant role, or do national welfare states remain largely untouched? This is the question addressed in this chapter.

Accounts of European social policy generally present a minimalist interpretation of EU involvement.[1] The sovereign nation-state, so the argument goes, allows no relevant role for the EU in social policy. The Union's sphere is market building, leaving social policy to the citizen-focused, national welfare state, its sovereignty formally untouched though perhaps endangered indirectly by growing economic interdepen-

---

1. Peter Lange, "The Politics of the Social Dimension," in Alberta M. Sbragia, ed., *Euro-Politics: Institutions and Policymaking in the "New" European Community* (Brookings, 1992), pp. 225–56; Abram De Swaan, "Perspectives for Transnational Social Policy," *Government and Opposition*, vol. 27 (Winter 1992) pp. 33–52; and Abram De Swaan, "Perspectives for Transnational Social Policy in Europe: Social Transfers from West to East," in Abram De Swaan, ed., *Social Policy beyond Borders: The Social Question in International Perspective* (Amsterdam University Press, 1994), pp. 101–15.

dence. "Welfare states," Abram De Swaan writes, "are national states."[2] On the face of it, the European welfare state does indeed look national. There is no EU welfare law granting individual entitlements from Brussels; there are no direct taxes or contributions funding a social budget that would back such entitlements; there is no Brussels welfare bureaucracy to speak of. Territorial sovereignty in social policy, as conventional wisdom has it, is alive and well.[3] We disagree. The process of European integration has eroded both the sovereignty (by which we mean legal authority) and autonomy (by which we mean de facto capacity) of member states in the realm of social policy. National welfare states remain the primary institutions of European social policy, but they do so in the context of an increasingly constraining multitiered polity.

We maintain that a moderate version of the neofunctionalist view of European integration can be applied to social policy development.[4] Although the extensive barriers to EU action have prevented any true federalization of European social policy, the dynamics of creating a single market have made it increasingly difficult to exclude social issues from the EU agenda. The emergence of a multitiered structure is less the result of attempts by Eurocrats to build a welfare state than it is a consequence of spillovers from the initiative to build a single market. By *spillovers* we mean the process through which the completion of the internal market produces growing pressures for the EU to invade the domain of social policy. Recall that the single-market initiative was based on a deregulatory agenda and assumed that initiatives to assure "free movement of goods, services, capital and labor" could be insulated from social policy issues, which would continue to be the bailiwick of member states. This is a dubious assumption.[5] Already there is significant evidence that the

2. De Swaan, "Perspectives," p. 102.

3. For a historical overview of social policy at the EC level, see Doreen Collins, *The European Communities: The Social Policy of the First Phase*, vol. 1, *The European Coal and Steel Community, 1951–1970*, and vol. 2, *The European Economic Community, 1958–1972* (London: Martin Robertson, 1975); Bernd Henningsen, "Die schönste Nebensache Europas—Zur Geschichte der EG-Sozialpolitik," *Sozialer Fortschritt*, vol. 41, no. 9 (1992), pp. 204–12; and Patrick Kenis, "Social Europe in the 1990s: Beyond an Adjunct to Achieving a Common Market?" *Futures*, vol. 23 (September 1991), pp. 724–38.

4. Ernst Bernhard Haas, *The Uniting of Europe: Political, Social and Economic Forces, 1950–1957*, 2d ed. (first pub. 1958) (Stanford University Press, 1968); and Leon N. Lindberg and Stuart A. Scheingold, *Europe's Would-Be Polity: Patterns of Change in the European Community* (Prentice Hall, 1970).

5. In fact, it runs directly contrary to the central tenets of political economy, which stress the embeddedness of economic action within dense networks of social and political institutions. See Peter Hall, *Governing the Economy: The Politics of State Intervention in*

tidy separation between market issues and social issues is unsustainable. No matter what the outcome of "high politics" struggles over social charters and treaty revisions, the movement toward market integration will be accompanied by the gradual erosion of the autonomy and sovereignty of national welfare states; national regimes will become more and more enmeshed in a complex, multitiered web of social policy.[6]

This transformation of sovereign welfare states into parts of a multitiered system of social policy occurs through three processes. "Positive," activist reform results from social policy initiatives taken at the center by the European Commission and Council of Ministers, along with determinations by the European Court of Justice (ECJ) of what those initiatives mean. "Negative" reform occurs through the ECJ's imposition of market compatibility requirements that restrict and redefine the social policies of member states. Finally, the process of European integration creates a range of indirect pressures that do not legally require but nonetheless strongly encourage national welfare states to adapt their social policies to avoid the potential negative consequences of economic integration. We consider each of these processes in turn. In the first section of this chapter we briefly review the EU's rather feeble direct efforts to develop an activist social policy. Like others, we stress the formidable obstacles: institutions that make reform difficult, limited fiscal capacity, jealous member-state protection of "state-building" resources, and an unfavorable distribution of power among interest groups. In the remainder of the chapter, however, we turn to the processes through which European integration is gradually transforming national welfare states into components of a unique, multitiered framework for social policy. The next section reviews the development of market compatibility requirements—legal challenges to those aspects of national welfare states that conflict with the single market's call for unhindered labor mobility and open competition for services. The following part considers the de

---

Britain and France (Cambridge: Polity, 1986); and Douglass C. North, *Institutions, Institutional Change and Economic Performance* (Cambridge University Press, 1990).

6. It might be useful at the outset to contrast this analysis with the Streeck and Ross chapters in part 3. Like Streeck, we accept that the ability of EU decisionmakers to dictate the course of social policies is quite limited. The absence of a strong central authority is one of the most distinctive features of the emerging system. We also agree with Ross that the history of EU politics has involved the subordination of a social policy agenda to more pressing (and politically feasible) ambitions of market integration and monetary union. Nonetheless, we conclude that this very process of building the single market not only touches on welfare-state sovereignty but also significantly erodes the autonomy of national welfare state regimes.

facto rather than de jure pressures on national regimes, resulting from factors such as competitive demands for adaptations of national economies to a single market and, potentially, a single currency area. The last section pulls together these arguments to highlight some of the distinctive features of this emerging multitiered system of social policy.

The Limited Success of Activist Social Policy

Direct attempts by the European Commission to construct a significant "social dimension"—areas of social policy competence where uniform or at least minimum standards are set at the EU level—have come in fits and starts during the past few decades. It has been a saga of high aspirations and modest results, marked by cheap talk proffered in the confident knowledge that the unanimity required for Council votes would never be reached and that ambitious blueprints would remain unexecuted. This story has been well told elsewhere, and much of the record is considered in other chapters in this volume.[7] Here we only broadly review that story, for our main argument is that the analytical focus on efforts to foist an activist social dimension on a reluctant Council has been a mistake. European integration has in fact eroded national welfare-state sovereignty, but mostly through quite different mechanisms.

As the introduction to this volume states, the obstacles to an activist role for Brussels in social policy development have always been formidable. EU institutions make it much easier to block reforms than to enact them, and they generally offer what would seem to be only narrow, market-related openings for social legislation. The member states themselves, which serve as gatekeepers for initiatives that require Council approval, jealously protect their prerogatives in social policy. In a context of competitive state-building, national governments will only reluctantly cede control over one of the most important remaining domains of national authority. Further barriers include the relative weakness of the social democratic forces most interested in a strong social dimension, the absence of financial resources that would facilitate expansive social policies, the sharp conflicts between the interests of member states with

---

7. Hugh G. Mosley, "The Social Dimension of European Integration," *International Labour Review*, vol. 129, no. 2 (1990), pp. 147–64; Wolfgang Streeck and Philippe C. Schmitter, "From National Corporatism to Transnational Pluralism: Organized Interest in the Single European Market," *Politics and Society*, vol. 19 (June 1991), pp. 133–64; and Lange, "Politics."

differing social wage costs, and the tremendous difficulties of harmonizing widely divergent and deeply institutionalized national social policies.[8]

Substantive policy enactments therefore have been rare. As George Ross and Wolfgang Streeck discuss in chapters 11 and 12, expansive visions of Union social policy have had far lower priority than initiatives for an integrated market. Only in a few areas where the Treaty of Rome allowed more latitude—most notably through the gender-equality provisions of article 119—has the EU legislated extensively (see chapter 5 by Ilona Ostner and Jane Lewis).[9] Even for gender issues, the market-oriented nature of the Union and its restricted focus on the paid labor market have circumscribed EU interventions. Nevertheless, the ECJ has played a particularly activist role through its expansive interpretations of EU initiatives. To take just one example, ECJ decisions have had a dramatic impact on private pension schemes. When in *Barber* the ECJ required equal retirement ages for men and women, fear that the ruling might be applied retroactively to private pensions (at a cost estimated at up to £40 billion in Britain and 35 billion DM in Germany) fueled "what is probably the most costly and intense lobbying campaign yet seen in Brussels."[10] This pressure led the negotiators of the Maastricht treaty to explicitly limit retroactivity, but the prospective impact of the Court's rulings remains dramatic.[11]

In the past decade the institutional restrictions on social policy initia-

8. Stephan Leibfried and Paul Pierson, "Prospects for Social Europe," *Politics and Society*, vol. 20 (September 1992), pp. 333–66.

9. A second area of activity would be health and safety standards in the workplace, which has been the subject of extensive EU intervention. Since this chapter focuses on traditional welfare state issues, however, we leave that topic for other chapters in the volume. See Volker Eichener, "Social Dumping or Innovative Regulation? Processes and Outcomes of European Decision Making in the Sector of Health and Safety at Work Harmonization," Working Papers in Political and Social Sciences, SPS 92/28 (Florence: European University Institute, 1993).

10. Sonia Mazey and Jeremy Richardson, "Introduction: Transference of Power, Decision Rules, and Rules of the Game," in Sonia Mazey and Jeremy Richardson, eds., *Lobbying in the European Community* (Oxford University Press, 1993), p. 15.

11. The issue of retroactivity raised in *Barber* was thought sufficiently important (and costly) to warrant the attention of the Maastricht treaty writers. In Maastricht a somewhat less costly, but not the least costly, version of retroactivity was chosen. It took a lot—a unanimous treaty change—to recoup the initiative from the ECJ; the ECJ upheld the solution found in Maastricht in *Ten Oever* (ECJ Case 109/91, October 6, 1993). Estimated costs of full retroactivity for Germany are from Claus Berenz, "Hat die betriebliche Altersversorgung zukünftig noch eine Chance?" *Neue Zeitschrift für Arbeitsrecht*, vol. 11, nos. 9, 10 (1994), pp. 385–90, 433–38; for Britain, from Mazey and Richardson, "Transference of Power," p. 15.

tives have loosened somewhat. The introduction of qualified majority voting in some domains, authorized under the Single European Act (SEA), has made social policy the focus of a sharp conflict, which Martin Rhodes aptly dubs the "treaty-base game" (chapter 3). Struggles have been waged to determine the range of issues that can be decided by majority vote under article 100a (covering distortions of competition) or under the SEA exception for proposals governing the health and safety of workers. Members of the Commission, the European Parliament, and the European labor organization ETUC (European Trade Union Confederation) have pushed with some success for expansive readings of these clauses, while UNICE (Union of Industrial and Employers' Confederations of Europe), the main employers' organization, has strongly opposed such a move.[12] One indication of the growing room for social policy initiatives, however, was the enactment of the Maternity Directive of October 1992, passed under the SEA health and safety provisions allowing qualified majority voting. This legislation both requires more generous policies in several EU countries and prohibits other countries from cutting back their existing regimes. Many proposals connected to the Social Charter, a "solemn declaration" signed by every member state except Britain in May 1989, have been watered down or stalled, but the combined impact of what has been passed is far from trivial.[13]

The Maastricht Treaty also may have lowered the institutional barriers to social policy enactments, although the creation of a separate institutional track for social policy has caused much uncertainty. Faced with an impasse between British unwillingness to expand majority voting to social policy and France's refusal to sign a treaty that did not do so, the Netherlands and Germany together with the Commission's Jacques Delors engineered a complex compromise.[14] All twelve member states agreed to allow the countries other than Britain to go forward on social policy issues under the new Social Protocol, which expands the scope for qualified majority voting.[15] Britain will not participate in such deci-

---

12. See Lange, "Politics," pp. 235–56.

13. For some estimates of the impact on firms and governments—with particular emphasis on the effects on Britain—see John T. Addison and W. Stanley Siebert, "The EC Social Charter: The Nature of the Beast," *National Westminster Bank Quarterly Review,* February 1993, pp. 13–28.

14. In addition to the chapters in this volume, see Peter Lange, "The Maastricht Social Protocol: Why Did They Do It?" *Politics and Society,* vol. 21 (March 1993), pp. 5–36; and George Ross, *Jacques Delors and European Integration* (Oxford: Polity Press, 1994).

15. Qualified majority voting will now be satisfactory for "improvement in particular of the working environment to protect workers' health and safety; working conditions; the

sionmaking, nor will it be governed by any policies taken within this framework.

How this unprecedented solution will affect social policymaking is unclear. The ECJ will need to rule on the legality of an arrangement that employs the Union's governing apparatus for a subset of the EU membership. Britain may face pressures to rejoin the other member states, either because of a change in government in London or growing perceptions that the costs of being the odd man out are too high.[16] It is not obvious, however, that being outside the new social policy framework will impose significant costs; it may in fact confer certain competitive advantages. British prime minister John Major, for one, claimed a victory: "Europe can have the social chapter. We shall have employment. . . . Let Jacques Delors accuse us of creating a paradise for foreign investors; I am happy to plead guilty."[17]

In principle, then, efforts to implement aspects of the Social Charter should be facilitated: Britain's capacity to obstruct legislation has been diminished, and the four "poor" states (Greece, Ireland, Portugal, and Spain) do not command enough votes to block reform under qualified majority vote. A European Works Council directive has already been approved under the Social Protocol.

But though some parts of the Social Charter may move forward, further activism in the near future will probably be modest. The Commission is itself involved in intensive soul-searching concerning its proper social policy role.[18] Efforts to combat stubbornly high European unemployment have taken center stage, and the Commission seems to have accepted at least part of the British argument about the need to promote "flexibility." The Commission's 1993 White Paper on "Growth, Competitiveness, Employment," for example, revealed a change in emphasis

---

information and consultation of workers; equality of treatment between men and women with regard to labour market opportunities and treatment at work; the integration of persons excluded from the labour market." *Social Protocol*, art. 2 (1, 2).

16. Both Labour and the Liberal Democrats made an issue of Britain's status in the recent European Parliament elections, asking why Portuguese and Greek workers should have access to higher standards of social protection than British workers. The Conservatives did abysmally in the election, though it is doubtful that the protocol itself was of much significance.

17. Quoted in Gerda Falkner, "Die Sozialpolitik der EG: Rechtsgrundlagen und Entwicklung von Rom bis Maastricht," in Max Haller and Peter Schachner-Blazizek, eds., *Europa—Wohin? Wirtschafliche Integration, soziale Gerechtigkeit und Demokratie* (Graz, Austria: Leykam, 1994), pp. 221–46, quote at p. 241.

18. Ross, *Jacques Delors*, pp. 221–26.

toward reducing labor costs, calling for tax reforms that would generate a substantial reduction of nonwage labor costs (between 1 and 2 percentage points of gross domestic product), particularly for the least-skilled workers.[19] Furthermore, the member states will be reluctant to allow the Commission to take the lead on social issues, suggesting that the immediate prospect is for consolidation, with the completion of current items on the agenda but few new initiatives.

The dismissal of claims that the EU possesses a significant role in social policy is based largely on the outcomes of these struggles at the level of high politics over center-imposed social policies through devices like the Social Charter; indeed, the results of activism have been limited. Developments such as the maternity directive suggest that there may now be room for some European initiatives, and EU legislative activity is probably as extensive as, for example, federal social policy activity in the United States on the eve of the New Deal.[20] Nevertheless, it is processes other than the efforts of EU officials to develop social policy legislation that have caused member states to lose considerable control over social policy in the European Union.

European Integration and Market Compatibility Requirements

Sovereign states control their welfare states. They may limit benefits to their own citizens (control over beneficiaries); insist that benefits be consumed on their own territory (spatial control over consumption); prevent other welfare-state regimes from competing within their territory (exclusivity); choose any policy design, whether based on monetary or in-kind transfers (regime control); demand that their agencies—and not the agencies of other nation-states—determine beneficiary status (administrative case control); and exercise a final say on who, in the case of services, may produce the benefits (control over access to the status of benefit producer). If all these conditions hold for member states, the argument

---

19. Commission of the European Communities, *Growth, Competitiveness, Employment: The Challenges and Ways Forward into the 21st Century* (Luxembourg: Office for Official Publications of the European Communities, 1993), pp. 136–41.

20. David Brian Robertson, "The Bias of American Federalism: The Limits of Welfare State Development in the Progressive Era," *Journal of Policy History*, vol. 1, no. 3 (1989), pp. 261–91.

that welfare-state institutions are still essentially national would be strong. But the conditions do not hold. The last three decades, and especially the most recent one, have witnessed a gradual, incremental expansion of EU-produced regulations and, especially, court decisions that have seriously eroded the sovereignty of national welfare states. Political scientists have paid scant attention to this area of "low politics," entranced by the world of high politics and high conflicts (reports of Mrs. Thatcher's allegedly pounding her handbag in Bruges, for example). The topic has been left to a small set of European welfare lawyers who have monitored another center of policymaking: the courts.[21]

The ECJ has delivered more than 300 decisions on social policy coordination, enough to incite pleas for a specialized EU welfare court for which the ECJ would function as a court of appeals. The ECJ's caseload has been escalating rapidly, and social policy cases account for a growing share of this rising total. The Court's overall caseload increased from 34 cases filed in 1968 to 280 in 1980 and 553 in 1992. A comparison with core common-market topics such as the customs union, free movement of goods, competition (including taxation), and agriculture is instructive. While social cases accounted for only 6.3 percent of the total in these four categories in 1968, that share had increased to 22.8 percent in 1992. By 1992 only competition cases outnumbered social ones, and the rate of growth for social policy cases was faster.[22]

The EU's social dimension is usually discussed as a corrective or a counter to market building, but it has proceeded instead as part of the market-building process. It is this market-building process that spurred demand for court decisions. The nexus between the market and social policy was at least partially acknowledged at the EC's inception, as the Community set about reducing restrictions on labor mobility, which involved tackling social policy. Articles 48–51 of the Treaty of Rome deal with the freedom of movement for workers, with article 51 stating:

---

21. For broad discussions of the Court's influence, see Joseph H. H. Weiler, "The Transformation of Europe," *Yale Law Journal*, vol. 100 (May 1991), pp. 2403–83; and Anne-Marie Burley and Walter Mattli, "Europe before the Court: A Political Theory of Legal Integration," *International Organization*, vol. 47 (winter 1993). For a good discussion of the myopia toward courts within political science, see Martin Shapiro and Alec Stone, "The New Constitutional Politics of Europe," *Comparative Political Studies*, vol. 26 (January 1994), pp. 397–420.

22. James A. Caporaso and John T. S. Keeler, "The European Union and Regional Integration Theory," paper presented at the third biennial International Conference of the European Community Studies Association, Washington, D.C., May 27–29, 1993, table 1.

"The Council shall, acting unanimously on a proposal from the Commission, adopt such measures in the field of social security as are necessary to provide freedom of movement for workers."

That a labor-mobility regime of coordination would restrict welfare state sovereignty was on the minds of treaty makers in 1957.[23] At that time, however, such impacts were neither very visible nor contentious since an already entrenched intergovernmental consensus existed on which the treaty could build: bilateral and multilateral social security treaties, drafts of a European Coal and Steel Community Social Security Treaty for miners and steelworkers, and standards of the International Labor Organization.[24] These embedded international legal norms facilitated fast and silent supranationalization.[25] The new regulations, along with the obligations they created for member states, gradually became more deeply institutionalized—mostly in the quiet of the Court's chambers. It was not until the end of the 1980s that member states began to wake up to the full import of coordination and to struggle with it.

In line with the Union's agenda of market integration, the EU also has an original competency to regulate and ensure the freedom of services (articles 59–66). At first sight this does not seem to allow much room for social policy. The treaty's signators saw no real connection between freedom of services and their sovereign welfare state building, in contrast to their concerns about coordination. But developments in recent times have shown that this constitutional principle and its implementation have far-reaching consequences for national social policy regimes, guaranteeing both the freedom of movement to consumers of social policy to shop where they want, and the right of service providers to deliver their services across the border into another welfare state. In the future this

23. See Frederico Romero, "Migration as an Issue in European Interdependence and Integration: The Case of Italy," in Alan S. Milward, Frances M. B. Lynch, Frederico Romero, and Vibeke Sørensen, *The Frontier of National Sovereignty: History and Theory, 1945–1992* (London: Routledge, 1993), pp. 33–58, 205–08. Romero traces the history of the "mobility of labor" clause in the Rome treaty and the specific contributions of Italian politics to it, with Italy being the prominent labor exporter of that period. The example shows that in particular circumstances, member states may push hard for expanded European competence. Without Italy the European Union might be missing freedom of labor mobility altogether. To take another example, without France the gender aspects of the social dimension (article 119, for example) would probably be absent.

24. Bernd Schulte, "Sozialrecht," in Carl Otto Lenz and others, eds., *EG-Handbuch, Recht im Binnenmarkt*, 2d ed. (Berlin: Verlag Neue Wirtschafts-Briefe, 1994), pp. 407–78.

25. Coordination law originally was specified in regulations 3 and 4 of 1958; it thus belongs to the "constitutive phase" of building the European Community.

spillover could become the major terrain for European conflicts over social policy reform.

Coordination, Labor Mobility, and the Remolding of Income Transfers

One crucial locus of tension between national welfare states and the developing common market has been the regulations governing the mobility of labor across the jurisdictional boundaries of member states.[26] Two regulations designed to ensure that the social policies of member states do not impede mobility constitute the core of an expanded domain of social welfare law.[27] The legally binding decisions of the ECJ pervade all of social security in all fifteen member states. Intra-European migration, compared with interstate migration in the United States, is small: only 5 million workers, including their dependents, actually exercise this freedom.[28] But these numbers have surpassed the critical mass necessary to generate ever-increasing litigation at the ECJ. In legal terms, the adaptation of social policy to a context of "interstate commerce" does not require a quantum leap in intra-European migration itself. The individual litigants and national (mostly welfare and labor) courts that refer cases to the ECJ are, together with the ECJ itself, the central actors in shaping this multitiered EC policy domain. They have given rise to a large corpus of national—and, especially, supranational—adjudication since 1958.

On the whole, labor mobility is a field of well-established administrative and legal routines, requiring EU decisions (politics) only if the rou-

---

26. The level on which primary Community (i.e., treaty) law is implemented usually is labeled secondary Community law. It consists of regulations, which are directly binding at the citizen level; directives, which specify goals and some standards, leaving implementation to the nation-states (this instrument has been interpreted by the ECJ to be binding insofar as it contains rules that are by themselves operational); recommendations and opinions, which have no legal force; and decisions, which have legal force for the parties designated (article 189).

27. The legal norms of coordination are documented in Bernd Schulte, ed., *Soziale Sicherheit in der EG, Verordnungen (EWG) Nr. 1408/71 and 574/72 sowie andere Bestimmungen*, 2d ed. (München: C. H. Beck, 1993).

28. In contrast, there are some 8 million third-country nationals living on EU territory. Quantitatively, immigration dominates the intra-European mobility issue. In terms of EC state building, immigration is much less relevant than migration. Bernd Schulte, "Einführung in die Schulßdiskussion," in Bernd Schulte and Hans F. Zacher, eds., *Wechselwirkungen zwischen dem Europäischen Sozialrecht und dem Sozialrecht der Bundesrepublik Deutschland* (Berlin: Duncker and Humbolt, 1992), pp. 237–52.

tines are to be changed. In the last decade or so, however, conflicts in this area have become more visible in a number of countries.[29] The 1958 coordination requirements to promote labor mobility mean that national welfare regimes have partially lost control over beneficiaries. Member states may not target benefits at their citizens only; they must include all EU "foreigners" employed in their territory. Since the ECJ interprets this principle strictly, in the sense that any de facto discrimination against nationals of other EU members is illegal, a traditional means of excluding noncitizens is no longer at the disposal of the national legislator.[30] Member states may still decide whether to provide benefits at all, but most forms of discrimination against EU nationals are supranationally precluded, and that preclusion is tightly policed.[31] The use of welfare state building for nation building—a common continental tradition—has thus become more difficult.

A second element of national control is *spatial control over consumption*. Traditionally, welfare state benefits were to be consumed within the nation-state. Their conjunctural macroeconomic effects, for example, depended on benefit consumption occurring within national markets. Only under exceptional circumstances could benefits be "exported" elsewhere. Benefits were not just *for* nationals but also *nation-bound*. With coordination however, benefits have been made portable within the European Union. All of EU Europe is to be treated as if it were part of one's own national territory. Thus in principle exportation is unlimited. Major ECJ

29. Quite a few examples of legal conflict have to do with Germany, since it was a major receiving country for migration in the 1950s and 1960s. The United Kingdom and France also figure heavily in the ECJ caseload, although the courts and legal professions of smaller member states were often more active in the early supranationalization of their cases. For practical reasons we focus largely on German examples in the following discussion. To treat the impact of EU law in a comprehensive way would require a team of legal experts from each member state.

30. This principle holds for all public outputs, not just for social policy. See P. von Wilmowsky, "Zugang zu den öffentlichen Leistungen anderer Mitgliedstaaten (Das Integrationskonzept des EWG-Vertrages in der Leistungsverwaltung)," *Zeitschrift für ausländisches öffentliches Völkerrecht*, 1990, pp. 231–81.

31. In keeping with the EU's focus on labor markets, beneficiary control through coordination is addressed not to citizens but to employees. The scope of this category has gradually expanded, however. *Employment* is defined broadly, and includes the self-employed; coverage is now usually extended to the preemployed (trainees) and formerly employed. The final step would be expansion to all citizens—from which a universal coordination regime would follow, since the employment nexus would be broken. See Hans F. Zacher, "Wechselwirkungen zwischen dem Europäischen Sozialrecht und dem Sozialrecht der Bundesrepublik Deutschland—Einführungsreferat aus sozialrechtlicher Sicht," in Schulte and Zacher, eds., *Wechselwirkungen*, pp. 11–26.

social cases have involved many member states, among them Belgium and Italy (concerning minimum social pensions), France (child benefits), Germany (child allowances, stipends, services), and the United Kingdom (occupational pensions).[32]

Exportability is fairly unproblematic for permanent, long-term benefits, like pension rights of all sorts, although enhanced portability does produce pressures to harmonize access formulas (age limits, definitions of invalidity, and so on).[33] Additive company pension benefits, which are now regulated at the national level, are becoming a challenge for European legislation, because they hinder the movement of the most mobile in today's European labor market: managers and professionals. There is no easy coordinating solution, however, without extensive interference in the benefits market. Furthermore, the southward mobility of EU pensioners, particularly from Denmark, Germany, and the United Kingdom, is beginning to make itself felt, especially when the southern country has to confront the costs of caring for the aged.[34] At the other end of the age spectrum, portability is guaranteed for family allowances, which are considered social security even though they may be organized as universal benefits for all citizens.[35] Legal problems have also arisen in connection with Germany's attempt to count child rearing as if it were paid work for the purpose of calculating pension entitlements.[36]

32. *Frilli*, ECR 457 (1976). Also, Belgian cases (*Defrenne I* and *II*) were central in developing gender equality rulings according to article 119. See also ECR 1427 (1983); ECR 1745 (1985); *Pinna I*, ECR 17 (1986); and Case 359/87, *Pinna II*.

33. Franz Ruland, "Rentenversicherung," in Schulte and Zacher, eds., *Wechselwirkungen*, pp. 47–81; and "Der Europäische Binnenmarkt und die sozialen Alterssicherungssysteme," *Deutsche Rentenversicherung*, 1989, pp. 605–29. On invalidity, see Rolf Schuler, "Soziale Sicherung für den Fall der Invalidität, des Alters und des Todes unter Zurücklassung Hinterbliebener," in Deutscher Sozialrechtsverband, *Europäisches Sozialrecht* (Wiesbaden: Chmielorz, 1992), pp. 79–113.

34. Diana Seiler, "Sozialpolitische Aspekte der internationalen Mobilität von Rentnern—insbesondere von deutschen Rentnern in Spanien," Ph.D. dissertation, Bremen University, 1994.

35. Since the EU regulation focuses on the place of employment, the family benefit regime in the country of employment applies even if some part of the family lives outside the country of employment. In a series of ECJ decisions concerning Germany and France, the ECJ has defended the exportation of family benefits. France had long sought to protect its high family benefits and to territorialize its pronatalist policy by relying on the residence principle—see *Pinna I* and *II*, cited in n. 32. The 1971 regulatory compromise, later dislodged by the ECJ in its *Pinna* decisions, introduced the principle of "country of employment" for all member states except France, where the country of residence still held. The ECJ found this exception to be discriminatory.

36. The policy was to be limited to children raised in Germany, even if the child-rearing parent was employed in Germany before and after child rearing in another country. This

Despite considerable administrative difficulties, exportability also applies to health insurance, although the "Europatient" with a "Eurocard" is not yet on the horizon.[37] Two categories of nonnationals seeking medical treatment have to be distinguished: (1) the tourist falling sick; and (2) the already sick person touring for a cure. In the first case, all treatment that is "immediately necessary" may be obtained. The foreign service provider must recover costs from the insurance institution in the country of employment, and the EU is working on a Europewide medical card to facilitate access.[38]

In the second case, which potentially has much more far-reaching consequences, national law usually requires permission from the consumer's insurance institution. The ECJ initially held that permission could be refused only if treatment was deemed medically unnecessary or inappropriate, but now, under national law, permission can be denied except for medical services that cannot be obtained in due time in the consumer's national territory. Whether this broader restriction conforms to EU law regarding free mobility of services remains undecided.[39] Impediments to mobility for social service consumers seem to be collapsing, however, not only because of the ECJ's liberal interpretations of the treaty but also because of the competitive pressures among the different insurance carriers. Furthermore, concern about the mobility of consumers merges at this point with the doctrine of "freedom of services," which in the view

---

issue has been taken up by the Commission. The German federal government's position: "The new transfer cannot be extended to all of Europe. The Federal Republic is only responsible for the welfare of births taking place on its territory. . . . Welfare reform would become generally impossible if such transfers had to be extended Europe-wide." Ruland, "Rentenversicherung," p. 55.

37. An EU sickness insurance passport, designed to be an instrument for easy access, is currently under discussion. Regarding place of employment versus citizenship as a qualifier for access, Voirin says: "In the EC context it is not possible to rely on the national passport as an access key (as is the practice in the northern countries in their interrelationships and vis à vis Great Britain since social security protection in these countries is universal and recoupment procedures among these countries are not provided for)." Michel Voirin, "Die Freizügigkeit zwischen den Mitgliedsstaaten der Europäischen Wirtschaftsgemeinschaft: praktische Auswirkungen auf die Träger der sozialen Sicherheit," *Internationale Revue für soziale Sicherheit*, vol. 45, no. 3 (1993), pp. 61–77, quote at p. 68; and Voirin, "Soziale Sicherheit und Europäischer Binnenmarkt: Welche Gemeinschaftsmaßnahmen im Hinblick auf 1993?" *Internationale Revue für soziale Sicherheit*, vol. 43, nos. 1, 2 (1991), pp. 47–84.

38. Voirin, "Freizügigkeit," p. 68.

39. Case 117/77, *Pierik*, ECR 825 (1978); and Case 182/78, *Pierik II*, ECR 1977 (1979).

of the ECJ generally includes the freedom of consumers to choose where and from whom they want to be served.

If exportability requirements have become a modest issue for long-term benefits, they raise more significant difficulties for short-term benefits. Truly sovereign welfare states may freely choose any policy structures, including any mix of monetary or in-kind transfers (*regime control*). Though these maxims still hold sway within the European Union, coordination requirements have made large cracks in the wall.[40] National control over social policy is limited by the need to accommodate the coordination doctrine. Welfare state benefits that can be construed as "earned" rights can be more easily coordinated without massive leakage to other member states. Coordination requirements work best with individualized, earned social rights of the employed, and worst with collective provision of services to all citizens. Policymakers are thus encouraged to follow the program designs of Bismarck (benefits based on contribution) rather than Beveridge (universal, flat-rate benefits). These requirements for coordination are likely to restrict many national social policies. In particular, member states will not be permitted to offer minimum unemployment or pension benefits based on past employment to their own citizens without also extending those benefits to other EU citizens who have worked in the country or who moved there in search of work. Payments must be exportable—they cannot be made conditional on residence or job seeking in a specific member state. In contrast, in-kind transfers (public housing, for example) may be more easily targeted on "locals."

This restriction will make it more difficult for member states to employ a significant part of their policy repertoire for combating low incomes. National income transfer programs (child allowances, minimum pension benefits) that do not rely on worker contributions are likely to lose favor. To escape the dilemma created by EU requirements, national welfare states may turn to contribution-based transfers and increase their emphasis on in-kind programs. In Germany, for example, the exportability

40. This mushiness is also noted in Schulte and Zacher, eds., *Wechselwirkungen*, p. 15: "Coordination originally dealt with systems explicitly addressed to social security proper ('acquired rights'). The borders to other social policies (housing assistance, college aid, welfare) and between social and general administrative services (as in a national health service) have become very diffuse over time. Also, in recent times, 'income packaging' between public and private security schemes have come to the fore, putting pressure on the coordination of private schemes (e.g., company pensions) too."

requirement was a major reason for the failure in the 1980s of a reform initiative to set minimum pension levels.[41]

Exportability rules may entail only incremental adjustments in those European welfare states relying mainly on contributory systems. Still, the rules will affect child allowances, youth welfare, welfare, and parts of unemployment insurance in many member states. Some smaller member states, like the Netherlands and Denmark (and now Sweden), which have a long-standing universalist tradition, will be under EU-induced pressure for more substantial reforms. One general effect observable in many countries and cases is that national welfare reforms are restructured to evade requirements of equal access and, especially, portability. If minimum pensions can be reorganized as welfare, they will not go to a Portuguese migrant worker who has returned to Portugal. If transfers for old-age care are made in the form of in-kind services and not as monetary transfers, they can be attached to national territory and need not be provided to those who have moved to Spain or Italy. Germany's new long-term care insurance (*Pflegeversicherung*), introduced in 1994, is a good example. The novel program provides payments to the care giver rather than to the beneficiary. This procedure circumvents the possibility of benefits leaking over German borders, unless the ECJ chooses to object.[42] Coordination thus affects national welfare regimes partly by encouraging shifts toward service structures. In contrast to the comprehensive effects mentioned above (loss of beneficiary control and loss of control over spatial consumption), these effects appear incrementally as member states consider social policy reforms.

National control over the design of social policy is stymied also where social policy packages combine income transfers with social service strategies. Since only the cash transfers, and not the in-kind benefits or services, can be exported, these packages fall apart when applied to migrant workers. Prominent examples include disability benefits, which are often

---

41. The writings of German officials on social policy abound with free-rider prognoses vis-à-vis other EU citizens, especially those from peripheral EU countries. See, for example, Peter Clever, "Soziale Sicherheit im Rahmen der europäischen Integration—Perspektiven nach dem Maastrichter Gipfel," in *Die Angestelltenversicherung*, vol. 39 (1992), pp. 296–304; and Peter Clever, "Grundsätzliche Bemerkungen zur Rechtsprechung des EuGH," *Deutsche Angestelltenversicherung*, no. 2 (1993), pp. 71–75. On the limits to German pension reform, see Manfred Zuleeg, "Die Zahlung von Ausgleichszulagen über die Binnengrenzen der Europäischen Gemeinschaft," *Deutsche Rentenversicherung*, no. 10 (1989), pp. 621–29.

42. The comments of a German labor ministry official make this motivation clear. Gerd Meyering, "Der internationale Bezug," *Bundesarbeitsblatt*, nos. 8, 9 (1994), pp. 58–60.

tied to rehabilitative services, and unemployment benefits linked to various job training programs.[43]

Unemployment insurance (UI) remains the main exception to exportability requirements for short-term benefits. Social policy regimes here still restrict mobility, leaving the unemployed under the authority of the regime of the country of last employment. Free movement of the employed, as guaranteed in articles 48 and 51 of the Treaty of Rome, is hindered rather than enhanced by EU regulation. Unemployment transfers may be exported for just three months, and only if certain conditions obtain and the UI administration grants permission.[44] If a person does not return after three months, all further benefits are forfeited. The restrictive legal structure for unemployment benefits, often defended as necessary to ensure control over a recipient's "availability to work," provides a clear indication that the single European labor market still has significant internal barriers to labor mobility. This is a likely area for change, be it through initiatives of the Council or of the ECJ.[45] The change might move the responsibility for coordination from the country of last employment to the country of actual residence, which would imply the creation of an EU-wide control mechanism for the legitimate use of benefits.[46]

Other effects of mobility requirements are, so far, less widespread but indicative of the same trend. *Exclusivity* is lost when the national welfare state no longer automatically applies to all those employed in a national territory. Some major exceptions to coordination requirements are relevant here. "Posted and seconded workers"—workers contracted by a company in one country for jobs in another—can maintain the social security status and minimum wage standards of their country of origin for up to two years; an extension for five or even ten years seems possible.

43. Karl-Jürgen Bieback, "Harmonisation of Social Policy in the European Community," *Les Cahiers de Droit*, vol. 32, (December 1991), pp. 913–35.

44. Regulation 1408/71, art. 69. If permission is granted, the benefit—at the original level received in the member state of employment—is paid out by the unemployment agency of the country of residence and then refunded by the insurance agency in the member state of employment.

45. Eberhard Eichenhofer, "Themenbereich Arbeitsförderung/Soziale Sicherung für Arbeitslose: Einführender Diskussionsbeitrag," in Schulte and Zacher, eds., *Wechselwirkungen*, pp. 189–93; and Eberhard Eichenhofer, "Freizügigkeit und Europäisches Arbeitsförderungsrecht," *Zeitschrift für ausländisches und internationales Arbeits-und Sozialrecht*, vol. 5 (1991), pp. 161–93.

46. This is how U.S. unemployment insurance solves the conflict; for a comparison, see Eberhard Eichenhofer, *Recht der Sozialen Sicherheit in den USA* (Baden-Baden: Nomos 1990).

Here again national welfare states may face the much-feared competition with countries maintaining lower social wages, but in a new form. "Regime competition" takes place between different national systems at the sectoral level in one national social space rather than between whole societies occupying separate territories. So far, this has mainly affected the construction and transport industries and has led to considerable conflict in Germany over the past year.[47] The concept of a "European Company," still being worked out in Brussels, will also limit the application of national welfare law; instead of a business moving "outward," it can stay put and move upward into a new trans-European legal regime, further limiting the reach of national social policy.

These aspects of control (beneficiary control, spatial control over consumption and exclusivity) are relevant in the quite common case of divided families, meaning, in this instance, families with a wage earner working in one member state and other family members residing in another. EU law considers it an unwarranted hindrance to mobility to expect that all conditions for an entitlement must be met within the national territory. To take some examples from Germany, child-rearing benefits in German pension insurance (which treats child rearing as if it were paid work) are granted even if the child is raised outside Germany, provided the mother is tied to the German labor market before and after child rearing. When unemployment benefits are calculated, family members resident in other EU states have to be treated as if they were living in Germany.[48] German child allowances paid for unemployed youth must also be paid to unemployed children not resident in Germany, whether they are in Italy or any other member state (*Bronzino* and *Gatto*).[49] Educational stipends are granted to foreign residents in Germany even if

---

47. See Mosley, "Social Dimension." An EU directive on minimum standards for posted or seconded workers is being discussed, which would require that workers who are in a member state for longer than three months be treated to the same minimum vacations and minimum wages. See Karl-Jürgen Bieback, "Marktfreiheit in der EG und nationale Sozialpolitik vor und nach Maastricht," *Europarecht*, no. 2 (1993), pp. 150–72; he points to KOM (91) 230 endg., BR-Drs. 547/91; see also Case C-113/89, *Rush Portuguesa*, ECR 1417 (1990).

48. This issue is controversial and remains unsettled.

49. ECR I 531 (1990). Eberhard Eichenhofer takes this to be a crucial case, as the ECJ overruled expressly contradicting EC regulation. It applied the treaty (article 51) as higher law, to the end that conditions stipulated in the substantive welfare law of one member state and fulfilled in another member state always have to be treated as fulfilled in the stipulating state. Eichenhofer, "Die Rolle des Europäischen Gerichtshofes bei der Entwicklung des Europäischen Sozialrechts," *Die Sozialgerichtsbarkeit*, vol. 39, no. 12 (1992), pp. 573–80.

their children want to study in their home country, on the same terms that they are granted to German students who want to study in a foreign country (*di Leo*).[50]

Finally, labor mobility requirements are undermining *administrative case control*. A sovereign welfare state decides who is to get its benefits; these decisions are never entrusted to foreign welfare states. But here too coordination rules, as understood by the ECJ, have lessened such control over benefits in cases in which transfers and labor market concerns clearly overlap: disability, invalidity, and short-term sickness. As Karl-Jürgen Bieback observes:

> Exporting rights means that quite a few requirements for benefits like disability and invalidity and their degree have to be checked and decided by the social security administration of another Member State. . . . The foreign administration's decision has to bind all other administrations because it may affect requirements which are common to different benefits in different countries, it may cost too much to examine the claimant in all countries and the migrant worker may not be capable to undertake the necessary travelling. Therefore it makes much sense that the ECJ has, in a fairly generous interpretation of the regulations, strengthened the binding power of these decisions. However, such administrative practices demand a basic similarity of legal requirements, expressions and procedures. Otherwise this necessary coordination will not work effectively.[51]

These decisions have been heavily criticized in Germany as uncontrollable impositions of foreign authority over German social policy.[52] Yet the Court has strongly rebuffed this member-state resistance. In the case of invalidity, the Germans tried to block external controls by specifying in an annex to the relevant EU regulation that only the German insurance record would be relevant for determining the claimant's "obtaining profession." The ECJ annulled this exemption on the grounds

50. ECR I 4185 (1990); an Italian woman who grew up and lived in Germany applied for a German government stipend to study medicine in Italy. For the expansive realm of EC activity in the field of education, see Klaus Sieveking, "Bildung im Europäischen Gemeinschaftsrecht," *Kritische Vierteljahresschrift für Gesetzgebung und Rechtswissenschaft,* vol. 73, nos. 3, 4 (1990), pp. 344–73; and Bruno de Witte, ed., *European Community Law of Education* (Baden-Baden: Nomos, 1989).

51. Bieback, "Harmonisation," p. 934.

52. Rüdiger Neumann-Duesberg, "Krankenversicherung," in Schulte and Zacher, eds., *Wechselwirkungen,* pp. 83–109.

that it conflicted with EU constitutional (treaty) principles.[53] Similarly, in a case involving an Italian working in Germany who had been on vacation in his home country, the Court held that the German sick fund had to accept an Italian doctor's finding of "inability to work" (*Rindone*), even if there were indications of fraudulent practice (*Paletta I*).[54] Thus doctors in other member states become administrative gatekeepers for German welfare state benefits.

There is still quite a gap to be filled before access to the welfare state is granted to anyone with EU member-state citizenship who moves across any EU border, a situation which obtains in most fully federalized states.[55] Coordination applies only to those attached to a national labor market (or to the families of those so attached), and not to EU citizenship per se. The ECJ has tried to bridge this gap in two ways. First, it introduced a definition of employment that goes far beyond national social security regulations.[56] Second, and more radically, the ECJ has used "free

---

53. *Roviello*, ECR 2805 (1988). The ECJ regards this as indirect discrimination against foreign workers, since upward professional mobility in another member state would have been precluded by such an exception.

54. ECR 1339 (1987). *Paletta II* is now pending as Case 206/94, *Brennet AG v. Vittorio Pannetta*, by request of the German Federal Labor Law Court of 1994; see "Arbeitsunfähigkeit im Ausland attestierbar?" *Euroreport 1994*, vol. 2, no. 5 (1994), pp. 10–11.

55. This is the situation in the United States, for example. Bryant G. Garth sees this as the threshold to a truly federal welfare state; see Garth, "Migrant Workers and Rights of Mobility in the European Community and the United States: A Study of Law, Community and Citizenship in the Welfare State," in Mauro Cappelletti, Monica Secombe, and Joseph Weiler, eds., *Europe and the American Federal Experience*, vol. 1, *Methods, Tools and Institutions* (Berlin: de Gruyter, 1986), pp. 85–163. One might note, however, that this comparison is biased. In the United States few welfare rights flow from the right to movement, because universal rights to welfare in the United States are only marginally institutionalized. In Europe, by contrast, the full crossing of this threshold would open access to a broad range of policies. The access achieved in Europe—through coordination (and the ECJ's wide definition of *employed*) and the "free mobility of service consumers"—may be worth as much to potential beneficiaries as what is currently obtainable to those crossing state lines in the United States.

56. This too involves a loss of sovereignty for the nation-state, namely, the loss of national control over the definition of legal categories that have traditionally ordered national social relations. EU law, for example, treats both civil servants and other wage earners as employees. This is similar to English law but quite different from that of Germany and France, which draw a distinction between civil servants and other employees and have quite different welfare-state and labor-market arrangements for each category. Also, EU welfare law comprises labor and social security law, areas which in the German tradition are distinct disciplines with separate court tracks. Germany must again incorporate a more comprehensive view. The EU also forces equal access to much of the civil service, devaluing the service's privileged social security status. Finally, the concept of *indirect discrimination*, that is, discrimination by outcome, which the ECJ introduced into discrimination by na-

movement of services" as an entering wedge at the individual level.[57] All EU citizens—"service consumers"—are free to consume services in any member state, and their lives and security have to be protected by that member's welfare state just as it protects the lives and safety of its own citizens. To take a prominent case, an Englishman visiting France to see his children was mugged in the Paris Métro. The ECJ, overruling the French courts, saw him as relying on French services and awarded him the same right to public indemnities against damages that a French citizen would have had.[58] Thus mobile member-state citizens are also connected to the welfare state in which they make use of their service consumption rights, entitled like any citizen of that state to basic protective transfers.

The individual consumer's freedom to shop out of state, once it is extensively exercised, could be quite consequential.[59] Bieback's example of the interface between market and national health systems may demonstrate the effect. Prices for hospitals in Germany do not reflect real costs, but only costs for services and materials associated with actual treatment. Investment costs, such as hospital construction, are paid by the *Länder* and the federal government. An EU citizen from another member state should therefore find it quite attractive to seek treatment in a German hospital at German prices. According to EU law, charging the full price only to EU foreigners constitutes discriminatory pricing. The full price could be charged only if the health provision regime itself were changed so that German and non-German alike paid the full costs. As Bieback concludes, since "the right of free access to all goods and services within the common market does not allow charging persons from Member States more than one's own citizens, the free common market will jeopardize all systems of subsidies for social services."[60]

Over the past thirty years a complex patchwork of regulations and court decisions has partially abridged the principle of member-state sovereignty over social policy. In the interests of encouraging mobility in the European labor market (and now consumer mobility as well), national

---

tionality and by gender, did not fall on hospitable ground in the German legal culture and thus forced a reconsideration of national views on equal treatment.

57. The ECJ distinguishes between passive and active freedom of services. The passive freedom, covering consumers, was developed in *Luisi* and *Carbone*, ECR 377 (1984). We treat this issue here since it is used to fill gaps in coordination. Active freedom of services, which concerns producers, is treated separately below.

58. Case 186/87, *Cowan*, ECR 195 (1989).

59. See Hans Sendler, "Themenbereich Krankenversicherung. Einführender Diskussionsbeitrag," in Schulte and Zacher, eds., *Wechselwirkungen*, pp. 169–76.

60. Bieback, "Harmonisation," p. 931.

capacities to contain transfers by territory have been curtailed.[61] The implications are the following:

—A member state may no longer limit social benefits to its citizens. The state no longer has any power to determine whether EU foreigners have a right to benefits or not. Benefits must be granted to all or withheld from all. This development is remarkable because citizen making through social benefits—the demarcation of outsiders—was a watershed in the history of state building on the continent, especially in France and Germany.

—A member state may no longer insist that its benefits apply only within its territory and thus must be consumed only there. As a result, today's member state can exercise its power to determine the territory of consumption only to a limited extent—basically when providing in-kind or means-tested benefits.

—A member state is no longer entirely—though it is still largely—in a position to prevent other social policy regimes from directly competing with the regime it has built on its own territory. Thus the state has lost its exclusive power to determine how the people living within its borders are protected.

—Member states do not have an exclusive right to implement claims to welfare benefits. Rather, the authorities of other nations may also have a decisive say in adjudicating benefit status in individual cases.

If complete de jure authority in these respects is what sovereignty in social policy is all about, it has already ceased to exist in the European Union. This has been a complex process in which supranational efforts to broaden access and national efforts to maintain control go hand in hand and are calibrated from conflict to conflict, court case by court case.

This transformation has not occurred without member-state resistance. Individually, member states have balked at implementing particular facets of coordination, although the ECJ has effectively taken them to task for this. Collectively, the member states have recently sought to roll back some aspects of coordination, unanimously agreeing to revisions that will allow member states, after giving proper "notification," to restrict portability in a range of cases.[62] The impact of this shift re-

61. Bernd Baron v. Maydell, "Einführung in die Schlußdiskussion," in Schulte and Zacher, eds., *Wechselwirkungen*, pp. 229–36. For an overview on the future of coordination, see Eberhard Eichenhofer, ed., *Die Zukunft des koordinierenden Europäischen Sozialrechts* (Köln: Carl Heymanns, 1992).

62. Notification must be approved by unanimous vote of the member states, although so far there seems to be a gentleman's agreement to allow such self-exemptions. To date,

mains unclear, though it may partially offset some loss of sovereignty. The notification agreement must still pass muster from the ECJ.

Nonetheless, coordination has become the catalyst for an incremental, rights-based, homogenization of social policy. Neither supranationalization nor harmonization seems an appropriate label for this dynamic, because each implies a stronger policy center than currently exists. The process is more a marketplace of coordination, with the ECJ acting as market police, enforcing the boundaries of national autonomy. It structures the interfaces of fifteen national social policy systems, with potentially far-reaching consequences for the range of policy options available to national welfare states.

The Common Market for Services and the Reshaping of Social Policy

The doctrine of free movement of services directly affects national welfare states, though the scope of its impact remains opaque. Although coordination issues have been worked out in hundreds of ECJ decisions spanning almost four decades, the real influence of the doctrine of free movement of services surfaced only with the passage of the Single European Act of 1986. It has generated only a few leading cases and comparatively little secondary Community law, but—judging from the general impact of the single market, the pervasive effects on the private insurance industry, and the high level of agitation in the specialist literature—prospects for remolding national policies in the social services, especially in health care, appear to be significant.[63]

In principle, so it used to be thought, each state may choose its own policies for social services. European law grants all qualifying member-state nationals only "access rights" to the given national structure. However, as Bieback notes, "national regulations of markets can be subject to control by community law with regard to their function as a nontariff barrier of free trade [articles 30 and 36]. Therefore they have to comply

---

these have been exercised largely by the "Latin rim" countries and by Britain. This change of coordination law represents an interesting contrast to the "lock-in" procedures and ratchet effects that are common at the EU level. Bernd Schulte, "Comments on Articles 4, 10a, and 5 of Regulation 1408/71," in Maximilian Fuchs, ed., *Nomos Kommentar zum Europäischen Sozialrecht* (Baden-Baden: Nomos, 1994).

63. Schulte, "Einführung in die Schlußdiskussion," pp. 237–52. For a view that suggests greater stability in health care systems, see Christa Altenstetter, "Health Policy Regimes and the Single European Market," *Journal of Health Politics, Policy and Law*, vol. 17 (Winter 1992), pp. 813–46.

with the principle of proportionality, i.e., they have to be necessary and appropriate for attaining the goals of the national regulatory system."[64] The ECJ may subject system characteristics themselves to a proportionality test. As a result, particular policy designs may face pressure to allow open competition in service provision.

The freedom of services doctrine may have considerable effects on national service delivery systems, limiting member-state control over access to the status of benefit producer. Here the divergent characteristics of the policy structures of member states become crucial. For example, some member states (Britain and Italy among them) have national health care programs with marginalized markets or nonmarket systems. In other insurance systems (in Germany, France, and the Netherlands, for example) the state supplies funds for goods and services, which are bought from private providers. As Bieback observes, "According to the ECJ the free movement of services clause in Article 59 of the Treaty of Rome applies only to services dealt with in markets and supplied for money, but not for services which are usually delivered as part of a 'national service.' Thus countries which organize their health service systems on the basis of private markets where public and private suppliers may compete and access is free, like the systems of social insurance in France and Germany, are open for competition from suppliers from other countries, whereas the 'National Health systems' are closed, except if they incorporate competitive structures like parts of the British system."[65]

Whereas access of foreign providers in nonmarket systems is a nonissue, access of foreign private deliverers in quasi-market systems is buttressed by Community law.[66] This may create a deregulatory dynamic, especially when regimes rely on closed national producer markets for social services.[67] These "closed shops" in welfare state production are

64. Bieback, "Harmonisation," p. 929.

65. Bieback, "Harmonisation," p. 932.

66. Some producers are more likely than others to take this route: "The Single Market for social services should be most valuable for private, international service organizations in fields such as hospitals, old age care and rehabilitation institutions, drug store chains and other providers of medical equipment, as seems to be the case in the US welfare state. The large organizations will then compete with national, nonprofit organizations, which have fewer resources and a smaller capacity for rationalization at their disposal. In addition, these nonprofit organizations will compete with each other across borders. Both tendencies will not be without effect on their structure and their outlook or orientation." Bieback, "Marktfreiheit," p. 171; authors' translation. Such producers are likely to become strong actors at the EU level through dealings with the Commission or the Courts.

67. The process seems to have moved furthest with national drug markets. Directive 89/105 has already set Unionwide minimum standards regarding price controls and price

not just market-access issues. Regulations protecting the homogeneity of provider groups are also important because they underpin national welfare cultures, stabilizing the large differences among the fifteen EU welfare states.

For the medical profession, the impact of freedom of services is most visible at the borders of countries.[68] Where Germany borders the Netherlands, for example, a number of Dutch dentists have offered their services on German territory because the Dutch *numerus clausus* limits the number of dental-service providers to one doctor for every 3,250 inhabitants; Germany has no similar restriction. Since EU regulation eroded Germany's original defense mechanism (nonrecognition of non-German medical degrees), Dutch doctors can freely settle across the border. From 1983 to 1987, the number of Dutch dentists on the German side of the border increased from 11 to 387.

Such effects are not limited to health care. The ECJ in April 1991 decided that the "monopoly of labor market placement" granted to German Federal Unemployment Insurance conflicts with EU law by infringing on the right of service entrepreneurs to sell their services in the market. The ECJ ruled that the German UI agency, though public, is subject to EU regulation of competition and that the placement of highly qualified labor, managers, and so on should rightfully be open to EU-wide as well as to German private competition.[69]

The developing free market of services can be seen in most dramatic form in the rapidly evolving private insurance market. On July 1, 1994, national private insurance was turned into a common market of the twelve EU member states. The furious pace of cross-border mergers and acquisitions made newspaper headlines. What is emerging is a more

---

fixing. Because equivalent pharmaceuticals are much cheaper in some other European countries, sickness-fund administrators in Germany are quite interested in importing such drugs. In addition, the Commission has developed proposals for a "Single Drug Market," which would strongly, though indirectly, harmonize national health insurance systems (by, for example, undoing price controls and introducing significant copayments). In 1994 the European Pharmaceutical Agency began its oversight and licensing work, under European law. "EuGH: EG-Recht regel Arzneimittelzulassung abschließend," *Euroreport 1994*, vol. 2, no. 2, pp. 3–4; and "Europäische Arzneimittelagentur nimmt Arbeit auf," *Euroreport 1994*, vol. 2, no. 5, p. 3.

68. Neumann-Duesberg, "Krankenversicherung," p. 103.

69. ECJ Case C-41/90, *Höfner and Elsner*, April 23, 1991; and *Europäische Zeitschrift für Wirtschaftsrecht* (1991), p. 349. This court decision tilted a long-standing German national debate in the direction of loosening the monopoly through a federal program of experimentation with private provision (*Frankfurter Allgemeine Zeitung*, August 10, 1993, p. 11). Since August 1, 1994, private provision has been allowed in Germany.

heavily concentrated insurance sector operating at the European level. This integrated private sector now confronts fifteen national, internally segmented public insurance domains. The results of the public-private interplay in the context of a radically altered private sector are difficult to anticipate. There is, however, considerable evidence from studies of national welfare states that the reform of private sector markets can have dramatic effects on public service provision.[70] Public and private insurance compete mainly in areas such as occupational pensions, life insurance, and supplemental health insurance. Permanent turf quarrels between the public sector and private firms seem likely about where basic (public) coverage should end and additional (private) insurance should begin. The ongoing struggle over the introduction of European Mutual Societies, a special European welfare company statute, points in the same direction.[71]

The balance between a free market in services and institutionally autonomous national welfare states, two principles embedded in the EC constitution, is thus not static but dynamic.[72] Here is open terrain for Brussels, an area with the potential for restructuring the delivery of national social services. The question of balance is likely to be particularly problematic for the Nordic countries that have just entered the Union, for they have systematically tried to marginalize private competition in social service provision. Kåre Hagen argues that the

political ambitions of providing high- and equal-quality health care to all segments of the population have required the extensive use of public monopolies that may militate against enterprise freedoms guaranteed by Community legislation. The same applies to state restrictions on private pension insurance and on how their funds are to be managed. In general, any kind of state welfare policy which is deliberately designed to prevent private purchasing power from being reproduced in the consumption of welfare goods sup-

70. See, for example, Martin Rein and Lee Rainwater, eds., *Public-Private Interplay in Social Protection: A Comparative Study* (Armonk, N.Y.: M. E. Sharpe, 1986).

71. See Hans F. Zacher and Francis Kessler, "Die Rolle der öffentlichen Verwaltung und der privaten Träger in der sozialen Sicherheit," *Zeitschrift für ausländisches und internationales Arbeits- und Sozialrecht*, vol. 4 (1990), pp. 97–157.

72. Some states have gone much further than others. Luxembourg is probably the first and only country that systematically arranged for "shopping" from many of the stationary health services of its neighboring countries.

plied by the market, will run counter to the freedoms of the common market.[73]

Since the two principles of a free market in services and national autonomy over social policy contradict each other, it is up to the EU to fix, again and again, an ever-shifting balance. Although coordination has been the main social policy item for the ECJ in the last three decades, other issues are coming to the fore. Freedom to supply social services (article 59), freedom to consume social services, and freedom of settlement are all issues tied to this newer challenge to the national welfare state.[74] As Bieback states, "As long as the Community opens the free market for social services there are only three options. Either the competence of the EC is extended to control and regulate the market for social services, or the Member States coordinate and harmonise their systems voluntarily, or finally all national systems of social services opt out of market systems into 'national' systems. Evidently, all options tend to increase the pressure towards harmonisation."[75] Two more points, then, need to be added to the list of restrictions on member-state sovereignty and autonomy:

—Member states may no longer mix market and state components at will in providing welfare, nor may they impose their preferred welfare mix of monetary transfers, in-kind payments, and services. Their power to determine the makeup of the welfare state is being reduced.

—Member states can no longer exclusively decide who may provide social services or benefits. They cannot determine the nature of social service professions, because mutual recognition of degrees and licenses from other member states intervene. And their capacity to protect their national service organizations from the competitive efforts of similar groups in other member states is circumscribed.

Relying only on cases concerning labor mobility and freedom of services, we have been able to document a wide range of market compatibility requirements through which either EU regulations or ECJ decisions impinge on the design and reform of national social policy. Examples related to the single market—restrictions on firm subsidies, for instance—

73. Kåre Hagen, "The Social Dimension: A Quest for a European Welfare State," in Zsuzsa Ferge and Jøn Eivind Kolberg, eds., *Social Policy in a Changing Europe* (Boulder, Colo.: Westview Press, 1992), pp. 281–303.

74. Bernd Schulte, "Europäisches Sozialrecht: Juristische Einführung und Überblick," in Deutscher Sozialrechtsverband, *Europäisches Sozialrecht*, pp. 7–50.

75. Bieback, "Harmonisation," p. 932.

also abound. The central government in Italy, for example, had used abatements of social insurance taxes to attract investment to the Mezzogiorno. The Commission agreed to permit this strategy until the end of 1993, but initiated ECJ proceedings against the continuation of the practice on the grounds of "unfair competition."[76] Social policies for particular sectors (for example, miners or farmers) are facing increasing scrutiny. Changes in Germany's social insurance system for farmers, for instance, now require Brussels' approval since such insurance is considered a sectoral subsidy. Examples could be multiplied. The broader point is clear: a whole range of policy designs that would be available to sovereign welfare states are prohibited to member states within the EU's multitiered polity.

European Integration and de Facto Pressures on National Welfare States

The European Union now intervenes directly in the social policies of member states in two ways: by enacting some significant social policy initiatives of its own and by striking down features of national systems that are deemed incompatible with the development of the single market. In addition, the process of European integration has consequential, though less direct, effects on the social policies of member states; the economic policies of the European Union and the responses of social actors to those policies pressure national welfare states to adapt their social programs. Because these effects are indirect they are difficult to measure, but they nonetheless add to the general picture of increasing supranational constraints on the design of national social policy.

The most frequently cited source of pressure on welfare states within the EU is the possibility that heightened integration may lead to "social dumping." The term refers to the prospect that firms operating where social wages are low may be able to undercut the prices of competitors, forcing higher-cost firms to either go out of business, relocate to areas where social wages are low, or pressure their governments to reduce social wage costs. In extreme scenarios, these actions could fuel a downward spiral in social provision, eventually producing national welfare states with rudimentary, lowest-common-denominator policies.

76. "Rom-Brüssel: Entlastung von Sozialkosten im Visier," *Euroreport 1994*, vol. 2, no. 5, p. 9.

There is some evidence that these kinds of pressures have indeed restricted social expenditures in the United States, where labor (and capital)
mobility is far greater than in the EU.[77] Despite widespread attention to
this issue, however, there is little evidence that European integration will
fuel social dumping. As several observers have noted, the social wage is
only one factor in investment decisions, and firms will not invest in
countries with low social wages unless worker productivity (relative to
wages) justifies such investments. Neoclassical trade theory suggests that
countries with high social wages should be able to continue their policies
as long as overall conditions allow profitable investment.[78] One sign of
the ambiguous consequences of integration is the fact that northern Europe's concerns about "sunbelt effects" are mirrored by southern Europe's concerns about "agglomeration effects," in which investment
would flow toward the superior infrastructures and high-skilled work
forces of Europe's most developed regions.[79]

Some analysts have criticized the neoclassical perspective for ignoring
the fragility of the institutional networks that sustain the high-wage,
high-productivity economies (see Streeck, chapter 12). Rather than producing a flood of investment in the periphery countries and a race to the
bottom in social regulation, economic integration may lead to a more
gradual, indirect erosion of national social policy. There is little doubt
that the enhanced exit option for businesses strengthens their hand in
bargaining with governments and employees. Furthermore, even if maintenance of existing standards is collectively rational for business, it may

77. See chapter 9 in this volume for an fuller discussion of this issue. See also Paul E.
Peterson and Mark C. Rom, *Welfare Magnets: A New Case for a National Standard* (Brookings, 1990).

78. Though nominal wage costs vary dramatically, with the Netherlands and Portugal
marking the two extremes, unit labor costs—and therefore productivity—diverge much
less and point toward some advantages for low-wage, periphery member states. See Loukas
Tsoukalis, *The New European Economy: The Politics and Economics of Integration* (Oxford
University Press, 1st ed., 1993), p. 145, fig. 6.1.

79. Wolfgang Streeck, "The Social Dimension of the European Economy," paper prepared for the meeting of the Andrew Shonfield Association, Florence, European University
Institute, 1989; Jørn Henrik Petersen, "Harmonisation of Social Security in the EC Revis-
ited," *Journal of Common Market Studies*, vol. 29, no. 5 (1991), pp. 505–26; and Lange,
"Politics," pp. 239–44. In the third yearly report of the Commission on the Community's
employment situation, Social Policy Commissioner Vasso Papandreou stressed that regional
disparities in the single market between the center (the North) and the periphery have
increased slightly. Two factors in the periphery account for the increase: stronger demographic growth and job loss in the agricultural sector. Per capita buying power in Ireland,
Portugal, Spain, and Greece was less than 70 percent of the northern average, a return to
the distributional situation of 1975. *Frankfurter Allgemeine Zeitung*, July 19, 1991, p. 12.

not be rational for individual firms. Increased mobility may generate free-rider problems. Emboldened firms may use the threat of regime shopping to force the renegotiation of national or local bargains with unions and governments. In turn, such efforts could introduce a dynamic that gradually undermines tightly coupled systems of social policy and industrial relations, such as the German one. This is a more restricted scenario for social dumping, but it nonetheless implies growing pressure on national welfare state regimes.

Although social dumping may prompt greater fears than current evidence warrants, the opposite could be the case for some of the other ways that economic integration indirectly constrains national social policy. The single market is forcing a gradual movement toward a narrowed band of value-added tax (VAT) rates.[80] In theory, governments that find that their VAT revenues have been lowered will be free to increase other taxes, but this may be no simple task. Because indirect taxes are politically easier to sustain than direct levies, the new rules may create growing constraints on member-state budgets, with clear implications for national social policies.[81] This is likely to be a problem particularly for Denmark, which relies heavily on indirect taxes rather than payroll taxes to finance its generous welfare state.[82] To take two extremes, only 14 percent of the Danish social budget was financed by payroll taxes in 1990, while 79 percent came from state-tax revenues and 9 percent from other sources; for Germany the distribution is far different: 71, 26, and 3 percent.[83]

The move toward monetary union, with its tough requirements for budgetary discipline, may also encourage downward adjustments in welfare provision.[84] For example, to participate in the final stage of monetary

---

80. Pekka Kosonen, "The Impact of Economic Integration on National Welfare States in Europe," paper presented at the thirteenth World Congress of Sociology, Bielefeld, Germany, July 1994, pp. 15–21.

81. Harold J. Wilensky, *The "New Corporatism,"* Centralization and the Welfare State (Sage, 1976); and Douglas A. Hibbs and Henrik Jess Madsen, "Public Reactions to the Growth of Taxation and Government Expenditure," *World Politics*, vol. 33 (April 1981), pp. 413–45.

82. Petersen, "Harmonisation," pp. 514–22; Jørn Henrik Petersen, "Europäischer Binnenmarkt, Wirtschafts- und Wahrungsunion und die Harmonisierung der Sozialpolitik," *Deutsche Rentenversicherung*, nos. 1, 2 (January–February 1993), pp. 15–49; and Gerda Falkner, "Die Sozialpolitik im Maastrichter Vertragsgebäude der Europäischen Gemeinschaft," *SWS-Rundschau*, vol. 33, no. 1 (1993), pp. 23–43.

83. Schulte, "Sozialrecht," p. 409.

84. Full monetary union by the year 2000 now seems improbable in the extreme, though the movement of a core group of EU countries to further monetary integration is

union, Italy would have to reduce its budget deficit from 10 percent of gross domestic product to 3 percent of GDP by the end of the decade. This has served to legitimate the Italian government's intense pursuit of major cuts in old-age pensions and other social benefits. Although other countries face less radical adjustments, the convergence criteria present formidable problems for almost all of them. Here again there is tremendous uncertainty about these effects. Monetary union remains an uncertain proposition at best, and governments would have faced pressure for austerity in any event. The convergence criteria do not, of course *require* budget cuts—tax increases would also be possible—but they do enhance the position of those seeking such cuts.

Monetary union would not only put pressures on national social programs; it also could prod the Union into a more active role in efforts to combat unemployment. Analysis of the prospects for monetary integration in Europe has frequently been coupled with discussion of the need for accompanying social policies to address the likely emergence of regional imbalances. Monetary union would strip national governments of significant macroeconomic policy levers, and a Unionwide macroeconomic stance would spawn significant regional unemployment problems. Should monetary union occur, there are certain to be demands for a greater level of fiscal federalism.[85]

Evaluating the consequences of these various indirect pressures on national welfare states is not easy. Many of the potential problem areas lie in the future, and some of the others, such as social dumping, would be difficult to measure even if they were occurring now. The pressures for reform have to be weighed against the welfare state's evident resiliency.[86] Yet the picture that emerges is one in which national governments possess diminished control over many of the policies that have traditionally supported national welfare states—macroeconomic policies, tax pol-

---

possible. For good discussions of the status of the European monetary union, see Barry Eichengreen, "Should the Maastricht Treaty be Saved?" *Princeton Studies in International Finance*, no. 72 (December 1992); and David R. Cameron, "British Exit, German Voice, French Loyalty: Defection, Domination, and Cooperation in the 1992–93 ERM Crisis," paper presented at the annual meeting of the American Political Science Association, September 1993.

85. See Eichengreen, "Maastricht," pp. 32–37. As Ross notes, the Spanish stressed this implication of monetary union during the run-up to Maastricht and made it clear that they would not sign a new treaty unless it included a major expansion of regional redistribution. Ross, *Delors*, pp. 152–53.

86. Paul Pierson, *Dismantling the Welfare State? Reagan, Thatcher and the Politics of Retrenchment* (Cambridge University Press, 1994).

icies, perhaps industrial relations systems. These developments challenge the dominant view of a European market-building process that supposedly advances relentlessly while leaving the evolution of welfare states a purely national affair.

Social Policy in Europe's Emerging Multitiered System

Although the case is easier to make for issue areas such as regional policy or agriculture, even in traditional parts of social policy the member states of the European Union now constitute part of a multitiered system. Scholarly attention has focused mostly on Commission efforts to establish a "social dimension" of Unionwide policies, or at least minimum standards. To date, these efforts have modified member-state social policies in only a few areas. More important, though far less visible, are the social policy effects of the development of the single market. These have occurred either indirectly (through pressures on national welfare states) or directly, as the Commission, national courts, and the ECJ have sought to reconcile the policy autonomy of member states with the effort to create a unified economic space.

We are living in a period of rapid change in the relations between nation-states and a global market. According to David Held, "The central question to pose is: has sovereignty remained intact while the autonomy of the state has diminished or has the modern state faced a loss of sovereignty?"[87] In the European Union, member-state sovereignty and autonomy have diminished in tandem.[88] The process has been subtle and incremental, but developments within the Union as a whole increasingly constrain national welfare states. Member states now find their revenue bases under assault, their welfare reform options circumscribed, many of their service regimes under threat of new competition, and their administrators obliged to share control over policy enforcement.

What is emerging is a unique multitiered system of social policy with three distinctive characteristics: a "hollow core," a prominent role for courts in policy development, and an unusually tight coupling to market-making processes. The hollow core receives particular emphasis in chap-

87. David Held, "Democracy, the Nation-State and the Global System," in David Held, ed., *Political Theory Today* (Stanford University Press, 1991), pp. 197–235.

88. Stephan Leibfried, "The Social Dimension of the European Union: En Route to Positively Joint Sovereignty?" *Journal of European Social Policy*, vol. 4, no. 3 (1994), pp. 1–24.

ters 12 and 13 and requires only brief comment here. Compared to any other multitiered system, the European Union's social policymaking apparatus is extremely bottom-heavy.[89] The quite weak center has limited capacity to formulate positive social policy. Social policy evolution is therefore more likely to be the result of mutual adjustment and incremental accommodation than a consequence of central guidance. From the center come a variety of pressures and constraints on social policy development, but little in the way of clear mandates for positive action.

The influence of the constituent member states, their incentives for competitive state-building, and the legacies of preexisting national welfare regimes are likely to remain crucial in this context, but the hollow-core depiction of the EU reveals a weakening of the member states' position as well. With the gravitation of authority, even of a largely negative kind, to the European level, the capacity of member states to design their welfare states as they choose decreases. The role of the member states at this juncture is multifaceted, if not contradictory. Member states lost significant autonomy and sovereignty without paying a great deal of attention. In some cases—Italy's push for enhanced labor mobility, for example—member states championed sovereignty-eroding initiatives. Member states may now fear some of the single market's implications for their own power, but their capacity to resist is limited by their reluctance to jeopardize the hard-won benefits of European integration.

Member states have to choose from an increasingly restricted menu. Because control over social policy often means responsibility for announcing unpopular cutbacks, member-state governments sometimes are happy to accept arrangements that constrain their own options. Given the unpopularity of retrenchment, governments may find that blaming the EU allows changes that they would otherwise be afraid to contemplate. The movement toward a multitiered political system opens up new avenues for the politics of blame avoidance.[90] Some have suggested that this dynamic strengthens national executives at the expense of domestic opponents, and this may be the case.[91] Yet in the process of escaping

89. Mark Kleinman and David Piachaud, "European Social Policy: Conceptions and Choices," *Journal of European Social Policy*, vol. 3, no. 1 (1992), pp. 1–19; see also their analysis of "Britain and European Social Policy," *Policy Studies*, vol. 3 (Autumn 1992), pp. 13–25.

90. R. Kent Weaver, "The Politics of Blame Avoidance," *Journal of Public Policy*, vol. 6 (October–December 1986), pp. 371–98.

91. Alan S. Milward, *The European Rescue of the Nation State* (University of California

domestic constraints, national executives have created new ones that profoundly limit their options. Decisionmaking bodies at the supranational *and* the national levels must cope with institutional arrangements that circumscribe their capacity for social policy intervention.

The second distinctive characteristic of social policymaking in the EU is that the constraints and requirements that do come from the center are remarkably court-driven. It is as much a series of rulings from the European Court of Justice as initiatives from the Commission and Council that directly impinged on national welfare states. The ECJ's institutional design fosters activism. In contrast to the Council or Commission, the ECJ cannot, once confronted with litigation, escape making what are essentially policy decisions; the Court may also rely on secret majority votes, which further removes it from the political immobility typical of other European actors. Moreover, it generally takes a unanimous vote from the Council to undo an ECJ decision.[92] The structure of EU institutions puts the ECJ on center stage. Attempts at corporatist policymaking have generated much of the drama surrounding Europe's social dimension, but businesses and unions have had little direct involvement in many of the decisions that created legally binding requirements for the social policies of member states.[93] Such a court-led process of social policy development is likely to have its own logic, reflecting demands for doctrinal coherence as much or more than substantive debates about the desirability of various social policy outcomes.

Finally, this multitiered system of social policy is uniquely connected to a process of market building. Of course, social policies in mixed economies always intersect in complex ways with market systems. Nowhere else, however, has the construction of markets so visibly and intensively shaped the development of social policy initiatives. EU interventions in the traditional spheres of social policy have not, on the whole, taken the form of Polanyi's "protective reaction" against the expansion of market relations.[94] Indeed, initiatives of this kind (the Social Charter, for example) have usually been dismal failures. Instead, as the centrality

---

Press, 1992); and Andrew Moravcsik, "Why the European Community Strengthens the State: Domestic Politics and International Cooperation," Department of Government, Harvard University, 1994.

92. Eichenhofer, "Rolle," p. 578.

93. This is not to say that the activities of economic actors are irrelevant to the development of EU social policy. The influence of business has been considerable in restricting Commission efforts to pursue a more activist social dimension, for example, and in advancing the deregulatory agenda that has set the framework for ECJ decisions.

94. Karl Polanyi, *The Great Transformation* (Rinehart, 1944).

of decisions regarding labor mobility and free service markets reveals, EU social policy interventions have grown out of the market-building process itself. These interventions have been, we emphasize, extensive. They have created a structure in which national welfare state regimes are now part of a larger, multitiered system of social policy. This arrangement is peculiar, different in many respects from traditional federal welfare states. It is, however, clearly one whereby the governance of social policy occurs at multiple levels. Member states profoundly influence this structure, but they no longer control it.

CHAPTER THREE

A Regulatory Conundrum: Industrial Relations and the Social Dimension

Martin Rhodes

D URING THE DIFFICULT negotiations that preceded the Maastricht summit of December 1991, Jacques Delors expressed his concern that an "organised schizophrenia" was emerging in the Treaty on European Union (TEU).[1] In the final draft of the Dutch presidency, as modified at the summit and signed on February 7, 1992, his fears were realized. For while efforts were made to ensure that progress in market integration was accompanied by parallel advances in nonmarket spheres such as social and labor market policy, Maastricht's main achievements related to European Monetary Union (EMU). Innovations in other areas were more modest and clumsily hedged with conditions and qualifications. Leaving aside the complicated relationship between the European Union (EU) and the distinct intergovernmental "pillars" of foreign and security policy and home and judicial affairs, the alterations to the "Communities" pillar alone reveal for one critic "more of a *bricoleur's* amateurism than a master brick-layer's strive for perfection and attention to detail."[2] Attempts to correct the Community's democratic deficit through constitutional reform were heavily constrained by the need for compromise between the desire for greater legitimacy and the political reality of the Community's power structure.[3] The complexity of the new rules and

---

1. *Financial Times*, December 12, 1991.
2. See Deidre Curtin, "The Constitutional Structure of the Union: A Europe of Bits and Pieces," *Common Market Law Review*, vol. 30 (1993), p. 24.
3. See Philip Raworth, "A Timid Step Forward: Maastricht and the Democratisation of the European Community," *European Law Review*, vol. 19 (February 1994), pp. 16–30, for a useful discussion of this issue.

decisionmaking procedures contributes neither to the democratic nature nor to the efficacy of the Union's institutions.[4]

The Maastricht arrangements raise more questions than they answer for social and labor market policy, and they complicate the creation of a regulatory regime. This reflects a more general feature of the TEU: it sets up a variegated regulatory structure—and a pragmatic, à la carte approach to integration—through its special case protocols. These include the Danish second home protocol; the Irish abortion protocol; the Barber protocol on the equalization of pension payments; and the EMU opt-out for the United Kingdom as well as the special social and labor market provisions contained in the Social Policy Protocol and Agreement, which allows eleven member states (Britain is excepted) to continue along the path laid down in the 1989 Social Charter.

The resulting potential for "variable geometry" in the integration process may be no bad thing, given the complications that could arise from enlarging the EU to include members of the European Free Trade Association (EFTA) and, eventually, some of the central and eastern European states. As *Financial Times* columnist Samuel Brittan remarked: "Even those who are not particularly enamoured of free-market thinking can surely see that there is absolutely no prospect of anything like a Social Charter, with harmonized social security and similar provisions, being applicable in an enlarged Community of more than twenty countries, taking in the former communist countries, with widely varying living standards and productivity levels."[5]

Nevertheless, powerful interests within the European Union —including Europe's unions, the governments of a majority of the member states, and the European Commission itself—remain committed to the construction of a "Social Europe" to ensure the preservation of workers' rights and entitlements and the creation of a higher degree of social cohesion and solidarity among the citizens of Europe. On the one hand, a European welfare state with harmonized social security structures is, as Brittan implies, clearly infeasible, not least because the European Union lacks the resources required to engage in large-scale redistributive policies. But on the other hand, this does not prevent the Union from undertaking

4. An in-depth analysis of the significance of the treaty reforms and their significance for efficacy, transparency, and democracy can be found in Jean-Claude Piris, "Maastricht, les institutions communautaires sont-elles plus efficaces, plus démocratiques et plus transparentes?" *Revue trimestrielle de droit européen*, no. 1 (January–March 1994), pp. 1–37.

5. Samuel Brittan, "A Better UK Road to Maastricht," *Financial Times*, October 31, 1991, p. 19.

ambitious programs of social and economic regulation, provided the political and administrative costs of the regulatory programs are borne by the regulated (firms and individuals) rather than by the regulators (in this case, the institutions of the European Union).[6] The future of the social dimension will therefore necessarily be one in which the core features of welfare state regimes remain nationally specific, with supranational influence restricted to a limited number of areas deemed crucial for market integration.

But the question remains of exactly how that regulatory structure is to be built. What are the political and practical limits to the creation of a pan-European policy regime in this area? How effective can a structure of regulation or governance in this sector be, given the diversity of historical, legal, and institutional traditions among the EU nations, as well as the infinite scope for discord over two key regulatory issues: (1) the desirability of new regulation in labor markets at either the national or supranational level, and (2) the assumption of EU competence in this domain, with all that that implies for the hallowed, if notoriously imprecise, notion of subsidiarity?

The regulatory conundrum produced by this discord has been both evident and inevitable since the Treaty of Rome. Despite the predictions of the early theorists of the European Community that the integration of the European market would lead to the integration of social security and labor market organization, social integration has proven to be anything but spontaneous. Nor has there ever been consensus even on the desirability of social integration. Interpretations of the legal underpinnings for Union action in this domain (principally articles 117 and 118 of the Treaty of Rome) have been divided from the outset over whether they establish the basis for a common social policy. Indeed, article 117 stated both that harmonization should result automatically from the functioning of the common market and that regulation and "administrative action" were required to ensure that outcome.[7] The consequence has been that, throughout the history of what was originally the Common Market, then the European Community, and now the European Union, advances in social and labor market policy at the European level have been gradual

6. See Giandomenico Majone, "The European Community between Social Policy and Social Regulation," *Journal of Common Market Studies*, vol. 31 (June 1993), pp. 160–61.

7. For a discussion of the treaty foundations of European social policymaking, see John Holloway, *Social Policy Harmonisation in the European Community* (Farnborough, England: Gower, 1981), pp. 11–39.

and piecemeal—and mostly unsatisfactory, for their supporters as much as for their opponents.

This chapter portrays the process of regulatory policymaking in the social dimension as an ongoing attempt to resolve this regulatory conundrum. It begins by describing the context for European-level social and labor market policy, that is, the actors, competing interests, institutions, and pressures and counterpressures that have simultaneously helped and hindered the construction of the limited regulatory regime that currently constitutes the social dimension. It then considers the emergence of an embryonic system of governance in this area in light of three essential characteristics of a regime: the *substantive* (the cluster of rights and rules associated with the regime), the *procedural* (the forms of decisionmaking), and the *mode of implementation*.[8] This is carried out by examining the twin pillars of the social dimension (see figure 3-1). The first, the legislative pillar, comprises substantive and procedural developments (involving EU legislative acts and treaty arrangements); the second, the social dialogue pillar, comprises a potentially important instrument of governance, namely, agreements between the so-called social partners. Developments since the Maastricht summit of December 1991—especially the attempt to reform the procedural and implementation components of the nascent regime—are then addressed.

There are two main arguments in the analysis that follows. The first is that the creation of a transnational regulatory regime for industrial relations and the labor market has not been easy: it has proceeded only through a complex process of intergovernmental bargaining in which the European Commission has been a critical, entrepreneurial policy actor, promoting alliances with and among member states and exploiting to the limit both its own powers and the latitude allowed by the treaties for Community competence in this domain. The second is that, despite the many impediments in its path, a transnational regulatory regime is nonetheless being constructed, with important implications for national sovereignty (which is gradually being surrendered), traditional interest-group activity (which has assumed a significant transnational dimension), and labor market policy (which is steadily being "Europeanized"). The future is uncertain, however. The greatest challenge now for the EU is combating high levels of unemployment. Confronting this problem will

---

8. Oran Young, *International Cooperation: Building Regimes for Natural Resources and the Environment* (Cornell University Press, 1989).

Figure 3-1. *The Twin Pillars of the Social Dimension*

	Legislation	*Social Dialogue*
1970s	Equal pay Equal treatment Collective redundancies	Sectoral joint committees of workers and employers (from 1955 in iron and steel industries)
1987	Single European Act (SEA)	New commitments with 1984 social action program and article 118B of the SEA
	Article 118A (health and safety) Article 100A (excludes workers' rights)	Val Duchesse social dialogue (intersectoral) *Phase one:* 1986–89
1989	Social Charter and Social Action Program	Val Duchesse *Phase two:* 1990 onward
	Treaty-base game	

	Under article 118A:
	  Third directive on atypical work
	  Health and safety
	Under "hybrids":
	  Working time directive
	  Pregnancy directive
	Under article 100A:
	  Second directive on atypical
	  work
	Under article 100:
	  First directive on atypical work
	  Proof of employment
		European Company Act, article
		54(3) (9) of Treaty of Rome
		
		European Works Council
		directive, article 100
		
		September 1990 CEEP and ETUC
		framework agreement
		
		October 1991 CEEP, ETUC, and
		UNICE agreement on "law by
		collective agreement"

1992	Maastricht and the Social Policy Protocol and Agreement	
With the United Kingdom	Without the United Kingdom	
QMV and unanimity, based on SEA and Treaty of Rome	QMV	Unanimity	Article 4 of the Social Policy Agreement, "Euro-agreements"
	Health and safety Work conditions Equality at work	Social security Representation and collective defense	Council decision	Implementation via col- lective bargaining and "national practice"

require creative, complex regulatory innovation in striking a balance between policies to protect employment and policies to create it.

Building a Regulatory Regime:
Actors, Interests, and Institutions

Taking Stephen Krasner's definition of a regime as a set of "implicit and explicit principles, norms or rules [and] decision-making procedures,"[9] Paul Teague and John Grahl have argued that a European industrial relations regime—based on more than guidelines, but on less than legally binding obligations—offers a superior regulatory model to either a constitution-based system or a decentralized, neoliberal mode of market regulation. While the former would be too rigid to accommodate the diversity of European industrial relations, the latter would fail to coordinate labor markets and would foster dysfunctional Hobbesian competition among agents and rules, leading to social dumping or regime shopping and to competitive deregulation.[10] A similar argument made elsewhere justifies European solidarity in social security provision, on the grounds that the free play of market forces would lead to social imbalances and underprovision.[11] In any event, the fragmented social policy framework of the European Union and the absence of interest-group cohesion and common behavioral norms have impeded the creation of such a regime. Political fragmentation appears to be the principal obstacle to transnational governance.[12]

In order to understand fully the regulatory problems in this domain, the existence of a deep-seated conflict must be appreciated. From the very beginning, any attempt by the European Commission to set an agenda for the harmonization or approximation of rules and regulations, or to promote supranational decisionmaking, has provoked a two-way con-

9. Stephen D. Krasner, *International Regimes* (Cornell University Press, 1983), p. 14.

10. See Paul Teague, "Constitution or Regime? The Social Dimension to the 1992 Project," *British Journal of Industrial Relations*, vol. 27 (November 1989), pp. 310–29; John Grahl and Paul Teague, "Integration Theory and European Labour Markets," *British Journal of Industrial Relations*, vol. 30 (December 1992), pp. 515–27; and Paul Teague and John Grahl, *Industrial Relations and European Integration* (London: Lawrence and Wishart, 1992).

11. See Mark Kleinman and David Piachaud, "European Social Policy: Conceptions and Choices," *Journal of European Social Policy*, no. 1 (1993), pp. 3ff.

12. See Beate Kohler-Koch, "Changing Patterns of Interest Intermediation in the European Union," *Government and Opposition*, vol. 29 (Spring 1994), pp. 166–67.

ceptual clash: between the competing philosophies of collectivism and liberalism in labor market regulation, and between solidarity and subsidiarity in the framing of Community policies. As elsewhere in the integration process, preferences for integration or decentralization tend to be closely related to attitudes toward markets.[13] This clash, which has become particularly acute since the 1986 Single European Act (SEA), underpins an ongoing debate and conflict of interests within a highly heterogeneous and fragmented policy community. It has been complicated still further by the diversity of Europe's national labor market regimes, among which there has been little hard evidence of genuine convergence.[14]

Consequently, despite the pressures for integration in industrial relations—which includes market integration, transnational union and business structures, and, arguably, the need for a more developed form of European social citizenship—there has been no simple process of spillover.[15] Instead, supporting the argument that "successful spillover requires prior programmatic agreement among governments,"[16] there has been a sclerotic process of intergovernmental bargaining, spurred on in fits and starts by a European Commission that has always played the role of initiator, formulator, and promoter of legislation, but which became increasingly entrepreneurial under the aegis of Jacques Delors.

Four major impediments to the creation of a full-fledged industrial relations regime therefore stand out: the low level of legitimacy attached to the project and the uncertain status of the regulator (the European Commission); the clash of philosophies and interests; the fragmentation of the policy community; and the complexity of the regulatory arena, stemming from the national (and even subnational) diversity of European labor market regulation.

---

13. See, for example, Michael Shackleton, "The European Community between Three Ways of Life: A Cultural Analysis," *Journal of Common Market Studies*, vol. 29 (December 1991), pp. 575–601; for a discussion of conflict-based analyses, see Simon Hix, "Approaches to the Study of the EC: The Challenge to Comparative Politics," *West European Politics*, vol. 17 (January 1994), pp. 21–22.

14. For recent refutations of the convergence hypothesis and evidence of persistent diversity among national institutional arrangements, see Christopher Baldry, "Convergence in Europe—A Matter of Perspective?" *Industrial Relations Journal*, vol. 25 (June 1994), pp. 96–109; and Richard Hyman, "Industrial Relations in Western Europe: An Era of Ambiguity," *Industrial Relations*, vol. 33 (January 1994), pp. 1–24.

15. See Teague and Grahl, *Industrial Relations*, pp. 85–91.

16. Robert O. Keohane and Stanley Hoffman, "Conclusions: Community Politics and Institutional Change," in William Wallace, ed., *The Dynamics of European Integration* (London: Pinter, 1990), p. 287.

The Legal Basis: The Commission as Policy Entrepreneur

The creation of any system of regulation depends in large part on the legitimacy of the project and the status of the regulator. The first problem encountered by the Commission is that its powers in this area have always been weak and its dependence on the support—usually, unanimous support—of the member states has been strong. Because the legal basis for an EU role in social and labor market policy is ambiguous, the Commission—which has always interpreted its powers broadly—has been forced to forge alliances with member-state governments and, where possible, interest groups, to fill the gap between formal competence and actual influence. If this has occasionally allowed the Commission to make great leaps forward with social action programs (the most recent after 1987), it has also made it heavily reliant on working groups and consultative committees for its expertise, a dependence reinforced by the expansion of its policy interventions.

Intergovernmentalism, some argue, has been a major obstacle to progress; this, rather than the fragile, inexplicit legal foundations in the Treaty of Rome, accounts for the difficulty of creating a regulatory regime for social policy.[17] It may well be the case that intergovernmentalism (and the need for compromise between irreconcilable positions) was originally responsible for weakening these legal foundations. Nevertheless, the legal framework subsequently became extremely important both in constraining the range of opportunities and in expanding them. Articles 117 and 118 can be interpreted two ways: as establishing harmonization as one of the aims of the treaty (without, however, providing the Commission with the instruments necessary to achieve it); or as doing nothing to restrict the autonomy of the member states (and, accordingly, giving few clearly defined powers in this domain to the Commission).[18]

Shifts in interpretation allow changes in the role of the Commission. In alliance with the Council of Ministers, the Commission has attempted

17. See Laura Cram, "Calling the Tune without Paying the Piper? Social Policy Regulation: The Role of the Commission in European Community Social Policy," *Policy and Politics*, vol. 21 (April 1993), p. 136.

18. See Holloway, *Social Policy Harmonisation*, pp. 11–32. Article 117 of the European Economic Community treaty states that the member states agree that the development of improved working conditions and an improved standard of living for workers, as well as their harmonization, will flow from the functioning of the common market (implying some sort of neofunctionalist spillover). But according to the same article, they will also be developed from the procedures provided for in the treaty and from the approximation of provisions laid down by law, regulation, or administrative action.

to push forward its regulatory project, endeavoring to bridge the gap between official competence and actual powers by relying on other treaty articles—the so-called treaty-base game (discussed below). Thus the 1972 Conference of Heads of State in Paris emphasized the importance of more vigorous action in the social policy field, and the Council of Ministers approved the use of articles 100 and 235 of the Treaty of Rome in helping produce directives regarding dismissals (December 1974) and workers' rights in the event of mergers (1975).[19] More recently the Commission played upon the ambiguity of its mandate to push forward its 1987 proposals for a social action program in an effort to bypass the British veto. By the mid-1990s, however, the replacement of Jacques Delors and member-state resistance to the Commission's entrepreneurial style of policymaking signaled the beginning of a new and much more cautious era of Commission activity.

The Commission and its bureaucrats play a less dramatic but often more consequential role by promoting relations between other organizations, which may assist voluntarist regulation (as in the case of the social dialogue, discussed below), or by exerting incremental bureaucratic pressure and advocating nonbinding instruments, such as opinions and recommendations.[20] As Laura Cram points out, "It may be that EC soft law and Euro-rhetoric ultimately create their own dynamic, eventually leading to an expansion in policy activity."[21] Cram also shows that the Commission has been especially successful in promoting sorts of regulatory legislation that are relatively costless to the Community as a whole or to its member-state governments, such as health and safety legislation. Nevertheless, progress in some policy areas, such as the freedom of movement of workers, is not matched by progress in others. The clash of philosophies and interests helps explain why.

19. Articles 100 and 235 allow measures not otherwise provided for in the treaty to be adopted and empower the Council of Ministers, by unanimous vote, to issue directives and regulations for the approximation of member-state laws, regulations, and administrative instruments, insofar as they directly affect the establishment and functioning of the common market.

20. On the importance of bureaucratic politics and policymaking in the Community, see B. Guy Peters, "Bureaucratic Politics and the Institutions of the European Community," in Alberta M. Sbragia, ed., *Euro-Politics: Institutions and Policymaking in the "New" European Community* (Brookings, 1992), pp. 75–122.

21. Cram, "Calling the Tune," p. 144.

The Clash of Philosophies and Interests

A clear division between the continental countries and the British government over the promotion of a European system of labor market regulation and industrial relations has been apparent since the late 1970s. The cleavage stems not only from the contrasts between the Anglo-Saxon and Romano-Germanic legal traditions but also from competing notions of national sovereignty and philosophies of economic organization. At the same time, there has been a clear clash of interests—and ideology—between Europe's employers and trade unions. The subsequent conflict has made the regulatory project more complex still.

The two-way clash between solidarity and subsidiarity and between the market and collectivism is especially acute in labor policy, partly because of the diversity of Europe's national systems of labor market regulation. Such diversity generates different conceptions of regulation and, more generally, makes policy implementation and enforcement problematic. As for the clash between different conceptions of labor market organization, broadly speaking, since the late 1970s the British government and Europe's employers have become increasingly concerned about the creation of supranational *regulation* while they are promoting national-level *deregulation*. They argue that economic efficiency and employment generation are hampered by excessive and ill-advised regulation; pointing to the dismal record of job creation in the Union, they state that the Commission should be leading the debate on making labor markets more flexible, not seeking an approximation of rights and entitlements across Western Europe.

The parallel clash between conceptions of solidarity and subsidiarity is a complex and probably unresolvable one, although it has been argued that there may be no contradiction since solidarity itself is a contestable concept and does not necessarily imply collective and universal provision. Thus, in principle, solidarity in shaping Unionwide norms and standards should be able to accommodate diversity.[22] This is precisely what a regime for the labor market could achieve, either by setting common minimum standards from which national departures are acceptable (the intention, after all, of much EC labor market legislation to date) or by creating rules within the framework of European agreements, which would be implemented by way of further agreements at lower levels,

22. See Kleinman and Piachaud, "European Social Policy," p. 14.

thereby preserving national traditions. This innovation is contained in the Maastricht Social Protocol and Agreement.

More generally, it has been argued that the strengthened subsidiarity clause in the Maastricht treaty (article 36) could reasonably be interpreted to mean that the EU should act to support the social protection activities of the member states and to fill the gaps at the national level, in line with the Catholic doctrine of subsidiarity. However, the abstract nature of this theoretical debate translates crudely into the political arena, where it focuses once again on the competence of the Union to act in an area in which—according to the opponents of a strengthened social dimension—it lacks the legitimacy to do so.

Fragmentation of the Policy Community

The problems of building a proregulation coalition derive as much from the fragmentation of the policy community as they do from disagreement on the form and extent of regulation. The task of the Commission in building the alliances required for progress has been made all the more difficult by rudimentary interest-group organization and by divisions within the European Commission itself. The clash of regulatory philosophies is replicated in the Commission between DG-5 (social affairs) and DG-2 (economic and financial affairs). As for interest groups, both UNICE (Union of Industrial and Employers' Confederations of Europe) and ETUC (European Trade Union Confederation) have lacked negotiating mandates from their affiliate organizations.[23]

And despite recent reforms by both organizations to increase their lobbying capacity, they remain weak by comparison with other actors, such as large companies (especially multinational ones), which use an increasing array of channels and access points to influence EU policy. Labor is especially disadvantaged, regardless of claims by employers that Europe's union representatives enjoy special privileges (Commission

23. UNICE was formed in 1958; its membership comprises thirty-two national employer and industrial federations from twenty-two countries. The ETUC was established in 1972 and has forty affiliated confederations from twenty-one countries, including all of the most important EU national union confederations, apart from the Communist French CGT (Confédération Générale du Travail) and the Portuguese CGTP-IN (Confederação Geral dos Trabalhadores Portugueses-Intersindical). The third important interest organization, CEEP (European Centre of Public Enterprises), was formed in 1965; it represents 260 of the European Union's public enterprises (from all member states except Britain and Denmark) and provides them with information and research on EU activities.

funding, for example).[24] While there has been growing confidence among business interests in using the direct route through Brussels for access to EU decisionmaking—as part of a multifaceted strategy including direct representation as well as lobbying through national- and European-level trade associations and other ad hoc organizations—there is little evidence of organized labor following suit.[25]

Although it seems logical that the internationalization of capital would have to be dealt with by an international labor movement, that is not necessarily the case. Indeed, as Barbara Barnouin points out, international agreements may well weaken the historically developed thrust with which labor unions pursue their objectives at the national level without strengthening international bargaining power.[26] Nevertheless, given the emergence of transnational structures of governance in the Union, it is clear that the labor movement must become transnational if it is to be part of the future. The main impediment is less the loss of national strength than the lack of an effective transnational structure, for whatever level of international coordination and centralization exists has come only from external pressure. The reform of the ETUC in the early 1990s—the result of developments in EC policymaking—aims to facilitate coalition building among its member confederations and to preempt any challenge to its role posed by European sectoral-level bargaining. The first goal is to be achieved by creating a management committee between the ETUC's executive council and its secretariat, with ten delegates representing the forty confederations on its executive council. The second is to be won by giving the International Industry Committees sectoral representatives on the ETUC's governing body. Although these changes fall short of transforming the ETUC into a genuine supranational actor, they begin to make it more than simply a mediator of nationally

24. See Jelle Visser and Bernhard Ebbinghaus, "Making the Most of Diversity? European Integration and the Transnational Organisation of Labour," in Justin Greenwood, Jürgen R. Grote, and Karsten Ronit, eds., *Organised Interests and the European Community* (London: Sage, 1992), pp. 214 ff.

25. See Justin Greenwood, Jürgen R. Grote, and Karsten Ronit, "Introduction: Organised Interests and the Transnational Dimension," in Greenwood, Grote, and Ronit, eds., *Organised Interests*. On employers' strategies for influencing decisionmaking, see Lynn Collie, "Business Lobbying in the European Community: The Union of Industrial and Employers Confederations of Europe," in Sonia Mazey and Jeremy Richardson, eds., *Public Lobbying in the European Community* (Oxford: Clarendon Press, 1993), pp. 222 ff.

26. Barbara Barnouin, *The European Labour Movement and European Integration* (London: Frances Pinter, 1986), p. 126.

based organizations.[27] They will also make it a more effective interlocutor both for the Commission and for Europe's employer organizations.

Creating greater cohesion in the employer camp may prove more difficult, simply because European business organizations have less immediate interest in coordination. It is precisely the proliferation of organizations and points of access for business lobbying that gives employers their strength as the most overrepresented interest group in EU affairs, enjoying superior financial resources, a highly trained professional staff, and a dense network of personal contacts and channels of information.[28] Keeping UNICE weak has allowed business interests to avoid its co-option into a corporatist policymaking process, and the Union's complex, multilayered structure has encouraged diversity.

But changes stemming from the development of the single market will have important implications for business as well as for labor. Luca Lanzalaco suggests that the creation of the internal market will cause more conflicts within the business community, making the management of diversity more difficult, especially between the national and sector-specific associations that constitute a dual channel of access to decision-making and weaken UNICE as the voice of Euro-business.[29] Business may be forced to rationalize its lobbying structures, and the new post-Maastricht procedures for social dialogue will require business to give greater weight to UNICE. Now that the Commission is pressuring UNICE to draw up Union-level collective agreements with the ETUC, the issue of UNICE resources will have to be seriously tackled.[30] Nevertheless, large multinational companies (MNCs) are unlikely to accept UNICE as their sole channel of influence, because they already wield important power through the European Roundtable and the European Enterprise Group and lobby directly and through national- and European-level trade associations.[31]

27. See Visser and Ebbinghaus, "Making the Most of Diversity," pp. 210ff.

28. Kohler-Koch, "Changing Patterns," p. 169.

29. Luca Lanzalaco, "Coping with Heterogeneity: Peak Associations of Business within and across Western European Nations," in Greenwood, Grote, and Ronit, eds., *Organised Interests*, pp. 173–205.

30. Collie, "Business Lobbying," pp. 222ff.

31. Jane Sargent, "The Corporate Benefit of Lobbying: The British Case and Its Relevance to the European Community," in Mazey and Richardson, eds., *Lobbying in the European Community*, p. 244.

Diversity of European Labor Market Regulation

A more coherent set of relationships between the regulatory authorities and social actors may assist the creation of a regulatory regime, but the complexity of the regulatory task presents another set of problems. This can be illustrated by briefly examining the diversity of the national systems of regulation that a transnational regime must accommodate. National labor market regimes in Western Europe are embedded in diverse social, political, and economic systems, which makes harmonization extremely difficult; the policy space of labor market regimes is already occupied by national behavioral norms, vested interests, and organizations.[32] Their rules—derived from both law and collective bargaining—differ considerably, as does the combination of arrangements that underpins the organization of the firm and determines its cost structure and position in the marketplace. The firm is also linked in different ways to national welfare-state traditions, which affect, for example, the ratio between its direct wage and nonwage costs and its willingness to engage in consensual, as opposed to adversarial, relations with the labor force.

There are considerable analytical problems in categorizing European labor market regimes, a task made all the more difficult by evidence that the decentralization of collective bargaining and the emergence of either regional or plant-level productivity coalitions is eroding distinctive national systems of industrial relations.[33] One way to group the different countries of the Union is to focus on state and legal traditions. Thus in the Roman-Germanic system (covering Belgium, France, Germany, Greece, Italy, Luxembourg, and the Netherlands), the state plays a central role through the constitutional provision of basic workers' rights (the right to collective bargaining, to form and join trade unions, and so on) and through comprehensive labor market legislation. In the Anglo-Irish tradition (Britain and Ireland), by contrast, the state has abstained from regulating the industrial relations system by either legislation or a labor code. In the Nordic system (represented by Denmark and now Sweden) the role of the state is less formal than in the Roman-Germanic system, but industrial relations have been regulated by agreements between employers and unions that function much like the constitutional and legis-

32. See chapter 1 in this volume.
33. See Harry C. Katz, "The Decentralisation of Collective Bargaining: A Literature Review and Comparative Analysis," *Industrial and Labor Relations Review*, vol. 47 (October 1993), pp. 3–22.

lative frameworks of the Roman-Germanic countries. The state has frequently mediated between the two parties, creating a tripartite or corporatist element in the system.

These differences partly explain the tendency of the British and Danes, in particular, to resist the extension of the continental law-based system of regulation to their traditionally voluntarist systems; they fail, however, to capture the role played by labor market management and organization in creating national regulatory systems. Accounting for this dimension produces a rather different configuration, one that helps explain important differences among the member states in types of labor market flexibility and in their views of European-level innovations.

Employers in the northern group of countries (Germany, the Netherlands, Belgium, and Denmark) are constrained by rules and regulations governing external flexibility (their freedom to hire and fire and employ a wide variety of contracts). These external constraints, however, are offset by a high level of skills, a highly educated work force, a lower level of hierarchy within the firm, and a consensual treatment of some issues (the introduction of new technology, restructuring of production, and employment adjustment, for example), which together promote a higher degree of internal (within-firm) flexibility than in other member states. Active labor market policies to reintegrate the unemployed into the work force tend to receive greater emphasis than passive compensatory support (employment benefits), although there are important differences in this respect among the northern countries. Their governments and unions wish to preserve their high-pay, high-productivity systems, which explains their fear of social dumping (relocation by employers seeking lower wage and nonwage costs) in a European labor market with diverse labor market standards and few impediments to "competitive deregulation."[34] Hence their support for a strong social dimension to European economic integration and disappointment with the failure to achieve it.

Employers in the Anglo-Saxon group (the United Kingdom and Ireland) enjoy a high degree of external flexibility (that is, there are few

---

34. The fear of social dumping, which is based on wide disparities in labor costs, has probably been exaggerated, as have the fears of employers in countries with high labor costs (such as Germany), who think that their competitiveness will be threatened unless these costs are lowered. Competitiveness depends on a host of factors other than labor costs, including education, training, the domestic financial system, and the degree of consensus in industrial relations. See Commission of the European Communities, *Employment in Europe, 1993* (Luxembourg, 1993); and "Labor Costs and International Competitiveness," *European Industrial Relations Review* (London), no. 241 (February 1994), pp. 13–17.

constraints on their powers to hire and fire and employ workers on fixed-term or temporary contracts). Because of a deficit in skills and a poorly educated work force, however—and, in the United Kingdom, a tradition of adversarial industrial relations—their internal or organizational flexibility has been low and their capacity for adjustment weak. The solution has been to pursue a low-skilled, price-oriented adjustment path whereby employers' costs are lowered by reducing the level of labor market regulation. This prevents British unions from working successfully for the adoption of the German "skills-oriented" strategy, which they admire and which underpins their support for a strengthened social dimension. Ireland has followed a different path from that of the United Kingdom by sustaining the role of the trade unions in bargaining and by extending rather than reducing protective regulation. Consequently, its government has been much less hostile than its British counterpart to a strengthened social dimension.

Employers in the Mediterranean group of countries (France, Italy, Greece, Portugal, and Spain) have typically enjoyed neither a high level of external flexibility nor a high level of internal flexibility. If on the one hand there have been strict limitations on their freedom to hire and fire and use part-time or temporary contracts, on the other a low level of skills provision and inadequate training systems, combined with an adversarial relationship between management and labor, has deprived them of organizational flexibility, except perhaps in the largely unregulated small-firm sector. More recently the expanded use of fixed-term contracts in these countries has compensated for a lack of flexibility elsewhere, but at the cost of producing a dual labor market that divides the insiders (the full-time, permanent, older workers) from the younger outsiders (those with insecure, fixed-term employment).

Union support for a strengthened social dimension is not hard to explain, since these labor markets are already rather heavily regulated, and a floor of rights and entitlements established at the European level would help prevent their erosion in these countries. Mediterranean governments, too, aware of the price of maintaining a high level of labor market regulation—in terms of costs and employment as barriers to competition with other countries fall—have supported the idea of a strengthened social dimension (as well as the strictures of EMU convergence), in part because of the prospect of an increase in regional aid.[35]

---

35. Indeed, the cohesion fund established by the Maastricht Treaty (to which the Commission wants to allocate some ECU 2.6 billion by 1997 for assisting those member

Impeding an industrial relations regime, then, are not only the intricate, multilayered, overlapping, and disordered structure of the European Union itself but also problems of legitimacy, clashes between philosophies, fragmentation of the policy community, and the sheer complexity of the regulatory task. Nevertheless, over the last twenty years, the twin pillars of a regulatory regime—legislation and social dialogue—have undergone gradual construction, albeit in fits and starts, subject to long delays, and, because of their weak foundations, beset by occasional subsidence. That process of construction is the subject of the next two sections.

The Legislative Pillar of the Social Dimension

The Commission has had to take an entrepreneurial role as initiator, formulator, and promoter of legislative and other developments in industrial relations because the legal foundations for a specific EU role are fragile. In alliance with some (usually a majority) member states, the Commission has attempted to bolster these weak foundations with recourse to controversial treaty provisions, because the Treaty of Rome made no specific provision for a EU social policy and articles 117–122 were vague and repetitive and conferred no real powers upon the Community institutions and little by way of direct rights upon Community citizens.[36]

It was only in the early 1970s, when the Council of Ministers approved recourse to other treaty articles (article 235, in particular), that the EC's first social action program of labor market measures made significant advances, producing directives on equal pay and equal treatment for men and women, on rules for collective redundancies, and on employee rights in the case of transfers of undertakings or employer insolvency. Some modest initiatives for formulating EC standards in health and safety also succeeded: between 1970 and 1985 the Commission proposed and the Council adopted six specific directives in this area.[37] Further initiatives,

---

states with a per capita gross domestic product that is less than 90 percent of the Community average) was the price for the assent of the poorer countries to the program of integration in the Treaty on European Union.

36. See Philippa Watson, "Social Policy after Maastricht," *Common Market Law Review*, vol. 30 (June 1993), p. 483.

37. See R. F. Eberlie, "The New Health and Safety Legislation of the European Community," *Industrial Law Journal*, vol. 19 (June 1990), pp. 81 ff; and, more generally, Phil

however, on more controversial issues—common regulations on part-time and temporary work and parental leave, for example—were blocked by British vetoes in the Council of Ministers. The European Commission's most ambitious projects—the Vredeling proposal of 1980 on employees' rights to information and consultation in multinational companies and the Fifth Company Law Directive on board-level employee participation—were defeated by a campaign conducted by European employers, multinational companies, and some member states. The American MNCs were especially influential, contesting the "principle of extraterritoriality" by which the EC intended to extend its jurisdiction to cover non-EC companies.[38]

Market-oriented initiatives that posed no threat to the autonomy of the firm—such as policies to increase the freedom of movement of labor in the Community and the use of the structural funds (especially the European Social Fund) to assist training in less-developed regions—have encountered far less resistance from member-state governments; they have been widely supported by unions, employers, and governments alike. However, even in those areas in which policy was market oriented and the grounds for Community action were more solid, progress has been slow because of the need for a complex process of intergovernmental bargaining. Although the creation of a common market for goods should have produced pressure for a common policy to increase labor mobility, intermediation by a complex policymaking process ensured delays. Regarding freedom of movement, for example, the Treaty of Rome obliged member states to remove domestic legislation that discriminates in employment terms against citizens from other parts of the Community. Despite the lack of open opposition, legislative progress was relatively slow: it took nearly a decade of debate and policy formulation before most legal discrimination against migrant workers within the member states was eliminated in the late 1960s. Thereafter, workers were entitled to apply for jobs in any member state, to settle there with their families, and to enjoy the same rights and entitlements as national workers.[39]

The conjuncture of two circumstances allowed the next major step: a favorable economic climate in 1986-90, a period of renewed economic and employment growth in the European Community; and the emergence

James, "Occupational Health and Safety," in Michael Gold, ed., *The Social Dimension: Employment Policy in the European Community* (Macmillan, 1993), pp. 135–54.

38. See Barnouin, *European Labor Movement*, pp. 102–41.

39. For an extended discussion of policies to promote the free movement of labor, see Teague and Grahl, *Industrial Relations*, pp. 142–62.

of a coalition of member states and the Commission against the attempted shift of Community policy in the direction of a liberal market, during the British presidency of 1986. The opportunity for this shift arose from the policy vacuum created by the announcement made by Jacques Delors in 1984 that no new social policy initiatives would be undertaken unless they were sanctioned by the social dialogue between representatives of Europe's trade unions and employers. The attempt to stimulate bargaining between the European "social partners" succeeded only in producing a deadlock, given the polarization of the employers and unions on most labor market issues. Then, between 1987 and 1989, the Commission engaged in coalition building and agenda setting for a relaunch of social and labor market policy, which eventually brought most of the member states on board.[40]

The Community Charter of Basic Social Rights—a "solemn declaration" adopted by eleven of the twelve member states at the Strasbourg summit in December 1989—was the result of a compromise to accommodate the concerns of the British, Spanish, and Portuguese governments. They remained uncertain about the desirability of a floor of social rights and entitlements that the Commission was promoting in league with the Belgian, German, French, and Greek governments, whose presidencies had been critical in moving the agenda forward. In the end it was the British government that rejected the Social Charter, claiming that "it did not satisfy criteria which were unanimously agreed by the Heads of Government at the Madrid Summit in June 1989": priority to job creation, adequate regard to subsidiarity and respect for the diversity of practice among member states.[41] Great Britain's decision to not sign gave formal expression to an already well-established breach with its eleven EC partners who, regardless of their differences on details, had reached a consensus on the need for progress. It also set a precedent for the Maastricht summit in December 1991: in effect, the British succeeded in diluting the substance and modifying the spirit of a document to which they did not subscribe.

As far as substantive rights were concerned, the Social Charter was an immense disappointment for those seeking to enshrine citizenship rights

40. For a fuller discussion of the genesis of the Social Charter, see Martin Rhodes, "The Social Dimension of the Single European Market: National versus Transnational Regulation," *European Journal of Political Research*, vol. 19 (March 1991), pp. 256ff.

41. British Department of Employment, *People, Jobs and Progress* (London, February 1992), p. 4.

at the center of the project for closer political and economic union. Most seriously for those seeking a Community commitment to high common standards of social welfare, the final draft no longer referred to the fundamental rights of *citizens*: the use of that word in earlier drafts was replaced by *workers*. This was of more than symbolic importance. It meant that the prospect of a "people's Europe" began to fade from the outset, to be replaced by a much more limited—not to say minimalist—set of provisions. Thus the charter focused overwhelmingly on policies required for the completion of the single market (primarily economic and industrial rights), with only limited reference to *social citizenship* rights.[42] Falling well short of the measures required to underpin a European welfare regime, the charter betrays the more general tension in EC social policy between the provision of rights as an adjunct of economic policy (primarily to enhance the mobility of labor) and the more comprehensive conception of social rights as advanced by the European Court of Justice (ECJ), which stems from a citizen's membership in the Union. Support for subsidiarity, and its conflation (especially by the British) with sovereignty, has served only to undermine the principle of universal rights and entitlements.[43]

Even so, the British government was concerned over the scope and the legality, under treaty provisions, of the social action program that followed. UNICE, Europe's employers' organization, complained that around a quarter of the program's measures fell outside the Community's legitimate sphere of influence. Both the British and Europe's employers have broadly supported social policy measures that secure the operation of the internal market (common health and safety standards, portable pensions, and the mutual recognition of qualifications), but they have consistently opposed measures concerning the relationship between cap-

42. In Marshall's sense, these would entail for all EU citizens "the right to share to the full in the social heritage and to live the life of a civilised being according to the standards prevailing in society." See Thomas H. Marshall, *Class, Citizenship and Social Development* (Westport, Conn.: Greenwood Press, 1964), p. 96. For a useful discussion of citizenship and the Social Charter, see Patrick Kenis, "Social Europe in the 1990s: Beyond an Adjunct to Achieving a Common Market?" *Futures*, vol. 23 (September 1991), pp. 724–38. Kenis uses the work of Eduard Heimann to assess the Social Charter in terms of three types of social policy: measures that secure the course of the economy, or change that course, or promote social citizenship rights. Kenis argues that the charter, in focusing on the removal of barriers to labor mobility, supports especially the first category of measures.

43. See Paul Spicker, "The Principle of Subsidiarity and the Social Policy of the European Community," *Journal of European Social Policy*, vol. 1 (1991), pp. 3–14.

ital and labor (such as rights to consultation and information) and the "equal protection of laws" in social security.[44]

They find support for their stance in the Treaty of Rome and in the Single European Act of 1987, which set precise limits on the procedural component of any emerging regulatory regime but resolved none of the ambiguity of the original legal bases for Community action. SEA article 118A did extend the scope of social policymaking—it granted the Commission the power of proposition after consultation with the Economic and Social Committee, gave the European Parliament a second reading of proposals through a new cooperation procedure, and allowed the Council to act under qualified majority voting—yet several provisos constrained Commission initiatives. Critically, only health and safety measures fell unambiguously under the new majority voting system, and directives were to avoid imposing burdens, be they legal, financial, or administrative, on small and medium-size firms. And although article 100A introduced majority voting for measures essential for the single market, those relating to the free movement of persons and the rights and interests of workers were specifically excluded. Thus the fragile legal bases for a Community role in social integration were barely strengthened by the SEA.[45]

Of course, Britain's resistance to legislative interference in the sphere of labor market policy revealed the distinction between the British legal tradition and that of its continental counterparts—the British tradition features voluntarism in labor market regulation (which it shares with Ireland and Denmark) and contractual relationships between employees and employers rather than ones enshrined in legal statute. This distinction raises another problem in building a regulatory regime in this policy area, that of implementation. Both the Anglo-Saxon and Nordic legal families give preeminence to enforcement through collective agreement rather than through social legislation (even though the United Kingdom has moved away from the voluntarist mode of regulation under the Conservative government, with a proliferation of restrictive labor legislation since the early 1980s).[46] But even in the continental countries (which can

---

44. In other words, type 2 and type 3 social policies in the schema presented by Kenis, "Social Europe," pp. 725–26.

45. See Eliane Vogel-Polsky, "L'Acte unique ouvre-t-il l'espace social européen?" *Droit Social*, no. 2 (1989), pp. 177–89.

46. See, for example, Barry Fitzpatrick, "Community Social Law after Maastricht," *Industrial Law Journal*, vol. 21 (September 1992), pp. 210–11. It is ironic that the Anglo-Saxon and Nordic countries have been more efficient than their continental counterparts in implementing social legislation.

broadly be described as belonging to a Romano-Germanic family, with a common tradition of individual, substantive rights in labor law), recent trends in industrial relations show modifications of national labor regulation through bargaining at the company or even plant level.[47] Thus the appropriate form of implementation of new labor regulations has also become an issue of debate, one which has been complicated by the clash over the principle of subsidiarity. A key question immediately preceding the 1991 Maastricht conference was whether EU labor regulation should be implemented through collective bargaining to both encompass diverse legal traditions and avoid disputes over regulatory competence.[48]

Hence the regulatory impasse at the turn of the decade. On the one side, the British, backed by European employers, opposed any encroachment on national sovereignty and demanded observance of treaty law to the letter; on the other, the Commission, backed by the European labor movement and a majority of the member states, began seeking ways to evade legal constraints. The substantive and the procedural foundations of the new regulatory regime were therefore weak and based on shifting ground. In the background, the viability of the entire project was threatened by uncertainty over implementation and enforcement. However, in an attempt to force a solution to the procedural problems in the first half of 1990, Jacques Delors, the European Parliament, and the Irish president of the Labor and Social Affairs Council all expressed support for the adoption of as many of the action program measures as possible by a qualified majority.[49] Gaining adoption would require a "creative" formulation of the program measures, which would link contractual rights with more limited entitlements in labor law. Predictably, both the substantive and procedural issues of regulation became embroiled in controversy.

Creative Regulation: Playing the Treaty-Base Game

Thus began some eighteen months of tactical maneuvering as an entrepreneurial Commission sought to outwit the British government (and to evade its veto power) by playing the "treaty-base game"—attempting,

47. See Katz, "Decentralisation of Collective Bargaining."
48. For a discussion of this debate and the potential problems of implementation of directives via collective bargaining, see Adelina Adinolfi, "The Implementation of Social Policy Directives through Collective Agreements?" *Common Market Law Review*, no. 2 (1988), pp. 291–316.
49. See Rhodes, "Social Dimension," p. 264.

that is, to push its legal competence to the limit by a skillful (and at times rather devious) interpretation of treaty provisions. For the Commission, this was its only option, pending a clarification of the EC legal framework. Maastricht, it was hoped, would achieve that clarification.

In the interim, legislation that fell unambiguously under article 118A proved the least problematic. This was the case, for example, with the third draft directive on atypical work, which sought to improve health and safety requirements at temporary or mobile work sites: the twelve member states formally adopted a common position in December 1991. Such legislation significantly extends both the entitlements in place in most European countries and the regulatory scope of the European Union in this area of employment policy. But, as mentioned above, Europe's employers and the British government view these advances as important for securing the internal market: after all, comparable health and safety costs are essential for creating a level playing field for competition among EU firms.

Contractual rights are viewed differently. Other Commission proposals therefore had to be more creative: they took the form of hybrid directives, which combined contractual rights with what were strictly health and safety entitlements, and they became open to challenge. The draft directive on working time, which set minimum requirements for daily and weekly rest periods and for night and shift work, as well as the draft directive on pregnant women in the workplace, fell into this more controversial category.

The British challenged the legal basis of the directive on working time, arguing that the regulation placed financial and other burdens on employers—which paragraph 2 of article 118A excludes—and that it stretched the meaning of "health and safety" beyond recognition. In the event, however, the British employment minister, Gillian Shephard, accepted the directive at the Lisbon summit in June 1992, but only after she had won a number of concessions. These included a seven-year period of grace for its implementation in Britain (the other member states were permitted three years) and an agreement that the forty-eight-hour limit agreed for the working week could be exceeded voluntarily in Britain. Moreover, several sectors, including continuous process work and the fishing, transport, and security industries, would be exempted entirely from that limit. The Council of Ministers reached a common position on June 30, 1993 (with the British government abstaining), and the Working Time Directive was formally adopted on November 23, 1993. In March 1994 the British government initiated action against the directive in the

European Court of Justice, challenging the use of article 118A as the directive's legal base. The Commission's legal service maintains that "the legal base was 100% correct," and fully expects a ruling in its favor.

In the case of pregnant women in the workplace, the British challenged the attempt to combine contractual employment and social security rights with more conventional health and safety measures: alongside protective provisions on exposure to toxins, for instance, the directive sought to regulate maternity leave and pay, presenting both together under article 118A. A common position was adopted in December 1991, with Britain abstaining to express its disapproval at the Commission's sleight of hand and once again gaining some key concessions: a fourteen-week entitlement to pregnancy leave was agreed to, but a minimum allowance equivalent to the sickness benefit replaced the full pay specified in an earlier draft; and eligibility was made conditional on national legislation, not on the length of time employed before the pregnancy (Britain currently requires two years' employment for eligibility for pregnancy leave; the originally proposed term of service was one year).[50]

The more controversial directives hit a solid wall of opposition constructed, as one would expect, from mainly British bricks and mortar. Playing the treaty-base game in the case of the second draft directive on atypical work—which affects employers' variable costs by granting part-time and temporary workers the same rights, prorated, as full-time workers to social protection, holidays, and dismissal procedures—was bound to be difficult. The Commission promoted this directive under article 100A, arguing that a lack of harmonization would distort competition; this article specifically excludes workers' rights, however, leaving the Commission wide open to challenge. Apart from its procedural objections, the British government claimed that, together with the first atypical work directive (which would extend prorated rights to occupational pensions, sick pay, and training), the new substantive rights provided by the second directive "would cost employers in the UK around £1 *billion*" and "imperil tens of thousands of jobs."[51] The structure of employment in the United Kingdom is the basis for British alarm, for Britain has one

50. In its second reading of the draft directive, the European Parliament tried to reclaim some of these concessions, calling for improved protection on night work and for maternity pay of at least 80 percent of normal pay (rather than the equivalent of sickness benefit). Only Italy supported the Parliament's proposed revision. See *European Industrial Relations Review* (London), no. 222 (July 1992), p. 2.

51. British Department of Employment, *People, Jobs and Progress* (London: HMSO 1992).

of the highest proportions in the EU of employees on part-time contracts and, with the exception of Belgium since 1990, the highest proportion of women on such contracts. The Commission under the Belgian presidency attempted to revive both the first and second draft directives on atypical employment in the second half of 1993 by merging them into a new compromise text on nonstandard employment. But this has not prevented further disagreements—mainly between the British and the rest—which have blocked further progress. Other highly controversial items of legislation have had to accommodate British objections. The draft directive on young workers (protecting children and adolescents from exploitation in the workplace), for instance, contains a controversial exemption to allow fourteen- and fifteen-year-olds in Britain to continue to work more than twelve hours a week. While the British government has celebrated this exemption as an "opt-out," the Commission maintains that it amounts only to a temporary concession.

The Commission has also attempted a creative interpretation of the treaty with the European Company Act (which, strictly speaking, falls outside the Social Charter program). Promoted by DG-15 (the Commission's Directorate-General for Financial Institutions and Company Law), the social clauses of this proposal would require transnational companies in Europe opting for a Union legal statute rather than a national one (and thereby obtaining certain tax concessions) to implement one of three types of workers' consultation: West German-style codetermination, internal workers' committees (along Belgian, French, or Italian lines), or a model established through bargaining between workers and management. In this case the Commission has invoked article 54(3)(g) of the Treaty of Rome, which permits qualified majority voting on coordinating safeguards that member states require of companies or firms. The act's company law provisions have been linked to article 100A, however, and can be passed only by a unanimous Council vote.

The Commission's approach to other directives has been more conventional but, for the British at least, no less controversial. The proposals of DG-5 (Directorate-General for Employment, Social Affairs and Education) for a European Works Council (EWC) have been linked, like the first atypical work directive and the proof-of-employment directive (discussed below), to article 100 of the Treaty of Rome; once again, unanimous support is required. The EWC directive in its original form would have demanded that companies with 1,000 or more EC employees and operations with more than 100 workers in two or more member states establish procedures for consultation on job reductions, new working practices, and the introduction of new technology. Regardless of the proliferation of voluntary forms of works councils in numerous large European MNCs (primarily German and French, reflecting the lobbying strength of the German unions and the influence of French Socialist government legislation in the early 1980s), this directive has been opposed by Britain and by UNICE because it "would impose a form of collective arrangement" and undermine the government's efforts to limit employee involvement to share-ownership, team briefings, and "quality circles." Britain, like UNICE, wanted instead a nonbinding recommendation or resolution that "would emphasise the need for effective employee involvement practices based on flexibility."[52]

The Commission had one clear, uncontested success under pre-Maastricht procedures in introducing binding legislation on broad employment rights. Passage of the directive on proof of an employment relationship was eased considerably by the fact that British law, unlike that in a number of other member states, already required a written statement from an employer. After successfully demanding several changes to the Commission's original draft, the British government nevertheless abstained from the Council vote in protest against the use of article 100 as the treaty base for the directive.[53]

Progress with these proposals has been agonizingly slow, and many of the most important draft directives became dead letters under the pre-Maastricht procedures. But although in heavily modified form, and despite the legal constraints and the opposition of the United Kingdom (which often allows those who share British misgivings to conceal them and seem more *communautaire*), the Commission and most of the member states have been creating a patchwork of minimum social standards. These clearly move beyond measures strictly required for the freedom of

52. See British Department of Employment, *People, Jobs and Progress*, p. 11; and Mark Hall, "Legislating for Employee Participation: A Case Study of the European Works Council Directive," *Warwick Papers in Industrial Relations*, no. 39 (March 1992), p. 9. This became the first directive to be dealt with under the new regulatory procedures of the Maastricht Social Protocol and Agreement, adopted by all of the member states except Britain.

53. Modifications to British labor law will still have to be made: most notably, the time period for providing an employment statement must be reduced from thirteen weeks to two months, and employees working between eight and sixteen hours a week must be granted the same rights to a statement as those working more than sixteen hours (until now there has been a five-year service condition). For a detailed analysis, see John Clark and Mark Hall, "The Cinderella Directive? Employee Rights to Information about Conditions Applicable to Their Contract or Employment Relationship," *Industrial Law Journal*, vol. 21 (June 1992), pp. 106–18.

movement toward an approximation, if not harmonization, of certain limited *industrial* citizenship rights.

The entrepreneurial work of the Commission under Jacques Delors and the pursuit of alliances with a majority of the member states contributed to this outcome. Absolute sovereignty in this domain is being gradually eroded, even if national preoccupations (and the scope for variable geometry) have thus far prevailed over the supranational ardor of the Commission. In the process—even before the reforms of the Treaty on European Union—the bare bones of a pan-European regulatory regime were being slowly laid down.

The Social Dialogue Pillar of the Social Dimension

The debates on procedures and implementation have been complicated further by an ambitious effort to complement the EU legislative process with pan-European collective bargaining. After all, every national industrial relations system embraces both legislation and law to one degree or another; and in the Anglo-Saxon and Nordic traditions, rule setting by collective bargaining has been fundamental. But introducing collective bargaining at the EC level provoked the hostility of capital, which is quite an impediment for any regime of social regulation dependent on economic agents for its operation. By the time of the Maastricht negotiations, however, employers had accepted—at least in principle—the procedural importance of rule setting at the EC level through the social dialogue. That acceptance represented a major advance, even if the social dialogue as a form of policymaking introduces an untried, potentially counterproductive, procedural element into the regime.

If the British veto has been the biggest stumbling block to legislative progress, Europe's employers have successfully kept the social dialogue in check. UNICE has consistently opposed both EC collective bargaining and any *legislative* enhancement of workers' participation rights in transnational companies. Thus, while the Commission promoted discussions among UNICE, the European Centre of Public Enterprises (CEEP), and the ETUC within the framework of the social dialogue (the Val Duchesse discussions launched in 1985), employers before Maastricht refused to be party to any statement that might be used for legislation. UNICE's member employer associations have refused to make (and still generally oppose making) UNICE an effective bargaining authority.[54]

54. See Martin Rhodes, "The Future of the 'Social Dimension': Labor Market Regu-

Yet article 118B of the Single European Act envisages just that in obliging the Commission to "endeavour to develop the dialogue between management and labor at the European level which could, if the two sides consider it desirable, lead to relations based on agreement." The vague and open-ended nature of this obligation has been criticized, but it has provided treaty support for the European trade unions, which do want to make collective agreements integral to a European industrial relations system. National union confederations no longer oppose (as they did in the 1970s) having the ETUC advance the collective rights of European workers at the EU level. However, the ETUC, like UNICE, does not now have a mandate for negotiating agreements; even if ad hoc solutions to the problem of mandates could be found, neither ETUC nor UNICE has the organizational strength or legitimacy to become a major actor in industrial relations.

It would be easy to draw up a negative balance sheet for the social dialogue, but it would be inaccurate to say that nothing has been achieved since the mid-1980s. Although the achievements of the social dialogue have been limited, they may form the basis for a more substantial process of negotiation between management and labor at the EU level in the post-Maastricht period. Certainly they were critical in creating the environment in which, by October 1991, UNICE and the ETUC could agree on a joint proposal for a new form of bargaining over the content of social action program directives. It is true too that the first steps were cautious. Phase one of the Val Duchesse dialogue (1986–88) saw the formation of two working parties—one to monitor economic developments and employment (the macroeconomic working party), the other on social dialogue and new technologies—and agreement on three rather imprecise joint opinions. Two of these came from the macroeconomic working party, the first on the need for a cooperative growth strategy (November 1986) and the second supporting the Commission's strategy for the European economy (November 1987). The third, on "training and motivation and information and consultation," came from the new technology working party (March 1987); it proposed the introduction of EC mutual recognition of qualifications, an enhanced dialogue with employees on the introduction of new technologies, and a more sophisticated training system in member states.

---

lation in Post-1992 Europe," *Journal of Common Market Studies*, vol. 30 (March 1992), pp. 40–46; and Wolfgang Streeck and Philippe C. Schmitter, "From National Corporatism to Transnational Pluralism: Organised Interests in the Single European Market," *Politics and Society*, no. 2 (1991), pp. 133–64.

Phase two began in 1989, when Jacques Delors relaunched the dialogue after two years of inertia attributable to discord between the social partners. This phase proved more productive, in part because of stimulation by a new steering committee (composed of representatives of the employer and union organizations), but also because of the Commission's agreement to consult the social partners on its draft directives for the action program. Also, phase two coincided with the beginning of a new Commission's term in office and the arrival of Vasso Papandreou as the new commissioner responsible for labor and social affairs.

The second phase of the dialogue was much more focused, placing priority on education and training. Four joint opinions were issued during this period: on the creation of a European occupational and geographical mobility area, advocating measures to reduce the barriers to labor mobility in the Community (February 1990); on education and training (June 1990), emphasizing the importance of initial and continuous training and the role of the collaboration between the social partners in this area; on the transition from school to adult and working life (November 1990), defining priorities in educational and vocational guidance and stressing, once again, the importance of bipartite arrangements; and on access to training (September 1991), noting the need both for management and labor partnerships in promoting synergies among company training programs and for a Community role in affirming the right to vocational training.

A system of neocorporatist policymaking it is not: the social partners have no formal role in the policy process, and the joint opinions do not amount to real and consequential agreements—even if they did, neither UNICE nor the ETUC has the means to deliver members' support for them. Nor do they have sufficient organizational strength to engage in a genuine process of neocorporatist bargaining, for employer and union representatives alike are subordinate to the authority of their member associations and federations. Similarly, despite Commission encouragement of a sectoral social dialogue,[55] the joint committees composed of employer representatives and union delegates from the fifteen European industry committees (sectoral union organizations linked to the ETUC) have produced only opinions and recommendations. The absence of effective employer organization at this level and the lack of interest in going beyond diffuse joint opinions hamper Commission efforts to pro-

55. See "The Sectoral Social Dialogue," *European Industrial Relations Review* (London), no. 224 (September 1992), p. 14.

sought to extend Community competence in the area of substantive rights, including influence over contractual rights and provision for workers' representation and consultation. Third, it included a new decision-making procedure—the formulation of EC policy through collective bargaining—for dealing with two related issues: the implementation of EC labor policy in member states with diverse legal traditions and the need to respect the principle of subsidiarity, which had been strengthened in the TEU at the insistence of the British. Finally, it attempted to make the implementation of social legislation more effective by empowering the European Court of Justice to enforce Community law by imposing fines or penalty payments.

The draft of the TEU's social chapter was largely the work of member states in the northern camp of labor market management. Both the Luxembourg and Dutch presidencies of 1991 were instrumental in drawing up a set of provisions that would extend QMV to several areas, among them "working conditions" and "the information and consultation of workers." In principle, this would help fill the gaps in the Commission's powers and exclude the single member-state veto, thereby making the treaty-base game redundant. The Germans, keen to ensure that their own high labor market standards were protected, sought to bring under EC jurisdiction such issues as redundancy conditions and the representation and collective defense of workers and employers, including codetermination.[62] By November 1991 the social chapter also contained the proposal from the social partners on European collective agreements.

The intransigence of the British Conservative government, founded on a potent mix of neoliberal ideology and expediency—anything that might undermine Britain's position as a low-cost location for foreign investors must be avoided—was unlikely to be softened by attempts at accommodation. Yet the final draft of the Maastricht Treaty did make genuine concessions to the British position. British hostility to federalism (a synonym for centralization for the British Conservatives) was accommodated by replacing the word *federal* with *union* in article A of the Treaty's common provisions and inserting a strengthened subsidiarity clause, article(3)(b), which stated that the Community should take action only when its objectives could not be better achieved by the member states themselves.[63] Advocates of a strengthened social dimension fear that this

62. On the background to the German position, see Wolfgang Streeck, "More Uncertainties: German Unions Facing 1992," *Industrial Relations*, vol. 30 (Fall 1991), pp. 317–49.

63. *Treaty on Political Union, Final Draft by the Dutch Presidency as Modified by the*

clause will severely constrain social policy, given the tendency, especially on the part of the United Kingdom, to interpret subsidiarity with regard to absolute sovereignty, not to diversity within a framework of Union solidarity. It also runs counter to the emphasis elsewhere in the Treaty on extending EC competence in social affairs, where hitherto the primary responsibility lay with the member states.[64] Both subsidiarity and the need to consider competitiveness are stressed also in the revised article 117 of the treaty (which became article 1 of the Agreement on Social Policy): "The Community and the Member States will take account of the diverse forms of national practices and the need to maintain the competitiveness of the Community economy." The limits on Community intervention are reiterated in the revised article 118(2) (article 2(2) of the final agreement): minimum requirements must avoid "imposing administrative, financial and legal constraints in a way which would hold back the creation and development of small and medium-sized undertakings."[65] More generally, the explicit aim of "upward harmonization"—which has underpinned much of the Community's social policy over the years—was dropped from the new Agreement.[66]

As for voting procedures, the social chapter excluded social security and the social protection of workers from the extended list of measures falling under QMV (along with protection of redundant workers, representation and collective defense of workers, conditions of employment for third-country nationals, and financial contributions for promoting employment and job creation). Collective work rights (pay, the right of association, the right to strike or impose lock-outs) were explicitly excluded from Community competence. Yet the British government was not prepared to accept *any* revisions that would extend majority voting or EC competence. Nor was it prepared to accept the social partners' proposal for collective bargaining on the content of EC legislation, despite the fact that it further strengthened the spirit of decentralization and flexibility evident elsewhere in the social chapter.[67] Indeed, the new

Maastricht Summit, reproduced as a supplement to *Europe*, no. 1750/1751, December 13, 1991.

64. Elaine Whiteford, "Social Policy after Maastricht," *European Law Review*, vol. 18 (June 1993) p. 207.

65. See Spicker, "Subsidiarity," pp. 9–13.

66. See "Maastricht and Social Policy—Part Two," *European Industrial Relations Review* (London), no. 239 (December 1993), p. 19.

67. See Michael Gold, "Social Policy: The UK and Maastricht," *National Institute*

role for the social partners helps bridge the divide between the legalism of continental industrial relations and Britain's voluntarist approach, which is often cited as an obstacle to Britain's full participation in an emerging social community based on the equivalence of laws.

The dialogue between social partners spans the gap in several ways. First, all directives, whether adopted by qualified majority or unanimity, may be entrusted "at their joint request" to management and labor for implementation by collective agreement (article 2, paragraph (4) of the Final Social Agreement). Second, under the new procedures the Commission is obliged to consult management and labor "on the possible direction of Community action" before submitting proposals, and to consult on the content of those proposals if it "considers Community action advisable." In response, management and labor "shall forward to the Commission an opinion, or, where appropriate, a recommendation." And third, the social partners may opt for contractual relations (that is, bargaining) with each other, wherein they negotiate the content of Commission proposals; they may then proceed, should they wish, to agreements. These agreements can be implemented by negotiation (providing further flexibility) "in accordance with the procedures and practices specific to management and labor and the Member States." This is the voluntarist path. But in those areas in which the EU has competence, the agreements can also be implemented "at the joint request of the signatory parties, by a Council decision on a proposal from the Commission." This course is much more problematic because Commission decisions are binding on the specified parties. Although the British government had much else to object to, this new procedure made the social chapter quite unacceptable, given its combination of EC-level collectivism and the possibility of Council imposition of law.

The sheer quantity of political capital invested in the social chapter excluded either further dilution or abandonment. Two weeks before the Maastricht summit the ETUC threatened a campaign of industrial action if Community leaders watered down the Dutch draft to accommodate British opposition. The unions would be prepared to pressure national parliaments to throw out a diluted treaty, the ETUC claimed.[68] An opt-

---

Economic Review, no. 1 (February 1992), p. 99; and Michael Gold, "Overview of the Social Dimension," in Gold, ed., *Social Dimension*, pp. 10–40.

68. Ivo Dawney, "Major to Urge General Opt-Out Clause on EMU," *Financial Times*, November 27, 1991.

out clause seemed the only answer, even if this entailed the danger, evoked by Jacques Delors, of setting up one country as a paradise for foreign investment, particularly Japanese investment.[69]

The solution to the "British problem" left the United Kingdom within existing treaty arrangements (which remained unrevised by Maastricht), while the rest opted "up and out" into the separate Agreement on Social Policy appended to the TEU. The protocol preceding the agreement—which was signed by all twelve member states—excludes the United Kingdom from involvement "in the deliberations and the adoption by the Council of Commission proposals" and from "any financial consequences other than administrative costs entailed for the institutions." The other eleven members are authorized "to have recourse to the institutions, procedures and mechanisms of the Treaty" to give effect to the Agreement on Social Policy. In a derogation from the treaty, proposals on social policy require a qualified majority, or at least forty-four out of a possible sixty-six votes, as against fifty-four out of seventy-six under standard QMV procedures. This formula is fundamentally different from that adopted for the United Kingdom on monetary union, which allows Britain (and Denmark) to opt out while the other members proceed under treaty provisions.

The Treaty on European Union therefore provides for twin-track policymaking in social affairs. Since the Maastricht Treaty retains the provisions of the Treaty of Rome and the Single European Act, the twelve member states can still make policy together, but with majority voting limited to health and safety measures (and yet more treaty-base game controversy) and a British veto threatening any other proposals. The eleven Agreement signatories can avoid British obduracy by taking the second track, however, allowing QMV in several new areas (most notably, work conditions and the information and consultation of workers) and the involvement of management and labor in policymaking (figure 3-1 depicts the newly opened policymaking paths).

At least in theory, the procedural, substantive, and implementation components of the regime have been clarified and strengthened. Procedurally, the Council of Ministers has a much wider basis for decision-making through QMV. With regard to substantive rights, the notion of social justice has replaced (under article 2 of the Social Agreement) the pursuit of an integrated market as a rationale for legislation and future

---

69. David Goodhart, "Social Europe: Opting Out and Cashing In," *Financial Times*, December 11, 1991.

progress. And as far as implementation is concerned, the exclusion of Britain makes the Romano-Germanic legal tradition prevalent within the "social Community," creating greater potential for consensus on individual rights, facilitating enforcement, and simplifying the relationships among the different legal traditions of the Union.[70] Finally, the European Court of Justice has been given new powers to ensure compliance with legislation.

But where will the second track lead the "Social Agreement eleven"? In principle, although the protocol's provisions fall legally outside the new treaty, the EU institutions are on loan to the eleven, and legislation adopted by those members can be enforced through the European Court of Justice. Also in principle, this will allow certain blocked Union proposals to proceed, including the two most controversial draft directives: one would give part-time and temporary workers the same employment protection and social security rights, prorated, as full-time and permanent workers; the other would require European works councils in companies with 1,000 or more EC employees and in operations with 100 or more workers in two or more member states. As it happened, the works council proposal became the first piece of legislation to advance under the new procedures. Thus, with Britain marginalized, the other member states could shore up the pillars of the social dimension. The construction of a full-fledged regime for European industrial relations could proceed unopposed.

At any rate, that was the expectation. The reality will very likely be more complicated. Existing treaty provisions may have been clarified and the legal bases for regime construction thereby strengthened, but the new arrangements are full of loopholes, contradictions, and ambiguities.

The Implications for Social Legislation

The scope for legal controversy is nearly infinite. Some lawyers initially argued that the Social Protocol and Agreement amounted only to an intergovernmental agreement without status under EU law; consequently, the Commission and the Court of Justice (which could have been awarded explicit competence by the contracting parties) may be prevented from making or implementing policy under the agreement. Measures would therefore have none of the force of EU directives and

---

70. See Fitzpatrick, "Community Social Law," pp. 210–12, for a discussion of these issues.

would have to be transferred into law through ratification by national parliaments, which could create serious delays in implementation and the potential for dilution.[71] According to other legal commentators, however, the fact that all twelve member states—including the United Kingdom—have agreed to the Social Protocol means that the protocol and the agreement are definitely part of the treaty.[72] But even if this legal problem can be resolved (which seems likely, given the lack of controversy surrounding the adoption of the Directive on European Information and Consultation in June 1994), there are clear conflicts of law between the Social Agreement and the treaty.

First, the boundaries are blurred between areas subject to QMV, those subject to unanimity, and those where the agreement eleven have no competence at all. Thus, while article 100A(2) of the treaty states that provisions relating to employee rights are subject to unanimous voting in the Council, article 2 of the agreement allows QMV on working conditions and the information and consultation of workers, both of which are clearly in the realm of employee rights. And while pay is excluded from Community competence in the treaty, there are specific provisions on equal pay in the agreement. All in all, treaty-base problems have not been resolved: there is ample scope (perhaps even more than before the adoption of the agreement) for member states to contest EU competence and for the Commission to engage in "creative regulation." For example, the phrase *working conditions*—an area subject to QMV— could apply to virtually any employment-related matter.[73]

There are also potential political problems. For the Commission, the pursuit of social policy reform along the Social Agreement track would undermine its efforts to ensure a united, cohesive approach to integration and set precedents for variable geometry. This would defeat the entire objective of the Treaty on European Union. For this reason the Commission may well prefer the slower but more consensual path involving all twelve member states, while using the treaty-base game to avoid the British veto. As progress with the Working Time Directive shows (Britain eventually accepted the principle of a forty-eight-hour workweek), this strategy may occasionally pay dividends, even if the most controversial

---

71. See the arguments in Eliane Vogel-Polsky, "I maghi di Maastricht, ovvero come sparì la carta sociale europea," *Politica ed Economia*, no. 3 (1992), pp. 23–25.

72. See Fitzpatrick, "Community Social Law," p. 202. For a discussion of the constitutional aspects of the question, see Curtin, "Constitutional Structure of the Union," pp. 52–62.

73. See "Maastricht and Social Policy—Part Two," p. 23.

Commission proposals remain blocked. For the agreement eleven, legal ambiguities may also make member states reluctant to take the agreement track; they may prefer instead the much more limited but more certain option of operating alongside the British under existing treaty arrangements.[74]

The Implications for the Social Dialogue

Important claims have been made for the new social dialogue as a means of building a new consensus on employment. Indeed, at the end of 1993 Padraig Flynn, the commissioner responsible for social affairs, argued that the social dialogue could provide the basis for a pan-European social pact. It is nevertheless unlikely that the provisions of the agreement will produce a European-level regulatory regime for industrial relations in the short term.

The relationship between the Commission and the social partners is not clearly defined: Do the legislative process and the social dialogue proceed in tandem, or does the social dialogue preempt the legislative process? What is the contractual status of "Euro-agreements"? Can the social partners sue each other for breach of agreement? And although UNICE says that it is committed to creating new structures for the "broad consultation of business circles," its motives differ from those of the ETUC. Initially concerned at the loss of their British ally should the eleven take the agreement path, the employers can now replace the British veto with their own. Not only is the UNICE membership internally divided on the desirability of bargaining (with the British and Dutch the least enthusiastic), but there is little sign of a moderation in its position on most of the Commission's proposals. And as Zygmunt Tyszkiewicz, president of UNICE, remarked before the Maastricht summit, his organization still intends to put strict limits on the scope of EC intervention in this area, whether by law or by agreement.[75]

Even if other intractable problems can be resolved—including the still

---

74. There have been numerous complaints about the dual legal framework now in place. The recent Commission white paper on the future of social policy (the details of which became available in July 1994) explicitly calls for a return to a single structure, a change considered vital if the integrity of the law and the principle of equal opportunities for all in the Union are to be upheld. This suggests that the treaty discussions scheduled for 1996 will seek to bring the United Kingdom back into the fold.

75. Andrew Hill and David Goodhart, "Countdown to Maastricht: Unions Fire Warning Shot over EC Treaty," *Financial Times*, November 11, 1991, p. 2.

uncertain status of the social partners as negotiating authorities—there is a high risk of paralysis under social agreement arrangements.[76] Moreover, some of the agreement eleven may well oppose costly new social provisions now that they cannot rely on the British veto to prevent their high-minded espousal of principles from coming to expensive fruition; their agreement to new legislation is heavily linked to compensation by way of side payments (the structural and new cohesion funds).[77] The new social dialogue arrangements also exclude the European Parliament from the legislative process, which creates yet another problem. The powers of the Parliament may have been generally strengthened by the new codecision procedure for EU decisionmaking, but members of the Parliament remain concerned.[78]

There is the additional question of exactly how meaningful the new collective bargaining process will be. One of the two declarations annexed to the Agreement would seem to limit its potential. The declaration on article 4(2) states that "this arrangement implies no obligation on the member states to apply the agreements directly or to work out rules for their transposition, nor any obligation to amend national legislation in force to facilitate their implementation."[79]

In fact, the problems of actually making the new arrangements work may mean that—far from being resolved—this component of the regu-

76. Apparently the issue of mandates for the European social partners from their national members is now much less problematic than hitherto. UNICE amended its statutes (June 1992), allowing it to seek specific mandates on an issue-by-issue basis from its members, who will then have to abide by the results of negotiated Euro-agreements. The ETUC is adopting a similar process for obtaining ad hoc mandates. For further details, see "Maastricht and Social Policy—Part Three," *European Industrial Relations Review* (London), no. 241 (February 1994), p. 31.

77. See Peter Lange, "The Social Protocol: Why Did They Do It?" *Politics and Society,* vol. 21 (March 1993), pp. 5–36.

78. The new codecision procedure applies to areas previously covered by the cooperation procedure (the free movement of workers, freedom of establishment, and mutual recognition of qualifications). Other articles on which draft employment legislation is normally based (articles 100 and 118A) remain covered by the consultation and cooperation procedures, respectively. Provision for the use of the cooperation procedure under article 100A does not apply to provisions relating to "the rights and interests of employed persons," which are also therefore excluded from the new codecision procedure. In addition, the Parliament can ask the Commission to submit any appropriate proposal on matters on which it considers a Community act is required; this could lead to numerous requests for proposals in social areas. But the Parliament has the power only to specify the subject of a proposal, not the proposal's content, and it may only request a proposal, not demand one. See "Maastricht and Social Policy—Part One," *European Industrial Relations Review* (London), no. 237 (October 1993), pp. 14–20.

79. See Whiteford, "Social Policy after Maastricht," p. 209.

latory regime has been rendered practically meaningless.[80] This derives from the complexities of introducing a new instrument of European policymaking (law by collective agreement)—especially if, as outlined in the social agreement, policies are to be implemented by *national* collective bargaining. This approach may in principle accommodate national diversity, but in practice it will encounter other impediments. These include conditions placed on the representativeness of workers' organizations (Belgium, Spain, and France); requirements for ratification of collective agreements by vote of the membership (Denmark); agreements that are not legally enforceable (the United Kingdom and Ireland); the growing practice of union derecognition (the United Kingdom); and regionalization of sectoral bargaining (Germany and Spain). And, unlike the other member states, Denmark, Ireland, Italy, and the United Kingdom have no provision for extending agreements to nonunionized workers. Together these issues severely constrain the role and potential of social dialogue at Union and sectoral levels.[81]

The new arrangements have also provoked new discord between the social partners. Both UNICE and the ETUC have strong feelings on the role that Euro-agreements will play. While UNICE stresses that the relationship between legislation and agreements should be dealt with at the EU level to ensure that national traditions are not violated, the ETUC emphasizes that agreements should not be viewed as alternatives to directives. Specifically, the ETUC wants workers' rights to be covered by legislation (thereby preempting problems of implementation caused by diverse national arrangements) and negotiations to be restricted to specific employment and social policies.[82]

So what can be expected under the new regulatory arrangements? The passage of the first major piece of legislation adopted under the post-Maastricht procedures—the European Works Council Directive (renamed the Directive on European Information and Consultation)—offers a first sign. As discussed above, the works council directive was fiercely opposed by both the British government and Europe's employer organizations, despite the proliferation of works councils among large Euro-companies. Showing clear evidence of policy entrepreneurship, the Com-

---

80. Fitzpatrick, "Community Social Law," pp. 204–06.

81. See Brian Bercusson, "European Labor Law and Sectoral Bargaining," *Industrial Relations Journal*, vol. 24 (December 1993), p. 258, for a discussion of the potential for regulation via the social dialogue. More generally, for a discussion of the problems of "law by collective agreement," see Adinolfi, "Implementation of Social Policy Directives."

82. See "Maastricht and Social Policy—Part Three," pp. 32–33.

mission managed to break the deadlock in late 1993 by preempting legislation and encouraging transnational meetings of workers' representatives from European MNCs (it made available ECU 31 million—US$37.5 million—for this purpose),[83] and by shifting the directive from its original treaty base (article 100, which requires unanimity) to the new social policy procedures established at Maastricht.

There followed two rounds of consultations with the social partners in late 1993 and early 1994, when they were given the option of negotiating an agreement. They were unable to agree to do so, however, and talks broke down in acrimony: the ETUC claimed that UNICE and CEEP still rejected the notion of workers' transnational information and consultation rights (indeed, the Confederation of British Industry effectively scuttled the negotiations by withdrawing), and UNICE accused the ETUC of wanting legislation instead of an agreement.[84] The Commission therefore had no choice but to submit a new draft directive, which the member states (excluding Britain) agreed to in June. Beginning in 1996 companies employing more than 1,000 people with more than 150 in at least two member states will have to ensure that workers' representatives are consulted and informed on cross-border business decisions.[85]

The successful passage of this directive proves the potential of the Maastricht innovations. They not only allow the British veto to be evaded but also allow an unprecedented degree of consultation with employers and unions. However, the desire of the Commission (and the Belgian presidency, under which the new directive was drafted) to achieve consensus resulted in significant dilution of the original proposals. Thus the requirement for a works council was replaced by a "European Committee" or an unspecified "procedure for informing and consulting," and employees based in the United Kingdom were removed from the threshold at which the directive applies (a measure the European Parliament unsuccessfully attempted to reinstate). Moreover, the breakdown of talks between UNICE and the ETUC suggests that the dialogue route to policymaking will remain blocked.

---

83. See "EC Funding for Transnational Meetings—Part One," *European Industrial Relations Review* (London), no. 238 (November 1993), pp. 15–19.

84. For details, see "Information and Consultation Talks Fail," *European Industrial Relations Review* (London), no. 243 (April 1994), pp. 3–4.

85. The operations of British companies outside Britain but within the Union will be covered by the directive.

The Implications for Enforcement

Finally, what of enforcement? Quite apart from the problems of implementation by collective agreement, there are already gaping holes in regulatory compliance across the EU, due to either intentional evasion or inadequacy of national enforcement mechanisms. Wide disparities have been recorded in the implementation of health and safety legislation, for example, and this has much to do with the diversity of regulatory styles and machinery among the member states. Italy has been particularly poor at ensuring compliance.[86]

Notification of implementation measures has also been very poor in some countries. By the end of 1993 only Denmark, Ireland, and the United Kingdom had notified the Commission of implementing measures for over 90 percent of the social directives applicable to them; Germany, Italy, and Luxembourg had provided notification for less than 70 percent of the relevant directives. Infringement proceedings began in 1992 against six countries that failed to notify the Commission of measures to implement the 1986 directive on equal treatment in occupational security, and against Belgium and France for their notification failure regarding the 1976 directive on equal treatment.

But notification does not necessarily signify a genuine application of the law. Also in 1992, proceedings started against the United Kingdom (for failure to properly implement the 1975 directive on collective redundancies and the 1977 directive on the transfer of undertakings) and against Greece (for failing to comply with the 1980 directive on insolvency).[87] Until lately there has been no way to ensure compliance, even when the ECJ has ruled that a member state violated the treaties or legislation. The TEU empowered the ECJ to impose fines to rectify this problem, but the main power lies with the Commission: it must bring before the Court of Justice any member state that fails to take the necessary compliance measures within a set time limit and specify the amount of the fine or penalty payment that it considers appropriate.[88] Nevertheless, the diversity of national regulatory styles and enforcement mechanisms is likely to prevent an even application of EU law.

---

86. See Duncan Matthews, "Enforcement of Health and Safety Law in the UK, Germany, France and Italy," paper presented at a research meeting of the Economic and Social Research Council, Noordwijk, The Netherlands, October 27–28, 1993.

87. See "Application of Social Legislation," *European Industrial Relations Review* (London), no. 237 (October 1993), p. 3.

88. See "Maastricht and Social Policy—Part One," pp. 17–18.

Conclusion

This chapter began by asking how effective a structure of regulation or governance for the European labor market could be, given the diversity of historical, legal, and institutional traditions among the EU member states and the infinite scope for discord over two key regulatory issues: the desirability of new regulation in labor markets at either the national or the supranational level, and the acceptability of the assumption of EU competence in this domain. The answer is that the future of the social dimension will continue to be constrained by diversity and discord, with little prospect of their being overridden by the spillover effects of market integration. Regardless of the Treaty on European Union and its Protocol and Agreement on Social Policy, the supranational authorities still lack the legitimacy to act as a regulator of the labor market beyond a number of limited areas; and the European social partners are not yet in a position to participate in a system of voluntary, joint regulation with the institutions of the Union. But important progress has been made in setting up a regulatory framework and in resolving some of the regime's procedural and implementation problems; significant advances have been made also with its substantive elements. Although many of the more ambitious pieces of social legislation have been blocked, an impressive corpus of minimum rights has been put in place, not just in the area of health and safety (where consensus among the member states is greatest) but also in more controversial areas of workers' rights and entitlements.

The future of the regulatory regime is difficult to predict. In the second half of the 1990s, the greatest challenge to the European Union and to its member states will be to find an adequate response to the European employment crisis. Rising unemployment and its associated income disparities, social divisions, and threats to stability and cohesion have major policy implications. In mid-1993 some 17 million people were out of work in the European Union; 1.4 million jobs had been lost since 1990. This policy challenge is especially difficult because of the absence of any clear relationship between economic growth and employment creation in the 1980s. The ensuing debate has given new support to the deregulatory position of the British and Europe's employers, and numerous member states have embarked on radical labor market reforms to reduce labor costs, improve competitiveness, and boost employment. Because of these circumstances, the Commission has had to address the issue of employment creation head-on, and it has sought a compromise between its traditional emphasis on improving worker protection and a new concern with labor market flexibility.[89]

Moreover, the agenda for the European labor market at the national level is being set increasingly by the twin constraints of market integration—the EMU convergence criteria are demanding austerity policies throughout the Union—and intensified international competition. Systems of social security and labor market organization are beginning to compete openly with each other, placing a premium on increased efficiency and the reduction of labor costs. This explains the recent position of the Commission, which combines a concern to consolidate and implement the advances already made while taking greater account of labor market flexibility.

The European social dimension could follow either of two disparate directions, although reality is likely to lie somewhere between the two. On the one hand, the Social Agreement eleven, the Commission, and the social partners might manage to clear the many legal, political, and institutional hurdles in their path and succeed in building a Social Europe that will extend to the new members of the European Union—Austria, Sweden, and Finland. In this optimistic scenario, a limited social pact would be achieved on broad principles of employment policy at the European level, and corporatist bargains (other limited social pacts) would be struck in those member states with the institutional prerequisites. This consensus would be conditional, however, on an EU commitment to an expanded budget and more spending to assist the poorer member states with economic and social convergence. It would also require some adjustment to the EMU convergence criteria and timetable to allow a more flexible and expansionary policy in those countries whose social consensus has been fragile and undermined by austerity policies.

Such a path would be neither cheap nor rapid, and it would require a long-term, Unionwide commitment to labor market harmonization and a concomitant investment in training and skills provision. Common standards could conceivably be put in place through EU legislation and framework agreements, allowing a degree of flexibility and subsidiarity in the industrial relations regime. The United Kingdom (probably under a Labour government) could then be brought under the Social Agreement,

---

89. See Martin Rhodes, "The Social Dimension after Maastricht: Setting a New Agenda for the Labor Market," *International Journal of Comparative Labor Law and Industrial Relations*, vol. 9 (Winter 1993), pp. 297–325.

ending the procedural—and increasingly substantive—bifurcation of the regulatory structure.

A more pessimistic scenario is one in which the Social Agreement eleven and the Commission would refrain from using the social policy fast track because of their reluctance to break European unity and the concern of the poorer member states over any costly upward approximation of employment rights. The new procedure for reaching collective agreements between the social partners would be deadlocked because UNICE would reject opposition to measures that imposed costs or constraints on employers. The debate on employment protection versus labor market flexibility would become more intense. Austerity policies linked to the achievement of EMU convergence criteria would frustrate the search for a social consensus on economic policy, and many member states would experience an upsurge in industrial militancy.

Under these circumstances, Social Europe would be most solidly anchored in the northern group of countries, but market integration would have destabilizing effects on traditional levels of workers' rights and entitlements, as well as on systems of corporatist or tripartite decision-making, even in those countries.[90] In the rest of the Union pressures would be strong for adopting à la carte social policy measures. Britain would follow an insular path, providing an attractive location for inward investment not just from Japan but also from firms in other EU member states, provoking conflict over social dumping and regime shopping.

90. For a discussion of the possible threats to the German system, see Streeck, "More Uncertainties."

CHAPTER FOUR

Structural Funds and the Social Dimension of EU Policy: Springboard or Stumbling Block?

Jeffrey J. Anderson

T HE EUROPEAN UNION has a regional problem. Spatial disparities in per capita income are at least twice the level of those in the United States, stretching from 40 percent of the Union average in Alentejo, Portugal, to 195 percent in the German city-state of Hamburg. Regional variations in unemployment are likewise considerable. Between 1991 and 1993 the average unemployment rate in southern Spain was almost three times the Community average of 9.4 percent, whereas tiny Luxembourg and parts of Bavarian Germany posted rates of less than 2.5 percent.[1] These figures should hardly elicit surprise; the Union's regional diversity is a function of the diversity of its member states. Thus the plight of the Greek rural periphery appears much worse when the reference point is the Île de France rather than Athens. Nevertheless, these disparities have taken on added significance precisely because the Union aspires to be more than a mere collection of nation-states.

Regional inequalities in income, employment, investment, and growth have held a prominent place on the EU agenda. In the early 1970s the Community turned to the structural funds to address these worrisome problems. Since then, the EU has tried to bring about an improvement in the economic prospects of underdeveloped and declining regions with

Research for this chapter was funded in part by the Younger U.S. Scholars to Germany Fellowship Program of The German Marshall Fund of the United States. I would like to thank the editors of this volume and Gary Marks for their helpful comments and suggestions.

1. All figures are taken from Commission of the European Communities, *Competitiveness and Cohesion: Trends in the Regions, Fifth Periodic Report on the Social and Economic Situation and Development of the Regions in the Community* (Luxembourg: Office for Official Publications of the European Communities, 1994), pp. 192–97.

targeted financial assistance to business enterprises, local authorities, and individual workers. With the completion of the internal market, the phased (and quite likely delayed) introduction of economic and monetary union, and the recently completed enlargement of EFTA (European Free Trade Association), the scale of the regional problem facing the EU is likely to grow. For this reason alone, the implications—past, present, and future—of the structural funds for EU social policy demand close attention. In this chapter, I examine the two most significant funds operated by the Community through 1993: the European Regional Development Fund (ERDF) and the European Social Fund (ESF).[2]

This chapter addresses two distinct yet interrelated sets of questions. First, what are the structural funds, and how can one account for their emergence? The structural funds are policies of social integration that lack an explicit social citizenship dimension. To explain this feature (or rather, the lack thereof), one must interpret the structural funds as a political response to a concrete bundle of problems, one that selected certain policy options while ignoring or excluding others. Second, what are the implications of the structural funds for the social dimension of EU policymaking and, specifically, for social policies based on the principles of entitlement and social citizenship? Do they provide a springboard or a stumbling block for such programs? This line of inquiry seeks to identify the links between the cohesion approach and the existence or creation of purer forms of social policy.

The argument can be summarized as follows. Regional problems present EU actors with formidable political challenges. The predominant policy response, embodied in the structural funds, defines both the problems and the solutions in territorial terms and borrows liberally from national programs to aid distressed regions. Since their inception, the structural funds have been the preferred option for many (but not all) actors at the supranational, national, and subnational levels, a fact that results in the crowding out of plausible, alternative social policy solutions to the Union's regional problem. Nonetheless, the empirical evidence reveals hints of a more benign relationship between the structural funds and an emergent EU social dimension. To achieve a bridge between the structural funds and social policy, however, two rather stringent conditions will have to be met: (1) the initiatives will have to originate with

---

2. Elmar Rieger discusses the third structural fund, the guidance section of the European Agricultural Guarantee and Guidance Fund (EAGGF), in chapter 6.

entrepreneurial policy elites at the local level; and (2) the salience of territory in the EU will have to abate at some point.

Structural Funds and Social Policy

Economic growth, income, and employment prospects are not distributed equally across territory. Constraints on capital and especially labor mobility, as well as the cumulative advantages of market access and lower transaction costs, lead to stable, regional concentrations of prosperity and poverty, belying the predictions of neoclassical economic theory.[3] The availability of infrastructure, skilled labor reserves, supplier firms, and markets for intermediate and consumer goods influences whether business enterprises invest in certain regions. Regional stagnation or growth results from the negative or positive accumulation of these location factors. The composition of the region's economy is also important. Through multiplier effects, a preponderance of high-growth sectors, particularly those with on-site research and development capacity, will propel expansion of the regional economy; conversely, declining industrial sectors, to the extent that they are geographically concentrated, will pull down the economic performance of the region.

Regional economic problems set up serious political challenges for a host of actors.[4] They can contribute to macroeconomic inefficiencies, as when high-growth regions suffer inflation arising from shortages of labor and production capacity, while depressed regions have underused plant and labor reserves. A regional pattern of boom and bust has an obvious social impact as well: it creates spatial disparities in unemployment rates, contributes to the breakdown of communities as the young and skilled leave the area in search of work, and results in unequal life chances across the nation. National and subnational politicians are not alone in feeling the pressures of regional economic crisis. Trade union officials confront membership demands to protect wages and jobs as regional economies contract and plants close. Firms must contend with crumbling markets and uncertain investment horizons. Regional and local governments face fiscal problems as their tax bases shrink.

---

3. Harry W. Richardson, *Regional Growth Theory* (Macmillan, 1973).
4. Jeffrey J. Anderson, *The Territorial Imperative: Pluralism, Corporatism, and Economic Crisis* (Cambridge University Press, 1992).

Any number of policy instruments could be employed to alleviate geographical concentrations of decline or underdevelopment.[5] Regionally differentiated tax policies, public investment programs, sectoral policies, and social policies based on individual entitlement could conceivably address some or all of the weaknesses that afflict the typical disadvantaged region. The range of instruments employed in Western democracies, however, is actually quite narrow. Regional economic policy focuses on the regional market and targets certain *functional* actors—capital, subnational governments, occasionally labor—that operate within it.[6] Typically, regional policies seek to bring work to workers; that is, they create spatial market biases that induce capital to locate in areas that otherwise would not be selected.[7] Instruments take the form of direct financial incentives, such as capital grants, soft loans, accelerated depreciation allowances, tax concessions, and labor subsidies. Infrastructure provision is another favored instrument; eligible local authorities and public utilities receive financial assistance to build new roads, rail links, communications, and sites for industrial development.

Why regional policy tended to win out over other policy options in national campaigns against spatial economic disparities is difficult to answer. In the first place, it can be justified on both economic and social

5. Some, of course, are not at all suited to the task. For example, monetary and exchange rate instruments are difficult, if not impossible, to use in a spatially differentiated manner, although their regional impact is undeniable. As a case in point, the economic and monetary unification of Germany on July 1, 1990, eliminated the exchange rate as an adjustment mechanism for the eastern German economy, which intensified the industrial collapse of the region. See Leslie Lipschitz and Donogh McDonald, eds., *German Unification: Economic Issues* (Washington: International Monetary Fund, 1990).

6. Governments occasionally resort to sectoral policies to achieve spatial economic objectives, but this is usually done in an episodic, ad hoc manner. See the discussion of British policy toward the automobile industry in Stephen Wilks, *Industrial Policy and the Motor Industry* (Manchester University Press, 1984). Sectoral economic policies can have pronounced regional effects, some of which work against the stated objectives of regional policy. For example, British urban policy and German technology policy in the 1980s tended to undercut regional assistance programs by channeling resources to regions not designated as assisted areas. Anderson, *Territorial Imperative*, pp. 73, 89. On the general subject of regional policy, see Harvey Armstrong and Jim Taylor, *Regional Economics and Policy* (New York: Philip Allan, 1985).

7. There are numerous examples of the alternative approach. Britain's first regional policy, the 1928 Industrial Transference Scheme, encouraged unemployed workers in the "distressed areas" to seek employment in the Midlands and the South. The abandonment of this policy in the early 1930s reflected a growing awareness of the political and social disruptions that accompanied a "workers to work" approach. See D. W. Parsons, *The Political Economy of British Regional Policy* (London: Croom Helm, 1986). The European Social Fund in its early years also focused principally on improving labor mobility.

grounds, and can therefore attract a broad coalition of support. Regional policy may further macroeconomic goals, particularly lower inflation and greater overall growth, by channeling excess demand from prosperous to poorer areas. And, through the reduction of unemployment differentials and outward migration, regional policy can stabilize communities, promote interregional equity, and improve the distribution of life chances. Regional policy holds an advantage over alternative approaches, such as industrial policies or social programs directed at individuals as citizens; unlike industrial policies, it targets structural obstacles to investment and thus is less likely to degenerate into an expensive holding operation designed to keep lame ducks afloat. Unlike social entitlement programs, regional policy directly addresses the sources of spatial economic disparities and poses no threat to established social policy networks.[8]

The EU structural funds share many features with programs operated at the national level across Europe; thus their potential social effects are also quite similar. As a collection of instruments designed to redress market-generated inequities, the funds seek to influence the distribution of life chances across space. Yet in terms of content and rationale, the policies differ from entitlement-based social policies that target individuals as citizens: the ESF and the ERDF define *eligible* (but not *entitled*) policy beneficiaries as specific functional actors—labor, capital, and the local state—in scheduled assisted areas. In the mid-1970s the ESF departed from its original emphasis on individual workers defined solely as factors of production and began to target subcategories of labor defined in a purer social sense: unemployed youth, women, and the handicapped, for example. However, the continuing strength of the territorial principle in the administration of the funds has held in check the ESF's gravitation into policy based on social citizenship.

Structural funds and entitlement-based social policy could interact in several ways. The funds may contribute to the emergence of entitlement-based approaches at the EU level either by evolving in that direction

8. This point requires further elaboration. If one were to employ these kinds of social policies to address regional disparities, several problems would arise. First, channeling resources to people and not to places has the disadvantage of indirectness. It focuses on the demand side, not the supply side, and thus does not address the catalog of weaknesses identified by regional growth theories. Second, a regional social policy would require a potentially nettlesome modification to the principle of individual entitlement—namely, a regional premium for citizens living in certain areas of the country. The fact that regional and social policies tend to work in the same direction anyway further simplifies the choice. On the regional impact of social policy in Canada, see chapter 8 by Keith Banting in this volume.

themselves or by eliciting independent initiatives through a classic "spill-over" dynamic.[9] Conversely, the structural funds may hinder such policies by weakening the impetus to supply or to demand EU social initiatives. Finally, the operation of the funds may be neutral with respect to social policy, in which case the main factors that shape the horizons of EU social policy must lie elsewhere.

Needless to say, it is a tall order to confirm the precise nature of the relationship between the funds and social policy, which is likely to be highly complex. It is therefore all the more important to depict the interactions in a manner that lends itself to empirical verification. In effect, at issue is the role of the structural funds as an independent variable: what is their impact on the probability that a distinctive policy approach will be adopted at the Union level? This question connects with the study of the effects of policy feedback. In a recent article, Paul Pierson describes two conceptualizations of the impact of public policies on politics: resource and incentive approaches and interpretive approaches.[10] The former method generally explains policy effects in terms of the resources distributed and the incentive structures created by government programs. The latter approach looks to the cognitive effects of policy, which influence political action by shaping the way actors think about the world and the various options available to them.

These various feedback effects are suggestive of the potential impact of structural policy on the supply of and demand for EU social policy. For example, the resources and incentive structures generated by the structural funds may influence the capacity and inclination of EU policymakers to *supply* new social initiatives alongside the funds or to substitute social for structural policy in the campaign against regional disparities. The structural funds could also represent a particular intellectual approach to problem solving that either encourages or crowds out individual entitlement-based initiatives at the EU level. Similarly, both types of feedback effects might condition the strategies, alliance possibilities, demands, and preferences of national and subnational actors; the question, of course, is whether these effects are conducive to a heightened *demand* for EU social policy.

The experiences of two Western European countries indicate that feed-

9. For a discussion of this term, see Paul Taylor, *The Limits of European Integration* (Columbia University Press, 1983), chap. 1.

10. Paul Pierson, "When Effect Becomes Cause: Policy Feedback and Political Change," *World Politics,* vol. 45 (July 1993), pp. 595–628.

back effects are likely to emanate from the structural funds. German and British regional policies share a number of properties, and these generate similarities in the politics of uneven regional development. For example, policymakers in both countries confront comparable territorial demands and conflicts because of the way in which conventional regional policies structure interests on the periphery. In both cases two distinct policy clienteles form in the regions: direct beneficiaries of policies, principally firms and individual local authorities, and territorial interest coalitions. The latter consist of two conflicting camps: those in current or emerging problem areas, who are intent on securing the fruits of regional policy, and those in prosperous regions, who seek to limit the scope and strength of regional policy.

These feedback effects, which are principally of the resource and incentive variety, are accompanied by others that reveal the impact of ideas. Standard interpretations of the regional problem appear to narrow significantly the range of acceptable modifications to government policy approaches vis-à-vis crisis regions. Both at the center and in the provinces, conventional policy solutions hold intellectual sway. Perhaps more telling, variations in regional policies across Britain and Germany lead to differences in the strategies and alliance options available to subnational actors. The British policy delivery system, which is highly centralized, encourages the formation of bilateral relations between Whitehall and affected groups in declining regions, which in turn limits the formation of interregional coalitions on the British periphery. Regional policy in Germany, on the other hand, brings together the federal government and the *Länder* in a joint policymaking framework; this increases the possibility of cross-regional alliances and logrolling strategies.[11]

The demonstrable feedback effects that regional policy generates at the national level could be reproduced by the structural funds on a Union-wide basis. The task is to identify the existing (if any) and potential links between these effects and the prospects for a European social policy. The EU's definition of the regional problem, the content of the claims that national governments and subnational actors place on the funds, and the ensuing political conflicts may create or close off openings for a supranational social policy.

---

11. Policy feedback, while important, is not as central as the constitutional order in shaping the politics of regional decline in these two countries. For an extended discussion of these issues, see Anderson, *Territorial Imperative*, chaps. 1, 6.

Table 4-1. *Structural Fund Allocations, 1989–93*

Millions of European currency units, 1989 Prices

Country	Objective (1) regions				Objective (2) regions			Objective (5b) regions				Total
	ERDF	ESF	EAGGF[a]	Subtotal	ERDF	ESF	Subtotal	ERDF	ESF	EAGGF	Subtotal	
Belgium	0.0	0.0	0.0	0.0	211.3	67.4	278.7	11.3	9.7	11.5	32.5	311.2
Denmark	0.0	0.0	0.0	0.0	30.2	9.8	40.0	12.2	6.3	4.5	23.0	63.0
France	406.0	322.0	160.0	888.0	948.0	283.6	1,231.6	335.0	176.0	449.0	960.0	3,079.6
Germany	0.0	0.0	0.0	0.0	441.5	173.8	615.3	248.1	95.1	181.8	525.0	1,140.3
Greece	3,662.0	1,728.0	1,277.0	6,667.0	0.0	0.0	0.0	0.0	0.0	0.0	0.0	6,667.0
Ireland	1,646.0	1,372.0	654.0	3,672.0	0.0	0.0	0.0	0.0	0.0	0.0	0.0	3,672.0
Italy	4,942.0	1,700.0	801.0	7,443.0	285.6	133.7	419.3	145.4	54.7	184.9	385.0	8,247.3
Luxembourg	0.0	0.0	0.0	0.0	24.0	0.4	24.4	0.9	0.2	1.4	2.5	26.9
Netherlands	0.0	0.0	0.0	0.0	118.0	62.1	180.1	24.9	6.6	12.5	44.0	224.1
Portugal	3,757.0	2,028.0	1,173.0	6,958.0	0.0	0.0	0.0	0.0	0.0	0.0	0.0	6,958.0
Spain	6,199.0	2,348.0	1,232.0	9,779.0	1,057.9	303.1	1,361.0	61.1	39.0	184.9	285.0	11,425.0
United Kingdom	348.0	315.0	120.0	793.0	1,980.1	619.9	2,600.0	267.8	48.3	24.9	350.0	3,743.0
Total	20,960.0	9,813.0	5,427.0	36,200.0	5,096.6	1,653.8	6,750.4	1,115.7	435.9	1,055.4	2,607.0	45,557.4

Source: Commission of the European Communities, *Die Durchführung der Strukturfondsreform 1992 (Vierter Jahresbericht)* (Luxembourg: Office for Official Publications of the European Communities, 1994), pp. 87–91.

a. EAGGF refers to the guidance section of the Common Agricultural Program.

The Development of the Structural Funds

Since 1958 the structural funds have grown in size and importance (see figure 4-1), and their broader objectives, assistance criteria, and implementation frameworks have become increasingly territorialized. As the figure makes clear, an aggregate picture of the structural funds obscures important variations among the three components. The ESF took the lion's share of the structural fund budget until 1976; thereafter the regional fund assumed preeminence.

If the funds were not created equal, neither were the recipients of their largesse. The Commission estimates that between 1975 and 1988, 93 percent of all ERDF grants went to seven countries, led by Italy (32.5 percent) and the United Kingdom (20.9 percent), with France, Greece, Spain, Ireland, and Portugal rounding out the list. The largest grants per capita went to Greece, Ireland, Italy, and the United Kingdom. Since 1988, which marked the end of the second major accession wave in the Community and the beginning of the new cohesion regime, approximately one out of every two cohesion ECUs has gone to the newcomers, Greece, Spain, and Portugal (see table 4-1).

The patterns in figure 4-1 depict a shift in EC policy priorities over the years. The figures do not lie; still, they are frugal with the truth, insofar as they conjure up the image of a policy growing mightier by the year. The structural funds have had an undeniable impact on the economic landscape of the Union; the Commission estimates that 1,800,000 jobs were created or safeguarded by ERDF assistance between 1975 and 1988, half directly and half indirectly.[12] Nevertheless, in light of the worrisome stabilization of regional disparities across the Community during the 1980s, the structural funds have at best helped maintain a holding pattern in the depressed areas. Moreover, their contribution to this outcome has in all likelihood been rather modest. ERDF assistance as a percentage of EC gross fixed capital formation (GFCF) rose from 0.4 percent to a mere 0.6 percent between 1989 and 1993; even in the poorest regions with the highest assistance priority, the ERDF attained just 5 percent of GFCF in 1993.[13]

Generally speaking, three distinct periods define the development of

12. All figures are taken from Commission of the European Communities, *European Regional Development Fund: Fourteenth Annual Report, 1988* (Luxembourg: Office of Official Publications of the European Communities, 1990), p. 63.

13. Commission of the European Communities, *Competitiveness and Cohesion*, p. 131.

Figure 4-1. *Structural Funds Share of the EC Budget, 1974–92*

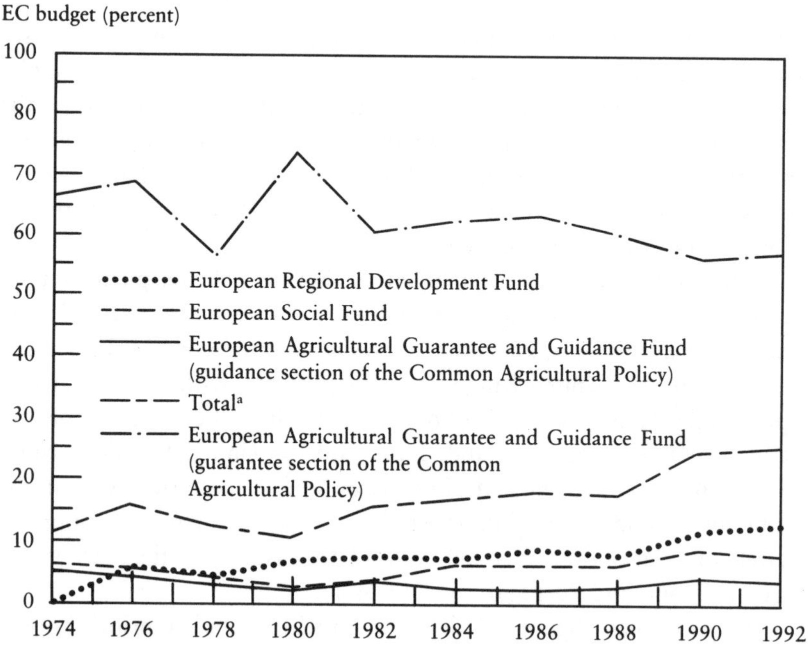

EC budget (percent)

Source: Commission of the European Communities.
a. Total comprises the three structural funds: ERDF, ESF, and the guidance section of the EAGGF.

the structural funds. The first began with the Treaty of Rome and ended in the early 1970s; it was characterized by forceful expressions of concern about the Community's regional and labor market problems but by few concrete initiatives. The second period, which lasted until 1979, encompassed the first major reform of the social fund and the creation of the regional fund. The final period began in 1979, and to date has introduced a series of unprecedented reforms that have enhanced the effectiveness of the funds.

In the introduction to this volume, Pierson and Leibfried argue that one of the perennial policy questions in a multitiered system is "Who should do it?" The structural funds exemplify the point. Debates often have centered as much on the distribution of competencies among Community institutions, national governments, and—increasingly—subnational authorities as they have upon the content of policy. With the evolution of the structural funds, the powers and responsibilities of the European Commission grew dramatically, a development that has yet to occur in the realm of social policy. Several circumstances account for the Commission's success in the 1980s: intractable Communitywide regional disparities, which threatened to worsen as a result of important integration initiatives; the accession of new members with huge regional problems, which shifted the balance of power within the Council of Ministers in favor of interstate transfers through the structural funds and which, because of the general weakness of their bureaucracies, offered the Commission key allies in its quest for greater administrative competence; the Commission's capacity to turn the member governments' general recommendations for action into specific administrative arrangements that conferred on it an important role; and the ability of the Commission to position itself as the actor best able to meet the demands of the member states for enhanced efficacy of the fund.

The Early Years: 1958–70

The six countries that signed the Treaty of Rome in March 1957—Belgium, France, Italy, Luxembourg, the Netherlands, and West Germany—were well aware of the spatial dimension of economic activity. Although each member qualified as an advanced capitalist democracy, their levels of industrial development and prosperity varied widely, and tended to run along a north-south axis, both intranationally and cross-nationally. Although most officials in the Commission and in the member governments believed that the European Economic Community (EEC) would produce net gains for all its members, they also recognized that the common market could preserve—even exacerbate—regional differences in growth, employment, and overall economic vulnerability.

The original text of the Treaty of Rome expressed these basic concerns. The signatories pledged in the preamble to reduce the economic gap among the various regions and to address the specific problems of the underdeveloped regions of the Community. Article 2 required harmonious development within the Community, while the articles dealing with agriculture, competition, and transportation acknowledged the need to take account of different regional interests and requirements in the execution of common policies. For example, article 92 granted certain exceptions to the prohibitions on state aid, provided that the member government could demonstrate that the assistance was necessary to benefit an underdeveloped or otherwise disadvantaged region.

The spatial goals expressed in the Treaty of Rome were not accompanied by commensurate actions. Two EEC policy instruments, the ESF and the European Investment Bank (EIB), were expected to alleviate Community regional problems, which were concentrated primarily in the

Italian Mezzogiorno.[14] The social fund, anchored in article 123, aimed to retrain or to resettle individual workers who had lost their jobs because of the formation of the common market. In other words, the ESF encouraged both occupational and geographical mobility, either of which could reasonably be expected to benefit distressed regions. Articles 129 and 130 established the EIB. The bank's objective was to promote the balanced development of the Community by granting loans and guarantees on a nonprofit basis. Specifically, article 130 defined three types of eligible projects: those that furthered the economic development of the less-prosperous regions; those that enhanced the competitiveness of industry in the Community; or those that were of common interest to several member states or to the Community writ large. Furthermore, the framers attached stringent conditions to the loans—namely, that projects be economically viable and that applicants provide adequate collateral.

The ESF and the EIB suffered from conceptual, financial, and administrative shortcomings that limited their effectiveness. During its first ten years of operation, the social fund was "too small, too slow, and lacking in a coherent strategy."[15] The fund paid out a mere $421 million during this period to schemes involving 1.43 million workers, or approximately 15 percent of the unemployed pool. Cumbersome administrative provisions prevented rapid take-up by eligible applicants; the fund paid up to 50 percent of a project's costs, but the money could be disbursed only *after* a worker had been retrained or resettled and subsequently reemployed. Most ESF assistance ended up going to projects that encouraged labor migration, notably from Italy to Germany and France. No mechanisms existed to match the content of retraining programs with the labor requirements of the disadvantaged regions. And finally, the individual member states, not the Commission, set the eligibility criteria and implemented policy decisions. In effect, the ESF did little more than offer member states a way to partially offset the costs of their own labor market policies.[16] As for the EIB, it served "as a useful complement to

14. Helen Wallace, "Distributional Politics: Dividing up the Community Cake," in Helen Wallace, William Wallace, and Carole Webb, eds., *Policymaking in the European Community* (John Wiley and Sons, 1983), p. 82.

15. Taylor, *Limits of European Integration*, p. 202. This brief analysis of the early years of the ESF is based in part on Taylor's account.

16. P. K. Hatt, "Dreißig Jahre Arbeit des ESF," *Soziales Europa*, February 1991, p. 80. The distribution formula of the ESF budget, based on country size, reveals again the centrality of national interests in the operation of the fund: Germany (32.0 percent), France (32.0 percent), Italy (20.0 percent), Belgium (8.8 percent), the Netherlands (7.0 percent), and Luxembourg (0.2 percent).

the private sector" by financing Community-oriented projects passed over by commercial institutions.[17] The bank's stringent loan criteria, its focus on large, capital-intensive projects, and its broad definition of eligibility (two project descriptions allowed funds to be channeled to prosperous regions) limited its usefulness in the fight against regional disparities.

Fifteen years would pass before members decided to move beyond a largely symbolic, indirect attack on spatial inequality to an explicit regional economic development policy carried out at the Community level. Why this gulf between words and deeds? First and perhaps foremost, the period was one of relative prosperity for most EC members, which limited the political salience of regional economic disparities. Italy possessed the only clear-cut example of a region in crisis. Although underdeveloped and declining regions existed elsewhere in the Community, they did not amount to a critical mass of member governments with pressing regional problems.[18]

Second, the six were, as a rule, extremely reluctant to consider a strong Community role in spatial policies, especially in an economic climate devoid of political urgency. The dictates of "competitive state-building" applied here with remarkable intensity. Each Community member had developed national regional assistance programs in the postwar period, and the officials who administered these policies resisted any significant transfer of authority to the European Commission. The ability to allocate spatially targeted policy benefits lay close to the hearts of elected officials in these countries, and the thought of losing all or even part of their discretionary powers was simply too much for them.[19] With arguments

17. Neill Nugent, *The Government and Politics of the European Community* (Duke University Press, 1989), p. 191. For a comprehensive account of the bank's organization and loan practices, see Jeffrey Harrop, *The Political Economy of Integration in the European Community* (Brookfield, Vt.: Gower, 1989), pp. 116–18.

18. Gary Marks, "Structural Policy in the European Community," in Alberta M. Sbragia, ed., *Euro-Politics: Institutions and Policymaking in the "New" European Community* (Brookings, 1991), p. 194. The irony of this situation should not go unmentioned. In the aftermath of the first OPEC crisis, low growth and widespread unemployment paved the way for a reform of the ESF and the creation of the ERDF. Yet the prevailing economic conditions militated against an effective policy response. In fact, economic growth correlates positively with the number of firms willing to move and/or invest. Thus the political salience of regional problems and the efficacy of regional policy appear to be inversely related.

19. See Jeffrey J. Anderson, "Skeptical Reflections on a Europe of Regions: Britain, Germany, and the ERDF," *Journal of Public Policy*, vol. 10 (October–December 1990), p. 427.

that foreshadowed the rallying cry of "Subsidiarity!" some three decades later, member governments maintained that they were in a better position than the Commission to identify, evaluate, and act upon regional claims for assistance. Finally, Community members held an overly sanguine view of the self-regulating powers of the common market. In a setting of overall economic growth, they reasoned, backward regions, aided by decentralized, loosely coordinated measures that focused primarily on the labor market, would catch up with more prosperous areas.

These obstacles notwithstanding, the decade of the 1960s was a time of profound reassessment within the Commission. Officials responsible for the ESF developed alternative proposals that envisioned a much more active role for the Commission and addressed the broader structural weaknesses of labor markets in backward regions. Huge strides were taken toward a Community regional policy; indeed, with great care and considerable foresight, the Commission prepared the ground for the decisions of the early 1970s by building both an intellectual case and a constituency for a Community regional policy.[20] The Commission outlined the link between a large common market and regional economic disparities, and warned that the resulting political tensions would threaten further integration. Its definition of the regional problem was quite orthodox, focusing on suboptimal industrial mix, infrastructural weaknesses, and skill shortages. Its proposed remedies borrowed liberally from the "tool kits" employed at the national level throughout Europe.

The Commission's problem-solving exercises took place within a network of national expertise and support created by the Commission itself. In 1961 the Commission sponsored a Conference on Regional Economies, which brought together politicians, bureaucrats, interest group representatives, local and regional officials, and academics to discuss the regional problem. In conjunction with national officials, the Commission undertook studies of specific regions, the objectives and instruments of national regional policies, the boundary demarcations of distressed areas, and the sources of spatial economic disparities.

These early efforts would eventually bear fruit, although the ripening process was both long and arduous. In 1965 the Commission placed before the Council, the European Parliament, and the Economic and Social Committee a proposal for Community coordination of national

---

20. The following analysis is based on H. von der Groeben's narrative account in *The European Community: The Formative Years* (Luxembourg: Office for Official Publications of the European Communities, 1987), pp. 81–83, 214–16.

regional policy programs. This proposal, which was grudgingly accepted by the member governments, left primary responsibility for the conduct of regional assistance in the hands of national authorities. Voices within the Commission had pressed for a more assertive role for their institution, but they made little headway. Coordination never advanced much beyond declarations of common aims and pledges to coordinate national policies so as not to disadvantage the less prosperous regions. In the aftermath of the merger of the Community executives in 1967, the EC Commission created a Directorate-General for Regional Policy (DG-XVI), and instructed that office to draft a proposal for a regional policy operated out of Brussels. The resulting document, which would serve eventually as the basis for an EC-wide regional assistance program, was presented to the European Council in 1969.

A European Regional Policy Takes Shape: 1971–78

By the early 1970s the obstacles to a Community regional policy looked much less formidable. Economic growth slowed dramatically, unemployment was on the rise, and countries with substantial regional problems—namely, the United Kingdom and Ireland—were knocking on Brussels' door. Moreover, Council deliberations over the Werner proposal for economic and monetary union highlighted the disadvantages for distressed regions under a system of fixed exchange rates.[21] This transformation of the political and economic context led many Community members to set aside some of their misgivings about an EC regional policy, thereby creating an opening for an expansion of the Community's role in this area. Others, like the United Kingdom, seized the opportunity to reduce their net transfers to Brussels. The Commission's presentation of a policy model that acknowledged existing political realities in the Council eased the process of reevaluation among the member governments. Two outcomes connected with this period are of particular importance: the overhaul of the social fund between 1971 and 1974 and the creation of the ERDF in 1975.

In 1971 the Council decided to increase expenditures for the social fund and to actively direct those resources to projects in sectors (textiles and shipbuilding, for example) and regions disadvantaged by the operation of the common market and by Community policies. In a break with past practice, the Commission assumed responsibility for the setting of

21. Wallace, "Distributional Politics," p. 91.

eligibility criteria, which were modified to increase the take-up of assistance. The fund was to devote special attention to the long-term unemployed and to groups with special vocational training needs, such as the handicapped, the young, women, and the aged. Youth unemployment became the number-one priority of the fund after 1976. Especially on the financial side, these reforms brought considerable advances. The fund expanded by nearly 500 percent between 1972 and 1976, becoming the second-largest budget item after agriculture.[22] Another expenditure increase in 1978 further consolidated the fund's evolving focus on youth unemployment and disadvantaged regions. Between 1971 and 1978 over 90 percent of budget outlays flowed to vocational training and other educational projects; the bulk of recipients resided in Italy and the United Kingdom.[23]

These improvements notwithstanding, the social fund failed to realize the aspirations of Commission reformers. By the end of the 1970s, the sheer scale of Community unemployment outstripped available resources. Moreover, the Commission found itself still hamstrung by administrative inefficiencies and the opposition of many member states, which jealously guarded their prerogatives during difficult economic times.[24]

The growing regional emphasis of the ESF can be attributed in large part to the ERDF. The 1972 Paris summit set December 1973 as the target date for the commencement of regional fund operations, yet a considerable delay resulted from the decision of the British Labour government to renegotiate the terms of accession and from Council disagreements over the size of the fund. After protracted bargaining rounds lasting into early 1975, the EC formally established a regional fund of approximately ECU 3.5 billion over the period 1975–77. The compromise delivered less than the original British, Irish, and Italian demands, but considerably more than the Germans—the principal underwriters of the Community budget—desired.[25] The ERDF provided assistance in the form of investment grants and loans at subsidized interest rates to both capital investment and local authority infrastructure projects. The initial

22. Taylor, *Limits of European Integration*, p. 204.
23. Hatt, "Dreißig," p. 82.
24. Taylor, *Limits of European Integration*, pp. 206–12.
25. For those interested in the negotiations leading up to the creation of the ERDF, see Wallace, "Distributional Politics"; and Simon Bulmer and William Paterson, *The Federal Republic of Germany and the European Community* (London: Allen and Unwin, 1987), pp. 204–14.

Table 4-2. *ERDF Quotas and Margins, 1975–86*

Percent

Country	1975–77	1978–80	1981–84	1985 Minimum	1985 Maximum	1986+ Minimum	1986+ Maximum
Belgium	1.49	1.39	1.11	0.90	1.20	0.61	0.82
Denmark	1.29	1.20	1.06	0.51	0.67	0.34	0.46
France	14.87	16.86	13.64	11.05	14.74	7.48	9.96
Germany	6.34	6.00	4.65	3.76	4.81	2.55	3.40
Greece	. . .	. . .	13.00	12.35	15.74	8.36	10.64
Ireland	6.46	6.46	5.94	5.64	6.83	3.82	4.61
Italy	40.00	39.39	35.49	31.94	42.59	21.62	28.79
Luxembourg	0.10	0.09	0.07	0.06	0.08	0.04	0.06
Netherlands	1.69	1.58	1.24	1.00	1.34	0.68	0.91
Portugal	. . .	. . .	. . .	. . .	. . .	10.66	14.20
Spain	. . .	. . .	. . .	. . .	. . .	17.97	23.93
United Kingdom	27.76	27.03	23.80	21.42	28.56	14.50	19.31
Total	100.00	100.00	100.00	88.63	116.56	88.63	117.09

Source: Edward Nevin, *The Economics of Europe* (New York: St. Martin's Press, 1990), p. 295.

size of the fund can only be described as modest; over the first four years of operation, its share of the total Community budget averaged just under 5 percent.

In its early incarnation, the ERDF afforded the Commission few opportunities to exercise policy leadership. DG-XVI was able to rely on a 1971 competition policy decision by the Council of Ministers that set limits on the level, instruments, and terminus of state aid granted on the basis of regional considerations; the ruling required that all regional aids be transparent (that is, subject to measurement) and stated that the Commission would henceforth distinguish between "central" and "peripheral" areas of the Community and apply restrictions on regional state aid in the former.[26] Nevertheless, the member governments remained not just active but preeminent participants in the policymaking process. States received fixed annual quotas that were negotiated by their representatives in the Council (see table 4-2).

Although ERDF allocations were supposed to supplement, not replace, national regional policy expenditures—thus raising aggregate spending on regional assistance throughout the Community—members showed little respect for this principle of additionality.[27] The Commission had

26. Wallace, "Distributional Politics," p. 92.

27. Britain was the worst offender; Whitehall officials openly confessed that the ERDF subsidized domestic regional policy. In February 1992 the British government finally acceded to the EC's request that Whitehall maintain a separate bookkeeping entry for ERDF allocations to the United Kingdom.

little or no say in the shaping of project proposals or in the designation of regional boundaries. Rather, proposals were submitted directly to Brussels by national governments, and eligible regions consisted of those areas identified in national regional assistance programs. In short, the initiative rested with national governments, leaving the Commission to play a largely passive role.[28] Furthermore, the insulated policymaking process effectively shut out subnational interest groups and regional lobbies, which in any event were indifferent to the new, underfunded program.[29]

The Years of Reform: 1979–94

The European Commission, chafing under these constraints, began a concerted effort to reform the ERDF and to bring about a closer coordination of the three structural funds. This initiative produced its first dividends in 1979 and steadily gained momentum during the 1980s.[30] As a result, the structural funds grew more significant from a budgetary standpoint (see figure 4-1) and became oriented to Communitywide objectives and criteria set largely by the Commission. This period also ushered in a thorough territorialization of the funds.

A conjunction of events, some of which are reminiscent of those that paved the way for the regional fund in the early 1970s, helped the Commission's case. The Community's efforts during the 1980s to rein in expenditures for the guidance section of the Common Agricultural Program (CAP) created the requisite budgetary opening for a shift of resources into the structural funds.[31] More directly, the accession of Greece, Spain, and Portugal increased both the sheer scale of regional disparities within the Community and the political weight assigned by the Council

28. Edward Nevin, *The Economics of Europe* (New York: St. Martin's Press, 1990), p. 294. Helen Wallace argues that the ERDF's characteristics during this period, particularly the quota system, underscore the fact that to national governments, intermember distributive issues overshadowed substantive policy concerns. Wallace, "Distributional Politics," p. 96.

29. Wallace, "Distributional Politics," pp. 97–98; and Taylor, *Limits of European Integration*, p. 42.

30. Invariably the gains were less than the Commission originally envisioned. In short, although member governments were more predisposed toward positive action at the Community level, they continued to whittle down Commission proposals. See Nevin, *Economics of Europe*, pp. 294–300; and John Mawson and others, "The Development of the European Community Regional Policy," in Michael Keating and Barry Jones, eds., *Regions in the European Community* (Clarendon Press, 1985), pp. 37–51.

31. See chapter 6 by Elmar Rieger.

to its reduction. Widening brought other salutary effects for the structural funds. The Iberian accession led to the 1985 Council decision to implement Integrated Mediterranean Programmes (IMPs) for Italy, Greece, and parts of southern France. These regions, which were most vulnerable to Spanish and Portuguese agricultural competition, received coordinated assistance for agriculture, fisheries, energy, industry, public infrastructure, and tourism. Furthermore, the multiyear programs expressly provided for the active participation of local and regional authorities in their formulation and implementation. The 1988 reform of the structural funds, which stressed among other things the participation of subnational authorities and the coordination of fund activity over several years, took its cue from the IMPs.[32]

The claims of the underdeveloped regions gathered strength as concern mounted over the regional implications of the Single European Act (SEA). Gary Marks offers a convincing explanation of the decision to double the structural funds in 1988, one that turns on the notion of a modified side payment: Weaker member states like Spain, Greece, and Portugal, whose approval was required for passage of the 1992 package, received compensation through the structural funds to offset the economic and political risks associated with completion of the internal market.[33] As testimony to the salience of the regional dimension of the SEA, the regional fund was incorporated into the Community treaty framework for the first time (article 130c).[34]

A similar dynamic led to the decision taken at the Maastricht summit in December 1991 to proceed with a phased introduction of economic and monetary union. The poorer EC members argued that once the devaluation option was taken away from them, their only means of achieving competitiveness would be through wage reductions or tight fiscal policies, which are likely to result in increased unemployment.[35]

32. See Marks, "Structural Policy," pp. 199, 209; and Commission of the European Communities, *European Regional Development Fund*, p. 21.

33. Marks, "Structural Policy," pp. 202–04.

34. The entrepreneurial role of the Commission should not be overlooked. Delors and his associates took up the regional fund commitments set out in the Single European Act and wove them into the ambitious and ultimately successful reform package passed a few years later. With a rationale based on cohesion and subsidiarity, the Commission turned back many of the standard objections of member states to an increased role for the Community in this policy area. For a detailed analysis of the Commission's strategy, see Marc E. Smyrl, "Cohesion, Subsidiarity, and Partnership: Reform of the European Community Structural Funds," paper presented at the annual meeting of the Northeastern Political Science Association, November 12, 1992.

35. This assessment of economic and monetary union is by no means universally

The price of support for the economic and monetary union (EMU) package involved a commitment to increase structural fund expenditures and to create a new "cohesion" fund by 1994, which would focus on environmental and transport projects.[36] This time the rationale advanced by "the poor four" (Spain, Portugal, Greece, and Ireland) was tied explicitly to integration. Structural fund assistance was essential to help these countries meet the stringent entry criteria for EMU. The linkage between convergence and cohesion is generally rejected by member countries like Germany and Britain, but the objections did not prevent yet another effort to expand the funds.

The anticipated spatial effects of the single-market initiative provided the main impetus for the sweeping reform of the structural funds in 1988. By this time, however, significant changes in the operation of both funds had already occurred. The territorial dimension of the ESF continued to develop; in 1983 the Council decided to further concentrate resources on underdeveloped regions, stipulating that at least 40 percent of available aid was to flow to areas in Greenland, Greece, the French Overseas Departments, Ireland, Northern Ireland, and southern Italy. This figure increased to 44.5 percent with the accession of Spain and Portugal.[37] The

---

shared. Unpublished research by economists working within the European Commission suggests that in the long run, these countries stand to gain the most from a system of fixed exchange rates, principally through lower inflation and interest rates coupled with expanding trade and investment. Similar findings have been published with respect to the impact of the single market; most of the medium- to long-term efficiency gains for producers will go to southern Europe. These studies have done little to diminish the force and urgency with which poorer members advance their arguments. National leaders in these countries are quite naturally fixated on the short-run costs of adjustment and, once again, they have pursued a strategy of linkage. A full discussion of these arguments can be found in Commission of the European Communities, *Regions in the 1990s*, pp. 67–72.

36. The relevant decisions represented a compromise between Spain and Germany. Spain, backed by other less-prosperous EC members, had announced well before the summit that it would veto EMU unless it received satisfaction on two demands: a shift in the burden of EC financial contributions onto the wealthier members, and an increase in the structural funds to address the economic costs that Spain was likely to incur in meeting the admission criteria for EMU. Several wealthier countries, notably Germany, were opposed to these demands in light of the cost and the proposed linkage between convergence and cohesion. The Commission, led by Delors, was open to the proposals on budget financing, but opposed compensation through the structural funds because this route would have permanent effects on the budget. Since the Commission viewed any economic problems generated by EMU as transitional in nature, it favored at most some form of transitional assistance in the form of a new fund. The expenditure commitments were accompanied by a decision, stated in a legally binding protocol to the treaty, that the poorer members would pay less into the EC budget in future years.

37. Hatt, "Dreißig," p. 88.

targeted recipients remained the unemployed and the untrained, particularly those among younger age groups; but a preliminary set of regional eligibility criteria determined by the Commission and based on per capita GDP (gross domestic product), the unemployment rate, migration rates, and economic structure played an increasingly important role in the distribution of aid. Even the remaining 55.5 percent of ESF resources after 1986 was disbursed on a territorial basis—that is, the aid went to *regions* with high long-term and youth unemployment rates. One of the self-proclaimed goals of the social fund was to assist regions of high unemployment that were not covered by ERDF or programs of the ECSC (European Coal and Steel Community).

The regional fund also made strides between 1979 and 1988. The relative weight of the Commission in the policymaking process began to shift with the 1979 reform package. Member governments were required to submit to the Commission detailed regional development programs containing profiles of problem regions, lists of project proposals from local authorities and other public bodies, and medium-term development targets. The 1979 reforms also modified the allocation formula of the regional fund by introducing a nonquota section controlled by the Commission. Since the nonquota section accounted for only 5 percent of fund appropriations and its final allocation required the unanimous approval of the Council of Ministers, the scope for Commission influence remained constricted. The Commission's options expanded considerably after the 1984 reforms, which abolished the distinction between quota and nonquota assistance and replaced it with a system of "margins," or maximum-minimum share ranges, for member states (table 4-2). Governments are guaranteed their minimum share in any one year; award amounts between the minimum and maximum are made at the discretion of the Commission on the basis of its own priorities and aid criteria.

In 1984 the Commission introduced a "programme contract" approach with the intent of replacing one-time, ad hoc assistance to individual projects with multiyear, integrated schemes based explicitly on direct relationships between the Commission and subnational governments. The 1984 reforms distinguished between programs organized by the Community and those organized by the national governments (National Programmes of Community Interest, or NPCI), and specified that priority was to be given to the former.

In 1988 the Community undertook its first comprehensive reform of the structural funds. The reforms achieved two basic objectives: to increase the size of the funds so as to enhance their efficacy, and to concentrate resources in the less-prosperous areas of the Community. Structural fund expenditures were to double in real terms over the period 1989–93; although still well below the amount devoted to the CAP, the increase represented a significant upgrading of Community regional assistance at a time when real spending on national regional policy was declining across much of Europe.[38]

To concentrate fund assistance, the Commission identified five objectives that are underpinned by a strong territorial principle: (1) promote the development and structural adjustment of lagging regions, defined as those in which per capita GDP is 75 percent or less of the Community average; (2) convert regions seriously affected by industrial decline;[39] (3) combat long-term unemployment; (4) facilitate the occupational integration of young people; and (5a) promote the adaptation of agricultural production and (5b) promote the development of rural areas.

For the first time, the Commission was empowered to draw up its own list of assisted areas.[40] To address Commission concerns about the stalling of economic convergence among the regions of the EC, the Council stipulated that up to 80 percent of structural fund outlays could be concentrated in the regions covered by the first objective. In fact, the Commission slated almost two-thirds of structural fund assistance for these regions between 1989 and 1993. Objective (1) regions, situated on the western and southern periphery of the Community, encompassed approximately 22 percent of the EC population during this period.[41] Three countries (Ireland, Portugal, and Greece) were classified in their respective entireties as Objective (1) regions; five member countries (Germany, Belgium, the Netherlands, Luxembourg, and Denmark) contained only (2) and (5b) regions. The amount allotted to the highest priority areas for the period 1989–93 was ECU 36.2 billion (table 4-1). In Objective (1) regions, the goal of the ERDF was to assist in the construction

---

38. Commission of the European Communities, *Regions in the 1990s*, pp. 60–61.

39. These regions are designated according to three criteria: (1) average unemployment rates above the EU average over the last three years; (2) a percentage of the regional work force employed in manufacturing above the Community average since 1975; and (3) a decline in the number of industrial jobs, compared with a 1975 benchmark. Commission of the European Communities, *Community Structural Funds, 1994–99* (Luxembourg: Office for Official Publications of the European Communities, 1993), p. 14.

40. These areas did not overlap perfectly with the assisted areas designated in national regional programs. In 1992 the Commission began to consider aligning national assisted-area maps with the Community's, a move that would significantly enhance its standing vis-à-vis the member governments.

41. Commission of the European Communities, *Regions in the 1990s*, p. 94.

of basic infrastructure, while the social fund concentrated on the development of human capital as well as on the provision of special infrastructure to carry out vocational training programs for the long-term and youth unemployed.

Objective (2) regions, which contained approximately 16 percent of the EC's population, received ECU 6.75 billion between 1989 and 1993. In these highly developed regions the ERDF focused less on basic infrastructure projects and more on capital investment projects to promote the diversification of the regional economy. The social fund again targeted human capital development, but with a special emphasis on high technology and environmental technology in the small- and medium-size firm sector. Objective (5b) regions contained approximately 5 percent of the EC's inhabitants, yet covered 17 percent of the Community's territory. The goal of (5b) expenditures, which totaled ECU 2.6 billion for 1989–93, was to complement (5a) assistance under the guidance section of the EAGGF, which seeks to improve the food processing and product marketing sectors in these regions. The Community viewed the development of tourism, craft production, and employment alternatives to agriculture as especially important goals.

It is not surprising that the ERDF played the lead role across the various objectives; its rationale and policy instruments dovetail with the fully articulated territorial thrust of the post-1988 structural funds. Yet even Objectives (3) and (4), which were within the exclusive purview of the social fund and ostensibly devoid of formal regional criteria, revealed a territorial dimension just below the surface. Over 40 percent of ESF expenditures on these objectives flowed to Objective (1) regions between 1989 and 1993.

To improve vertical coordination, the Community intensified its program approach and sought to develop lasting partnerships with regional and local authorities. In fact, the Commission pursued partnerships with vigor; it regularly sent official delegations to eligible regions to drum up interest in fund applications, and it required national governments to consult with local and regional authorities in the drafting of program applications. These actions were not always well received by national officials, who resented the disruption of sheltered relations with their provinces and, perhaps more important, the avalanches of new claims for assistance.

The partnership principle received new institutional backing during this period. In conjunction with national, regional, and local actors, the Commission drew up Community support frameworks (CSFs) for EC-assisted areas. These established medium-term development priorities and outlined the types of assistance that were to be used as well as the financing obligations of national, regional, and local authorities, the Community, and the private sector. The CSFs were designed to help the Commission target expenditures above the minimum margins. The Commission also created the Consultative Council of Local and Regional Authorities (CCLRA). Composed of forty-two current officeholders at the subnational level, the CCLRA was to be consulted on general questions of regional development and on the regional implications of Community activities.

The 1988 reforms also strengthened the shift toward Community initiatives. The Commission announced the creation of Resider, a program to assist regions affected by the decline of the steel industry, and Renaval, a program to aid declining shipbuilding regions. In 1989 five additional Community initiatives, totaling ECU 2.1 billion, were approved for 1990–93: a program to assist areas adversely affected by the decline in the coal-mining industry (Rechar); a program to address environmental problems in Objective (1) regions (Envireg); a program to improve capacities for regional research and technological development (Stride); a transfrontier cooperation program; and a program to develop the more remote regions of the Community. Community initiatives funded solely by the ESF include Comett (vocational training in new technologies), IRES and ILES (local employment programs for women), Helios (employment programs for the handicapped), and ERGO (for the long-term unemployed).[42]

In the aftermath of Maastricht, the members of the Union commenced arduous and protracted negotiations that eventually culminated in a decision to expand the overall cohesion budget (the three original funds, plus the cohesion fund); by the end of the EU's next financial period (1994–99), cohesion spending will reach ECU 141 billion in constant 1992 prices, or one-third of the total EU budget. The Commission pushed through a modest redefinition of Objectives (3) and (4) to allow for a revamped role for the ESF. In 1995, in the wake of the accession of Austria, Finland, and Sweden, the Union created a sixth objective targeting thinly populated regions in the Arctic Circle. Despite these changes, as well as others designed to stream-

42. P. K. Hatt, "Der ESF im Rahmen der Gemeinschaftsinitiativen," *Soziales Europa,* February 1991, p. 50.

line the implementation process, the core of the 1988 reforms remains intact in the post-Maastricht period.[43]

During the 1980s the Commission buttressed the structural funds with a vigorous application of its competition regulations. Article 93 empowers the Commission to monitor national regional assistance programs and to nullify any in violation of EU rules. Member governments must inform the Directorate-General for Competition (DG-IV) in advance of their intentions to create new aid policies or to alter old ones, and must receive approval from Brussels before proceeding. If the DG-IV office determines that distortions to competition would result from assisting a specific project or from the general provisions of a program, it may demand cessation or modification of the aid measure; it may also refer the case to the European Court of Justice in the event of noncompliance. The court has backed the Commission consistently, putting additional muscle behind the structural funds.

In keeping with the overall priority accorded to the less-developed regions in the EC, DG-IV concentrated its efforts on limiting the geographical coverage of regional policy and the level of award rates in the wealthier member countries. For example, Germany was the target of repeated efforts by the Commission to regulate both federal and state regional assistance programs, with special emphasis on area coverage and award rates; between 1988 and 1994 the German government reduced the percentage of the population covered by federal- and state-assisted areas from 45 percent to 22 percent. The interaction of EC regional and competition policies thus constrained the options available to several member governments.

Analysis

The Union's regional problem translates into a political problem for EU policymakers, whose incentives to act are every bit as robust as those that operate at the national level. To central governments, subnational authorities, and business interest associations, EU regional assistance represents yet another means to an end; the rationales that move them to respond at the national level therefore apply at the supranational level

---

43. For a description of these changes, see Commission of the European Communities, *Community Structural Funds.*

as well. Members of the European Parliament have taken a keen interest in matters regional, in part to nurture supportive constituencies that will assist them in expanding the competence of the legislature. For the European Commission, other motives apply. Integration often exposes economically vulnerable regions to politically intolerable pressures. Member governments may balk at the regional costs, or they may raise thorny distributive issues by demanding compensation. Either way, the EU policymaking process becomes strained. Because regional disparities are a formidable economic and political obstacle to integration, the Commission has had to pay close attention to this issue.

To combat uneven regional development the Community has defined the problem, adopted objectives, and employed instruments in ways that, apart from the level of subnational involvement in the policy process, are scarcely distinguishable from national approaches employed throughout Europe.[44] As such, the structural funds possess several characteristics of social policies broadly conceived. They address the needs of the losers in the common market. The funds also have a demonstrable social impact: they enhance skill levels, provide infrastructure, attract inward investment, and create or preserve jobs, all of which both directly and indirectly influence the welfare of individual citizens and the distribution of life chances across the EU space. Many ESF programs that focus on human capital development possess an unmistakable social component.

Yet the structural funds are grounded in principles quite distinct from those that underpin social policies based on the principle of citizen entitlement. Eligible beneficiaries within designated assisted areas are not citizens per se, but functional economic entities such as firms, local authorities, and labor. The unit of analysis is an administrative region or labor market, with *need* defined by statistical indicators such as per capita GDP, unemployment rates, and migration flows. This territorial dimension has come to dominate even the ESF, which is technically not a regional policy and, of the three funds, comes the closest to a positive integration policy based on social citizenship. Moreover, as the territorial dimension of the structural funds grew over the years, the Community eschewed a dirigiste channeling of investment to needy areas. In other words, regions are not entitled to a predefined minimum level of prosperity and employment; rather, the structural funds seek to modify the

---

44. Although the "preempted regional policy space" did not prevent the Community from developing a cohesion policy, it forced the adoption of a particular model once the decision was made to proceed at the supranational level.

incentive structure facing capital so that the poorer regions become more economically attractive. The structural funds influence probabilities but provide no guarantees.

Why, at critical junctures in the development of the EC, have member states and the Commission selected this particular approach to uneven regional economic development over plausible entitlement-based social policy options? This is by no means a rhetorical question—Keith Banting shows in chapter 8 that social policy has been used effectively in Canada to produce interregional transfers. And what impact do the structural funds have on the development of EU social policy?

Why the Structural Funds?

The structural funds emerged as a preferred alternative to social policies for three interrelated reasons. First, they jibe with the fundamental institutional characteristics and broader aims of the EU. Second, the structural funds, once in place, have presented Union policymakers with preexisting frameworks for interpretation and action. Therefore the marginal costs—financial, political, and intellectual—of addressing the negative effects of integration through the structural funds are quite low in comparison with social approaches that have yet to be formulated, adopted, and implemented at the EU level. Finally, the structural funds have generated strong support networks at the national and subnational levels that maintain a strong interest in the expansion of the funds. Each of these constitutes a classic policy feedback effect.

The compatibility between the structural funds as a policy approach and the Union as a goal-oriented institution revolves around the notion of territory. With the demise of the federal approach to integration by the mid-1960s, scholarly understanding of the EC has been shaped almost wholly by theoretical variations on functionalism and intergovernmentalism. This is unfortunate, because these approaches obscure the extent to which the Community was and is a territorial entity of the first order.[45] It is a collection of democratic states, each increasingly less

45. See Taylor, *Limits of European Integration*, for a discussion of these approaches. On the tension between functional and territorial politics, see the introductory chapter in Sidney Tarrow, Peter J. Katzenstein, and Luigi Graziano, eds., *Territorial Politics in Industrial Nations* (Praeger, 1978). For an excellent discussion of the territorial dimension of the Community, which can be traced to the central role accorded to the nation-states, see Alberta M. Sbragia, "Thinking about the European Future: The Uses of Comparison," in Sbragia, ed., *Euro-Politics*, pp. 257–91.

sovereign in the traditional, nineteenth-century sense but acutely aware of its basic territorial prerogatives and obligations to its citizens. Many of the EU's most significant conflicts are territorial in nature, if only because the member governments sit at the bargaining table, trying to secure outright advantages or, at a minimum, fair shares for their respective populations. Across a broad range of Union activities, problems and claims are defined in terms of territory. Indeed, even the language of the Union conjures up the image of two- and three-dimensional space: the common *market* (the ancient locus of trade and commerce); the removal of *barriers* to the free flow of goods, services, and people; the *deepening* and *widening* of the Union.

Given that a powerful territorial principle lies at the heart of the EU, it follows naturally that members have chosen to define a certain class of economic problems, which they see as intimately bound up with the integration process, as territorial in nature. Economic integration produces net efficiency gains for the Union as a whole, but the gains and losses are distributed unevenly across the EU space. Existing and anticipated inequities are more likely to be addressed through policies that can be justified in terms of what has been described as *developmentalism* within the Community[46]—in other words, enabling regional economies to compete more effectively in an integrated common market. They are also more likely to be addressed through policies that offer clear territorial gains to the main protagonists: the member states. The decisions to employ and to expand upon the structural funds resonate with the overarching ideology, preferred policy instruments, and institutional interests of the main actors in the European Union. Once in place, the structural funds exerted a powerful interpretive feedback effect on the preferences and goals of EU policymakers and domestic actors.

If problem solving and political compatibility have allowed regional policy to prevail over certain broad categories of social policy in the competition of ideas within EU policymaking circles, the clienteles that benefit from the structural funds have reinforced this success. Stable networks of national and subnational actors support the existing policy framework. At the subnational level, the direct recipients of structural funds—specifically, local authorities, business firms, and unemployed workers—are backed by a much broader array of actors who reap the indirect benefits of assistance: elected members of local councils and

46. Peter Lange, "The Politics of the Social Dimension," in Sbragia, ed., *Euro-Politics*, pp. 230–33.

regional, national, and supranational parliaments; trade unions; business interest associations; civic associations; research institutes; and universities. The extent to which diverse territorial coalitions actually mobilize varies from country to country, but their incidence is ubiquitous.[47] Indeed, these domestic networks are likely to become more important with the move toward multiyear EU support frameworks and the input from the CCLRA. A more capable policy clientele has taken shape as a result of the 1988 reforms, one that has both a demonstrable interest in the funds *and* an improving capability to maintain the focus of Brussels policymaking on the structural fund alternative. In short, the funds are now supported by reservoirs of expertise and interest that enjoy increasing access to the EC policymaking process. This, of course, is no accident: the Commission has pursued this objective actively since the 1960s, in a way reminiscent of the competitive state-building that Pierson and Leibfried discuss in the opening chapter.

The Structural Funds, Feedback Effects, and the EU Social Dimension

Is there any evidence that the structural funds can spill over, through policy feedbacks, to generate supply of and/or demand for entitlement-based social policies at the EU level? This could occur, for example, as the result of intellectual problem solving within expert policymaking circles, most likely lodged within the European Commission. As specialists grapple with existing problems that prevent regional policy from working effectively or with new problems generated by EU regional policy, they may look to social policy for solutions and begin to formulate and to advocate such initiatives. The spillover process could also unfold in a more interest-based manner. Through positive or negative effects, the structural funds may prompt member governments, functional actors, and even individual citizens to demand Europeanwide social policies directed at entitled individuals, either as complements or alternatives to the regional approach. The previous section of this chapter points both to a good deal of evidence that the structural funds will inhibit the emergence of an EU social policy to address the regional problem and to hints of a more positive relationship between the two approaches.

National governments and domestic interests, linked in a variety of ways to the EU decisionmaking machinery in Brussels, are in a position

47. See Anderson, "Skeptical Reflections"; and Marks, "Structural Policy."

to ensure that, as a means of combating regional economic disparities or as compensation for future integration initiatives, scarce Union resources flow not to social policy alternatives but into the coffers of the structural funds. The wealthier countries generally view the funds as an acceptable approach to the Union's regional problem, provided the resources are used efficiently, the overall burden on the EU budget does not escalate beyond reason, and the administrative constraints imposed by the Commission remain tolerable. For the less-prosperous members, the structural funds provide a supplement to national regional policies as well as a compensatory mechanism to deal with the known and potential costs of integration. Furthermore, as Leibfried and Pierson underscore in chapter 2, the funds present the poorer member countries with the opportunity to capitalize on one of the few advantages they hold over countries such as Germany and the Netherlands: an abundant supply of relatively cheap labor.[48] Since the ERDF and the ESF enable the underdeveloped regions of Spain, Greece, and Portugal to offer greenfield development sites, comprehensive infrastructure, *and* inexpensive semiskilled labor to investors, the attractions of this policy model to the less-prosperous members are considerable. Thus they have every reason to actively ignore or to block social policy proposals, for these would threaten their low-wage growth strategies in a way that the structural funds do not.

For members of subnational networks, there is probably less overt instrumentalism involved in rejecting entitlement-based social policy alternatives. A local authority official, business leader, or trade union representative pondering the future of the local economy probably will think primarily of investment and jobs. In terms of the available options and politically feasible time horizons, these are more likely to result from the structural funds, which speak directly to the issues of capital and labor, than from direct transfers to individual citizens by way of policies that have yet to be formulated. This is not to suggest that the two approaches could not coexist—clearly they could. Rather, specific claims based on social policy criteria are unlikely to emanate from the direct and indirect clienteles of the structural funds. Interpretive and resource/incentive feedbacks serve to keep their gaze fixed on existing EU regional policy. So, although Pierson and Leibfried are surely correct in highlighting the additional dimensions of strategic action that institutional fragmentation

---

48. As an indication of just how ephemeral such advantages can be, recent evidence suggests that low-cost production areas in the Union are losing out to even cheaper locations in Eastern Europe.

presents in multitiered systems, one should not underestimate the degree to which existing policy frameworks generate islands of order that narrow actors' preferred range of options.

The structural funds therefore present a politically attractive policy formula and generate a loyal policy clientele, both of which strengthen tendencies to opt in the future for structural measures to cope with regional adjustment problems and their attendant economic and social effects. The result, willed or otherwise, is to crowd out broad categories of social policy options in the eyes of the actors involved with the structural funds.[49] This, of course, does not in any way sound the death knell for a European social policy. Clearly, other EU policy arenas and networks, such as the European Court of Justice, can and do provide independent thrusts for the development of an EU social dimension. What is more, there are at least two ways in which the structural funds themselves could provide a thin wedge for the introduction of policies based on the principle of social citizenship.

First, the prospects for a Union social policy may be closely linked to the ultimate success or failure of the structural funds. To the extent that the regional and social funds fail to equip regions to compete in the single market, these areas may lose their most mobile citizens at an accelerated pace, as the young and qualified depart for the greener pastures opened up by the 1992 initiative. The Objective (1) regions would appear to be the most vulnerable, and the negative effects of outmigration would be compounded by underlying demographic trends already documented by experts. Because of declines in birth and mortality rates across much of Europe, older people will constitute an increasingly larger percentage of the citizenry in many parts of Europe, especially in the poorer regions.[50] Should the gap between the rich and the poor regions widen still further, then considerable political pressures within the Commission and the affected member states may build for more of the same—that is, for upgrading the structural funds.

If the structural funds do work as intended, however, they could

49. Margaret Weir employs a "crowding out" argument in her contribution to this volume (chapter 10).

50. See European Foundation for the Improvement of Living and Working Conditions, *Mobility and Social Cohesion in the European Community: A Forward Look* (Dublin: Loughlinstown House, 1990), pp. 20–23; and Commission of the European Communities, *Long-Term Regional Demographic Developments up to the Beginning of the Next Century and Regional Policy* (Luxembourg: Office for Official Publications of the European Communities, 1988), p. 3.

enable these regions to escape the worst consequences of economic integration. Indeed, few hope for much more; historically, regional structural policies have only slowed, not reversed, market-driven processes of economic change. Efficacy is measured in terms of the second derivative, and success is defined as preventing the collapse of the regional economy. Should the structural funds play a role in securing this outcome, then the horizons for social policy may broaden, if only slightly.[51] By helping to place a floor beneath the regional population, the structural funds may keep disadvantaged communities intact by enabling them to retain the young and qualified, who tend to be the most economically and politically engaged inhabitants.[52] These individuals may then voice demands for direct, individually targeted social transfers from the EU. By slowing or even arresting the disintegration of disadvantaged communities, and thereby holding together potential social policy constituencies and minimizing economic heterogeneity within the Union, the structural funds may create preconditions for the development of social policy initiatives.[53]

However, the political effectiveness of such constituencies will depend on factors outside the structural fund networks. In other words, the mobilization of disadvantaged communities around social policy claims on the EU is not likely to originate with local authorities, business firms and associations, or trade unions. In the absence of automatic spillover from the structural funds to social policy, a certain element of political entrepreneurship will be required to forge a link between the funds and a social dimension. Political parties would appear to be best suited to the task of bridging, especially party officials whose careers are intimately bound up with the EU—namely, members of the European Parliament. And this, of course, hinges on the further strengthening of the European Parliament.

Second, the ESF's social policy affinities, which have been held in check by inexorable territorialization, could enable the social fund to function as a bridge between the structural funds and social policies directed at entitled individuals. The social fund finances numerous programs aimed

---

51. The financial role is likely to be quite modest; it will be effective only in conjunction with the continued application of industrial and regional assistance by the member governments themselves.

52. See European Foundation for the Improvement of Living and Working Conditions, *Mobility and Social Cohesion*, p. 23.

53. See chapter 2 of this volume.

at equipping the long-term unemployed to reenter the labor market, and many of these projects are grass-roots operations that address more than just the technical aspects of vocational training. These programs, which vary widely from country to country and city to city, often provide individual participants with knowledge and skills that extend beyond the workplace to the educational, health, and psychological spheres of life.[54]

EU support for such programs could have two salutary effects on the development of European social policy. First, the social fund becomes linked through such programs to the much broader problem of poverty, which has increasingly become a manifestation of unemployment.[55] This opens up the possibility that two quite different policy models, one that addresses human capital development and others that address the problems of poverty, can be joined. There is already some evidence for this: witness the Council's decision in July 1989 to establish a medium-term action program to foster the economic and social integration of the least-privileged groups in the Community. This program seeks to combine a focus on poverty, particularly the new forms associated with unemployment and single (female) parenthood, with a territorial emphasis on declining or late-developing regions. It draws an explicit connection to the structural funds, arguing that "although the fight against poverty is not one of the specific tasks of the structural funds, their action serves as a safety net to prevent the impoverishment of categories or regions at risk."[56]

Second, social fund resources, by supporting local programs and the community activists who run them, contribute to the creation of new subnational networks that are more inclined to make social policy claims on the Union. The medium-term poverty action program mentioned above envisions a close partnership among the Commission, national and subnational governments, voluntary and private bodies, and the individual beneficiaries themselves in the thirty-odd pilot schemes it intends to

---

54. For example, see European Foundation for the Improvement of Living and Working Conditions, *Taking Action about Long-Term Unemployment in Europe: The Experience of 20 Locally Based Projects* (Dublin: Loughlinstown House, 1988).

55. European Foundation for the Improvement of Living and Working Conditions, *Mobility and Social Cohesion*, p. 57.

56. Commission of the European Communities, "Medium-term Community Action Programme to Foster the Economic and Social Integration of the Least Privileged Groups," *Bulletin of the European Communities: Supplement*, April 1989, p. 13. A summary of EC measures through 1989 to fight poverty is contained in annex 1 of that supplement, pp. 13–15.

support. Thus the ESF holds out the promise of creating social policy claimants that can draw sustenance from the territorial networks organized around the structural funds.

The Way Forward

Will the structural funds play midwife to an EU social dimension, or will they continue to overshadow fledgling social policy initiatives? Recent and future developments at the Union level suggest that the territorial dimension will strengthen in the coming years, and with it the role of the structural funds as both policy instrument and bone of contention. A difficult road lies ahead for those advocates of social policy who look to the structural funds for a push. The Maastricht summit demonstrated that the Community is capable of taking quite respectable steps forward on the path of integration, yet the bargaining and outcomes invariably reflect territorial clashes of interest. In fact, the twelve member nations and the Commission embarked on the rocky road to European union in the midst of a flowering of regionalist sentiment in the Community, the roots of which go much deeper than the feedback effects emanating from the structural funds. Subnational interests, emboldened by the prospect of nation-states squeezed from above and from below, have begun to stake claims for independent representation and even decisionmaking competence within the Union. Many regional authorities, like the German *Länder*, have their own "embassies" in Brussels to monitor and, where possible, influence the flow of Union business. Since 1989 representatives of regional governments from eight member countries have convened several "Europe of Regions" conferences to formulate demands for direct participation in EC affairs. The Maastricht summit responded to these demands by creating an advisory Committee of the Regions, which will serve as a liaison between Brussels and subnational governments. There is every reason to believe that national governments will remain actors of considerable consequence, thus placing limits on the development of a Europe of regions.[57] Nevertheless, the subnational dimension of EU interest representation and, one would presume, policy formulation is becoming increasingly salient.

The territorial dimension of Union policymaking will grow with the

57. On this point, see Anderson, "Skeptical Reflections"; and Marks, "Structural Policy."

ongoing enlargement of the EU. The accession of Austria, Finland, and Sweden in 1995, with more countries to come in future years, will challenge the existing balance of spatial economic interests within the Union, which up until now has favored the underdeveloped Mediterranean countries. Indeed, many observers believe that the southern members used the negotiations over the Commission's 1994–99 financial plan as their last opportunity to beef up the structural funds, since expansion will touch off an inexorable decline of southern political influence within the EU. As such, center-periphery conflicts within the Union are likely to sharpen over the course of the next decade.

Competition for territorial assistance and compensation will probably intensify once the EU has been widened. Even the wealthy EFTA entrants are not without distressed areas, and current disadvantaged regions may eventually have to contend with the claims of declining Eastern European industrial regions. In Poland, Hungary, and the Czech and Slovak republics, the four most probable candidates for EU membership, the share of manufacturing employment exceeds the Union average of 33 percent.[58] Yet their industries are outmoded, centered around heavy manufacturing, and regionally concentrated. Problems of industrial mix are compounded by serious environmental and infrastructural weaknesses. Doubtless these countries face long, wrenching adjustment processes accompanied by high levels of unemployment. Even if these countries make considerable progress in rebuilding their economies before they gain admittance to the EU, they will still place formidable demands on the regional and social funds. Indeed, if the wrangles over the terms of eastern Germany's inclusion in the Union and its status as an Objective (1) region for the period 1994–99 are any guide, then members like Spain, Portugal, and Greece will fight bitterly to protect their respective shares of the EU budget, including of course structural fund assistance.[59] Indeed, as the financial burdens of assisting the newcomers are redistributed, some of the poorer countries—for example, Spain—may experience a move from the net receiver to net payer camp, which will only intensify spatial conflicts. Regardless of the eventual outcomes, the issues and remedies will be defined in territorial terms.

According to this scenario, the structural funds will continue to crowd

58. Commission of the European Communities, *Regions in the 1990s*, p. 73.
59. See Jeffrey J. Anderson, "Germany and the Structural Funds: Unification Leads to Bifurcation," in Liesbet Hooghe, ed., *European Cohesion Policy and Subnational Mobilization* (Oxford University Press, forthcoming 1995).

out entitlement-based social policy alternatives to the Union's regional problem. The combination of new problem regions and new member states will only accentuate the territorial dimension of EU problem solving and distributive politics, pushing the structural funds even further into the foreground. Furthermore, in light of the increased costs of the 1992 CAP reform over the medium term, as well as the reluctance of net contributors such as Germany and Britain to approve yet another major expansion of the EU budget, untried and expensive social initiatives will face an uphill battle to secure the attention of Union policymakers and domestic clienteles.

Assume for a moment that bridges between the structural funds and social policy are constructed along the lines detailed above. It is still improbable that they will be uniformly distributed across the Union. Rather, depending on the distribution of political skills, resources, and degrees of deprivation, cross-policy links will emerge in some parts of the EU and remain dormant in others. Whether a checkerboard pattern of bridging between the social fund and claims for Union social policies— or what Pierson and Leibfried characterize as "policy innovation and emulation"—can form the political basis for a Europeanwide social policy is problematic. In fact, it may prove to be anything but helpful, insofar as it prompts a less than holistic response from Brussels.[60] Member states, with the encouragement of the Commission, may support EU initiatives that merely "top off" national social programs in selected regions, using existing national implementation frameworks. The Community has been willing to take this more cost-effective and politically less controversial route in the past; witness the original ESF framework. This outcome could land the incipient EU social dimension in a cul-de-sac and simply confirm the dominant territorial impulse within the Union. In short, the regionalization of European social policy could preempt the Europeanization of social policy.

---

60. This would be consistent with the thrust of the Social Protocol reached at Maastricht, which represented a retreat from holism.

CHAPTER FIVE

Gender and the Evolution of European Social Policies

Ilona Ostner and Jane Lewis

T HE WEAKENING OF MEMBER-STATE power as EU policymaking expands has only recently become an issue for those studying gender policy.
This new tier of governance affects women's lives considerably as member states go about relegitimating—and often redesigning—their social
policies to meet supranational standards.[1] The European Commission
and the European Court of Justice (ECJ) have had much success in promoting, monitoring, and interpreting the rights of working women, forcing major revisions of national practice. Possibilities for social policy
initiatives have been eased by article 119 of the Treaty of Rome, which
addresses equal treatment for women. Although the provision essentially
lay dormant for almost two decades, the article created an opening for
both the Court and the Commission when they began to take a more
activist approach in the mid-1970s. Gender policies have evolved through
the intricate interplay between these two supranational bodies, within
the range of outcomes tolerated by member states. By the late 1980s the
Court's interpretations of article 119, Commission-fostered directives
that give the article concrete form and extend it, and the Court's subsequent rulings about the meaning of the directives yielded a body of
gender-related policies of substantial scope.

Treaty amendments and changed decisionmaking rules resulting from
the Single European Act (SEA) have further limited national sovereignty.
Article 100a, which allows qualified majority voting on issues linked to
creating a single market, curbed the veto power of member states. In

1. Elizabeth Meehan, *Citizenship and the European Community* (London: Sage, 1993);
and Catherine Hoskyns, "Gender Issues in International Relations: The Case of the European Community," *Review of International Studies*, vol. 20 (July 1994), pp. 225–39.

addition, the introduction of a provision calling for a "second reading" (which allows a second review) of proposed legislation has significantly strengthened the position of the European Parliament.[2] Consequently, the future of member-state sovereignty, the interplay of Community and national institutions—their sharing, pooling, ceding, and reclaiming of power in the policy process—and the problematic liaison of supranationality and subsidiarity have become key issues for social and political scientists, as well as for legal scholars.[3]

The Union's successes, however, occur within strict limits. Students of gender issues have repeatedly stressed the problems of treating labor-market issues in isolation from the broader environment that encompasses gender relationships.[4] The EU builds on a narrow notion of equality that implies treating working women like working men. The Union does not fully address the diversity of women's life courses. EU law applies only to the working population or to people "actively seeking employment." Only the family concerns of continuously employed wage earners attract political attention. Work interruptions to fulfill family care obligations have not reached the political agenda. In short, as two observers put it, the EU's nondiscrimination policy is "tantamount to asserting that the Ritz is open to all—the availability of a facility does not mean that everyone has the wherewithal to take advantage of it."[5]

This chapter examines the scope and limits of EU equal-treatment policy. First, we hold that the Commission and the ECJ have exploited successfully the principle of equal pay and equal treatment, forcing mem-

---

2. David R. Cameron, "The 1992 Initiative: Causes and Consequences," in Alberta M. Sbragia, ed., *Euro-Politics: Institutions and Policymaking in the "New" European Community* (Brookings, 1992), pp. 23–74; and "Special: The European Parliament," *The Economist*, May 21–27, 1994, pp. 19–22.

3. As evidenced in Sbragia, ed., *Euro-Politics*.

4. Nancy Fraser distinguishes two strategies to achieve gender equity. Promoting "universal breadwinning" means granting women equal and viable access to the paid labor market. Furthering "carers' parity" involves acknowledging the value of women's work outside the paid labor market and detaching economic rewards from continuous participation as a wage earner. See Fraser, "After the Family Wage: Gender, Equity and the Welfare State," paper presented at the conference "Crossing Borders: International Dialogues on Gender, Social Politics, and Citizenship," Saltjoebaden, Sweden, May 27–29, 1994, pp. 27–29. See also Ann Shola Orloff, "Gender and the Social Rights of Citizenship: The Comparative Analysis of Gender Relations and Welfare States," *American Sociological Review*, vol. 58 (June 1993), pp. 303–28.

5. Anne E. Morris and Susan M. Nott, *Working Women and the Law: Equality and Discrimination in Theory and Practise* (London: Routledge, 1991), p. 193.

ber states to give up many discriminatory practices. Nevertheless, both the Court and the Commission have consistently refrained from family policy per se—indeed, from any policy that was not "clearly stated or unambiguously implied in the Treaty."[6] Transforming the gendered division of labor in households has not been a goal of EU social policy.

Even within the Union's restricted gender agenda, reforms are constrained. In a multitiered EU, supranational policy is filtered through distinctive national social policy regimes, and differences in political and cultural attitudes toward social problems influence the interpretation and implementation of supranational rules. Social policy is often highly contested in member states, particularly as one moves beyond the issues of social security for typical workers. The distinctive mixes of social policies in different countries bolster particular gender orders:[7] member states still wish to determine which institution is to provide for whom, how much, and how, and they are likely to resist new policies that challenge existing national patterns.

Thus gender-related policies must pass through two separate "needles' eyes" to be discussed, adopted, and implemented. Supranationally, such policy generally has to be cast as employment-related, limiting it to individuals in the world of paid work. The welfare regime of each member state and the gender order underlying it constitute the other needle's eye that influences how EU directives are implemented. As Guy Peters suggests, "Losing at the policymaking stage may not be so important if there is a second round at the implementation stage when the national government . . . has an opportunity to determine what will actually happen in the policy area in that country."[8]

This chapter first summarizes the history of Community gender policy development before outlining the scope of current initiatives. Finally, we look in more detail at the two needles' eyes that constrain reform: the principles underlying EU policy and the preexisting policy and cultural frames that influence implementation at the national level.

6. Desmond Dinan, "The European Community, 1978–1983," *Annals of the American Academy of Political and Social Science*, vol. 531 (January 1994), pp. 10–24, 11.

7. *Gender order*, or *regime*, refers to the norms, principles, and policies informing the allocation of tasks, rights, and life chances to both sexes. Paid work, unpaid care, and their allocation are not neatly separated, but are located in a complex system of subordination and precedence. Gender regimes differ as to who should provide for a family's income or who should take care of the baby or the frail grandmother.

8. B. Guy Peters, "Bureaucratic Politics and the Institutions of the European Community," in Sbragia, ed., *Euro-Politics*, pp. 75–122, 104.

The Development of EC Gender Policy

Community gender policy is closely linked to the development of the Community's social dimension.[9] From 1957 to 1972 the EC intervened in social policy only when the link to creating a common market was obvious, but this period set the critical foundation for future gender-related initiatives. In drafting the Treaty of Rome, experts and politicians had considered whether competition among member states with divergent social policies might justify EC regulation. Conflicts between France and Germany revealed fundamental differences over women's paid work and the EC's proper role in social policy. For France, social protection schemes were integral to wages, and indirect labor costs called for harmonization across the Community. Germany countered that indirect labor costs were only one factor among the many—including taxation, productivity, labor relations, and location—that determine competitiveness. Given this multiplicity of factors, Germany saw no reason to focus particularly on harmonizing social policy. The International Labour Organisation (ILO) was asked to investigate, and the majority of ILO experts supported the German point of view.

Urged on by employers who traditionally paid for social security and family allowances, France nonetheless insisted that the member states insert article 119 into a treaty section on social policy: "Each member state shall . . . ensure and maintain the application of the principle that men and women should receive equal pay for equal work. For the purpose of this article, 'pay' means the ordinary basic or minimum wage or salary and any other consideration, whether in cash or kind, which the worker receives, directly or indirectly, in respect of his employment from his employer." Though concerns about France's competitiveness—not women's interests or some quest for social justice—gave rise to article 119, it has become the entering wedge for gender-related EU social policy. At first, however, the Community did little to implement or to further member-state implementation of article 119.

The second stage of development of the social dimension comprises

9. For historical overviews, see Chris Brewster and Paul Teague, *European Community Social Policy: Its Impact in the UK* (London: Institute of Personnel Management, 1989); Hortense Hörburger, *Europas Frauen fordern mehr* (Marburg: SP-Verlag Norbert Schüren, 1990); Jos Berghman, "1992 and Social Security: Critique and Proposals," in Graham Room, ed., *Towards a European Welfare State?* (Bristol: SAUS, 1991), pp. 91–104; and Jane Keithley, "Social Security in a Single Market," in Room, ed., *European Welfare State*, pp. 72–90.

the decade between 1973 and 1983 and coincides with the rise of new political and social movements, the ascendance of labor and social-liberal governments, and the EC's enlargement to include the United Kingdom, Ireland, and Denmark. The Community began to confront employment policy issues such as full and better employment, gender equality in the workplace, improvement of worker health and safety conditions, and industrial codetermination. At the same time the ECJ started to interpret article 119 imaginatively and extensively, deciding the first of three *Defrenne* cases (discussed below). Also, the EC's first social action program (1974) included a section on women.[10]

Many social policy directives were drafted at this stage. The most ambitious ran into immediate trouble. Significant legislation on a number of issues crucial to women—work hours, prorated social benefits for people working less than full time, and measures to accommodate work and family obligations—was blocked in the Council of Ministers. Faced with strong opposition from member states, the Commission failed to push a comprehensive memorandum regarding working conditions through the Council in 1975. The proposals, which would have affected collective bargaining, were considered a major intrusion on national sovereignty.[11] Germany and the United Kingdom rejected extending equal treatment to social security, which they felt went beyond "working conditions." Denmark, the Netherlands, and Germany opposed a directive on positive discrimination. The Commission regrouped around a more piecemeal strategy, however; step by step, five directives were proposed and adopted, detailing some of the legal and procedural implications of equal pay and equal treatment.

In spite of failures and often stiff opposition from member states, this was far and away the most active period for EC women's policy. The Council of Ministers passed five equality directives between 1975 and 1986, which may be divided into two groups: the *equal-pay* directive only details the scope of article 119; the four subsequent *equal-treatment* directives go beyond article 119.[12] The Council also adopted three action

10. Catherine Hoskyns, "Working Women and Women's Rights: The Development and Implications of EC Policy," in Susan Milner and Linda Hantrais, eds., *Workers' Rights in Europe*, Cross-National Research Papers (Birmingham: Aston University, 1994), pp. 23–32.

11. Peter Lange, "The Politics of the Social Dimension," in Sbragia, ed., *Euro-Politics*, pp. 225–56; and Hörburger, *Europas Frauen*, p. 28.

12. "Directive (75/117) on Equal Pay for Men and Women, February 10, 1975," OJEC (Official Journal of the European Communities) L 45, February 19, 1975, pp. 19–20; "Directive (76/207) on Equal Treatment, February 9, 1976," OJEC L 39, February 14,

programs on equal opportunities, covering the period 1982–95.[13] Equality legislation was accompanied by nonbinding political instruments, such as recommendations, resolutions, and proposals, that transcended employment-related issues.

But by the early 1980s the tide had turned. As Fritz Scharpf argues, many of the goals that could easily justify extensive Court intervention had been attained. Barriers to free mobility of capital and labor were removed.[14] Legal intervention that would go beyond market-related concerns posed greater challenges to national policy and national identities. At the same time, the Left-liberal governments most supportive of gender initiatives were either out of office or on the defensive in much of Europe. Economic pressures further reduced the enthusiasm for social reform; so did the member states' growing recognition of the complex and extensive implications of previous initiatives. The Commission's proposed directive on parental leave for family reasons was vetoed several times by the

---

1976, pp. 40–42; "Directive (79/7) on Equal Treatment in Matters of Social Security, December 19, 1978," OJEC L 6, January 10, 1979, pp. 24–25; "Directive (86/378) on Equal Treatment in Occupational Security Schemes, July 24, 1986," OJEC L 225, August 12, 1986, pp. 40–42; "Directive (86/613) on Equal Treatment Engaged in an Activity, Including Agriculture, in a Self-employed Capacity, and on the Protection of Self-employed Women during Pregnancy and Motherhood, December 11, 1986," OJEC L 359, December 19, 1986, pp. 56–58. We have abbreviated the official titles of the directives somewhat.

13. These measures are summarized in "Community Action to Promote the Employment of Women," in Commission of the European Communities (hereafter EC Commission), *Employment in Europe* (Luxembourg: EC, 1991). The first action program (1982–86) was to consolidate the impact of new directives and to improve rights of individual women workers by preparing additional legislation. In 1984 the Council passed a resolution on "Action to Combat Unemployment among Women" and a recommendation "On the Promotion of Positive Action," as well as the European Community Support Program for Local Employment Initiatives for Women, intended to encourage women to start their own businesses; EC Commission, *Employment*, pp. 146, 147, 151. In 1988, under the second action program (1986–90), the Commission issued a report on the implementation of the Council recommendation on positive action (see "Action to Promote The Employment of Women," in EC Commission, *Employment*, pp. 147–48); interpretation and measures were shown to differ widely among member states. The NOW (New Opportunities for Women) initiative was enacted with the third action program on equal opportunities for women and men (1990–95), and was to entrench equality policy as integral to Community economic and social policy. NOW is funded by the European Social Fund and the European Regional Development Fund, so resources must be targeted on less-developed regions; see Susan Cox, "Equal Opportunities," in Michael Gold, ed., *The Social Dimension: Employment Policy in the European Community* (Macmillan, 1993), p. 55.

14. Fritz W. Scharpf, "Wege aus der Sackgasse, Europa: Zentralisierung und Dezentralisierung," *WZB* (Wissenschaftszentrum Berlin) *Mitteilungen*, vol. 56 (June 1992), pp. 24–28.

United Kingdom.[15] Also, in 1984 the ECJ, dealing with gender-specific maternal leave, stated that "it was not the job of the Court to settle questions concerned with the organization of the family or to alter the division of responsibility between the parents."[16]

These incidents mark the transition to the third stage of the development of EC gender policy, which lasted from 1983 to 1991, roughly corresponding to the internal market initiatives of the Single European Act and to the emphasis of the Delors presidency on the "politics of social dialogue" (see chapter 11, by George Ross, in this volume). Delors hoped to foster negotiations and agreements among the main political actors, with social policy initiatives generally relegated to bargaining between employers and trade unions.[17] The Delors approach shifted the orientation of policy from monolithic harmonization to "lowest-common-denominator" and consensual standards, leaving implementation to member states.[18]

Such caution was encouraged by vigorous resistance from the United Kingdom, which limited Community social policy to a small band of issues regarding employment-related rights. As Peter Lange notes, in the context of a unanimity requirement the predictable U.K. veto became "a screen behind which the other member states could avoid responsibility for not doing what they did not want to do."[19] Member states could practice "cheap talk," offering purely rhetorical support for expanding Community social standards without having to confront the complex structure of interests that would have been affected had such standards been implemented.

Progress during the current fourth stage, marked by neopluralist and highly fragmented interest policies, is slow and unlikely to proceed unless social measures are highly consensual or subject to qualified majority voting.[20] Both Margaret Thatcher's fall in 1990 and the Maastricht summit of 1991 seemed to increase the potential for EC social interventions. Opportunities for cheap talk vanished. However, the recent period has

15. The "Directive on Parental Leave" would have given a working parent a right to at least three months of leave to take care of a child under the age of two and a right to stay home for a minimum number of days should there be serious family reasons, such as the sickness or death of a close family member; see Cox, "Equal Opportunities," p. 55.

16. *Hofmann* v. *Barmer Ersatzkasse,* Case 184/83, ECR 3047 (1984).

17. Dinan, "European Community," p. 17.

18. Giandomenico Majone, "Regulating Europe: Problems and Prospects," *Jahrbuch zur Staats- und Verwaltungswissenschaft,* vol. 3 (1989), pp. 159–78.

19. Lange, "Politics," p. 246.

20. Lange, "Politics," p. 256.

generally confirmed the changing priorities already evident in the late 1980s. For example, the draft directive on atypical work was not considered a gender-equality issue, although in most member states the proposals would affect mostly women. Furthermore, the social fund no longer addresses women as a special-needs group for training purposes.[21] Contentious regulations flowing from the Commission's action program to implement the Social Charter, such as draft directives on atypical work or proof of work contracts, are still blocked in the Council.

An important exception in the recent period concerns the directive on the protection of pregnant women at work, which establishes minimum requirements for maternity leave within the Community. The directive was stalled for years, but a watered-down version of the Commission's proposal finally became law in October 1992. The directive seeks "to encourage improvements in the safety and health at work of pregnant workers and workers who have recently given birth or are breastfeeding." This wording reflects the remedy found to break the impasse: pregnancy and maternity were treated not under the rubric of gender equality but as matters concerning working conditions, under the label of "sickness." Because health and safety in the workplace is the stated rationale, no "similarly situated comparator" is necessary—the talk of such a comparator made pregnancy issues difficult to tackle under the Community's regulations on equal opportunity.[22] Also, and crucially, the use of article 118a allowed the proposal to be decided by a qualified-majority vote.[23]

To summarize, the Union has adopted five equality directives and the recent directive on pregnant women's health and safety in the past two

21. Elizabeth Meehan, "Women' Rights in the European Community," in Jane Lewis, ed., *Women and Social Policies in Europe: Work, Family and the State* (Brookfield, Vt.: Edward Elgar, 1993), pp. 194–205.

22. Centre for Research on European Women (hereafter CREW), "Maternity," *CREW Reports* (Brussels), vol. 12, no. 10 (1992), pp. 3–7. The equation of pregnancy with sickness caused some outcry. While prohibiting "any reduction in levels of protection already achieved," the directive states that the right may not be made conditional on having worked for longer than twelve months before giving birth. This will considerably improve the situation of women in Portugal, Ireland, and the United Kingdom. The United Kingdom therefore consistently opposed the proposal and abstained during the final vote. Italy had previously vetoed the proposal, proposing instead the (much longer) Italian leave paid at 80 percent of previous salary. Italy also abstained on the final vote; CREW, "Maternity," p. 4.

23. Article 118a states that the Council shall adopt, by means of directives, minimum requirements for encouraging improvements, especially in the working environment, to protect the safety and health of workers. On how social policy advocates use shifting rationales to create the most favorable rules for initiating social policies, see Martin Rhodes's discussion of the treaty-base game in chapter three of this volume.

decades.[24] Many proposals were either watered down or rejected outright.[25] A closer look at success and failure reveals that most of the proposals that were fiercely disputed, modified, or rejected would have had a major impact on women's socioeconomic status in many member states. But even the policies that have been enacted have had important consequences, especially given the generally expansive interpretations applied by the ECJ. The next section explores these points in more detail.

The Scope of EC Gender Policy

In a literal sense, article 119 addresses only the most overt discrimination: different pay for identical work. Read thus, additional national or supranational standards specifying "comparable worth" would be superfluous.[26] In the absence of ECJ instructions, however, it was unclear whether article 119 applied only to equal pay for the *same* work, or also to equal pay for *equal* work. It was also unclear to what extent fringe benefits constituted pay and which standards should apply. A combination of Council decisions and ECJ adjudication has gradually resolved these ambiguities. Until the mid-1970s the ECJ construed article 119 narrowly as equal pay for the same work. The Court refused to deal with more troublesome issues such as "equal value" (comparable worth) claims, indirect discrimination, or social security matters.[27] Over time, however, the Court's stance has become more assertive. Almost fifty equal-treatment cases have reached the ECJ, forty-four in the 1980s

24. "Directive on the Introduction of Measures to Encourage Improvements in the Safety and Health at Work of Pregnant Workers and of Workers who have Recently Given Birth or Are Breastfeeding," *Tenth Individual Directive within the Meaning of Article 16(1) of Directive 89/391/EEC;* see *CREW Reports,* vol. 12, no. 10 (1992), pp. 5–7.

25. See Susanne Schunter-Kleeman, "Das Demokratiedefizit der EG und die Verrechtlichung der Frauenfrage," in Susanne Schunter-Kleeman, ed., *Herrenhaus Europe: Geschlechterverhältnisse im Wohlfahrtsstaat* (Berlin: Sigma, 1992), pp. 29–58. According to Schunter-Kleemann (p. 43), the Council's intervention transformed the following draft directives into weaker recommendations or announcements (all dates refer to the year of first proposal): women's unemployment (1984), equal treatment in taxation (1991), family policies (1991), child care (1991), and sexual harassment at the workplace (1991). The Council rejected the following draft directives: part-time work (proposed 1983), parental leave (1984), social security (1989), widow[er]'s pensions (1989), additional benefits for families (1989), age of retirement (1989); reversal of burden of proof (1989), organization of working time (1991), and atypical employment (1991).

26. Morris and Nott, *Working Women,* p. 113; and Cox, "Equal Opportunities," pp. 47–48.

27. Hörburger, *Europas Frauen,* p. 26.

alone. In the past two decades the Commission has played an important enforcement role, initiating twelve infringement complaints against member states.[28] Equally important has been the Council's enactment of new directives that clarify and expand the implications of article 119.

In 1968 two Belgian women helped to bring the *Defrenne* case before the ECJ—against the advice of Belgian trade unions and Commission officials.[29] The Belgian airline Sabena expected stewardesses to change jobs within the company, at a loss in wages, at the age of forty; Sabena imposed no such requirement on cabin stewards doing the same work. The ECJ held that this policy was discriminatory and required Sabena to compensate Defrenne's loss of income. Sabena's personnel policy also permitted a lower pension for women, but this issue was considered at the time to be beyond the scope of article 119.

Through the treaty member states have surrendered some of their sovereignty to the Community. Treaty provisions have direct effect and take precedence over domestic law in conflicting cases.[30] The Court, sometimes at the Commission's behest, may review whether national legal practice conforms to treaty standards. Generally, supranational legislation cannot be relied on directly by citizens in national courts, and directives usually do not have direct effect. But in *Defrenne* and similar cases, the ECJ held that article 119 is directly enforceable and grants rights to an individual if remedies do not exist under national law (as they do, for example, under the British equal-pay act).[31] Such remedies

28. Hoskyns, "Working Women," p. 25.

29. *Defrenne v. Sabena*, Case 43/75 ECR 547 (1976). Catherine Hoskyns stresses that progress in gender equality depends on women's own efforts in going to court, as in *Defrenne*, or in forming strong pressure groups, as was the case with British Invalid Care Allowance (for the context of this allowance, see the discussion of *Drake* below); Hoskyns, "Gender Issues," pp. 234–36. Women have had to fight the resistance of employers and trade unions to the extension of equal protection to working individuals who did not conform to the "normal worker" standard.

30. Martin Shapiro, "The European Court of Justice," in Sbragia, ed., *Euro-Politics*, pp. 113–56.

31. Being a part of the treaty, article 119 belongs to EC *primary legislation*. Regulations and directives are *secondary legislation*. The latter must be justified as "means to a goal" by reference to the treaty. Directives bind insofar as the result to be achieved is concerned, while they leave a choice in the means employed by member states. Overt pay discrimination, however, distorts competition and therefore falls within the bounds of article 100, which allows a promulgation of directives if their subject directly concerns establishment or functioning of the common market. The equal-pay directive fell under article 100 because it clarified the content of article 119. Shapiro, "European Court," p. 146; and Bernd Schulte, "Einführung," in Bernd Schulte, ed., *Soziale Sicherheit in der EG: Verordnungen sowie andere Bestimmungen* (München: Beck, 1993), p. xxviii.

exist only in some member states and do not comprehensively cover discriminatory practices.[32]

Equal-Pay and Equal-Treatment Directives: Direct and Indirect Discrimination

In 1975—the International Women's Year—the Council passed the equal-pay directive, which introduced a broader interpretation of article 119 itself.[33] Article 1 of the directive calls for equal pay for the same work or for work to which equal value is attributed and for the elimination of all discrimination on grounds of sex with regard to all aspects and conditions of remuneration. In particular, where a job classification system is used for determining pay, it must be based on the same criteria for both men and women and so drawn up as to exclude any discrimination on grounds of sex. Article 2 requires member states to introduce legal procedures through which individual complaints may be processed.[34] The concept of equal value allowed "for broader comparisons across jobs," at least for occupations in which an employer hires both women and men.[35] Various Court decisions extended that scope of com-

32. Germany, for example, lacks such a remedy. To save time and energy, and to promote optimal outcomes, sympathetic judges of lower German courts tend to refer cases directly to the ECJ, thus bypassing German federalism's own multitier judiciary. Sibylle Raasch, "Gleichberechtigung im EG-Binnenmarkt," *Kritische Justiz*, vol. 23, no. l (1990), p. 65.

33. The four equality directives passed after the equal-pay directive were based on article 235 of the treaty, which deals with "unforeseen needs." Acting unanimously on a Commission proposal and after consulting with the European Parliament, the Council may take appropriate measures to attain Community objectives when the treaty does not otherwise provide necessary powers. Ninon Colneric maintains that the change from article 100 to article 235 points to the weakening significance of gender equality; Colneric, "Gleichberechtigung von Mann und Frau im Europäischen Gemeinschaftsrecht," *Der Betriebsberater*, vol. 43, no. 14 (1988), pp. 968–76. According to Shapiro, the ECJ has interpreted article 235 narrowly, "as providing only for the creation of particular instruments or devices that were not specifically provided for in the treaties"; Shapiro, "European Court," p. 145. Furthermore, Community action rarely is justified by article 235 alone; rather, its justification is as an appropriate means to explicit treaty goals. In contrast, Raasch claims that in referring to article 235 the Court and EC social policy have broken away from rights strictly related to employment and moved toward a broader understanding of the social dimension; Raasch, "Gleichberechtigung," p. 65.

34. For an overview on enforcement procedures, see Angela Byre, "Applying Community Standards on Equality," in Mary Buckley and Malcolm Anderson, eds., *Women, Equality and Europe* (Macmillan, 1988), pp. 20–32; and Jennifer Corcoran, "Enforcement Procedures for Individual Complaints: Equal Pay and Equal Treatment," in Buckley and Anderson, eds., *Women*, pp. 56–70.

35. Byre, "Applying Community Standards," p. 22.

parison. In 1986 the European Court of Justice held in *Rummler v. Dato-Druck* that member states were to develop schemes for job classification, relying on average standards for the work performance of *both* sexes.[36]

Although neither article 119 nor the equal-pay directive specifically mentions different forms of discrimination, the ECJ has ruled that article 119 does apply to indirect discrimination. *Direct* discrimination means formally and expressly treating two equally situated individuals differently, whereas *indirect* discrimination refers to certain practices that generate different outcomes for men and women. Whether such a practice constitutes indirect discrimination depends on the answers to two questions: Is the group disadvantaged by some measure significantly larger than the group advantaged? And, if so, is the discriminatory measure an effective means to a justifiable end?[37] For example, "Bilka, a German department store, excluded part-time employees, mainly women, from its occupational pension scheme. The ECJ maintained that a company may use its wage policy to minimize part-time employment, but this is legitimate only if the enterprise proves that its measure addresses a real need and that the chosen policy properly serves such a need. This *Bilka* failed to prove."[38]

In *Bilka* the ECJ significantly expanded the meanings of *discrimination* and *pay*. The Court indicated its willingness, absent a clear justification, to strike down the exclusion of women from any employer-provided benefits, be they pensions or free travel bonuses for retired railway employees.[39] The Court held that all elements of pay are due to all employees in a particular field, without regard to the hours worked. In Germany, for example, employees who worked fewer than ten hours a week for a commercial cleaning company did not receive statutory sick pay; mainly women were affected.[40] The ECJ saw this as indirect discrimination

36. *Gisela Rummler v. Dato-Druck GmbH*, Case 237/85 ECR 1201 (1986); and Colneric, "Gleichberechtigung," p. 970.

37. Colneric, "Gleichberechtigung," p. 971.

38. *Bilka-Kaufhaus GmbH v. Karin Weber von Hartz*, Case 170/84 ECR 1607 (1986).

39. *Susan Jane Worringham and Margaret Humphreys v. Lloyd Bank Limited*, Case 69/80 ECR 768 (1981); and *Eileen Garland v. British Rail Engineering Limited*, Case 12/81 ECR 359 (1982). Susan Cox lists some of the benefits now included under *pay* in EU law: postretirement *ex gratia* payments; statutory sick pay; payments under a private occupational pension scheme contracted out of a state earnings-related one; redundancy payments, whether statutory, contractual, or *ex gratia*; rules that govern the automatic passage to a higher salary grade; and paid leave or overtime pay for staff members attending educational events in the course of duty; Cox, "Equal Opportunities," p. 43.

40. *Ingrid Rinner-Kühn v. FWW Spezial-Gebäudereinigung GmbH Co KG*, Case 171/88 ECR 2757 (1989).

against women and a violation of article 119, "unless the discriminatory impact the hours requirement had on women" was justified by objective standards. In this case, the member state setting the hour limits (not, as in *Bilka*, the individual employer) had to legitimate the practice "on the basis of objective gender-neutral factors, rather than generalized statements."[41] Since Germany did not provide such legitimation, Ingrid Rinner-Kühn won her case. By interpreting pay broadly and deciding that excluding part-timers from pension and sick-pay schemes indirectly discriminated against women, the Court also extended the meaning of work beyond the "standard (full-time) worker" to encompass part-time employees.

However, a proposed regulation that would improve standards for part-time work—later changed into a draft directive on atypical work—has been blocked repeatedly in the Council. Thresholds defining a worker (and, therefore, who is entitled to social security) vary between twenty-five hours (Belgium) and eight hours a week (Britain and the Netherlands). The European Parliament proposed a relatively low threshold of twelve hours.[42] Since higher thresholds can easily be justified on the grounds that social security costs would be unsustainable if thresholds were lower, the Court can do little more than ask for good reasons and minimum means.[43]

Article 119 and the equal-pay directive do not eradicate different treatment; instead they oblige member states to justify discrimination in detail. The treaty and the four equal-treatment directives allow different treatment only for legitimate reasons, such as the protection of local health, safety, morals, or welfare. The Court tests discrimination in two ways: first, it discerns the intent of the party discriminating; it then uses a "balancing standard" (also termed a minimum-means or proportionality test).[44] Let us take the example of flexibility—that is, an employee's

41. Morris and Nott, *Working Women*, p. 116.

42. Catherine Hakim, "On the Margins of Europe? The Social Policy Implications of Women's Marginal Work," in Margaret O'Brien, Linda Hantrais, and Steen Mangen, eds., *Equal Opportunities and Welfare*, Cross-National Research Papers, no. 3 (Birmingham: Aston University, 1990), pp. 21–28.

43. In Germany, SPD proposals to cover "atypically employed" in social security are strongly opposed by the social insurance agencies. Such legislation would enormously increase the number of claimants to old-age pensions without proportionally increasing contributions.

44. Shapiro refers to free movement of *goods* within the Community and to relations among member states and between justifiable local and supranational interests; Shapiro, "European Court," p. 130. The relevant EEC article 36 justifies prohibitions and restrictions on imports "on grounds of public morality, public policy or public security; the

readiness to comply with a company's shifting schedule. The need for flexibility is sometimes used implicitly to exclude certain categories of workers from employment, and women, who generally have greater family responsibilities, might easily be disadvantaged. If such a criterion informs pay scales, as in the *Danfoss* case, the employer must prove its importance for performing the job in question.[45] Second, flexibility must be proven to be the means of reaching the firm's goals that will least conflict with EU regulations and aims (the minimum-means test). This rule also applies to other potentially discriminatory criteria such as seniority and completion of vocational training.[46]

The Court thus examines whether an employer's concern is legitimate and whether the means chosen to address it are the least destructive ones to treaty goals and article 119. Permitting an employer to "justify" discriminatory practices, though, has narrowed the equalizing potential of equal-treatment legislation for women, allowing national legislators "to override the social good of equality" through references to fiscal scarcity and market forces.[47] Nevertheless, the effects of ECJ decisions under article 119 and the equal-pay directive should not be underestimated. Employers may not simply persuade a token male to accept a lower "female" wage for a certain job. Rather, they have to examine the effects of their pay structure statistically and justify any adverse impacts on women.[48]

"Good reason" and minimum-means rules are especially relevant for the four equal-treatment directives. The first directive on equal treatment, which was issued in 1976 shortly after the equal-pay directive, covers a wide range of sex discrimination regarding work.[49] Although these di-

---

protection of health and life of humans, animals and plants; the protection of national treasures; or the protection of industrial and commercial property." Such reasons and similar principles for justification can also be found in social policy matters.

45. *Handels-og Kontorfunktionaererners Forbund i Danmark v. Dansk Arbejdsgiveforening (for Danfoss A/S)*, Case 109/88 ECR 3199 (1989).

46. Cox, "Equal Opportunities," p. 49.

47. Morris and Nott, *Working Women*, p. 196.

48. Changes in the labor market, however, may gradually weaken this approach. As men themselves increasingly find nonstandard or atypical employment, women and their lobbies will have a harder time proving indirect discrimination.

49. Directive 76/207 on equal treatment extended the principle of equal treatment for men and women to access to employment (including promotion), vocational training, and working conditions. There was to be no further discrimination on grounds of sex either directly or indirectly, in particular by reference to marital or family status. Legal and administrative practices contradicting the equal-treatment principle were voided, regardless of whether they concerned collective agreements or individual employment contracts.

rectives cite the general Community goal of improving and equalizing living and working conditions of the employed, they allow different treatment for "good reason." Regarding night labor, for instance, the Court has refused to accept women's family responsibility as a good reason for unequal treatment; it judged night labor to be equally harmful to men and women, and different treatment to be unjustifiable distortion of competition.[50] Therefore in July 1991 the ECJ, referring to the equal-treatment directive, voided the article in the French labor code that prohibited night labor for women only. France and six other member states retracted their regulations prohibiting women's night labor in industrial enterprises. The Court made its stance even clearer in adjudicating claims based on two subsequent directives, which require equal treatment in social security and occupational security schemes.

To sum up, Community law enacted through the equal-pay and equal-treatment directives has often had direct effect when the member state offered no legal remedy, as well as indirect effect by broadening the definitions of pay and work. Job classification and evaluation schemes must exclude overt discriminatory practices; by extending the scope of comparison, indirect discrimination not supported by good reason is also prohibited. These principles apply both to individual contracts and to collective agreements. Once evidence of discrimination has been established, the burden of proof falls on the employer, and Community law requires that member states develop enforcement measures and remedies. If court claims are successful, the ECJ obliges member states to compensate claimants in proportion to the damages they incurred.[51] On the national level, however, the fragmented policy process, arduous legal procedures, and scarce resources of equal-opportunity agencies (leading to insufficient financing and support of individual claimants) have hindered successful legal representation. Furthermore, these rules apply only to equal-pay cases. Draft directives on burden of proof, which would extend these rules, have made no progress in the Council.

The Social Security Directives

Through two directives the Community sought to introduce equal treatment in social security—a tricky matter, given the diversity and

---

50. Sibylle Raasch, "Nachtarbeitsverbot für Frauen?" *Kritische Justiz*, vol. 25, no. 4 (1992), pp. 427–36.

51. Cox, "Equal Opportunities," p. 50.

complexity of national social security regimes. Article 3(1) of the directive on social security enumerates the areas to be covered: statutory schemes that protect against sickness, invalidity, old age, accidents at work, and occupational diseases, as well as unemployment. Survivor's pensions and family benefits that do not supplement compensation for the risks mentioned in article 3(1) are not covered. According to article 4, any discrimination, either direct or indirect, on the grounds of sex is outlawed (indirect discrimination refers in particular to marital or family status); this prohibition holds for coverage of a scheme, conditions of access, and calculation of benefits. Maternity benefits, states article 3(2), do not contravene equal treatment. The occupational social security directive extends equal treatment to schemes not covered by the other directive. Member states were allowed six years, from 1978 until 1984, to implement both directives.[52]

These directives restrict equal treatment to workers and to those with some relationship to work (the involuntarily unemployed and pensioners, for example). The directives do not distinguish between full-time and part-time work, enabling the ECJ to extend the meaning of *worker* as it did in the *Bilka* and *Rinner-Kühn* cases; nonemployed and unpaid workers are excluded, however. While the social security directive explicitly prohibits indirect forms of discrimination, proof is often hard to establish. Disadvantages in social security often result from complex social divisions and inequalities, such as the general difficulty of combining employment with family care obligations.[53]

Both social security directives seem ambiguous regarding equalization of pension and retirement ages. In many member states women traditionally were forced to, or had the right to, retire earlier than men, based on the rationale that male breadwinners married somewhat younger women, who presumably would be supported in their early retirement by their husbands' pensions. Article 7(a) of the directive on social security expressly states that pension age is outside its domain. Consequently, the ECJ held in *Burton* that men and women's attainment of pension rights at different ages does not in itself conflict with the treaty.[54] Yet the directives do affect policies governing *retirement* age. In *Marshall* the

52. Linda Luckhaus, "The Social Security Directive: Its Impact on Part-time Work," in O'Brien, Hantrais, and Mangen, eds., *Equal Opportunities*, pp. 11–20.

53. Karl-Juergen Bieback elaborates this argument in "Mittelbare Diskriminierung der Frauen im Sozialrecht," *Zeitschrift fuer ausländisches und internationales Arbeits- und Sozialrecht*, vol. 4, no. 1 (1990), pp. 1–33, especially p. 33.

54. *Arthur Burton v. British Railways Board*, Case 19/81 ECR 555 (1982).

Court maintained that, although article 7(a) of the social security directive had to be narrowly interpreted, compulsory earlier retirement for women was an unjustified violation of equal treatment.[55] Because member states now run early retirement schemes—complete with pensions—mainly for men, retaining differing age thresholds for pension eligibility is unjustified, many observers argue.

The *Barber* case, in which the Court extended the meaning of article 119 to cover age thresholds for pension eligibility, demonstrates the complex impact of EU gender policy. Mr. Barber was made redundant—let go from his job—at age 52. Although a participant in an occupational pension arrangement (which was partly a contracted-out state scheme), he was denied a pension that would have been available immediately to female employees. Instead, Barber received only a lump-sum payment. According to the ECJ, his treatment was illegal, since pensions are pay and therefore are within the scope of article 119.[56] The decision, which required massive restructuring of pension schemes, caused an uproar. Following furious lobbying, a "Barber protocol" was included in the Maastricht treaty, to the effect that *Barber* was not to be applied retroactively. Nonetheless, the implications for future pension policy are considerable.

The issue of different retirement ages for women and men has been fiercely debated since then. As Anne Morris and Susan Nott point out, it is uncertain whether women profit from the *Barber* decision and, in general, from the social security directive.[57] Where women were previously treated preferentially, they may now have to work longer for their right to pension benefits. In the long run, widow's pensions may be delegitimated unless "good reasons" can be advanced for retaining them. Although article 117 explicitly states that living and working conditions must be progressively improved, the equal-treatment directives may trigger lowest-common-denominator adjustments, as they did for preferen-

55. *M.H. Marshall v. Southampton and South-West Hampshire Area Health Authority (Teaching)*, Case 152/84 ECR 723 (1986); and Colneric, "Gleichberechtigung," p. 974.

56. Morris and Nott, *Working Women*, pp. 115, 155; Philippa Watson, "Social Security," in Gold, ed., *Social Dimension*, pp. 153–71; and *Barber v. Guardian Royal Exchange Assurance Group*, Case C-262/88 (1990). Since Barber was about a contracted-out state scheme (SERPS, State Earnings Related Pension Scheme), some argue that "pay" was inappropriately applied. See Peter Clever, "Rechtsprechung des EuGH im Sozialbereich auf dem Prüfstand," *Sozialer Fortschritt*, vol. 41 (1992), pp. 1–6.

57. See Winfried Schmähl, "Die europäische Dimension der Alterssicherung," *Hamburger Jahrbuch für Wirtschafts- und Gesellschaftspolitik*, vol. 38, no. 3 (1993), pp. 137–54.

tial treatment of male employees.[58] In countries traditionally biased toward male wage earners, equal treatment may be established through a process of leveling down.[59] As governments become preoccupied with the high cost of social spending, they may use equalization requirements as a relatively palatable way to cut expenditures. Recently, the U.K. Tory government announced plans to set the retirement age for British women at sixty-five, the usual retirement age for men. The new policy will become effective in 2010 for women now aged forty-four and younger. The alternative—lowering the retirement age for men—was rejected as excessively costly.[60]

The British response is but one example of the significant, complex effects of EC gender policy. The equality directives and the ECJ rulings forced member states to adapt their legislation on some important employment-related issues. They influenced national legislation and legal practice by outlawing direct and indirect discrimination both in individual and collective agreements and in outcomes, as well as by questioning legal restrictions placed on the type of work women could do, on retirement ages, and on women's working time and hours—all of which had seriously limited women's access to jobs, to promotion, and to social security.[61]

On the other hand, although Community principles stress that disadvantaged groups should be incorporated under improved national standards, member states have frequently opted to remove discrimination by reducing the benefits of privileged groups. "Husbands-only" benefits were abolished in Germany and in Ireland; married male employees had to adapt to the less privileged situation of their female counterparts. Women who once enjoyed more favorable working conditions with re-

---

58. Some German employers granted male employees a "wife benefit" (Ehefrauenzulage), while women could not claim a "husband benefit." When the case went to court (Arbeitsgericht Berlin), some expected that the benefit would be extended to women workers. While the court maintained that unjustified discrimination obtained, it held that payments referring to sex and marital status are illegal and should be abolished altogether; Colneric, "Gleichberechtigung," p. 969. Ina Sjerps lucidly elaborates the possible impact of a "politics of equalization" for women in the Netherlands; Sjerps, "Indirect Discrimination in Social Security in the Netherlands: Demands of the Dutch Women's Movement," in Buckley and Anderson, eds., *Women*, pp. 95–106. The revision of the tax system according to the principle of equal treatment was costly for married women, who still are the majority of women, while "the traditional breadwinner underwent a considerable improvement."

59. Sjerps, "Indirect Discrimination," p. 101.

60. See *The Economist*, December 4, 1993, pp. 42–43.

61. Cox, "Equal Opportunities," p. 52.

gard to retirement age or night labor had to adjust to male standards. Some member states have used the leveling-down potential of equal treatment to restructure social security, as did the Netherlands and the United Kingdom, where "equal treatment reform took place against a background of severe cost-cutting in the social security system as a whole."[62]

Two Needles' Eyes: Limits on the EU Agenda and Policy Implementation

Equal treatment has supported policies that treat women as wage earners and tax payers. Treating women equally in these respects, however, papers over gender inequalities outside employment. Because women's involvement in the paid labor market is circumscribed, gains for women have been restricted despite the considerable success of EC law. Two general reasons for this limited impact stand out. First, the philosophy behind EC equality laws, the decisionmaking rules of the Community, and the lack of member-state consensus confine EU intervention to issues related to paid employment. Second, different gender orders in Europe—national structures of labor markets, social policies, and patterns of unpaid "caring" work—influence implementation of gender-equity policy at the national level. The diversity of gender regimes in the EU's emerging multitiered structure not only creates barriers to the formation of supranational gender policies but also constrains the prospects for effective implementation.

The First Needle's Eye: The Paid Employment Nexus

The directives and ECJ decisions seek to reconcile variants of two principles, liberty and equality. Creating a common market, an area without barriers, has meant the promotion of egalitarian liberalism— "the Ritz open to all." This version of liberalism implies that dependency is by choice, resulting from the interactions of free individuals. Participants in the common market are seen as free agents (invisibly backed by supportive families) who contract at will. *Direct* discrimination then amounts to coercion. It obstructs choice through the direct intervention of others, as when women are forced to accept lower wages or poorer social security simply because they are women or wives. Article 119 and

---

62. Schunter-Kleemann, "Implementation," p. 53.

the first directive on equal pay address this issue, protecting the *formal* conditions of freedom.

Dealing with *indirect* discrimination has raised complex problems for European policymakers. Some people have little alternative but to do *X*, although nobody demands *X* from them. Nobody forces women to accept part-time jobs with lower career prospects and poorer social security. By focusing on indirect forms of discrimination, the equal-treatment directives began to address the difference between obstruction by others and a general lack of means and opportunity.[63] These directives allow positive, affirmative action programs for "those who start the race with differing and/or unequal abilities."[64] So far, however, these positive efforts have been limited, and the Union lacks both the fiscal resources and the political inclination to provide more meaningful support.

The EU is reluctant to confront those social circumstances that weaken women's position in the labor market. In liberal philosophy, preferences are said to be matters of individual taste that are beyond public scrutiny. Moreover, the EU's stance reflects the common-market orientation of the Treaty of Rome, which focuses scrutiny on the paid labor market. The ECJ has maintained this view strictly and abstained carefully from touching on the private, domestic sphere (the family) and dealing with its impact on women's choice. The division of labor by gender in a household is regarded as a matter of free choice, left to the privacy of the couple, or as a matter for national—not supranational—policy. As Kirsten Scheiwe observes, while the family is not always beyond the Court's purview, family is acknowledged solely as a nonmarket appendage of a labor-market participant who moves across the borders of EU member states.[65] Family is relevant only as a possible hindrance to a worker's labor mobility.

EU policy addresses working women or women seeking work, who are or should be similarly situated to working men. The ECJ stated in

63. Ernst Tugendhat, "Liberalism, Liberty and the Issue of Economic Human Rights," in Ernst Tugendhat, ed., *Philosophische Aufsätze* (Frankfurt: Suhrkamp, 1992), pp. 352–70.

64. Ian Forbes, "Equal Opportunity: Radical, Liberal and Conservative Critiques," in Elizabeth Meehan and Selma Sevenhuijsen, eds., *Equality, Politics and Gender* (London: Sage, 1991), pp. 17–35. The Commission has expressly recommended positive action programs for women. In contrast, positive discrimination, the preferential treatment of women to overcome starting-gate inequality, requires a comprehensive set of directly intervening policies, which has normally been rejected.

65. Kirsten Scheiwe, "EC Law's Unequal Treatment of the Family," *Social and Legal Studies,* vol. 3, no. 1 (1994), pp. 243–65.

Achterberg and other cases that article 119 is about equal treatment of the working population only; the Court does not address equality in general.[66] Therefore how work is defined becomes crucial.[67] The *Bilka* and *Rinner-Kühn* cases mentioned above reveal that the Court wants to include all shades of paid work, but it has never swayed from defining work solely as paid work.[68] *Johnson* clearly demonstrates what the Court defines as work under the treaty and what this implies for unpaid care-takers: "In *Johnson*, a woman had interrupted work to take care of her child. The woman could not reenter employment since she became se-verely disabled. The U.K. claims adjudication officer rejected her appli-cation for a disability pension, arguing she had left work voluntarily. According to the ECJ the Social Security Directive applies only to the working population and to people actively seeking work. Mrs. Johnson, so the ECJ held, belonged to neither category when she claimed the benefit."[69] EU policy does not apply to those who never worked in the labor market or to those who did but left employment to raise children. However, the social security directive covers the search for work and outlaws direct or indirect discrimination by reference to sex, marital, or family status.

Issues closely related to labor-market prospects for women, such as extending the notion of work to include unpaid care, have received only sporadic and symbolic attention. Peter Moss maintains that the EC's commitment to equal treatment for working men and women reveals its "longstanding interest in childcare," dating back to the 1974 social ac-tion program.[70] Yet substantive steps have not matched the rhetoric. The

66. *Achterberg* case and joint cases 48, 106, and 107/88, ECR 1963 (1989); and Schulte, "Einführung," p. xxvii.

67. The following section owes a lot to Scheiwe's detailed analysis in "EC Law's Unequal Treatment," although Scheiwe does not always arrive at our conclusions; see also Meehan, "Women's Rights," pp. 200–01.

68. Only *Drake* seems to suggest the opposite. On *Jacqueline Drake v. The Chief Ad-judication Officer 150/85 (1986)*, I-1995–2012, see Scheiwe, "EC Law's Unequal Treat-ment," p. 256; and Luckhaus, "Social Security Directive," p. 15. The Court held that the invalid care allowance, because it is part of a statutory scheme that provides protection against invalidity, falls under the scope of the directive on social security even though it is paid to a third party (the care giver) and not to the disabled. The case was brought before the Court as part of a U.K. social movement campaign. The Child Poverty Action Group successfully claimed that excluding married women from the invalid care allowance violated the social security directive; Hoskyns, "Working Women," p. 27. The Court does not even implicitly refer to unpaid care, however.

69. *Johnson v. The Adjunction Officer*, Case C-31/90 ECR (1991), as summarized in Scheiwe, "EC Law's Unequal Treatment," pp. 257–58.

70. Peter Moss, "Childcare and Equality of Opportunity," in Linda Hantrais, Steen

Social Charter of December 1989 and its attendant action program prompted the Commission to draft a nonbinding recommendation on child care, which the Council of Ministers finally accepted in 1991. The recommendation notes that the lack of child-care facilities in most member states is a serious impediment to employment equity, and urges corrective measures such as parental leave and public child care.[71] *Binding* legal measures, however—a revised parental leave directive or a framework directive on child care—are not likely to appear on the EU's agenda. The variety of national mixes of paid and unpaid care for the elderly has attracted even less attention, although many women interrupt employment or reduce their working hours to care for an elderly parent.[72] The Council and the ECJ have generally left to the member states the questions of whether and how to provide for those performing unpaid work or not actively seeking work.

This reflects not only article 119's focus on employment but also the difficulties of establishing common policy positions at the EU level. Political actors have vastly differing opinions on women's work, family life, and equality. The content and direction of women's issues are also highly debated among women's groups, which weakens lobbying and coalition-building efforts at the supranational level. For the most part, German, Irish, and Italian feminists have always been reluctant to identify independence with employment. Egalitarian policies that promote full-time paid work for women have never been wholeheartedly welcomed by a majority of German feminists or by many Irish. Although women's groups in societies in which Christian Democratic norms and values prevail may be critical of women's subordinate position, they nevertheless emphasize motherhood and advocate social rights for mothers; they opt for parity for care givers. On the other hand, feminists who grew up with, or who have become familiar with, ideas like autonomy of the (gender-neutral) individual seek policies that promote self-reliance and

---

Mangen, and Margaret O'Brien, eds., *Caring and the Welfare State in the 1990s*, Cross-National Research Papers, 2d series, no. 2 (Birmingham: Aston University, 1990), pp. 23–31.

71. See Caroline Steindorff and Christiane Heering, "Familienpolitik und Recht im Europäischen Integrationsprozeß," in Erika Neubauer, Christiane Dienel, and Marlene Lohkamp-Himmighofen, eds., *Zwölf Wege der Familienpolitik in der Europäischen Gemeinschaft* (Stuttgart: Kohlhammer, 1993), pp. 131–61.

72. Anne Jamieson, "Care of Older People in the European Community," in Hantrais, Mangen, and O'Brien, eds., *Caring*, pp. 32–45; and Anne Jamieson, "Community Care for Older People," in Room, ed., *European Welfare State*, pp. 107–26.

self-determination of each individual in work and in the family; they favor universal breadwinning.

Even some gender-related issues with clear ties to the paid labor market have proven difficult to handle. In the EU framework, treating people the same requires that they be "similarly situated" in the market place. To proponents of liberal equality, providing for, say, pregnant women raises a special problem, because no comparable situation exists for males.[73] Conflicts over *equal* versus *special* treatment stalled the directive on the protection of pregnant women at work, which was finally treated as a health and safety issue. This solution simultaneously sidestepped the difficulties of establishing equal treatment for pregnant women and permitted qualified majority voting. One result, however, was that the required minimum maternity benefit was set at the level for sickness pay in the various member states, not at the full-pay level proposed in an early draft.

Those issues not linked to the labor market but of tremendous importance to women cause even more problems for EU policymakers. Controversial issues are pushed from the agenda or treated rhetorically, as happened with abortion, homosexuality, and sexual harassment. Abortion, in particular, is such a difficult issue within the member states that compromise at the supranational level hardly seems possible.[74] Abortion laws differ widely in the EU, from prohibition (Ireland) to obligatory counseling and justification (Germany) to "on-demand" rules during the first three months of pregnancy (Denmark). Often regulations at the national level were passed only after much compromise and logrolling and long struggles among various social actors.

Despite the expansion of European women's movements in the 1970s and German (and later Irish) concerns about "abortion tourism," there have been only feeble efforts to harmonize abortion laws in the EU.[75] Dutch and British abortion laws have been very liberal in practice. Many German women have traveled to the Netherlands, and Irish women to the United Kingdom, to have abortions. Attempts to reconcile national laws thus attracted the interest of both pro- and antiliberalization Coun-

73. *Equal treatment* in the context of constitutional equal rights always meant to adjust women to an already existing male standard. *Discrimination* presupposes some comparison with a better standard.

74. Joyce Outshoorn, "Abortion Law Reform: A Woman's Right to Choose?" in Buckley and Anderson, eds., *Women*, pp. 204–19.

75. Outshoorn, "Abortion Law Reform," p. 213.

cil members. In a context marked by high controversy and unanimity requirements, however, such discussions were unlikely to go very far, and they did not.

In 1980 the Ad Hoc Committee on Women's Rights prepared a resolution on the position of women in the European Community, which included two paragraphs on abortion under the heading of "health and care."[76] Although already a carefully drafted compromise, these paragraphs instigated a heated debate, revealing different cultural attitudes toward abortion—and, more generally, toward motherhood and women's roles—among and within member states. Different European parties, often represented by women members of Parliament, expressed widely divergent views while forming cross-national alliances.[77] The resolution was finally adopted by the European Parliament with only few amendments, none of them concerning abortion. The 1981 Parliament debate reflects how difficult it is to translate important women's concerns into a broadly shared agenda, even on the national level. The difficulties recur in similarly agonizing struggles on the supranational level. This is especially true for the peculiar case of abortion, but it holds generally for family issues. Therefore, while the successful passage of even a resolution on this issue seems remarkable, there should be no expectation of meaningful EU action on such matters.

Efforts to enact EU gender policy therefore face serious constraints. EU policy on equal opportunity is limited by an assumption of the readiness and capacity of women to take part in paid work on equal terms with men. Even the equal-pay directives will become less effectual for women as more men begin to work in flexible, low-paid jobs, thus providing an increasing pool of male comparators.[78] Equity policy has to

76. Outshoorn, "Abortion Law Reforms," p. 213. Resolution and parliamentary debate are documented as follows: "Debates of the European Parliament," 1980–81 session; and "Report of the Proceedings from 9 to 13 February, 1981," no. 266. A full report of the Parliament hearing was issued in document EP 68.457; European Parliament, ed., *The Position of Women in the European Community: European Parliament Debates* (Luxembourg: Office for Official Publications of the European Communities, 1991).

77. This information is taken from Catherine Hoskyns' draft chapter on implementation, in which she refers to many personal communications she had with women representatives. The chapter is part of a comprehensive project on EC gender politics. Catherine Hoskyns, *Integrating Gender: Woman, Law and Politics in the European Union* (London: Verso, forthcoming 1995). See also Outshoorn, "Abortion Law Reform," p. 214; and *Official Journal of the European Communities*, p. 42.

78. Some have therefore argued in favor of directives that guarantee basic universal rights for all kinds of (paid) work. See Jill Rubery, "Equal Pay and Institutional Systems of Pay Determination: A Comparative Study for the Commission of the European Commu-

square a circle to be successful: it must treat women the same as men, while acknowledging that special measures are needed to assure equal access to the labor market. Even if women's education were to become more similar to men's, this would not make up for the discontinuity of many women's work careers and for their consequent weaker position in the labor market. Despite a general increase in female qualification levels and employment rates, in most member states many women who wish to work could not be absorbed without major changes in economic institutions and in the family. On the many issues beyond the paid labor market nexus, activity will be far more limited. Lack of a clear treaty mandate and the diversity of member-state practices and preferences are sure to constrain policymaking. Indeed, this member-state diversity is pivotal even in those areas where the Union is actively involved in gender policy.

The Second Needle's Eye: Diverse National Regimes and the Problem of Implementation

The strength or weakness of two norms filters equality policies at the member-state level: one holds the male to be the breadwinner and the other deems the family to be the primary care giver. These norms give a peculiar meaning to gender equality and influence how EU directives are implemented. Thus the Union's promotion of employment equity can be seriously impeded and diverted through the second needle's eye: a diverse array of national policy frameworks, preferences, and underlying cultural attitudes.

National social policies rest on underlying assumptions about who is the primary and who the secondary breadwinner or care giver. These assumptions are crystallized in the various institutions that constitute a member state's welfare regime. In the multitiered process of EU policy-making, a member state's gender order serves as a filter for both the incorporation of directives into national law and the transformation of the reformed laws into everyday practices. Unfortunately, not much research has been done on the implementation of EU social policy. Considerable time must go by following the passage of directives, and studying

---

nity," Contract 900547 (January 1991). Aspects of the Social Charter, such as the atypical work proposals, seek to diminish existing differences between full-time and part-time work by providing for a common floor of employment rights. So far such efforts have been to no avail, and even a common floor will not compensate for the part-time worker's more limited earnings and career prospects.

detailed outcomes in several distinct political systems is a daunting challenge. Therefore the following argument is sketched in broad terms, buttressed by case materials drawn mainly from Germany and Ireland. Both countries belong to what we call strong male-breadwinner countries; both emphasize the value of a family based on marriage. Germany, however, has been a strong promoter of the EC from the outset, whereas Ireland as a latecomer has had a more peripheral role.

All member states outlaw overt discrimination—some as a result or even a precondition (as in the case of Ireland) of EU membership. But *equality* can be interpreted in different ways: it can mean sameness (as it does in the United Kingdom and, increasingly, the Netherlands), or it can denote equality of difference (as in Ireland and Germany). Correspondingly, the idea of *family* differs, from families based on marriage (again, Germany and Ireland, and the Mediterranean countries) to any form of parenting (France and Denmark). Thus a member state can easily interpret equal treatment as treating women and men differently but equally, especially in the field of social security.[79] In this case, social provisions for women would derive largely from a male breadwinner's employment and his primary income, maternity protection and benefits would be relatively generous, and parental leave programs and incentives for part-time work would be prevalent.

Throughout this century the majority of women have received more (and often better) social rights as family members (that is, as wives or mothers) than as independent workers. In some member states, for instance, widow's pensions make up the bulk of elderly women's income, predominating over pensions earned by their own contributions. Because so many women interrupt their work career and work shorter hours—some out of free choice, some for family reasons—dependence on a partner's employment record has continued.

None of the member states has fully championed breadwinners' equity, which means men and women both would have a fair share of labor market opportunity and related rights. Although some countries, like Denmark or France, have moved toward treating women as citizen-

---

79. Different treatment of German full-time and part-time public employees (for lump-sum compensation in case of dismissal, for example) traditionally has been justified by arguing that part-time workers do not fully contribute to their own living costs and to those of their family. While outlawing discrimination against part-timers, the ECJ has not commented on such justifications. See Ninon Colneric, "Neue Entscheidungen des EuGH zur Gleichbehandlung von Männern und Frauen," *Europäische Zeitschrift für Wirtschaftsrecht*, vol. 2, no. 3 (1991), pp. 75–79.

workers and working mothers and reached relatively high rates of mothers' employment, none have come close to gender equity in the combined realm of work and family. While EU gender policy is unambiguously focused on employment as far as principles and intended outcomes are concerned, national policies are not. Member states are ambivalent about whether to promote equity for breadwinners or parity for care givers. All states have developed specific mixes of allowances and benefits for care givers and breadwinners.

In most societies women's concerns are closely tied to highly sensitive questions of whether to provide for families and how best to do so. National policies for women often must reconcile conflicting principles, such as a woman's right to choose a career versus the needs of a child. Political parties are often split about the means and ends of women's policy. Straightforward answers are rare, and the consensus they must be built upon is precarious, even at the national level. Policy toward women therefore tends to lack coherence.

As matters stand, assumptions about the existence of a male breadwinner and a dependent family consisting of a female and child are built into welfare provision to varying degrees in EU member states.[80] Although the vast majority of countries recognize the male-breadwinner role, they differ significantly in the extent to which women are confined to homemaking and motherhood and are recognized also as workers.

We distinguish among strong, moderate, and weak male-breadwinner states. Patterns of caring and family obligations vary systematically according to the strength or weakness of the breadwinner norm. Starting from the various breadwinning regimes and their underlying principles, it is possible to predict the nature, especially, of married women's participation in the labor market. We can also predict policymakers' support for or resistance to EU policies that encourage universal breadwinning. Countries that rely particularly heavily on the family and on women's unpaid caring role expect women to depend on a male breadwinner. These are the states that are most likely to mount the strongest challenges to EU gender policies, and to be the most resistant to effective implementation.

---

80. For greater detail, see Jane Lewis, "Gender and the Development of Welfare Regimes," *Journal of European Social Policy*, vol. 2, no. 2 (1992), pp. 159–74; Jane Lewis, "Introduction: Women, Work, Family and Social Policies in Europe," in Lewis, ed., *Women and Social Policies*, pp. 1–14; and Jane Lewis and Ilona Ostner, "Gender and the Evolution of European Social Policies," Working Paper 4/94 (Centre for Social Policy Research, Bremen University, 1994).

Though different in the particular composition of their policies, Britain, Germany, and Ireland are all *strong* male-breadwinner countries.[81] All tend to treat adult women as dependent wives for the purpose of social entitlements. They differ, however, in the extent to which they develop social policies to promote marriage and family life, thus compensating for the risks and disadvantages that women face in the labor market. France and Belgium, by contrast, have traditionally recognized and promoted the position of women as wives and mothers *and* as workers, and are therefore categorized as *moderate* male-breadwinner countries. Although the household is the unit of measurement determining need, the roles of family members are assumed to be significantly different from those in strong male-breadwinner countries. Each of the family's members is treated as a "corporate individual" to be nurtured by social policy. Denmark is categorized as a *weak* male-breadwinner country, because—at least in the last two decades—social policy has tended to define women primarily as workers, though mainly part-time workers, and not as wives and mothers.

How do gender regimes affect the policy process? To illustrate the answer, in the following sections we focus on two member states, Ireland and Germany, which are considered to be strong male-breadwinner regimes. These countries might well be expected to face major adjustments in adopting nondiscriminatory practices in employment and social security. And their dominant collective actors, who are mostly male groups— legislators, churches, parties, employers, and trade unions—might in turn be expected to openly or quietly resist a significant weakening of the male-breadwinner model.

THE FEDERAL REPUBLIC OF GERMANY. During the past thirty years Germany has slowly developed and implemented sophisticated gender policies promoting "equality of difference"; these policies counteract both national and EU equal-employment rules and measures. During the negotiations over the equal-pay and the first equal-treatment directives in Brussels, Germany was concerned primarily with legal issues. New regulations should not violate *Tarifautonomie* (autonomous collective bargaining between employers and trade unions). The German delegation resisted broad interpretations of *pay* and *equal pay for work of equal value*. A broad reading would, in their view, go beyond the intent of

81. Admittedly, diversity in the group of strong male-breadwinner countries is rather large, especially if the Mediterranean countries are included.

article 119.[82] German bureaucrats and representatives of the "social part-ners" (employers and employees) at the national and EU levels saw no need for detailed equal-pay regulation. Employers and lawyers, in partic-ular, thought that article 3 of the Basic Law (the German constitution), which prohibits discrimination by sex, race, ethnicity, and religion, was sufficient. The Basic Law, however, contains potentially conflicting arti-cles that protect freedom of contract *and* equal treatment *and* marriage and the family *and* a basic right to social protection. Article 9 of the Basic Law also guarantees *Tarifautonomie*.

The principles of the Basic Law support a "social-market economy," promoting undistorted competition buffered and completed by "social" elements. Undistorted competition aims primarily at creating consumer sovereignty, while restricting state intervention vis-à-vis the family or the market; collective labor law strengthens the ongoing dialogue between the social partners. Marriage and family are considered intrinsically valu-able institutions with distinctive though complementary gender roles.

Labor and capital were to be solely responsible for determining a male breadwinner's wages, which were supposed to be sufficient to support a family with a little help (wage work) from his wife. Accordingly, the wage agreements produced through autonomous collective bargaining have always safeguarded the male breadwinner, and, because they must comply with only the Basic Law, they allow ample room for discrimi-nation.[83] The aim of supplementary allowances and family benefits was to enable women—married ones—to stay at home as housewives and mothers, as well as to acknowledge both the importance of women's work at home and the need to raise the value of such nonwage labor.[84]

The implications of this gender order became evident when the 1975 and 1976 directives had to be transformed into German law. Business and labor, along with some feminists, rejected comprehensive implemen-tation. As on the European level, employers in Germany resented restric-tions on the freedom of contract. Trade unions emphasized that equality

82. Catherine Hoskyns, "'Give Us Equal Pay and We'll Open Our Own Doors': A Study of the Impact in the Federal Republic of Germany and the Republic of Ireland of the European Community's Policy on Women Rights," in Buckley and Anderson, eds., *Women*, pp. 33–55.

83. This point is extensively documented in Heide M. Pfarr and Klaus Bertelsmann, *Diskriminierung im Erwerbsleben: Ungleichbehandlung von Frauen und Männern in der Bundesrepublik Deutschland* (Baden-Baden: Nomos, 1989). Our German case is based on this study.

84. Ilona Ostner, "Back to the Fifties: Gender and Welfare in Unified Germany," *Social Politics*, vol. 1, no. 1 (1994), pp. 39–59.

measures should be negotiated by the social partners and not dictated by the state. Women's groups, if they focused on legal rights at all, did so not for equity reasons but for better accommodation of work and family obligations, with positive action as an attendant goal.[85]

But Germany was obligated to comply. Despite considerable resistance, a law on equal treatment was passed in August 1980.[86] Given its context, it is hardly surprising that the law was a complex compromise with evident problems. First, to protect *Tarifautonomie*, changes in articles 611 and 612 of the civil code apply to individual employers exclusively. They do not address the parties of collective bargaining, for whom only article 3 of the Basic Law applies. Second, German policymakers have fought hard to diminish the impact of the directives, forcing a long and tangled legal battle. German labor law traditionally excludes women from many occupations, and from certain operations within an occupation. Employers (including the state as employer) and labor courts have justified these exclusions for "indisputable" and "sensible" reasons, broadly interpreted.[87] The European Commission, however, held that Germany had failed to detail *conclusive* reasons for the exclusions, which they should have provided in a detailed code of practice. In 1987 Germany complied with the ECJ standards by promulgating a list of exceptions.[88]

The equal-treatment law still disadvantages women in "economically unavoidable" dismissals and in future reemployment. Firing women first is permissible after considering three criteria: the existence of an employed spouse, seniority, and age of the employee. The employed-spouse standard is rarely applied to men. The other two criteria often discriminate indirectly in promotions, where they are used to disadvantage women. Dismissals executed according to these criteria can be appealed

85. Hoskyns, "'Give Us Equal Pay,'" pp. 41–42.

86. "Gesetz über die Gleichbehandlung von Frauen und Männern am Arbeitsplatz (Arbeitsrechtliches EG-Anpassungsgesetz)"; as the phrase in parentheses ("EC Adaption Law") indicates, the law changed title six ("Work Contract") of the German civil code and inserted articles 611a (equal treatment in employment, promotion, and dismissal), 611b (advertisement of vacancies), and 612, para. 3 (pay).

87. In Germany "indisputable" reasons relate to clear nondiscretionary categories such as the military or Catholic priesthood. "Sensible" reasons relate to all other trades; they allow considerable discretion in excluding women from certain occupations or occupational segments, such as mining, construction, and the automobile industry.

88. *Commission v. Federal Republic of Germany*, Case 248/83, ECR 1474 (1985). The list is documented in Pfarr and Bertelsmann, *Diskriminierung*, pp. 70–71.

only under article 3 of the Basic Law, not under the 1976 equal-treatment directive. According to Heide Pfarr and Klaus Bertelsmann, although the federal labor court formally rejected discrimination based on family status in 1956, it maintained that married women are generally hurt less by dismissal than are male heads of households.[89] The 1980 German law adapting the civil code to the equal-pay and equal-treatment directives did not abolish this interpretation, and lower courts readily took it up. Finally, there are still many practices in public employment that disadvantage part-time employees, the majority of whom are women. Each practice has to be taken to court, often to the ECJ, because a court decision applies only to the individual case tested.

Germany's response included often subtle efforts at meeting the letter of EC requirements while subverting the spirit of the directives. For example, the government transformed its maternity leave, which had excluded fathers, into gender-neutral parental leave. During the 1960s the German constitutional court held that housework and employment are different but are of equal value, and that pension schemes should therefore attach some value to women's unpaid work in the family. The government responded in 1986 with child-rearing legislation allocating pension rights for time devoted to care-giving work at home. The policy was worded in gender-neutral terms, but it serves largely to facilitate labor-market exit and reentry for working women.

The distinctive structure of Germany's gender regime has shaped the implementation of EC directives in crucial ways. Pointing to its constitution and its basic principle of gender equality, Germany has argued repeatedly that there was no need to adapt national law and practice to EC standards. The German government did adjust article 611 of the German civil code, which deals with equal pay, to ECJ requirements, but it did so only reluctantly and in some ways superficially (for example, existing structures were left largely unchanged). In spite of its long-standing reputation as a paragon of European integration, Germany has consistently ignored the Commission's critique on this topic.[90] Catherine Hoskyns concludes that "Germany has the reputation of being the country which has done least to implement the European policy and

89. Pfarr and Bertelsmann, *Diskriminierung*, pp. 185–88.

90. Simon Bulmer and William Paterson, *The Federal Republic of Germany and the European Community* (London: Allen and Unwin, 1987), p. 7; and Lily Gardner Feldman, "Germany and the EC: Realism and Responsibility," *Annals of the American Academy of Political and Social Science*, vol. 531 (January 1994), pp. 25–43.

where the situation of women shows least change. . . . The effects . . . have been limited, mainly it would seem because it has not so far connected with any real mobilization by women."[91]

IRELAND. Until recently Ireland was an extreme version of the strong male-breadwinner model. Despite a growing, export-oriented economy, the employment rate of women has remained far below the EU average. The social security system severely disadvantaged women: until finally complying with certain EC requirements in 1984, married women were entitled to fewer benefits, at lower rates, and for a shorter duration than were men. Until the early 1970s married women could not work in the civil service. And, similar to Germany, Ireland paid a wife's benefit regardless of the wife's employment status.[92] The Irish constitution assumes that different social groups have different but equal capacities and, consequently, gender roles are also different. In line with this conception, mothers should not be forced by economic necessity to earn a living and thereby neglect their duties at home.[93] Irish policymakers cultivated a strong notion of the family as the "basic unit of society with rights and responsibilities to be left untrammelled and unfettered by state interference."[94] Implementing EC equality laws thus required major revisions in Irish policy.

Beginning in the 1960s, women's rights groups formed to fight for equal pay and legalized contraception.[95] Ireland's preparation for entry into the EC, which occurred in 1973, gave the women's movement a prime opportunity to push for equal pay. Irish legislation mandating equal pay for equal work was enacted in 1974, before the 1975 EC directive on equal pay. It provided for equality officers, who were to

91. Hoskyns, " 'Give Us Equal Pay,' " p. 46. It may be that German feminists side with the many "family-centered" women who leave employment or reduce work hours and take care of a family. For these women, a sudden move away from the existing division of labor by gender is risky. Consider the case of abolishing restrictions on women working night shifts: some women gain through the creation of new job opportunities, but many women lose because employers can now require them to work at night.

92. Lewis and Ostner, "Gender," pp. 162–63.

93. Hoskyns, " 'Give Us Equal Pay,' " p. 47. The article in the Irish constitution is fully quoted in Pauline Conroy Jackson, "Managing the Mothers: The Case of Ireland," in Lewis, ed., *Women and Social Policies*, pp. 72–91.

94. Jackson, "Managing the Mothers," p. 80. As in the German case, nonintervention in the family and numerous measures to protect all kinds of women—such as those for deserted women and lone mothers, and comparatively generous maternity legislation—do not contradict one another. They all support the institutions of motherhood and family.

95. Jackson, "Managing the Mothers," p. 79.

investigate complaints and make recommendations. Although designed to minimize disruptions to the existing economic and employment order, the act upset Irish employers. The government's lack of enthusiasm is evidenced by its unsuccessful efforts, backed by employers' organizations, to lobby Brussels for derogation from implementation of the directive.[96] The 1976 equal-treatment directive has proven even more significant for women and problematic for Irish policymakers, because it prohibits discrimination based on marital or family status. As in Germany, however, implementation of the directive permitted exclusion of women from occupations and operations for "sensible" reasons.

Ireland faced a fundamental challenge to its discriminatory practices with the passage of the 1979 EC directive on equal treatment in social security, which prohibited the payment of different levels of unemployment benefits and the automatic payment of a wife's allowance to married men. The dependent's (wife's) allowance was abolished; its loss severely harmed many low-income families. The government responded by redesigning the allowance as a supplementary benefit for those with low incomes.[97] Although a bill aimed at implementing the 1979 directive was introduced, progress in removing discrimination against married women was slow. Throughout, the government showed tremendous reluctance. As Ita Mangan summarizes, "In spite of having six years to prepare, the date for implementation passed without any action by the government. The method of implementation which was finally decided upon was, in some respects, discriminatory and the government has been accused of being negligent in its handling of this issue. . . . The so-called 'compensating payments' which were introduced to quell the outcry resulting from the loss of benefits by married men were themselves discriminatory. Following a decision of the European Court of Justice, the Government was obliged to pay retrospective payments to the women affected by the failure to implement the Directive."[98]

The Irish experience reveals a decidedly mixed picture. The European Community initiated and accelerated gender equity in Ireland. Despite considerable foot-dragging and attempts to narrow the scope of the EC directives, Ireland has had to make fundamental changes in its policy. A

---

96. Hoskyns, "'Give Us Equal Pay,'" p. 48. Ita Mangan, "The Influence of EC Membership on Irish Social Policy and Social Services," in Seamus O'Cinneide, ed., *Social Europe: EC Social Policy and Ireland* (Dublin: Institute of European Affairs, 1993), pp. 60–81.

97. Hoskyns, "'Give Us Equal Pay,'" pp. 50–51.

98. Mangan, "Influence of EC Membership," p. 75.

report compiled by Ireland's Joint Committee on Secondary Legislation of the EC concluded that "the Community has brought about changes in employment practices which might otherwise have taken decades to achieve. Irish women have the Community to thank for the removal of the marriage bar in employment, the introduction of maternity leave, greater opportunities to train at a skilled trade, protection against dismissal on pregnancy, the disappearance of advertisements specifying the sex of an applicant for a job and great equality in the social welfare code. After farmers, Irish women in employment have probably benefited most from entry to the EEC."[99]

Yet progress has been hampered by the failure of the Union to effectively police equal treatment in social security. Furthermore, the EU's failure to confront issues such as contraception and abortion, which are extremely important for the status and citizenship of Irish women, further limit the possibilities for policy change. Indeed, the EU's growing relevance for Irish social policy prompted an aggressive effort to solidify core aspects of Irish gender policies on these controversial subjects. Seeking to limit the possible impact of membership in the Community, Ireland added a prohibition of abortion to its constitution. In response to growing indications that the ECJ was willing to review Irish policy on the grounds that abortion was a "service" subject to EC common-market requirements, Ireland obtained a specific exemption for its ban on abortion in the Maastricht treaty.[100]

Both Germany and Ireland rose to the challenge of EC equality legislation, introducing important legal changes related to women's position in the labor market. Each, however, continued to distinguish between women as "equal citizens" and women as a "social category of different moral and physical capacity," though in somewhat different ways. The diversity of breadwinner and care regimes within the EU thus not only hinders the formulation of coherent women's policies on a supranational level; it also means that even where EU action succeeds, implementation

99. Joint Committee on the Secondary Legislation of the EC, *Report on Proposals relating to Equality of Opportunity* (Dublin: Stationary Office, 1984), quoted in Mangan, "Influence of EC Membership," p. 72. Mangan maintains that the EC's role is overstated, but that "the general thrust of this statement is correct." That conclusion is echoed by Jackson, "Managing the Mothers"; and Hoskyns, "'Give Us Equal Pay.'"

100. See Diarmuid Rossa Phelan, "Right to Life of the Unborn v. Promotion of Trade in Services: The European Court of Justice and the Normative Shaping of the European Union," *Modern Law Review*, vol. 55 (September 1992), pp. 670–89. On the enforcement of a single market for services and national social policy, see chapter 2, by Stephan Leibfried and Paul Pierson, in this volume.

may take a different shape from country to country. On the national level, gender regimes operate as gatekeepers, favoring policies compatible with culturally transmitted assumptions and tenets about gender roles.

Conclusion

The Union's interventions in gender policy remain constrained. Two severe tests—the needles' eyes of the employment nexus at the supranational level and national constraints on implementation—narrow the focus of EU gender policies. But these constraints should not be exaggerated. By transforming the ECJ and the Commission into prominent actors, article 119 created a unique opportunity for developing Unionwide social policies on gender equality.

Several important changes in member-state policy have already resulted from developments at the EU level. EU policy initiated a forceful process of situating working women similarly to men. By extending the scope of its legislation to women who are seeking work or who work atypical hours, the ECJ has come close to treating most women of working age as men are treated. The history and content of the maternity directive suggest that women will profit most from EU policy if their concerns can be either presented as those of "similarly situated" workers entitled to equal economic and social rights or couched in terms of health and safety or improvement of working conditions.

Some have anticipated that the exit from the Maastricht accord of Britain, with its strong history of vetoes, will open up new avenues for social—and therefore women's—issues. This projection overlooks the prominence of cheap talk in the past pronouncements of member states, however, and thus exaggerates their eagerness for action in this area. What is actually evident is hesitancy to increase social regulation of the labor market (for example, through atypical work regulations, which would significantly benefit women workers). EU policy toward women seems to have reached the limits of what may be expected in the current framework, and any new proposals are likely to be merely the unexpected or unintended byproducts of the increasingly complex politics of logrolling. The existing body of directives and rulings is sufficient to generate a continuing stream of important policy adaptations, but the two needles' eyes—the employment nexus and the constraints of member-state cultural and political diversity—greatly narrow the space for EU policymaking.

CHAPTER SIX

Protective Shelter or Straitjacket:
An Institutional Analysis of the Common
Agricultural Policy of the European Union

Elmar Rieger

T HE COMMON AGRICULTURAL POLICY (CAP) of the European Union
is a unique experiment in policymaking and social engineering. First, it
is the only centrally financed and directed policy domain of the Union
that is comprehensive in scope, in the sense of having responsibility for
the welfare of the entire agricultural population. Despite the long tradition in Western Europe of state intervention in the agricultural sector
and its institutional legacies, the Common Agricultural Policy and its
agencies have grown into the largest domestic repository of resources for
rural economic development and rural social welfare in only a few years.
EU institutions and interventions have become a major factor in the
creation, formation, and distribution of life chances in the agricultural
sector. This fundamental fact has altered the relationship between the
agrarian population and the Union, on the one hand and the relationship
between the farmers and the governments of the member states, on the
other. Nevertheless, the EU has not supplanted the national state as the
basic focus of farmers. Instead, the Union has increasingly become a
passive instrument of the member states in the highly protective regulation of international agricultural trade.

Second, with regard both to its aims and to its organizing principles,
the CAP follows the logic of "positive" integration, whereas the basic
idea behind European integration is the creation and maintenance of an

This chapter was originally prepared for the CES workshop on "Emergent Supranational Social Policy: The EC's Social Dimension in Comparative Perspective." I want to
thank Stephan Leibfried and Paul Pierson, who organized the workshop, for their helpful
suggestions and Jeffrey Anderson, who served as a commentator on the paper. If the paper
is readable and comprehensible, this is due in no small part to the careful and competent
editing of Margaret Herden.

essentially intervention-free common market. As the sector that receives the most regulation and support from the Union, then, agriculture stands in sharp contrast to its economic and institutional environment. Although EU institutions have no direct links to farmers, they nonetheless complement the different forms of government regulations in agriculture that have evolved in Europe since the interwar years.

Third, the CAP is remarkable also for its size: it now consumes almost two-thirds of the EU budget. Partly because of its size and complexity and partly because of its international repercussions, the CAP has developed from an important source of internal and external stability into a source of crises that have transformed the agenda of policymaking for member states, the Union, and international trade relations. The CAP is therefore far more than simply an agricultural policy. It has been—and still is—a political battleground for forces both for and against European integration. Thus attitudes toward the CAP often have very little to do with agriculture.

In this chapter the politics of agriculture in the European Union are understood as a succession of attempts, carried out in a volatile environment, to solve the basic problems of the agricultural sector in the developed industrial societies of Western Europe. The first section focuses on the emergence of the institutional arrangements found in the political structures of agricultural policymaking in the Union. Because the institutions of the Union—not the market economy—are the central mechanism for the allocation of resources and the principle source of conflicts and tensions, it is legitimate to speak of the "welfare dimension" of the CAP. The basic criterion governing the CAP has never been economic rationality alone, but also economic and social security and distributive justice. For this reason the institutional structure of this field of EU activity can be compared with developments on the national level, that is, the emergence and institutionalization of welfare regimes, especially in Western Europe and in the United States. Yet as discussed below, the institutional structure of the CAP and the way in which it is governed prevent the CAP from measuring up fully to these criteria.

Described simply, the introduction of the CAP transferred the responsibility for market regulation in the field of agriculture from national authorities to a new supranational organization. The (relatively) easy administration of uniform systems of price support through market intervention meant a division of labor in agricultural matters between the Community and national authorities: the Community became responsible for systems of price support for an increasing number of agricultural products, whereas the member states controlled all those policies aimed at problems stemming from a noncompetitive farm structure, regional imbalances, rural infrastructure, and so on.

As discussed below, two developments turned this division of labor between two tiers of governance (three tiers in member states with a federal political system) into a major problem. First of all, the CAP followed the well-known law of the "pull of the superior budget": the Community enlarged its responsibility for agricultural matters and provided more and more financial support for the agricultural policies of the member states. Second, because of the peculiar institutional structure of the CAP and the nature of the division of labor between the Community and the member states, the CAP favored farmers already in a good position and brought about a sharp increase in the heterogeneity of the agricultural sector with regard to farm size, output, and income. The second section of this chapter deals with this development in some detail. In particular, this transformation of rural social structures called into question the very compromise that lays at the heart of the division of labor between the CAP and the member states, because it led to proliferation of new categories of policies that quite radically changed the institutional structure of the CAP.

But the CAP increasingly lost its meaning as a cornerstone for European integration after the launching of the "single European market." Its strong reliance on market intervention simply no longer fit the general climate of economic and social thinking. In addition, because of the drastic reduction of the economic importance of agriculture—its contribution to the gross domestic product declined and employment in the sector decreased—the CAP also lost its meaning as a major supplier of legitimacy for the Community in the eyes of the politicians. This holds true both for the Community and, although to a lesser extent, the member states. Therefore, triggered by increasing criticism of the new role of the Community as a major exporter of agricultural products, a fundamental shift in the aims of the CAP took place: income security for most farmers was replaced by concerns over the market, international free trade, and the wealth of the more commercially oriented farmers. Pressure built for a renationalization of the CAP because the governments of the member states are still dependent on the farm vote, and only they have the institutional and administrative capabilities to help their agricultural sectors adjust so that existing inequalities are not deepened or surplus production prolonged.

But there was a change also in the international environment of the

Community and its CAP. The Community became indispensable in the defense of the agricultural interests of the more important member states in the new round of negotiations on the General Agreement on Tariffs and Trade (GATT) starting in 1984. In fact, all of the member states increasingly recognize that only the Union, as the most powerful and legitimate spokesman for the entire agricultural sector, can counter the strong demands of the United States and other major exporters of agricultural products. So there is pressure both to preserve the present system of governance—including sharing the financial burden of agricultural support—and to shift the general direction of the CAP. The main argument of the first section of this chapter—and, insofar as consequences are concerned, also of the second and third sections—is, first, that this ambivalent situation has exacerbated the economic position of most farmers; and, second, that national governments, especially in countries with a large agricultural sector dominated by small-scale farming, use the Union to block agreements in the GATT that would further damage the farming sector.

Therefore the Union has reached an impasse over the future shape of the CAP. These two developments—the internal transformation of the CAP and the change in its political environment—mean that the central elements of this policy domain no longer serve the interests of the majority of farmers, but, increasingly, only those of a relatively small number. Much more important, they serve the interests of politicians at the Union and member-state levels who are concerned about conflicts resulting from the costs of the CAP and the consequences for international trade regimes.

It came as no surprise, then, that the agreement between the Community and the member states, reached in the summer of 1992, consisted of a compromise that preserved the status quo: drastic reductions in the institutional prices of most products—up to 33 percent over the course of the following five years—to be accompanied by direct payments to all farmers to compensate for income losses. This solution simultaneously addressed concerns about the GATT negotiations and the income problems of the majority of farmers and rural social structures. The overall effect, however, was a massive increase in the costs of the CAP. From 1989 to 1993 total per capita expenditures on the CAP rose from 72 ECU to 101 ECU.[1] Considering the problems inherent in the complex

---

1. Kommission der Europäischen Gemeinschaften, *Die Lage der Landwirtschaft in der Gemeinschaft* (Luxembourg, 1993), p. T84.

multitier system of the CAP, a significant change will quite probably come about only after the structural transformation of agriculture is complete: over the next five to ten years, old age will force almost half of the farmers within the Union to give up farming, and undoubtedly, they will not find successors in their field.

The Making of the Common Agricultural Policy of the European Community

> Agriculture does not necessarily require peasants. . . . In France 150,000 peasants now leave the land every year. The economic planners of the EEC envisage the systematic elimination of the peasant by the end of the century. For short-term political reasons, they do not use the word elimination but the word modernisation. Modernisation entails the disappearance of the small peasants (the majority) and the transformation of the remaining minority into totally different social and economic beings.[2]

To understand more clearly the rationale and the objectives of the agricultural policies of the Community, it is necessary to look first at both the particular features and problems of modern agriculture and the historical trends in the development of the institutional framework of government activities in this area.[3] Doing so is important for two reasons. One, the outcome of the institutionalization of a specific public policy is the result of the dynamic interplay between the characteristics of the social structure of the sector, on the one hand, and the peculiar quality

2. John Berger, "Introduction," *Into Their Labours: A Trilogy* (London: Granta Books, 1992), p. xxv.

3. For an overview of the historical development of agriculture in advanced industrial societies, see Ulf Jonsson and Ronny Petterson, "Friends or Foes? Peasants, Capitalists, and Markets in West European Agriculture, 1850–1939," *Fernand Braudel Center Review,* vol. 12 (1989), pp. 535–71; Paul W. Barkeley, "A Contemporary Political Economy of Family Farming," *American Journal of Agricultural Economics*, vol. 58 (1976), pp. 813–19; and Vernon Ruttan, "Agricultural Policy in an Affluent Society," *American Journal of Farm Economics* 48 (1966), pp. 1100–20. For a discussion of the special problems of the agricultural sector in capitalist market economies, see Susan Archer Mann, *Agrarian Capitalism in Theory and Practice* (University of North Carolina Press, 1990).

of the policy, on the other.[4] Two, the making of the Common Agricultural Policy was not determined exclusively by the obvious social and economic problems of the agricultural sector or by the pressing need for recovery of agricultural production after the Second World War, but also by the existing apparatuses of national systems of protection in the member states of the Community. The founders of the CAP had to design a new overarching tier of common programs and regulations, which meant that they had to confront the problems of finding adequate rules for the governance of the new programs as well as solutions for potential conflicts with existing policies at the national and, sometimes, even regional levels.

The peculiar dynamics of the development of the CAP and the consequences of its institutionalization must be seen in the context of significant differences between agriculture and industry in modern societies. First of all, agriculture in Western Europe is chararacterized in large part by small-scale, owner-operated family farms.[5] Second, agriculture in Western Europe is distinguished by the atomistic nature of its economic and social organization. The main decisionmaking entities are tens of thousands of individual farmers operating independently; the market power of one single farmer therefore is infinitely small. The uniformity and homogeneity of agricultural products further diminish the impact farmers can have on the market. Third, around the turn of the century in both Europe and the United States most farms were still in some respect subsistence units. The primary link between the farm and the nonfarm sector was the product market—that is, the market for things farmers sell. In the course of the development of modern agriculture, the markets for purchased inputs (manufactured capital equipment and current inputs) have become increasingly important, which has brought about a radical change in the structural positioning of agriculture in the market economy. Fourth, besides the instability stemming from its interrelationships with a market economy and an industrialized society, agriculture

4. The term *outcome* refers both to the structuring of conflicts between social groups—that is, social and system integration—and to the allocation of resources—that is, welfare (or its absence).

5. For a description of ideal family farming, see Marty Strange, *Family Farming: A New Economic Vision* (University of Nebraska Press, 1988), pp. 32ff. For an attempt to explain the persistence of family farming in the European Community, see Günther H. Schmitt, "Warum ist Landwirtschaft eigentlich überwiegend 'bäuerliche Familienlandwirtschaft'?" *Berichte über Landwirtschaft*, vol. 67, no. 2 (1989), pp. 161–219.

has certain unique instabilities of its own: the vagaries of nature cause fluctuations in yields and total production; and for certain farm products, production ("pig") cycles grow out of the cumulative effect of false price expectations of thousands of independent producers.[6]

Agriculture in Western Europe has changed, of course, in the past thirty years. There has been a gradual transformation from family farming to specialized, intensified industrial agribusiness. But, to say the least, this development is extremely uneven and far from complete. Small-scale family farming still coexists with commercial farming and industrial agribusiness. The persistence of small-scale farming and the evolution of a broader stratum of commercially directed farms are attributable to the shape and the functioning of the CAP.[7] A few remarks on the social structure of agriculture and its economic implications may help explain this outcome.

The formation of nation-states, the Industrial Revolution, and the establishment of national markets gave rise to national agriculture and to the industrialization of agriculture and food. The competition of cheaper grains from settler regions, especially the United States, Canada, and Australia in the second half of the nineteenth century, induced an agricultural crisis in Europe that eventually prompted all European states to adopt protectionist policies for their agricultural populations. The European national governments wanted to ensure self-sufficiency in food supplies, especially in times of war, and they were committed to maintaining a healthy and dynamic rural sector.[8] With very few exceptions, both national agricultural and international food regimes, especially in the wake of the Great Depression, became highly regulated.[9]

In the first ten years after World War II, austerity and a new Western European solidarity characterized the atmosphere in which the European Economic Community and the CAP were conceived and brought into the

6. See Susan Archer Mann, *Agrarian Capitalism in Theory and Practice* (University of North Carolina Press, 1990).

7. Further elaboration on this topic can be found in Elmar Rieger, "Der Wandel der Landwirtschaft in der Europäischen Union," *Kölner Zeitschrift für Soziologie und Sozialpsychologie*, vol. 47, no. 1 (1995), pp. 65–94.

8. For the history of these developments, see Harriet Friedman and Philip McMichael, "Agriculture and the State System: The Rise and Decline of National Agricultures, 1870 to the Present," *Sociologia Ruralis*, vol. 29, no. 2 (1989), pp. 93–117; and Michael Tracy, *Government and Agriculture in Western Europe, 1880–1988* (New York: Harvester Wheatsheaf, 1989).

9. For an overview, see the study by Karl Schiller, *Marktregulierung und Marktordnung in der Weltagrarwirtschaft* (Jena: Fischer, 1939).

world. European agriculture was subjected to severe dislocations. Facilities had been damaged, and the flow of trade between Eastern and Western Europe, especially between Eastern and Western Germany, had been disrupted or had ceased altogether. Most European countries therefore continued to control production and distribution of agricultural products in order to increase production. Under the influence of the Marshall Plan and other foreign aid programs, additional measures were directed toward improving efficiency and quality.[10]

The rapid but uneven recovery brought no return to free markets. And dependence on substantial American food imports after the loss of traditional food-surplus areas in Eastern Germany and Russia fostered plans for harmonizing interests in the field of agriculture: "The need of integration in this field is incontestable. During 1946 and early 1950, a situation like that of the thirties began to develop in Europe, with agricultural surpluses in some countries and scarcity in others. . . . Integration of European Agriculture is the plain answer. The creation of a large area without trade barriers would provide for greater stability in markets and prices, would tend to redirect production to the areas most suited for various products and bring higher production at lower cost. In this respect, integration in agriculture is based on the same principles as industrial integration."[11] Lack of space does not permit a detailed account of the European discussions on how to organize a common agricultural market and harmonize systems of national protection.[12] Let it suffice to say that the concept of an integrated market and the liberalization of trade among the member countries of the new organization was robust enough to include agriculture in the "economic community."

At the same time, the distinctive features of Western European agriculture and the existence of broad systems of government support to farmers singled out the agricultural sector for special treatment. This point was acknowledged in 1952 by Sicco Mansholt, then Dutch minister of agriculture: "The application of the principle of economic liberalism,

10. See Naum Jasny, "Decline and Recovery in European Agriculture: World Wars I and II," *Foreign Agriculture*, vol. 10 (May 1946), pp. 66–75; J. H. Richter, "The European Recovery Program: Programs, Developments and Prospects in Agriculture," *Journal of Farm Economics*, vol. 32 (November 1950), pp. 541–52; and G. J. Dobson, "Government Aid to Agriculture in Some Western European Countries," *Economic Analyst*, vol. 26 (June 1956), pp. 55–59.

11. S. L. Mansholt, "Toward European Integration: Beginnings in Agriculture," *Foreign Affairs*, vol. 31 (October 1952), pp. 106–13, quotation at p. 110.

12. A very good historical analysis is in Alan S. Milward, *The European Rescue of the Nation-State* (London: Routledge, 1992), pp. 224–317.

suitable for the industrial sectors of the economy, cannot be applied to farming."[13] This position, shared by all member states of the prospective community, resulted in agriculture's peculiar position in the Treaty of Rome. Another cornerstone in the building of the CAP was the settlement of France and Germany's diffferences over economic interests: the less industrialized France opened its market for German industrial products and in exchange got access to the German market for its agricultural products.[14]

The implication of these agreements—the necessity for strong elements of supranational governance—contrasted sharply with the restricted authority of the organs of the new Community.[15] The European Economic Community was far less supranational than the European Coal and Steel Community. This feature of the new Community is of crucial importance, because the Community's responsibility for agriculture was much greater than for other fields of economic integration, where the logic of "negative" integration prevailed: the abolition of trade barriers, tariffs, and quotas to create a framework for more dynamic economies. The commitment of the six founding member states to establish a common set of policies in agriculture was therefore a large one, since it implied the withering away of strictly national agricultural policies. Yet the governments of the member states did not relinquish their authority and decisionmaking power: the institutional dominance of the Council of Ministers put the member states in a much stronger position than the Commission of the EC.

This structural imbalance, or structural error, with regard to decisionmaking explains why the CAP with its rather costly features now seems to be totally out of kilter with the contemporary mood.[16] Its institutional features reflect social, economic, and political conditions that are long gone. Those features arose mostly from the intergovernmental character of the new organization, which ensured that important decisions about the institutional structure of the CAP were fully sensitive to national

---

13. Mansholt, "Toward European Integration," p. 110.

14. Wilfried Loth, *Der Weg nach Europa: Geschichte der europäischen Integration, 1939–1957* (Göttingen: Vandenhoeck und Ruprecht, 1990), pp. 128 ff.

15. For the supranational character of the High Authority, see Ernst B. Haas, *The Uniting of Europe: Political, Social, and Economic Forces, 1950–1957* (Stanford University Press, 1968), pp. 451 ff.

16. The implications of this "structural error" were already acknowledged at the beginning of the debate on the agricultural policy after the acceptance of the treaty. See Heinrich Niehaus, "Effects of the European Common Market on Employment and Social Conditions in Agriculture," *International Labour Review*, vol. 77 (1958), pp. 289–312.

interests. In addition, the strong position of the Council of Ministers, operating in crucial matters more like an international conference of national delegates than as the governing organ of a community, provided agrarian interest groups with easy access to the center of decisionmaking. Intensifying this situation were the substantial electoral salience of farm issues in the national systems, especially in the larger member states; strong national party ties; and—especially important for the implementation of policies—national bureaucratic links between national farm groups and national government agencies.[17] The activities of agricultural interest groups on the national level therefore reinforced the intergovernmental character of decisionmaking in the Community. They played a minor role in the creation of a genuine supranational political system.[18]

Because each of the original six members of the Community had a complex set of agricultural policies, the Treaty of Rome could outline a common plan for agriculture in only very broad terms, and only after a long period of exploratory negotiations.[19] The significant point of the provisions of the Treaty of Rome is that policy was designed deliberately to promote the general welfare of the farmers of the Community in a direct way, by new, centrally governed and financed agencies. Equally important as the broad and, for that matter, contradictory statements on social and economic ends was the choice of administrative institutions, because they also define and defend interests and values.

One basic requirement for the introduction of the CAP was an agreement on the mode of regulation and the level of support of the farm economy. The treaty remained vague on the nature of the common agricultural policy. It could consist of common rules of competition or of coordination of national market organizations or of a European market organization. Not surprisingly, considering the strong position of the

17. For an overview of this topic, see Derek W. Urwin, *From Ploughshare to Ballotbox: The Politics of Agrarian Defence in Europe* (Oslo: Universitetsforlaget, 1980). For a historical and comparative view, see Hans-Jürgen Puhle, *Politische Agrarbewegungen in kapitalistischen Industriegesellschaften. Deutschland, USA und Frankreich im 20. Jahrhundert* (Göttingen: Vandenhoeck and Ruprecht, 1975).

18. On this point, see William F. Avery, Jr., *Agropolitics in the European Community: Interest Groups and the Common Agricultural Policy* (Praeger, 1977), pp. 114ff.

19. For the history of the CAP, see Leon N. Lindberg, *The Political Dynamics of European Economic Integration* (Stanford University Press, 1963); Rosemary Fennell, *The Common Agricultural Policy of the European Community: Its Institutional and Administrative Organisation* (Oxford: BSP Professional Books, 1987); and Antonio Fernando Alvarez and Donato Fernandez Navarrete, "Agrarian Policies and Agricultural System of the European Community: A Historical Overview," in Alessandro Bonanno, ed., *Agrarian Policies and Agricultural Systems* (Boulder, Colo.: Westview Press, 1990), pp. 76–105.

Council of Ministers, it took nearly three and a half years of debate to settle the basic principles of a common policy after the treaty was signed. In the end, the three guiding principles of the CAP were free trade of agricultural products within the Community, Community preference in trade, and common financial responsibilities. By the end of 1960 the Council of Ministers had accepted a system of market support consistent with these principles.

The hard bargaining among the member states over the details of applying the common policy, however, produced an agricultural price policy that was more protectionist and provided higher levels of income support than the national policies it replaced.[20] The reasons for this course of development were, first, countries with already high levels of price support wanted high common prices; second, the range of products covered by the CAP had to be expanded because each country had special interests in particular commodities; and third, the principle of common financing reduced pressure on individual countries to limit price increases. The vehicle the Community used to achieve its aims has turned out to be price policies, with target prices designed to maintain a stable income for producers, rather than a combination of economic and social policies.

Taking into consideration the institutional features of Community decisionmaking—intergovernmentalism and unanimity rule—it is obvious that systems of common institutional prices are more easily agreed upon and administered than are specific policies. These became the main pillar of the CAP. The principal instruments with which the CAP supports market prices are intervention buying on domestic markets by government agencies and variable import levies and export refunds on trade with third countries.[21] These instruments are supplemented or replaced by a host of others, depending on the commodity, including producer subsidies, slaughter premiums, consumer and processor subsidies, production quotas, import quotas, and aids for private storage. Over 70

20. This outcome, especially the high institutional prices, owed a good deal to the strong bargaining powers of national interest groups. See Paul Ackermann, Der Deutsche Bauernverband im politischen Kräftespiel der Bundesrepublik (Tübingen: Mohr, 1970); and Ulrich Weinstock, "Der zu hoch festgesetzte Getreidepreis und die Folgen: Rückschau auf ein Vierteljahrhundert deutscher Politik in der Gemeinschaft," in Winfried von Urff and Heino von Meyer, eds., Landwirtschaft, Umwelt und Ländlicher Raum: Herausforderungen an Europa (Baden-Baden: Nomos, 1987), pp. 63–86.

21. For the details, see Fennell, Common Agricultural Policy; and Julius Rosenblatt and others, The Common Agricultural Policy of the European Community: Principles and Consequences (Washington: International Monetary Fund, 1988).

percent of final agricultural output is subject to these instruments, which dictate common prices with varying degrees of support; for 25 percent regulations exist, but not common prices. The only significant commodity not covered by the CAP is potatoes—and this may change in the immediate future if the Commission has its way.

From the beginning of the evolution of the CAP institutional framework, the bedrock principle has been to stabilize farmers' incomes with institutional prices and an artificially insulated market. The need to maintain farm incomes was the rationale put forward for price determination; to satisfy the income needs especially of small farmers, which represented the majority of farmers, prices had to be fixed at a high level.[22] Commodity programs with fixed institutional prices, however, benefit not farmers but farms. As the Commission and independent observers foresaw, these programs encouraged increased production and rewarded expansion because their benefits are tied to the volume of commodities a farm produces, with large farms benefiting the most. Moreover, the institutional structure of the CAP and the peculiar framework of decision-making in agricultural matters—prices set annually by the Council of Ministers tend to stay high because unanimity is required for such decisions[23]—was another cause of huge surpluses in agricultural products and an explosion of the Community budget.[24] In the years 1973 to 1982 nominal Community budget growth was about 25 percent annually, with about two-thirds of total spending going to agricultural price supports. Even in following years when the size of the farming sector had declined, the growth rates of the budget of the CAP were quite high (see figure 6-1).

But common and uniform programs of price support are only half of the picture. Because of the overall backwardness of their farm sectors,

22. See Tracy, *Government and Agriculture*, pp. 258–63. For a general discussion, see Theodor Heidhues and others, *Common Prices and Europe's Farm Policy*, Thames Essay 14 (London: Trade Research Centre, 1978).

23. For a more detailed analysis, see Fritz W. Scharpf, "The Joint-Decision Trap: Lessons from German Federalism and European Integration," *Public Administration*, vol. 66 (Autumn 1988), pp. 239–78.

24. The two basic features of the institutional arrangements in agricultural matters are the unanimity rule for decisions made by the Council of Ministers and the requirement that the Council make annual decisions on agricultural prices. Deadlines ensure that decisions are ultimately made. In addition, there is no "exit option" for member states. It is not possible simply to return to national price policies and commodity regimes. See Carlisle Ford Runge and Harald von Witzke, *The Market for Institutional Innovation in the Common Agricultural Policy of the European Community* (Kiel: Wissenschaftsverlag Vauk, 1986).

Figure 6-1. *Expenditure on Agriculture under the Community Budget,*
1973–91

Billions of European currency units

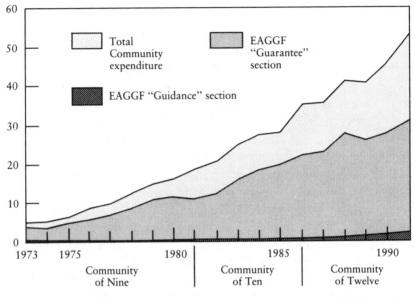

Source: Authors' calculations, using data from European Commission, *The Agricultural Situation in the Community*, various years.

all member states of the European Community had their own policies in
place to increase farm efficiency and to support the transition from small-
scale farming to commercial farming. This common aim became part of
the CAP, in the form of so-called structural measures which range from
land drainage to vocational training, and from eradication of cattle diseases to providing aid for producers of olive oil. There was another
reason, too, to introduce structural measures at the Community level:
Because prices are institutionally fixed and because they are on a high
level, there is no market to weed out the weak and reward the efficient.
Farmers who are "efficient" and want to enlarge their business have no
chance to do so, since less efficient farmers have, because of high institutional prices, no incentive to give up farming. Thus the former cannot
buy extra farm land. Now structural policy steps in by giving efficient
farmers extra means (vocational training, credit) to enlarge, and by giving
less efficient, small-scale farmers bigger incentives to leave ariculture
altogether (payments for "outgoers"). The bulk of the expenditure on
structural measures has, in fact, gone to farm modernization measures,

improvement of infrastructure in disadvantaged areas, and, increasingly, direct income payments.[25]

At the outset CAP structural measures were based solely on the idea of making farms more competitive—to help farmers consolidate and enlarge their holdings, thus becoming able to specialize and intensify production and thereby increase their income.[26] An important precondition for this course, however, is the willingness of farmers with small holdings to give up farming and to move to other sectors of employment. To that end, the Mansholt Plan, which was supposed to force small, inefficient holdings out of production, was proposed at the end of the 1960s. This proposal for an active Community policy was enacted only partly and it did not achieve its goal of substantially increasing labor and land mobility.

Beginning in the mid-1960s, new programs were introduced to supplement the structural measures; these were aimed at assisting small-scale farming, especially in regions with structural and natural disadvantages for farming. This second source of Community structural policies—the *regional policies*—reflected the changed economic environment surrounding the restructuring of the agricultural sector: high unemployment rates, which meant only scarce employment possibilities for the rural labor force, and growing concern about the depopulation of rural areas, with negative consequences not only for farmers but for the entire region.

Because agriculture was a major fact of social integration and economic well-being in many regions of the Community, the common denominator of the regional measures was the provision of compensatory allowances to farmers in mountain, hill, and other "less-favoured areas." The regional policies therefore are essentially a social instrument rather

25. Both price support measures and structural measures are financed from a special fund, which is an integral part of the Union budget. The European Agricultural Guidance and Guarantee Fund (EAGGF), the mechanism through which the CAP is financed, was set up in 1962. Expenditures on export funds and on domestic market intervention are financed from the guidance section of EAGGF; regulation 17/64 provides that expenditures on structural measures also should be financed from the guidance section. Under regulation 25/62, expenditures from the guidance section should correspond—as far as possible—to one-third of expenditures under the guarantee section. However, the amount of money spent on structural measures is less than 5 percent of the money spent on price support. This is already a clear indicator of the nature of the CAP, since the only way to direct more Union resources to disadvantaged regions and sectors of the agricultural community is through guidance section schemes. See Fennell, *Common Agricultural Policy*, pp. 75 ff.

26. For a general discussion of this policy domain, see John S. Marsh, "Agriculture and Structual Policy," in Kees Burger and others, eds., *Agricultural Economies and Policy: International Challenges for the Nineties* (New York: Elsevier, 1991), pp. 95–118.

than a means of structural adjustment.[27] These policies gained importance after the third enlargement of the Community, because they seemed to provide the means to deal with the increased heterogeneity of the agricultural sector and the structural disadvantages of southern European member states vis-à-vis northern member states.[28]

The development of these apparently more social policy–like measures owes as much to the institutional dynamics of the CAP and to increasing pressure to reform as to deliberate attempts to develop genuine, full-blown social policies. Gradually the recognition grew that the income problem of western European farmers could not be solved with a common price policy alone.

The adverse economic and social effects of the Community shift from mainly permissive mechanisms in agricultural regulation (high institutional prices, investment aids, occupational training) to more bureaucratic control mechanisms (quotas, levies, set-aside regulations) triggered the need for compensatory measures. The distinctive aspect of these new policies—first the horizontal measures, and later the targeted regional measures—is their more explicit social policy–like character. They were at least in part consciously designed to counter the unequal distribution of social and economic disadvantages resulting from attempts to curb expenditures under the CAP. Like the original commodity regimes of the 1960s, they have to take into account the various national mechanisms of compensation for income reductions and increased social insecurity in the agricultural sector.[29] At least at their inception, they could be seen as an attempt to institutionalize Community-based competencies and administrative capacities to achieve a more just distribution of resources based on autonomous criteria of distributive justice and social security.[30] From the standpoint of the member states, however, these efforts implied a serious encroachment upon their own prerogatives in the field of agri-

---

27. See Tracy, *Government and Agriculture*, p. 328.

28. In addition, these policies proved to be extremely helpful in package agreements in the context of annual price reviews. See Tracy, *Government and Agriculture*, p. 329.

29. This is in sharp contrast to the first structural measures of the CAP, which were designed to reinforce member states' structural spending. See Marsh, "Agriculture and Structural Policy," p. 101.

30. An important indicator stressing this point is the reform of the structural funds, which enabled the Community "to link agriculture with other sectors of the economy and make joint use of various Community funds to create an economic environment in which treasured rural characteristics are retained but combined with incomes for the rural community that are acceptable in comparison with those enjoyed elsewhere." Marsh, "Agriculture and Structural Policy," p. 106.

cultural policies. But even more important, social policy-like measures depend on a different and much more elaborate implementation structure than that required for broad systems of price support. As the Community does not have such an administrative apparatus, these new policies have to be organized in the same ways as commodity regimes—that is, in a way that discounts the specific income situation of farmers.[31]

Yet the evolving picture is not just that of organic growth and diversification of policy instruments. The CAP is not now, and never has been, a monolithic policy. It comprises numerous commodity regimes that differ in the details of their implementation. The common denominator of the commodity regimes is the maintenance of high internal prices. Structural measures, on the other hand, are not as easy to summarize; in some cases they use fundamentally different mechanisms to achieve their goals, so no common denominator is evident. Grasping the implications of the proliferation of policy instruments for the evolution of the CAP's social dimension requires a more analytical apparatus than the distinction between horizontal and regional structural measures.

What the evolving picture does show is that structural agricultural policies vary with respect to two dimensions of diversification: whether the criterion for benefit eligibility is the competitive capacity of farms in a market economy or the maintenance of farms irrespective of economic criteria, and whether or not the benefits provided by the Union have a structural link to economic criteria. Figure 6-2 shows the different paths the CAP has taken. The proliferation of policy instruments actually appears to be bifurcated with regard to the purpose of policies and to the way the policies provide benefits to farmers. And this bifurcation is the reason why the CAP has become a highly ambivalent policy.

As already noted, this system of classification is shaped by Union-induced changes in the agricultural sector. Surplus production, an explosion of CAP costs, and problems in the regulation of international agricultural trade increased public pressure for basic reform of the CAP. These changes have weakened the dominance of economic rationality in the governance of the CAP and have driven more differentiated and less universal policies. It has become extremely difficult to advocate faster structural change as the best solution to both the farm-income problem and the budget problem that the CAP presents to the Union.

Against this background it became easier for the Commission to ad-

31. Certain exceptions regarding the application of quota regulations and the administration of mandatory fallowing are made for small farms.

Figure 6-2. *Social Welfare Qualities of the Various Policies of the CAP*

Criteria for eligibility

		Making farms competitive	Maintaining agricultural activity
Type of provision	Linkage with economy	Investment aid to farmers; installation grants for young farmers *premiums on efficiency*	Direct income support ("less-favoured" areas, hill farming) *maintenance of an appropriate living standard; compensation for structural disadvantages*
	No linkage with economy	Early retirement payments *compensation for improving economic structure*	No mechanism *maintenance of an appropriate living standard: securing a basic income*

vocate decoupling income support from price support. For instance, in 1988 the Commission proposed a radical break with the "classic" CAP of high institutional prices and investment aids: the introduction of a Community-financed system of direct income aid "for families whose income from farming is less than 100% of the average national income (or 75% of the regional income), with Community contributions on a scale related to the level of development and the importance of agriculture in the region."[32] Implementing this policy (or something similar) would be a concrete example for the last cell of figure 6-2, securing a basic income for farmers. So far it has not been possible to get such a scheme through the Council. Aside from the political difficulty of compromising on such a proposal, the existing social policy–like measures suffer from problems that limit their possible significance.

Community-based social policies within the framework of the CAP are limited and closely circumscribed because this area of Community activities, unlike price support measures, lacks a legally prescribed monopoly of action. The consequences of this arrangement can be seen in the way the Community introduced structural and regional measures as

32. Tracy, *Government and Agriculture*, p. 330.

well as in the interplay between Community-based policies and member-state policies.

In the series of compromises involved in the bargaining that accompanied the three enlargements of the Community, the EC was forced to introduce special measures outside the existing framework of the CAP. The most important example concerned the program for less-favored areas, which was introduced to supplant a similar British scheme that, as a purely national measure, could not be brought into the Community. The "Mediterranean Package," which included aids for irrigation and infrastructure improvement, resulted from Italy's dissatisfaction with the distribution of benefits under the CAP. Similarly, the ambitious "Integrated Programmes" became the price the Community had to pay to Greece for the accession to membership of Spain and Portugal.[33]

But more important than these developments were Council decisions on the admissibility of specific national measures. To make a long story short, Council decisions about compensatory mechanisms on both the Commmunity and member-state levels have created a jigsaw pattern of social policy–like regulations and exceptions. These decisions take into acount only the immediate problem at hand, with very little regard to more general criteria of rationality.

Under article 92 of the Treaty of Rome, the Commission, member state, or any other interested party can challenge any program of national aid to farmers that is not explicitly addressed in Community agricultural legislation. To prevent renationalization of the CAP and to maintain the common agricultural market, the Commission attempts to regulate national aid, in most cases by using article 92 to block the efforts of agriculture ministers to compensate their farmers for the effects of restrictive price policies. Since 1974 the member states are legally bound to register with the Commission any national measure that either directly or indirectly supports agricultural incomes and to report annually on changes in those regulations. Thus the Commission has an important means of controlling national activities that could endanger the common agricultural market and increase the existing inequality among agricultural regions in different member states.

Nevertheless, the Commission is in a weak position vis-à-vis the Council of Ministers—the former prepares proposals but the Council decides them—and national income aids can be made a political issue in Council bargaining. It has therefore proved extremely difficult to harmonize

33. See Tracy, *Government and Agriculture*, pp. 328 ff.

national income aid in a way that satisfies Community-oriented and Community-defined goals of distributive justice.[34] A further difficulty lies in the fact that national systems of income support vary widely across the Union. The differences in national institutional structures of agricultural policies and the uneven capabilities of national administrations result in distortions with serious consquences, despite a formal harmonization of policies.

The administrative apparatus of the Union does not provide a direct link with farmers. EU structural measures depend on the member states for their implementation, yet member states sometimes lack an adequate implementation structure. They are therefore unable to make use of EU programs, which helps explain the low status of social policy–like measures in the present framework of the CAP: these measures do not present a workable alternative to high institutional prices. The price cuts of the last years have not been accompanied by a social policy that discriminates among farmers on the basis of need. Indeed, the summer 1992 agreement to cut institutional prices included a plan to make direct payments to *all* farmers.[35]

The overall position of social policy in the institutional structure of the CAP is not the only indicator of the significance and the value of the CAP as a collective achievement, however. The CAP's bearing on the actual lives of men and women in Western European agriculture also needs to be evaluated, as do the large-scale consequences of the CAP. The next section outlines those consequences, and the following one turns to the welfare-state implications of the Union's agricultural policies.

34. For a more detailed discussion, see Eckard Seebohm, *Nationalstaatliche Landwirtschaftsförderung und Europäische Agrarpolitik: Zum Problem der Kompatabilität nationaler Beihilfen mit der gemeinsamen Agrarpolitik* (Hannover: Strothe, 1981). On the problems of harmonization of national structural programs, see E. Pabsch, "Zur Harmonisierung von Strukturbeihilfen in der EWG," in Winfried von Urff, ed., *Der Agrarsektor im Integrationsprozeß* (Baden-Baden: Nomos, 1975), pp. 173–88. For an overview of national systems of income support, see *Landwirtschaftliche Einkommensstützung: Der Rat genehmigtedie veröffentlichung der Berichte* (Organization for Economic Cooperation and Development, 1983).

35. For details on the implementation of the CAP reform, starting in Summer 1993, see Bundesministerium für Ernährung, Landwirtschaft und Forsten, *Die Agrarreform der EG*, Publication B 242/93 (Bonn, 1993). In particular, an unprecedented level of administrative difficulties has been caused by the introduction of payments to farmers based on livestock numbers and hectarage and the bureaucratic control of the accompanying introduction of quotas and mandatory fallowing.

Western European Agriculture under the CAP

It has ... to be recognized that structures of social inequality of both condition and opportunity—or, in other words, systems of social stratification—are inherently highly resistant to change. ... This is not, of course, to suggest that change in stratification systems cannot, or does not, occur; but rather that any significant reduction in the degree of inequality will require purposive, well-designed and politically forceful action to this end—that it is unlikely to come about simply as the unsought-for consequence of technological advance, economic growth, or any such like secular trends. Such developments may well modify certain forms of inequality; but they appear just as likely to accentuate others.[36]

Improvements in agricultural technology coincided with, and often were stimulated by, the introduction of the CAP. Since most commodity regimes entailed fixed prices and various measures of price support, farmers responded to the new CAP environment by increasing output. The volume of agricultural output grew rapidly, without increases in the area of land farmed or in livestock numbers. Not surprisingly, with respect to economic performance the CAP has been eminently successful. Western European agriculture has not only reached self-sufficiency in almost all farm products but moved from being an importer of many agricultural commodities to becoming an exporter in a very short time span.[37]

One of the most obvious results of the transformation of Western European agriculture under the CAP is the rapid decline of the agricultural labor force. Though there is an overall trend toward a reduction of employment in agriculture, important differences among member states persist. In addition, the second and third enlargement of the Community led to even more diversity in European agricultural structures (see table 6-1). The still-high level of employment in agriculture is a clear indicator of the (relative) failure of attempts by the Union to change its agricultural structure through the creation of larger and more effective farms, but

36. John H. Goldthorpe, "Social Inequality and Social Integration," in Lee Rainwater, ed., *Social Problems and Public Policy: Inequality and Justice* (Chicago: Aldine, 1974), pp. 33 ff.

37. For a more detailed analysis, see Denis R. Bergmann, "The Transition to an Overproducing Agricultural System in Europe: An Economic and Institutional Analysis," in Gilberto Antonelli and Alberto Quadrio-Curzio, eds., *The Agro-Technological System Toward 2000: A European Perspective* (New York: North-Holland, 1988), pp. 53–74.

Table 6-1. *Social Structure of Agriculture in the Member States of the European Community, 1987*

Indicator	Belgium	Denmark	Germany	Greece	Spain	France	Ireland	Italy	Luxembourg	Netherlands	Portugal	United Kingdom
Farm size (number of hectares per holding)	14.8	32.2	16.8	4.0	13.8	28.6	22.7	5.6	30.2	15.3	5.2	64.4
Agricultural workers as a percentage of total civil employment	3.0	6.4	4.2	27.0	15.1	7.0	15.4	10.5	3.7	4.9	22.2	2.4
Family members as a percentage of total workers in agriculture	32.8	32.2	52.0	54.0	44.6	43.0	39.0	44.6	53.0	42.2	56.6	36.4
Paid laborers as a percentage of total workers in agriculture[a]	9.4	33.4	23.6	3.7	31.8	16.8	13.4	37.9	11.2	33.2	16.7	49.4
Percentage of farm holders for whom agriculture is the principal activity	29.5	10.4	38.1	26.6	22.0	11.9	25.0	20.5	13.5	15.6	31.7	14.0
Percentage for whom agriculture is a secondary activity	3.0	22.6	4.7	6.5	5.8	19.9	10.1	3.4	4.1	8.1	6.3	9.6
Percentage of farmers whose spouses have other gainful activity	8.5	44.4	8.0	8.3	11.5	27.7	55.8	13.9	6.6	1.3	n.a.	22.5
Percentage of farm holders who are 55 or more years old	44.3	45.1	33.0	56.0	58.3	48.6	50.7	59.7	45.2	42.1	58.3	48.9

Source: Author's calculations, using data from Komission der Europäischen Gemeinschaften, *Die lage der Landwirtschaft in der Gemeinschaft, Bericht, 1990;* (Luxembourg, 1991), p. T20; and Eurostat, *Farm Structure: 1987 Survey: Main Results* (Luxembourg, 1991).
a. Figures are for 1988.

what is more apparent is the emergence of a dual structure with quite efficient agricultural sectors in northern Europe and rather large, economically inefficient, and socially vulnerable agricultural sectors in the southern European member states.

The information provided in table 6-1 should give an impression of the task facing the Union.[38] Without doubt, the CAP's strong reliance on price support has increased the heterogeneity of agricultural structures. As already noted, these measures benefit larger farms and encourage increased production; at the same time, high institutional prices effectively provide protective shelters for small farmers. In addition, in some member states conditions allow farmers (or their spouses) to engage in a second job, and dual activity works also as a cushion against market pressures and falling agricultural incomes.[39] Clearly then, the CAP and the agricultural policies of the member states—many of which remain outside the CAP—are not the only response to the specific problems and needs of the agricultural component of society. Agrarian social structures have adjusted in their own ways to changing social and economic environments, following their own logic, according to their institutional capabilities. Sometimes these adjustments have been in line with the structural policies of the Union; sometimes they have worked against them. The persistence of small farmers is a case in point.

And sometimes, as argued before, differences in the institutional structures of member states contribute to inequalities in agriculture. Differences in the distribution of age classes in the member states are an important example. In 1987 in all countries but Germany, more than 40 percent—near 60 percent in some countries—of the farmers were older than fifty-five. The specialized pension system for farmers in Germany accounts for its relatively good position. Retirement payments form part of the structural policies of the CAP at the Union level: directive 72/160 provides for payments to outgoers, either as annuities or as lump sums

---

38. It should be borne in mind that the picture becomes much more complex if the regional level is taken into account. The dual structure of marginal and efficient farming can be detected in both northern and southern countries. See CEPS CAP Expert Group, *New Directions for European Agricultural Policy,* Paper 49 (Brussels: Centre for European Policy Studies, 1990), pp. 1–6.

39. The emerging picture, a dual structure of agriculture, is due to the disappearance of farmers with middle-sized farms: either farms grow larger to accommodate increased production and income, or they get smaller and farmers take up outside employment to supplement their agricultural income. For a general view, see Peter Hamilton, "Small Farmers and Food Production in Western Europe," *International Social Science Journal,* vol. 37 (1985), pp. 345–60; and *GeoJournal,* vol. 6, no. 4 (1982).

to elderly farmers.[40] But until the end of 1986 only Germany, and to a lesser degree France, made use of the EC funds.[41] All other countries were either unwilling or unable to offer their farmers such alternatives because they lacked an adequate implementation structure.[42]

Differences among member-state policies notwithstanding, one fact stands out: the Union has continued to pump more and more money into agriculture, despite the shrinking of the agricultural labor force.[43] At the same time, member-state expenditures on agriculture have, in most cases, been decreasing (see table 6-2).

The most important reason for this development is the strict division of labor between the Union and its member states. The Union is footing the bill for pricing policies, while the bulk of member-state expenditures on agriculture goes to structural and regional programs, which often have some connection to Union programs.[44] Because the Union has a monopoly of action in price policy—that is, the introduction of common institutional prices, which are financed by the Union—member states simply shifted that burden to the Community and concentrate instead on structural policies. The data provided in table 6-3 show, in the aggregate, the social consequences of the sharp separation of agricultural policymaking in the Community. The dominant focus on prices and commodity regimes did nothing to prevent declining standards of living in the peripheral regions of the Community. Because price policies are tied to commodities

40. Tracy, *Government and Agriculture*, p. 326.

41. Under directive 72/160, Germany got 5 million ECU and France 1 million until the end of 1986. See Tracy, *Government and Agriculture*, p. 327, table 14.5.

42. It must be said that such payments, to become a real alternative to farming, have to be substantial. Without a considerable financial contribution by the state, a social security system for independent farmers is not feasible. This is especially true in countries with large agricultural sectors dominated by a majority of small farmers. For an overview of the emergence and history of social security regimes for farmers, see Herbert Pruns, "Soziale Sicherung im Bereich der Landwirtschaft: Versuch eines internationalen Vergleichs," in Hans Pohl, ed., *Staatliche, städtische, betriebliche und kirchliche Sozialpolitik vom Mittelalter bis zur Gegenwart* (Stuttgart: Steiner, 1991), pp. 295–358.

43. For a general dicussion, see Brian Ardy, "The National Incidence of the European Community Budget," *Journal of Common Market Studies*, vol. 26 (1988), pp. 401–29.

44. This is an additional reason for the low take-up rate of Community programs, especially in the early years of the CAP. See the comment on Italy by Paul Ginsborg: "Italian agriculture . . . did less well out of the Common Market than its French counterparts, but those benefits which were offered to Italy were often unused. It has been calculated that by the end of 1974, of the grants given to Italy by the orientation section of the EAGGF for structural projects for the decade 1965–74, only 15 per cent has been spent, compared to 37 per cent in France, 53 per cent in Germany and 55 per cent in Holland." *A History of Contemporary Italy: Society and Politics, 1943–1988* (Penguin, 1990), p. 286.

Table 6-2. Spending on Agriculture as a Percentage of Total Government Expenditure, 1972–88[a]

Country	1972	1975	1978	1979	1980	1981	1982	1983	1984	1985	1986	1987	1988
Belgium	1.4	0.8	0.8	1.1	0.9	0.8	0.7	0.7	0.9	1.0	0.7	0.7	...
Denmark	3.5	5.0	...	0.9	0.9	1.0	1.9	1.8	1.0	1.3	1.0	...	...
France	...	1.8	...	1.2	1.2	1.3	1.1	1.1	0.7	0.7	...	...	...
Germany	1.6[b]	0.7[b]	...	1.1	1.9	1.8	2.0	2.4	2.4	2.1	...	...	...
Greece	8.7	7.8	6.6	6.3	5.3	6.3	...	...	...	...	...	...	...
Ireland	...	...	...	...	...	...	7.0	6.6	6.1	5.4	5.4	6.6	...
Italy	2.4[c]	2.8	...	0.9	1.1	1.2	1.6	1.1	1.5	1.0	1.1	1.2	1.1
Netherlands	...	...	...	1.0	1.1	0.9	0.8	0.9	0.8	0.9	0.7	0.8	0.8
Portugal	...	...	...	2.8	2.1	1.7	1.6	1.1	1.4	1.6	2.0	...	...
Spain	5.8	4.4	...	...	3.4	3.3	3.1	3.5	2.6	2.3	...	...	...
United Kingdom	2.3	3.4	...	1.1	1.2	1.2	1.1	1.3	1.2	1.3	1.1	0.9	...
United States	2.9[b]	1.0	...	...	1.3	2.5	1.6	2.3	1.6	2.3	2.7	2.4	...

Source: Author's calculations, based on data from *International Monetary Fund*, Government Finance Statistics, and OECD, National Accounts.
a. Total government expenditure equals general government expenditure for Germany and the United States; for all other countries, central government expenditure is meant.
b. Central government.
c. Figure is for 1973.

Table 6-3. *EAGGF Expenditures, 1986*

Percent

Country	EC total (ten member states) = 100			EC total (twelve member states) = 100		
	Expenditure per annual work unit	Related to gross value added	Related to GDP	Expenditure per annual work unit	Related to gross value added	Related to GDP
Belgium	170	105	78	190	98	68
Denmark	185	115	143	239	123	156
France	107	99	111	145	111	118
Germany	125	110	61	153	112	58
Greece	64	123	590	78	123	510
Ireland	67	113	321	76	107	298
Italy	70	82	136	80	79	129
Luxembourg	96	89	67	113	87	67
Netherlands	208	97	131	222	86	104
United Kingdom	147	110	59	207	129	65
EC totals (ten member states)	100	100	100	125	104	98
Portugal	...	...	...	10	78	146
Spain	...	...	...	55	75	122
EC totals (twelve member states)	...	...	...	100	100	100
Average of the ten lowest regions	42	66	24	13	38	20
Average of the ten highest regions	231	154	592	311	161	552

Source: Kommission der Europäischen Gemeinschaften, *Die Regionen der erweiterten Gemeinschaft: Dritter periodischer Bericht über die sozio-ökonomische Lage und Entwicklung der Regionen der Gemeinschaft: Zusammenfassung und Schlußfolgerungen* (Luxembourg, 1987), p. 166.

and levels of output, most of the money spent under the CAP is going to countries with large agricultural sectors.

A closer look at the table shows, however, that "large" means not the number of farmers but the level of productivity and the type of commodity. Hence the center regions of the Community receive preferential treatment, a legacy of the historical development of the CAP with its concentration on the major commodities of the original six member states and strong reliance on pricing policies. Mediterranean agricultural products normally do not receive the high institutional prices of the traditional products of the core regions (milk products, beef and veal, cereals).[45]

45. For more detailed information on the distribution of CAP expenditures according to commodities, see Tracy, *Government and Agriculture*, p. 310.

Consequently, the bulk of expenditures under the CAP, in relative terms, goes to the northern European member states.

Benefit distribution in this policy domain is therefore eccentric—there is no consistent relationship between the economic and social needs of agricultural regions and CAP spending.[46] The expenditure pattern of the guidance section of the European Agricultural Guarantee and Guidance Funds (EAGGF), however, shows a shift in the center of gravity from the northern countries to the southern countries, which mirrors the new emphasis in agricultural policymaking on problems of rural development—that is, the maintenance of agriculture in disadvantaged regions. The 1975 directive addressing mountain and less-favored areas exemplifies the new approach. Especially after the enlargement of the Community and the reduction of institutional prices, this compensatory measure became increasingly attractive.

In recent years the measure has been extended to additional regions. Now more than half of the Union's agricultural area under cultivation—in contrast to about one-third in 1976—is classified as less-favored. This implies a transformation of the measure: no longer does it merely compensate for serious natural handicaps; it is fast becoming a broad measure to support farm incomes that are declining because of price adjustments. For this reason the eligibility criteria for compensatory allowances are still mainly economic, that is, size of farms and number of livestock. This economic rationale proved to make the directive much more attractive politically than one that hinged on social objectives.[47]

Of course, expenditures under the guidance section of the EAGGF are still only a small proportion of expenditures under the guarantee section. On the other hand, because of the greater purposefulness of regional measures, their influence on standards of living and rural development is surely greater than the aggregate figures indicate.

---

46. For a more detailed picture, see Bernard Roux, "Les régions mediterranéennes de la CÉE et la logique capitaliste de la marginalisation territorial," *International Review of Community Development*, vol. 22 (1989), pp. 87–100.

47. Characteristically, despite heavy criticism, farms with fewer than three hectares were not eligible. This means that a large proportion of small farmers in peripheral regions were unable to apply for money under this scheme. The criterion was changed in 1985 (directive 797/85, article 14) for the Mezzogiorno, Spain, Portugal, and Greece. In these countries or regions the threshold is now two hectares. See Hermann Priebe, "Gestaltungsmöglichkeiten der Agrarstruktur- und Regionalpolitik," in Hermann Priebe, Wilhelm Scheper, and Winfried von Urff, eds., *Agrarpolitik in der EG: Probleme und Perspektiven* (Baden-Baden: Nomos, 1984), pp. 217–50.

Making Sense of the CAP: Toward a Sociology of Sectoral Integration and Community Building

> A survey of society will probably convince him that one of the things generally necessary to human happiness is security, and that men can neither shape their own lives nor co-operate with one another unless they know what to expect and what is expected of them under given conditions, unless, that is, they have recognized rights and duties. At the same time he will see how important it is that rights and duties should be modifiable by a regular and agreed procedure in accordance with the changing requirements of human happiness.[48]

The CAP was intended to accompany the building of a common market for agricultural products. Thus from the very beginning agriculture stood outside the institutional framework of the common market, which was conceived more or less in purely market economic terms. This put the CAP in an awkward position and attracted increasingly heavy criticism. After the enactment of the Single European Act, which again underlined the overall objective of the Community as a basically intervention-free economic space, it became even more difficult to defend the CAP and its purposes. Yet it is of crucial importance to see that the CAP forms an institutional sphere that is structured differently from the prevailing mode of economic and social integration of the Union, its general dynamics, and its logic.

Any attempt to dismiss the peculiarity of this policy domain as something marginal and transitory will fail to grasp the significance of the autonomous dynamics of the CAP. This dismissive reading of history and the persisting problems of the CAP owe a lot to the explanatory framework of neoclassical economic analysis, yet in this instance that framework is part of the problem rather than part of its solution. Instead, one has to look at the actual structures and forms of agricultural policies of the Community. Its contradictory elements are not accidental: they are the result of attempts to solve the problems it originally had to confront.

This chapter has stressed, first, the proliferation and diversification of the policy instruments of the CAP, and, second, despite this growing comprehensiveness and complexity, a deepening of the social and eco-

48. L. T. Hobhouse, *The Elements of Social Justice* (New York: Henry Holt and Company, 1922), p. 7.

nomic problems the CAP was intended to solve. To understand this seeming paradox, it is necessary to examine the institutional particularities of the CAP. In this respect it is important to see that social policy, broadly interpreted, is not just at the periphery of the CAP—it was at the core of the integration of the agricultural sectors of the member states of the Community. The creation of a common market for agricultural products was less important.[49] The CAP was created and used for specific social purposes in a specific historical setting.[50] Its main purpose was to enable farm incomes to keep pace with other incomes, even given the relatively low income elasticity of demand for agricultural products. Within the framework of this organization, prices have come to be regarded primarily as implements for the maintenance of farm income, not as a mechanism for continuous, efficient direction of productive resources to meet changes in consumer demand and in production techniques.

Experience from the CAP shows that a central agency charged with managing prices in a capitalist society is so pressured by producer groups for special concessions that rational management of prices is impossible. Price control inevitably becomes a political football, with those groups aggregating the most power in moments of decision receiving the most advantageous prices. The idea of a self-regulating market therefore increasingly appeals to policymakers. Strong reliance on market forces would make it easier for them to achieve some legitimacy for their actions, especially when the market appears better able than their own measures to allocate resources and to achieve a higher degree of societal integration.[51]

With the institutionalization of the CAP and, especially, the introduction of highly regulated commodity regimes and the rapid proliferation of structural policies, the independence of farmers and peasants in West-

---

49. For this reason the CAP survived the introduction of "compensatory monetary amounts," which in fact brought about a renationalization of agricultural markets with widely differing levels of prices among the member states. For an overview, see Joachim Friedrich Heine, *Die agrarmonetären Regeln des Gemeinschaftsrechts: Eine systematische Darstellung* (Regensburg: Walhalla und Praetoria, 1988.

50. As Susan Strange states, "Those who attack the CAP do not always understand that the protection it has given has been protection against the uncertainty of volatile world prices as much as protection against more efficient foreign producers. It is not entirely accidental that the two commodities in which the CAP has been most protectionist—grain and sugar—have also been those marked by the most violent changes in world prices." Susan Strange, *Casino Capitalism* (Oxford: Blackwell, 1986), p. 113.

51. For a general discussion of these problems, see Walter W. Wilcox and Willard W. Cochrane, *Economics of American Agriculture* (Prentice-Hall, 1960); and Willard W. Cochrane, *Farm Prices: Myth and Reality* (University of Minnesota Press, 1958).

ern Europe eroded and reached unknown levels of legal and bureaucratic control. Farming has been transformed into an estate, directed by an amalgam of EU agencies, member-state politicians, officials, and professional agricultural organizations that determine prices and control access to markets, production quotas, grants, credits, and various forms of supplementary allowances. The farmers, for their part, are left with the sense of a pervasive organization of coercive power operating beyond their immediate control, intruding into all aspects of their lives, and deeply affecting the day-to-day management of their farms.

This dependence is not voluntary. While for some farmers—above all, the more commercial and efficient ones—the CAP constitutes a golden cage, it is nevertheless a cage. In other words, the common agricultural market and the CAP can be seen as a social order of a special kind, one with a peculiar structure of programs, expectations, and political and economic relationships.

This unique social order was neither masterminded by people with unfailing precognition (the founding fathers of the Treaty of Rome), nor is it a direct response to the particular problems prevailing in Western European agriculture. As the previous sections have shown, it involves very different institutional features; it grew slowly, not according to one dominating principle but following different, and at times competing and contradictory, objectives. It also expresses the public's general notions about the kind of rural society it wants to live in, how food is produced, how soil and animals are treated, and what values the Union and the governments of the member states should nurture or protect. How can one make sense of the resulting structure?

If social structures are thought of as arrangements of life chances (in Weberian terms, market chances, price chances, supply chances, chances of acquisition, exchange chances, interest chances, and so on),[52] the overwhelming influence of the CAP is obvious. Establishing common rules for competition and European market organizations produced a new institutional system, which influenced and formed life chances in the field of agriculture in a way unparalleled in other fields of Community activity. As for its economic and social *consequences*, the CAP functions as an agent of "decommodification" of agricultural markets, where decom-

---

52. See Ralf Dahrendorf, *Life Chances: Approaches to Social and Political Theory* (University of Chicago Press, 1979).

modification is construed as the use of social rights to make farmers' income more independent of market forces.[53]

Decommodification works through several mechanisms. First of all, commodity regimes protect farmers' incomes against sudden rises and falls in market prices. Second, the level of institutional prices was set high enough to secure adequate incomes for peasants and small-scale farmers. Third, schemes have been introduced to uncouple direct aid to agricultural incomes from price supports, thereby increasing the gap between market incomes and real incomes.

These institutional features of the CAP constitute a wedge between market forces and the life chances of the agricultural labor force. One of the most interesting questions therefore concerns the emergence of social rights in agriculture on a European level—that is, the entitlements and financial mechanisms that supersede markets. What are the legal and sociopolitical foundations of this veritable "European welfare state," which consumes the lion's share of the Union budget, and what is it doing to its citizens?

Two theoretical approaches designed for analyzing industrial welfare structures in Western Europe may cast some light on the dynamics of the institutional structures of the Union's agrarian policies, as well as on the vertical division of labor between the Union and the member states. The first comes from T. H. Marshall, especially his work on the "moral economy" of the welfare state. The second is Max Weber's analysis of the creation and the nature of rights in modern society.

Income maintenance problems and rural poverty are salient features of agriculture in advanced industrial societies. In such societies, employment in agriculture has become structurally similar to that in other sectors of the economy; therefore demand for income security and material welfare has grown.[54] Since agriculture is now much more intertwined with the national and international economies, it is also more vulnerable to general economic changes and more dependent on institutionalized income maintenance. Paradoxically, this is particularly true for the com-

53. See Gøsta Esping-Anderson, *The Three Worlds of Welfare Capitalism* (Princeton University Press, 1990), pp. 35 ff.

54. The beginning of this development was noted by Karl Kautsky at the turn of the century: "I have reached the conclusion that we should not expect, in agriculture, the end of the small farm nor the end of the big farm. At one pole, we have the universally true tendency toward proletarization, but, at the other we have a continous swinging in the development of small and big farms." Quoted in Alessandro Bonanno, *Small Farms: Persistence with Legitimacy* (Boulder, Colo.: Westview Press, 1987), pp. 9 ff.

mercial farmers in the Union. Subsistence farming is a thing of the past; it is no longer a fallback in hard times. The institutionalization of commodity regimes with fixed prices and the introduction of various forms of direct income payments have to be seen as a straightforward consequence of the socioeconomic changes in Western European agriculture. Not only in these countries but also in almost all other developed industrial societies, the marginalization of agriculture was accompanied by a plethora of state measures that tried to shelter peasants and farmers from the full impact of a dominant market economy.

Even though economists and most politicians concerned with the CAP want to regain the efficiency—and, of course, the legitimacy—that flows from a market mechanism, most persons actively engaged in agriculture are not disposed to return to the laissez faire of the nineteenth century. More than the economics of agriculture has changed; the moral environment has as well. All industrial societies have become welfare states, and the perception of social inequality has changed. In the Western European states, with their big public sectors and comprehensive welfare policies, the not-so-blind forces of the market are no longer the only factor in the distribution of life chances. The institutionalization of welfare policies for the poorer segments of society (and later, for the middle classes) separated market incomes from disposable incomes. T. H. Marshall described this process as incorporating social rights into the status of citizenship, "and thus creating a universal right to real income which is not proportionate to the market value of the claimant."[55] For Marshall, "Social rights are no longer merely an attempt to abate the obvious nuisance of destitution in the lowest ranks of society. It has assumed the guise of action modifying the whole pattern of social inequality."[56]

In addition, social policy in the welfare states focused on the social status of citizens: "What matters is that there is a general enrichment of the concrete substance of civilized life, a general reduction of risk and insecurity, an equalization between the more and the less fortunate. . . . Equalization is not so much between classes as between individuals within a population which is now treated for this purpose as if it were one class. Equality of status is more important than equality of income."[57] In line with this reasoning, one latent (and sometimes even

55. T. H. Marshall, "Citizenship and Social Class," in T. H. Marshall, ed., *Class, Citizenship, and Social Development* (Doubleday, 1964), p. 96.
56. Marshall, "Citizenship," p. 96.
57. Marshall, "Citizenship," p. 102.

manifest) aim of the creation of agricultural commodity regimes was the security of a steady flow of income in the agricultural community. The same rationale lies at the heart of social policy measures in the industrial sector of advanced societies, which eventually gave rise to broad income maintenance systems.

Because of the particularities prevailing in agriculture—especially the independence of farmers and the individual ownership of land—commodity regimes can be seen as equivalents to social insurance programs. Without doubt these measures, in the form of market organizations that often provide guaranteed minimum prices, operate in this direction. The CAP in its original design relied solely on high institutional prices as the means to provide income security and material welfare. Its policies resulted in the transformation of "market incomes" (that is, income gained through the selling of products in a market that can freely adjust to changing patterns of supply and demand) into incomes that reflect overall standards of living and household consumption needs. This goal was from the very beginning an official aim of the CAP and of the majority of governments in the member states.

Although the income-maintenance aspects of agricultural price policy have been paramount since the introduction of the CAP and have dominated most community legislation concerned with agriculture, public attention focused mostly on the resulting surplus production and its accompanying budgetary problems. But the social objectives of the CAP need to be viewed in a wider context. The very issue of income security, income maintenance, and the promise of higher standards of living in agriculture provided the common denominator enabling the creation of a common policy that could substitute for existing national-income support systems. This aspect of the CAP has not lost its significance. On the contrary, the need for more social protection and for a more differentiating social policy has grown in the last decades. So also, as a result of the GATT negotiations, has the pressure to cut the high level of CAP institutional prices.

Despite this crucial shift in the basic needs of the agricultural labor force, the "moral economy" of the welfare state did not take hold in agriculture. Whereas in the welfare states quite a solid consensus exists on the proper functions of government, the relative weight of market forces and the equality encompassed in common citizenship, especially its social rights, there is no similar agreement on the balance of different value and policy outcomes in the field of agriculture.

Why not? Marshall's analysis of the development of the institutional structure of welfare state gives some hints, but there is another way to contrast the institutional development of the CAP with the more familiar development of national welfare regimes. Here some observations by a second sociologist, who concentrated on the institutional structure of modern social and political systems, will serve as a starting point.

Max Weber conceived the expansion of state administration and the subsequent rationalization of its activities, institutions, and values as a fusion of all those organizations that had engendered their own bodies of law into one compulsory association of the state, now claiming to be the sole source of all "legitimate" law. Weber was especially interested in law because the development of monopolies of legitimate authority changed the way in which the law serves private interests and, above all, economic interests. For Weber, the existence of a right ensures nothing more than a higher probability that a certain expectation of the right-holder will not be disappointed. He saw the creation of a right as the normal way to increase such probability.[58]

It should be clear by now that the dependence of the farmers and their households on the CAP is tremendous. But is the CAP in fact a "welfare state for farmers" in the midst of Europe, as it is often claimed? Despite the dominance of social aims, especially until the beginning of the 1980s, there are some problems with this interpretation. The earlier discussion of the CAP as a social order in which life chances were created and distributed meant, in Weberian terms, the creation of rights: farmers could expect to sell their products for a fixed price, and in a certain quantity at that price; they could expect certain subsidies if they enlarged their farms, changed the products of the farms, modernized their build-ings, or bought new equipment; they could anticipate the amount of money they would get for their disadvantaged location or for the set-aside of parts of their land; and so on.

The important question, then, is whether this structure of programs and expectations is *actually* the creation of rights. What security do farmers have that a certain program will continue to exist, that the price or the production quota received this year will be the same as for the next year? What chances do farmers have to resist changes in commodity regimes that affect their economic situation and the well-being of their families?

Again, the field of social welfare policies outside agriculture demon-

---

58. See the discussion in Guenther Roth and Claus Wittich, eds., *Economy and Society: An Outline of Interpretive Sociology*, vol. 2 (New York: Bedminster Press, 1986), pp. 666 ff.

strates a broad range of measures designed to secure the right of clients to certain benefits, that is, legal and administrative remedies in the form of special kinds of courts and tribunals. Commodity regimes and the other measures of the CAP have apparently not experienced the same juridification that took place in the social welfare domain—or at least not in respect to the individual farmer. Therefore, in Weberian terms, the legally secured interests of the farmers are but the "reflex" of a "regulation"; farmers do not possess a *right* in the strict sense of the word.[59]

Since the CAP affects not only farmers but also traders and food processing companies, it is interesting to note the differences in the political and juridical treatment of farmers and these likewise concerned categories. The governing of the CAP by the Community provided several occasions for traders and food processing companies to seek and to secure legal redress, yet, as my research shows, the European Court of Justice was reticent to admit the emergence of rights and specific Community responsibilities vis-à-vis farmers. More concretely, since the Treaty of Rome entails different and, with regard to their social and economic consequences, contradictory objectives the CAP has to meet, the European Court of Justice tends to maximize the discretion of the Commission and Council of Ministers. Therefore it is possible to justify sudden changes in the calculation of levies, quotas, and tariffs with the balance of markets, the interests of commercial producers, or, increasingly in recent years, the necessity to come to terms with the United States and other export nations.

The existing literature on the subject seems to suggest that the interests of the Union outweigh the interests of the farmers. It comes as no surprise, then, that one of the leading scholars of Community law in Germany and director of Max-Planck-Institut maintains that there is no legal protection of the social and economic rights of farmers "because this would endanger the entire system of the CAP."[60] Such a conclusion indicates an important departure from other policies of the Union, which became much more responsive to the interests of EU citizens through decisions of the European Court of Justice.[61]

59. See Max Weber on the creation of rights, in Roth and Wittich, eds., *Economy and Society*, pp. 667ff.

60. See Ernst-Joachim Mestmäcker, "Die Wiederkehr der bürgerlichen Gesellschaft und ihres Rechts," *Rechtshistorisches Journal*, vol. 10 (1991), pp. 177–92, especially p. 191. For a detailed discussion of the legal and administrative system of the Community, see Jürgen Schwarze, *Europäisches Verwaltungsrecht: Entstehung und Entwicklung im Rahmen der Europäischen Gemeinschaft*, 2 vols. (Baden-Baden: Nomos, 1988).

61. For an view on the evolution of female citizenship rights in the European Com-

This departure is perplexing, given that in other fields of state and goverment activity, more contacts with ever-growing segments of the population and increasing state control of economic resources have led to new individual rights, termed "new property" by Charles Reich.[62] These rights are a source of power and, naturally, income and status. So why has the Union not legislated such new property in the field of agriculture, despite the dominance of the CAP and the dependence of the farmers on the management of the CAP?

The restrictive features of the CAP reveal much about the social and political nature of the Union. Social rights, in general, acknowledge the status of individuals within a community and recognize them as full legal members of that community for social and political purposes. In important aspects, then, the peasants and farmers affected by the CAP lack the same citizenship status that members of nation-states enjoy. The CAP, despite its legal autonomy and formal authority, is not "available" to the individual farmer: the national tier intervenes between the individual farmer and the institutional tier on which the CAP is located, blocking direct links and contacts.

Within the national context, the availability of courts, admininstrative agencies, and elected officials is, to say the least, a real opportunity. But in matters concerning the Union and its CAP, *availability* refers solely to national actors and national social forces. In addition, powerful private interests—namely, traders and food processing companies—have entrenched themselves within the political and economic framework of the CAP. These interests do not represent the concerns of most farmers; instead, the special interests, which organized alongside specific commodity regimes, direct their forces to maintain the status quo. This is another reason why it seems quite unlikely that market-oriented policies will lose their dominance in the CAP to policies more sensitive to the needs of economically weak but socially important groups in the agricultural labor force.

It has to be kept in mind that the very success of the Community in the field of agriculture was attributable to the narrow circumscription of its competencies. Strong reliance on broad economic measures such as price supports ensured that all member states and all farmers could ben-

---

munity, see Elmar Rieger, "Frauenrechte und Staatsbürgerstatus," in Ilona Ostner, ed., *Ehefrau, Mutter, Erwerbstätige* (Frankfurt: Campus, forthcoming).

62. Charles Reich, "The New Property," *Yale Law Journal*, vol. 73 (1964), pp. 733–87.

efit from the Community. To introduce programs that narrowly targeted low-income farmers and severely handicapped regions would threaten the political support the CAP still enjoys. For this reason alone—setting aside for the moment the problem of an inadequate implementation structure—it is difficult to envisage in the CAP policy mix any further separation between rights-oriented, social policy–like measures, on the one side, and modernization measures, on the other. Yet the challenge of countering the effects of the price cuts and preventing a further increase in the depopulation of rural areas while avoiding major trade wars produced new interest in policies that could substitute for commodity regimes with high institutional prices. Most important are proposals to enlarge the role of direct income support.

This is not the first time the Commission and a few independent observers have supported direct income aid as a solution to the CAP's problems.[63] But the chances for a policy of "lower institutional prices plus direct income aids" have not improved over time, because the constellation of important actors is still the same. And these actors, especially the powerful farmers' organizations of France and Germany, are heavily biased toward big farmers, who have already suffered from price cuts in recent years. Already in the mid-1970s the COPA (Comité des Organisations Professionelles Agricoles de la Communauté européenne) rejected a policy switch to generalized income aid, which "besides running into psychological problems by putting all farmers on public assistance . . . is expensive to apply and difficult to administer. It makes farmers directly dependent on budgetary decisions."[64] The point is not, of course, dependence on budgetary decisions—something farmers will be unable to escape in any event—but the ineligibility of the leading stratum of farmers' organizations for targeted income aid. Nor are these proposals very attractive to politicians in the member states, because such programs would benefit only a small proportion of farmers.[65]

63. See Edmund Neville-Rolfe, *The Politics of Agriculture in the European Community* (London: Policy Studies Institute, 1984), pp. 10–17; Günther Schmitt and Harald von Witzke, "Minimum Income Policy: Elements and Effects of an Alternative Instrument of Farm Policy in the European Community," in Margot A. Bellamy and Bruce L. Greenshields, eds., *The Rural Challenge: Contributed Papers Read at the seventeenth International Conference of Agricultural Economists* (Aldershot: Gower, 1981), pp. 258–61; and U. Koester and S. Tangermann, "Supplementing Farm Price Policy by Direct Income Payments: Cost-Benefit Analysis of Alternative Farm Policies with a Special Application to German Agriculture," *European Review of Agricultural Economics*, vol. 4 (1977), pp. 7–31.

64. Quoted in Neville-Rolfe, *Politics of Agriculture*, p. 14.

65. In addition, commodity regimes with institutional prices provide invisible income transfers, whereas direct incomes are highly visible payments.

Greater reliance on targeted policies would mean a major redistribution of the benefits and the costs of the CAP. Some countries would receive far less money from the CAP in relation to their contribution than they now do, whereas other countries, especially those with large numbers of peasants and small farmers, would benefit more. There is therefore much to say in favor of the thesis that the reform initiatives, especially the policy changes from 1988 to 1992, were designed to maintain the status quo without further increasing spending for agricultural support.

Solving budgetary crises and problems encountered in the GATT negotiations is still more important to policymakers than improving the social efficiency of the CAP. Although there are attempts to tackle the problem of increasing divergence of incomes within the agricultural sector of the Union, the means employed and the money spent to achieve this objective are still, in most cases, insignificant. In the agricultural policies of the Union, it seems that all-encompassing regulations in the form of commodity regimes with institutional prices will—like the poor—always be with us, and partly for that reason.

The institutionalized division of labor between the Union and the member states is mostly responsible for this situation. Although the member states would be in a much better position than the EU to counteract the highly uneven consequences of price cuts and adjustment to world markets, they are afraid to take back full responsibility for the farming sector, particularly the heavy financial burden of agricultural policies. Another reason for the likely persistence of the CAP in its present form lies in the simple fact that only the Union can protect, in some measure, the interests of the majority of Western European farmers in GATT negotiations. No single member state could defend its agricultural interests equally as well as the Union.

In short, the implications of the last GATT negotiations and budgetary constraints will have economic consequences for the institutional structure of the CAP, but the CAP is unlikely to change with regard to its social consequences. In its most vital aspects the CAP will remain a welfare policy. It will fulfill this function in a way that is bound to be destructive to farmers, especially small- and middle-scale farmers, because of the ambivalence inherent in its multileveled institutional structure.

CHAPTER SEVEN

Migration, Free Movement, and Immigrant Integration in the EU: A Bifurcated Policy Response

Patrick R. Ireland

SOCIAL POLICY IN THE European Union, as much of the analysis in this volume attests, involves intense wrangling and horse trading over the responsibilities of national governments and EU institutions. Perhaps no issue area illuminates this complex meshing and friction as clearly as the knot of challenges associated with migration. Europe's large, diverse foreign population—comprising migrants from former colonies, foreign workers and their families from within and outside the Union, political asylum-seekers, illegal migrants, and refugees—constitutes both a threat and a spur to the building of "Social Europe."

Even while working to remove remaining restrictions on the free movement of persons within Union boundaries, the EU is presently struggling to define its social dimension. This latter project, linked to the first, is unlikely to succeed unless Europe develops a more coordinated approach both to regulating migration and the influx of refugees and to integrating those who do not return to their country of origin. Member-state migration and immigrant policies cannot help but directly and indirectly affect the employment picture and, more generally, living and working conditions in the Union.[1] Worries have grown that if EU and so-called third-

The author is grateful for the generous financial assistance from the German Marshall Fund of the United States and the University of Denver that made the research for this article possible. Thanks, too, to Stephan Leibfried, Michael Marks, Paul Pierson, Alberta Sbragia, Nina Tannenwald, and Madeleine Tress for commenting on earlier drafts.

1. I use *migration policy* as a general term to denote EU and member-state governments' efforts to regulate population movements both within and into the EU. *Immigrant policy* refers to governmental actions that affect resident migrants' (or immigrants') living and working conditions and their social, economic, and political integration. For a similar distinction, see Stephen Castles and Mark J. Miller, *The Age of Migration* (New York: Guilford Press, 1993).

country workers (those from outside the Union) do not enjoy freedom of movement and equality of treatment with national labor in every member state, threats to European firms' competitiveness and risks of a form of social "dumping" could well mount.

As Peter Lange has observed, the EU social sphere includes all policies providing for "rights, opportunities, benefits, or protections to actual, potential, or former participants in the labor market."[2] Across Europe, industry, which depended vitally on foreign workers for its postwar reconstruction and expansion, is undergoing a drawn-out, painful period of post-Fordist restructuring. A host of newly shared problems spawned by deindustrialization, welfare state retrenchment at the nation-state level, and social marginalization argue for the extension of social issues to the European level. Migrant laborers and their families are a living, visible byproduct of this postwar evolution of industrial capitalism.[3] The European Commission has lobbied in no uncertain terms for an "integrated and coherent response . . . to the challenges that migration pressures and the integration of legal immigrants pose for the Union as a whole." "Failure to meet those challenges," warns the Commission, "would be to the detriment of attempts to promote cohesion and solidarity within the Union and could, indeed, endanger the future stability of the Union itself."[4]

Despite strong pressures for a common strategy and wide agreement on the need for it, however, collaboration on migration and the "transnationalization" of migrants' social rights have only been partially achieved.[5] For citizens of EU member states, something approaching complete freedom of movement and a bona fide Union-level social policy have emerged.[6] But this development has been an incomplete one, because for third-country nationals, conversely, the EU has not yet been

2. Peter Lange, "The Politics of the Social Dimension," in Alberta M. Sbragia, ed., *Euro-Politics: Institutions and Policymaking in the "New" European Community* (Brookings, 1992), pp. 229–30.

3. See Patrick R. Ireland, *The Policy Challenge of Ethnic Diversity: Immigrant Politics in France and Switzerland* (Harvard University Press, 1994).

4. *Migration News Sheet*, no. 132 (March 1994), pp. 1–2.

5. See Thomas Faist, "Transnationalizing Labor Markets and Social Rights in Europe," Universität Bremen, Zentrum für Sozialpolitik, 1994.

6. Stephan Leibfried and Paul Pierson, "Prospects for Social Europe," *Politics and Society*, vol. 20 (September 1992), p. 338. Of course, the marginalizing forces of poverty and inequality are such that full mobility does not truly exist even for citizens of a given member state; Paul Teague and John Grahl, "The European Community Social Charter and Labour Market Regulation," *Journal of Public Policy*, vol. 11 (April–June 1991), p. 230.

able to legislate substantively; policy here remains largely under the control of member-state governments and intergovernmental arrangements and organizations outside the EU structure. What has produced this bifurcated policy reponse? What has prevented the Union from developing truly European policies on "external" migration of the type seen, for instance, in agricultural or regional policy?

Serious political and structural obstacles, I argue in this chapter, have stymied complete EU-level collaboration on migration. The multitiered institutional architecture of the EU has directed the pressures to align policies along certain channels: the member states are the major players in this multilevel game, and there has been too much diversity of conditions and interests across them for real policy harmonization to materialize. Member states experience migratory inflows in different degrees. Their non-EU populations vary in size, regional concentration, and ethnic composition. Their policy responses to these people have diverged in key respects, and the extremist movements and political parties that have risen up in reaction to them vary in intensity and effectiveness.

Thus, although migration has generated undeniable pressures for common policies, it also poses the ultimate threat to efforts to forge Social Europe. National governments are loath to relinquish control over access to their territory and their domestic labor markets, "which constitute an essential attribute of sovereignty."[7] And the massive, ethnically diverse, and unexpectedly permanent immigration of the postwar period is defying traditional conceptions of a common citizenship molded by identity-shaping experiences and grounded in an underlying social homogeneity. Accordingly, how extracommunitarian foreign workers and their families are incorporated socially and politically into Western Europe speaks to primordial, visceral notions of identity and membership in these societies: who belongs, who does not, and who decides? If Europe is to become a society, the EU will have to respond to such formidable questions.

Typically, EU policy intervention has proved problematic and politically infeasible except where and when no alternative solution presents itself. National governments have retained their ultimate control and veto power over EU migration, refugee, and immigrant policies—a politically explosive dossier leading to "joint-decision traps" that have stalled move-

---

7. Federico Romero, "Migration as an Issue in European Interdependence and Integration: the Case of Italy," in Alan S. Milward and others, eds., *The Frontier of National Sovereignty: History and Theory, 1945–1992* (New York: Routledge, 1993), p. 39.

ment in this important sector. Such dangerous stagnation has prompted a series of "end-run" efforts to escape.[8] With EC encouragement, international organizations like the Council of Europe and the International Labour Organisation (ILO) have stepped into the breach. Even more significantly, the activist approach of the European Court of Justice (ECJ) in Luxembourg has propelled the Union forward on divisive migration issues. The ECJ's "judicial creativeness" has broken several policy logjams,[9] albeit at least initially at the cost of establishing "reactive" rights that member states often fail to implement fully.[10]

Optimistic observers, like the Commission's Giuseppe Callovi, argue that such forces are prodding the Union to structure a more coherent approach to migration and refugee issues: "Within the European Community, we are witnessing the shaping of a new political decision-making landscape which involves in some cases the sharing of sovereignty among member states."[11] My objective in this chapter is to explain which factors have fragmented EU migration and immigrant policies and hindered sovereignty sharing. After an initial overview of migration in postwar Europe, the focus shifts to the origins, evolution, and limits of Union-level policy in this field. Excessive optimism regarding coordinated efforts to integrate non-European immigrants is not in order, at least not in the near future. On the other hand, the outlook for further intergovernmental policy convergence—possibly even ending in common EU policies on controlling access to the Union by migrants and refugees—does seem reasonably certain.

Postwar Immigration and the Impetus for EC Involvement

One major reason why migration has resisted full inclusion in the EU structure concerns the nature of population movements into Europe after

8. See Fritz Scharpf, "The Joint-Decision Trap: Lessons from German Federalism and European Integration," *Public Administration,* vol. 66 (Autumn 1988), pp. 239–78.

9. G. Federico Mancini, "The Making of a Constitution for Europe," *Common Market Law Review,* no. 26 (1989), p. 599.

10. Bryant G. Garth, "Migrant Workers and the Rights of Mobility in the European Community and the United States," in Mauro Cappelletti, Monica Secombe, and Joseph Weiler, eds., *Integration through Law,* volume 1: *Methods, Tools and Institutions,* book 3: *Forces and Potential for a European Identity* (New York: Walter de Gruyter, 1986), pp. 141–46.

11. Giuseppe Callovi, "Regulation of Immigration in 1993: Pieces of the European Community Jig-Saw Puzzle," *International Migration Review,* vol. 26 (Summer 1992), p. 354.

the Second World War. Different from prewar flows, they have produced a strange new ethnic diversity and explosive social tensions that have revived an "anxious nationalism" and raise the political risks for governments as they attempt to devise appropriate migration policies.[12] Indeed, Europe has transformed itself into an immigration continent since 1945. By the early 1990s the total foreign population in the EC member states was estimated at around 13.7 million, or 4.28 percent of the EC's total of 320 million. EC citizens represented some 5 million of that number (36.5 percent); foreign workers and their families from outside the EC, some 8 million (58.4 percent). Of the 140 million people employed in the Community, 2 million worked in another EC member state, and 5 million were third-country nationals.[13] Adding to the foreign presence were asylum-seekers, whose ranks continued to grow (over 500,000 applied in the EC in 1990 alone), and illegal migrants and refugees, for whom no reliable estimates exist.[14]

Before the war migrants had arrived primarily from neighboring countries, to which the bulk of them eventually returned. Those laborers and refugees who did settle permanently in the receiving societies underwent a thorough process of individual assimilation and "melted" into their new country. Postwar migration has proved different. France, the Netherlands, and Britain became home to many of their former colonial subjects. By the mid-1960s those societies, along with Germany and the rest of the Benelux, welcomed large numbers of manual workers from southern Europe, North Africa, and Turkey in order to meet the labor requirements of their rebuilding industries.

The host societies, largely unwittingly, allowed a severe sociopolitical crisis to develop, one that today defies national-level solutions. Seeing the phenomenon as temporary, Western European authorities implemented no comprehensive, proactive policies for coping with the social and political effects of the mass recruitment of immigrant workers after the war.[15] The situation reached a turning point in the 1970s, as oil

12. See John Kenneth Galbraith, "The New Dialectic," *American Prospect*, no. 18 (Summer 1994), pp. 9–11.

13. Bichara Khader, "L'Immigration maghrébine face à l'Europe 1992," *Migrations-Société*, vol. 3 (May–June 1991), p. 17.

14. Kai Haibronner, "Perspektiven einer europäischen Asylrechtsharmonisierung nach der Maastrichter Gipfelkonferenz," *Zeitschrift für Ausländerrecht und Ausländerpolitik*, no. 2 (1992), pp. 51–59.

15. See Mark J. Miller, "Policy Ad-Hocracy: The Paucity of Coordinated Perspectives and Policies," *Annals of the American Academy of Political and Social Sciences*, vol. 485 (May 1986), pp. 65–75.

shocks precipitated a rapid deterioration in economic conditions in the labor-importing countries. The host societies all prohibited additional immigration during this period of rising unemployment.

But that action did not remove the problem. Instead of leaving for their homelands when Europe's postwar economic growth sputtered, most of the "guests" stayed. In fact, more of them were bringing their family members to join them. Meanwhile, illegal immigrants took the place of legal ones. What was once a cheap, temporary work force and a manageable collection of asylum-seekers metamorphosed into permanent resident ethnic communities. Host-society officials faced the task of integrating these variegated communities, even as they labored to restrict additional inflows. Divergent national policy responses resulted. What all the member states save Ireland shared, even so, was a sizable foreign-origin population. Social tensions in each were escalating and leading to a policy impasse.

European governments seemingly lacked the political will or the resources, or both, to respond individually to what was becoming a continental problem. National officials were learning that every government's actions affected the nature of migratory pressures on its neighbors. Consensus was building for some kind of joint action. Yet at the same time European states recoiled at challenges to their control over entry into domestic labor markets. There were some exceptions: in the 1950s the Council of the Organization for Economic Cooperation and Development effected a relaxation of rules governing the issuance of work permits; the Nordic Employment Market (1954) promoted labor mobility; the Benelux Economic Union was formed in 1958; and Ireland and the United Kingdom set up a special arrangement for worker movement across the Irish Sea.

More notable and far-reaching in this regard have been developments in the EU. The Treaty of Rome, which laid the foundations for the European Economic Community in 1958, included provisions for the progressive acceptance of complete labor mobility among the signatory states. The inclusion of this principle should not be surprising: "A common economic market could not do without the free movement of workers, at least as a support measure, when it wanted to introduce the free circulation of three other economic factors—goods, services and capital."[16]

The Community took steps in subsequent years to advance toward

16. Callovi, "Regulation of Immigration," p. 355.

that ideal. Geographical mobility accrued to nationals of the member states not on the basis of their citizenship status but when they traveled as workers, for economic purposes. Several regulations and directives in the 1960s and 1970s provided for the implementation of articles 48–51 of the treaty (free mobility and equal treatment and labor market access for workers from member states) and articles 52–58 (equal access for EC workers to unremunerated activities and the provision of services, and equal treatment in the establishment and running of businesses).[17]

By the mid-1960s "independent, individual movements inside the liberalized framework of the European Community" became possible for EC workers.[18] They gained considerable protections: equal treatment in housing and social assistance, trade-union rights, the right to remain in another member state after suffering permanent disability (unrestricted, if the injury was work-related) or involuntary unemployment, the right to retire in another member state (after three years' continuous residence and having worked the preceding year), and the right to remain and look for work for a limited time (between three and six months). Articles 48 and 51 of the Treaty of Rome also allow for the aggregation of social security contributions and limited "exportability" of pensions. Upon demand, legal EU workers receive a residence permit, valid for five years and automatically renewable.[19] True, member states can restrict the freedom of movement and establishment for reasons of public safety and order, national security, and public health; nevertheless, directive 221 of 1964, as well as ECJ case law, defined these limitations very narrowly.[20]

17. One of the most important directives issued under article 48 has been 1612 (1968). EU law can take the form of three instruments: regulations, which are binding on member states in all respects and have general applicability; decisions, which address specific situations and are binding only on those to whom they are addressed; and directives, which establish the outcome or results that the member states concerned must achieve through means of their own choosing. Recommendations, or opinions, are nonbinding declarations of EU policy. The Council of Ministers implements these various instruments, acting on proposals originating with the Commission, with the express goal of realizing the principles of the Treaty of Rome. See Jon Viner, "Turkey, the EEC and Labor Law: Is Harmonization Possible?" *Northwestern Journal of International Law and Business,* vol. 13 (Fall 1992), pp. 445–76.

18. Romero, "Migration," p. 57.

19. These and other protections cover the family members of such workers, even after their death; Commission of the European Communities, *Compendium of Community Provisions on Social Security,* 1st ed. (Luxembourg: Office for Official Publications of the European Communities (hereafter OOPEC), 1980). A migrant from elsewhere in the Union can have even more rights than a national: in Britain, for instance, EU law (not British law) has secured the right to live with one's family.

20. Martin Baldwin-Edwards, "The Socio-Political Rights of Migrants in the European

Apart from voting rights—which only Denmark, Ireland, and the Netherlands granted to all noncitizens meeting certain residency requirements—EC migrants and their families gradually came to receive close to the same treatment as nationals throughout the Community.

This development of common policies on intra-EC migration and of a powerful set of social rights has been gradual and has yet to reach its completion. Much of it occurred during the economic boom years before 1973, when both labor demands and welfare-state spending were escalating in a common market composed of the six founding members. Then, free movement meant that Italy's surplus labor could serve as a "temporary and fluctuating shift of single male workers" to meet the needs of neighboring member states. Even this testimony to Western Europe's growing interdependence, however, took place "on the basis of a coordination and actual convergence of national necessities" and "lacked any common policy and external protection."[21] The central elements of labor policy resisted any real transfer or erosion of member-state authority. Governments could freely exercise veto power in the Council of Ministers, the most intergovernmental EC institution, which holds responsibility for all consequential decisions on migration policy.

National sovereignty reigned supreme when it came to recruiting labor from third countries—initially including Spain, Portugal, and Greece—and offering political asylum. Third-country nationals did not win freedom of movement, and their entry into the Commmunity and its labor market remained firmly dependent on member-state prerogatives. Only after Europe moved to close its borders to non-EC workers in the early 1970s did they finally capture serious political interest from the Community. The Council of Ministers adopted a resolution concerning the EC's "foreign" work force in 1974. The Commission responded that December with an "Action Programme for Migrant Workers and Their Family Members." It aimed to encourage consultation on policies dealing with workers from non-EC countries, to develop common standards for their treatment, and to find ways to control illegal migration. This pro-

---

Community," in Graham Room, ed., *Towards A European Welfare State?* (Bristol: School for Advanced Urban Studies, 1991), p. 207. The ECJ ruled in *Bouchereau* (case 30/1977) that to deport EC workers on public policy grounds, there must exist "a genuine and sufficiently serious threat to the requirements of public policy affecting one of the fundamental interests of society"; Elspeth Guild, "Protecting Migrants' Rights: Application of EC Agreements with Third Countries," CCME Briefing Paper 10 (Brussels: Churches' Committee for Migrants in Europe, 1992), p. 9.

21. Romero, "Migration," pp. 36, 57, 58.

gram was the first in a series of well-intentioned but toothless pronouncements that did little to reduce the control of national governments.

In 1975 civil servants from the Justice and Interior ministries of the nine member states met together for the first time as the Trevi Group.[22] In secret, regular conferences it has acted as an intergovernmental coordinating and planning body. On top of its original objective of fighting terrorism, the Trevi Group gradually set up several working groups to cope with drugs, threats to public order, crime, and immigration.[23]

It was concern over this rather telling juxtaposition of issues that provoked EC interest in the social integration of resident immigrants, especially the potentially disruptive second generation—in other words, immigrant policy. The only text dealing with the children of foreign workers to result, however, was a 1977 Council directive that urged the member states to undertake special, concerted efforts to improve educational opportunities for them. The Council, rebuffing the Commission's proposal to include *all* children, excluded those of third-country nationals from coverage under the directive. Even at that, years passed before national governments moved to implement the measure. The pilot projects that resulted suffered from "confused thinking and practice" and "contradictions . . . between stated aims and actual practice."[24]

EC policies to promote the political integration of both EC and non-EC migrants suffered a similar fate. "Denial of civic and political rights seems to be inconsistent with the spirit of the principle of free movement of persons and with the political objectives of the Community with regard to European union," the Commission reasoned in 1976.[25] It argued in favor of limited local-level suffrage by 1980 for immigrants meeting certain residency requirements. As a preparatory stage, member states were urged to involve migrants in decisionmaking in the communities where they resided, by immediately establishing local-level consultative

22. Trevi is usually described as a French acronym for "Terrorisme, Radicalisme, Extrémisme, Violence Internationale." Though appropriate—those are its major issues of concern—the group actually received its name from the Trevi fountain in Rome, where it held its first meeting under the leadership of Dutch Minister Fontejne (pronounced like *fontaine*, French for fountain); Antonio Cruz, "Schengen, Ad Hoc Immigration Group and Other European Intergovernmental Bodies," CCME Briefing Paper 12 (Brussels: Churches' Committee for Migrants in Europe, 1993), pp. 18–19.

23. Baldwin-Edwards, "Socio-Political Rights," p. 220.

24. Euen Reid and Hans Reich, *Breaking the Boundaries: Migrant Workers' Children in the EC* (Philadelphia: Multilingual Matters, Ltd., 1992), p. 229.

25. Commission of the European Communities, "Action Programme in Favour of Migrant Workers and Their Families," *Bulletin of the European Communities,* supplement (Luxembourg: OOPEC, March 1976), p. 20.

bodies based on Belgium's well-developed network of Consultative Commissions for Immigrants (CCI). The European Parliament (EP)—which could advocate through "initiative reports" that legislation become the subject of formal Commission proposals—strongly supported the Commission's call for migrant participation in local elections and for the establishment of CCI. In a 1975 report the EP also came out strongly in favor of widening the political rights of migrants from EC member states in preparation for the first election of the Parliament by direct suffrage in 1979.[26] Yet while the Council of Ministers accepted the general outlines (if not all of the specifics) of the positions taken by the Commission and the EP, member-state sensitivities precluded progress on that front, too.[27]

Challenges to Immigration Policy Convergence in a Multitiered System

Never very effective, the push for greater migration and immigrant policy coordination completely lost its momentum by the end of the 1970s, as did the entire process of European integration. In a context of skyrocketing unemployment and inflation, social tensions over immigration flared across the continent. Strongly worded calls for concerted action never amounted to much, because EC member states were determined to protect their own interests.

Special problems arose from the multitiered structure of the EC policymaking system. Such an institutional arrangement has allowed domestic interests and national sovereignty to retain their salience and much of their power. During the economic troubles of the late 1970s and early 1980s, irresistible temptations grew for member states to adopt a devil-take-the-hindmost approach: they acted unilaterally to tighten their borders and thereby to direct disproportionate numbers of would-be migrants and refugees to their neighbors with more liberal legislation. There was a general recognition of the need to attenuate such potentially harmful discrepancies in national migration and refugee policies. Nevertheless, that awareness did not translate into agreement on how to achieve co-

26. European Parliament, *Working Documents, 1975–76*, Document 160/75 (July 31, 1975), p. 22.
27. Catherine Wihtol de Wenden, *Les immigrés dans la cité* (Paris: La Documentation Française, 1978), p. 33.

ordination or whether it should entail "centralised bargaining procedures" or "institutionalised links between decentralised bargaining units."[28]

When external migration was the issue, then, nation-states remained largely autonomous actors in the EC. Over and above the important, enduring contrasts in member states' social welfare systems in general, the disparities among their migration-related policies and in the extent and quality of social rights that migrants enjoyed persisted and even widened. And each host society had its own migratory history and traditions. In each a different constellation of immigrant-origin communities had become established over the course of the postwar boom years. Such heterogeneity complicates the framing of any common Community policies in the social sphere, all the more so with respect to migration and freedom of movement: controlling borders and membership in the polity has always been a prime means of protecting national identity and sovereignty.

The acquisition of citizenship represents a crucial barometer here. EC member states have never offered foreigners uniform routes to joining the national community, holding to their very different citizenship laws and naturalization procedures. In attributing citizenship at birth, Belgium, Denmark, Germany, Ireland, and Portugal have tended to emphasize parentage and blood ties (the principle of *jus sanguinis*). In the other member states, birthplace has more or less determined citizenship (*jus soli*). Naturalization procedures, too, have ranged from extremely liberal (the Netherlands: five years' residence, minimal knowledge of Dutch, and no criminal offenses) and fairly liberal (France and Spain) to somewhat stringent (Belgium and Greece) and highly protectionist (Germany: ten years' residence and strict requirements regarding language skills, employment history, and "attitude").[29] Britain, France, Ireland, and Italy have allowed dual citizenship, whereas countries such as Germany and Denmark have forced people to drop their old one when naturalizing.[30]

Nonnationals' length of residence abroad has largely determined what labor and other social rights they have enjoyed in any given member state. Restrictions on choice of employer, occupation, location, and length of stay usually fall away the longer third-country nationals reside in a host society. The relationship between length of residence and rights

28. Teague and Grahl, *European Community,* p. 211.
29. Baldwin-Edwards, "Socio-Political Rights," pp. 213–15.
30. "What Is a European?" *The Economist,* August 17, 1991, pp. 42–43.

varies for each country, though. Host societies have also set aside categories of "privileged" foreigners, those from former colonies or otherwise favored countries, who face less stringent obligations. Residence permits have varied widely in their duration within the Union, often changing over time even in a single member state. They have sometimes been linked to work permits (for example, France) and sometimes not (Denmark, Greece, Ireland). National policies have likewise diverged with respect to visa requirements for non-EU citizens, civil and voting rights, family reunification, access to public education and state-subsidized housing, efforts to control illegal migration, and measures to combat racial and ethnic discrimination.[31]

Nor have laws on the granting of political asylum been close to identical. All EU member states except Italy have accepted the Geneva Convention on Refugees of 1951, but each has interpreted its provisions differently. The numbers of applications—with Germany and France together accounting for more than three-fourths of the EU total—and the national and ethnic origins of the petitioners—a majority from sub-Saharan Africa in Britain, from North Africa in France, and from eastern Europe (including ethnic Germans) in Germany—have differed significantly across Western Europe. There has also been a wide range of acceptance rates.[32]

Confronted with such dissimilar, entrenched policies, it is hardly surprising that the EC's moves to harmonize them ran aground in the 1970s. Callovi has remarked on the dichotomy separating member states' declarations from their policies: "On one hand they seem to admit the necessity of a common immigration policy, on the other hand they seem to jeopardize the results by reducing the Community's powers and responsibilities. . . . This is why the work on abolition of internal borders is carried out in intergovernmental forums and tends to be embodied in a series of international Conventions rather than in a Community legally binding instrument."[33] Attempting to do more in such a highly sensitive policy realm would have been political suicide.

Struggles over the locus of policy control, typical of federal and other multitiered systems, further hobbled EC efforts to hammer out an ac-

---

31. Baldwin-Edwards, "Socio-Political Rights," pp. 209–20.

32. Detlev Samland, "Asylrecht in Europe," *Information zur Ausländerdienst*, no. 1 (1992), pp. 26–29.

33. Giuseppe Callovi, "Regulating Immigration in the European Community," paper presented at the International Conference of Europeanists, Washington, March 23–25, 1990, pp. 15–17.

ceptable European-level solution. For example, the Commission proposed in 1976 (and revised in 1978) a directive to fight clandestine
immigration. The Council of Ministers, representing member-state governments, blocked it for years. The European Parliament argued earliest
and most strenuously for harmonized immigration and refugee policies
and stressed the need to fight racism and to integrate non-EC workers
and their families into European society. The EP harshly criticized the
Commission, and especially the Council, for foot-dragging and allowing
social tensions to escalate dangerously.[34] These institutional differences
"clearly reflect the strains on any 'communitarian' policies during economic recession, but they also underline the lack of an institutional basis
to resist Member State efforts to concentrate above all on maintaining
their own welfare states for their own nationals."[35]

The Sharpened Imperative of Policy Coordination

Even if the EC proved unable to develop common migration policies that
reconciled national and Community interests, pressures to coordinate
policy, at a minimum, were building. The shortcomings and negative
effects of national solutions to the challenge of migration fed the search
for European options. By shutting their doors to additional inflows in
the mid-1970s, the host societies had not eliminated the "push" factors
in Africa and Asia that produced them. Family reunification added to
legally resident, foreign-origin populations, and much of the remaining
influx was simply diverted into illegal and refugee channels. The result
was increasingly virulent, organized anti-immigrant reactions, especially
in France, where Jean-Marie Le Pen and his National Front made their
electoral breakthrough in the early 1980s.

The EC's project for a unified European market in the mid-1980s,
which threatened to reduce further national control over member-state
labor markets, heightened fears that non-EC migrants might exploit the
different national regulations if internal Community borders were
opened. Migrants from within the Community did not provoke serious
upset: once Greece, Spain, and Portugal joined the EC in the 1980s, there
was no flood of migrants northward. Free mobility for their citizens was

34. "Entschließung zur Bekämpfung von Rassismus und Fremdenfeindlichkeit," *Information zur Ausländerdienst,* no. 1 (1991), p. 4.
35. Garth, "Migrant Workers," p. 135.

introduced only gradually—it was not completely accomplished until the early 1990s.[36] By then southern Europe was becoming a magnet for illegal migrants and refugees from North and East Africa and elsewhere in the developing world.

Southern Europe's porous borders generated anxiety in the rest of the EC. They threatened to make all of Europe vulnerable to illegal migration. Lord Cockfield's White Paper, which the Commission published in 1984, enumerated the major areas in which the EC should forge common policies. The list included removing controls and border formalities within the Community as a step toward complete freedom of movement and coordinating policies on political asylum, visa policies, and the legal status of third-country nationals. The Single European Act (SEA) of 1985-86 consequently stated in its article 8A that "the internal market comprises an area without internal frontiers in which the free movement of goods, persons, services, and capital is ensured in accordance with the provisions of this Treaty."

The Council of Ministers acknowledged in a resolution that same year that the economic and social changes that the single-market project would effect made common migration policies necessary. Otherwise the forces of competition risked serious distortion. If third-country nationals did not face the same totally free labor market as EC workers, job openings and jobseekers would be unlikely to match up in the way that the Commission forecast. Further complicating matters, companies with non-EC employees were bound to win contracts for projects outside their national base as the European market approached complete unification and bidding on government procurement opened up.[37]

EC leaders realized that migration policy had to include projects to foster integration. They were showing increasing awareness of the social consequences of a barrier-free Europe, and the SEA clearly legitimated EC action in the social sphere. Since 1981 the Commission had acknowledged that the Community had "to be seen to have an active social

36. In the years since, the "stimulative effects of trade and investment, which have raised living standards and increased employment opportunities in the less-developed countries of the south," have actually induced a mass return of southerners to their homelands; James F. Hollifield, "Migration and International Relations: Cooperation and Control in the European Community," *International Migration Review,* vol. 26 (Summer 1992), pp. 587–88.

37. See W. S. Siebert and J. T. Addison, "Internal Labour Markets: Causes and Consequences," *Oxford Review of Economic Policy,* vol. 7, no. 1 (1991), pp. 76–92.

policy" that addressed the situation of immigrant workers.[38] "How," asked Commission President Jacques Delors, "could we conceive of an effective freedom of movement and settlement of persons within the Community without defining progressively the bases of a common immigration policy, without adopting a comparable and positive attitude toward accepting and integrating the already established immigrant populations?"[39]

If Delors and the Commission had their way, then, it would eventually become possible for someone who had managed to enter EC territory anywhere and by any means to move freely throughout the Community, doubtless heading (or so many northern Europeans feared) for the more generous welfare states. Likewise, one member state's liberal or restrictive citizenship laws and naturalization procedures would necessarily affect the entire Community. Many observers began to conclude that policies concerning resident immigrants had to be coordinated so that countries could not "dump" their problems on their neighbors or lower their own social welfare benefits and labor standards to compete as production sites.[40] Refugee dumping was also deemed a threat, since political asylum-seekers with the same application could be turned down in one member state and accepted in another.[41]

In the end, however, national governments exercised their prerogatives and reserved the right to take appropriate measures to control migration from outside the Community's boundaries. They inserted into the SEA (at articles 13–19) a statement that dissipated any notion that drastic change was afoot: "Nothing in these provisions shall affect the right of Member States to take such measures as they consider necessary for the purpose of controlling immigration from third countries."[42] No other reference to non-EC migrants appeared. The SEA's focus fell almost

38. Quoted in Garth, "Migrant Workers," pp. 135–36.
39. Jacques Delors, "L'Europe en mouvement," *L'Événement Européen* (Paris), nos. 3–4 (1988), p. 22. It should be noted that though foreign policy considerations were not as critical, the EU's failure to grant third-country nationals freedom of movement and equal rights and combat anti-immigrant violence has drawn criticism from homeland governments, Morocco and Algeria in particular; Khader, "L'Immigration maghrébine," pp. 23–24.
40. Faist, "Transnationalizing," p. 23.
41. In 1992, to cite one example, 65 percent of applications for asylum by Tamils were approved in France, but only one out of a hundred in Germany; Samland, "Asylrecht in Europe," p. 27.
42. Quoted in Callovi, "Regulation of Immigration," p. 358.

exclusively on the challenges that the removal of physical barriers would create within the Community. Votes on measures affecting free movement and migration still had to be unanimous. The EC's multitiered institutional framework therefore made it impossible to take the affirmative steps toward managing legal and illegal migration that were clearly becoming imperative.

Ways Out of the Joint-Decision Trap

The EC thus kept butting up against the same "structural limitations" that had long forestalled the development of coordinated migration and immigrant policies.[43] A number of efforts emerged to compensate for the Community's failure to protect and integrate resident immigrants and to control migratory and refugee flows. International organizations, member-state governments, and EC authorities devised strategies to circumvent the blockages in Brussels.

International Organizations and Treaties

In the absence of sustained, harmonized EU action, many migrants' rights have their basis in international human rights law. The United Nations (UN) Universal Declaration on Human Rights, plus the binding agreements that have constituted the "International Bill of Rights" since 1976 and a pair of additional conventions in 1985 and 1990, have required contracting states to ensure nondiscrimination before the law and in education and employment for all resident aliens. The International Labour Organisation, likewise, has since the 1920s issued binding conventions and nonbinding recommendations calling for equal treatment in the workplace, including trade-union rights, social security benefits, and protections for illegal workers. And a number of conventions concluded by the Council of Europe—which was set up in 1949 in large part to watch over human rights in post–World War II Europe—have contained clauses that apply to migrant workers and their families: the European Convention on Human Rights (ECHR, 1950), the European Social Charter (1951), the Convention on Establishment (1955), the European Convention on Social Security (1972), and the Convention on the Legal Status of Migrant Workers (1977). The Council has also been

---

43. See Garth, "Migrant Workers," p. 136.

active in developing projects to improve the education and training of migrant children.[44]

Not all EU member states have signed onto the various conventions and recommendations of the UN, ILO, and Council of Europe. Even so, a majority of the twelve have signed the ECHR, which is a legal instrument of the Council (with its own commission and court to serve as control machinery) and applies to citizens of signatory and nonsignatory states.[45] Its provisions protect migrants' family life, freedom of expression and assembly, right to nondiscriminatory treatment, and free movement and settlement. Also, every EU member state has signed the European Social Charter, which came into effect in 1965 and guarantees equal social rights to legally resident nationals of the contracting parties.

These multinational treaties and accords approach (even if they do not reach) the level of protection for all noncitizens that the EU's "system of mobility and social rights" offers to citizens of its member states.[46] The ECHR, the European Social Charter, and the Convention on the Legal Status of Migrant Workers have helped to blur the distinction between the foreign worker and the resident immigrant. But they, as well as other like-minded initiatives that have emerged, amount to "soft law." Vaguely worded and with no real enforcement mechanisms, their goal is really to pressure governments to change their policies.

Even when EU member states have signed on, their national authorities can exercise great discretion. Some have attached reservations to their obligations. Martin Baldwin-Edwards points as well to crucial effects of the different legal systems in the Union. "Monist" systems like those in Belgium, France, Greece, Luxembourg, the Netherlands, Portugal, and Spain "incorporate a treaty automatically once approved by the competent state bodies"; "quasi-dualist" systems like those in Germany and Italy "require a transforming legislative act for treaty incorporation but can approach the level of applicability of monist systems"; and "dualist" systems like those in Britain, Ireland, and Denmark make "implementa-

44. Sources here include Council of Europe, *European Convention on the Legal Status of Migrant Workers,* European Treaty Series, no. 93 (Strasbourg: Council of Europe, April 1985); Giovanni Kojanec, "The UN Convention and the European Instruments for the Protection of the Migrants," *International Migration Review,* vol. 25, no. 4 (1991), pp. 818–30; and Franco Millich, "Social Protection of Migrants in the Normative Instruments of the European Council," *Forum,* no. 3 (Brussels: European Communities Migrants' Forum, 1993), p. 11.

45. Debate still rages, though, over whether the EU itself will adhere formally to the ECHR, a move opposed most strongly by France and the United Kingdom.

46. Garth, "Migrant Workers," p. 118.

tion dependent upon the provisions of separate domestic legislation addressed [by the state] to subjects."[47] In the monist and (sometimes) the quasi-dualist systems, international law can be invoked in domestic courts. Even then, treaties must be "self-executing," or domestic legislation is still necessary. The various conventions and charters therefore have direct effect in some EU member states but not in others. Normally, it is easiest to invoke international law in Belgium, the Netherlands, and France. Britain, at the other extreme, virtually ignores such international treaties.

The European Court of Justice

A burgeoning specialized literature demonstrates that in a number of policy areas an activist stance by the European Court of Justice has charted a "rights-based, court-led" path out of the joint-decision traps into which the EU has fallen.[48] An "ingenious, teleologically oriented" ECJ has transformed the rather ambiguous Treaty of Rome into a veritable Union constitution.[49] The ECJ's lawmaking role is no secret, and scholars have spoken of "integration by judicial fiat"[50] and the "juridication of politics in the European Community."[51] The ECJ has in many ways become the "principal motor for the integation of Europe."[52]

EU law generally has direct effect, which means that it becomes part of the *acquis communautaire* that domestic courts must enforce (*Simmenthal*, case 106/1977). The Treaty of Rome charges the ECJ with interpreting and applying its provisions. The Court reviews the legal status of acts undertaken by EU institutions (articles 173 and 175), supervises member-state compliance with the founding treaties and secondary Union legislation (articles 169 and 170), and interprets EU law for domestic courts. If a member-state government fails to implement EU law, any EU national who suffers a loss as a result is entitled to seek redress (*Francovich*, cases 6/1990 and 9/1990). When national courts have reason to believe that a piece of domestic legislation contravenes

47. Baldwin-Edwards, "Socio-Political Rights," pp. 203–04.
48. For an overview, see Mary L. Volcansek, "The European Court of Justice: Supranational Policy-Making," *West European Politics*, vol. 15 (July 1992), pp. 109–21.
49. Garth, "Migrant Workers," p. 97.
50. W. Andrew Axline, "Legal Integration through Judicial Fiat," *Journal of Common Market Studies*, no. 7 (1969), p. 217.
51. Volcansek, "European Court of Justice," p. 109.
52. G. Federico Mancini, "Attivismo e Autocontrollo nella Giurisprudenza della Corte di Giustizia," *Rivista di Diritto Europeo*, no. 30 (April–June 1990), p. 229.

Union law, they can grant interim relief pending an ECJ opinion (*Marleasing*, case 106/1989; and *Factortame*, case 221/1989).

ECJ case law has been responsible for expanding the Union's definition of *worker* and for developing the quasi-right of EU citizens to travel, as discussed above.[53] Largely with the blessings and encouragement of the Commission, the ECJ has strengthened the fundamental EU rights of entry and settlement, favored social security coordination, and advanced the aggregation and exportability of benefits.[54] The ECJ has been steadily extending the principles of free circulation to cover students, participants in vocational training programs, pensioners who have not worked in the country where they want to settle, tourists, self-employed and white-collar professionals, part-time workers, some public-sector employees, and (in the so-called Playboy guidelines) those who are not part of the economically active population but have funds sufficient to prevent them from receiving social welfare assistance.[55] It has even risen above and mitigated the interinstitutional squabbling that has so often paralyzed the EU. In 1977, for instance, the European Parliament, Commission, and Council of Ministers were in fact yielding to the ECJ when they issued a joint pledge to make it a Community priority to honor the European Convention on Human Rights.[56]

Recalling the role of the American Supreme Court during the civil rights period, the ECJ has concerned itself more and more often with the fight against not only direct but also indirect discrimination in the Union. It has interpreted EU law more and more inclusively. Since the mid-1970s, in fact, the ECJ has repeatedly referred to the Treaty of Rome and related Council regulations (especially the 1968 regulation no. 1612) in decisions that have secured non-EU workers many of the same social, employment, and fiscal rights as EU nationals, all in the name of removing barriers to free entry, mobility, and establishment.[57]

53. For a comparison with the complete right to travel in the United States, see Garth, "Migrant Workers," pp. 103–08.

54. It has done so through such cases as *Michael S.* v. *Fonds national de reclassement social des handicapés* (Belgium) (76/1972), *Rutili* v. *Minister for the Interior* (France) (36/1975), *Cristini* v. *Société nationale des chemins de fer français* (France) (32/1975), and *Levin* v. *Staatssecretaris van Justitie* (the Netherlands) (53/1981).

55. Commission of the European Communities, *Freedom of Movement* (Luxembourg: OOPEC, 1991).

56. Marcel Zwangborn, "Human Rights Promotion and Protection through the External Relations of the European Community," *Netherlands Quarterly of Human Rights*, no. 7 (1989), p. 13.

57. Judith Reicherzer, "Arbeit Ohne Grenzen," *Die Zeit*, November 20, 1992, p. 42.

A series of international treaties signed by the EC made this activism possible, although national governments were for a long time not compelled to abide by their provisions. Over the years the governments of Western Europe's labor-importing societies had entered into bilateral agreements with their labor-exporting counterparts, based on the prototypical Franco-Italian Accord of 1947. Such agreements focused on labor recruitment, but they generally included vaguely worded provisos concerning the host society's responsibilities in terms of family reunification, housing, and equality of treatment of the workers and their dependents.[58] As many of them began to lapse or fall into disuse in the mid-1960s, the EEC stepped into the breach. The Treaty of Rome (article 238) empowered it to reach treaties with third countries.

The EEC entered into five agreements that dealt with worker mobility and economic and social rights. Each set up a council composed of the EEC Council and Commission and representatives of the governments of the countries in question, with the decisions of these councils legally obliging all parties. In cases where member states had already made bilateral arrangements to grant citizens of third countries more favorable benefits, those agreements took precedence. The EEC thus worked toward setting a uniform, minimum social security regime to protect third-country workers in several Community member states.[59]

Still, for a long time these treaties did little to override national interests. The 1963 EEC Association Agreement with Turkey foresaw free movement for Turkish workers in the Community by 1986, but member states' misgivings have pushed off implementation at least until 1997. In 1980 the Association Council did institute for legal Turkish workers the gradual elimination of employment restrictions (there are none after four years); the same rights and responsibilities as member-state nationals regarding social security benefits; free access to the labor market for family workers after five years' residence; equal educational, apprenticeship, and vocational training opportunities; and a prohibition against new restrictions on Turks' access to employment. Meanwhile, the EEC

See also L. Neville Brown and Francis G. Jacobs, *The Court of Justice of the European Communities* (London: Sweet and Maxwell, 1983), chap. 4.

58. Mark J. Miller and Philip L. Martin, *Administering Foreign-Worker Programs: Lessons from Europe* (D.C. Heath and Co., 1982), p. 43.

59. The Lomé conventions that the Community has signed with developing countries mandate mutual respect for basic freedoms, equal pay and working conditions, and reciprocal social provisions. Not yet recognized as having direct legal effect, however, these provisions have remained effectively unenforceable.

signed cooperation agreements with the former Yugoslavia (effective in 1983, abrogated in 1991) and the Maghreb countries of Algeria, Tunisia, and Morocco (effective in 1978). Though not as extensive in scope as the agreement with Turkey, they were similar in spirit and forbade discrimination on the basis of nationality.

In the 1980s the ECJ began to take these treaties and their provisions on social rights seriously. Thus in the *Kupferberg* case (104/1981), the ECJ recognized that the EEC association agreements have direct effect and that member states must apply them consistently and uniformly.[60] In the *Demirel* case (12/1986) the Court nevertheless added a key nuance: it specified that since the requisite legal instrument to implement the free-mobility provision of the EEC/Turkey Association Agreement had never materialized, the treaty did not have direct effect in that area. In its 1990 ruling in *Sevince* (case 192/1989), however, the ECJ found that decisions of the Association Council promising equal access to employment and education did. In July 1987 it ruled that collaboration among member states in the social realm, as foreseen in article 118 of the Treaty of Rome, extended to migratory policies vis-à-vis third countries and empowered the Commission to set up enforceable regulations in the area. In 1991 the Court ruled in the *Kziber* case (18/1990)—which arose from the EEC-Morocco Cooperation Agreement—that lawfully employed and resident workers from the Maghreb countries (and by extension Turkey), as well as their families, may claim social security benefits on the same terms as citizens of EC member states. Moreover, provisions of the third-country accords dealing with working conditions and salaries have direct effect.[61]

In other areas as well the ECJ has been narrowing the gap between the rights of EU and non-EU nationals that member-state governments and the Council have worked so hard to preserve. Hence third-country nationals who are family members of an EU citizen may rely on that person's rights to achieve and maintain access to the Union and its labor market (*Singh*, case 370/1990). EU companies have won some ability to move non-EU workers from one member state to another in order to provide legally contracted services (*Rush Portuguesa*, case 113/1989).[62]

---

60. This condition holds only when third-country agreements contain a clear and precise obligation to ensure its application and enforcement, a stipulation that likewise applies to Union directives; H. Gacon-Estrada, "L'Europe des étrangers à petits pas," *Plein Droit,* special issue (1989–90), p. 82.

61. Guild, "Protecting Migrants' Rights," pp. 12–16.

62. Guild, "Protecting Migrants' Rights," p. 1.

There has been movement in Luxembourg toward codifying the same narrowly defined justification for deporting Turkish and North African workers as applies to EU nationals.

The *Kus* case (237/1992) represents one of the most recent and possibly the single most stunning example of ECJ policymaking. A German court asked the ECJ whether Mr. Kazim Kus, a Turkish national, could renew his work permit for the same employer in Wiesbaden after one year's work, even though he had lost his residence permit as a result of his divorce from a German woman. On December 16, 1992, the ECJ referred to the *Sevince* case—which involved a Turkish worker who had managed to prolong his residence and employment in the Netherlands by successfully appealing a deportation order—to argue that, having legally entered Germany and obtained work and residence permits, Mr. Kus was entitled now to renew both of them. It did not matter that he had come to Germany under the family reunification program.[63]

Bryant Garth, for one, has seen in the ECJ's rulings a reactive defining of rights that play mostly a symbolic and face-saving role for the Union: "The rights that are extended to migrant workers . . . are not the product of a widely supported social program but instead reflect a response to criticism based on liberal values."[64] The ECJ, he argues, has drafted rights, but implementation has lagged. For him the good news is that this process helps legitimate the EU without overtaxing its capabilities. Too much enforcement would risk exacerbating opposition to Union institutions and initiatives over the long run.

In truth, proclamations of noble-sounding principles have far outnumbered actual efforts to improve migrants' lot, and perhaps that has been all the better for the institutional stability of the Union. But then again, the Luxembourg Court has not hesitated to criticize member-state governments or to condemn domestic legislation impeding free movement within the Union. France, to cite one noteworthy example, had long withheld family allocations from any workers whose children resided abroad. Though the law applied equally to French citizens and foreign workers, it clearly affected the latter more frequently and to greater detriment. Even children of noncitizens from elsewhere in the Community received benefits (generally lower) from their parents' homelands,

---

63. Simultaneously, the ECJ reiterated its 1990 *Sevince* ruling that the Turkish Association Agreement had direct effect. See Antonio Cruz, ed., *Migration News Sheet*, no. 118 (Brussels: Churches' Committee for Migrants in Europe, January 1993), pp. 1–2. The British and Dutch governments both submitted advisory briefs in this watershed case.

64. Garth, "Migrant Workers," p. 141.

and not from France. Yet in two decisions reached in 1986 and 1989, the *Pinna* rulings, the ECJ found that the French restrictions (as well as the 1978 article in EC regulation 1408 that had allowed national courts to uphold them) violated the equal-treatment and free-mobility clauses in articles 48 and 51 of the Treaty of Rome. French authorities feared the costs that would accrue from the ruling and the possibility that the ECJ might eventually mandate a uniform system that included third-country nationals. The French government subsequently used its presidency of the Council in 1989 to delay implementation of the rulings and to limit the future exportability of social welfare benefits.

The ECJ, in short, has not been able to force the Council to accept its decisions. Some French courts have nonetheless begun to base their rulings on these and other points of ECJ case law. With EU member states unwilling to grasp the nettle of fundamental, patently necessary immigration reform, the Court has stepped in, supplied a policy, and at least forced them to react.[65]

Intergovernmentalism Triumphant

And national governments have reacted. While the ECJ's activism has pierced the migration and immigrant policy blockage by widening the reach of the Union's legal protections, national governments have for their part responded to ECJ and migratory pressures by developing lowest-common-denominator strategies that preserve their veto power over policy. Cooperation among governments, outside the ambit of EU institutional control, has become the preferred mechanism to reconcile national sovereignty and European interests.

The governments of Germany, France, and Benelux worried that Europe was moving too slowly in implementing freedom of movement and decided to move ahead on their own. In June 1985 they agreed in Schengen, Luxembourg, to remove all controls at their common frontiers by New Year's 1990. This treaty operates under international, and not Union, law; it provides for harmonized immigration and security policies.

65. Isabelle Ypsilantis and Nicolas Brun, "L'Affaire Pinna," *Plein Droit,* special issue (1989–90), pp. 88–93. The Commission, to cite another example, has applied the ECJ's famous ruling in the *Cassis de Dijon* case, which established the principle of mutual recognition, to the freedom of movement and settlement of the self-employed and professionals: "If a person is fit to practise a professional activity in one Member State, he should, in principle, be fit to practise it in any other." Commission of the European Communities, *Opening Up the Internal Market* (Luxembourg: OOPEC, 1991), p. 40.

It foresees a system of international border controls and checks, information exchanges on asylum-seekers and undesirable aliens, and even sanctions on private air carriers who transport illegals into the Union. As has been the case under the Benelux Economic Union, resident third-country nationals are to be able to travel freely through the participating nations for up to three months, albeit for tourist purposes alone. The five original Schengen states began writing up a common list of countries—over 120 at latest count—whose nationals will need a visa to enter any of them. The regime's "backbone" is to be the Schengen Information System (SIS), based in Strasbourg, which will hold data on foreigners, asylum-seekers, criminals, firearms, vehicles, and people under police surveillance.

The Schengen countries failed to meet their original deadline. Undaunted, they signed a supplementary convention in June 1990. This text enumerated and put in place all measures needed to effect the removal of internal frontiers in "Schengenland"—since enlarged to include Austria, Greece, Italy, Portugal, and Spain. Technical problems with the SIS, Southern Europe's still sievelike borders, liberal drug policies in Spain and the Netherlands, and the reluctance of several signatory states to ratify the supplementary convention have since pushed back the deadline for implementation of the Schengen system several times.[66]

The EU Commission has used the Schengen countries as a model or laboratory, watching how they work out the technicalities of eliminating internal borders. It has also learned that member-state resistance makes Union action increasingly unrealizable. In March 1985, for instance, the Commission sent a communication to the Council entitled "Guidelines for a Community Policy on Migration." In it the term *Community* was found alongside *migration policy* for the first time.[67] Citing article 118 of the Treaty of Rome, which gives it general competence in the realm of social policy, the Commission issued a decision that summer that required member states to notify and consult with the EC before adopting policies on migration from third countries. But national sovereignty still ruled supreme when it came to immigration: Germany, France, the Netherlands, Denmark, and Britain saw the decision as an unwarranted af-

---

66. The Schengen convention has finally been applied, as of March 26, 1995, in the five original signatory states, Spain, and Portugal. Austria, Italy, and Greece are to follow "soon," but they have yet to announce a date. "Convention is Finally Applied," *Migration News Sheet*, no. 145 (April 1995), p. 1.

67. Callovi, "Regulation of Immigration," p. 356.

front to their authority in this domain and appealed to the European Court of Justice, which annulled it in 1987.[68]

At first, ironically, that legal challenge seemed to open up new possibilities for EC action. For in its ruling the Court recognized the need "to facilitate the adoption of a common position by the member states; to achieve progress toward harmonization of national legislation on foreigners; to promote the inclusion of common provisions in bilateral agreements; and to improve the protection of Community nationals working and living in nonmember countries."[69] The Commission, in short, was competent to issue enforceable decisions on labor from third countries.

The member states had a different interpretation, though, and it would prevail. At the insistence of the British government, which held the presidency of the Council of Ministers in the second half of 1986, intergovernmental policymaking received another fillip: an Ad Hoc Immigration Group, buttressed by several committees, appeared within the Council secretariat to work toward the removal of internal border controls; the desirability of harmonizing migration policies would be evaluated in light of that goal.[70] Areas deemed of immediate joint concern resembled Schengen's laundry list: control over external Community borders and the influx of asylum-seekers; judicial coooperation; the development of a common visa policy; a bilateral exchange of information on migrants and people under security surveillance; and the fight against drug trafficking, terrorism, crime, and illegal migration. The group's work was to proceed behind closed doors; the Commission had merely observer status.[71]

Like it or not, then, the Commission was compelled to accept a supporting role. At the 1988 Rhodes summit of the European Community heads of government—the European Council—Jacques Delors announced that decisions governing common visa and asylum policies would come before the Commission only when intergovernmental agree-

68. The ECJ ruled that the Commission could not mandate use of consultation to ensure that proposed national measures conformed to Community guidelines. The Commission revised (read: softened) and reissued its decision in 1988.

69. Callovi, "Regulation of Immigration," p. 357.

70. This incident shows that a key to policy developments has become the priorities and interests of the member-state government holding the rotating presidency of the Council of Ministers for any given six-month period.

71. T. Bunyan, "A Europe Steeped in Racism," *Manchester Guardian*, January 28, 1991, p. 8.

ments proved impossible to reach. "States rely on national border controls for their own security," he conceded, and "if they loosen this instrument, they have to compensate through another mechanism that tightens-up controls at the Community's external borders."[72]

That European Council meeting also yielded agreement that coordination was necessary among the various groups responsible for migration.[73] What resulted was the Rhodes Group of Coordinators, composed of high-level civil servants from member-state interior ministries, supported by working groups on asylum, police and customs coordination, and judicial cooperation. The coordinating group has undertaken the preparatory work for the Union on migration and has written up position papers. The dossiers it has prepared have passed first to the Permanent Representatives Committee (COREPER) and then to the Council of Ministers and the Ad Hoc and Trevi groups.

The European Council continued to take the lead in the years that followed. In 1990 in Dublin, its summit produced a convention on political asylum. If ratified by all member states—Denmark, France, Germany, Greece, Luxembourg, Portugal, Spain, and the United Kingdom have so far—the convention will become a legally constraining text. An asylum-seeker will be able to apply only in the first EC member state or "safe" third country that he or she enters.[74] A planned accompanying agreement that would have established common policies on crossing the Community's external borders fell apart over the conflict between Spain and Britain over Gibraltar. Nation-state privileges still oblige.

Enlargement and the prospect of adding even more members to the Union have further reduced the likelihood that the role of member-state governments will wane. In Luxembourg in 1991, the Community reached an agreement with the seven members of the European Free Trade Association (EFTA) to create what has become known as the European Economic Area (EEA). The EEA, which came into effect in early 1994, gives nationals of any EU or EFTA state (save Switzerland, whose voters rejected EEA membership in December 1993) the right to move freely throughout all of them. (Austria, Finland, and Sweden, of course, joined

72. Callovi, "Regulating Immigration in the European Community," p. 11.

73. The Single European Act made first official mention of the European Council, but it is not really a Union institution.

74. If the application were refused there, no further attempts could be made to secure asylum elsewhere in the Community. The safe countries are Austria, the Czech Republic, Finland, Norway, Poland, Sweden, and Switzerland; "Asylum Refugees," *Migration News Sheet,* no. 119 (February 1993), p. 6.

the EU on January 1, 1995.) The Union has also signed Association Agreements with the "Visegrad Four"—Poland, Hungary, the Czech Republic, and Slovakia—and, more recently, with Bulgaria and Romania.

Those accords with central European nations do not contain the same free-mobility provision as the EEA. Fear is nonetheless great in North Africa that the EU's opening to both EFTA and the east will be accompanied by a closing off to the south.[75] And indeed, advancing the rights and integration of third-country nationals has been downgraded to a very long-term objective. Those with a permanent residence permit valid for at least four months have gained free movement within the Union, but only for tourist purposes.[76]

The European Council did commission a series of studies of national migration policies in the late 1980s. They all came to the same conclusions that most host societies did in the mid-1970s: it is incumbent upon the Community to integrate the legally resident foreign population, and success in that area depends on gaining control over migratory movements. European Council meetings since the mid-1980s have issued, mantralike, denunciations of racism and antiforeigner violence and calls for the social integration of immigrants. A genuine European-level response has had to wait, however. The Dutch President-in-Office of the Council of Ministers, Hans van den Broek, noted in response to a question from an MEP (Member of the European Parliament) in November 1991 that "as regards the way in which immigrants from third countries are treated in the Community, this matter is still something for which individual Member States remain competent. . . . The Council firmly believes that all Member States of the Community will adopt a stance towards immigrants that is in keeping with their long tradition of humanism and of respect for human beings as persons, irrespective of their origin, race or philosophical or religious beliefs."[77]

In the migration and immigrant policy area, as in others, the EU has thus moved to implement the "subsidiarity" principle: "The Commission proposes that Community legislation in this field be applied only to those cases where the legal security and uniformity provided by Community law constitutes the best instrument to achieve the desired goal."[78] The Maastricht Treaty, drafted by the European Council in December 1991,

---

75. Rémy Leveau, "Inquiétudes du Sud," *Esprit*, vol. 7 (July 1992), pp. 134–39.
76. Baldwin-Edwards, "Socio-Political Rights," p. 56.
77. *Debates of the European Parliament*, no. 3–411 (November 20, 1991), p. 184.
78. Callovi, "Regulation of Immigration," p. 360.

effective in November 1993, officially confirms the commitment of EU member states to "formal and actual harmonization" to confront the challenges of migration and asylum. Articles K.1–9 of title 6 of the accord lay out the three main areas in which common policies will be necessary and appropriate for its implementation: a common policy on visas, asylum, and the crossing of external Community borders; institutionalized judicial and police cooperation (Europol); and a protocol on social policy. The latter, accepted by all of the member states except Britain, built on the nonobligatory 1988 Community Charter of the Fundamental Social Rights of Workers. For Europe's non-EU migrants the charter promised official recognition of their right to freedom of movement and association and an action program to facilitate their integration. The Maastricht Social Protocol includes mention of "conditions of employment for third country nationals legally residing in Community territory" as an area in which the Council would act unanimously on proposals emanating from the Commission. Yet it drops earlier references, including those in the 1988 charter, to "living conditions" (that is, housing, education, health, and social rights). In the realm of third-country migration, in other words, immigrant policy is to stay off the Union docket.[79]

In its final form the Maastricht accord says nothing about the institutional framework within which joint action on migration is to be produced; therefore intergovernmental compromises on issues of "common interest"—those rooted in the principle of free mobility—are still the major vehicle for migration policy. Though the document provides some new institutional capacity for the Commission to take the policy initiative in certain areas, at bottom it does not weaken the veto power of national governments over any unwanted action. Three new steering committees are to supersede the existing intergovernmental committees, yet the same people will sit on the new bodies: Steering Committee 1 (replacing the Ad Hoc Group) will treat migration and asylum, committee 2 (replacing the Trevi groups) will deal with police and security issues, and committee 3 will oversee judicial cooperation. The steering committees will send their statements and proposals to a new coordinating committee (replacing the Rhodes group), and COREPER will be more directly involved than before. The member states rejected a proposed clause that would have mandated an ECJ review of any conventions on migration. Article K.7 stipulates that the treaty does not compromise or create any obstacles

---

79. "Maastricht et la libre circulation," *Forum,* no. 2 (Brussels: European Communities Migrants' Forum, 1994), pp. 14–17.

to the development of closer cooperation between two or more member states—a clear reference to the Schengen agreement.[80]

The European Parliament, which at the Maastricht summit gained an important say in budgetary matters and greater consultative input in general, did not receive a like boost in its influence on migration and immigrant policies. Still, the EP has exhibited more consistent interest in integrating immigrants and tackling the structural causes of migratory and refugee flows from the developing world. It has tried to find a European solution to these challenges that respects human rights, and it stands as the only EU institution to speak of the "moral and historical responsibility of the member states of the European Community toward asylum-seekers and refugees."[81] The EP has repeatedly demanded that matters pertaining to third-country nationals be brought under EU competence. At the same time, it has retreated from its fruitless insistence on extending local-level voting rights to them, opting instead to "invite" member-state governments to do so.[82] Maastricht, furthermore, has enabled EU and legally resident third-country nationals to seek judicial redress in any member state, direct a petition to the European Parliament, and register complaints with the EP's Ombuds(wo)man.

Meanwhile, a report on fascism, racism, and xenophobia presented to the EP in 1985 by the late Greek MEP Evregenis sparked the idea of assembling a forum where people of migrant origin could find their political voice and enter into a dialogue with European institutions. Drawing on that report, as well as from those submitted by MEPs Heinz-Oskar Vetter (Social Democratic Party, Germany) in 1987 and Glyn Ford (Labour, Britain) in 1991, the EP passed a resolution to set up such a body. The EC Commission surveyed migrant associations across Europe and then assembled a constituent assembly that elected a preparatory committee. In May 1991 the EC Migrants Forum resulted. It has begun to employ the Forum's annual subsidy (estimated at 500,000 ECUs) to establish a dialogue and exchange information between EU institutions and migrant communities; work to improve interethnic relations in the

---

80. Personal interview with Jan Niessen, General Secretary, Churches' Committee for Migrants in Europe, Brussels. Under the Maastricht treaty, immigration and asylum come under the third and final "pillar"—justice and home affairs—on which the European Union is to be built. See Ann Dummett and Jan Niessen, "Immigration and Citizenship in the European Union," CCME Briefing Paper 14 (Brussels: Churches' Committee for Migrants in Europe, November 1993), pp. 15–20.

81. Margit Gottstein, "Asylpolitik im Schatten des Binnenmarktes," *Information zur Ausländerdienst*, no. 1 (1992), p. 32.

82. Assane Ba, "Le Rapport Vetter," *Plein Droit*, special issue (1989–90), pp. 72–73.

Union; promote the interests of migrants and refugees in Brussels; and lobby for equal employment and social rights, free movement, and the right to vote.[83]

Here the hardening dichotomy between the status of EU and non-EU migrants becomes glaring. When the forum was being developed, southern European migrant associations argued that their status as EC nationals did not perforce guarantee them equal treatment or eliminate discrimination against them. The Commission refused their demand for inclusion, charging that it could not grant special status to EC citizens. The 110 migrant organizations from throughout the Union who participate in the forum represent more than fifty nationalities and most political persuasions, but all of them mobilize only third-country nationals.

Several major provisions of the "Union citizenship" that the Treaty on European Union advances have similarly aggravated the segregation of migrants by nationality. Maastricht envisions granting migrants the right to vote and run for office in local and European elections—but only migrants who hold the nationality of an EU member state and who meet certain residency requirements. In the name of promoting a "European consciousness," the Union has underscored the differences between EU and third-country nationals.[84]

Conclusion: Future Scenarios

Prodded by migratory forces, the dynamics of economic integration, international organizations, and the European Court of Justice, therefore, the EU has been approaching complete freedom of movement for citizens of Union member states. It has also been developing a set of social rights for

83. Personal interview with Taha Mellouk, EC Migrants' Forum, Brussels.

84. Patrick Weil, "Immigrés: Les risques d'une dérive," *Le Monde,* September 9, 1992, p. 2. Union institutions have been moving haltingly toward implementation of this aspect of European citizenship. National-government resistance has occasionally been fierce. Even tiny Luxembourg, which has the EU's largest nonnational European population, has managed to have a "derogatory measure" inserted into the Commission's proposal for a Council directive on the matter: the derogation applies to any member state whose proportion of resident EU nationals who are not nationals of that state and who have reached voting age exceeds 20 percent of the total number of EU nationals residing there who are of voting age. Such a member state—only Luxembourg qualifies—may require from nationals of the other member states a minimum period of residence before being allowed to excercise the right to vote and stand as a candidate in local elections; "European Parliament Report on the Right to Vote in Local Elections for EU Nationals," *Migration News Sheet,* no. 134 (May 1994), pp. 7–8. Belgium has also recently won a derogation.

these "internal" foreigners. Of course, with member-state social policies themselves continuing to diverge, there are limits to the harmonization of immigrant policies. Through intergovernmental bargaining, meanwhile, a consensus is emerging on external migration and refugee policies. The social rights of third-country nationals, however, vary greatly across the Union, and their freedom of movement remains circumscribed. The dangers that such partial policy convergence poses for the EC's economic and social integration seem likely to produce changes in the status quo. This evolution could take three possible directions.

A Fortress Europe?

As a first policy option, the member states could try to close the Union off from the problems of the world around it. All energies could go into preventing the further influx of unwanted migrants and refugees and forcing resident non-EU nationals to assimilate or return to their homelands. EU citizenship would become the passport to the rights of free mobility and equal treatment.

Such a policy of exclusion is neither feasible nor desirable. Those close to the Commission, like Giuseppe Callovi, insist that the Union will not become "a self-contained and inward-looking fortress, if only because of its commitments to respect basic human rights . . . and [its] foreign and trade policies."[85] The European Council reaffirmed at its summit meetings that Europe will not retreat from its defense of human rights and the rule of law and its fight against racism and xenophobia.[86] Besides their public relations value, such pronouncements speak to the liberal and democratic ethos that underpins the Union, which should not be underestimated. Without it, foreign workers and refugees and their families from outside the EU could hardly have won the important social rights and legal protections that they already enjoy.

There are also practical obstacles to a fortress Europe. Highly skilled European workers now move about the Union more and more frequently and easily as the EU removes the final barriers to their mobility and as European business undergoes further internationalization.[87] Projections are hotly disputed, yet it seems likely that lower-skilled migrant workers,

85. Callovi, "Regulation of Immigration," p. 365.
86. See, for example, "Ruling Confirms More Rights for Turks Working in a Member State," *Migration News Sheet*, no. 118 (January 1993), pp. 1–2.
87. See John Salt, "Migration Processes among the Highly Skilled in Europe," *International Migration Review*, vol. 26 (Summer 1992), pp. 484–505.

too, will become increasingly necessary to meet labor demand in certain sectors and to pay for social programs supporting rapidly aging populations. In fact, influential business interests are already lobbying for access to cheap labor. Germany has signed bilateral agreements that permit eastern European companies in labor-hungry sectors like health care, construction, food processing, and agriculture to operate with their own workers in the Federal Republic. These seasonal and contract laborers remain subject to home-country social security systems and labor standards, thereby saving the German economy and government money and, officials in Bonn argue, reducing migratory pressures at the source.[88]

Meeting in Luxembourg on June 20, 1994, the EU Justice and Home Affairs Council resolved that, since the "present high levels of unemployment in the Member States increase the need to bring Community employment preference properly into practice," it approves of such arrangements for the temporary employment of foreigners "only where vacancies in a Member State cannot be filled by national and Community manpower or by non-Community manpower lawfully resident on a permanent basis in that Member State and already forming part of the Member State's regular labour market." Still, national governments could not bring themselves to restrict definitively their freedom of maneuver: the text of the resolution stipulates that its principles "are not legally binding on the Member States and do not afford a ground for action by individual workers or employers."[89]

Policy Harmonization?

If exclusion is not likely, then neither is the elaboration any time soon of truly common immigrant policies for member-state or third-country nationals, or totally free movement for non-Europeans. To a large extent the same dynamics that led to joint-decision traps in the 1970s are still at play in the multitiered EU policy system. National policies continue to diverge. Fights over the locus of policy rage on. The Gibraltar conflict, for example, still holds up the convention on external borders. And for a few weeks early in 1994, Belgium even threatened to grant political asylum to a Basque couple wanted in Spain, a fellow member state, for suspected terrorist activities![90]

88. See Faist, "Transnationalizing," pp. 16–24.
89. Quoted in "Resolution on Immigration Contains Hardly Anything New," *Migration News Sheet*, no. 136 (July 1994), p. 1.
90. "Citizen's Europe," *Europe*, no. 5892 (January 7, 1993), pp. 5–6.

Take the institutions of citizenship as another, even more telling example. Belgium changed its nationality law in 1992, giving automatic citizenship to Belgian-born, second-generation immigrants with at least one Belgian-born parent and easing the process for those whose parents were born in the homeland. The Belgians eliminated the possibility of holding dual nationality, however, and naturalization is difficult and costly. Spain, similarly, has moved to strip Spanish nationality from most people who have acquired another one. Yet the Netherlands—which has pushed more generally for liberal immigrant policies in the Union—has eased its naturalization procedures and has considered allowing dual nationality. In the meantime the French government of Édouard Balladur enacted a stricter nationality code in 1993, even as Germany was taking its first tentative steps away from *jus sanguinis* and strict naturalization procedures. Germany and the Netherlands want more Union involvement in migration-related issues, while Britain, Denmark, and Ireland refuse any EU role in "internal security."[91]

Furthermore, institutional squabbles have not subsided and still impede EU action. The Parliament has stayed faithful to its reputation as the Union institution with a conscience. It has come out in favor of a far-reaching and ambitious community system for the protection of human rights, including economic, social, and cultural rights. It has also accepted yet another report, prepared by MEP Cesare de Piccoli (ex-Communist, part of the Socialist group, Italy) on the resurgence of racism and anti-migrant violence in Europe. The Piccoli report implores the Council of Ministers, Commission, and member states to set up a Union program to fight groups and associations that incite racial and ethnic hatred, to extend local-level voting rights to foreigners resident for five years in an EU host society, and to introduce a European resident's statute to protect non-EU nationals.[92]

The EP's impatience with secret, intergovernmental policymaking in the EU has escalated. To the Commission's dismay, it has taken the issue of free movement in the Union to the European Court of Justice. The Parliament demands that it be given a more important role in the application and interpretation of the future convention on external borders and insists that the Commission use its enhanced powers to ensure im-

91. See, for example, Yvan Mayeur, "Code de la nationalité," *MRAX Information*, no. 70 (May 1993), p. 37; and Hermann Bleich, "Ausländer in den Niederlanden," *Frankfurter Rundschau*, June 24, 1993, p. 2

92. "EP/Human Rights," *Europe*, no. 5939 (March 13, 1993), pp. 3–4.

plementation of article 8A of the Single European Act. In a joint resolution presented by the Socialist, Christian Democratic, and Liberal groups and adopted on February 10, 1994, the EP condemned the inadequacy of the purely intergovernmental procedure.[93] MEPs want national parliaments and Union institutions to exercise more control over the application of the Schengen agreement.

Europe as Schengenland?

"Is the Schengen Agreement a Way Out?" asked the *Kölner Stadt-Anzeiger* in a front-page headline on November 28, 1991. Indeed, since the drafting of the Maastricht treaty, the EU's migration policies have gradually converged with the Schengen system. Though an intergovernmental convention will be needed before final implementation, the European Information System (EIS), a version of the Schengen Information System covering all twelve member states, is taking shape.

The reason for this convergence is clear: member states may try to go their own way on migration, but the negative effects of doing so are gradually forcing greater policy coordination. As of July 1, 1993, for instance, Germany no longer guaranteed a constitutional right to political asylum; and Britain, Portugal, and Spain have recently tightened up their asylum laws as well.[94] Such strict new policies, enacted unilaterally, have threatened to shift flows to neighboring countries like Belgium and Denmark. Meeting in Copenhagen within the framework of the Ad Hoc Immigration Group in June 1992, the interior ministers of the EC responded. They agreed to conduct tighter identity checks on migrants, to move more quickly to expel illegal migrants, and to rationalize family reunification. Hovering over the Danish capital was the "spirit of Schengen, times twelve."[95] Explicitly in the name of following that spirit, the French government convinced the National Assembly to amend the constitution and restrict the right of foreigners to ask for asylum in France in 1993. Hence, EP upset notwithstanding, the intergovernmental approach has seemingly prevailed over Community action: member states have pooled sovereignties while rejecting any obligation to transfer sov-

---

93. All of the following are from various issues of *Migration News Sheet*: "European Parliament," no. 117 (December 1992), pp. 2–3; "Attempts to Dissuade Parliament," no. 122 (May 1993), p. 1; "Migration Policies," no. 132 (March 1994), p. 2; and no. 134 (May 1994), p. 1.

94. Baldwin-Edwards, "Socio-Political Rights," p. 53.

95. "L'Europe se disperse sur l'immigration," *La Libre Belgique,* June 1, 1993, p. 6.

ereignty to Brussels. The EU's "territorial dimension" maintains its importance, and national boundaries remain "key organizers of political power and economic wealth within the Community."[96]

Through the back door of intergovernmental bargains, however, member states are inching toward de facto policy harmonization on those issues where unanimity and common interest prevail, that is, controlling external and illegal migration and refugee flows. Agreed on this priority, member-state governments are enacting institutional modifications that will eventually remove barriers to its realization and effectively transfer some sovereignty to the EU. Thus the Council of Ministers will be able to adopt decisions concerning third countries whose nationals require a visa to enter the Union by a qualified majority as of January 1, 1996. The trend, therefore, is actually toward a form of supranationality. For Ernst Haas, who developed the concept, supranationality did not mean that Union institutions would exercise authority over national governments. Rather, it is a style of policymaking, "a cumulative pattern of accommodation in which the participants . . . seek to attain agreements by means of compromises upgrading common interests."[97]

As for harmonizing immigrant policies and granting free mobility to third-country nationals, common interests in this realm appear less urgent to national governments and the likely compromises more unsettling for national sovereignty. Over the medium term, chances seem great that the Union will rely on habitual mechanisms for escaping policy deadlocks in these areas. The European Court of Justice persists in advancing the rights of EU and non-EU nationals alike: in April 1994 the justices ruled (in case C-58/93) that the Cooperation Agreement between the EEC and Morocco entitles a Moroccan national, Mr. Z. Yousfi, to a disability allowance in Belgium; and German authorities are bracing themselves for expected ECJ condemnation of illegal but widely practiced restrictions on Turkish workers' rights of mobility and settlement in the Federal Republic.[98] With its own house divided, moreover, the EU today welcomes even more enthusiastically than before the initiatives of the Council of Europe, the ILO, the Conference on Security and Cooperation in

96. Alberta M. Sbragia, "Thinking about the European Future: The Uses of Comparison," in Sbragia, ed., *Euro-Politics*, p. 274.

97. Quoted in Robert O. Keohane and Stanley Hoffmann, "Conclusions: Community Politics and Institutional Change," in William Wallace, ed., *The Dynamics of European Integration* (London: Frances Pinter, 1990), p. 280.

98. "Racism/Discrimination," *Migration News Sheet*, no. 135 (June 1994), pp. 7–8. See also *Der Spiegel*, no. 32 (1994), pp. 34, 36.

Europe, and the United Nations to find ways to manage migration and refugee issues, such as the joint migration conferences in Berlin (1991), Budapest (1993), and Prague (1994).[99]

Ultimately, if the Union hopes to avoid social dumping without betraying its liberal and democratic values, immigrant policy—including the integration and free mobility of third-country nationals within the EC—will need to be harmonized and thereby subject to supranational decisionmaking. Such a shift would represent a sea change in EU social policy, since basic social structures and definitions of membership would be in free play. In a sense, then, the EU should see the migration and immigrant policy sector as something akin to the canary in the mineshaft: if efforts to develop common policies die, then the outlook for the building of a unified European society will be bleak indeed.

99. EP President Egon Klepsch has gone so far as to lobby actively for a "worldwide coordinated immigration policy"; "EC/Migrations," *Europe*, no. 5914 (February 6, 1993), p. 5.

Part Two

Social Policy Integration in
North America

The Welfare State as Statecraft: Territorial Politics and Canadian Social Policy

Keith G. Banting

T HE POWER OF territorial politics represents an enduring feature of modern societies. Despite predictions in the 1960s that allegiances to local or regional communities would fade away, to be displaced fully by identities rooted in class or functional interests, territorial conflict remains a core element of the politics of Western nations. "It is through the territorial units they live in," Sidney Tarrow reminds us, that citizens "organize their relations with the state, reconcile or fight out conflicts of interest, and attempt to adapt politically to wider social pressures."[1] Territorial politics is particularly salient when regional boundaries within a nation coincide with cultural and linguistic divisions or when countries are marked by sharp economic inequalities among regions. The resurgence of substate nationalism and the strength of regionalist, autonomist, or separatist political movements in several Western nations are simply the most dramatic examples of the continuing importance of local political communities in the modern world. Even efforts to construct supranational political systems cannot fully escape an impulse to define political interests in territorial terms. Certainly, territorial politics, as represented by the power of member states, constitutes the dominant feature of politics within the European Union.[2]

Despite the durability of regional identities and interests, territorial politics has not been adequately incorporated in our understanding of the determinants and role of the welfare state. The existing literature

1. Sidney Tarrow, "Introduction," in Sidney Tarrow, Peter J. Katzenstein, and Luigi Graziano, eds., *Territorial Politics in Industrial Nations* (Praeger, 1978), p. 1.
2. Alberta M. Sbragia, "Thinking about the European Future: The Uses of Comparison," in Alberta M. Sbragia, ed., *Euro-Politics: Institutions and Policymaking in the "New" European Community* (Brookings, 1992), pp. 257–91.

provides sophisticated interpretations of the importance of class forces in shaping the social role of the state, directing attention to the strength of organized labor and Left political parties, or the pattern of class coalitions at critical junctures in the historical development of social programs.[3] Although the insights that emerge from this tradition are powerful, they do not fully capture the experience of large countries characterized by deep regional divisions, socially heterogeneous populations, and fragmented political institutions. Territorial politics can leave a clear imprint on the shape of the welfare state in such countries, and that role needs to be acknowledged in interpretations of the determinants of social policy.

The same is true when attention shifts to the broader functions of social policy. The welfare state has long been recognized as an instrument of social integration, capable of mediating conflicts and preserving stability in divided societies. For the most part, however, attention has focused on the role of social policy in mediating class divisions, which has been traced in detail from the days of Speenhamland and Bismarck. Many commentators on modern social policy argue that the welfare state has integrated labor into a capitalist world, reduced the scope for radical politics, and legitimated an inegalitarian social order.

In contrast, the potential of the welfare state as an instrument of national integration on a territorial basis is underexplored. National social programs create a network of intimate relations between citizens and the central government throughout the country, helping to define the boundaries of the national political community and enhancing the legitimacy of the state. In countries whose territorial integrity is not questioned, this integrative role of social policy goes largely unnoticed. In countries that are deeply divided along regional lines, however, the territorial role of the welfare state is highly salient, and much depends on the locus of program control. Social programs controlled by the central government can become instruments of nation building, helping to mediate regional tensions and strengthen the state against centrifugal forces rooted in territorial politics. Alternatively, social programs designed and controlled at the regional level can become instruments for strengthening regional cultures and enhancing the significance of local communities in

3. Gøsta Esping-Anderson, *The Three Worlds of Welfare Capitalism* (Princeton University Press, 1990); M. Shalev, "The Social Democratic Model and Beyond: Two 'Generations' of Comparative Research on the Welfare State," *Comparative Social Research*, vol. 6 (1983), pp. 315–51.

the lives of citizens, thereby reinforcing differentiation and centrifugal tendencies at the national level.

Canada is a rich case study in the subtle interplay between territorial politics and the welfare state. The combination of federal institutions, linguistic and cultural pluralism, and regional conflicts has important implications for the design of Canadian social programs. The complexity of territorial pressures makes policy outcomes particularly dependent on the attributes of formal institutions of the state and on decision rules that vary from one sector of social policy to another. In some sectors, territorial politics and multitiered institutions have increased the opportunities enjoyed by reformist forces and facilitated the expansion of the state; in other sectors, complex decision rules have created joint-decision traps that deeply constrain change.

Canadian experience also highlights the reciprocal nature of the relationship between the welfare state and territorial divisions by pointing to the potential of social policy to act as an instrument of national integration across regional and linguistic divisions. National social programs developed in the postwar years quickly emerged as important instruments of legitimation for a federal system facing serious regional challenges, and some of the most bitter battles in subsequent decades were fought over which level of government would control these levers of cultural definition. The issues surfaced again with a vengeance during the 1990s as the result of a renewed struggle over the Canadian constitution, a battle in which the continued existence of a single Canadian state seemed repeatedly at risk.

Thinking about social policy as an instrument of statecraft, to be employed in defining political communities and legitimating the structures of the state, broadens contemporary perspectives on the integrative role of welfare. This shift does nothing to deny the importance of social policy in mediating class conflicts in Western nations. It does insist, however, that state structures as well as economic systems require legitimation, and that the pervasive interactions between state and citizen implicit in modern social programs have important implications for both. Such a perspective is consistent with recent neoinstitutionalist literature, and it provides additional insights into the politics of social policy in multitiered systems, including the European Union, where an emergent supranational social policy is constrained by the massive legitimation of member states that comes from national systems of social security.

This chapter explores the relationship between territorial politics and the welfare state in Canada. In particular, it examines three broad historical periods. The first section examines the influence of federalism and territorialism on the development of the Canadian welfare state during the postwar era. The second section explores the role of the welfare state as an instrument of integration in a divided society and the resulting intergovernmental battles over control of social programs during the 1960s and 1970s. The third section turns to the contemporary period, exploring the tension between territorial conflict and the politics of conservatism in the restructuring of the Canadian welfare state. A concluding section draws together the lessons implicit in Canadian experience for our wider understanding of the role of multitiered political institutions and territorial politics in shaping the welfare state in Western nations and in supranational organizations such as the European Union.

Territorial Politics and the Postwar Welfare State

In many ways Canadian politics resembles that of other Western nations. The politics of class and new social movements gives shape and substance to debates over the social role of the state and the evolution of public policy. In addition, a new language of rights—given constitutional expression in the Charter of Rights and Freedoms adopted in 1982—increasingly conditions Canadian discourse over social issues. Nevertheless, Canadian politics is also defined by ethnic and regional divisions. The tension between English- and French-speaking communities has been an elemental feature of politics in northern North America for over two centuries; wider conflicts among the various regions of the country are as old as the federation itself.

These ancient lines of division retain contemporary force. The French-speaking community, centered primarily in the province of Quebec, remains a distinctive society that is constantly concerned about its capacity to resist the pressures for assimilation inherent in an overwhelmingly English-speaking North America. The resurgence of *Québécois* nationalism and the emergence of a potent separatist movement during the last thirty years have sometimes represented a serious threat to the survival of a single Canadian state, and inevitably welfare policy has been swept up in the constitutional struggles generated by this challenge. Regional divisions are also kept fresh by the natural conflicts of interest between the industrial heartland in central Canada and the resource-based economies of the west, and by the economic underdevelopment of Atlantic Canada. However, uneven economic development has produced different consequences for Canada than for the United States, where the low-wage economy of the South has been a brake on the development of national social programs throughout the twentieth century.[4] In Canada, poor regions have supported an expansive federal role as a means of preserving their traditional economies and communities against the forces of modernization. Their interests and expectations constitute a significant force in national welfare politics.

Federal institutions reflect and give added life to territorial politics in Canada. The constitution divides authority over social policy between the federal and provincial governments in complex ways, and responding to the social needs of a modern society has involved elaborate intergovernmental diplomacy and agreements. The crucible in which many of the country's social programs have been forged is the network of federal-provincial meetings, at the apex of which sits the First Ministers' Conference, a meeting of the prime minister and provincial premiers which in many ways resembles the Council of Ministers of the European Union. Such a decisionmaking process tends to be particularly responsive to the bureaucratic interests of governments themselves and to social and economic interests that can be defined in territorial terms. In contrast to this inbuilt sensitivity to regional claims, other social interests such as labor, women's groups, and welfare rights organizations have long complained about their relative exclusion. Canadian social programs bear the imprint of these institutions and processes, as a closer look at their development in the postwar years illustrates.

Two theories of the relationship between federalism and the role of the state compete for acceptance. The first theory sees federalism as a form of institutional fragmentation that constrains the role of the state. Independent action at the regional level is restrained by interregional economic competition and by the recurring fiscal imbalance to which federations are prone; and joint action by the central and regional governments requires complex intergovernmental decisionmaking, which favors those least interested in change. According to this interpretation, then, federalism in effect is another form of checks and balances that limits bold action and entrenches an incremental approach to reform. The second theory holds that innovative policies can be introduced more

4. Jill Quadagno, *The Transformation of Old Age Security: Class and Politics in the American Welfare State* (University of Chicago Press, 1988); Jill Quadagno, "Race, Class and Gender in the United States Welfare State," *American Sociological Review*, vol. 55 (1990), pp. 11–28; and Margaret Weir, Ann Shola Orloff, and Theda Skocpol, eds., *The Politics of Social Policy in the United States* (Princeton University Press, 1988).

rapidly in federal states than in unitary ones. The regions of a large country are always at different stages of economic and political development, and innovative ideas are more socially appropriate and politically acceptable in some parts of the country than in others. The genius of federalism is precisely that such regions can experiment with innovations, and the seeds of radicalism can then spread as other regions become convinced by example.[5]

Both of these interpretations find resonance in the history of the Canadian welfare state. In the early years divided jurisdiction was a barrier to broad-scale reform. In 1937 the courts struck down a package of social insurance programs, finding them beyond the authority of the federal Parliament, and a similarly broad package foundered on the shoals of wider federal-provincial conflicts in 1945. However, the federal system did accommodate incremental expansion during the war and postwar decades, largely through an expansion of the role of the central government. The political and financial resources of the provincial governments had been sapped, first by the depression and then by the centralizing impulses of the Second World War. Compared with earlier periods in the nation's history, provincial leaders were less committed to, or capable of, resisting an expansion of the federal role. The constitution was amended on three occasions to give the federal government jurisdiction over unemployment insurance and pensions, and the federal government effectively exploited the mechanism of conditional grants to initiate a succession of nationwide programs in health care, social services, and welfare, all of which were provincial areas of jurisdiction.

The social policy regime that was built up in this way has several distinctive characteristics that flowed in part from the structures of federalism. Most important is what might be described as the ideological bifurcation of the Canadian welfare state.[6] Income maintenance programs are predominantly liberal in conception. Public benefits provide a basic floor of social protection, but leave considerable scope for the development of private benefits through collective bargaining and per-

---

5. For a more general discussion of these two views, see Keith Banting, *The Welfare State and Canadian Federalism*, 2d ed., (McGill-Queen's University Press, 1987). The classic Canadian statement of the second interpretation remains Pierre Trudeau, "The Practice and Theory of Federalism," in Michael Oliver, ed., *Social Purpose for Canada* (University of Toronto Press, 1961).

6. For an effective statement of this feature of the Canadian welfare state, see Carolyn J. Tuohy, "Social Policy: Two Worlds," in Michael Atkinson, ed., *Governing Canada: Political Institutions and Public Policy* (Harcourt Brace Jovanovich, 1993).

sonal savings, which are further encouraged through substantial subsidies delivered through the tax system. The structure of pensions, in particular, reflects this liberal ethos. The pattern in health care, however, is different. Canada has a universal system of public health insurance that covers all essential medical and hospital services without deductibles, user fees, or significant out-of-pocket expenses. As a result, there is no parallel private sector in basic health care; private health insurance is limited to supplementary items not covered by the public program. The basic organizing principle is therefore universal, comprehensive public health insurance.

This striking contrast between health care and pensions is explained in part by the different forms of multitiered decisionmaking through which the country makes choices in these two sectors. Health care is governed by a system of *multiple, independent action points,* which allows both the national and provincial governments to take independent action, without the concurrence of other governments. Contributory pensions, however, are governed by a system of *joint decisionmaking,* which requires the agreement of a substantial number of governments before any action can be taken. The implications of these two systems differ significantly.

The multiple, independent action points in health care created opportunities for innovation at the regional level.[7] Under the terms of the constitution, health care is a provincial responsibility, and proposals for federal action have always centered on shared-cost programs. During the Federal-Provincial Conference on Postwar Reconstruction in 1945, the federal government presented proposals for a shared-cost national health insurance program, but the proposal sank when provincial governments rejected the associated proposals on intergovernmental finances. Yet national failure did not block action. Three provinces—Saskatchewan, British Columbia, and Alberta—acted unilaterally to establish public insurance for hospital services and mounted a protracted campaign for federal support. When more provinces moved toward the model established by these provincial leaders, Ottawa finally agreed. In 1957 it established a

7. For a fuller discussion of federalism and Canadian health insurance, see Gratton Gray, "The Politics of Stealth," *Policy Options,* vol. 11 (1990), pp. 17–29; Carolyn J. Tuohy, "Federalism and Canadian Health Policy," in William M. Chandler and Christian W. Zöllner, eds., *Challenges to Federalism: Policy-Making in Canada and the Federal Republic of Germany* (Queen's University, Institute of Intergovermental Relations, 1989); and Malcolm G. Taylor, *Health Insurance and Canadian Public Policy: The Seven Decisions that Created the Canadian Health Insurance System,* 2d ed. (McGill-Queen's University Press, 1987).

national hospital insurance program, with cost-sharing between the two levels of government.

A similar cycle extended public insurance to all medical care, including physician services. In 1962 the left-wing New Democratic Party government of Saskatchewan introduced a comprehensive medicare plan, despite a determined doctors' strike. This cathartic experience set the model for national action. The right of patients to choose their own doctors and the preservation of a fee-for-service system, essential elements of the compromise that ended the strike, became the starting point for subsequent debates in the country. More important, however, the Saskatchewan experience soon demonstrated that such a plan was feasible in practice, easing the intensity of opposition elsewhere. In particular, because they no longer had to provide uncompensated care, doctors' incomes in Saskatchewan rose significantly in the early years of the program, which reduced the likelihood of militant resistance to a national program.[8] The early success of the Saskatchewan plan reinforced the commitment of reformist forces in national politics to universal health insurance. The stage was set with the 1963 election of the federal Liberal Party, which was committed to universal medicare on a nationwide basis.

Conservative interests continued to oppose universal public health care, but the intergovernmental decisionmaking rules did not give them additional leverage at the national level. Private insurance plans were expanding rapidly at the time, and the Canadian Medical Association and the private insurance industry advocated that government action be limited to the "hard to insure," such as the elderly and the poor. Had this position prevailed, medical health insurance in Canada would closely resemble the current system in the United States. This approach received powerful support from a number of conservative governments in the country, including the government of Ontario, the largest province. Ontario actually introduced a plan for the hard to insure, and the premier denounced the federal medicare plan as "a Machiavellian scheme that is . . . one of the greatest political frauds that has been perpetrated on the people of this country."[9] Nevertheless, the rules and norms of the intergovernmental process did not give Ontario a veto. Once the federal plan was in place and Ontario residents were paying federal taxes to support the program in other provinces, Ontario had little choice but to accede and adopt the universal model.

8. Tuohy, "Federalism."
9. Taylor, *Health Insurance*, p. 375.

On balance, then, institutional fragmentation facilitated the expansion of public health care after 1945. Federalism provided opportunities for the political Left to innovate at the regional level, and the structure of intergovernmental decisionmaking at the national level did not provide any strategic advantages to conservative forces.

Joint decisionmaking over contributory pensions in Canada shows the opposite face of federalism. This sector is characterized by formidable institutional barriers, which do give conservative forces additional protection from expansionist pressures. In 1951 Canada adopted a universal flat-rate retirement benefit known as Old Age Security. The universal flat benefits tended to be low, however, and could not meet the retirement income expectations of the better organized elements of the working class and the growing middle class. As a result, organized labor and other interests began to campaign for the addition of a contributory pension with earnings-related benefits.

In this case multitiered institutions limited the scope of policy innovation. Once again the same federal Liberal government that introduced medicare took the lead in the mid-1960s, and once again the Conservative government of Ontario became an important rallying point for conservative forces, including the private-pension industry which is overwhelmingly based in that province. In contrast to the case of health care, the decision rules that governed the pension sector placed Ontario in a much stronger position. A prior constitutional amendment expanding federal jurisdiction was needed before the full contributory plan could be implemented. According to the conventions governing constitutional changes at the time, unanimous provincial consent was required. Ontario therefore had a veto over the constitutional change and consequently over the pension plan. The province accepted the desirability of a contributory plan, but balked at the more expansive and redistributive plan that the federal government and Quebec wanted. Negotiations produced an outcome that was much more congenial to Ontario than that for health care. The new Canada Pension Plan was a limited program that left substantial room for the private sector, and—more important—Ontario won a complex set of rules that would constrain future changes in it.

The rules governing reform of the Canada Pension Plan create a process analogous to the joint-decision trap analyzed by Fritz Scharpf.[10] Change requires the agreement of the federal government and at least

---

10. Fritz W. Scharpf, "The Joint-Decision Trap: Lessons from German Federalism and European Integration," *Public Administration*, vol. 66 (1988), pp. 239–78.

seven provinces representing two-thirds of the population, making the Canada Pension Plan more difficult to amend than most sections of the constitution of the country.[11] The federal government has a veto over changes to the Canada Pension Plan; Ontario also has a veto by virtue of its share of the Canadian population; and several combinations of other provinces can block change. In addition, because Quebec decided to operate its own pension plan, the Canada and Quebec plans need to be coordinated, giving Quebec additional weight in the process. Here is a joint-decision process of withering complexity. Its effects are compounded by another feature: any surplus in the Canada Pension Plan fund is loaned to provincial governments at an attractive rate of interest, making them especially cautious about benefit increases that would reduce the size of the fund.[12]

These decision rules have tended to insulate contributory pensions from political pressures for expansion, pressures that in the United States led to a substantial expansion of the role of social security after its adoption.[13] In Canada, increases in benefits have been minor and focused primarily on supplementary payments for the disabled and survivors, rather than on the core retirement benefit; changes in contribution rates have been designed to stabilize the fund rather than to expand the program's role.[14] In Canada, electoral pressures are displaced onto the Guaranteed Income Supplement (GIS), an income-tested supplement that is fully under federal control. The GIS was introduced initially as a temporary measure that was expected to fade away naturally as the Canada Pension Plan matured. The supplement was repeatedly enriched in real terms, however, usually just before or after an election, and it now represents a major component of the system, providing some support to close to half of the elderly population, including many who had average earnings before retirement. Nevertheless, an income-tested supplement is

11. Under the constitutional amending formula adopted in 1982, most changes require the approval of the federal government and seven provinces representing *half* of the population. As a result, the formula does not give a veto to any individual province.

12. For a fuller discussion of this joint-decision process, see Keith Banting, "The Decision Rules: Federalism and Pensions Reform," in David W. Conklin, Jaclynn H. Bennett, and Thomas J. Courchene, eds., *Pensions Today and Tomorrow: Background Studies* (Toronto: Ontario Economic Council, 1984); and Keith Banting, "Institutional Conservatism: Federalism and Pension Reform," in Jacqueline S. Ismael, ed., *Canadian Social Welfare Policy: Federal and Provincial Dimensions* (McGill-Queen's University Press, 1985).

13. Martha Derthick, *Policymaking for Social Security* (Brookings, 1979).

14. These institutional constraints were most visible during the battle over the "child rearing drop-out clause" in the 1970s and the "great pensions debate" in the late 1970s and early 1980s. See Banting, "Institutional Conservatism."

a much more limited instrument than a broad, earnings-related insurance program such as the Canada Pension Plan.

A complete explanation of the differences between the evolution of health care and pensions in Canada would require a fuller analysis of the structure of interests and ideologies that shaped the aspirations of the contending forces in the two sectors.[15] Nevertheless, the multitiered structures of the federal system are clearly an essential part of the story. In health care, multiple independent action points gave invaluable opportunities to reformist forces; in the pensions sector, joint decisionmaking entrenched a limited role for government with almost constitutional firmness.

The Welfare State and National Integration

During the 1970s and 1980s, territorial politics became more intense in Canada. The separatist party, the *Parti Québécois*, took power in Quebec in 1976, as economic problems fueled bitter battles between the federal government and the provinces in western Canada, especially over energy policy. Increasingly, the national agenda was dominated by a deadly serious struggle over constitutional reform, in which the powers of the federal government and the unity of the country were at risk. In this context, the welfare state that had emerged in previous decades was increasingly seen as an instrument of national integration. Medicare, pensions, and unemployment insurance created a set of benefits and rights that were founded not on language or region but on a common national citizenship. They represented spheres of shared experience in a society marked by considerable regional diversity, and they tied the interests of individuals across the country to the federal state. Consequently, national social programs could engage a pan-Canadian constituency. Given the economic structure of the country, monetary policy, trade policy, and energy policy inevitably pit one region against another; given the ethnic and linguistic structure of the country, cultural policies can generate similar conflicts. On social policy, however, Ottawa can fashion appeals that cut across territorial divides and reinforce the legitimacy of the federal state.

This integrative dynamic can be seen in the different responses of two regions of the country to the postwar expansion of the federal role in

15. Tuohy, "Social Policy."

social policy. Atlantic Canada and Quebec represent different forms of territorial distinctiveness: economic and cultural. For the poor provinces of Atlantic Canada, federal social programs are an instrument of interregional equality, providing a level of benefits and services that could not be sustained without federal intervention. These provinces therefore have long been staunch defenders of a strong role for the central government in the federation. In contrast, Quebec has seen federal social programs as an "external" cultural instrument that mutes its social distinctiveness. The result has been an intergovernmental struggle between Ottawa and Quebec City for control of the state-building potential inherent in modern social programs, a war that has been waged intermittently for twenty years. Both of these reactions deserve fuller attention.

Atlantic Canada and Interregional Redistribution

Social programs and the taxes that support them alter the distribution of the nation's product in a variety of ways. Income is shifted over the life cycle of a single individual; among individuals in the same social class; among different social classes; between men and women; among ethnic, linguistic, and racial groups; and among people living in different regions of the country. Which dimensions of this complex pattern become the subject of debate and conflict depends on the underlying pattern of political cleavages in the society. In most Western nations, controversy focuses primarily on redistribution among social classes, and a rich body of literature tracks this dimension of the welfare state. Much less attention is paid to patterns of interregional redistribution. Yet as Gunnar Myrdal pointed out almost forty years ago, the development of social security and the advent of income taxes are "two mighty policy trends which have forcefully contributed to equalization between regions" in Western nations generally.[16] Stuart Holland makes the same point: the welfare state "is the submerged but massive part of the iceberg of state interventions" that favors poor regions.[17]

The intensity of linguistic and regional divisions in Canada ensures that this side of the welfare state does not go unnoticed. In the words of a 1940 royal commission report, "The unequal distribution of the national income as between people of different regions may excite feelings

16. Gunnar Myrdal, *Rich Lands and Poor: The Road to World Prosperity* (Harper and Row, 1957).
17. Stuart Holland, *Capital versus the Regions* (New York: St. Martin's Press, 1976).

Table 8-1. *Per Capita Federal Income Expenditures, Canada and the Provinces, 1991–92*

Canadian dollars

Province	Income support programs	Insurance programs	Total
Newfoundland	1,137	2,262	2,473
Prince Edward Island	1,334	2,188	2,524
Nova Scotia	1,171	1,621	2,049
New Brunswick	1,199	1,749	2,207
Quebec	939	817	1,305
Ontario	846	1,200	1,440
Manitoba	1,214	1,097	1,717
Saskatchewan	1,270	1,035	1,680
Alberta	820	989	1,361
British Columbia	979	1,259	1,816
Canada	947	1,139	1,540

Source: Data supplied by Human Resources Development Canada (Ottawa).

quite as dangerous to national unity as those aroused between different income groups."[18] The expansion of the role of the central government during and after the Second World War transformed social policy into a powerful instrument of interregional redistribution. As long as welfare was a municipal or provincial responsibility, redistribution took place within the confines of the local economy; the poorest regions always had the greatest needs but the fewest resources with which to respond. Centralization of responsibility has generated significant interregional flows: the population of poor regions has larger proportions of needy people who benefit from federal social programs, whereas taxpayers in those same regions provide a smaller proportion of the taxes that support them.

Interregional transfers are implicit in several federal social programs. First, as table 8-1 indicates, direct income transfers to individuals (such as pensions, family benefits, and unemployment insurance) provide higher per capita benefits in the poorer provinces of Atlantic Canada, that is, Newfoundland, Prince Edward Island, Nova Scotia, and New Brunswick. This is particularly the case for unemployment insurance, which has been a much larger program than its counterpart in the United States.[19] Unlike the American program, unemployment insurance in Can-

18. *Report of the Royal Commission on Dominion-Provincial Relations*, bk. 2 (Ottawa: Queen's Printer, 1940), p. 10.

19. For example, in 1987 government expenditures for unemployment benefits represented 3.2 percent of gross domestic product in Canada, but only 0.4 percent in the United States. See Organization for Economic Cooperation and Development, *OECD in Figures: Statistics on the Member Countries*, supplement to *OECD Observer*, no. 158 (June–July 1989), pp. 16–17.

Table 8-2. *Net Interprovincial Transfers Implicit in Unemployment Insurance, 1992*[a]

Province	Total net transfer (millions of dollars)	Per capita net transfer (dollars)
Newfoundland	+818.5	+1,415
Prince Edward Island	+149.0	+1,142
Nova Scotia	+326.7	+360
New Brunswick	+478.4	+656
Quebec	+1,538.7	+222
Ontario	−1,701.0	−168
Manitoba	−132.2	−112
Saskatchewan	−86.1	−87
Alberta	−366.4	−143
British Columbia	+41.7	+13

Source: Data supplied by Human Resources Development Canada (Ottawa).
a. Net transfers calculated as expenditures in each province minus premiums collected in that province. Gains and losses do not balance as the Unemployment Insurance program operated at a deficit in 1992.

ada is an exclusively federal program. It provides extended benefits in regions with high unemployment, and it does not rely on experience rating by industry, a feature that further increases the implicit transfer to poor regions with highly seasonal employment. Unemployment payments therefore go well beyond the role of insurance in poor regions—they have become a general program of income supplementation. Benefits paid under unemployment insurance are a significant part of the annual income of many workers in forestry, fishing, and tourism, and they are critical to the survival of many of the smaller communities that dot Atlantic Canada. Table 8-2 outlines the role of the program in the different provinces.

Federal transfers to provincial governments also benefit poor regions disproportionately. Part of this dividend flows through federal support for provincial social programs, including social assistance, welfare services, health insurance plans, and postsecondary education. The largest contribution, however, flows through a program of equalization grants, which provides untied federal payments to the governments of the seven poorer provinces, so that they can provide average levels of public services without resorting to above-average levels of taxation. Table 8-3 shows the equalizing effects of these federal grants on the fiscal capacity of the provinces. The powerful redistribution of fiscal capacity accomplished by these grants protects provincially delivered social programs from exclusive dependence on the strength of the regional economy.

Just as the welfare state mitigates the extent of class inequality generated by a market economy, social programs also mitigate the regional

Table 8-3. *Index of Fiscal Capacity of Provincial Governments,*
1990–91[a]

Percent

Province	Before equalization	After equalization (preceiling)	After equalization (postceiling)
Newfoundland	62.4	92.5	91.2
Prince Edward Island	63.8	92.5	91.2
Nova Scotia	75.0	92.5	91.2
New Brunswick	70.4	92.5	91.2
Quebec	85.6	92.5	91.2
Ontario	110.9	103.2	104.2
Manitoba	79.3	92.5	91.2
Saskatchewan	85.8	92.5	91.2
Alberta	133.0	123.8	125.0
British Columbia	105.2	97.9	98.8

Source: Paul Hobsen and France St Hilaire, *Reforming Federal Arrangements: Towards Sustainable Federalism* (Montreal: Institute for Research on Public Policy, 1993), table 2.
a. The growth in total annual equalization grants is subject to a ceiling corresponding to the rate of growth in the Gross Domestic Product. *Actual* fiscal capacity is therefore represented by postceiling figures.

inequality inherent in uneven economic development. Such interregional flows are hardly unique to Canada, but the political salience of the Canadian pattern does appear distinctive. The interregional transfers implicit in social programs undoubtedly preserve occupations and entire communities that would otherwise disappear. This is especially true for the fishing industry in Atlantic Canada and the many small communities that dot the eastern shores of the country. The welfare state has altered the patterns of labor adjustment in the Canadian economy, preserving a "stay" option for thousands who would otherwise have to leave Atlantic Canada. Not surprisingly, these programs have come under substantial criticism for that very reason, but they are nonetheless deeply embedded in the politics of Canadian social policy.

It is also not surprising that Atlantic Canadian politicians have been among the leading proponents of a strong central government within the federal system. During the recurring negotiations over constitutional reform and the division of taxing authority, when federal authority has been under sustained pressure, the Atlantic provinces repeatedly resisted proposals that would weaken the central government. Indeed, as one analyst of federal-provincial diplomacy noted in the early 1970s, poorer provinces often advocate a stronger federal government than do federal officials themselves.[20] The same instinct was alive in the late 1980s during

20. Richard Simeon, *Federal-Provincial Diplomacy: The Making of Recent Policy in Canada* (University of Toronto Press, 1972).

debate over a set of constitutional proposals known as the Meech Lake Accord, when political leaders from the poorer provinces again worried about elements of the package that would weaken the federal government; one proposal would have restricted federal spending power, making it more difficult for Ottawa to initiate new conditional-grant programs.[21] The poorer provinces know that the well-being of their regions and the strength of their own provincial governments depend on the redistributive capacities of the federal state.

Quebec and Competitive State-Building

Governments in Canada have long recognized the potential of social programs as instruments of statecraft, to be harnessed to nation-building agendas. This can be seen most clearly in the protracted struggle between the federal government and the province of Quebec for the commanding position in the politics of welfare during the second half of the 1960s and continuing into the 1970s. The intensity of these disputes can be understood only by appreciating the extent to which the two governments vied to retain the loyalty of Quebecers and to protect and enhance their institutional power. In short, Ottawa and Quebec were engaged in a process of competitive state-building.

Quebec's challenge to federal leadership in social policy built steadily through the postwar period. In 1956 a Quebec royal commission described federal social programs as a form of cultural imperialism that, unless checked, would erode the province's distinctive character: "As far as the assimilation of French Canada is concerned, thirty years of social history will thus have had more effect than a century and a half of political history."[22] The commission recommended the transfer of all social programs to the province, together with appropriate fiscal compensation. Although the traditional Catholic conception of social policy that had underpinned the commission's views was soon swept aside, all Quebec governments since then have subscribed, with more or less intensity, to the view that social policy is important to the protection of the distinctive French-speaking community in North America. In the words

---

21. Simeon, *Federal-Provincial Diplomacy*; and Donald L. Brown, "Sea-Change in Newfoundland," in Ronald L. Watts and Douglas M. Brown, eds., *Canada: The State of the Federation, 1990* (Kingston: Queen's University, Institute of Intergovernmental Relations, 1990).

22. Royal Commission of Inquiry on Constitutional Problems, *Report*, 3 vols. (Quebec: Editeur officiel, 1956), p. 130.

of the Quebec premier in 1971, "Income security is far from being merely a means of redistributing wealth; it touches the very fibre of a culture."[23] Beginning in the mid-1960s, the province struggled to recapture jurisdiction lost to the federal government during previous decades, and insisted that it have exclusive control over any new programs.

The federal government was equally conscious of the power of social policy. In rejecting Quebec's early demands for the transfer of federal income security programs to the province, the federal government emphasized the importance of social policy in sustaining a pan-Canadian political community: "The sense of Canadian community is at once the source of income redistribution between people and regions in Canada and the result of such measures. It is the sense of community which makes it possible for Parliament to tax residents of higher income regions for the purpose of making payments to persons in lower income regions. And it is the willingness of people in higher income regions to pay these taxes which gives additional meaning in the minds of those who receive the payments to the concept of a Canadian community."[24] Federal authorities were deeply conscious of the extent to which the power of the central government was rooted in the welfare state. Since virtually all other public services are provincially delivered, income transfers represent one of the few direct links between Ottawa and the public, a link that ties millions of Canadians to the strength of the federal government rather than to their provincial governments. Deprived of these client relationships, the federal presence in the everyday life of Canadians would fade even more. In addition, Ottawa's economic power is embedded in the welfare state. Social expenditures and the associated taxes constitute a substantial portion of the federal government's fiscal role, and to transfer these responsibilities and taxes to the provincial level would represent a transfer of economic power as well.

With institutional agendas on both sides clearly set, it was jurisdiction over social policy—not the actual substance of programs—that sparked some of the sharpest conflicts in the postwar era. In a succession of major battles, usually accompanied by press headlines predicting that the survival of the country was at stake, the two sides clashed repeatedly over control of the welfare state. During the mid-1960s the fight centered on existing conditional-grant programs and the new contributory pensions plan; in 1971 a major package of constitutional reforms known as the

23. Quoted in Banting, *Welfare State*, p. 130.
24. *Income Security and Social Services* (Ottawa: Information Canada, 1969), p. 68.

Victoria Charter fell apart over the issue of formal authority over social programs; in the mid-1970s jurisdictional skirmishing plagued intergovernmental negotiations over a guaranteed annual income; and in the late 1970s another round of constitutional discussions got stuck on elements of family policy.

As often happens in political life, the series of adjustments that resulted from these protracted battles satisfied neither side. The federal government did accommodate itself to a significant degree of decentralization in shared-cost programs. In 1965 Quebec opted out of a number of national shared-cost programs, including hospital insurance, social assistance, and vocational training, and received additional tax room so that it could operate those programs on its own.[25] The victory was largely symbolic, however, since the arrangement was deemed an interim one and the province agreed to maintain its existing obligations under the various programs and to account for expenditures to Ottawa. Yet it was a harbinger of the future: by the late 1970s federal support for health care and postsecondary education in all provinces had been transformed into a block grant, with less detailed federal scrutiny of provincial actions.

Quebec also exercised its constitutional authority in 1965 to mount a contributory pension plan separate from the Canada Pension Plan. The Quebec Pension Plan illustrates the ways in which control of social policy advanced the economic and not only the cultural agenda of Quebec nationalists. The province established a partially funded plan so that it could build a pool of public capital in the early years to invest in the economic development of the province. The government agency that manages the fund, the *Caisse de dépôt et de placement du Québec*, soon emerged as a critical purchaser of the bonds of public corporations engaged in major development projects in the province, especially *Hydro Québec*; it also became the owner of the largest portfolio of common stocks in Canada. For Quebec nationalists, the *Caisse* symbolized a growing *Québécois* role in the world of finance—a world previously dominated by English-speakers—and a key element in a larger provincial industrial strategy. Control over social security, then, became a component of state-building at the provincial level.

In other areas, however, the federal government resisted Quebec de-

25. The financial compensation for any province opting out of a shared-cost program mostly took the form of a transfer of tax points, according to which the federal government reduced its tax rates in the province and the provincial government simultaneously raised its taxes by the same amount.

mands, including demands that Ottawa surrender formal jurisdiction over a number of income security programs. Income transfers are instruments of statecraft, and states do not surrender such instruments willingly. Their political importance was etched more sharply during a referendum on Quebec sovereignty in 1980. The *Parti Québécois* government called the referendum to seek support for its policy of "sovereignty-association," according to which Quebec would become a sovereign state but maintain close economic ties to Canada. During the referendum campaign, federal ministers charged that independence would threaten the standard of living of Quebecers, and that a sovereign Quebec would not be able to sustain the social programs that Quebecers enjoyed as citizens of Canada. The federal minister of National Health and Welfare pointed to the interregional transfers implicit in federal social programs that would disappear, and plunged on to warn elderly voters that their guaranteed income supplement would probably disappear. The *Parti Québécois* protested these tactics vehemently, but still found itself on the defensive.[26] The politics of social policy represented only part of the federalist campaign during the referendum, and it is difficult to assess its contribution to the defeat of the proposal for sovereignty. In any event, however, the battle highlighted the strategic role that politicians attribute to social policy in the life and death of states.[27]

Territorial Politics and Restructuring the Welfare State

The 1980s and 1990s have witnessed major changes in the politics of social policy in Western nations. Economic restructuring on a global level, the emergence of strong regional trading blocks, a shift in the political balance between business and labor, the fiscal weakness of the state, and the election of conservative governments have all combined to redefine political discourse and redirect the evolution of social policy. Canadian politics have been reshaped by these forces as well. The election of a Conservative federal government in 1984 brought to power a party

26. In fact, the "White Paper on Sovereignty-Association," published by the *Parti Québécois* government, pledged to maintain "acquired rights" to family allowances and old age pensions, but no similar commitment was made to maintain standards under unemployment insurance. See *Quebec-Canada: A New Deal* (Quebec: Editeur officiel, 1978).

27. Social programs also played an important role in the only other referendum on the territorial dimensions of the country, namely, when Newfoundland voted to join Canada in 1949.

that was committed to an agenda that gave priority to international economic competitiveness, tax reform, and deficit reduction; it was less enthusiastic about social programs. During its first term in office, the government's social policy was relatively muted, but this tentativeness faded with its reelection in 1988. The Conservatives dropped plans for expansion of child care, reduced unemployment benefits, clawed back some pensions from upper-income recipients, restructured child benefits, froze transfers to the provinces for health care and postsecondary education, and restrained the rate of growth in its support for provincial social assistance programs.[28]

As always, however, the Canadian version of the contemporary ethos has also been shaped by territorial conflicts and the politics of national unity. At one level, territorial politics have constrained the impact of conservatism and protected the interests of poor regions in several sensitive programs. But at a deeper level, the forces at work in Canada threaten to weaken the larger integrative role of national social programs. The combined weight of conservatism and fiscal weakness in Ottawa, added to the continuing jurisdictional struggles in key policy areas, is narrowing the federal dimension of the welfare state. These pressures did not suddenly disappear with the defeat of the Conservative government in 1993, and the politics of expenditure restraint continues to shape social programs under the Liberals. The result has been an anxious search for mechanisms to reinforce the integrative dimension of social policy, one sign of which was the sudden transfer of the idea of a Social Charter from the European context to the heart of Canadian political debate in the 1990s.

Territorialism and Conservatism

Unlike their British counterparts, conservatives in Canada cannot hope to construct a winning national coalition without heavy support from poorer regions, which rely on the redistributive power of the federal

28. For fuller discussions of the social policies of the federal Conservative government, see Keith Banting, "Neoconservatism in an Open Economy: The Social Role of the Canadian State," *International Political Science Review*, vol. 13 (1992), pp. 149–70; Ken Battle and Sherri Torjman, *Federal Social Programs: Setting the Record Straight* (Ottawa: Caledon Institute of Social Policy 1993); Gray, "Politics of Stealth"; and James J. Rice and Michael J. Prince, "Lowering the Safety Net and Weakening the Bonds of Nationhood," in *How Ottawa Spends, 1993–94: A More Democratic Canada?* (Ottawa: Carleton University Press, 1993).

government. Even the most conservative caucus and cabinet in Ottawa have senior members from poorer parts of the country who must protect the interests of their regions if they wish to survive politically.[29] Moreover, conservative provincial governments invariably fight hard—and effectively—against cuts in federal social programs that would hurt their regions. Clearly, Canada's territorial dimension precludes a neat polarization of the politics of social policy along the axes of class and ideology alone.

The contradictions between territorialism and conservatism are illustrated by the battle over unemployment insurance. In other countries, proposals to reduce unemployment benefits tend to pit conservative politicians against organized labor; in Canada, the primary opponents of such cuts are politicians from poor regions. A federal advisory committee in 1986 recommended a radical restructuring of unemployment insurance, including the elimination of benefits targeted to areas of high unemployment. The proposals were attacked ferociously in poorer regions, especially Atlantic Canada, and senior ministers from that region quickly distanced themselves from the recommendation.[30] After considerable delay the government did limit benefits, but in ways that actually *increased* regional differentials. In regions with low levels of unemployment, individuals were required to work for twenty weeks before becoming eligible for benefits, and benefits were limited to thirty-five weeks. In areas of high unemployment, the minimum qualifying period remained at ten weeks, the maximum benefit at fifty weeks. As one commentator observed, "From a neo-conservative point of view, this pattern is the exact opposite of what is desirable. UI benefits are collected most easily in the areas of the country with the lowest labor demand, thereby reducing the movement of workers to areas of higher demand for labour."[31] Unemployment insurance was subjected to further incremental reductions in the early 1990s, but the basic principle of regionally varied benefits has remained. In Canada, conservative logic bends to regional politics.

Sensitivity to regional inequality also constrained retrenchment in some intergovernmental transfers. Federal equalization grants to poorer

29. This pattern is not restricted to social policy. Regional concerns also constrained the enthusiasm of the federal Conservative cabinet for proposals for sweeping privatization and expenditure cuts more generally. See Donald J. Savoie, *The Politics of Public Spending in Canada* (University of Toronto, 1990), pp. 141–45, 264–66.

30. Savoie, *Politics of Public Spending*.

31. Bruce Smardon, "The Federal Welfare State and the Politics of Retrenchment in Canada," *Journal of Canadian Studies*, vol. 26 (Summer 1991), p. 130.

provinces, which enable those provinces to supply public services in line with national norms, have survived reasonably intact. A ceiling on the rate of growth in these payments has had only a marginal impact on the extent of fiscal equalization, as table 8-3 indicates. Moreover, equalization grants were the only social program exempt from cuts in the very tough budget introduced by the Liberal government in 1995. Similarly, when the Conservatives placed a cap of 5 percent on the annual rate of growth in federal support for provincial social welfare programs in 1990, the poorer provinces were exempted from the restriction. Admittedly, the rate of increase in welfare costs was actually greatest in the richer provinces, especially in Ontario, where programs were expanding and unemployment was serious during the recession of the early 1990s. Nevertheless, the fact that federal support for social assistance in poorer provinces remained open-ended throughout the Conservative years is a testament to the power of territorial politics in Canada.

The Fading of the Federal Role

Although territorial politics have protected the interests of poorer provinces in several critical programs, there is growing unease about the future of federal social programs as integrative instruments that bind a divided nation together. Fiscal constraint at the center and continued federal-provincial jurisdictional battles together have begun to narrow the federal presence in social policy.

Federal expenditure restraint is in tension with the politics of national integration. As part of the effort to control the deficit, every federal budget after 1986 increased transfers to the provinces for health care and postsecondary education by less than the rate of inflation; the 1991 budget went further and announced that support would be frozen completely until 1994–95, and the 1995 budget shows even sharper cuts over the next couple of years.[32] In the words of Tom Courchene, Canadians are living through a "profound *de facto* change in the division of powers" in the federal system.[33]

Fiscal decentralization weakens the nationalizing role of the welfare state. At the level of program design, restraint clearly limits federal influ-

32. *Budget Plan: Including Supplementary Information and Notice of Ways and Means Notions* (Ottawa: Ministry of Finance, 1995).

33. Thomas J. Courchene, *In Praise of Renewed Federalism* (Toronto: C. D. Howe Institute, 1991), p. 83.

ence over provincial policies. In the health sector, for example, federal transfers are conditional on provincial acceptance of five basic principles that guarantee universal accessibility to a comprehensive, public system of health care. In 1984, amid concern that growing extra-billing by doctors and user fees in hospitals was undermining universal access,[34] Parliament adopted the Canada Health Act, which reinforces the five principles of medicare and authorizes the federal government to withhold part of the cash transfer to any province that does not uphold them. The legislation stemmed a trend toward extra-billing and hospital user fees in basic medical services.[35]

The decline in federal support for health care is likely to weaken Ottawa's ability to enforce these principles. If the formula governing the size of the transfer in recent years is continued by the Liberal government, the federal cash payment to the provinces will slowly disappear altogether.[36] Figure 8-1 shows the projected decline in the cash payment under the existing assumptions.[37] Critics fear that the disappearance of the leverage implicit in the cash payment will lead to the erosion of the national health system, with some regions opting for user fees, restricting the range of covered medical services, and expanding the role of private insurance. During the summer of 1995 an active debate emerged within the Liberal government about the wisdom of allowing the cash contribution to fall to zero. Even if the transfer is stabilized at some point in the future, however, the federal share of total provincial health expenditures will have been considerably eroded, inevitably reducing Ottawa's infuence over provincial decisions.

This pattern is being replicated in the area of social assistance. The federal Canada Assistance Plan, which until recently provided support to

34. *Extra-billing* is a term of art, referring to bills sent to the patient by the physician, *on top of* the bill to the provincial medical plan.

35. Carolyn J. Tuohy, "Medicine and the State in Canada," *Canadian Journal of Political Science*, vol. 21 (1988), pp. 267–96.

36. Federal support for health care and postsecondary education has two parts: a tax transfer and a cash transfer. The tax transfer took effect in 1977, when the federal government lowered its taxes and the provinces simultaneously raised their taxes by the same amount. The cash transfer is calculated each year by determining the total entitlement and then subtracting the revenues raised by the province from the transferred taxes. The important point is that the cash portion is a residual. As the value of the tax transfer rises, the annual cash transfer shrinks. For a succinct explanation, see National Council of Welfare, *Funding Health and Higher Education: Danger Looming* (Ottawa, 1991).

37. Under the existing formula, the cash payment disappears first for Quebec, because of a special intergovernmental agreement that weights its transfer more heavily toward the tax component.

Figure 8-1. *Total Federal Cash Transfers to the Provinces for Health, Postsecondary Education, Welfare, and Social Services, 1980–2012*[a]

Billions of constant 1995 dollars

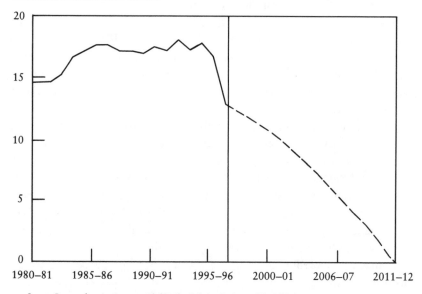

Source: Data and projections provided by the Caledon Institute of Social Policy.
a. Data for 1980–81 to 1996–97 combine expenditures under the Established Program Financing and the Canada Assistance Plan. Projections beyond 1996–97 are for the combined block grant, the Canada Health and Social Transfer, announced in the 1995 federal budget.

provincial welfare programs, was a more flexible instrument than the Canada Health Act, imposing less comprehensive conditions on provinces. Nevertheless, it did require provinces to offer support to all persons in need, to establish formal appeal procedures for recipients, and to avoid residency requirements for social assistance. Following the 1995 budget introduced by the Liberal government, however, this conditional grant was folded into a new general block grant, known as the Canada Health and Social Transfer; only the prohibition against residency requirements in social assistance was retained.[38] The ability of the federal government to enforce even this condition over time depends on the Liberals' willingness to reverse the decline in the federal cash contribution that also threatens the Canada Health Act.

Fiscal decentralization thus raises the prospect of growing regional diversity in Canadian social programs, but an even more fundamental outcome stands out: the erosion of federal support for major social pro-

38. *Budget Plan.*

grams such as health care, university education, and social welfare reduces the stake that Canadians have in the continued strength of the central government and of the federation itself. Federal ministers would have greater difficulty today in convincing Quebecers that the quality of their health care and postsecondary education hinges on remaining part of Canada. Decentralization of responsibility for the social needs of the country inevitably weakens the integrative role of the welfare state.

Fiscal decentralization is reinforced by continuing battles over jurisdiction. In many fields, the competitive expansionism that fueled intergovernmental conflict during the 1960s and 1970s has faded, as both federal and provincial governments seek to limit their expenditures and, where possible, to transfer their financial burdens to the other level. Jurisdictional tensions between the federal and Quebec governments endure, however, and have increasingly focused on labor market programs, especially training, a sector critical to the nation's competitive advantage in the wider global economy.

The struggle over jurisdiction reemerged during a new round of constitutional struggles in the early 1990s, which were designed to resolve Quebec's long-standing grievances. Once again the survival of the federation seemed in doubt, with public opinion polls in Quebec showing a majority of the electorate in favor of a sovereign state and the *Parti Québécois* well ahead in popular support.[39] Once again the federalist forces in Quebec provincial politics responded with demands for decentralization, including the transfer of all federal social programs to the province.[40] The federal government came back with a more modest package, but even those proposals would have eliminated Ottawa's role in labor-market training and curbed any new shared-cost programs in areas of provincial jurisdiction.

In the end, the constitutional package known as the Charlottetown Accord was defeated in a national referendum, yet jurisdictional pressures did not cease. They simply flowed into nonconstitutional politics, with the Quebec government demanding an administrative agreement consolidating control of labor-market training in its hands. In the last weeks before the 1993 election, the federal Conservatives agreed to the idea in principle, but they were defeated before the agreement could

39. For a useful introduction to the roots of the constitutional struggle in its most recent manifestations, see R. Kent Weaver, ed., *The Collapse of Canada?* (Brookings, 1992).

40. Quebec Liberal Party, "A Quebec Free to Choose: Report of the Constitutional Committee of the Quebec Liberal Party," submitted to the twenty-fifth convention of the Quebec Liberal Party, 1991.

be consummated. The victorious Liberal government has resisted the demand so far, but the strong showing in the federal election of the *Bloc Québécois*, a new separatist party, and the subsequent victory of its sister party, the *Parti Québécois*, at the provincial level strengthen Quebec's hand.

For many English-speaking Canadians, the dilution of the integrative role of national social programs caused by the fiscal weakness of the central government and continued jurisdictional tensions in the federal system strikes at their very conception of the country. They see the curtailed social role of the federal state as a weakening of the social glue that holds the country's fissiparous tendencies in check. The result has been an anxious search for instruments to preserve both the redistributive and integrative roles of federal social programs.

National Integration and the Social Charter

The most graphic symptom of this anxiety was the sudden emergence of the idea of a social charter as an instrument to protect social programs and their integrative role in Canadian life. At the beginning of 1991, proposals for a social charter were virtually unheard of in Canada; by the end of the year, such a charter had become an important component of the constitutional debate. The quest attracted support on the political Left from both intellectuals and social advocacy groups.[41] Its real political credibility, however, came from the province of Ontario, which was governed by the left-wing New Democratic Party. The Ontario premier made a social charter the primary goal of his government in the round of constitutional negotiations that unfolded in the early 1990s.[42]

The essential idea of the social charter was to entrench in the constitution of the country a commitment to maintain the existing framework of social programs. Different versions of a social charter were advanced by different advocates, with important variations in the substantive content of a charter and in the balance between the courts and political

41. Havi Echenberg and others, *A Social Charter for Canada? Perspectives on the Constitutional Entrenchment of Social Rights* (Toronto: C. D. Howe Institute, 1992); Robin W. Boadway, Kenneth H. Norrie, and Lars Osberg, "The Constitution and the Social Contract," in Robin W. Boadway, Thomas J. Courchene, and Douglas D. Purvis, eds., *Economic Dimensions of Constitutional Change*, vol. 1 (Queen's University, John Deutsch Institute, 1990); and Canadian Council on Social Development, "Constitutional Reform and Social Policy," *Overview* (Fall 1991).

42. *A Canadian Social Charter: Making Our Shared Values Stronger* (Toronto: Ministry of Intergovernmental Affairs, 1991).

institutions responsible for its enforcement. Nevertheless, the enthusiasm for the idea in any form was visible evidence of deep unease about the weakening of the role of the central government. Ontario feared that the decentralization demanded by Quebec would trigger a competitive downward spiral, with provinces reducing benefits and taxes in an effort to attract private investment, and that the regional variations in social benefits and residency requirements would act as barriers to interprovincial labor mobility. Ontario argued that a social charter would help to preserve the integrative potential of the welfare state. Indeed, the most forceful arguments advanced by this social-democratic government were premised not on the politics of class but on the politics of national integration: "Where once Canada was linked from sea to sea chiefly by its railways, we are now linked by common values that are expressed most clearly in our institutions of social policy. For Canadians, Confederation has come to mean not only the creation of a single, transcontinental economy, but the creation of a nation where the social fabric is strengthened by shared values and by a network of social programs."[43]

The idea of a social charter remained a symbol of, rather than a solution to, the problems of territorial integration in Canada. No such charter was included in the constitutional accord that went down to defeat in the national referendum. Nevertheless, a social charter has now entered the constitutional agenda of reformist political forces in Canada, and it will undoubtedly resurface in the next round of constitutional conflict.

Canadian Conclusions and European Echoes

Canadian politics remain, in many significant ways, territorial politics. Despite all of the homogenizing forces implicit in modernity, linguistic and regional divisions continue to represent core features of the Canadian political economy. These territorial divisions prevent polarization of social debate solely along the axis of social class and introduce important contradictions into the social agenda of the nation. In addition, federal institutions reflect and refract these political impulses, channeling them through complex decision routes and conditioning the policy decisions that emerge at the end of the day. As a result, Canadian experience has

43. *Canadian Social Charter.*

important lessons for a wider understanding of the role of territorial politics and multitiered institutions in Western nations generally.

Multitiered Decision Processes and Policy Outcomes

Theories of the state that place heavy emphasis on the structure of political institutions find compelling support in the experience of multitiered political systems. Policy and process become deeply confounded, and linkages between state and society become highly complex. Admittedly, this complexity vitiates efforts to establish simple propositions about the impact of political institutions on policy outcomes.[44] Nevertheless, the development of the Canadian welfare state offers clear testimony to the importance of understanding the institutional dynamics of the politics of social policy.

Several lessons stand out. First, a political system does not necessarily establish a single set of decisions rules for all policy sectors; the constitutional framework in Canada leaves considerable latitude for quite different decisionmaking rules to evolve in different policy domains. Second, these different decision rules contribute to different policy outcomes. Canadian experience points to a critical distinction between two forms of multitiered decisionmaking, namely, multiple independent action points and joint decisionmaking. The policy consequences of these two processes differ significantly.

Considerable controversy rages over the multiple independent action points implicit in federations. Many observers insist that such systems inherently constrain the social role of the state, as the mobility of capital and labor forces regions to compete for investment by lowering their social benefits and tax rates, providing strategic opportunities for those opposed to redistribution; there is certainly evidence for this proposition in the United States, and examples can be found in Canada, as well.[45] This view notwithstanding, the development of the Canadian health care system points to the *expansionist* potential of multiple independent action points. Decentralization gave invaluable opportunities to reformist

44. R. Kent Weaver and Bert Rockman, eds., *Do Institutions Matter? Government Capabilities in the United States and Abroad* (Brookings, 1993).

45. The disappearance of wealth taxes in Canada is a classic example. See Keith Banting, "The Politics of Wealth Taxes," *Canadian Public Policy*, vol. 17 (1991), pp. 351–67. On the United States, see the chapters by Paul Pierson and Margaret Wier in this volume; see also Paul Peterson and Mark Rom, *Welfare Magnets: The Case for a National Welfare Standard* (Brookings, 1990).

forces, allowing innovation to take place at the regional level and enhancing the pressure for national action. Moreover, when the central
government moved toward a national program, conservative interests
derived no significant advantage from multitiered decisionmaking.

The effects of multiple independent action points may be contingent
on the balance of political forces in each situation, but the impact of joint
decisionmaking is more predictable. The rules governing changes in contributory pensions in Canada have created a classic joint-decision trap,
with consequences similar to those found elsewhere: strategic advantages
for those opposed to change; policy proposals that reflect the lowest
common denominator; a tendency toward delay, blockage, and immobility; and a search for alternative policy instruments that are governed
by more flexible decision rules.[46] In the case of Canadian contributory
pensions, joint decisionmaking entrenched a limited conception of social
policy, protecting conservative interests from the expansionist potential
of democratic politics.

Competitive State-Building

Canadian experience also highlights the role of the welfare state as an
instrument of statecraft that can be turned to the historic task of nation
building. This dimension of social policy often goes unrecognized in
societies that are fortunate enough to take their territorial integrity for
granted. Canada does not enjoy that luxury. Canadian political elites
have tended to see social policy as an instrument that helps to define the
boundaries of political community and to legitimate the central state.
The intensity of the competition between the federal and Quebec governments for control over this instrument has long reflected the larger political stakes involved. Moreover, the erosion of national social programs
in the contemporary period carries implications for the territorial integrity of the Canadian state, a dimension that need not trouble most other
countries.

There are echoes of Canadian experience, however, in other multitiered systems. For example, the long-term intergovernmental balance
in any sector depends heavily on which level of government preempts
that policy space. The first level to establish significant social programs
has the strategic advantage: it builds strong linkages with affected
social interests and the wider public, and captures for itself the political

46. Scharpf, "Joint-Decision Trap."

support inherent in social policy. Where constituent governments have already seized the dominant position in social policy, as in the European Union, the central authorities are pushed to the margins of the sector, where they are forced to rely on supplementary programs and to concentrate on newly emerging issues. Canada represents the opposite pattern. The federal government established a strong social role when the provinces were politically and financially weak, during and after the Second World War; since then, Quebec and some other provinces have waged a thirty-year war to recapture their surrendered ground in social policy, by freeing themselves from detailed federal controls over shared-cost programs and working to transfer some federal programs to provincial control.

Canadian experience also demonstrates that the propensity of constituent governments to engage in jurisdictional combat varies. Culturally distinctive Quebec has led the campaign to capture control over the welfare state; the economically disadvantaged provinces of Atlantic Canada have defended a strong federal role and the interregional redistribution implicit in it; and the other provinces have shifted their support between the two camps, depending on the issue in dispute. These patterns are not replicated in every multitier system, to be sure. For example, the contrast between Atlantic Canada and the U.S. South is striking. Southern states believed that a strong federal role in welfare programs would jeopardize their labor arrangements and social institutions, whereas Atlantic Canada has regarded expansive federal social programs as a mechanism for protecting traditional occupations and communities.

Moreover, Canadian experience suggests that the overall intensity of any battles over control of social policy waxes and wanes with the economic calendar. The period of sharpest engagement came during the expansive days of the 1960s and 1970s when governments were confident of their fiscal capacity to occupy newly won policy space. In this period Quebec could often find allies among the more affluent provinces, especially in western Canada. During the 1980s and 1990s, when both levels have been retreating from existing policy commitments, the key issue for many governments has shifted from jurisdiction to revenues, as Ottawa began cutting financial transfers to the provinces. Quebec has remained committed to greater control over social policy, especially in the fields of labor-market programs and training; other provinces, however, find the enhanced policy autonomy implicit in a weaker central role to be poor compensation for fewer federal dollars.

Territory, Class, and Legitimacy

Theories that focus on the class basis of the welfare state obviously need to be broadened to accommodate territorial politics. Although the territorial dimensions of welfare are particularly acute in Canada, the basic dynamics are hardly unique to the northern half of the North American continent. Presumably the territorial dimensions of welfare are irrelevant only in countries that meet several conditions: the territorial integration of the state was definitively settled well before the emergence of modern social programs; there is no significant regional differentiation in either cultural or economic terms; and political institutions are highly centralized. Even in such countries the role of the welfare state in territorial integration would not be absent, but it would be redundant and of little political import.

The territorial role of social policy is worth exploration, for many countries fail to meet these conditions. Such analysis can enrich our understanding of the history of the welfare state. In some countries, for example, the historical processes of territorial consolidation and welfare development took place in similar periods. Germany in the second half of the nineteenth century stands as an example. Although Bismarck's initiatives in social policy were clearly part of an agenda of class integration, their role in the consolidation of a unified state also merits examination. In other countries, territorial boundaries were settled before the advent of modern social programs, but regional divisions certainly played an important role in their historical development. In the United States, questions of national unity were resolved in the blood and anguish of the Civil War, yet the distinctiveness of the South still helped shape the development of U.S. social policy.

The territorial politics of welfare is of more than historical significance in Europe as well. For example, in 1991 Belgium headed into another round of constitutional debates, the terms of which sounded hauntingly familiar to Canadian ears. At the time, the *Economist* predicted that "social security may prove the most contentious issue. The Flemings, who resent subsidizing poor Wallonia, would give responsibility for social security to the regions. Mr. Martens [the prime minister] shares Wallonia's hostility to the idea, fearing it could lead to the end of the Belgian state."[47] Similarly, the implications of regional economic in-

47. *Economist*, October 12, 1991, p. 53.

equality in Italy for the politics of social policy would represent fertile ground for comparison.

Finally, many of the Canadian patterns find echoes in the European Union. The politics of the EU has powerful territorial elements, which are rooted in nationality, linguistic heterogeneity, and uneven economic development; the EU operates through fragmented political institutions that can create joint-decision traps of daunting complexity; and the issues the EU faces as it strives for closer economic integration parallel those confronted by Canada both internally and in its relationship with the larger North American economy.[48] Not surprisingly, parallels abound in the politics of social policy in the two systems, from the debates over the role of a social charter to the ways in which important social policy decisions are made. For example, the role of dissenting units in joint-decision processes reveal intriguing similarities: the role of Ontario in the development of pensions policy in Canada parallels that of Britain in European social policy before the agreement at Maastricht, whereas the pattern of Quebec opting out of pan-Canada arrangements at various points parallels Britain's stance after Maastricht. More important for present purposes, the experience of the European Union testifies to the role of the welfare state in defining political communities and allegiances. The political legitimation of member states inherent in the existing national welfare systems stands as an important check on the ambitions of the Union and on the hopes for a deeper sense of European citizenship.

Contemporary attention often focuses on the forces that seem to be pushing power beyond the grasp of the nation-state into global economic relationships and supranational political organizations. Such forces are palpable, and they are reshaping the world in which we live. Yet their influence does not go uncontested. As long as citizens define their communities locally and nationally, as long as ethnic and linguistic groups are geographically concentrated, as long as regional economic inequalities persist within political communities, territorial politics will inform social policy, and the welfare state will be an instrument of statecraft as well as an instrument of social justice.

48. The similarities between Canada and the European Community led some Quebec nationalists to see the institutions of the EC as a model for Canada in the most recent round of constitutional negotiations. The interest was sufficiently widespread that the federal government's 1991 proposals for constitutional reform were accompanied by a cautionary study entitled The European Community: A Political Model for Canada? (Ottawa: Minister of Supply and Services, 1991).

CHAPTER NINE

The Creeping Nationalization of Income Transfers in the United States, 1935–94

Paul Pierson

T HE HISTORY OF THE European Union has been brief and turbulent, but the United States is a mature, relatively stable multitiered system. Its institutions are reasonably well understood, and both the processes and outcomes of policymaking are more routinized and predictable. Yet even in such a comparatively static context, the changes in public policy over time are bound to be dramatic. This chapter focuses on one aspect of social policy change that is particularly relevant for this volume: the balance between state and federal responsibility for programs of income maintenance.

Conventional wisdom holds that the American welfare state's basic structure was established in a single stroke, the "big bang" of the 1935 Social Security Act (SSA).[1] The SSA established most of the core programs of American social policy: old age insurance (OASI), old age assistance (now supplemental security income, or SSI), unemployment insurance (UI), and aid to dependent children (now aid to families with dependent children, or AFDC). This policy structure had a number of distinctive characteristics, including the omission of any programs based on a conception of shared social citizenship, the sharp bifurcation between targeted and universal programs, and a markedly decentralized orientation.

These initial policy choices have profoundly influenced the evolution of American social provision. Yet there has been tremendous change from these original patterns, most obviously in the sheer scope of government

1. For a clear statement of this view, see Christopher Leman, "Patterns of Policy Development: Social Security in the United States and Canada," *Public Policy*, vol. 25, no. 2 (1977), pp. 261–91. For an important corrective focused on the pre–New Deal era, see Theda Skocpol, *Protecting Soldiers and Mothers: The Political Origins of Social Policy in the United States* (Harvard University Press, 1993).

Table 9-1. *Expenditures on National and Shared Programs*

Type of program	Expenditures (billions of 1993 dollars)	Rate of growth, 1975–93[a] (percent)
National programs		
OASDI (social security)	302.0	2.3
Food stamps	24.6	2.9
Earned income tax credit (EITC)	6.6	not applicable
Supplemental security income (SSI)	21.2	3.5
Shared programs		
Unemployment compensation	35.4	−0.7
Aid to families with dependent children	22.3	0.1[b]

Source: Committee on Ways and Means, U.S. House of Representatives, *1994 Green Book: Background Material and Data on Programs within the Jurisdiction of the Committee on Ways and Means* (Government Printing Office, 1994), pp. 1263–65.
a. Annual rate, adjusted for inflation and population growth.
b. Includes child support enforcement.

efforts to transfer economic resources across income and generational lines. This chapter's subject, however, is a second, rarely observed shift in the structure of the American welfare state: the gradual if incomplete nationalization of income transfer programs between 1935 and 1994.[2] The New Deal system of income security retained an extensive role for state and local governments. Only one program introduced in the Social Security Act, old age security, was fully national. All other income transfers were either left to states and localities or, in the case of unemployment insurance, old age assistance, and aid to dependent children, treated as joint responsibilities of the state and national tiers of government. As table 9-1 indicates, the current system, by contrast, is far more centralized.

This creeping nationalization has occurred through three processes: (1) Washington's gradual assumption of authority over previously shared programs; (2) the creation of new national programs; and (3) the more rapid growth of national programs as opposed to shared programs. The first process, nationalization of existing programs, has been rare. Despite frequent attempts at nationalization, AFDC and unemployment insurance remain quite decentralized. Old age assistance (along with aid for the blind and disabled), however, became the nationalized SSI program

2. Rather than considering the entire range of American social policies, the scope of this chapter is limited to cash and "near-cash" programs (that is, food stamps). Confining the analysis in this way makes the discussion manageable. It also excludes those cases of service provision (for example, health care, housing) in which the distributional impact of policies may be less clear-cut and the dynamics of multitiered decisionmaking are probably most complex. I make no claim that the arguments developed here could be extended to these other areas of social policy.

in 1972. Food stamps (enacted as a fairly decentralized, experimental program in 1961) emerged as a fully national and extensive system of income support for the poor in the 1970s. Also important has been the addition of new national programs to the structure. The earned income tax credit (EITC), adopted with little fanfare in the mid-1970s, was fully national from the outset. In the past decade it has been transformed from a tiny, virtually unknown program into a central component of income support policy for the working poor. Finally, the major national programs (especially OASI, and, more recently, the EITC) have had significantly higher rates of expenditure growth than shared programs. Both among means-tested and universal income transfer programs, the absence of shared decisionmaking has meant higher spending.

In combination, these three trends produced an income transfer system that was not only more generous but far more centralized than the system of the 1930s. Although variation in benefits across states and regions remained quite substantial by comparative standards, it was greatly reduced. The degree of discretion of local authorities over benefit and eligibility rules was substantially curtailed. This chapter investigates the transformation of income support policies, seeking to understand, in particular, why income provision shifted toward the national level and why some programs proved easier to nationalize than others.[3]

One way to account for failures to nationalize would emphasize the institutionalization of preexisting, state-level programs. *Policy preemption*, as noted in the introduction to this volume, may lead to the development of dense institutional networks involving organized interests and bureaucrats. "Competitive state-building" would then induce state-level resistance to nationalization efforts. Theda Skocpol and John Ikenberry, for example, suggest that existing state-level initiatives helped to forestall a more fully national unemployment insurance scheme during the New Deal.[4]

Yet the focus of my argument is not on clashes between state and national governments eager to claim credit for administering popular

3. The more rapid growth of national programs will receive less attention. Part of the connection may be spurious. Programs may become national because they are popular, and popular programs will tend to grow faster. But as discussed below, decentralized programs are also likely to grow more slowly *because* they are decentralized.

4. Theda Skocpol and John Ikenberry, "The Political Formation of the American Welfare State in Historical and Comparative Perspective," *Comparative Social Research*, vol. 6 (1983), pp. 87–148. See also G. John Ikenberry and Theda Skocpol, "Expanding Social Benefits: The Role of Social Security," *Political Science Quarterly*, vol. 102, no. 3 (1987), pp. 389–416.

social policies. Administering programs of income maintenance for the poor, after all, is rarely the road to political popularity. Resistance has come not because state officials have preempted and then jealously guarded social policy space. Rather, the *substantive* consequences of nationalization for the operation of social policy have often led powerful economic interests, along with sympathetic political representatives, to fiercely oppose national programs. At the heart of political struggles has been the shifting role of what may be called the "veto coalition" in American social policy. American political institutions make it extremely difficult to legislate significant policy changes in the absence of broad consensus.[5] Such consensus for extensive, national income transfers has been rare. The core opposition has included most segments of American business, the Republican party, and—most critically—southern Democrats. This veto coalition has generally fought generous social programs, and has (rightly) associated nationalization with liberalization. It has been especially skeptical about social policy initiatives that offer assistance to the able-bodied poor, which might decrease work incentives or increase demands for higher wages. The coalition is far from monolithic, and the alliances that developed in legislative struggles over the welfare state have varied across issues and over time. But when the coalition has held together, nationalizing reforms have failed.

Nonetheless, there was a slow but steady shift in policy outcomes over time, a shift that is of considerable interest to those concerned with how social policy authority is allocated among different tiers of government. The political power of the veto coalition has diminished somewhat (especially that of the South). Yet the main openings for the nationalization of existing programs or the adoption of new ones have appeared where members of the veto coalition, especially southern Democrats, chose not to fight legislation. Such opportunities arose either because the interests of the veto coalition had changed (as with SSI), because new policy designs met their concerns (the EITC), or because nationalizers found a way to buy off potential opponents (food stamps). Where members of the veto coalition stood firm—as they have when reform would have provided an income maintenance alternative for the able-bodied, working-aged population—nationalizing efforts failed. Thus by the end of the Reagan and Bush years the federal government had taken almost complete responsibility for all income transfers except those to the able-

5. Margaret Weir, Ann Shola Orloff, and Theda Skocpol, eds., *The Politics of Social Policy in the United States* (Princeton University Press), 1988.

bodied poor: even for that group it assumed a more extensive role (through expanded EITC and food stamps programs) than it had in the past.

The Veto Coalition and the Politics of American Social Policy

Opposition to the nationalization of income transfers generally has been concentrated within three groups: business, representatives of the Republican party, and southern Democrats. The opposition of the first two groups has been fairly consistent and easy to understand. Republicans have long been sympathetic to business views on issues of economic management, and business in the United States has generally favored minimalist social policies. Generous social provision, especially for potential labor market participants, is likely to strengthen labor's bargaining position, raising the level of wages and working conditions employers must provide to find workers.[6] The exceptions to this rule are firms in relatively high-social wage areas that are unable to relocate at low cost. Such firms may well support nationalizing reforms as a way of creating a level playing field with their low-social wage competitors.[7]

If business support for restricted social policies is understandable, so too is the manner in which that support encourages resistance to nationalization. The general logic was laid out in the introduction to this volume. Decentralization of social policy, combined with capital mobility, enhances the ability of business to play off one political jurisdiction against another. Because jurisdictions are eager to maintain business investment, the result is likely to be lower levels of spending for decen-

6. This view of the preferences of business and conservative politicians underlies the "power resources" analysis that has been influential in comparative studies of welfare state development. See, for example, Walter Korpi, "Social Policy and Distributional Conflict in the Capitalist Democracies," *West European Politics*, vol. 3 (1980); and Gøsta Esping-Andersen, *Politics against Markets: The Social Democratic Road to Power* (Princeton University Press, 1985). For broadly similar arguments about the United States, see Francis Fox Piven and Richard A. Cloward, *Regulating the Poor: The Functions of Public Welfare* (Random House, 1971); and Jill Quadagno, *The Transformation of Old Age Security: Class and Politics in the American Welfare State* (University of Chicago Press, 1988). This argument oversimplifies business social policy preferences, but it is an adequate approximation for this discussion. For a more subtle view, see Cathie Martin, "Together Again: Business, Government and the Search for Health Care Cost Containment," *Journal of Health Politics, Policy, and Law*, vol. 18 (Summer 1993), pp. 359–93.

7. See Colin Gordon, "New Deal, Old Deck: Business and the Origins of Social Security, 1920–1935," *Politics and Society*, vol. 19, no. 2 (1991), pp. 165–207.

tralized social programs than would otherwise be the case.[8] Only if social programs offer significant offsetting benefits, such as the promotion of human capital or the quelling of social unrest, is business opposition likely to be muted.

The crucial role of southern Democrats requires some discussion. The policy preferences of southern politicians fundamentally affected the shape of the American welfare state.[9] At critical junctures, U.S. institutional structures made southern politicians the gatekeepers for social legislation. During and after the New Deal, the South was economically marginal but politically pivotal; the region possessed only a quarter of the nation's population and little more than a tenth of its taxable income, but these figures fail to capture its influence.[10] The New Deal political base consisted of an alliance among farmers, northern workers, and the southern ruling elite. Because of long-standing Democratic dominance in the South and the congressional rules governing seniority and committee autonomy, southern Democrats generally chaired key congressional committees. Southern interests thus had a key institutional foothold throughout the New Deal, and they have often held the balance of political power since then.

The interplay of the South's distinctive interests and America's federal institutions dictated the strategy of southern politicians, encouraging them to favor policy designs that would turn the dynamics of interstate competition to their advantage. To be blunt, a programmatic agenda of nationalized social policies has always been anathema to the southern wing of the Democratic coalition. The South during the New Deal constituted a distinctive political economy in the truest sense of the term. Networks of political and economic domination, backed up by the volatile element of racial hatred, were tightly linked and mutually reinforc-

8. The dampening effect of decentralization has been a consistent finding of econometric studies of AFDC in the United States. See Paul E. Peterson and Mark C. Rom, *Welfare Magnets: A New Case for a National Standard* (Brookings, 1990). On the restraining effects of decentralized social policy before the New Deal, see David Brian Robertson, "The Bias of American Federalism: The Limits of Welfare-State Development in the Progressive Era," *Journal of Policy History*, vol. 1, no. 3 (1989); and Gordon, "New Deal, Old Deck."

9. The following account is based primarily on Richard Franklin Bensel, *Sectionalism and American Political Development, 1880–1980* (University of Wisconsin Press, 1984), chap. 3; Kenneth Finegold, "Agriculture and the Politics of U.S. Social Provision: Social Insurance and Food Stamps," in Weir, Orloff, and Skocpol, eds., *Politics of Social Policy*, pp. 199–234; and Jill Quadagno, "From Old-Age Assistance to Supplemental Security Income: The Political Economy of Relief in the South, 1935–1972," in Weir, Orloff, and Skocpol, eds., *Politics of Social Policy*, pp. 235–63.

10. Robertson, "Bias of American Federalism," p. 273.

ing. Race and class were inextricably entwined in this system, and both led southern politicians, who represented the ruling white oligarchy, to fiercely guard local prerogatives, particularly when it came to policies governing the labor market. Ruling interests in the South were hostile to any national policies that might weaken black sharecroppers' dependence on the labor market.[11]

Southern politicians also objected to policies that might threaten the low-wage, nonunion environment that made the region attractive to potentially mobile capital. Just as interjurisdictional competition opened up opportunities for business, it held considerable promise for the South. Southern Democrats therefore continued to oppose nationalized social policies long after the demise of the sharecropping economy, which had motivated Southern rejection of aspects of the Social Security Act; they had no desire for an integrated labor market or for nationwide social policies.[12]

The persistent posture of southern politicians over the past half-century is striking. Proposals for a more national system of welfare, for example, would have produced considerable net public transfers to the South, where poverty rates were highest and federal taxes were lowest. But these proposals also would have jeopardized the South's major competitive advantage within the American economy: the availability of a cheap, nonunionized work force. Southern politicians were, in short, pursuing a strategy of "competition through laxity" in social policy.[13] Southern politicians opposed, while Northern interests supported, proposals that would have paid disproportionate benefits in the South from taxes on the rest of the country. This paradox clearly reveals how multitiered institutional settings can generate quite distinctive conflicts over social policy provision.

---

11. See, for example, Lee J. Alston and Joseph P. Ferrie, "Labor Costs, Paternalism, and Loyalty in Southern Agriculture: A Constraint on the Growth of the Welfare State," *Journal of Economic History*, vol. 45 (March 1985), pp. 95–117.

12. Ira Katznelson, Kim Geiger, and Daniel Kryder, "Limiting Liberalism: The Southern Veto in Congress, 1933–1950," *Political Science Quarterly*, vol. 108, no. 2 (1993), pp. 283–306; and Bruce J. Schulman, *From Cotton Belt to Sunbelt: Federal Policy, Economic Development, and the Transformation of the South, 1938–1980* (Oxford University Press, 1991), especially chap. 3.

13. On the concept of competition through laxity, see William L. Cary, "Federalism and Corporate Law: Reflections upon Delaware," *Yale Law Journal*, vol. 83 (March 1974), pp. 663–705. For a general discussion of the impact on social policy, see Miguel Glatzer and Paul Pierson, "Competition through Laxity or National Standards? Social Policy Preferences of Poor States in Federal Systems," paper presented at the 1994 annual meeting of the American Political Science Association, New York.

Table 9-2. *Evolution of Income Transfers in the United States*

Program (year enacted)	Initial structure	Evolution
Adopted as national programs		
Old age insurance (1935)	National	Incremental but massive expansion
Earned income tax credit (1974)	National	Major expansions in 1986, 1990, 1993
Successful nationalizations		
Old age assistance and supplemental security insurance (1935)	Shared; strong state role	Nationalized, 1972
Food stamps (1961)	Shared; limited state role	Nationalized and greatly expanded, 1970, 1974
Failed nationalizations		
Aid to families with dependent children (1935)	Shared; strong state role	Failed efforts to nationalize, 1970, 1977, 1988 Failed effort to decentralize, 1982
Unemployment insurance (1935)	Shared; strong state role	Failed efforts to nationalize, 1954, 1958, 1966 Marginal expansion of federal role 1961, 1970 (partially reversed in 1981–82)

Divergent Fates of Individual Programs

In the past half-century the trend toward expanded national authority in the provision of income transfers was slow but steady. Benefit packages became more uniform, something resembling a national floor of benefits emerged, eligibility rules became more regular, and local administrative discretion was reduced. The trends for individual programs, however, were quite diverse. Dramatic cases of expanded national competence coincided with repeated failures in other programs to increase the national role in policy formation and implementation. These trends are summarized in table 9-2.

The veto coalition was pivotal in determining these divergent outcomes. Business groups, Republicans, and southern Democrats remained strongly opposed to reform in AFDC and UI. This coalition demonstrated that as long as it remained intact, reform was unlikely to be successful, even when Democrats controlled the White House and held substantial majorities in Congress. The virulence of the veto coalition's opposition derived from the character of these two programs—that is, both programs offered cash transfers to the able-bodied unemployed. Employers and many Republicans resisted strengthening these programs because of the anticipated impact on wage rates, work incentives, and workers' bargaining power. Not surprisingly, these same implications led organized labor and most Democrats outside the South to consistently favor proposals for increased centralization.

In other social policy arenas the veto coalition proved less durable, and nationalizing reforms were possible. Demographic shifts and the demise of sharecropping led to a change in southern attitudes toward old age assistance, facilitating the nationalization of that program in 1972. In other cases innovative policy designs limited traditional opposition. Food stamps, which evolved out of a complex logrolling arrangement between rural and urban interests, found a unique institutional niche for providing nationally uniform transfers to the poor, including those who were unemployed. The earned income tax credit, targeted exclusively on working poor families, sidestepped traditional resistance to cash subsidies for the able-bodied.

Failed Nationalizations: The Evolution of UI and AFDC

Unemployment insurance, enacted as part of the SSA, represents a clear case of enduring, shared authority over a social program. As Murray Rubin observes, "In no other public program were responsibilities so thoroughly shared between two levels of government."[14] Despite repeated efforts to create a more nationalized system, all but the most limited steps in that direction were rebuffed between 1935 and 1980; moreover, much of the modest increase in the federal role that did occur was reversed in the 1980s. As a result, the U.S. unemployment insurance system remains a patchwork of disparate state programs, providing benefits that are much lower, of much shorter duration, and far less widely available than is generally the case in Europe.[15] Cross-state variations in rules and benefit levels are dramatic.

The system of UI established in 1935 required a minimum degree of national uniformity and allowed for substantial state-level discretion. Designers of the system did acknowledge the possibility that decentrali-

---

14. Murray Rubin, "Federal-State Relations in Unemployment Insurance," in W. Lee Hansen and James F. Byers, eds., *Unemployment Insurance: The Second Half-Century* (University of Wisconsin Press, 1990), p. 207.

15. For a detailed comparison of benefits, see Gary Burtless, "Jobless Pay and High European Unemployment," in Robert Z. Lawrence and Charles L. Schultze, eds., *Barriers to European Growth: A Transatlantic View* (Brookings, 1987), pp. 105–62.

zation would encourage competition through laxity, and stressed the need for strong national incentives to establish and maintain programs. As the Roosevelt administration's Committee on Economic Security noted, "So long as there is danger that business in some States will gain a competitive advantage through failure of the State to enact an unemployment insurance law, few such laws will be enacted."[16] This problem was addressed by establishing a national unemployment tax that would be rebated only if states enacted laws that met national standards. In this way state failure to enact UI would impose a penalty on local business, not grant it a competitive advantage. Because the U.S. Department of the Treasury oversees the accounts set up for UI contributions from the individual states, the national government has been able to maintain some other restrictions on state-level programs, such as the prohibition of proposals to impose a means test on UI benefits.[17]

Yet within these constraints the committee sought to give states "broad freedom to set up the type of unemployment compensation they wish. . . . All matters in which uniformity is not absolutely essential should be left to the States."[18] The result has been continued variation in benefit levels and pressure on high-benefit states to keep their programs from being too much more generous than those in low-benefit states. Not surprisingly, the lowest benefits are found overwhelmingly in the South.

Two circumstances account for the establishment of such a decentralized UI system: the impact of policy preemption and strong resistance among southern Democrats to more national alternatives. Skocpol and Ikenberry make a strong case for the role of policy preemption.[19] Preexisting state unemployment insurance systems, they argue, created strong barriers to nationalization. Policy networks formed around state-level programs, especially the system developed in Wisconsin. Many of the Wisconsin reformers were active in the development of the Social Security Act, and, according to Ikenberry and Skocpol, they struggled to ensure that state autonomy would remain extensive so that Wisconsin could

16. Committee on Economic Security, *Report to the President of the Committee on Economic Security* (Government Printing Office, 1935), p. 16.

17. In a similar way, the federal government has maintained the availability of UI benefits for those working in one state but living in another, or crossing state lines to look for work. On these points, see Rubin, "Federal-State Relations," pp. 209–19.

18. Rubin, "Federal-State Relations."

19. Ikenberry and Skocpol, "Expanding Social Benefits." Ikenberry and Skocpol also note that those drafting the SSA feared that a more centralized plan would be ruled unconstitutional.

maintain its distinctive program. Furthermore, preexisting state policies strengthened the dynamics of competitive state-building, in which state-level actors sought to retain control over administrative resources and political credit for public social provision.[20]

Yet the influence of policy preemption can easily be exaggerated. As discussed below, the preexistence of state programs, or of a strong state role in shared programs, constituted only a limited obstacle to nationalizing reforms in food stamps and old age assistance. And there is little evidence that the states that had ushered in state-level policies before 1935 resisted proposals to nationalize unemployment insurance when those returned to the political agenda in the 1950s and 1960s—quite the contrary.

Nonetheless, nationalizing efforts have failed. Unions and liberal Democrats have fought hard on several occasions for increased centralization of UI. The closest that the federal government came to enacting a truly national program was in 1966, during the high tide of social policy reform, with a strong Democratic president and large Democratic majorities in both houses. Many state governments supported reform because of the prospect of fiscal relief, and Lyndon Johnson made the issue a high priority. Legislation did pass both chambers: the Senate approved Johnson's proposals, but the House proposed replacing Johnson's nationalizing provisions with a set of modest modifications that confirmed state-level control over the program. The House would not accept the Senate's more liberal version, and the reform possibility died in conference.

The most significant reform enacted came during the Nixon administration, with the introduction of extended benefits in 1970. Yet as Edward Harpham observes, "Unlike the Kennedy and Johnson administrations . . . the Nixon administration rejected the idea that a wholesale nationalization of the existing system through the imposition of federal standards was either desirable or necessary."[21] The extended benefit provisions did not radically change the nature of the system. In any event,

---

20. On competitive state-building, see in this volume Keith Banting, "The Welfare State as Statecraft: Territorial Politics and Canadian Social Policy"; and Paul Pierson and Stephan Leibfried, "Multitiered Institutions and the Making of Social Policy."

21. Edward J. Harpham, "Federalism, Keynesianism, and the Transformation of the Unemployment Insurance System in the United States," in Douglas E. Ashford and E. W. Kelley, eds., *Nationalizing Social Security in Europe and America* (Greenwich, Conn.: JAI Press, 1986), pp. 155–79.

they were effectively gutted by the Reagan coalition of Republicans and "boll weevil" southern Democrats in the early 1980s.[22]

The split between high-wage and low-wage regions has clearly been a critical factor in the failure to nationalize UI. From the beginning, national policymakers realized that southern politicians would fight against a more centralized program (as they did in the case of aid to dependent children, where preexisting policies were not an issue); that recognition had a substantial influence on the strategies of the Roosevelt administration.[23] Southern opposition to proposals that would have pushed UI in a more national direction has been remarkably consistent, even after the demise of the rural sharecropper economy. In a modest 1961 reform, the crucial vote was on a pooling arrangement that would give federal assistance to states providing extended benefits. The plan barely survived— the vote was forty-four to forty-two—an attempt by Senator Harry Flood Byrd (Democrat of Virginia) to have the pooling provision stripped from the bill. Republicans voted twenty-six to five in favor of Byrd's proposal. While Democrats opposed Byrd's amendment thirty-nine to sixteen, fourteen of the sixteen votes in favor were cast by southern Democrats.[24] In the crucial debate of 1966, southerners lined up largely against the Johnson proposals, working in the House Ways and Means Committee to water down reform. Southern Democrats in the Senate were also skeptical: a solid majority of them voted alongside Republicans on important votes, although Finance Committee Chair Russell Long carried just enough southern votes to slip through the main provisions of the administration's plan.

Business organizations have resisted nationalization proposals as well, although their record is more mixed. In the 1930s a few employers (especially those closest to the Roosevelt administration) favored nationalization proposals that would have created a more level playing field. Since then, however, major business organizations such as the Chamber of Commerce and the National Association of Manufacturers have strongly opposed such proposals.[25] The 1966 debate pitted organized

22. On these cutbacks, see Paul Pierson, *Dismantling the Welfare State? Reagan, Thatcher and the Politics of Retrenchment* (Cambridge University Press, 1994), chap. 5.

23. Ann Shola Orloff, "The Political Origins of America's Belated Welfare State," in Weir, Orloff, and Skocpol, eds., *Politics of Social Policy*, pp. 71, 77.

24. *CQ Almanac* (Washington: Congressional Quarterly Press, 1961), p. 278.

25. For evidence on the 1930s, see Ikenberry and Skocpol, "Expanding Social Benefits"; and Gordon, "Old Deal, New Deck." On the postwar period, see Harpham, "Transformation of Unemployment Insurance."

labor against business, with the president of the AFL-CIO, George Meany, arguing that stronger national standards were necessary: "Many states consciously pursue a policy of underfinancing as part of an industrial development program to attract new industry through low payroll taxes. . . . If unemployment insurance is to be insulated from interstate competition, either the tax rates must be standardized or there must be a minimum standard applied to benefits."[26] The Chamber of Commerce reportedly took the position that national standards were completely unacceptable, and its opposition carried a lot of weight with House participants in the conference committee on the bill. Observers at the time regarded the failure to reach an agreement as "a major defeat for organized labor and an important victory for business interests."[27]

Thus the result of combined opposition from Republicans, business lobbyists, and most southern Democrats has been the continuation of a quite decentralized system. National standards for benefits would have created a level playing field among the states, which would have encouraged more generous benefits that might have had significant effects on labor markets. That outcome was unacceptable to the veto coalition.

The struggle over AFDC has been equally sustained and more prominent. The federal role in AFDC gradually expanded, but efforts to establish a more centralized program with a national floor of benefits repeatedly failed. Southern opposition to such efforts remained a constant from the 1930s through the 1980s; the stance of business groups and Republicans has been a bit more erratic, but southerners managed to cobble together coalitions adequate to prevent nationalizing reforms.

There was never any real prospect that the Social Security Act would fully nationalize public assistance. Aid to dependent children was seen as a successor to mothers' pension programs, which were organized at the state and county levels. Financially strapped state governments were interested in receiving federal assistance, but not for programs that would establish minimum benefits or shift administrative discretion to the national level. The Roosevelt administration, concerned about exacerbating possible southern opposition to critical parts of the Social Security Act and predisposed to maintain local control over welfare in any event, had only modest ambitions. Federal assistance was limited to one-third of program costs (compared to one-half for old age assistance), and local officials were allowed wide latitude over program implementation.

26. *CQ Almanac* (Washington: Congressional Quarterly Press, 1966), p. 834.
27. *CQ Almanac* (Washington: Congressional Quarterly Press, 1968), p. 831.

The result was, predictably, dramatic variation in benefits across the country (with benefits remaining far lower in the South), considerable pressure on all states to keep benefits low, and widespread racial discrimination in program implementation.[28] Welfare benefits in the South have never come close to lifting family incomes above the poverty line. Because of the threats of interstate competition and the possibility that the poor might migrate to high-benefit states, low southern benefits have acted as a brake on policy expansion in other states.

Reform efforts have repeatedly targeted these state-level disparities. Through incremental policy changes, federal officials have tried bribery, whereby the federal government pays a higher percentage of benefits for low-benefit states. These attempts have had only a modest impact, and may have, perversely, rewarded states for keeping benefits low. The federal government paid 52 percent of state welfare costs, on average, in 1970 but over 70 percent of the costs for every southern state except Virginia (62 percent). Nonetheless, no southern state other than Virginia paid as much as three-quarters of the average state AFDC benefit.[29]

More promising, but also more radical, have been proposals to establish either a truly national system or at least one with a national floor on benefit levels. The first major attempt at nationalization was also the one that came closest to success.[30] Ironically, the Family Assistance Plan (FAP) was proposed by a Republican president, Richard Nixon. Nixon's position in the development of American social policy remains something of a puzzle.[31] Alone among Republican presidents, he was sympathetic to the nationalization of some social welfare programs.[32] Concerned about racial unrest and operating in a climate that was more liberal on

28. Piven and Cloward, *Regulating the Poor*; and Peterson and Rom, *Welfare Magnets*.

29. Schulman, *Cotton Belt*, p. 199.

30. On FAP, see Christopher Leman, *The Collapse of Welfare Reform: Political Institutions, Policy, and the Poor in Canada and the United States* (MIT Press, 1980); Daniel Moynihan, *The Politics of a Guaranteed Annual Income: The Nixon Administration and the Family Assistance Plan* (Random House, 1973); and Jill Quadagno, *The Color of Welfare: How Racism Undermined the War on Poverty* (Oxford University Press, 1994). For details on the movement of the bill in Congress, see *CQ Almanac* (Washington: Congressional Quarterly Press, 1970), pp. 1030–41.

31. For a good analysis see Timothy Conlan, *New Federalism: Intergovernmental Reform from Nixon to Reagan* (Brookings, 1988), pp. 19–91; see also Quadagno, *Color of Welfare*, chap. 5.

32. Reagan's decentralizing inclinations are discussed below. Eisenhower was equally unsympathetic: "I believe deeply that the State and local financial responsibility in these programs should be strengthened, not weakened." Quoted in Peterson and Rom, *Welfare Magnets*, p. 102.

social policy issues than the one faced by other Republican presidents, Nixon sought to reform rather than to repudiate the programs of Lyndon Johnson's War on Poverty. Spurred on by moderate advisors, including Johnson administration carryover Daniel Moynihan, Nixon saw a national welfare system, organized as a negative income tax with strong work incentives, as a rational piece of social engineering. Support from a Republican president significantly undercut the usual Republican resistance to nationalizing reform. Many Republicans in Congress, however, shocked by their president's backing for a guaranteed income proposal, continued to oppose the legislation.

Business, too, was fragmented.[33] Large, capital-intensive firms (represented by the National Association of Manufacturers) generally supported the FAP, but it was not a legislative priority for them. Smaller, more labor-intensive firms strongly opposed the plan and (through organizations such as the Chamber of Commerce) lobbied vigorously against reform. As Jill Quadagno observes, "With 3,800 trade associations and local chambers and a direct membership of more than 35,000 business firms, the Chamber wielded a mighty club."[34]

Only the South remained clearly and heatedly opposed. By the late 1960s the focus of southern concern was less on the position of black sharecroppers than on preserving the South's low-wage economy. FAP's high minimum benefits and requirement that families with unemployed heads be made eligible for assistance would have had a revolutionary impact in the South: according to estimates from the Department of Health, Education, and Welfare, the number of welfare recipients in the low-benefit states of the South would have increased by 250–400 percent.[35] Five of six southern Democrats on the House Ways and Means Committee opposed FAP. Even as FAP reached its high-water mark, passing the House in 1970, it was supported by only seventeen southern congressmen.[36] This strong opposition arose despite the fact that the South's low-benefit, low-tax, high-poverty status meant that FAP could deliver dramatic fiscal relief.

Yet passage of the FAP in the House indicated that southern opposition alone, given the ambivalence of business and the Republican party, was not enough to stop the bill. Southern opponents in the Senate, led

33. Jill Quadagno, "Race, Class, and Gender in the U.S. Welfare State: Nixon's Failed Family Assistance Plan," *American Sociological Review*, vol. 55 (1990), pp. 19–20.

34. Quadagno, *Color of Welfare*, p. 131.

35. Ibid., pp. 129–30.

36. Ibid., p. 130.

by Russell Long, proved more successful, but they relied heavily on support from liberal Democrats who found FAP insufficiently generous. In the crucial Finance Committee vote on FAP, three liberal Democrats joined conservative Democrats and Republicans to produce a ten to seven vote against reporting the bill to the Senate floor.

Liberal opposition to FAP had complex roots: contempt for Nixon, confidence that time was on their side and that a Democrat would soon be in the White House, and fear of alienating critics on the Left (including the National Welfare Rights Organization, which termed FAP "an act of political repression").[37] A desire to preserve state-level programs in more liberal states also played an important role. Northern liberals argued that, given their comparatively generous state-level programs, their constituents would gain nothing from FAP.

In retrospect, the liberals' arguments look seriously flawed. The anticipated liberal revival never arrived. Northerners badly miscalculated the prospects for maintaining generous benefits in a decentralized welfare system. At the time, however, liberals must have found it difficult to back a radical reform of welfare that appeared to promise so little for the northern poor.

FAP represents the one instance of post-1935 income maintenance policy that lends support to arguments about the role of state-level policy preemption. Both northern liberals and southern conservatives, because they preferred "their" state-level programs, organized to defend the status quo against nationalizing proposals. Yet it is important to emphasize that this was not an instance of competitive state-building, in which state governments and state-level bureaucrats fought to keep a program because of the political benefits conferred by program control. The alignment of state representatives highlights, again, the *territorial* basis for much of the politics of social policy in federal systems. Substantive policy preferences were at stake, and the issue was decided by politicians in the federal government who sought the substantive outcomes most favorable to politically influential constituents in their respective regions.

The strange alliances generated by FAP were unique, and by the late 1970s traditional coalitions had reformed. Jimmy Carter's Program for Better Jobs and Income, a more liberal version of FAP, failed to get out of the House Ways and Means Committee.[38] Eventually the administra-

---

37. Quoted in Moynihan, *Politics of a Guaranteed Income*, p. 514.

38. On the politics of Carter's proposed program, see Laurence E. Lynn, Jr., and David deF. Whitman, *The President as Policymaker: Jimmy Carter and Welfare Reform* (Temple University Press, 1981).

tion fell back on a simpler attempt to set a national floor for AFDC, first at 75 percent of the poverty line and later at 65 percent. This final attempt, which would have raised benefits in thirteen states (all in the South and Southwest), passed the House but died in the Senate Finance Committee. Throughout, southern, Republican, and business opposition was considerable. Most southern Democrats in the House moved into opposition after failing to strip the more liberal features from the bill. Southern Democrats voted 51 to 28 against passage; Republicans voted 118 to 29 against the bill.[39]

The 1980s saw a novel twist—the single major *decentralizing* social policy initiative of the period between 1935 and 1994. Following his successful tax and budget initiatives of 1981, Ronald Reagan made a brief, unsuccessful attempt to turn AFDC (along with food stamps) entirely over to the states.[40] But although the veto coalition that constituted Reagan's power base was capable of blocking centralizing reforms, it could not enact policy reversals of its own. State governments, exerting their influence in Congress, effectively blocked the way. Although the National Governors Association engaged in protracted negotiations with the Reagan administration, its members ultimately decided that the proposal had little to offer and that it would be costly to state budgets. The proposal died without legislation even being introduced.

By the late 1980s advocates of nationalization had regained the initiative, but they continued to run into the veto coalition. Democrats succeeded in including a national floor in the welfare reform proposals introduced in the House Ways and Means Committee in 1987. The plan to encourage benefit harmonization, however, produced the predictable outcry. In 1985 the average combined food stamp and AFDC benefit provided 68 percent of a poverty-line income in the United States, but average benefits in the South amounted to only 51 percent of the poverty line.[41] Southern Democrats insisted that the benefit floor, which would have reduced that discrepancy, be removed as the price of their support for the Family Support Act. Faced with this rebellion and the prospect of a certain veto from President Reagan, the House cut the national benefit floor from the welfare reform proposal that it passed.[42]

39. *CQ Almanac* (Washington: Congressional Quarterly Press, 1979), p. 6-c.

40. On Reagan's "new federalism" proposals, see Conlan, *New Federalism*, pp. 179–98; and Pierson, *Dismantling?* pp. 120–22.

41. Schulman, *Cotton Belt*, p. 199.

42. Peterson and Rom, *Welfare Magnets*, pp. 109–10; Mark Rom, "The Family Support Act of 1988: Federalism, Developmental Policy, and Welfare Reform," *Publius*, vol. 19

The repeated failure of nationalization efforts had little to do with competitive state-building efforts of bureaucrats at the state level. Evidence is scanty that state governments fought to hold on to their authority for its own sake. Facing fiscal pressures, they were in fact often eager for federal relief. As two close observers of the fight over the Program for Better Jobs and Income observed, the Carter administration saw state and local governments as the "only . . . powerful lobby for welfare reform."[43]

The heart of the problem was the veto coalition. No social policy proposals posed as much of a threat to low-wage industries and regions as initiatives that would have nationalized unemployment insurance and welfare. By providing a standardized and more generous benefit package for the nonworking but able-bodied poor, these proposals would have made it difficult for employers to keep wages down. National standards would also have made it impossible to sustain the low benefits that allowed southern officials to advertise the South as a low-wage haven for business. The veto coalition therefore fought hard to block these reforms. As the next section reveals, however, this resistance has not been so consistent in the case of other programs.

Successful Nationalization of Shared Programs: *SSI and Food Stamps*

The transformation of old age assistance into supplemental security income represents the clearest, most dramatic nationalization of an income transfer program.[44] Established in 1935 as a program with shared financing, wide variation in benefits from state to state, and considerable local discretion, public assistance for the aged, blind, and disabled became a fully national program in 1972. The main cause of this shift was the changed stance of southern Democrats, who moved from fierce opposition to nationalization to open support for it. Economic, demographic, and political changes all altered the incentives facing southern politicians.

(1989), pp. 57–73; and *CQ Almanac* (Washington: Congressional Quarterly Press, 1987), pp. 552–57.

43. Lynn and Whitman, *President as Policymaker*, p. 246.

44. My discussion here relies particularly on Jill Quadagno's excellent account of the political economy of reform, "From Old-Age Assistance to Supplemental Security Income." See also Jerry Cates, *Insuring Inequality: Administrative Leadership in Social Security, 1935–54* (University of Michigan Press, 1983); and Martha Derthick, *Agency under Stress: The Social Security Administration in American Government* (Brookings, 1990).

Coverage for the aged poor under the Social Security Act had been tailored to meet the concerns of elite white landowners in the South. Given the South's restricted political system, these landowners wielded enormous influence within rural districts. Their representatives, frequently occupying key committee chairs, had tremendous clout in Congress. Concerned that federal assistance would make black tenant farmers more independent—in the extended kinship networks of the rural South aid to the elderly poor could easily assist working-aged individuals and their families—Southern politicians succeeded in circumscribing the reach of new programs. Eligibility for old age insurance was defined in restrictive terms (omitting the self-employed, domestic workers, and farm workers) that excluded 90 percent of black workers. Old age assistance was made a joint state-federal program, with 50 percent federal financing, no minimum benefit (at the behest of southern congressmen), and considerable local administrative autonomy. These terms produced, of course, substantial variation in benefits from state to state and— especially in the South's cotton belt—widespread racial discrimination in administrative practices.[45]

From the perspective of Southern politicians, however, the rationale for this program structure had vanished by the 1960s. Mechanization of agriculture had largely ended the need of white landowners for tenant farmers. Younger blacks increasingly migrated to areas with more economic opportunity, leaving the rural South with a demographic structure that made local control over relief for the elderly an unattractive, costly arrangement. These demographic changes also meant that providing benefits to the elderly was less likely to adversely affect local labor markets. The civil rights movement began to give the poor, including the black poor, at least some political influence in southern elections. In this context southern opposition to nationalization proposals evaporated. Because the consequences for labor markets were minimal, business interests were relatively indifferent, and Nixon's support served to limit Republican anxieties. Thus support was widespread for the 1972 legislation ushering in supplemental security income, a program with national financing, uniform benefits, and tight constraints on local discretion. Policy responsibility for roughly one-quarter of the welfare population was quietly and uncontroversially shifted to the national government.[46]

45. Quadagno, "From Old Age Assistance to Supplemental Security Income," pp. 242–47.

46. Conlan, *New Federalism*, pp. 81–84; and Derthick, *Agency under Stress*, pp. 52–60.

Soon after Nixon's Family Assistance Plan was blocked, SSI became law. Indeed, as reform of welfare for the working-aged poor was first watered down and then blocked, the scope of proposed reforms of welfare for the aged became more rather than less extensive.[47] This contrast—and the combination of southern support for SSI with resistance to a national standard for the nonelderly—indicated the new, more restricted scope of southern opposition to national income transfers. Given shifts in the political economy and in the demographics of the South, national programs targeted at the elderly promised substantial fiscal relief to southern states without challenging the South's low-wage economic structure. FAP, which was more threatening to the South's low-wage economic structure, remained a cause for considerable concern. Russell Long was FAP's most powerful opponent. FAP, he complained, would leave no low-wage workers to iron his shirts.[48] Yet Long was a supporter of SSI. One-third of the elderly in Louisiana were on public assistance, a proportion exceeded only in Mississippi.[49]

As with SSI, the emergence of food stamps as a national program of financial assistance for the poor depended on a shift in the political position of southern Democrats. The food stamp program is unique: it is the only fully national social policy that offers benefits to all the working-aged poor, regardless of family status, including those who are unemployed. It is nationally administered and has a national benefit standard, indexed against inflation. How could this program be nationalized when UI and AFDC could not? The "agricultural" status of food stamps linked a distinctive programmatic structure to peculiar political institutions in a way that facilitated reform. The agricultural focus of the program created a perfect vehicle for logrolling arrangements between rural interests (including those represented by southern Democrats) and urban ones. Advocates for the poor utilized this program's advantages to transform food stamps from a tiny effort run by county-level decisionmakers into a central component of national income maintenance policy.[50]

---

47. Vincent J. Burke and Vee Burke, *Nixon's Good Deed: Welfare Reform* (Columbia University Press, 1974), pp. 188–204; and Robert M. Ball, "Social Security Amendments of 1972: Summary and Legislative History," *Social Security Bulletin* (March 1973), pp. 3–25.

48. Quoted in Burke and Burke, *Nixon's Good Deed*, p. 162.

49. Burke and Burke, *Nixon's Good Deed*, p. 197.

50. On the process summarized in the next few paragraphs, see especially Kenneth Finegold, "Agriculture and the Politics of U.S. Social Provision"; Jeffrey Berry, *Feeding Hungry People* (Rutgers University Press, 1984); Randall B. Ripley, "Legislative Bargaining and the Food Stamp Act, 1964," in Fredric N. Cleaveland, ed., *Congress and Urban Problems* (Brookings, 1969), pp. 279–310; and John Ferejohn, "Logrolling in an Institutional

The food stamp program was initially organized in 1939 as an experimental venture of limited scope, designed primarily to dispose of surplus commodities; purchases were limited to a restricted range of farm products. The program was clearly more oriented to the needs of farmers than to those of the impoverished. When surpluses vanished during World War II, the program was allowed to die. Because food stamps would subsidize only food consumption, they were somewhat less threatening to southern political elites than cash subsidies for the poor, but opposition was still strong. As Kenneth Finegold describes the situation from 1945 to 1960, opposition to proposals for a revived and expanded food stamp program was directed by "southern Democrats, who led and were over-represented on the House Agriculture Committee. Food stamps, like contributory social insurance, threatened southern planters' paternalistic control of their labor force. A subsidy to food consumption, moreover, would not directly benefit southern producers of cotton or tobacco."[51]

Beginning in the late 1950s, advocates of a federal response to the food needs of the poor became more aggressive in pushing a revival of food stamps on a reluctant Agriculture Committee. The committee structure of Congress, which made the agriculture committees the gatekeepers for legislation on food stamps, facilitated the eventual development of a complex logrolling arrangement.[52] The House Agriculture Committee had little interest in food stamps and generally kept such legislation bottled up in committee. Rural and southern farm interests, however, needed support on the House floor for their own legislation. Gradually, the mounting evidence that rural interests depended on urban votes for farm bills, changes in the composition of Congress, and weakening southern control over committee chairs led to an increasingly favorable bargaining position for supporters of food stamps. Over the course of fifteen years program advocates transformed food stamps from a modest program constrained by producer interests into an extensive social welfare program that was an "agricultural" policy only in symbolic and institutional terms.

This process involved a long sequence of negotiation, tactical shifts, and "mutual hostage taking."[53] By threatening the passage of bills sub-

Context: A Case Study of Food Stamp Legislation," in Gerald Wright and others, eds., *Congress and Policy Change* (New York: Agathon Press, 1986), pp. 223–53.

51. Finegold, "Agriculture and the Politics of U.S. Social Provision," p. 220.

52. See especially Ferejohn's excellent analysis linking the possibilities for a stable logrolling arrangement to the specific institutional structure of Congress; Ferejohn, "Logrolling in an Institutional Context."

53. See Ripley, "Legislative Bargaining"; and Ferejohn, "Logrolling in an Institutional

sidizing agricultural commodities, liberals first obtained an amendment authorizing the president to set up an experimental program in 1959. Eisenhower refused to act, however, noting that "this authority would simply replace the existing distributory system with a Federally financed system, further increasing the already disproportionate Federal share of welfare expenses."[54] President Kennedy, however, introduced pilot food stamp programs in several congressional districts in 1961. This began a gradual process of liberalization, with southern Democrats grudgingly giving way on reform proposals as they realized that their opposition to food stamps would threaten commodity programs. The program was expanded in 1964, though still on a relatively decentralized and limited basis. Counties were free to choose whether to participate in food stamps or alternative commodity distribution programs. Strict eligibility limits were maintained, requirements that recipients purchase stamps were designed to make sure that the program increased food consumption, and states and localities had to share in program costs.

As the logrolling arrangement took hold, accelerated by growing concern about hunger in America, major moves toward nationalization occurred in 1970 and 1974. By the late 1970s the program had been radically redesigned. Financing was fully federal, eligibility rules were much more liberal, and the purchase requirement was eliminated. The federal share of spending rose from 36 percent of the value of food coupons in 1968 to 100 percent in 1980; over the same period federal expenditures increased from $229 million to $8.7 billion, and monthly participation from 2.2 to 21 million people.[55] The food stamp story shows, as did SSI, that the right circumstances and policy designs could allow advocates of nationalization to overcome or placate traditional sources of opposition.

The EITC: Enactment of a National Income Support Program

The earned income tax credit has been the great political success among American social programs for the poor during the past decade.[56]

Context." The phrase *mutual hostage taking* is from R. Kent Weaver, *Automatic Government: The Politics of Indexation* (Brookings, 1988), p. 101.

54. Quoted in Ripley, "Legislative Bargaining," p. 288.

55. Finegold, "Agriculture and the Politics of U.S. Social Provision," p. 223. Before 1977 the program had a "purchase requirement," with recipients obligated to buy food stamps. This was designed to assure that expenditures represented additional spending on food.

56. Very little work has yet been done on the EITC. My discussion draws primarily on

Although not enacted until 1974, minuscule until 1986, and relatively unknown even today, this program has become a central component of national income maintenance policy. By 1994 the program benefited over 18 million families at a cost of $19.6 billion.[57] The further massive expansion introduced in the 1993 Deficit Reduction Act represented the largest increase in any program for low-income people in the past two decades.[58] The expansion of the EITC through successive enlargements in 1986, 1990, and 1993 has been surprisingly uncontroversial. Backed by Republican and Democratic presidents alike, the EITC failed to generate anything like the opposition of the veto coalition to other income transfer programs.

The design of the EITC—a refundable tax credit, available only to low-income *working* families with children—made it attractive to many of the political actors who opposed the expansion or nationalization of other income transfer programs. Because the program benefited only those who work, acting as a wage subsidy, it posed no threat to businesses or regions dependent on low-wage jobs. On the contrary, by making low-wage jobs more attractive to potential workers, the EITC was particularly helpful to industries and regions that rely heavily on low-wage labor. Thus the program had much to offer to those who traditionally sought to block national social policies for the working-aged population.[59] Republicans and moderate Democrats also have been enthusiastic about the program's strong work incentives and have helped assure broad, if intermittent, support for programmatic expansion.[60]

C. Eugene Steurle, *The Tax Decade: How Taxes Came to Dominate the Public Agenda* (Washington: Urban Institute Press, 1992); Pierson, *Dismantling?* chap. 5; and, especially, the excellent analysis in Christopher Howard, "A Truly Exceptional Social Program: The Politics of the Earned Income Tax Credit," paper presented at the 1992 annual meeting of the American Political Science Association, Chicago.

57. *Background Material and Data on Programs within the Jurisdiction of the Committee on Ways and Means*, Committee Print 102-9, House Committee on Ways and Means, 103 Cong. 2 sess. (GPO, 1991), p. 901.

58. Fundraising letter from Robert Greenstein, Center on Budget and Policy Priorities (Washington: Center on Budget and Policy Priorities Archives, October 6, 1993), p. 1.

59. For a general argument on the political economy of wage subsidies, see John Myles, "Decline or Impasse? The Current State of the Welfare State," *Studies in Political Economy*, vol. 26 (Summer 1988), pp. 73–107; and John Myles, "Can Liberal Welfare States Compete? Social Policy in Canada and the United States," Florida State University, Institute on Aging, 1994.

60. Republican support has been revealed on a number of occasions. The White House included EITC expansion in its initial tax reform proposals (key advisor Richard Darman reportedly "loved" the tax credit). Representative Thomas Petri (Republican of Minnesota) spearheaded an effort to substitute EITC expansion for a Democrat-proposed increase in

Piecing together an explanation for the enactment and growth of the EITC is difficult, because at every stage the program's fate has been joined to broader budget or tax legislation.[61] With no votes on the EITC itself, the paper trail that would enable clear identification of political cleavages over the program does not exist. What is clear is that the tax-credit aspect of the program was tremendously helpful. It made the program a compelling response to concern about rapidly rising payroll taxes on the working poor, and it rendered higher program spending less visible to a deficit-conscious Congress and electorate. Finally, it meant that the credit could be used flexibly to create a distributional balance in the periodic broad tax and budget deals that became a staple of American politics after Reagan's election in 1981; all three of the EITC's expansions came in the context of major package deals, namely, the Tax Reform Act of 1986 and the budget agreements of 1990 and 1993.[62]

Yet the most striking feature contributing to the EITC's long ascendancy is an innovative policy design that transformed traditional opponents into allies. The support of Russell Long—a strong opponent of poverty programs that might have adversely affected the willingness of workers to take low-wage jobs—was crucial to the program's initial enactment.[63] Since then southern Democrats have often supported an income transfer program that provided benefits in a form highly favorable to their regional political economy. Thus in his successful effort to expand the EITC, President Bill Clinton was loyal to his geographic roots.

Explaining the Nationalization of Income Transfer Policies

In discussing the design of the Social Security Act, Ann Orloff notes that "the tension between national standards and coordination and state-level

---

the minimum wage in 1987. Petri and others succeeded in persuading the party to endorse EITC expansion in the 1988 Republican platform. Howard, "Exceptional Program," pp. 28, 30–31.

61. See James Milton Harmon, "Mega-bills and Ideas in the Growth of the Earned Income Tax Credit," undergraduate thesis, Harvard University, Department of Government, March 1994.

62. On the causes and consequences of these budget-centered "megabills," see Joseph White and Aaron Wildavsky, *The Deficit and the Public Interest: The Search for Responsible Budgeting in the 1980s* (University of California Press and Russell Sage Foundation, 1989). On the case of the EITC, see Harmon, "Mega-bills."

63. Ways and Means Chair Al Ullman (Democrat of Oregon), another harsh critic of guaranteed annual income proposals, was also influential. Howard, "Exceptional Program," pp. 13–14.

autonomy and diversity was of overwhelming importance."[64] The struggle over the division of social policy responsibility between national and local officials has continued ever since. In the case of income maintenance programs, the clear trend between 1935 and 1994 was toward more generous provision, more centralized administration, and more uniform benefit and eligibility rules. Resistance to this trend, however, was often fierce. The opposition stemmed far less from the desire of state officials to amass and retain bureaucratic power than from the demands of many interests to prevent a nationalization of benefits that would hinder economic strategies based on low wages and stingy social provision.

Social policy development since the New Deal evidences little competitive state-building, in which state governments take the lead in enacting programs and then seek to prevent federal usurpation of cherished initiatives. Skocpol and Ikenberry's account of the energetic protection of Wisconsin's preexisting unemployment insurance policies from national encroachment in the 1930s finds no echo in subsequent events. State governments have either stood on the sidelines, or, when faced with particular budgetary pressures, clamored for federal assistance. In several cases fiscal stress on the states gave a big boost to nationalization pressures.[65]

Opposition to nationalization has been a matter of economic interest rather than institutional competition. The core of resistance has been a coalition based on business, the Republican party, and southern Democrats. Rightly, these groups identify nationalization with more liberal programs and with declining opportunities to restrain benefits and wages through the competitive pressures endemic to decentralized federal systems. This opposition was never monolithic for several reasons: large, capital-intensive firms sometimes were less concerned with wage rates than with social unrest; Nixon's attitude toward an expanded federal role was more complex than that of most Republicans; and some southern Democrats were progressive on social issues. The repeated pattern of alliances in the past five decades, however, is striking. Time and again the strength of this coalition proved critical to the fate of nationalizing reforms.

Nationalizing pressures have come from northern liberals, strapped

64. Orloff, "Origins of America's Welfare State," pp. 70–71.

65. On this factor in the development of SSI, see Quadagno, "Political Economy of Relief." For welfare reform, see Peterson and Rom, *Welfare Magnets*, p. 117; and Lynn and Whitman, *President as Policymaker*, pp. 240–55.

state governments, organized labor, advocates for the poor, and policy analysts seeking a more uniform and equitable system of social support.[66] Their success has depended on weakening the veto coalition—and, most critically, on the ability to minimize resistance from the South. The trend toward nationalization shows that southern opposition has, indeed, weakened over time. Shifts in the nature of the southern economy eventually made SSI and the EITC attractive to southern politicians. A weakening in the political position of southern Democrats and the peculiar institutional structure of congressional committees facilitated a logroll on food stamps. Nevertheless, southern politicians have continued to block efforts to nationalize AFDC and unemployment insurance.[67]

That the South continues to act as a brake on these particular programs indicates the powerful link between the structure of federal institutions and the expression of economic interests in politics. Southern politicians have sought to maintain decentralized control over the low-wage labor market. After World War II the mechanization of agriculture and the rise of the civil rights movement eroded the paternalistic, racist foundations of southern agriculture, but political representatives of low-wage regions continued to seek economic benefits from federalism. Avoiding generous, standardized benefits for the able-bodied poor allows regions to exploit a comparative advantage—low wages—in order to attract new investment. The voting records of southern representatives in Congress throughout the post–New Deal period reflect this strategy.[68]

66. For an analysis laying particular weight on the role of policy insiders in driving reform, see Peterson and Rom, *Welfare Magnets*, pp. 90–118.

67. Peterson and Rom argue that by 1990 the basis for the South's special role had all but ended, opening the way to a national welfare standard. Peterson and Rom, *Welfare Magnets*, pp. 135–37. The fate of a national standard in the evolution of the Family Support Act suggests some reason to doubt that the South's position has moved this far.

68. My emphasis on how social policy preferences are affected by the political economy of federalism explains an apparent conflict between this analysis and an important recent investigation of the "southern veto." In a persuasive review of rollcall votes from 1933 through 1950, Katznelson, Geiger, and Kryder argued that southern Democrats diverged significantly from their northern counterparts only on civil rights and labor issues, not on social policy ones. This chapter, however, argues only for a divergence on social policy issues that threatened to create a more national labor market—a small subset of the social policies considered by Katznelson, Geiger, and Kryder. My finding is in fact wholly compatible with their analysis, which also emphasizes the weight southern Democrats placed on blocking the creation of a national labor market. See Katznelson, Geiger, and Kryder, "Limiting Liberalism."

Comparative Implications

This investigation of nationalizing trends within the American welfare state does not provide a general model of social policymaking in multi-tiered systems, but the conclusions reached here about the American experience suggest several important implications for other polities. First is an observation about the role of competitive state-building within multitiered systems: this dynamic is much less prominent in the policy developments discussed in this chapter than in other cases considered in this volume.[69] Although regional interests often opposed nationalization initiatives, state governments seldom fought against reform simply because they wanted the bureaucratic and political resources associated with policy control. Indeed, state governments often advocated the transfer of policy authority to the national level. Resistance from other tiers of government, therefore, need not always be an obstacle to increased centralization of social policy.

This conclusion needs to be carefully qualified. The poverty programs considered here are among those least likely to generate scrambles for political credit. Furthermore, state-level support for nationalization often depended on the promise of fiscal relief—a promise that the tax-poor European Union is unlikely to be able to offer to member states. Nonetheless, the American experience suggests a need to hedge against predictions that constituent units in multitiered systems will never support the centralization of social policy administration.

Second, this study suggests that aspects of programmatic design have crucial implications for the politics of social policymaking.[70] All of the nationalization proposals considered in this chapter sought to provide cash (or near-cash) transfers to the poor, but only some of these proposals provoked sharp resistance. Part of the story of "creeping nationalization" in the American welfare state is one of Darwinian struggle among different program designs to find a niche in a harsh political environment. Only those programs that proved acceptable to the veto coalition (SSI, food stamps, the EITC) were able to succeed. Program advocates have gone through a trial-and-error learning process, eventually focusing on the programmatic designs least threatening to program opponents. A similar process is likely to operate over time in other multitiered systems.

---

69. See the chapters by Weir and, especially, Banting, as well as the chapters on the European Union in part 1 of this volume.

70. For an elaboration of this theme, see Pierson, *Dismantling?*

Some of the specific programmatic designs or strategies discussed in this chapter may also be relevant in other multitiered settings. Logrolling opportunities can make it possible to overcome anticipated resistance. More fundamentally, policy designs that do not threaten to upset regional wage differentials will find easier acceptance. In the European Union, for example, policy entrepreneurs at the center have emphasized regional programs and benefits to poor farmers (both of which encourage logrolling and pose only modest challenges to low-wage labor markets) because resistance to such programs is more limited.

Finally, and most important, this study indicates the importance of analyzing the *political economy* of social policymaking in multitiered institutional contexts. The interaction of economic interests and institutional setting requires careful examination. Economic interests have had a critical impact on struggles over the design of social policy, but institutional arrangements shape both the nature of those economic interests and the capacity to advance those interests through the exercise of political power. The possibilities for competitive deregulation in multitiered institutional environments influence the strategies pursued by both business groups and political representatives of low-wage regions. Territorial cleavages influence how social and political actors view various proposals for social policy reform.

The focus on the political economy of institutions suggests also that one must be attentive to how institutional features influence the ability to express particular economic interests. In political systems with few veto points, opposition from one region may be relatively easy to overcome. In the United States, however, features of the national government that gave disproportionate power to the South (a seniority-based congressional committee system, for example) allowed advocates of decentralization considerable say in policy development. A crucial question for the European Union, then, is the degree of leverage that low-wage member states have over policy design.[71] Where that leverage is considerable—as it is, for example, under unanimity voting rules—territorially based cleavages are likely to pose a major obstacle to policy initiatives. By the same token, just as changes in congressional rules enhanced the prospects for social policy legislation in the United States, changes in EU decision rules that limit minority veto power may have similar consequences.

---

71. On this point, see the discussion in Peter Lange, "The Social Protocol: Why Did They Do It?" *Politics and Society*, vol. 21 (March 1993), pp. 5–36.

CHAPTER TEN

Poverty, Social Rights, and the Politics of Place in the United States

Margaret Weir

T HE NEW DEAL is widely regarded as the pivotal nationalizing episode in American social policy. In addition to inaugurating national social programs, the New Deal enhanced the power of federal institutions and marked the beginning of a long decline in the ability of state governments to resist national initiatives. During the 1930s the undemocratic racial caste system in the South, and the power of the South in national politics, limited social policy in ways that especially disadvantaged African-Americans, the majority of whom lived in deep poverty. But even with the decline in southern influence from the 1960s on and the greater power of the federal government after the 1930s, new federal social policies could not bridge the social and economic gulf separating the black poor from the rest of American society. Indeed, the growing isolation of this group became a central theme in American politics during the 1980s.[1]

The weak response of American social policy to African-American poverty tells us much about the limits of social policy in the United States. It also highlights the limited and peculiar forms of federal government centralization after the New Deal. In contrast to those who emphasize a "bias for centralization,"[2] I argue that the failure of efforts to address urban black poverty stems from a reenergized strand of localism. The new racially based territorial divisions that accompanied postwar suburbanization, I stress, have national significance.

The development of social policy in the United States offers some

---

1. See, for example, William Julius Wilson, *The Truly Disadvantaged: The Inner City, the Underclass and Public Policy* (University of Chicago Press, 1987).

2. See John E. Chubb, "Federalism and the Bias for Centralization," in John E. Chubb and Paul E. Peterson, eds., *The New Direction in American Politics* (Brookings, 1985), chap. 10.

suggestive parallels to the obstacles that supporters of social policy will have to negotiate in the European Union. The size of the EU, its ethnic diversity, and its multitiered system of decisionmaking in which "local" (member-state) interests penetrate the highest levels of policymaking all resonate with the American experience. In addition, the EU, like the United States, has relied heavily on place-based policies and extensions of legal rights to achieve social policy goals. Both cases feature conflict over which governmental level should hold responsibility for policy and about which measures can be guaranteed as rights. Nonetheless, many differences in the terms of decisionmaking and in the incentives of policy actors indicate that the policy outcomes are unlikely to converge. The American comparison serves primarily as a means of illuminating the dynamics and potential problems of developing social policy in a decentralized, institutionally fragmented, and socially diverse setting.

Race, Localism, and the Politics of American Social Policy

Localism has long been a defining feature of American politics. The power that localities have to resist federal government intrusions, and the deference to local interests built into national institutions, have allowed local interests to play an unusually strong role when compared cross-nationally. The federal government had little authority or capacity to impose policies or restrictions on states before the New Deal. But even after the growth of federal capacities and the Supreme Court's affirmation of a broader scope for federal activity in the 1930s and 1940s, the decentralized organization of American political institutions ensured that local interests would continue to play a significant role in national politics and policymaking.

Thus the development of social policy after the New Deal can be understood as a product of two dynamics that emerge from the continuing importance of localities in American political life. The first concerns the rules and practices governing the creation of subnational political boundaries and the formation of geographically based interests. The struggles among political actors about what level of government should bear which responsibilities are the second. As Paul Pierson and Stephan Leibfried note in the introduction to this book, the "who should do it" and the "what is to be done" become intertwined.

This perspective contrasts with interpretations that emphasize the centralization in American politics after the New Deal. John Chubb, for example, contends that the emergence of the federal grant system in the 1930s and its expansion in the 1960s and 1970s created a strong force for centralization in American politics.[3] Because congressional careers depend on amassing and distributing resources from the national government, he argues, local governments have declined in importance and a strong federal role, mediated by Congress, has become self-reinforcing. This dynamic may capture the politics of existing grants to individuals, but it does not, I argue, accurately describe the politics of federal aid to *places*, which has played a central role in poverty policy. Moreover, the focus on congressional politics has little to say about the forces that determine which questions reach the national agenda and what form they take. Both of these issues are more adequately understood by reasserting the enduring importance of decentralization and localities in American politics.

Creating New Territorial Interests in Postwar America

For most of American history, region has provided the most significant definition of place-based interests. The division between the economically developed industrial North and the poor rural South marked the central rift in American society and politics.[4] The civil rights movement and the economic modernization of the South over the past forty years, however, attenuated much of the force of the North-South division. In its place, a new kind of geographically based difference has assumed political importance: the split between city and suburb. This division rests on two long-standing features of American politics and society: the laws that govern the formation and autonomy of independent political units and the racial divisions that have been woven into the fabric of American society since the founding of the country.

By cross-national standards, municipalities in the United States enjoy a great deal of autonomy.[5] Although local governments lack formal constitutional recognition (they exist at the discretion of state government), they have, over time, come to wield substantial powers. Among the most important of these is control over local land use. Through zoning and

3. Chubb, "Federalism."

4. See Richard Franklin Bensel, *Sectionalism and American Political Development, 1880–1980* (University of Wisconsin Press, 1984).

5. Edwin S. Mills, "Nonurban Policies as Urban Policies," Urban Studies, vol. 24 (1987), pp. 562–63; and Michael N. Danielson, *The Politics of Exclusion* (Columbia University Press, 1976), chap. 2.

other measures officially aimed at ensuring local health and safety, localities can determine what kinds of people can live within their borders and what kinds of business activities can be conducted there. Another fact contributes to the rift between suburb and city: the formation of new political jurisdictions is relatively easy in most states, but the expansion of older jurisdictions, via annexation or consolidation, is usually a much more difficult process.[6]

A second major impulse toward fragmentation has been racial antagonism. As a major and long-standing social division, race has played a central role in creating the specific urban forms that distinguish the United States from European nations. The salience of race for the metropolitan form grew after World War II, as African-Americans migrated to cities and whites moved to the rapidly growing suburbs.

Although racial zoning was outlawed in 1917, suburbs used a variety of land-use regulations to bar lower-income people, a group in which African-Americans were disproportionately concentrated. These measures were accompanied by informal practices ranging from racial steering to firebombing.[7] Where these tactics failed, the process of white flight was repeated in the suburbs. Black income rose in the 1960s and 1970s, but this did not translate into significant levels of suburban integration. Instead, separate black suburbs formed, often close to inner cities.[8]

Rather than counterbalancing local fragmentation, the federal government reinforced it in several ways. Washington's support for suburban life—building highways, promoting automobile use, and subsidizing private home ownership—is well known.[9] But the federal government also engaged in practices that encouraged racial exclusion. Most significant was federal sanction of discrimination in housing markets by promulgating rules that largely prevented blacks from receiving FHA (Federal Housing Administration) mortgages. Similarly, the federal government bowed to local opposition to subsidized housing that might promote integration; federal housing policies were predicated on local acceptance.

6. See Richard Briffault, "Our Localism: Part I—The Structure of Local Government Law," Columbia Law Review, vol. 90, no. 1 (January 1990), pp. 72–85.

7. On zoning and exclusion, see Danielson, *Politics of Exclusion*, pp. 69–74.

8. See Douglas S. Massey and Nancy A. Denton, *American Apartheid: Segregation and the Making of the Underclass* (Harvard University Press, 1993), pp. 67–74.

9. See Kenneth T. Jackson, *Crabgrass Frontier: The Suburbanization of the United States* (Oxford University Press, 1985), chaps. 11, 12; and John Mollenkopf, *The Contested City* (Princeton University Press, 1983), pp. 109–22.

As a consequence, subsidized housing was concentrated in cities; very little was located in the suburbs.[10]

The rules governing the creation and authority of separate political jurisdictions combined with federal policies to open numerous exit options for white Americans. In the space of thirty years, a major new territorial division was created. Metropolitan areas took on a distinctive shape, that of a multitude of political jurisdictions sharply segmented by income and race. By the 1980s these patterns had become deeply entrenched.

Central Institutions and Local Interests

These differences among localities carry great significance for political actors, since debates about which level or arena of government bears responsibility for social policy are a focal point of political competition in the United States. That competition can better be understood by assessing how actors in institutional sites that can cut across political boundaries—the presidency, Congress, and the courts—weighed local interests when considering national policies. During the postwar years, changes in the responsibilities and organization of central institutions altered the ways in which local interests could be mobilized and represented at the center. These institutions thus presented a shifting set of opportunities for political actors at different levels of government as they sought to define and locate social policies.

THE PRESIDENCY. Perhaps the most significant change in American political institutions since the New Deal was the growth of the presidency. Expectations of presidential leadership gave rise to a more energetic presidency and a much expanded executive bureaucracy; after the New Deal, the president's program set the agenda for congressional deliberations.[11] However, this stronger presidency was permeated by local interests. The presidency continued to be strongly attuned to local interests, because until the 1970s it was embedded in an electoral system in

---

10. Danielson, *Politics of Exclusion*, chap. 4; on the FHA, see Jackson, *Crabgrass Frontier*, pp. 203–18.

11. See Richard E. Neustadt, "Presidency and Legislation: Planning the President's Program," *American Political Science Review*, vol. 49 (1955), pp. 980–1021.

which parties were dominated by local organizations.[12] Moreover, from the New Deal on, presidents found that an enhanced federal executive did not translate into a flexible instrument for achieving their policy goals. This was particularly true in the domestic sphere where myriad interests located in state and local governments complicated the task of policy implementation. Thus the growth of the presidency and the federal executive expanded the president's capacity to initiate new social policies, but it did not erase the critical role of local interests and it increased the danger that the president would be unable to deliver promised initiatives in domestic policy.

CONGRESS. Local interests have always had a strong voice in Congress. Although American political parties have never been strong programmatic organizations, before the 1970s they played an important role in organizing congressional activity and in linking local interests to Congress. This gave local party organizations a vital presence in national politics. In the 1970s, however, congressional reforms augmented the power of individual congressional members and new forms of campaign finance increased resources at the center.[13] Consequently, congressional representatives became more independent of local parties.[14] In the traditional structure of American parties, power flowed from the local organization up to the national level. As local parties atrophied and congressional members created their own campaign organizations, critical links between local and national politics decayed. Congress continued to respond to local constituencies, but in a much more individualized way.

The changes in congressional organization also disrupted established modes of congressional deal making that had important implications for localities. As R. Douglas Arnold has argued, congressional logrolling provided a way to bring the concerns of distinctive localities together

12. On local party organizations and the presidency, see David R. Mayhew, *Placing Parties in American Politics* (Princeton University Press, 1986), chap. 11. As Mayhew notes, ties between the president and local party organizations did not dictate specific kinds of policies; presidents had a fair amount of freedom in translating this support into policy.

13. On the reforms of the 1970s, see Nelson W. Polsby, *Consequences of Party Reform* (Oxford University Press, 1983).

14. See Advisory Commission on Intergovernmental Relations (hereafter ACIR), *Transformations in American Politics: Implications for Federalism* (Washington, 1986); and Timothy J. Conlan, "Politics and Governance: Conflicting Trends in the 1990s?" *Annals of the American Academy of Political and Social Science*, no. 509 (May 1990), pp. 128–52.

under an umbrella compromise that permitted some geographical targeting.[15] But after reform, congressional leaders found it harder to legislate logrolls that involved geographic targeting. In Arnold's words, the decline of locally based parties "removes one of the few forces working to impede the politics of inclusion that now transforms every narrow program into one dispensing benefits universally and uniformly."[16]

THE COURTS. The final institution in which decisionmaking powers can cross state and local borders is the federal court system and ultimately, the Supreme Court. Court actions in the sphere of social policy and poverty, and in the domain of local versus central prerogatives, depend very much on the development of legal doctrine and the recruitment of legal personnel. The legal doctrine in the 1960s and 1970s as well as the appointment of liberal judges dramatically expanded the courts' intervention in social policy. Even so, the courts are loosely bound by their constitutional starting point and by established modes of legal decisionmaking.[17] Thus even the most activist courts of those decades fell far short of embracing economic rights; they also continued to uphold local power in ways that made it difficult to redress spatial inequalities with legal tools. Moreover, by the 1980s political checks had been put on the courts: the recruitment and appointment of more conservative judges sharply stemmed the flow of judicial activism.

To sum up, the American government was indeed more centralized after the New Deal, yet local interests had not lost influence at the center. The form of local voice, however, began to shift as local parties declined in power and lost the ability to dominate central-local relations. The replacement of party-organized links by more individualized ties between the federal government and local interests had great implications for policy. In the context of the new territorial divisions between cities and suburbs, these changes in central-local ties were especially significant. They particularly hurt cities, in which many of the strongest local party organizations were located.

15. R. Douglas Arnold, "The Local Roots of Domestic Policy," in Thomas E. Mann and Norman J. Ornstein, eds., *The New Congress* (Washington: American Enterprise Institute, 1981), pp. 285–87.

16. Arnold, "Local Roots," p. 286.

17. On the limits of the courts, see Gerald N. Rosenberg, *The Hollow Hope? Can Courts Bring about Social Change* (University of Chicago Press, 1991), chap. 1.

Figure 10-1. *Trends in Federal Grants to Poor Individuals and to Places, 1960–90*[a]

Billions of 1987 dollars

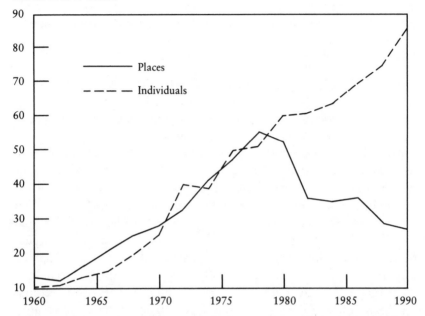

Source: *Budget of the United States Government*, Fiscal Year 1992, Part Seven, Historical Tables 11.3 and 12.3.
a. Grants to poor individuals include medicaid, housing assistance, welfare payments, low-income home energy assistance, earned income tax credit, supplemental feeding, food stamps, and the child nutrition program. Federal grants to places include general revenue sharing, public service jobs and job training, community development block grants, social services block grants, economic development assistance, the regional development program, urban mass transit, compensatory education, local public works, the Appalachian regional development program, urban development action grants, federal aid to highways and the highway trust fund, and general antirecession assistance.

Policies for Poor Places and the Politics of Rights

During the New Deal the major social welfare policies, embodied in the Social Security Act of 1935, provided benefits to individuals who qualified for them on the basis of contributions or a means test. Individually targeted benefits were extended in the 1960s to include medical care for the elderly and the very poor, but the federal government also introduced a new policy approach that focused on poor *places*, not poor *individuals* (see figure 10-1). At the same time social policy advocates were pressing a newly activist judiciary to elaborate social rights by expanding access to existing individual benefits.

Examination of the political underpinnings of place-based and legal strategies to alleviate poverty clearly shows how fragilely situated they were in the institutional context of American politics. When the distinctive demographic and organizational circumstances that supported these approaches faded in the 1970s, they faltered. As antipoverty strategies, legal and place-based initiatives generally produced narrow and piecemeal measures that not only failed to sustain favorable political circumstances but often actually provoked opposition. Once the immediate political circumstances became less favorable, such approaches could not survive for long, because they had no durable institutional protection.

Cities and the Politics of Place

By the 1950s poverty was no longer the widespread generalized condition that it had been in the Great Depression.[18] Instead, poverty appeared to concentrate in particular places. Governors and congressional representatives pointed to the "pockets of poverty" in both rural and urban areas of their states, where industrial change had left whole communities mired in chronic depression. This analysis provided the starting point for the place-based policies adopted in the 1960s.

The first efforts to address these pockets of poverty reflected the logic of congressional politics. In 1961 Congress approved the Area Redevelopment Act (ARA), the first full-fledged "regional" policy in the United States. The administration of the policy attested to the difficulties of distinguishing among regions in American politics: the ARA rapidly became a classic pork barrel program offering benefits to all states to promote economic development.[19]

The more pointed logic of the War on Poverty emerged from the executive branch. Although initially targeted at rural and urban areas, the War on Poverty very quickly came to focus on cities, where poverty had become more visible and more black. And, as riots engulfed city after city, the politics of poverty became inextricably linked with cities and minorities. Reflecting the national concern with cities and an ongoing commitment to place-based policies, President Lyndon Johnson created the Department of Housing and Urban Development in 1965.[20] The department supervised a range of new programs that extended and further institutionalized the idea of place-specific policies.

18. See James T. Patterson, *America's Struggle against Poverty, 1900–1980* (Harvard University Press, 1981), chap. 5.

19. On the ARA, see Randall Ripley, *The Politics of Economic and Human Resource Development* (Bobbs-Merrill Co., 1972), chap. 2.

20. See Mark Gelfand, *A Nation of Cities: The Federal Government and Urban America, 1933–1965* (Oxford University Press, 1975), chaps. 7, 10.

Why did place-based policies, targeted on cities, become a major route for combating poverty in the 1960s? One reason was congressional resistance to major expansions of social welfare spending in the early 1960s, which ruled out proposals for new income-support programs for poor individuals. By contrast, support for place-based policies in pockets of poverty, both urban and rural, had been building in Congress for years. Moreover, the targeted place-based distribution of benefits that became the hallmark of the War on Poverty was supported by administration economists who viewed geographic concentration of resources as a way to increase the effectiveness of limited funds.[21]

For a Democratic president, providing benefits for cities, in particular, was good politics. The urban vote—along with the South—had constituted the electoral core of the national Democratic party since the New Deal. The strong organization of political parties in many cities, especially in the East and the Midwest, magnified their importance in the electorate and gave city leaders special access to national policymakers. In places like Chicago, where the local party was particularly strong, local party leaders could control delegations to the state legislatures and to Congress.[22] The importance of urban interests within the Democratic party as a whole was clear in Congress, where Democrats from suburban areas in the North voted heavily in favor of measures to aid the cities.[23]

But the drawbacks of place-based attacks on poverty quickly became apparent. Even during the Johnson administration, geographic targeting was limited; both the president and Congress pressed for wider distribution of benefits. Moreover, even those benefits that were targeted to poor places did not automatically flow to the poor; in many cases benefits went to poor communities only after substantial mobilization. The struggle for control of these resources often encouraged urban, and particularly black, political mobilization. In many instances local communities were able to win reforms in federal programs that made them more responsive to the needs of poor people.[24]

21. James L. Sundquist, *Politics and Policy: The Eisenhower, Kennedy, and Johnson Years* (Brookings, 1968), p. 138.

22. On the changing relationship of local and national party organizations, see ACIR, *Transformations in American Politics*, chaps. 2, 4; on Chicago, see Milton Rakove, *Don't Make No Waves Don't Back No Losers* (Indiana University Press, 1975).

23. See Demetrios Caraley, "Congressional Politics and Urban Aid," *Political Science Quarterly*, vol. 91 (Spring 1976), pp. 19–45.

24. On the importance of local decisions about how federal funds should be spent, see Michael J. Rich, *Federal Policymaking and the Poor: National Goals, Local Choices, and Distributional Outcomes* (Princeton University Press, 1993). On community challenges to

When Nixon came to power in 1969, however, targeting became even more attenuated. The new president replaced the urban focus of place-based policies with less targeted general revenue sharing and block grants which made benefits available to a broader range of localities. In particular, benefits became more accessible to smaller localities, from which the Republican party drew its strength. In addition, a newly assertive Congress wrested control over the distribution of funds from the bureaucracy, replacing project grants with congressionally determined formula grants that spread funds even further.[25]

The place-based policies of the 1960s also created political problems. Rather than institutionalizing a broad national responsibility for poverty, the politics of poverty became more narrow and localized. This outcome was somewhat paradoxical because the War on Poverty was clearly national in its origins. It was devised in the executive branch and was pushed through Congress by a president recently elected in a landslide. It was administered by an independent agency in the Executive Office of the President. Yet at the heart of the program were incentives and resources designed to promote local mobilization of the black community. The limited resources devoted to the War on Poverty meant that it served far more effectively as a vehicle for black political empowerment than as a remedy for poverty.[26]

As racial tensions rose in the latter part of the 1960s, black political assertiveness translated into pressures for community control over the institutions that delivered social policy.[27] In the conflicts over community control, the broader national debates over expanding the scope of social policy gave way to narrow, piecemeal squabbles over dividing the shares.[28] Thus, although the War on Poverty started as an odd blend of centralization and localism, by the end of the 1960s its localizing impulses

---

urban renewal that helped to shift more resources to the poor, see John H. Mollenkopf, *The Contested City* (Princeton University Press, 1983), chap. 5.

25. See Arnold, "Local Roots," pp. 250–87; Margaret T. Wrightson and Timothy J. Conlan, "Federal Dollars and Congressional Sense: Targeting Aid to Poor People and Poor Places," in Michael E. Bell, ed., *Research in Urban Economics: State and Local Finance in an Era of New Federalism*, vol. 7 (Greenwich, Conn.: JAI Press, 1988), pp. 163–89; and Rich, *Federal Policymaking*.

26. Paul E. Peterson and J. David Greenstone, "Racial Change and Citizen Participation: The Mobilization of Low-Income Communities through Community Action," in Robert H. Haveman, ed., *A Decade of Federal Anti-Poverty Programs: Achievements, Failures and Lessons* (University of Wisconsin Press, 1977), pp. 248, 251–56.

27. On community control, see Alan Altshuler, *Community Control* (New York: Pegasus, 1970)

28. See Ira Katznelson, *City Trenches* (New York: Pantheon, 1981).

dominated. Government policies had mobilized new locally based interests, but the links between center and locality were not organized to channel or satisfy those interests.

In addition, federal aid to cities was less useful as an antipoverty tool in periods of recession. By the 1970s, when black citizens began to elect mayors, cities faced cross-pressures: they needed both to promote economic development and to assist poor constituents. What they could do for their poor citizens, then, was sharply limited.[29] Moreover, policies aimed at places did not challenge the growth of political boundaries that emerged in the 1950s and 1960s and divided the metropolitan population into separate political jurisdictions by income and race. Once cities began to lose their advantages in population and political organization, place-based policies were doomed.

The Politics of Social Rights

At the same time that the executive branch was creating policies for cities, the judiciary was taking a newly activist role in social policy. Prodded by civil rights activists, poverty advocates, and new legislative provisions for judicial review of social policy administration, the courts entered the realm of social policy in unprecedented ways. The assertion of rights offered a means for making political claims to social and economic benefits and a method for bypassing the power of localities and the limits of place-based policies: nationally confirmed rights were, by definition, available to citizens in all jurisdictions. But the rights strategy was inherently limited for addressing poverty.

Given the importance of law and lawyers in American politics, it is perhaps not surprising that the movement to extend social policy in the 1960s took legal expression.[30] But using rights arguments to broaden social policy and relying on the courts to make constitutional claims for extending social policy were novel. In the 1930s new social policies had rested on legislative majoritarianism, not on rights claims.

The turn to the courts and the politics of rights in the 1960s was in part a reflection of institutional receptivity. In the 1950s the Supreme Court reversed its refusal to consider economic distinctions as a subject

---

29. This is the theme of Paul E. Peterson in *City Limits* (University of Chicago Press, 1981)

30. On the importance of law in the early years of the American republic, see Alexis de Tocqueville, *Democracy in America*, vol. 1 (New York: Vintage, 1945), chap. 6.

for judicial deliberation, and in several rulings it suggested that economic distinctions were suspect classifications.[31] These rulings encouraged supporters of more egalitarian social policy to develop constitutional arguments likening social policy benefits to rights. Advocates for the poor, armed with new arguments that compared social benefits to "new property," looked to the courts to remedy the often discriminatory administration of social welfare programs and to assure fair and equal access to policy benefits.[32]

In contrast to the Court's new interest in social policy issues, Congress seemed reluctant to act. With the exception of the overwhelmingly Democratic 89th Congress (1965–66), the Democratic congressional majority, still dominated to a significant degree by southern conservatives, was unreceptive to proposals for extending social policy. This reluctance to endorse social spending was compounded after 1966 by budgetary pressures from the Vietnam War. Moreover, Congress actively pushed the courts to act in the sphere of social policy. Throughout the 1960s Congress passed legislation that specifically invited courts to review the administration of policy; it also approved laws so vague that courts were left with the final say about their meaning.[33]

Both of these institutional proclivities (the court's receptivity to social rights and the Congress's reluctance to approve social spending) stemmed from the politics of race. The civil rights movement and the growth of legal efforts to secure equal rights under the law provided the critical background to the judicial activism of the 1960s. The civil rights movement offered a new model of political activism that put legal claims at the center of politics. On the legislative side, the southern opposition to increased social spending had long been predicated on the desire to preserve the racial caste system on which the southern agricultural economy rested.[34] Social spending became particularly identified with African-Americans in the 1960s, when the civil rights movement cast the problems of black poverty into the national spotlight and President Johnson sought to justify increased spending for blacks by reference to the denial

31. See Rogers M. Smith, *Liberalism and American Constitutional Law* (Harvard University Press, 1985), p. 160.

32. See Charles A. Reich, "The New Property," *Yale Law Journal*, vol. 73, no. 5 (1964), pp. 732–87.

33. See Donald L. Horowitz, *The Courts and Social Policy* (Brookings, 1977), p. 5.

34. See Jill Quadagno, "From Old Age Assistance to Supplemental Security Income: The Political Economy of Relief in the South, 1935–1972," in Margaret Weir, Ann Shola Orloff, and Theda Skocpol, eds., *The Politics of Social Policy in the United States* (Princeton University Press, 1988), pp. 235–63.

of past rights.[35] During the course of the 1960s, efforts to secure social assistance for black communities confronted mounting opposition to "rewarding rioters." Federal spending aimed at reducing black economic inequality won temporary acceptance in the mid-1960s, at the height of the civil rights movement, but quickly lost favor as urban riots captured headlines across the nation.

The rights strategy achieved some important advances in social policy. On a number of issues, the courts defined the precise content of rights and extended the reach of social policy by mandating broader access. The Supreme Court outlawed many of the restrictions that states imposed on access to social benefits: residency requirements as a condition of eligibility for welfare were struck down, as were various life-style criteria, such as "man-in-the-house" rules.[36] And by defining more precisely the meaning of some legislation, the courts sparked activity in whole new areas of social policy. For example, a 1974 ruling that ordered the San Francisco school district to address the language needs of Chinese-speaking pupils created a flurry of activity in the field of bilingual education.[37]

For all their successes, legal strategies proved to be a tool of limited flexibility for extending social policies. The rhetoric of rights became attached to American social policy, but the rights so gained were far more narrow and legalistic than the social rights that were part of the rhetoric of many European welfare states. For example, in welfare policy the rights of clients had been meticulously and narrowly enumerated by 1968: in New York City, welfare recipients were entitled to slacks, kitchen can openers, toilet tissue holders, and other such items.[38] But the specification of such rights did little to ameliorate the stigma attached to receiving welfare in the United States; nor did it prevent substantial declines in real benefit levels during the 1970s, as welfare grants failed to keep pace with inflation.[39]

35. This was most evident in the president's 1965 address entitled "To Fulfill These Rights," delivered at Howard University. The text of the speech is reprinted in Lee Rainwater and William L. Yancey, *The Moynihan Report and the Politics of Controversy* (MIT Press, 1967), pp. 125–32.

36. See Michael R. Sosin, "Legal Rights and Welfare Change, 1960–1980," in Sheldon H. Danziger and Daniel H. Weinberg, eds., *Fighting Poverty: What Works and What Doesn't* (Harvard University Press, 1986), pp. 260–83.

37. Horowitz, *Courts and Social Policy*, pp. 15–17.

38. Richard M. Titmuss, "Welfare 'Rights,' Law and Discretion," in Brian Abel-Smith and Kay Titmuss, eds., *The Philosophy of Welfare: Selected Writings of Richard M. Titmuss* (London: Allen and Unwin, 1987), pp. 243–44.

39. On the declining value of AFDC payments, see *Overview of Entitlement Programs:*

Moreover, these narrow rights did not serve as a stepping-stone to acceptance of broader, more encompassing notions of social rights. The failure of the "rights revolution" of the 1960s to create broad social rights reflected not only the changing composition of the Supreme Court but also the character of the American Constitution. Despite vigorous attempts to find support for social and economic egalitarianism in the Constitution, social rights proponents were unable to persuade the Court to rule that unequal economic impacts of public policy outcomes were a constitutional matter.[40] Lawsuits argued on the grounds of "economic equal protection" ended in 1973, when the court ruled that the Texas school financing law did not violate the Constitution although it had a different impact on rich and poor students.[41] Similarly, challenges to states' rights to set different (and unequal) benefit levels in the federal-state social assistance programs failed, because the Court rejected fundamental tenets of the "new property" argument.

The rights strategy also encountered political problems. In many cases an emphasis on legal strategy and assertions of individual or group rights directed the energies of antipoverty activists away from a politics of coalition. And because legal decisions were framed as matters of rights, activists tended to ignore the costs of proposed remedies; they also seemed to lack a firm grasp of the broader ramifications of the decisions.[42] As Mary Ann Glendon notes, "In its simple American form, the language of rights is the language of no compromise. The winner takes all and the loser has to get out of town. The conversation is over."[43]

In fact, the rights strategy in social policy often engendered resentment, which reduced the prospects for building broad coalitions to support the substantive extension of social rights. The strategy of the National Welfare Rights Organization (NWRO) provides an example.[44] Formed in the late 1960s, the NWRO sought to mobilize welfare recipients to claim all

---

Background Material and Programs within the Jurisdiction of the Committee on Ways and Means, Committee Print, House Committee on Ways and Means, 102 Cong. 1 sess. (Government Printing Office, May 7, 1991), tables 10, 11, pp. 604–06.

40. See Smith, *Liberalism*, chap. 6. See also Lawrence Mead, "Comment," in Danziger and Weinberg, eds., *Fighting Poverty*, p. 284.

41. The case was *San Antonio Independent School District v. Rodriguez*. See the discussion in Smith, *Liberalism*, pp. 163–64.

42. Horowitz, *Courts and Social Policy*, pp. 262–63.

43. Mary Ann Glendon, *Rights Talk: The Impoverishment of Political Discourse* (New York: Free Press, 1991), p. 9.

44. On the NWRO, see Guida West, *The National Welfare Rights Movement: The Social Protest of Poor Women* (Praeger, 1981).

benefits they were entitled to by law. The focus on securing these particular benefits as a matter of right made supporters of welfare rights less willing to consider alternative forms of social support, such as proposals that would tie welfare to work. The broad and public assertion of rights by the NWRO made compromise around potentially more politically popular forms of economic and social assistance difficult to negotiate.

These rights issues are very much tied up with racial conflict in the United States. The legal strategy was often the only one that could force recalcitrant state governments to offer equal services and benefits to black citizens. And over the course of the 1960s and 1970s, advocates used legal remedies to address as many facets of black inequality as possible, whether these inequalities were the product of unequal treatment or the result of more general economic factors. In the inhospitable political climate of the 1970s, legal claims based on racial discrimination became the central means for addressing black poverty. In areas where elected officials feared to act or actually opposed action, such as in the provision of equal educational opportunities, the courts imposed controversial and aggressive judicial solutions, such as busing.

In the end the legal rights strategy could not be sustained. Despite their insulation from immediate political pressures, the courts are not immune to broader political changes. After Republicans won the presidency in 1980, judicial appointees evinced much less sympathy for activism in the realm of social policy or minority rights. Because the courts are ultimately tied to popular sentiments, which had grown particularly hostile to minority rights claims that entered the economic sphere, the courts proved to be a limited instrument for extending social policy.[45]

The New Politics of Localism and the American Poor

The politics of poverty and the policy options for the poor have narrowed since 1980. In the decades after the War on Poverty, the national will to

45. I am not arguing that the legal strategy *caused* racial backlash. There is sufficient evidence of harsh white responses to blacks in American cities during the 1950s and 1960s before the most contentious legal strategies were put into place. For the view that legal strategies were the main cause of backlash, see Thomas Byrne Edsall and Mary D. Edsall, *Chain Reaction: The Impact of Race, Rights, and Taxes on American Politics* (W. W. Norton, 1991). For an empirical examination of the contentious nature of local race relations around housing issues in the 1940s and 1950s, see Thomas J. Sugrue, "Crabgrassroots Politics: Race, Homeownership, and Anti-Liberalism in the Urban North, 1940–1964," University of Pennsylvania, Department of History, 1993.

address African-American urban poverty through broad public means eroded. This change in public sentiment has been fed by and in turn has nourished a "defensive localism" that circumscribes and particularizes the public sphere.

The changes in the politics of urban poverty in the 1980s can be understood by examining the partisan strategies that developed around assigning responsibility for social problems to different levels of government and arenas of policy. Less overt but equally significant was the role that law played in buttressing the legitimacy of localism. Legal rulings treated local jurisdictions as an expression of "natural" community that higher levels of government should leave alone.

The Political Decline of American Cities and the Abandonment of the Urban Poor

The political weakness of place-based antipoverty policies became evident in the 1980s when cities lost their pivotal political position. Demographic shifts and changes in party organization contributed to the political eclipse of cities, but it was the dynamics of partisan competition that left cities politically isolated: Republicans showed that national elections could be won without urban support. The consequences for poverty policy were significant. Republican policy strategies sought to reduce the national role in social policy, devolving power to the states.

The decline of cities was both political and economic. Federal policies that promoted suburbanization combined with economic shifts and technical advances to hollow out the older cities of the Northeast and the Midwest. In 1960 the nation's population was evenly divided among cities, suburbs, and rural areas; by 1990 both urban and rural populations had declined, leaving suburbs with nearly half of the nation's population. The urban population declined to 31 percent.[46] And as cities lost population, they became poorer and more minority in their racial composition. The shift of population into suburban areas made it possible to win national elections without the urban vote. In 1968 suburbs cast 35.6 percent of the nation's vote for president; by 1988 that figure had risen to 48.3 percent. By the 1992 election, suburbs constituted a majority of the electorate.[47]

46. These data are reported in William Schneider, "The Suburban Century Begins," *Atlantic Monthly*, vol. 270 (July 1992), pp. 33–44.

47. See the figures reported in Edsall and Edsall, *Chain Reaction*, p. 229; Schneider,

Demographic disadvantage was compounded by organizational changes in political parties. One feature of American party organization that had historically benefited cities in national politics was the strong organization of local parties, especially when compared to the weakness of their national counterparts. In the 1960s and 1970s, however, changes in the procedures for nominating candidates and the decline of urban machines turned this relationship on its head. As primaries replaced party nominations as the chief mechanism for selecting candidates, local parties were shunted aside by nationally organized financing sources, such as political action committees.[48] And as minorities took control of city government, racial divisions weakened former strongholds of Democratic politics.[49] With the atrophy of local parties, members of Congress representing urban areas had to assemble their own electoral machines; in the process they became more independent of mayors.[50] These developments significantly muted the voice of cities in national party politics. As Timothy Conlan notes, the growth of the intergovernmental lobby in the 1960s and 1970s, which looked like an increase in the power of localities, really indicated "an erosion in the unique political role once occupied by these officials and their party organizations in the political system."[51]

The terms of partisan competition did not take long to register these changes. During the 1980s a sharp disjuncture between urban and suburban voters in the North and the Midwest attested to Republican success in mobilizing a distinctive suburban political identity. In contrast to the pattern prevailing in the sixties and seventies, when central cities and suburbs tended to vote in similar directions, by 1980 there was a marked split between the suburban and urban vote. Central cities remained the only stronghold of the Democratic party, while the majority of suburban areas voted Republican.[52]

"Suburban Century"; and Robert Reinhold, "Chasing Votes from Big Cities to the Suburbs," *New York Times*, June 6, 1992, p. A1.

48. Conlan, "Politics and Governance."

49. James A. Barnes, "Creaky City Machinery," *National Journal*, November 3, 1990, pp. 2655–59; see also Charles J. Orlebeke, "Stress and Stalemate: Illinois State-Local Relations in the 1980s," in E. Blaine Liner, *A Decade of Devolution: Perspectives on State-Local Relations* (Washington: Urban Institute Press, 1989), pp. 122–23

50. Conlan, "Politics and Governance."

51. Conlan, "Politics and Governance," p. 134.

52. On the older pattern of suburban-urban voting, see Joseph Zikmund II, "Suburban Voting in Presidential Elections: 1948–1964," *Midwest Journal of Political Science*, vol. 12 (May 1968), pp. 239–58; and Robert C. Wood, "The Impotent Suburban Vote," *The Nation*, March 26, 1960, pp. 272–73. On the new splits in urban-suburban voting, see

This difference reflected a new presidential strategy. In 1968 Richard Nixon had feared the political repercussions of ignoring the cities; in 1980 Ronald Reagan demonstrated that a president could be elected without the support of cities, as well as that urban programs could be curtailed with few political consequences. Running against the trends of the last half century, Reagan fashioned a successful political appeal around the idea that the federal role in social policy should be minimized. Instead, he argued, initiative should be left with state and local governments, which had shouldered these burdens before the New Deal. Instead of using the presidency to support national policies that spanned local political boundaries, the new Republican strategy sought to reduce federal taxes and devolve social responsibilities to states and localities. The energies of the presidency would be focused on foreign affairs; the domestic responsibilities of the presidency would be reduced as much as possible by giving states more responsibility.

The pattern of success and failure that Reagan's initiatives experienced confirmed the political weakness of cities. The only programs totally eliminated during the 1980s were those that particularly benefited urban areas. For example, in 1981 Congress terminated the Comprehensive Employment and Training Act, which cities had used (unofficially) to bolster the ranks of their employees. General revenue sharing, which provided extra untargeted revenue for localities, ended in 1986. By the end of the Reagan administration, a major urban development program, Urban Development Action Grants lost funding. The area of social policy most severely hit during the 1980s was housing, which disproportionately aided cities.[53] Demetrios Caraley has estimated that grants for cities were cut some 46 percent between 1980 and 1990.[54] The federal government exacerbated the effects of these cuts by preempting various sources of local revenue. The 1986 Tax Reform Act, for example, extended restrictions on tax-exempt bonds, which localities had increasingly come to rely on to attract business.

The sharp cuts in these place-based policies stand in marked contrast to the relatively minor reductions made in programs targeted at individuals. Most congressional representatives had strong incentives to main-

Richard Morin, "Largest Downtowns Eluded Bush's Grasp," *Washington Post*, November 25, 1988, pp. A29, A30. See also Schneider, "Suburban Century."

53. See E. Blaine Liner, "Sorting Out State-Local Relations," in Liner, ed., *Decade of Devolution*, chap. 1.

54. See Demetrios Caraley, "Washington Abandons the Cities," *Political Science Quarterly*, vol. 107 (Spring 1992), p. 8.

tain the programs aimed at individuals, and not simply because policies toward individuals were more likely to be entitlement programs; after all, Congress did eliminate revenue sharing, the largest entitlement program for places. Rather, it was harder for Congress to claim credit for revenue sharing, which disappeared into the coffers of local government. Individually targeted programs, on the other hand, had more direct and tangible meaning for individual constituents. As John Chubb notes, the logic of constituent ties to Congress made these programs important elements in the congressional reelection process.[55] The same is not true of policies to places. Far fewer members of Congress had a comparable stake in these programs.

Cities fared only slightly better at the state level. Long dominated by rural interests, state governments instituted reforms in the 1960s and 1970s that equalized urban representation and modernized administration.[56] By the time the initiative for social policy devolved to the states, however, cities had lost ground to suburbs in state legislatures. Some states made up for federal cuts during the 1980s, but on the whole states did not compensate for the loss of federal support.[57] To the contrary, by the end of the decade many states, pressed by the recession, made further cuts in programs for the poor.[58]

The political isolation of the cities has had a disproportionately negative effect on the poor because place-based policies had provided a critical supplement to the coverage of social policies aimed at individuals. Poor people and minorities in cities had developed influence and won benefits by their relationship with the federal government. As cities lost federal sources of support, they found themselves shut out of national policy discussions and poorly equipped to compete for resources at the state level.

55. See Chubb, "Federalism."
56. The revitalization of state government is discussed in Ann O'M. Bowman and Richard C. Kearney, *The Resurgence of the States* (Prentice Hall, 1986); and Mavis Mann Reeves, "The States as Polities: Reformed, Reinvigorated, Resourceful," *Annals of the American Academy of Political and Social Science*, no. 509 (May 1990), pp. 83–93.
57. See Helen F. Ladd and John Yinger, *America's Ailing Cities: Fiscal Health and the Design of Urban Policy* (Johns Hopkins University Press, 1991), pp. 324–27.
58. See Iris J. Lav, Edward Lazere, Robert Greenstein, and Steven D. Gold, *The States and the Poor: How Budget Decisions Affected Low Income People in 1992* (Washington: Center on Budget and Policy Priorities, 1993).

The Political Logic of Defensive Localism

What underlies these national shifts in politics and policy? A look below the national level, at the political and spatial ordering of socioeconomic differences, suggests an answer. Clearly, racial antipathies have been a driving force dividing city and suburb, but how was this new form of racial politics cemented? The discussion below highlights the key role of law and the organization of social policy in legitimating and sustaining these race-based territorial divisions.

LAW AND TERRITORIAL DIVISIONS. The political and legal framework for defining localities and determining the extent of local autonomy helps explain the pace and extent of suburbanization and the extreme opposition of suburb to city. Despite growing concern about the costs and negative social consequences of metropolitan fragmentation in the 1950s, the political and legal framework was on the side of the forces dividing metropolitan areas.[59]

One reason was that the responsibility for these issues formally lay in the hands of the states. Despite the reforms to their legislative and executive structures, states were often dominated by suburban interests, which greatly benefited from the existing fragmentation of local land-use decisions. Most state laws worked against efforts to expand the political boundaries of cities. State laws regarding annexation typically required the approval of the area to be annexed. In the Northeast and the Midwest, this meant that city boundaries were essentially fixed by the first decade of this century. Added to the curbs on city expansion was the ease of creating separate political jurisdictions through incorporation. With the legal context favoring fragmentation and the political context favoring the suburbs that benefited from that fragmentation, political jurisdictions proliferated.[60]

In the early 1970s the cause of promoting more rational land use was taken up at the national level. Although the federal government did not have the constitutional authority to intervene in local land-use decisions, it could use its control over the purse strings of infrastruc-

59. See Briffault, "Our Localism: Part I"; and "Our Localism: Part II—Localism and Legal Theory," *Columbia Law Review*, vol. 90, no. 2 (1990), pp. 346–454. See also Oliver P. Williams, *Metropolitan Political Analysis: A Social Access Approach* (New York: Free Press, 1971).

60. Briffault, "Our Localism: Part I" and "Our Localism: Part II."

ture and economic development programs to encourage the states to exercise their authority over land use. The cause of local land-use planning was first proposed in the Senate and then embraced by the executive branch.[61] The legislation initially aimed to encourage states to plan, but it emerged from the House of Representatives—where locally based interests are represented—in a much diluted form. Even in this weakened form, the legislation did not pass. By the mid-1970s the federal government had withdrawn from any comprehensive effort to influence the organization of local space.

This failure in the United States can be contrasted with the successful efforts of many European nations to place local finances on a sound footing by instituting territorial reorganization.[62] In several countries the number of local governments was reduced, and as the boundaries of local governments expanded, so did their resources. For example, in Sweden the number of municipalities was reduced from about 2,498 in 1951 to 284 in 1989, in order to increase the revenue base for funding locally provided social services.[63] In 1970 the British government reduced the number of local authorities by two-thirds to rationalize the administration and financing of social policy.[64] Although such reforms did not prevent some fiscal distress in the 1970s and 1980s, they did reduce the disparities among localities and enhance the ability of local units to provide social services.

SOCIAL POLICY AND THE TERRITORIAL DIVIDE. The legal framework that governs the formation of localities is only part of the story of how the opposition of city and suburb became entrenched in the United States. The other piece of the story lies in the organization of social policy and taxation. Despite the growth of individual social policies in the New Deal

61. See Sidney Plotkin, "Policy Fragmentation and Capitalist Reform: The Defeat of National Land Use Policy," *Politics and Society*, vol. 9, no. 4 (1980), pp. 409–45.

62. On the general issue of comparative governmental reorganization, see Francesco Kjellberg, "Local Government Reorganization and the Development of the Welfare State," *Journal of Public Policy*, vol. 5, no. 2 (May 1985), pp. 215–39. See also the essays in *State Restructuring and Local Power: A Comparative Perspective*, edited by Chris Pickvance and Edmond Preteceille (New York: Pinter Publishers, 1991); and *Financing Urban Government in the Welfare State*, edited by Douglas Ashford (New York: St. Martin's Press, 1980).

63. On Sweden, see Ingemar Elander and Stig Montin, "Decentralisation and Control: Central-Local Relations in Sweden," *Policy and Politics*, vol. 18, no. 3 (1990), pp. 165–80.

64. On Britain, see L. J. Sharpe, "Modernising the Localities: Local Government in Britain and Some Comparisons with France," in J. Lagroye and V. Wright, eds., *Local Government in Britain and France* (London: Allen and Unwin, 1979).

and place-based policies in the 1960s, two critical areas of policy remained strongly tied to local prerogatives and local capacities: education and housing. Compounding these differences across political boundaries was the power of localities to raise a variety of taxes, including the property tax, income taxes, and fees. These arrangements are critical for understanding the locational decisions of individuals and businesses and their often fierce support for local autonomy.

Housing policies not only failed to provide much support for city residents but also reinforced the divisions between city and suburb. The centerpiece of American housing policy, the tax deduction for interest on mortgage payments, was of little use to the majority of poor urban dwellers, who were far more likely to be renters than owners. Suburban zoning sharply limited the availability of low-cost housing outside the city. Even during the 1960s and 1970s, the federal government devoted relatively few resources to low income housing or to support for rental housing. Perhaps most crucial, the construction of public housing remained contingent on local acceptance; middle-class communities could and did reject publicly subsidized low-cost housing in communities across the United States from the 1930s onward. The federal government had limited power to challenge such local preferences, and in the early 1970s it quickly retreated when its efforts provoked opposition.[65]

The local provision of public education, traditionally funded by local property taxes, has been a cornerstone of American democracy. The quality of local education is deeply connected to local financing capacities, despite considerable expansion of state funding for education since the 1960s. As metropolitan areas have segmented by income, stark inequalities in the provision of education have emerged across localities.[66] For example, in Texas in the early 1970s, despite a state equalizing formula for educational funding, the wealthiest school districts spent three times as much as did the poorest. In 1973 the U.S. Supreme Court rejected challenges to these funding arrangements, arguing that education was not a fundamental right and that relative differences between the rich and the poor were not constitutional issues. Although state courts have ruled more expansively in this area, legislative actions are far behind.

65. Danielson, *Politics of Exclusion.*

66. On inequities in educational funding, see William M. Taylor and Dianne M. Pinche, *A Report on Shortchanging Children: The Impact of Fiscal Inequity on the Education of Students at Risk*, Committee Print, House Committee on Education and Labor, (GPO, 1991), pp. 21–24.

DEFENSIVE LOCALISM. These features of social policy, together with the ability of localities to impose (or reduce) many taxes, made the costs and benefits of living in one political jurisdiction over another substantial. With the decline in federal aid to places in the 1980s, the trade-off sharpened. American politics and policy can now be described as "defensive localism," in which the aim is to reduce domestic spending by the federal government, push responsibilities down to lower levels of government, and contain the social problems associated with poverty—and their costs—within defined spatial and political boundaries.

Because questions concerning local political boundaries are not constitutionally part of American national politics, the problems that arise from resource fragmentation at the local level rarely enter national political discourse. Once this set of issues fell from the national agenda in the 1970s, the range of explanations and solutions for the problems of cities (and, by extension, urban poverty) was truncated. In this context it became easier to blame local politicians for mismanagement or to point to individual deviant behavior as the cause of the cities' social problems.[67]

Thus the organization of power across political boundaries in the United States made possible the policy strategy first pursued by the Republican party in the 1980s: to devolve social policy responsibility to lower levels of government and to encourage private solutions to social problems. This new approach to policy in turn redefined the problems of poverty and race in the United States. The federal government has abandoned these problems, treating them as inner-city issues that are the proper responsibility of the localities in which they occur. That abandonment accounts for the curious silence about poverty and race in American national politics, unbroken even in the wake of the most violent urban riots in American history in Los Angeles in 1992.

Conclusion: Multitiered Political Systems and Social Policy

The American experience highlights some of the ways a multitiered political system can affect social policymaking. In the United States the possibilities for isolating the poor politically and spatially offered a way to fragment the polity that severely handicapped proponents of a more expansive social policy. Key to this outcome was the way in which na-

---

67. See, for example, Lawrence M. Mead, "The New Politics of the New Poverty," *The Public Interest*, no. 103 (Spring 1991), pp. 3–20.

tional political institutions were linked to local interests and the different strategies that national political actors could pursue through national institutions. Thus differences in the organization of central institutions create distinct possibilities and perils in social policymaking.

A brief examination of the central institutions of the European Union indicates the ways that differences in decision rules and in the nature of the ties of central actors to the local level could create different political outcomes. As in the United States, the EU has relied heavily on policies for poor places and legalistic extensions of social protections; fiscal constraints make it likely that these will continue to be the main channels for extending European social policy.[68] Yet these policies fit into the politics of the EU quite differently than do their American counterparts.

The political strength of policies for poor places is closely related to the political significance of those places. In the United States, the political importance of poor places (cities) was a temporary phenomenon that disappeared as cities lost population and local party organizations atrophied and lost power at the center. In the EU, poor places—in this case, countries—are better positioned structurally. Because votes in the European Council are allotted by country, and because decisions require either unanimous or qualified-majority votes, shifts in population or party organization will not diminish the power of poor places. Their political importance is much more institutionally rooted than was the power of American cities after the New Deal.

A second difference suggesting that policies for poor places would be more secure in the Union than in the United States is the position of the executive. The head of the European Commission faces a set of incentives quite distinct from those of the American president. The Commission's institutional goal is to extend the reach of the European Union and to deepen the ties that bind its members. In this context the concentration of poverty in particular regions actually serves to heighten the importance of policies that aim to alleviate economic disparities. The EU's structural policies are the price paid for the other economic advantages that stem from the union and are essential for binding together the diverse elements of the community. Thus there is no real counterpart at the executive level in Europe to the American Republican strategy of ignoring poor places. Cities cannot affect the power and prestige of the presidency by threatening to secede. The American president needs simply to win the majority

---

68. See Stephan Leibfried and Paul Pierson, "Prospects for Social Europe," *Politics and Society*, vol. 20 (September 1992), p. 355.

of electoral votes to exercise the privileges of office. By contrast, the "executive" of the EU—the Commission—very much needs the cooperation of poor places to extend its own power and reach.

Legal strategies for extending social policy also fit into the European Union quite differently than in the United States. Like the American legal system, the European Court of Justice (ECJ) has played a crucial role in extending social policy when political channels have been blocked or sluggish. But there are crucial differences. In the United States, the constitutional barriers to basing legal arguments on economic inequality led to an increased emphasis on racial inequalities. Yet race is the deepest social cleavage in the United States, and perhaps the most politically divisive issue in American history. Legal decisions extending social policy on the basis of racial discrimination were therefore highly vulnerable politically. By contrast, the employment-based rationale on which the ECJ makes its decisions is far less likely to exacerbate existing cleavages. Indeed, this rationale heightens "the visibility of the benefits bestowed while obscuring the costs."[69] The crosscutting interests of national employers militates against a united employer counterattack on the courts.

The highly centralized welfare states of postwar Europe created a model for social policy that is not likely to be replicated in the more sprawling "federal" institutions of the European Union. But the more fragmented and decentralized organization of the EU does not mean that Europe will follow in the path of the United States; the political and social policy consequences of decentralization depend greatly on the social and political context in which institutions operate. The distinctive combination of race and localism in American history deeply affected the institutions that span subnational boundaries as they sought to define the balance between local and national responsibilities and authority. Because localities are organized along racial and income lines, the blend of national and local responsibility for social welfare inherited from the 1930s has not only sustained less generous policies for the poor; it has also institutionalized policy and political divisions between the poor and the rest of the nation. The limits of American social policy as a tool for social integration stem not just from its decentralized political structures but also from the localistic and racially divided context in which those institutions are situated.

69. Leibfried and Pierson, "Prospects."

Part Three

Prospects for Social Europe

CHAPTER ELEVEN

Assessing the Delors Era and Social Policy

George Ross

T HE EUROPEAN COMMUNITY (now the European Union) was founded on a liberal vision that did not embrace supranational social programs. Social policy matters were first seriously broached in the 1970s, but they were quickly shelved. They reappeared only under the Delors presidency after 1985, when two dynamics merged to allow a general renewal of European integration. Central member states changed their outlooks, particularly in economic policy. Next, an activist Commission used the "variable geometry" of European institutions—specifically, its own constitutionally flexible role—to set new agendas and mobilize new resources. Consequently, the European Community entered a renewed period of expansion and change. Moreover, perhaps for the first time the Community established a number of social policy bridgeheads. Not surprisingly, these were largely in the labor market and industrial relations sectors rather than in core welfare state matters.

The renewal of European integration after 1985 quickly captured the imagination of many scholars. Their enthusiasm sometimes obscured deeper dynamics, however, particularly in social policy. Some foresaw the contagion of integration leading to the construction of a federal European welfare state.[1] Others weighed prospects that the EC would build an industrial relations regime comparable to those of European nation-states.[2] Still others measured Community accomplishments against a need to provide collective goods to compensate for deterioration

---

1. Some of the original working papers for this volume took this approach.

2. The excellent work of Martin Rhodes provides the best examples. See, for example, Rhodes, "The Future of the 'Social Dimension': Labour Market Regulation in Post-1992 Europe," *Journal of Common Market Studies*, vol. 30 (March 1992), pp. 23–51.

of labor market regimes at national levels.[3] That such criteria were unrealistic should have been more evident. The EC was constitutionally barred from most welfare-state areas, and it was not a nation-state, let alone an instrument for the social democratic rebalancing of the international economy. The larger problem of such approaches was that they made the task of judging what the Community actually did accomplish very difficult.

Any discussion of social policy in the European Union should begin with a reminder of how explicit policy initiatives occur in the complex European political system. The European Commission must be at the center of any explanatory equation, since it is the institution explicitly charged with proposing policy to the Council of Ministers. But the opportunity structures governing its ability to make propositions constrain in three different ways. Constitutionally, the Commission can propose policy only in areas permitted by EC/EU treaties. Next, it can propose only what member states are likely to entertain, given that governments in the decision setting of the Council constitute the EU's legislature. Finally, it must itself have the capacities to find and exploit those limited opportunities that treaty prospects and the intergovernmental context do allow. It must be a skillful policy entrepreneur, astute enough to devise proposals that will maximize prospects for success.

The simple truth is that these three factors rarely combined positively in social policy. The treaty has never allowed much European social policy activity. Member states have seldom facilitated EC/EU activity even in those narrow areas allowed by the treaties. Opportunities for Commissions to act in the area of social policy have therefore been limited. And there have been very few Commissions with the entrepreneurial capacities to promote what these constraining opportunity structures did permit.

Over EC history, until the mid-1980s, policy successes and their legacies were very modest. This is what makes the social policy history after 1985 so interesting. The Delors Commissions generated considerable capacity to act. How well did they do within the limits of what was possible? This chapter will try to answer this question, first reviewing the settings and policy legacies that the Delors Commissions inherited in 1985, then scrutinizing what happened in the three social policy areas

---

3. See Wolfgang Streeck, "European Social Policy after Maastricht: The Social Dialogue and Subsidiarity," *Economic and Industrial Democracy,* vol. 15 (Spring 1994), pp. 151–77.

(regional redistribution to counteract social dumping, health and safety regulation, and broader industrial relations matters) where results might reasonably have been expected.

Policy Processes and Policy Legacies

The Treaty of Rome's most important social provisions were limited to interstate trading and agricultural policy and focused on issues of labor market mobility (articles 48, 52, and 59), training (article 128),[4] and equal opportunity for men and women (article 119).[5] In none of these areas was there much indication about how and when prescribed "harmonization and cooperation" should be achieved, rendering any Commission role very difficult. The treaty also created a European Social Fund (ESF, in articles 123-128) to make "the employment of workers easier, increasing their geographical and occupational mobility within the Community" and a European Investment Bank (EIB, in articles 129 and 130), an instrument with a certain regional equalization bent;[6] nevertheless, the scope of the programs and the amounts of money involved were relatively small.

The diplomatic setting constrained EC action in social policy as much as the treaty did. This was the era, par excellence, of the consolidation of modern welfare states. Opportunities for the Commission to act in

4. The best source for the early period is Doreen Collins, *The European Communities: The Social Policy of the First Phase* (London: Martin Robertson, 1975).

5. The first directive on equal pay for equal work (75/117) derived from article 119; it came in 1975 and was followed by two more in the 1970s, on access to employment (76/207) and on social security and professional certification (79/7). The intervention of the European Court of Justice in 1976 in response to a suit against Sabena (which established the right of individual appeal on the basis of article 119) opened new doors. See Eliane Vogel-Polsky and Jean Vogel, *L'Europe Sociale 1993: Illusion, Alibi ou Réalité?* (Brussels: Editions de l'Université Libre de Bruxelles, 1991); Sonia Mazey, "European Community Action on Behalf of Women: The Limits of Legislation," *Journal of Common Market Studies* (September 1988), pp. 63–84; and Catherine Hoskyns, "Women, European Law and International Politics," *International Journal of the Sociology of Law* (November 1987), pp. 299–316.

6. There had been a certain implicit regional intentionality in the ESF, along with its agricultural counterpart, the European Agricultural Guidance and Guarantee Fund (EAGGF), given the geographic localization of problems of industrial and agricultural restructuring in the original six member states. Article 130 also established a European Investment Bank, with the charge of supporting development projects in less advanced regions (the Italian Mezzorgiorno, in particular). See Paul Romus, *L'Europe et les Régions* (Paris: Fernand Nathan, 1979).

social policy areas were very small, not because the EC's architects and members did not believe in social policy but because they thought that social policy should remain at the heart of national sovereignty. The Community thus grew in coexistence with as wide a variety of social policy regimes as it had members.

This evolution had a deeper logic. Virtually all organized social forces—political elites and parties, employers, unions, and others—saw the nation as their essential location. Social policy became a fundamental mechanism for distributing available rewards. Underwriting this arrangement was the relative feasibility of nation-state strategies for economic development in the first decades after World War II. The common market, as it was constructed, was designed to aid and abet such national strategies, not transcend them.

EC heads of state and government attempted to reconfigure Community ambitions in the early 1970s, and this also brought new concern with EC social policy.[7] The moment turned out to be contradictory. Greater ambitions for Europe were stymied by changed economic circumstances that promoted divergent national responses, and new EC movement toward social policy faltered.[8] The treaty, unchanged, presented the same constraints as earlier; member-state willingness to go forward, even when the treaty allowed it, remained limited. The Council of Ministers adopted the first EC social action program in 1974,[9] but its implementation fell short of ambitions.[10] The creation of the European Regional Development Fund (ERDF) in 1975 was another product of this period,

7. This period brought first reflections about creating a single European market and "economic and monetary union." On social matters, see Collins, *European Communities*, pp. 212 ff.

8. For a rapid review, see Paul Teague, *The European Community, The Social Dimension: Labor Market Policies for 1992* (London: Kogan Page, 1989), chap. 4.

9. Member states agreed to adopt thirty measures over three years, largely in labor market areas (employment policy, improvement and harmonization of working conditions, workplace health and safety, and increased participation by "social partners" in the EC social decisionmaking processes and by workers in firms). Commission of the European Communities, "The Social Action Programme," *Bulletin of the European Community*, no. 2 (1974).

10. Implementation, through Community legislation and other instruments, involved proposals directed toward the "less favored"—migrant workers and their families, the handicapped, youth, and the poor. The first social directive (75/129) involved the coordination of member-state legislation on mass layoffs. The treaty base of this directive and others that followed in similar areas—on workers' rights and company relocations (77/187) and bankruptcies (80/297)—was article 100, which allowed the EC to act generally where member-state regulations affected the "establishment or functioning of the Common Market," with specific reference, via article 117, to social policy distortions.

signifying heightened recognition of problems of socioeconomic convergence in the Community; its scope turned out to be limited as well.[11] Only in health and safety was there the slow accretion of policy that became, over time, a new approach. New social policy activity in the 1970s was therefore modest.[12] Moreover, national governments increasingly began to subvert the workings of even those measures that had been adopted; meanwhile, as the 1970s went on, very little got through the Council of Ministers.[13]

In the 1980s circumstances began to change, however, ultimately changing the opportunity settings within which European institutions lived. Political and business elites in all the major EC states were looking for ways out of "Eurosclerosis," but they had few fixed ideas about solutions. The effects of economic crisis and, more specifically, those that flowed from the policy-induced deflation of the earlier 1980s (largely imported from the United States) led to a convergence of economic management outlooks, which was propitious for European integration. The more favorable setting did not guarantee success, of course. Political actors had to make it happen. Key member states provided one such set of actors.[14] The new European Commission appointed in 1985 constituted the other.

The Commission needed to outline strategies and set agendas. Its first task was to design a launchpad project that would gather support from

11. The main political reason for the ERDF was the enlargement of the Community in 1973 to include Ireland, Denmark, and Great Britain. ERDF resources remained small, largely because member states were reluctant to commit to genuine interstate transfers. More generally, member-state governments used new EC regional involvement for annual budget relief, deliberately leaving holes in national budgets to be filled in by EC payments, which were seen as counterparts to national contributions to the Community budget. Allocations were decided by a quota system at the level of the Council of Ministers. See Helen Wallace, "The Establishment of the European Regional Development Fund: Common Policy or Pork Barrel?" in Helen Wallace, William Wallace, and Carole Webb, eds., *Policy-Making in the European Communities* (New York: John Wiley and Sons, 1977).

12. The European Foundation for the Improvement of Working and Living Conditions, concerned essentially with health and safety matters, was set up in Dublin in 1975. The beginning of EC legislative involvement in health and safety matters also came in this period. Later directives protected workers against risks of chemical, physical, and biological agents at work (in 1980) and against lead (1982) and asbestos (1983).

13. Proposals for workers' participation (the Vredeling directive of 1980) were stopped, as well as a number of regulations on working time (for part-time and temporary work) in the early 1980s.

14. The complementary objectives of the "Franco-German" couple in the EC/EU diplomatic context were of immense importance. Changed economic policy perspectives of the French leftist government are correctly cited as fundamental.

business and other important interest groups, and in the process bring itself new institutional power and clout. The White Paper on completing the internal market filled the bill. Playing simultaneously to the needs and concerns of the most important member states, it began the renaissance of European integration. Placing a time limit on the implementation of the White Paper (two Commission terms) created a slogan—"1992"— and proved a stroke of political genius. Complex politicking then led member states to call an intergovernmental conference to update the Rome treaty to take into account the "1992" program, producing the Single European Act (SEA). Perhaps the shrewdest move in these negotiations was to link the single market to a change in EC decisionmaking procedures to liquidate the Luxembourg compromise. Council unanimity for all important decisions thus would give way to decisions by qualified majority voting in most policy areas covered by the White Paper.[15] It was logical also to propose new powers for the European Parliament in these areas through a cooperation procedure, which allowed the Parliament to propose amendments. Finally, the negotiators agreed on an extended list of EC "competences"—new areas in which the Community acquired a legal basis to act.[16]

Given the EC past, it was not surprising to find no mention of social matters in the White Paper. Member states were clearly not eager to give the Community new social policy latitude. In the SEA the application of qualified majority decisionmaking in the general area of harmonization (article 100a) was excluded for two single-market areas central in the EC's very thin social policy legacy: provisions "relating to the free movement of persons" and those "relating to the rights and interests of employed persons." Social policy concerns were not completely absent from the SEA, however.[17] Much stronger commitment to "economic and social cohesion" (regional development policies) came in a new article 130 of the treaty. Qualified majority voting on directives concerning health and

15. See Emile Noël, "The Single European Act," *Government and Opposition,* vol. 22 (Winter 1987), pp. 3–13. The best single account of the SEA period is to be found in Jean de Ruyt, *L'Acte Unique Européen: Commentaire* (Brussels: Editions de l'Université de Bruxelles, 1989).

16. In research and development, the environment, foreign policy cooperation, and, most important for this research, economic and social cohesion.

17. Delors had clearly announced his social policy concerns as early as his first program speech to the European Parliament in January 1985. "Europe," he noted, "will not modernize its structures of production solely by establishing a Single Market." The speech is reproduced in Jacques Delors, *Le Nouveau concert européen* (Paris: Odile Jacob, 1992), pp. 27–49.

safety issues (in article 118a) became possible, presumably because health and safety regulations might be used as nontariff barriers. Finally, a new "social dialogue" (article 118b) between capital and labor at the European level was encouraged. The SEA thus opened up prospects for limited new social policy activity.[18]

The Delors Commission approached its tasks using what its staff labeled the "Russian doll" strategy.[19] Forward-looking policy linkages were explicitly designed into each policy proposal, implying further-reaching new proposals later on. Next, each policy package was designed to maximize the political resources returning to the Commission, to give the Commission sufficient new clout to push the next packages forward. The deeper logic of Russian dolls involved building on the EC market-building mandates to move into state-building areas. In essence, the new Commission hoped to become the energizer of a cycle of Europeanization, beginning in market-building areas and extending toward more federalist and political matters. From the outset, however—given the treaty, member-state desires, and slim existing policy legacies—the place of social policy in this ambitious strategy had to be modest.

Russian Dolls, Social Policy, and Regional Redistribution

In keeping with its strategic concerns, the Commission hardly allowed the ink to dry on the Single European Act before agitating for new programs. Its next Russian doll was *Paquet Delors,* a dense budgetary program proposed in 1987 as the financial complement of the Single European Act.[20] That the Commission would ask for more money in the aftermath of the SEA and in the midst of a major budgetary crisis was not surprising. More unusual was how the Commission linked financial matters to more far-reaching concerns. It first proposed redefining the Community's procedures to ensure that general budgetary discussions among member states would occur only every five years, gaining greater year-by-year budgetary latitude and freedom from the bane of annual money fights. The package's second dimension proposed changes to the

18. For a juridical consideration of these questions, see Vogel-Polsky and Vogel, *L'Europe,* pt. 2, chap. 2.

19. I have written about this from the point of view of the Delors staff in George Ross, *Jacques Delors and European Integration* (Oxford University Press, 1995).

20. See Delors' speech to the European Parliament in February 1987 for his own framing of the package. Delors, *Le Nouveau concert,* pp. 50–60.

Common Agricultural Program (CAP), introducing budgetary stabilizers that would kick in as financial limits were approached. It was the Delors package's third dimension, however, that had an important social content. In the name of "economic and social cohesion," it proposed bringing Europe's less-developed areas up to levels comparable to those of the Community's rich core.

At first sight regional redistribution might not seem to be social policy at all, but it would be wise to look again. Regional blocs are formed out of national states, themselves usually at different levels of economic and social development. Socioeconomic divergence, in the absence of federalist-type regulation, is almost certain to enhance existing distortions and cause new ones, in particular to promote downward harmonization. There will obviously be a host of counteracting variables, including human capital, culture, the pull of successful regions, and the like, yet the odds are great that some form of social dumping will eventually occur. Well-constructed regional development policies can counteract tendencies to downward harmonization; since 1987–88 EC/EU regional policies have become the most significant instruments for preempting any "race to the bottom" in labor standards and labor-market regulation.

As of 1985 there existed a small policy legacy in regional redistribution to give the Commission its opening. The regionalizing intentions of the ERDF, the ESF, and the EIB were clear, even if their workings were poorly focused, organized, and financed. The intergovernmental situation had also changed favorably. Greece joined the Community in 1982, with negotiations on admitting Spain and Portugal quickly following (the two joined in 1986). With these three new less-developed members joining Ireland, the EC became an economically bimodal space, dominated by advanced industrial nations but including several less-advanced nations on its edges. Per capita income levels in Greece and Portugal, for example, were half those of the more advanced EC nations. There was considerable danger to the EC North that the new South might choose a low-wage, low-regulation development strategy. Moreover, these regional disparities had an important political dimension: they existed within a transnational space where basic decisions were taken intergovernmentally. The single-market program, for example, was meant to give northern Europe's firms the run of a much larger economic area. The means devised to do so—creating a genuine frontier-free EC internal market—would make it extremely difficult to protect inefficient industries in less-developed regions and, more generally, would cause serious adjustment problems for the EC's South. This asymmetry of costs and benefits also helped place regional redistribution on the agenda.

The "reform of the Structural Funds" introduced by the Delors package was the first substantial European-level attempt to confront regional inequalities by planned redistribution among member states. The reform increased Community resources, proposed using these funds more effectively, and, most important, sought to consecrate a long-term EC commitment to the kinds of interregional transfers found in federal systems. In absolute terms, general structural fund aid doubled over a five-year period, rising from roughly 7 billion ECU[21] in 1987 to over 14 billion in 1993 (in 1988 prices). To these numbers one should also add loans made by the EIB (almost 35 billion ECU over the same period). To get some idea what this represented historically, from 1975 to 1987 when the Delors package reforms were proposed, only 24 billion ECU had been disbursed in toto. But there was much more involved than money. The shift to interregional economic solidarity was accompanied by a commitment to medium-term regional development planning, in which the Commission itself gained a substantial new role.[22] The workings of separate Community instruments (the structural funds—ESF, ERDF, and EAGGF—plus the European Investment Bank) were to be coordinated to target a set of specific objectives and principles.[23]

A second Delors package was passed in December 1992 in the newly stringent setting of Communitywide recession. Using an accounting technique that included sums allocated to the new cohesion fund established at Maastricht, it proposed another doubling of regional policy money by 1999.[24] The first reform package of 1987–88 was meant to be a break-

21. At the time of this writing the ECU was worth US$1.33.

22. Commission of the European Communities, "Community Structural Funds: Assessment and Outlook," COM (92) 84 (Brussels, March 1992), p. 9.

23. Objective 1, in EC parlance, was aid to less-developed EC *regions* where per capita income was less than 75 percent of the Community average (largely in the South). Objective 2 was reconversion activities in regions with declining, usually Rust Belt, industries (mainly in the North). These first two objectives were to be attacked through combined use of at least two of the funds (the ERDF, plus at least one other). Objectives 3 and 4, training programs, were the prerogative of the ESF: objective 3 was targeted at overcoming long-term unemployment (for adults over twenty-five years old unemployed more than a year); objective 4 was to help unemployed young people (under twenty-five) and the disabled enter the labor market. Objectives 5(a) and 5(b), considerably smaller and largely the prerogative of the EAGGF, involved development and structural adjustment in rural areas. In 1990 a special arrangement was added to provide aid for the five new East German *länder*.

24. During the Maastricht negotiations in 1991, the Spanish insisted upon a quid pro

through toward consecrating the EC commitment to regional redistribution. Passage of the second package clearly deepened this new commitment, with the clear intention of inscribing regional redistribution so deeply in the *acquis communautaire* that it could not be removed.[25]

What have been the consequences of all this? The ostensible purpose of the programs is to promote a convergence in levels of development among regions by stimulating more rapid and successful growth in poorer areas. If equity is a central matter in these transfers, it is primarily equity among regions and zones in the European Union, not equity across populations and classes. The social policy goal is to buy backward EU regions into the "European model of society" and preempt races to the bottom. The most important result so far is political: the beginning of federalized relationships beyond simple market exchanges across the multinational community.[26] The regional transfer structures discussed thus far are probably the most important such breakthrough in the three and a half decades of EC/EU history.

In practical terms, pluriannual funding programs around more or less coherent goals were established during the first period, but without a great deal of precise projection of results.[27] Whatever else has hap-

---

quo to compensate for economic and monetary union, leading to a protocol to the Maastricht deal establishing a new "cohesion fund." This fund is designed to compensate the South for compliance with EC/EU environmental policies and for participation in the "trans-European networks" for integrated infrastructure in transport, telecommunications, and energy established by Maastricht. The fund will help undercut temptations to sabotage EC/EU environmental policies (another significant new federalist-type Union responsibility) and provide more incentives to less developed areas to participate in one of the more important industrial policy dimensions of the EU.

25. For an excellent discussion of the politics of the second Delors package, see Michael Shackleton, "The Delors 2 Budgetary Package," in Neill Nugent, ed., *The European Community 1992, Annual Review of Activities* (Oxford: Blackwell, 1993), pp. 11–26.

26. In addition, the design of the new regional policy approaches is quite explicitly directed toward producing stakeholders, particularly at the regional level, in their success and continuation. See Michael Keating and Liesbet Hooghe, "The Politics of EU Regional Policy," paper presented at the Conference of Europeanists, Chicago, 1994; and Gary Marks, "Structural Policy and Multilevel Governance in the EC," in Alan W. Cafruny and Glenda G. Rosenthal, eds., *The State of the European Community*, vol. 2, *The Maastricht Debates and Beyond* (Boulder, Colo.: Lynne Rienner, 1993).

27. Evaluative rigor is hard to achieve since it is difficult to reach firm conclusions about extraordinarily complicated policy innovations that are barely five years old. Not surprisingly, it has taken most of that period simply to get the new procedures for planned programming up and running. The Greek Community Support Framework (CSF), for example, structuring the entire EC/EU effort toward Greece, was not even approved until March 1990. It is clear, however, that thus far Brussels has been dependent upon member states and regions for the production and execution of the proposals; moreover, differences

Table 11-1. *ERDF and Structural Fund Contributions to Objective 1 Regions, as Percent of Country Investment and GDP, 1989, 1993*

Country	Investment		ERDF (percent of GDP)		Structural funds (percent of GDP)	
	1989	1993	1989	1993	1989	1993
Greece	6.8	7.8	1.3	1.7	2.3	2.9
Ireland	5.8	6.3	1.0	1.3	2.2	2.7
Portugal	4.9	6.0	1.4	2.1	2.7	3.7
Spain	2.5	3.0	0.6	0.8	1.1	1.2
European Union average	0.5	0.6	0.1	0.1	0.2	0.3

Source: Commission of the European Communities, *Les Régions Dans les Années 90*, Quatrième rapport periodique sur la situation et l'évolution socio-economiques des régions de la Communauté (Luxembourg, 1991), p. 63.

pened—and a lot has—resource transfers in relation to the investment needs of the poorer Union countries have been substantial, as table 11-1 shows.[28] These figures are impressive. The Commission claimed in 1993 that the transfers had made an important contribution to growth of aggregate demand in these areas.[29] In its evaluations the Commission is cautious, however, about supply-side improvement. The structural funds are Keynesian in essence, injecting into recipient regions new public spending capacities that otherwise would have not been present. As such, they cannot help providing additional growth or tax relief (or both); their precise multiplier effects may be unclear, but they clearly have some positive results, particularly in job creation. A 1992 EC document optimistically estimates that about 500,000 additional jobs could be attrib-

---

in willingness to cooperate and administrative capacities from country to country have been great. More sophisticated choices of targets, areas for emphasis, and the grounds for medium-term evaluation of effectiveness will come only in the second period, which has just begun. The first CSF under the second Delors package, for Portugal, has just been put together. See Commission of the European Communities, *Cadre Communautaire d'Appui, 1994–1999: Portugal* (Brussels, April 27, 1994).

28. See Commission of the European Communities, *Guide to the Reform of the Community's Structural Funds* (Luxembourg: Office for Official Publications of the European Communities (hereafter OOPEC), 1989). For detail, see yearly issues of Commission of the European Communities, *Annual Report on the Implementation of the Reform of the Structural Funds* (Luxembourg: OOPEC); and Yves Doutriaux, *La Politique Régionale de la CEE* (Paris: Presses Universitaires de France, 1991).

29. See European Commission, *Fourth Annual Report: The Implementation of the Reform of the Structural Funds, 1992* (Luxembourg: OOPEC, 1994), pp. 24–27. The training funds were allocated on a different geographical basis from the other funds, hence the difficulty of evaluation. The major changes with the coming of the second package were to enjoin stronger efforts at equal male-female allocation plus greater stress on training for new technologies.

uted to regional aids for Objective 1 areas (with Spain getting 120,000, Italy 85,000, and Portugal 70,000).[30]

More generally, there has been very little North-South social dumping in the European Union and remarkably few signs that southern EU member states are eager to exploit their relative economic and social policy backwardness as a competitive tool. By and large, the South seems persuaded that it should cast its low with the higher-wage, stronger welfare-state northerners. There are obviously many reasons other than EU regional redistribution programs for this attitude. But there is enough evidence about such programs—in particular, the magnitude of the sums involved—to ask, What would have happened had they not existed?

The "Social Dimension" and Health and Safety

Following the difficult passage of the Delors package, the Commission turned to economic and monetary union (EMU), its highest priority and the most important Russian doll.[31] Immediately on the heels of the submission of the Delors report on EMU to the European Council in 1989, however, when Commission power and prestige may have been at its highest point ever, Delors introduced the *Community Charter of Basic Social Rights for Workers*.[32] The charter was a "solemn commitment" on

30. Commission of the European Communities, *Community Structural Funds*, p. 16. The same document (p. 19) argued further that regional redistribution also paid off for the most advanced areas of the EC. For every 100 ECU invested in Portugal, it claimed, 46 came back to the rest of the Community in terms of Portuguese imports (with the return for the other Objective 1 areas ranging from 36 to 16 ECU). For more data, albeit extremely difficult to interpret, see Commission of the European Communities, *Employment in Europe, 1993* (Luxembourg: EC, 1993), especially chap. 5.

31. The Delors package was held up for several months. It finally took the willingness of the Germans to pay the lion's share of budget increases to get it through at a special Brussels summit in 1988.

32. The actual notion of a new *socle* (foundation) of social rights was first proposed in 1987 by the Belgian minister of labor. Delors then took the notion to the 1988 Stockholm conference of the European Trade Union Confederation, where he spoke of a set of basic social rights as "one of the . . . major axes of European social space," clearly implying that these rights would be enforceable. In the meantime, an internal Commission think tank, the Groupe Lacroix, worked through the issues. Patrick Venturini, future social policy adviser in the Delors cabinet, was charged with producing a proposal on social matters, later published as "Un Espace Social Européen a l'Horizon, 1992" (Luxembourg: OOPEC, 1988). The Economic and Social Committee and the European Parliament then sketched and debated an *enforceable* bill of social rights for citizens, and not only workers. This, the so-called Beretta report, is reprinted in "Opinion of the Economic and Social Committee on Basic Community Social Rights," *Social Europe* (January 1990). The Marin report—

the part of eleven member states—with Britain furiously opposed—to a set of "fundamental social rights" for employees. It made no legal addition to the Treaty of Rome or to the Single European Act; instead, it sought to gather together and make good on as many as possible of the unfulfilled social promises already contained in the Community's treaty base.

The Commission was clearly pursuing a number of agendas with the Social Charter. One essential concern was to mobilize political resources for itself by calming some of the fears that "1992" had aroused in the European labor movement. More important, however, it was hoping to generate the kind of public pressure for a *future* change in the EC treaty base needed for greater Community activism in social policy. In the meantime, there was one particular area in which the Social Charter meant considerable new legislation: that of workplace health and safety, a field in which the Delors Commission had already begun to act.

Workplace health and safety is unquestionably where the EC has had the greatest scope for regulating labor standards and the Delors Commission had a serious policy legacy (from before the mid-1980s) with which to work.[33] The 1974 social action program established a tripartite Advisory Committee on Safety, Hygiene and Health Protection at Work (ACSH), which became the source of initiatives for legislation in occupational health.[34] Despite considerable difficulty in the Council, some binding health and safety regulations, largely to harmonize rules concerning very specific problems, were enacted over the next decade.[35] The first general health and safety action program was adopted in 1978, projecting a large number of directives addressed to an entire gamut of risks.[36] Enacting it did not get far, however. The harmonization process

---

named after EC Commissioner Manuel Marin—indicated the general, less expansive directions which would be taken, however. It can be found in "The Social Dimension of the Internal Market," *Social Europe,* special edition (1988).

33. This section of the paper draws heavily on the work of Andrew Martin done in the context of a joint research project with the author for the U.S. Department of Labor; Andrew Martin and George Ross, "Lessons from Europe for NAFTA," Harvard University, Center for European Studies, 1994.

34. The ACSH consists of two representatives each from government, trade unions, and employer organizations, nominated by each member state and appointed by the Council. Its founding opened up a new forum for union participation.

35. Directives were enacted on safety signs at the workplace (77/576) and vinyl chloride monomer (78/610). Both were legislated under article 100.

36. Among the very few actually enacted, the 1980 framework directive on chemical, physical, and biological agents at work (80/1107) contained one ingredient of what would become the "new approach." Instead of dealing with a single hazard or remedial technique,

proved extraordinarily cumbersome—it took ten years after 1975 to pass a single directive on gas containers made of unalloyed steel, for example. But the snail's pace of harmonization prompted a search for an alternative method, leading to a new approach to product safety regulations (under article 100). Under this approach, directives about health and safety requirements for products were limited to defining "essential safety requirements" or other "requirements of general interest";[37] they no longer laid down technical specifications. These specifications were instead incorporated through a "general reference to standards" drawn up by European technical standardization bodies (CEN and CENELEC).[38] The legal force of these standards, once set, derived from their function in preventing technical barriers to the movement of products across member-state borders. The label established the presumption that a product was in compliance, putting the burden of rebuttal on the state seeking to bar the product.[39]

---

it identified a broad category of hazards and stated some principles for addressing all hazards in the category. The directive then listed eleven hazardous agents to be treated subsequently in individual directives. Only two of these were enacted—on lead (82/477) and on asbestos (83/477)—and the compromises required to get them enacted left the member states with a great deal of discretion in implementing them.

37. The new approach was developed in a succession of Community instruments. A precedent for using a general reference to standards was set by 1973 legislation to harmonize electrical equipment within certain voltage limits—that is, appliances and tools. A decade later the Commission proposed the extension of that method to all directives aimed at eliminating technical barriers to trade as a remedy for the very slow pace of progress at harmonization; the so-called information directive established "the procedure for the provision of information in the field of technical standards and regulations" (83/189). This was followed in 1984 by an agreement between the Commission and the European standardization bodies, the "general guidelines for cooperation," on procedures for setting standards referred to by directives, including commitments by the Commission to provide financial support and by the bodies to coordinate, increase resources, enable all interested parties to be involved, and improve information. The division of norm setting between directives and standardization thus accomplished by these procedures was consecrated as the "new approach" in a Council resolution on European standardization in 1984. And in May 1985 the Council adopted a "communication on technical harmonization and standardization: a new approach," which fully spelled out the principles described above.

38. Thus, once a directive aimed at providing protection against some specified hazards was enacted, the Commission gave the relevant European standardization body a mandate to draw up technical standards specifying the essential requirements of protection. Comité Européenne de Normalisation (CEN) and Comité Européenne de Normalisation Électrotechnique (CENELEC) were established in 1961 and 1962, respectively, as private, non-profit technical and scientific associations under Belgian law.

39. The binding effect is on the member states which are prohibited from preventing the entry of products in compliance with the directive. Any member state that does so can be taken to the European Court of Justice by the Commission.

The new approach promised a speedup in health and safety harmonization once legislation had been passed, but it did not eliminate the larger blockage, namely, unanimous Council voting. The SEA removed this by allowing qualified majority voting under a new article 118a.[40] Moreover, in a new article 100a, where decisions are still governed by unanimity rules in social areas, the Commission is required to "take as a base a high level of protection" whenever those measures concern "health, safety, environmental protection and consumer protection." Article 118a adds that "member states . . . shall set as their objective the harmonization of conditions in this area, while maintaining the improvements made." The SEA thus specifically enjoined the Commission to promote a "race to the top." The Commission used article 118a to formulate a third health and safety action program for the period 1988–93, whose directives were subsequently incorporated into the action program of the Social Charter.

The first measure under the new article 118a was the framework directive of June 12, 1989 (89/391 EEC), on the "Introduction of Measures to Encourage Improvements in Safety and Health at Work." The framework directive, a statement of principles concerning risk prevention and the general protection of health and safety, plus training and information and consultation of workers about such matters, was aimed at staking out a broad interpretation of the EC's enlarged competence in the field.[41] It spawned a dozen or more directives in specific areas.[42] It also was designed to be the social counterpart of a set of technical harmonization directives (under article 100a) to ensure that the prevention measures enjoined on equipment were carried out by "prevention in the workplace." The first and most important of these equipment directives was the 1989 machinery directive (89/392 EEC); it was followed by

40. As Martin points out, however, at the same time the SEA explicitly precluded the application of qualified majority voting to legislation concerning the "rights and interests of employed persons" (article 100a)—that is, the fundamental rights to organize, bargain collectively, and strike which underlie autonomous worker representation. As is well understood, the effectiveness of health and safety standards depends heavily on the extent to which compliance can be independently monitored and enforced at the workplace by workers and their representatives. Thus, by exempting European legislation on worker representation from qualified majority voting, the SEA left intact a major limit on the possibilities for regulating health and safety at the European level. Martin and Ross, "Lessons from Europe," p. 1.

41. For a more detailed description, see Roger Blanpain and Chris Engels, *European Labour Law*, 2d ed. (Boston: Kluwer, 1993), pp. 170–73.

42. Blanpain and Engels, *European Labour Law*, p. 301.

Table 11-2. *Health and Safety Directives Proposed under the Action Program*[a]

Directive	Date proposed	Result
Protection against asbestos	June 1990	Adopted July 1991 (91/382/EEC)
Minimal standards of medical care aboard ships	July 1990	Adopted April 1992 (92/29/EEC)
Minimum standards at temporary or mobile workplaces	August 1990	Adopted August 1992 (92/57/EEC)
Minimum standards for workplace signage (health and safety warnings)	December 1990	Adopted June 1992 (92/58/EEC)
Minimum standards in extractive industries—drilling	December 1990	Adopted November 1991 (92/91/EEC)
Proposal to create a European hygiene, health, and safety agency	September 1991	Pending as of November 1993
Minimal health and safety standards on fishing boats	November 1991	Pending as of November 1993
Minimum standards in extractive industries—mining	February 1992	Adopted December 1992 (92/104/EEC)
Minimum health and safety standards in transportation	November 1992	Pending as of November 1993
Minimum health and safety standards concerning physical agents	May 1993	Pending as of November 1993
Minimum health and safety standards concerning chemical agents	May 1993	Pending as of November 1993

Source: Annex 3 of Commission of the European Communities, "Green Paper: European Social Policy" (Brussels: EC, November 1993), annex 3, pp. 98–99.

a. All of these directives are subject to qualified majority voting.

several specifying measures.[43] Table 11-2 lists the specific health and safety directives grouped under the action program itself.

Like regional redistribution, health and safety regulation is new legislation, much of it going into effect only at the end of 1992. Its ultimate consequences thus cannot be clear until several complicated processes are completed. Member states must transpose the legislation and, once that is done, they must enforce it. Finally, what happens on the shop floor will be contingent on the commitment and skill with which management and workers strive for safe and healthy work environments. At

43. Specifying measures include personal protective equipment, nonautomatic lifting equipment, gas appliances, telecommunications terminals, equipment for heating combustible liquids and gases, and equipment in potentially explosive atmospheres. Pending are directives on lifts and pressure equipment. Directives on construction products were proposed before the passage of the SEA and adopted afterward.

this point even the Commission knows little about progress. Transposition and implementation in health and safety, as in other single-market areas, are questions just now capturing the attention of EU institutions.[44]

Whatever the outcomes—they may not be known until the end of the 1990s—significant steps have already been taken toward the construction of a broader set of EU labor standards.[45] There is already a solid body of European-level regulation enjoining a race to the top in health and safety. Pre-1985 health and safety policy legacies were slim, but the Delors Commissions worked energetically and resourcefully to build on them. To be sure, the Delors teams cannot take credit for the development of the new approach to harmonization, whose foundations were laid before 1985. They did refine this new approach, however, and then capitalize upon it to the fullest to produce new regulation. The second major innovation—removing unanimity rules and changing article 118a in the SEA—was an important contribution of the Delors Commission. Once it became possible to put together the new approach and changed decision rules, the Commission wasted little time. The new setting allowed the Commission considerable control and latitude in the legislative and standardization process, and the extent and quality of the products are clear.[46] It skillfully promoted high levels of regulation through extensive new legislation, while also consistently trying to strengthen the positions of labor and other interests, particularly in the standardization area where such groups had been underrepresented.[47] The Council has regularly enacted the Commission's proposals without much change.

The Social Charter and Social Dialogue

The teeth of the Social Charter were in the action program that followed (November 24, 1989), which produced a flood of new Community ac-

44. Preliminary Commission data on the application of the framework directive, for example, show a wide variety of different fits between EU injunctions and national health and safety arrangements.

45. The most elaborate argument to this effect is Volker Eichner, *Social Dumping or Innovative Regulation? Processes and Outcomes of European Decision-Making in the Sector of Health and Safety at Work Harmonization* (Florence: European University Institute, 1993)

46. Eichner's discussion of the Commission's role is important here; see Eichner, *Social Dumping*, pp. 39–64.

47. Eichner, *Social Dumping*, pp. 86ff; see also Martin and Ross, "Lessons from Europe." Among other things, the Commission funded and encouraged the work of the Trade Union Technical Bureau, the ETUC's standardization arm in Brussels.

tion.[48] Some forty-seven different instruments were to be submitted to the Council by January 1, 1993.[49] The bulk of proposals for "hard" Community legislation involved living and working conditions, freedom of movement, worker information, consultation and participation, equal treatment, and health and safety. In broader social policy areas there were proposals for recommendations—nonbinding opinions—on convergence of objectives in social protection and in Community floors for social assistance for the poor. In the same register was a proposal for a Community opinion on appropriate minimum wage levels.[50]

The Commission was on shaky political ground with the action program. The slim policy legacy from the 1974 action program legitimated Commission activities (indeed, the 1989 action program covered much of the same ground of the 1974 program), but, with the exception of health and safety, the decision rules that impeded progress in the 1970s had not been altered by the SEA. In areas beyond health and safety, then, passage of legislation was bound to be difficult, if for no other reason than that the British had already signaled their intentions by opposing the Social Charter in the first place.

Of the nine most juridically and politically contentious legislative proposals in the action program, three directives were proposed for "atypical" work (part-time and short contract work). The first aimed at equalizing access to benefits such as training and social services by prorating benefits to actual time worked, and sought to regulate certain operations of "temp"-type agencies. The second proposed granting atypical workers the same rights of vacation time, seniority, and severance pay as full-time workers, prorated by extent of service. The third directive (which passed) extended health and safety guarantees to temporary workers.[51] The directive on working time (passed in watered-down form)

48. It is of some interest here for historians that Delors himself was skeptical about an action program. It took his social policy adviser, Patrick Venturini (director-general of DG-5), Jean Degimbe, and others to persuade him to go ahead.

49. See Com (89) 568, Brussels, November 29, 1989, for the full text. A table of the proposed initiatives is in "Action Program Relating to the Implementation of the Community Charter of Basic Social Rights for Workers," *Social Europe* (January 1990), pp. 52–76.

50. Vogel-Polsky and Vogel carefully enumerates the changes between the Commission's proposed draft and the somewhat weakened document approved later by the Council. See Vogel-Polsky and Vogel, *L'Europe,* pp. 165–75.

51. The most important weakness of all three directives was that they excluded anyone employed for fewer than eight hours a week. For an excellent juridico-political review of action program measures, see Philippe Pochet, *Programme Social: Le Bilan* (Brussels: Observatoire Social Européen, 1993).

proposed minimum rest times and a maximum regular work week, sought to limit night and shift work hours, and imposed new health and safety rules on employers. Next came a directive on pregnant workers to prevent their dismissal, provide minimum levels of remuneration, and protect health and safety during pregnancy (the version that passed was cut back). The Council also quickly passed a directive concerning an employer's obligation to inform employees of the conditions of their employment contracts.[52] Another directive, unpassed because of opposition from southern member states, covered employment and working conditions of workers temporarily posted in another country in the "provision of services."[53] Such workers would retain the social protection schemes of their original countries, but would work under "imperative dispositions" governing pay and working conditions in the country where the service was being performed.[54] Another directive (passed), which updated a 1975 measure on collective layoffs (plant closures), dealt with employer obligations to provide certain timely information to employees, including transnational information. Perhaps the most significant proposal involved establishment of European works councils in transnational firms. It became the centerpiece of the most important social policy matter of the post-Maastricht period. Table 11-3 shows clearly that only proposals with a treaty base in article 118a (health and safety) and article 119 (equal treatment) had much of a chance of getting around a British government intent on stopping or downsizing action in any other area.[55]

Those responsible for producing the Social Charter and the action program—in rough order, the Delors staff, the Commission's Directorate-General for Social Affairs (DG-5), and Vasso Papandreou, then social affairs commissioner—were aware that their efforts were somewhat sacrificial. What could be produced in hard regulatory terms would turn out to be modest. To all but the most euphoric Euro-optimists, this was all that could have been expected, given the modesty of the Community's mandates and policy legacies in social policy. The Social Charter and

---

52. Its two-month grace period and weak enforcement provisions were a problem. Moreover, this directive, like those on atypical work, excepted those hired for eight or fewer hours a week.

53. This was in part prompted by labor mobility in the construction industry. The discovery of Portuguese workers who were building the new headquarters of the Council of Ministers in Brussels but being paid at the Portuguese level was important.

54. Excepting "detachments" of under three months made the measure less effective, however.

55. See "Premier Rapport sur l'Application de la Charte Communautaire des Droits Sociaux Fondamentaux des Travailleurs," *Social Europe* (January 1992).

Table 11-3. *The Most Important Action Program Measures*

Proposal	Date of introduction	Result
Atypical work 1: working conditions	June 1990	Pending as of November 1993
Atypical work 2: distortion of competition	June 1990	Pending as of November 1993
Atypical work 3: health and safety (qualified majority)	June 1990	Adopted June 1991 (91/383/EEC)
Working time (qualified majority)	September 1990	Common position adopted June 1993 (93/104/EEC)
Pregnant workers (qualified majority)	November 1990	Adopted October 1992 (92/85/EEC)
European works councils in transnational corporations	February 1991	Adopted under Maastricht Social Protocol, September 1994
Explicit employment contract	January 1991	Adopted October 1991 (91/533/EEC)
Regulating cross-border detachment of workers providing services	August 1991	None
Update of 1975 directive on collective layoffs	September 1991	Adopted June 1992 (92/56/EEC)

Source: Commission of the European Communities, "Green Paper: European Social Policy" (Brussels: EC, November 1993), annex 3.

action program did not stand alone, however. Interaction with social dialogue, another element in the social dimension, turned out to be very important in the particular context of the Maastricht treaty.

The Single European Act had included a new article 118b stating that "the Commission shall endeavour to develop the dialogue between management and labour at European level which could, if the two sides consider it desirable, lead to relations based on agreement." The launching of new social dialogue was in fact Delors' first step in social policy, taken in January 1985. The initial discussions among UNICE (the Union of Industrial and Employers Confederations of Europe), the employers' association (the European Trade Union Confederation, or ETUC), and the public sector employers' association (CEEP, the Confédération Européenne des Employeurs Publics) began conflictually and did not get very far.[56] Neither ETUC nor UNICE, both essentially Brussels lob-

56. See Janine Goetschy, "Le Dialogue Social Européen de Val Duchesse," *Travail et Emploi* (January 1991), for the antecedents of post-1985 "social dialogue." The two *avis communs* of the "new technologies and social dialogue" and "macroeconomics" groups of the Val Duchesse talks are reproduced in Venturini, *Un espace social*, annex 4.

bies based on confederated national organizations, was empowered to negotiate.[57]

Delors knew that the exercise would initially be more about confidence building than about immediate results. Thus the social dialogue was relaunched in 1989 amidst the élan accompanying the Social Charter. A new steering group (supplemented by a small ad hoc group) was convened, ostensibly to talk about education, training, and the evolution of the EC labor market. Discussion again revealed contradictory purposes. UNICE sought to frustrate Commission legislative purposes and to prevent any bargaining.[58] ETUC, in contrast, wanted as many concrete proposals as possible.

At the heart of the social dialogue strategy were efforts to provide carrots and sticks (collective goods and regulation) to seduce and to constrain the European-level social partners into bargaining. Until 1991 UNICE adamantly refused to contemplate anything of the sort; the Commission's first tactics therefore were to try to strengthen and encourage ETUC and national union movements to become stronger European actors. Thus the Commission systematically encouraged ETUC to take itself more seriously, and, in turn, be taken more seriously by its own constituents and by employers. In particular, it provided substantial funding to facilitate union training, research, and meetings at the European level; the Commission also financed the bulk of ETUC research work on health and safety, a great deal of ETUC internal education, and the costs of organizational get-togethers in Brussels and elsewhere. Meanwhile, it opened up privileged networks of communication between itself and ETUC.[59] As a result ETUC perked up, began to do a great deal more work, hire more people, and assume a higher profile.[60] In the context of

57. On the employers' side, the UNICE secretary general, Zygmunt Tyszkiewicz, could not have been clearer about disinterest in real negotiating; see "European Social Policy: Striking the Right Balance," *European Affairs* (Winter 1989). On the union side, the problem was more that ETUC was a resource-poor and largely ineffectual organization.

58. Nonetheless, an agreement between ETUC and the public-sector employers' association on training in the public sector was actually signed in September 1990.

59. Delors himself was an ex-unionist and knew many of the lead operatives of ETUC; his social affairs adviser, Patrick Venturini (the major architect of the Social Charter and action program), was a former researcher for the Confédération Française et Démocratique de Travail (CFDT) with long-standing and easy contacts with ETUC leaders (certain of whom were from the CFDT); and the director for industrial relations at DG-5, who gave out the money, had a wide range of similar contacts.

60. The ETUC had long settled into the stodgy Brussels routine. Growing concern among ETUC's national constituents about the importance of European-level issues led to substantial changes in ETUC organization at the May 1991 congress, which reconfigured

negotiations for Maastricht, however, new vitality on the union side weighed much less on UNICE than the consequences of the action program. The Commission's practice of consulting the social partners about pending Social Charter legislation, which it began to produce copiously in 1991, persuaded the employers to reconsider the negotiation option.

The Commission thought very carefully about its own social policy submission to the Maastricht intergovernmental conference. According to Delors' social policy adviser, the persistence of large disparities in the Community in wealth, systems of social protection, and systems of social regulation (meaning collective bargaining and industrial relations) had to be accepted as given. "Even if timid convergence appears here and there . . . attachments to national models are often stronger than political divisions." He added, however, that such things needed to be relativized, because intra-EC differences were much less deep that those between each member state and the United States or Japan, a fact that constituted "one of the paths to develop the theme of the 'European model of society.'" The second given was that economic integration would render certain new forms of social regulation necessary. "The debate is . . . on the size and nature of the social dimension and the method of putting it into place . . . but total harmonization is not demanded by anyone." Third, the social dimension at the EC level encompassed three different orders: universal rights enshrined in various charters (those of the International Labor Organization, Council of Europe, United Nations, and so on); an area of exclusive EC competence dealing with market integration, which the EC treaties imperfectly cover; and a gray zone between the EC and member states, where completion of the single market would eventually undermine certain member-state competences.

What should be the principles of new EC social regulation? "The problem is large; given the imperative of subsidiarity, we need to move forward, while respecting 'positive diversity' at member state level, to develop regulatory principles during a period when, in several countries, old forms have been strongly called into question while new ones have

---

ETUC top leadership. The new leadership more aggressively promoted European-level unionism, and the new presence of the industry committees in high EC matters—they were placed in ETUC's power structure at the congress—made transnational issues much more salient. There are fourteen European industry committees affiliated with the ETUC, usually European branches of the International Confederation of Free Trade Unions. The change was promoted largely by the Germans, who had become sufficiently concerned about social dumping to break ranks with their northern trade union allies, who feared European-level tampering with national collective bargaining institutions.

yet to be put into place."[61] It was important for the Community that it not introduce additional labor market rigidities or prevent fruitful experimentation by member states. The Community had a recognized, legitimate role to intervene to promote "space without borders" and "a space of solidarity" (helping to overcome regional differences, devise policies about migrant labor, and so on) and to address "problems common to all member states" (largely informational matters concerning demography, health, and poverty).

The treaty-changing strategy advised by the document was to derive specific proposals from a logic of Community functions flowing from single-market matters, rather than to make spectacular new departures. The biggest foot in the door for future EC social policy, if not necessarily for Maastricht, would come from the market itself. For Maastricht, however, the Commission proposed to broaden the Community purview over social policy matters, hoping for both an incremental growth of the social areas in the treaty and an extension of qualified majority decisionmaking in these areas.[62] A simple but ingenious suggestion accompanied these proposals: Where the Commission could legally propose action in the social policy area under the new provisions, it would first announce its intention to do so to the "social partners" (employers and employees). These partners could then decide, if they agreed, to negotiate in the area announced for legislation. If negotiations succeeded, their results could become a substitute for EC legislation. If the social partners were unable to negotiate, then the Commission could proceed with its legislation.

The Maastricht talks did not immediately comfort the Commission. Proposals to expand qualified majority voting were watered down, attempts to expand Community purview were cut, and the "negotiate or face legislation" clauses were disregarded. In the weeks leading up to Maastricht, however, the atmosphere changed. Discussions throughout most of 1991, nursed carefully by the Commission, saw different national employers' associations begin to shift their positions. Eventually UNICE concluded that if the Community and Commission acquired a wider legislative mandate, the barrage of legislation that it had confronted

61. Interview with Patrick Venturini, Brussels, June 1991.
62. The Community should thus make sure that, beyond the amelioration of living and working conditions, an "adequate level of social protection" was provided, that workers have new rights of "information and consultation," and that new actions were taken to promote employment and act against labor market "exclusions," to improve professional training, to enhance social dialogue, and to expand the provisions of article 119 beyond equal pay to equal treatment in the workplace and in the labor market.

under the Social Charter would only intensify. Accepting the offer to negotiate or face legislation appeared preferable to having meager consultation rights on proposals that would eventually become constraining regulation. The employers could always slow down negotiations and push for the least-damaging deals. To avoid legislation, however, they had to accept the possibility of European-level collective bargaining. Thus on October 31, 1991, the social partners wrote a joint letter to the Dutch Prime Minister proposing a version of the initial Commission proposal; their proposals were then incorporated into the working treaty draft. The October agreement was the first major bargain to be negotiated at European level.

UNICE was hedging its bets, because employers knew that the British had made refusal of the Maastricht social policy proposals their bottom negotiating line for the entire treaty. The British thus could save UNICE from actually having to negotiate. At Maastricht the Dutch presidency, anticipating the British position and perhaps in sympathy with it, proposed a much watered-down social clause to replace the October package. But British Prime Minister Major, in need of a symbolic stand to bring home, refused to accept it. Then the twelve member states agreed to a protocol to the Maastricht agreement, proposed at the very last moment by the Commission via Chancellor Kohl: eleven of them would accept the October package of social clauses. UNICE found itself outmaneuvered; some kind of collective dealing over European social matters seemed inevitable.

Here fate intervened. Had the Social Protocol gone into effect quickly, there might have been a rapid breakthrough to European collective bargaining. The Commission had prepared a list of pending social policy directives from the social action program to resubmit when Maastricht came into force. Ratifying Maastricht proved difficult, however, and did not happen until much later than expected, in November 1993. At this point a weakened Delors Commission with only one more year in power had to pick and choose its opening carefully. It first put out a document operationalizing procedures for the Maastricht Social Protocol.[63] Next

---

63. See Commission of the European Communities, "Communication Concerning the Application of the Agreement on Social Policy Presented by the Commission to the Council and to the European Parliament" (Brussels, December 14, 1993). Because *two* possible approaches to social matters existed (the treaty before Maastricht, which applied to all twelve member states, and the Maastricht protocol, which excluded Britain), the Commission announced that it would choose one or the other on a case-by-case basis, except for health and safety proposals, which follow the old procedures. Under the Maastricht pro-

it chose its best case—a reformulation of the European works council directive.[64]

The setting around the works council issue had changed positively. In some EC member states, France and Germany in particular, prior experience with information and consultation had led to proto-European works councils.[65] Moreover, unions had made considerable new efforts to prepare the way for more such experiments. In 1991 the European Parliament decided to appropriate 17 million ECU to allow European sectoral trade unions to prepare themselves for the eventuality of works councils.[66] In some sectors, particularly metals, there had already been quite a bit of activity, but the Euro-parliamentary money encouraged a number of other unions—chemical, construction, and food service workers, among others—to redouble their efforts. An important groundswell of support for a new directive thus preceded its proposal.[67]

The first version of a new directive (late October 1993) came from the Belgian government. It proposed that a European works council be established, on the basis of negotiations, in every "Community scale group of undertakings" (defined as a group with at least one thousand employees within the EC and two undertakings in different EC member states, with at least one hundred employees in each). Works councils would

---

tocol, there would be two preliminary consultations between the Commission and the social partners, the first about the general area for potential legislation and the second about the potential contents of such legislation, each lasting six weeks. The social partners could then decide between delivering recommendations to the Commission for legislation or opening negotiations.

64. Council of the European Communities, "Presidency Note for Labor and Social Affairs Council: Proposal for a Directive on European Works Councils," 8709/93 (Brussels, October 6, 1993). The proposal on information and consultation of workers had a long history, stretching back to 1980 when the Commission proposed the so-called Vredeling directive (named after the EC commissioner), only to see it buried because of opposition from the British, the American Chamber of Commerce in Europe, and UNICE. The Social Charter action program had also proposed a directive.

65. Paul Marginson, Mark Hall, and Keith Sisson list the twenty or so companies with proto-works councils in "European-Level Information and Consultative Structures in Multinational Enterprises," *Issues in People Management*, no. 7 (London: Institute of Personnel Management, 1993).

66. The money was to be supplied, through the Commission, to the fifteen European sectoral industry committees to bring together workers in transnational companies for preliminary meetings (that is, the money was to subsidize the meeting expenses).

67. Perhaps as important, this support was located primarily in Europeanwide sectoral industry committees. Such efforts had been pushed in the past mostly by the ETUC, as a European-level lobby and national union confederation. The enhanced strength of the industry committees, in large part derived from this mobilization, made them in turn more important players in ETUC and vis-à-vis national organizations.

encompass all of an undertaking's operations within the Community. The negotiations to establish the councils would specify, by written agreement, the scope, composition, powers, and term of office of the councils, and they would have to be held "in a spirit of co-operation with a view to reaching an agreement." The social partners would thus have latitude concerning arrangements, but minimum requirements would mandate that a works council be composed of no more than thirty members (drawn from existing employee representatives, or elected if such did not exist), meet at least annually, be informed of company activities and projects (accounts and strategic plans should be open), and told of any decision significantly affecting employees' interests before its implementation. Council competence would be limited to transnational, as opposed to national, matters concerning the group in question.

The initial step under the Social Protocol was for the Commission to consult the social partners about its intention to propose legislation. ETUC favored the Belgian proposal, while UNICE wanted "a broader voluntary approach" with maximal structural flexibility and without binding standard procedures. The next step, a six-week consultation, involved dialogue between the social partners to decide whether to negotiate or legislate.[68] From the first meeting (February 23, 1994), ETUC posed stringent conditions to be met before any negotiations occurred.[69] UNICE was cagier, willing to accept "appropriate arrangements," but again stressing flexibility and the need to examine alternative methods and procedures.[70] The conclusions of the first round of full talks listed key matters at issue. Was information and consultation of workers and their representatives a right, and should it become a right in transnational

68. Thus when the Commission reworked the Belgian proposal on February 8, 1994, into an official proposal, it tried to ensnare UNICE by mildly watering down the Belgian proposal. It removed the "European Works Councils" title, replacing it with the catchy "mechanisms for informing and consulting employees in Community-scale undertakings or groups of undertakings."

69. ETUC insisted that any bargain declare information and consultation to be a fundamental right at the European, general management, and all other decisionmaking levels, with workers' representation at each level. This representation should be structured, permanent, and involve a transnational bargaining committee composed of official employee representatives (usually union members) and the general management of the firm. Finally, if no agreement could be reached in particular firms on these matters, there should be minimum provisions applied to all "mechanisms." The ETUC also preferred that any agreement reached among UNICE, itself, and CEEP (the public sector employers' federation) be submitted by the Commission to the Council to become Community law. ETUC, "Draft Record of Conclusions" (Brussels, March, 9, 1994).

70. "UNICE Text," March 3, 1994.

undertakings? Should central management be required to negotiate with *representatives* of workers (that is, unionists) to set up such a mechanism or equivalent procedures? Third, should there be minimum provisions if transnational firm-level negotiations were refused or broke down once they had begun?[71]

UNICE and CEEP initially responded by denying any right to information and consultation at the transnational level and refusing to allow that "representatives of workers concerned" (union members) be implicated legally in the negotiation to set up the mechanisms. ETUC then threatened to break off the negotiations. In response, UNICE capitulated. Just at that point, however, the Confederation of British Industry announced that it disapproved of negotiating and would no longer participate, which led the ETUC to stop the talks. The process of legislation began soon thereafter on a fast track for the German Council presidency after July 1, 1994.

The result did not mean that there would be no further collective bargaining at the European level. In itself, a legislated directive on information and consultation obliged a substantial amount of new European-level negotiating to put the mechanisms of the works council into place.[72] From the trade union point of view, the ensuing changes will be important. Several thousand unionists from across the Union will eventually become official representatives on European works councils. They will have to think of the transnational implications of their union actions, develop new collaborative practices with unionists from other countries, and construct new linkages with union bases inside different national branches of the company. ETUC and its sectoral industry committees will have to generate the intellectual and financial resources to help train and support these new people.[73]

71. Both parties wanted the Council to make into Community law any agreement they reached. Both also agreed to limit negotiations to a shorter period than the one set out in the Social Protocol (ETUC two months, and UNICE three). See "Record of Conclusions (draft text discussed at 6:45 pm on March 17, 1994)," Brussels.

72. Several hundred transnational corporations (TNCs) qualify for inclusion under the new directive (at least one thousand employees in at least two member states). Moreover, even though the Commission's draft directive cut back on possibilities for capturing British multinationals, at least 100 U.K.-based multinational companies will also be included. TNCs not headquartered in the Union will also have to include British activities in the information-consultation mechanisms. Transnational corporations, including major U.S. firms, headquartered outside the EU will also be subject to the directives; forty-three TNCs so affected are listed in Marginson, Hall, and Sisson, "Information and Consultative Structures," p. 390.

73. For British unions, campaigning in the United Kingdom to get cooperation from

This story underlines the complexities of collective bargaining, as played out for the first time on the European level. ETUC was only willing to accept a bargain that was roughly equivalent to legislation. UNICE was willing to negotiate, but wanted to "flexibilize" the "mechanisms for information-consultation." The game thus turned upon how much dilution ETUC would be willing to accept in exchange for the precedent of European-level bargaining, versus how much UNICE was willing to sweeten its positions to avoid legislation. Background factors biased the outcome. Knowledge that the upcoming German presidency would push through the Commission's legislative proposal stiffened ETUC determination not to bargain downward and tempted UNICE to take a minimalist approach.[74] The heart of the story, however, is that ETUC wanted a directive more than UNICE wanted negotiations to avoid one.[75]

The sinuous track leading from the Social Charter and action program, via social dialogue and Maastricht, produced fewer tangible results than in regional redistribution and health and safety. Legislation for the action program passed only where qualified majority was possible, and even then it was diluted by the Council. Had Maastricht been ratified more rapidly, however, much more might have been accomplished under the Social Protocol, and some of this would undoubtedly have taken the form of bargained deals between the social partners. That these outcomes were not attained was almost accidental, certainly not the fault of the Commission. In the last analysis, therefore, the major product of the entire episode is an expanded policy legacy for future Commissions to use, particularly to promote European collective bargaining.

those British companies not directly falling under the legislation also quickly became a key demand.

74. Moreover, both organizations denied having a mandate to negotiate. This is a common bargaining ploy, of course, but for either there were all sorts of reasons for affiliates to want to slow down negotiations. UNICE clearly had a serious problem with its Irish, Danish, and British organizations, even if its Latin members (the Spanish, French, and Italians) and the Belgians were quite eager. ETUC had a German problem: the German unions favored legislation over negotiation.

75. Thus much of the maneuvering in the second stage of consultation that ended in March 1994 was about who would bear public responsibility for failure to negotiate. ETUC was very worried that it would be blamed if it broke off the talks. It even went to the extreme of offering UNICE a different set of matters to negotiate (on atypical work rather than the works councils). After intervention from the Confederation of British Industry, ETUC decided that it could break off the talks without too much bad publicity.

Conclusions

Those who expected—hoped?—that renewed European integration after 1985 would bring welfare-state innovation at the European level could not have been more off the mark. In constitutional terms, the core welfare state was not part of any conceivable Community mandate, except in indirect, long-term ways. In practical political terms, the bulk of conventional welfare-state matters remained solidly ensconced behind borders of national sovereignty in all EC member states. Moreover, despite the alarmism of social policy specialists, welfare states were surviving the change in general economic circumstances. To be sure, one could worry about budgetary squeezes, cringe at neoliberal rhetoric, and regret that there was little new expansion. At bottom, however, there was not much for the EC to fix in core welfare-state areas, even had it been possible for Europe to act at all.

Those who focused on EC actions on labor market matters were more on target, because this was where Europe had the most promising constitutional openings and where greatest change was occurring. The coming of substantial unemployment and considerable new social exclusion was evident; some labor market deregulation had taken place, although unevenly across the Community; and union strength was in serious decline in most member states. The notion that EC social policy development should be judged in comparison with national models of labor market regulation remained farfetched, however. Beyond the treaty and the differences among the industrial relations systems of member states—which made any harmonization a huge puzzle—these national models survived with sufficient vitality to persuade unions and employers to continue investing resources in them. It was therefore very hard to persuade them to risk these resources on a hypothetical European substitute.

The most stringent of these arguments concerning labor market regulation, advanced by Wolfgang Streeck in this volume, measured EC social policy efforts not simply against national models of labor regulation but against the most successful of them, the German one. In this light the European Union stands condemned for failure to counteract the labor deregulatory effects of its own market-building efforts, and for more general inadequacy in struggling against transnational tendencies toward labor market deterioration. What Europe ought to have done, the argument goes, was to begin providing the public goods needed to build something like a German model on the European level.

This argument is disturbing. First of all, its demands for EU action are vastly greater than anything Europe could realistically have been expected to produce. More profoundly, however, the argument is premised on a pessimistic vision of Europe's future, which data do not support. True, economic conditions have changed, and true, these changes have had their most pronounced effects on labor markets. But arguing that these tendencies flow into the de facto creation of an entirely new system of "neovoluntarism," which in turn portends the collapse of Europe's social distinctiveness, is premature.

The Rome treaty set the EC on a trade-market trajectory. Its social policy passages were ambiguous and restrictive. The narrow social policy mandate of the early years was also a product of the institutional stabilization of the Luxembourg compromise, which reflected deeply rooted accumulation strategies based in the nation-states. In this context, extensive spillover into Europeanized social policy areas was unlikely. Changed conditions in the early 1970s opened the door to EC social policy initiatives in the labor market and regional policy, but the persistence of rules from the Luxembourg compromise limited the practical scope of the EC commitment. In 1985 positive changes occurred in the EC central policy equation. Member states renewed their interest in European approaches, and the Commission was taken over by skillful policy entrepreneurs. Existing treaty prerogatives, the diplomatic situation, and the Community's history, however, meant that Europe's new opportunities would be seized first for market building rather than market correcting. Social policy was relegated to a secondary concern, while thin policy legacies from the earlier period ensured that what did occur would be confined to labor market questions and regional redistribution.

A number of outcomes were possible. The Commission might have chosen to do nothing at all—this was what the British desired. It might have decided to do no more than it had been doing before 1985, a course that would have avoided conflict. It might have done different, and more daring, things to expand the EC social policy mandate into new areas, but only at considerable risk to the economic concerns that had created the consensus for relaunching European integration in the first place. What it did do was focus its energies on making the most of the relatively narrow, specific social policy legacies it had inherited.

It is a mistake to minimize the significance of what was actually undertaken. Trying to block social dumping was an important endeavor, and this was what regional redistribution programs and much of the Social Charter and action program, particularly health and safety legislation, were about. Trying to tease out the beginnings of European-level collective bargaining was icing on the cake, a down payment on the future. The results demonstrate some success. Through Maastricht and the two Delors budgetary packages, firm principles of interregional solidarity were established. In the area of workplace health and safety, there now exists the legal framework for a functioning, high-level, European regulatory system. Progress has been much more limited in the remainder of the Social Charter and action program package. Nevertheless, social dialogue, whose purpose from the outset was to lay the foundations for genuine European collective bargaining, has moved further than anyone would ever have anticipated in 1985.

The Delors period leaves a considerably enlarged social policy legacy to its successors. Whether the new period will be propitious for maximizing this legacy is less clear, however. The broader context has been rapidly changing. The severe recession that began in 1992 revealed fundamental problems that had been discounted during the euphoric period of the 1992 program. In the words of the important 1993 Commission White Paper on Growth, Competitiveness, and Employment, "The truth is that although we have changed, the rest of the world has changed even faster."[76] Over the last two decades, according to the White Paper, the European economy's potential rate of growth had shrunk from 4 percent to around 2.5 percent annually; unemployment has been steadily rising from cycle to cycle; the investment ratio has fallen by 5 percentage points; and the Community's competitive position in relation to the United States and Japan has worsened in terms of employment, shares of export markets, research and development, and innovation and its incorporation into marketable goods and new product development.

Recognition of Europe's fundamental employment problem has become the major new element in the Union's social policy debate. The unspoken assumption behind the efforts of the Delors Commissions was that completing the single market and implementing economic and monetary union would be sufficient to stimulate new European economic growth, technological innovation, wealth, and job creation to levels competitive with other industrialized areas of the world. The assumption was clearly unrealistic. Indeed, the major criticism to be leveled at the architects of renewed European integration after 1985 should concern the miscalculations built into their market-building strategies much more

---

76. Commission of the European Communities, "Growth, Competitiveness, Employment: The Challenges and Ways Forward into the 21st Century," supplement 6/93 to *Bulletin of the European Communities* (Luxembourg, 1993), p. 10.

than the relative modesty of their social policy goals. These miscalculations have led to a new discussion about the need for further basic reforms and a new political wave in favor of deregulation, particularly of labor markets. Whatever the outcome, the social policy order of the day has shifted from constructing social regulatory policies at the European level to reconfiguring labor market and other arrangements to allow the European economy to compete in the world market. This, plus the important fact that a new European Commission—certainly less pro-labor and much weaker than the Delors Commissions—began its tenure in 1995, means that the Union agenda on matters of social policy may be different from the one that preoccupied Europe after 1985.[77]

77. The degree to which EC/EU reflections on social matters has changed is equally illustrated in the Commission's 1993 Green Paper on "European Social Policy, Options for the Union," whose contents are not a positive set of proposals but a set of vague options, very few of which involve new Commission activism.

CHAPTER TWELVE

From Market Making to State Building? Reflections on the Political Economy of European Social Policy

Wolfgang Streeck

T HE "RELAUNCHING OF EUROPE" was the response of European political and business elites to a number of predicaments that had befallen
their countries in the years following the second oil shock. Future research will sort out the details and undoubtedly will be divided over what
weight to attach to the various forces that contributed to the resurgence
of European integration.[1] But a major factor was clearly economic stagnation, accompanied by high unemployment, which was widely diag-
nosed as the result of a disease called "Eurosclerosis" that had given rise
to a widespread mood of "Europessimism."[2] Further in the background
was the fear among large European firms of falling irreversibly behind in
competition with Japan and, in part, the United States—not just because
Europe, unlike the two other regions, was still saddled with strongly
entrenched trade unions and welfare states but also because European
markets seemed too small to absorb the large production volumes
deemed necessary to underwrite rapidly rising research and development
costs.

In the political sphere, European governments had witnessed the failure of the French exercise in national-level Keynesian reflation; their
worst fears about the consequences of growing economic interdependence for the effective sovereignty of national states over their economies
had been confirmed. At the same time hopes for a return to some sort of

I am grateful to Catherine Farry and Sigurt Vitols for research assistance.

1. For an excellent initial account, see David R. Cameron, "The 1992 Initiative: Causes
and Consequences," in Alberta M. Sbragia, ed., *Euro-Politics: Institutions and Policymaking
in the "New" European Community* (Brookings, 1992), pp. 23–74.
2. The following relies heavily on Wayne Sandholtz and John Zysman, "1992: Recasting the European Bargain," *World Politics*, vol. 42 (October 1989), pp. 95–128.

orderly global economic coordination, under American leadership and together with Japan, were being crushed by U.S. high-dollar and high-interest policies, as well as by apparently inexorable Japanese penetration of European markets. On the brighter side was Margaret Thatcher's stunningly successful replacement of the postwar settlement between capital and labor with monetarist stabilization and neoliberal deregulation policies, demonstrating that containing inflation through unemployment, disengagement of public policy from the economy, and a return to the "free market" were again within the range of the politically and electorally possible. Also, several years of successful operation of the European monetary system under the de facto leadership of the German Bundesbank had flattened inflation rates and induced more convergent macroeconomic performance. Together, these and other developments pointed to practical possibilities for and potential gains from closer cooperation among European governments in their pursuit of monetary stability and improved competitiveness of the European economy; that cooperation, many thought, might serve as a regional substitute for worldwide coordination.

"1992," then, and the integration projects that emerged in its wake, were the result of a double compromise: first, among European governments and, second, between them and European business. Labor was not a party to what may be called the preconstitutional bargain on the post-1992 European Community. The nation-states participating in the deal—especially France, in the aftermath of the disastrous reflation experiment—had apparently concluded that European states, taken by themselves, had become too small not only to be successful players in the global economy but also to govern their own externalities-ridden national economies. With national sovereignty having lost its capacity to control the national fate, the logical answer seemed to be a pooling of sovereignties:[3] increased concertation and coordination among governments, drawing on and expanding the institutional resources of the European Community to create an economic and political entity large enough to enclose a wide range of previously external effects in its boundaries and, at least potentially, to compete with the United States and Japan on the same plane. In this way French nationalism, in particular, seems to have turned in the mid-1980s into European supranationalism.

---

3. Robert O. Keohane and Stanley Hoffmann, "Institutional Change in Europe in the 1980s," in Robert O. Keohane and Stanley Hoffmann, eds., *The New European Community: Decisionmaking and Institutional Change* (Boulder, Colo.: Westview Press, 1991), pp. 1–39.

The details of the second of the two rapprochements that underlay "1992," that between European political and economic elites, are less easy to reconstruct. Indeed, very few attempts to do so have been made, perhaps because the more theoretically ambitious analyses of European integration still take as their frame of reference the old controversy between neofunctionalist supranationalism and neorealist nationalism (see chapter 11, by George Ross, in this volume). I do not claim that this is a trivial subject, although it does seem true that most participants in that debate tend to end up with the somewhat unsatisfactory conclusion that both sides cover significant aspects of the phenomenon. For the fuller story, I suggest looking beyond the interaction between two kinds of institutions, national and supranational, to the relationship between the entire political-institutional complex that takes part in such interaction and results from it and the integrated internal-market economy that is embedded in it. The question behind this is, of course, the central one of any institutionalist political economy: how national and supranational institutions work together or against each other in shaping a polity that governs—or refuses to govern—a common market. Because the answer is so consequential, one cannot expect economic interests to be indifferent to it or to abstain from influencing it. Viewing the formation of the European economy's domestic institutional regime as taking place under a range of restrictive conditions imposed by economic on political forces, then, is at least as likely to aid understanding as yet another attempt to adjudicate between neofunctionalism and neorealism.

It bears note in this context that the relaunching of European integration had to take place on a background of considerable business disaffection with the European Community. Not only had the Community failed to assist European business in weathering the crises of the 1970s—being unable, for example, to organize a common European response to the energy shortage—but in fact it had proven increasingly impotent vis-à-vis the growing protectionist tendencies of national governments. Moreover, the Community apparently was on the verge of an industrial policy that centered on the preservation of jobs, not on the restoration of competitiveness and profitability. And although the political clout of unions and social-democratic parties was declining in national polities, the Community, in some sort of time lag, was still pursuing "Social Action Programme" projects dating back to the precrisis 1972 Paris summit (such as legal information rights for work forces in large firms, under the so-called draft Vredeling directive), which in the early 1980s pitched European and international business in a dramatic battle against an alliance between the Commission and the European trade-union movement.[4]

A short time later, however, perceptions changed and the European Community again came to be seen by influential business elements as potentially benevolent. New conditions in the world economy raised the expected benefits of market integration in Western Europe above its costs, or perhaps made continued recourse to national protectionist solutions more costly. Also, after the defeat of the Vredeling proposal in 1984, business associations and individual business leaders may have become more confident that they could "play" the Community successfully. The stabilization of conservative political majorities in core countries, such as Germany and Britain, and the reversal of French socialism in 1983 very likely contributed to this conclusion. "Farsighted" business leaders from large multinational firms, above all those organized in the European Business Roundtable, played a role. So did, probably, the efforts of go-betweens like the European Commissioner Etienne Davignon, who offered himself as organizer of a different kind of industrial policy aimed at restoring and safeguarding the competitiveness of world market-oriented European multinational companies.

It is not implausible—indeed, it is likely—that political strategists like François Mitterrand and Jacques Delors understood two basic points by the mid-1980s: first, if they wanted to restart Europe, they had to "bring business back in"; second, provided proper assurances were given and policy changes made, there was a realistic possibility for a coalition with business that would add fresh support to a renewed European project. Finding out the conditions for business cooperation cannot have taken much ingenuity. Business had long opposed what it saw as bureaucratic excesses in Brussels, including but by no means limited to the upward harmonization agenda of the social action program; over time it had become outright hostile to the interventionist-technocratic frame of mind hibernating in the Commission bureaucracy since the days of Monnet. To join a revived integration project, therefore, business needed credible assurances that the European Community's emerging economic regime would be significantly less *dirigiste* and more flexible—that is, market-driven—and that integration would proceed so as to help remedy that ominous European affliction, "Eurosclerosis." As political leaders began to work such demands into their emerging proposals for a new integra-

---

4. Tom DeVos, *Multinational Corporations in Democratic Host Countries: U.S. Multinationals and the Vredeling Proposal* (Brookfield, Vt.: Gower, 1989).

tion effort, the revival of European integration in the 1980s became bound up with a European deregulation project.[5]

Nobody has claimed that the relaunching of Europe was conceived by big business and implemented at its behest. But strong business influence—through direct lobbying, as well as through the hard facts that business attitudes and expectations constitute for political decisionmakers—can be seen especially in the selection of the political project around which the renewed push for integration came to be organized: the completion not of "Social Europe" but of the "internal market" (as the common market was renamed).[6] The method by which market integration was made both technically possible and politically safe was extensive application of a new, serendipitously discovered regulatory instrument, *mutual recognition*. Enough has been written about this to make the details dispensable; *Cassis de Dijon* has become a household word to even the most teetotalist of political scientists. What is important here are the implications of mutual recognition for the relationship between the integrated market and the polity that governs it. Where mutual recognition is used for market integration, it voids the need for supranational harmonization of national product regulations as a condition of free trade. As long as integration was governed by harmonization, the establishment of a common market for any good or service required agreement between governments on a common, centrally enforceable definition of the respective commodity. Among other things, this requirement offered opponents of integration, be they national governments or interest groups, rich opportunities to waylay the process.

5. Stanley Hoffmann, "The European Community and 1992," *Foreign Affairs*, vol. 68 (Fall 1989), pp. 27–47.

6. Since today any assertion of privileged business influence on political decisions seems to be suspect of having sprung from a "conspiracy theory," I hasten to reassure the reader that I am aware that business interests are far from monolithic (for proof, see "Interest Heterogeneity and Organizing Capacity: Two Class Logics of Collective Action?" in Wolfgang Streeck, *Social Institutions and Economic Performance: Studies of Industrial Relations in Advanced Capitalist Economies* (Newbury Park, Calif.: Sage, 1992)); that there are sectoral as well as national cleavages among European firms on important matters such as trade protection; and that some large European firms are only moderately interested in European integration because they have long operated on the global level. On the other hand, while caution against conspiracy theories is always advisable, sometimes there *are* conspiracies in the real world, and *excessive* caution might make one overlook them. In the present case, fashionable desires not to sound like a "vulgar Marxist" do not do away with the fact that an incoming president of the European Commission is more likely to return a phone call from the president of Philips, especially if he also happens to be president of the European Business Roundtable, than from one of the firm's assembly-line workers.

Mutual recognition, by comparison, automatically extends any product's national market into the common market. By establishing a general principle that, in the absence of an explicit political decision to the contrary, national markets are part of the common market, mutual recognition reduces the number of decisions intergovernmental or supranational bodies have to make for integration to proceed. It also promises to limit the proliferation of supranational law, while preempting a vast amount of national regulatory law. In principle, mutual recognition makes economic integration possible without replacement of national regulations at the supranational level and without supranational political institution building. It thus represents a sophisticated version of "negative integration": that is, economic integration through the mere removal of national trade barriers, offering a way to advance integration while leaving intact the sovereignty of nation-states and market forces and to separate market making from state-building.

The original intention seems to have been to base the renewed integration process entirely on a general presumption that from 1992 on, European nations would recognize one another's regulations unless they reached unanimous agreement on common supranational rules. This radical approach, however, turned out not to be feasible. Rather than creating the internal market entirely by default, the Single European Act (SEA) established a carefully bounded political process of market making. This involved identifying a narrowly specified range of issues for which harmonized regulation, as an alternative to national rules and their mutual recognition, was facilitated by lifting the unanimity requirement in the Council that had governed the European Community since the Luxembourg compromise. The result was the celebrated system of qualified majority voting.

The domain of qualified majority voting, however, was and remains very restrictively defined. The positive integration element of the 1992 process—its supranationalism, as vested in the qualified majority vote—was to apply to "all issues relating to the internal market,"[7] but to nothing else; indeed, it was only because it was entirely dedicated to the purpose of market making that qualified majority voting was acceptable in both European international relations and Europe's domestic political economy. Even determining the equivalence of national professional and vocational certificates remained subject to unanimity, and the same is

---

7. Michael Calingaert, *The 1992 Challenge from Europe: Development of the European Community's Internal Market* (Washington: National Planning Association, 1988), p. 11.

true for the proposed European Company Law. Although the free movement of capital would be advanced if firms could incorporate under European rather than national law, the SEA made no provision for facilitating Community-level decisionmaking in this area. Presumably, this was because mutual recognition, broadly defined, remains available as a fallback: if governments fail to agree on a European company statute, they, or the Court of Justice, may still decide that a firm incorporated in one country is ipso facto incorporated in all.

The result of all this was a peculiar configuration of national sovereignty and market autonomy. Under the ground rules of "1992," national sovereignty was curtailed by qualified majority voting only insofar as its exercise would interfere with the completion of the internal market, narrowly defined. From a liberal perspective this was not much of a sacrifice, because governments in principle should always deploy their sovereignty, or refrain from deploying it, in the service of the free play of market forces. And national sovereignty remained basically untouched—protected by the unanimity principle—by any intervention in market relations in excess of what one might call a neoclassical minimum of state activity. While market making was made easy, proceeding either by default or by majority vote, market correction—especially redistributive distortion of market outcomes along class lines—was made difficult by requirements of an improbably high level of consensus among national governments. Also, whereas market integration typically proceeded through or in spite of nondecisions, market correction called for decisions. In the constellation of decision procedures and policy areas that defined the internal-market process, and in the interaction between national politics, international relations, and economic interests inside the market, the act of defending a country's sovereignty in the councils of Europe and the act of defending the freedom of "market forces" in the integrated European economy thus came to be one and the same, with the objectives of liberal deregulation, or nonregulation, and of nationalist defense of sovereignty inextricably intertwined.

For some time this constellation was personalized, and thereby obscured, by Margaret Thatcher's vigorous simultaneous defense of British sovereignty against "French multinational bureaucrats" and of the "free market" in Europe against "socialism" creeping in through the back door. The imperious personal style with which she played the two themes, easily and opportunistically switching from one to the other in support of identical substantive demands, hid the fact that at the core of the political settlement that had enabled the relaunching of Western European integration was a historical convergence of nationalism and economic liberalism.

Defeat of the Social Dimension

The Single European Act was adopted to facilitate the completion of the internal market. But for some of the forces behind the *relance*, market completion in turn was to move the Community beyond its predominant intergovernmentalism of the mid-1980s onto a trajectory of supranational state formation. A crucial role in this was supposed to be played by social policy. Grafted onto the internal market as its presumably logical extension, and forced on hesitant member states as an allegedly inevitably consequence of economic integration, Community-level social policy was to give rise to interventionist-federalist institutions capable of superseding both national states and free markets, and legitimating the former by doing the latter. Taking off and "spilling over" from the internal market, social policy was to promote a twofold, mutually supportive, and inseparable evolution of the Community toward a *federal* state as well as a *welfare* state.

The problems such a project was bound to face were not new; indeed, the game had been played—and lost—before. The Community had always had a social policy, but it had been constitutionally limited to Communitywide labor market making, in particular by enabling the cross-border mobility of workers. Although there had been sporadic confusion as to what it would take to make a European labor market and how much supranational governance and international harmonization was required, centralized social welfare policies or the creation of supranational rights to collective bargaining were clearly outside the Community's original mission. Those who wanted social policy to go beyond market making—that is, to pursue positive integration and "politics against markets,"[8] in addition to removing barriers to cross-border mobility—therefore had to attach their projects to the narrow core of mobility-enhancing policies that had been placed under Community jurisdiction. They invoked a broad interpretation of Community powers in the hope of thereby expanding them.

Before the relaunching of the Community in the mid-1980s, there had

8. Gøsta Esping-Andersen, *Politics against Markets: The Social Democratic Road to Power* (Princeton University Press, 1985).

been two major attempts to saddle a more ambitious agenda onto the Community's market-making social policy mandate: the social-democratic "Social Europe" initiative of the 1970s and, less visible, a civil-rights project pursued by the European Court of Justice. The latter was in many respects successful; it extracted far-reaching antidiscrimination law from the treaty principle of free mobility of labor, and worked from there toward a judicially based, nonstatist construction of equal European citizenship. The former, however, associated with federal welfare state building and dependent on member-state approval, stalled in the early 1980s and contributed to the Community's stagnation. The Delors Commission's return to social policy after the internal market had been set on its way took place with this experience as its backdrop; it was therefore handicapped from the beginning.

The sole purpose envisaged in the Treaty of Rome for social policy was to make a Europeanwide labor market. Community jurisdiction on social protection thus was limited to work and employment-related matters, excluding "such classic social policy issues as pensions, unemployment, housing, family, the disabled and the young."[9] On the other hand, precisely because it was so narrowly focused on labor markets and employment, Community social policy was always easily identifiable as related to the regulation of class relations between labor and capital at the European level. In an almost pure social-democratic sense, and reflecting the dominant view in the postwar years that labor markets needed tripartite public intervention to be politically sustainable, social policy in the Community revolves around the creation of employment-related entitlements for workers, including not only social insurance and substantive labor standards but also rights to collective organization and representation. Any analysis of European social policy that addresses only social insurance schemes is therefore incomplete, as is one that omits industrial relations—not least because employment-related entitlements may be generated alternatively by direct state provision, government regulation of employer behavior, or delegated rule making under collective bargaining.

Labor markets and employment relations, and the entitlements that are related to them, raise very old questions of power. Indeed, T. H. Marshall defines social policy as the use of "political power to supersede, supplement or modify operations of the economic system in order to

9. Bernd Henningsen, "Europäisierung Europas durch eine europäische Sozialpolitik?" in Peter Haungs, ed., Europäisierung Europas? (Baden-Baden: Nomos, 1989), p. 56.

achieve results which the economic system would not achieve on its own, ... guided by values other than those determined by open market forces."[10] Social policy in this sense is redistributive and market correcting, generating entitlements for workers that the market would not provide on its own, including collective-status rights that change the relative power of the two classes in the labor market. Indeed, it is on the possibility that Community social policy might move from market making to changing the power structure and correcting the distributional outcomes of labor markets that the discussion and the politics of European social policy have centered in recent years.

Ambiguities in the Community's social policy mandate reflect initial uncertainty over how much homogeneity among national systems was needed to produce an integrated European labor market and to protect advanced national systems of social provision from destabilization by economic competition from systems with lower social costs. Language in the treaty demanding "an accelerated raising of the standard of living" and a harmonization of living and working conditions stems from this, and presumably so does the Community's mandate to foster "dialogue between management and labor." The same holds for treaty commitments to harmonization of national social security systems and equal pay for women and men, both of which responded to French government concerns that the social policies it required for domestic reasons might disadvantage its economy. It soon turned out, however, that differences in living standards did not obstruct market integration; that the common market worked well without tripartite concertation at the European level; that social security harmonization was not only unnecessary for keeping the more advanced countries competitive but also was intractable—the pertinent treaty article was soon conveniently forgotten; and that French laws on equal pay for men and women did not ruin the French economy.

Very early, then, Community social policy abandoned harmonization and limited itself to removing obstacles to mobility, especially of manual workers, among national—and still nationally governed—labor markets. Leaving national systems basically as they were, Community policy concentrated on building interfaces among them, in particular by obliging countries to let EC "foreign" workers enter freely to seek work and to eliminate any legal discrimination that impeded the free movement of labor as a production factor across national borders. It was to this developing core of minimalist, market-making European social policy that

10. T. H. Marshall, *Social Policy* (London: Hutchinson, 1975), p. 15.

the European Court of Justice later attached its own separate project, by interpreting individual and personal rights to equal treatment into the obligation of member states not to obstruct the free movement of labor. These rights, whose connection to employment and the functioning of the integrated labor market appears remote, have come to be perceived as the basis for some sort of common European citizenship.[11] Examples include strict equality and portability of social insurance benefits; rights of residence in Community countries before and after employment, or even unrelated to employment; rights of families of foreign workers to the same treatment and social benefits as citizens; and the same legal protection for travelers from other Community countries as for citizens, even if they are only tourists.

Much attention has been paid in the literature to the Court's impressive capacity to make supranational law that overrides national law and binds national policy, and to the sense of mission and the political acumen with which that capacity has sometimes been deployed. Still, it is important to note that the Court was never interested in social policy as such (for example, in transforming individual rights to labor market participation into collective rights to industrial or social citizenship); instead it used international commitments as a wedge to open national labor markets so that transnational individual civil rights could be inserted into European legal systems. Rather than equalizing protection *across* national regimes, the Court removed discrimination *within* them, and in doing so it remained well within the limits of intergovernmental commitments to joint market making.[12] Moreover, given the character of the Court's legal innovations as individual rights, and the Court's apparent ideological commitment to creating juridically guaranteed European civil rights for a European civil society waiting to be delivered from parochial national politics, such innovations make little contribution to Europeanwide institution building and political development.

Social-democratic attempts to take Community social policy beyond the limits of market making began in earnest in the early 1970s. The first project of a market-correcting Community social policy, the "Social Action Programme" of 1972, responded to the worker unrest of the late 1960s and, later, to the deep restructuring of the European economy in

11. Stephan Leibfried, "Wohlfahrtsstaatliche Entwicklungspotentiale: Die EG nach Maastricht," *NDV*, vol. 72, no. 4 (1992), pp. 107–19.

12. Bernd Schulte, "The Role of the Court of Justice of the European Communities," Max-Planck-Institut für ausländisches und internationales Sozialrecht, Munich, 1991.

the aftermath of the first oil shock. Drawing on long-dormant treaty commitments, such as harmonization of working conditions, as well as on a broad concept of barriers to cross-border mobility, the program aimed at centralized governance of labor markets, upward harmonization of labor standards, and Europeanization of collective representation rights and of individual entitlements.[13] The initiative was driven by social-democratic governments in key countries, as well as by unions as they intensified their efforts at international organization; the program also linked up well with an older federalist agenda harbored in particular in the Commission.

The first wave of attempts at a market-correcting Community social policy peaked in the early 1980s. It was successful only in two areas—equality of men and women in the labor market and health and safety—where Community intervention did result in upward harmonization and in supranational jurisdiction. But success in these two areas was for very specific reasons that do not apply elsewhere, making spillover to other social policy subjects improbable and continued encapsulation of federalism and upward harmonization in the two areas likely.

Three factors account for the exceptional effectiveness of Community policy on sexual equality. First, the Commission as "political entrepreneur" was able to draw on the by-then almost forgotten mandate of the Rome treaty to establish equal pay for women and men, and to deploy it for purposes never anticipated by the treaty signatories. Second, equality between men and women has not traditionally been central to national states' social policy concerns; the Community could relatively easily enter this unclaimed territory in an effort to expand its jurisdiction and enlarge its constituency. And third, sexual nondiscrimination fits a liberal agenda also, and may in fact be more market making than market correcting. In any case, its political support extended well into the professional middle classes; national governments therefore were not eager to be perceived as opposing Community initiatives.

Peculiarities with health and safety as well make replication of federalization in other areas doubtful. Mutual recognition of national health and safety regulations would have put pressure on some countries to lower their standards in order to remain competitive, which might very

13. It was at this time that European social policy first began to become involved in industrial relations, which was not controversial after the Europeanwide worker unrest of 1968 and 1969. The move could be justified legally by a broad reading of the treaty's commitment to dialogue between management and labor.

well have been welcomed in the Thatcherist spirit of the time as an economically although not physically healthy supply-side shake-up, or shake-out. But nationally different health and safety standards, combined with the post-Luxembourg unanimity requirement for Communitywide harmonization, acted as strong barriers to trade in an important product market, that for production machinery. As long as machines had to meet different national safety standards, there could be in effect no common market for them. Supranationalization of the issue through qualified majority voting under the Single European Act made it possible in 1989 to pass the machinery directive,[14] which harmonized health and safety standards for the design of new machinery and thereby created a Communitywide free market in production equipment.[15]

When the Delors Commission took office, it was clear that European integration could not come unstuck without a retreat from central elements of the social action program. The 1992 project with its supply-side economics solved this problem elegantly. Public attention during the first years of the *relance* was absorbed by the effort to complete the internal market, to the almost complete exclusion of social policy. As Bernd Henningsen notes,[16] the White Paper on the internal market never mentioned social policy, apart from the need to provide for free movement of workers and professionals inside the Community by, among other things, removal of residence permits, harmonization of standards for vocational education, and mutual recognition of degrees.[17] To the

14. Sean O'Cleireacain, "The Emerging Social Dimension of Europe 1992," Occasional Papers 4, City University of New York, Center for Labor Management Policy Studies, 1989, p. 17.

15. Note also that health and safety policy as such is not market correcting but what Peter Lange calls market-braking—policy designed to prevent an "overheating" of markets that would result in destruction of productive resources, or, in other words, policy that corrects not market outcomes but market failure; Lange, "Maastricht and the Social Protocol: Why Did They Do It?" *Politics and Society*, vol. 21 (March 1993), pp. 5–36. See also Giandomenico Majone, "The European Community between Social Policy and Social Regulation," *Journal of Common Market Studies*, vol. 31 (June 1993), pp. 153–70. This has little to do with promoting social citizenship; see Patrick Kenis, "Social Europe in the 1990s: Beyond an Adjunct to Achieving a Common Market?" *Futures*, vol. 23 (September 1991), pp. 724–38. Indeed, public intervention to protect the physical integrity of workers was compatible even with nineteenth-century Victorian liberalism. As the British example shows, early development of a health and safety regime at work does not foreshadow an early and stable transition to redistributive social policy. While it is probably true that even the Thatcher government did not want to be seen by voters as improving the competitiveness of the British economy at the expense of workers' health and safety, in all other areas of social policy it had no such compunctions at all.

16. Henningsen, "Europäisierung Europas?"

17. Beverley Springer, "The Social Dimension: Progress or Retreat?" paper presented

extent that the subject was addressed at all, the language offered was that the internal market itself, since it would create employment, was the best possible social policy; misguided attempts to improve on it would only detract from its benefits. Supply-side rhetoric of this kind was to be continue in subsequent years, when it was used to fight the Commission's social dimension program.

Social policy returned in 1988 with the Delors speech at the European Trade Union Congress, where he suggested adding a "social dimension" to the internal market by adopting a "platform of guaranteed social rights" as a baseline for national systems and a mandate for future European-level legislation.[18] The resurgence of social policy in the train of the internal market signaled the beginning of an attempt to break the stranglehold of the nationalist-neoliberal coalition on European integration by exploiting presumed functional needs, created by market integration, for institutional growth beyond both the nation-state and a deregulated market economy. It was in this strategic concept that the social dimension differed most from the social action program, which had been driven by lingering memories of industrial militancy and supported by favorable political majorities. Devoid of potent political allies and swimming against the current of the neoliberal *Zeitgeist*, the Delors Commission counted on the process of market integration itself to give rise to tensions and conflicts that would demonstrate to national governments that successful completion of the process required a rebuilding of Community institutions and policies from a regime geared to market making into one capable of market correction.

In reality, what turned out to control events was not a logic of functionalism but a lack of political resources at the disposal of the welfare-*cum*-federal state-building project. Three years after Maastricht there was little doubt that the battle for an EC social policy had been lost once more on all three fronts of the social dimension: legislation of meaningful Communitywide labor standards, extension of the Community's jurisdiction and legislative capacity on social policy, and development of European-level neocorporatism as an additional mechanism of social policymaking:[19]

---

at the inaugural conference of the European Community Studies Association, George Mason University, Fairfax, Va., May 24–25, 1989, p. 6.

18. Stephen J. Silvia, "The Social Charter of the European Community: A Defeat for European Labor," *Industrial and Labor Relations Review*, vol. 44 (July 1991), pp. 626–43.

19. For lack of space, most of the details must be assumed to be known; some are reported by Martin Rhodes in this volume.

—The Social Charter was adopted only as a nonbinding "solemn declaration" of the European Council.[20] Legal nonbindingness had been the principal demand of UNICE (Union of Industrial and Employers' Confederation of Europe). The original title, "Community Charter of Fundamental Social Rights," was changed to "Charter of Fundamental Social Rights of Workers," and references to *citizens* were replaced with references to *workers* to avoid the appearance of an expanded social policy mandate for the Community. The charter explicitly reminds the Community to stay "within the limits of its powers," and the preamble states that "the implementation of the Charter must not entail an extension to the Community's powers as defined by the Treaties." Almost all sections require that rights be enforced "in accordance with arrangements applying in each country" or with "national practice."

The Commission next issued an "Action Programme" proposing forty-seven separate social policy measures to implement the charter. Only twenty-eight of them at most, however, would involve binding legislation. Of these, ten are directives on health and safety at the workplace, two deal with freedom of movement for workers across national borders, and a number of others resemble in their scope and importance a proposed directive "on the introduction of measures aimed at promoting improvement in the travel conditions of workers with motor disabilities." No legislation was proposed in two core areas of the charter, namely, social protection and freedom of association and collective bargaining.[21]

—The intergovernmental conferences that resulted in the Treaty of Maastricht were to produce a package of institutional reforms, presumably flowing with functional necessity from the progress of the internal market, that would enhance the political capacities of the Community. In social policy, the main reform proposed by the Commission was to extend qualified majority voting to a range of subjects beyond health and safety. As it happened, social policy was not covered in the treaty at all; it was instead relegated to an attached "protocol." To sidestep British

20. See John T. Addison and W. Stanley Siebert, "The Social Charter of the European Community: Evolution and Controversies," *Industrial and Labor Relations Review*, vol. 44 (July 1991), pp. 597–625; Lammy Betten, "Prospects for a Social Policy of the European Community and its Impact on the Functioning of the European Social Charter," in Lammy Betten, ed., *The Future of European Social Policy* (Boston: Kluwer, 1991), pp. 107–61; Silvia, "Social Charter"; and Paul Teague and John Grahl, "The European Community Social Charter and Labour Market Regulation," *Journal of Public Policy*, vol. 11 (April-June 1991), pp. 207–32.

21. Addison and Siebert, "Social Charter," provide a useful synopsis.

opposition, the protocol allowed the United Kingdom to dissociate itself from Community social policy; in return, the United Kingdom was to allow the eleven countries that "wish[ed] to continue along the path laid down in the Social Charter of 1989" the use of Community institutions for making "the necessary decisions."[22]

Social policy was dealt with substantively in a separate "agreement" not signed by Britain. Its purpose is to "implement the 1989 Social Charter on the basis of the 'acquis communitaires.'" For this purpose alone the agreement amends the treaty to extend qualified majority voting among the Eleven to five subjects, including information and consultation of workers.[23] The agreement also specifies a category of issues that continue to require unanimous decisions, if only among the Eleven (for example, "social security and the social protection of workers," "protection of workers where their employment contract is terminated," and "representation and collective defense of the interests of workers and employers, including co-determination"). Finally, the agreement states that the treaty "shall not apply" to "pay, the right of association, [and] the right to strike or the right to impose lock-outs"; all of these remain excluded from supranational decisionmaking.

The Maastricht settlement was a decisive British victory over the federalist welfare state-building project. It reinforced the tendency in the Community toward a "Europe of variable geometries," whereby integration is subdivided by policy areas with varying sets of participating nation-states. The result is systematic deviation from state models, with a unified central government wielding identical, functionally integrated authority over a given territory.[24] The emerging arrangement, which gives member states the opportunity of partial exit as an alternative to voice or compromise, does not improve the capacity of supranational institutions to enlarge their jurisdiction. By creating a separate social policy Community of eleven member states, Maastricht also raised a host of

22. The protocol is reprinted in European Institute of Public Administration, *The Intergovernmental Conference on Political Union* (Norwell, Mass.: Kluwer Academic, 1992), pp. 484–85.

23. The two other subjects of significance are, not surprisingly, "improvement in particular in the working environment to protect workers' health and safety" and "equality between men and women with regard to labour market opportunities and treatment at work."

24. Philippe C. Schmitter, "Interests, Powers and Functions: Emergent Properties and Unintended Consequences in the European Polity," Stanford University, January 1992.

political and constitutional problems for "Europe's would-be polity."[25] The need to sort these out will for some time act as a powerful brake on Community social policy initiatives, as will domestic pressure on the governments of the Eleven to keep as narrow as possible the difference between the social obligations of their firms and those of their British competitors.

—Following adoption of the deregulatory single-market program, the Delors Commission embarked on a sustained effort to draw European employers' associations into political exchange with labor and the Commission, in the hope that this would extricate them from their negative alliance with the nationalist forces on the Council. The Treaty of Rome had established the Economic and Social Committee (ESC) for consultation with and between the "social partners," but by the late 1970s the employers had lost interest because too many ESC recommendations had been adopted over their objections. Bypassing the ESC, the Delors Commission started what it called a "social dialogue" at the European level (also known as the Val Duchesse talks), which included only the peak associations of European business and labor; in effect the arrangement guaranteed both groups a veto over the results. Although presented as a social-dimension project designed to increase union influence, in fact the change of venue to Val Duchesse was intended to strengthen the position of business and thereby raise its stake in supranational institutional growth.

The results, however, were disappointing. UNICE never changed its view that social matters should be dealt with exclusively at the national level. It also continued to argue for a narrow interpretation of the applicability of qualified majority voting to social legislation in the Council, and resisted the extension of binding status to agreements reached in the social dialogue. As a consequence, all that was produced was a number of "joint opinions" on matters such as "cooperative growth strategy" and vocational training as a key component of a European employment policy.

UNICE nevertheless agreed in late 1971 to a Commission proposal that the impending treaty revision award formal status to the social dialogue as a channel for joint participation of business and labor in Community social policymaking. Under the new codecision procedure, the Commission has to "consult" the European peak associations of

25. Leon N. Lindberg and Stuart A. Scheingold, *Europe's Would-Be Polity: Patterns of Change in the European Community* (Prentice Hall, 1970).

business and labor on any social policy initiative it may want to take. If the Commission thereafter decides to proceed further, management and labor must be consulted on the substance of the "envisaged proposal," and they may issue "an opinion or, where appropriate, a recommendation" to the Commission. Alternatively, the two sides "may inform the Commission" that they prefer to settle the subject between them through "contractual relations, including agreements." The latter may be implemented either by management and labor directly at the national level or "at the joint request of the signatory parties, by a Council decision on a proposal from the Commission."

The Maastricht codecision procedure was intended by the Commission as a step toward a neocorporatist organization of the internal market's emerging polity, devolving responsibility for public policy to organized capital and labor, granting them quasi-public political status, and thereby drawing them into tripartite governance of the European economy. However, like the agreement on social policy as a whole, codecisionmaking is confined to the implementation of the Social Charter and thus shares all of its weaknesses. And like the Charter, it does not apply to the United Kingdom. Most important, the codecision procedure can contribute to welfare-state federalism only with the assent of European employers, and UNICE has made clear that its inclusion in the treaty does not imply a change in its minimalist interpretations of EU jurisdiction over social policy and the proper scope of the social dialogue. As long as this position holds, employers will use their new formal participation rights not to promote but to obstruct supranational political and institutional development.[26]

The collapse of the social dimension replicates the defeat of its predecessor, the social action program. Outside the encapsulated federalism of workplace health and safety policy, the internal-market period added nothing to the social policy legislation that had been in place by the early 1980s; in fact, no progress was made even on equal treatment for men and women. Nor did the internal market and the ensuing treaty revisions extend the Community's capacity for future market-correcting social policy. Just as the British opt-out demonstrated the unbroken strength of national states, so did the codecisionmaking procedure confirm the veto

26. For more on the codecision procedure, see Wolfgang Streeck, "European Social Policy after Maastricht: The 'Social Dialogue' and 'Subsidiarity,'" *Economic and Industrial Democracy,* vol. 15 (Spring 1994), pp. 151–77.

power of business, and with it the deregulatory thrust of the mid-1980s integration process.

Students of European social policy tend not to let the obvious lack of progress at present disturb expectations of progress in the future. Those who point out that little was going on were told that good things always take time and that the glass would soon be almost half full. I argue that after the defeat of the second attempt to develop a European social policy, it is time to take the empirics seriously and, rather than dismiss them as accidental, search for the systemic pattern that produced, and will very likely reproduce, them. In the following I more explicitly address the functionalist fallacies that have all too often made observers treat the insignificance of Community social policy in the integration process as insufficient evidence of its insignificance. I then propose an analytical schema for examining really existing European social policy, conceiving it as a product of complex interactions between national and supranational actors and policies and focusing on the character of political resources in an integrated market without an integrated state. Finally, I attempt to identify the contours of what might be an emerging European social policy settlement under the post-1980s institutional structure of Europe's "would-be polity."

Functionalist Fallacies

To justify interpretations of past and present social policies as intermediate steps toward a supranational European welfare state, institutional, economic, and political reason—all with a distinctly functionalist flavor—are invoked to show that the Community's social deficit need not, cannot, and will not remain.[27]

Institutionalist reasoning, often beholden to neofunctionalist traditions of regional integration theory, assumes that integration in one policy area or sector must ultimately lead to integration in others. In a political economy version of the same line of thought, institutionalists

27. Notwithstanding the fact that the same reasons were put forward during decades of stagnation of Community social policy: "Bekanntermaßen ist aus den Initiativen der siebziger Jahre (fast) nichts geworden; alle Papiere, Artikel und Bücher der damaligen Zeit lesen sich heute angesichts der politischen Folgenlosigkeit so interessant (weil kaum ein Argument hinfällig geworden ist) wie grotesk (wegen der nicht erfolgten politischen Umsetzung)"; Henningsen, "Europäisierung Europas?" p. 67.

postulate that markets in general, and labor markets in particular, "need" market-correcting political intervention.

An alternative *economic* (or better yet, economistic) argument emphasizes the benefits of a redistributive, entitlement-creating European social policy for the competitiveness of the European economy in world markets for high-quality goods and services, claimed to require a highly skilled, highly motivated, and cooperative work force. The assumption is that "flexibly specialized"[28] European firms will not misinterpret their interests in such a way as to try to impose an American-style, market- and management-driven labor regime on their work forces. Rather than exploiting negative integration to cut costs, European business is expected to continue to support cooperative labor relations and social policy intervention, acting in its enlightened self-interest to avoid disruption of sensitive production processes. In fact, long-term, rational, self-interested benevolence, it is believed, will not only make European employers play fair even in the absence of Europeanwide social policy but also make them receptive to European-level joint regulation with unions, to trilateral bargaining between the "two sides of industry" and the Commission, and to European legislative backup of a cooperative industrial order.

Unlike the economic functionalism of cruder versions of flexible specialization, *political* arguments for the necessity and, consequently, the inevitability of European-level social policy suggest that European unity must be grounded in some form of popular European identity; that identity, in turn, is believed to require a policy of redistributive justice based on an advanced version of common European citizenship.[29] Implicitly or explicitly following the logic of T. H. Marshall's seminal work,[30] political constructions of European social policy assume an inherent tendency for citizenship to progress and expand from the civil right to enter in markets and contracts, to political rights of participation in governance, to industrial rights of collective bargaining, and finally to social rights defining a general floor of income and living conditions below which no member

28. Michael J. Piore and Charles F. Sabel, *The Second Industrial Divide: Possibilities for Prosperity* (New York: Basic Books, 1984).

29. "If a 'European identity' exists or should develop, it does not do so because of (expensive) common European markets for steel or agricultural products, but because of a policy of social justice." Bernd Henningsen, "Social Security and Health," in Carl-Christoph Schweitzer and Detlev Karsten, eds., *Federal Republic of Germany and EC Membership Evaluated* (London: Pinter Publishers, 1990), p. 189; see also Henningsen, "Europäisierung Europas?"

30. T. H. Marshall, *Class, Citizenship and Social Development* (Doubleday, 1964).

of the political community can fall. This argument maintains that it is through this evolutionary sequence, however modified in individual cases, that modern polities acquire legitimacy and achieve unity. If European national states have reasons to form a Community, they must therefore accept development of that Community into a "Europe for the citizen"—social policy and all—or else their integration project will die from lack of popular support.[31]

None of the three functionalist defenses of social policy optimism is convincing. By itself the observation that economies, including market economies, are inevitably, as Karl Polanyi has pointed out, "instituted processes" is less than instructive.[32] As can be learned from the same author, it is also true that markets, while certainly "instituted," are grinding "satanic mills" that pulverize social commitments and obligations unless placed under political control.[33] That "countermovement," however, does not occur automatically, nor in necessarily felicitous ways. While markets "need" rules, the rules that are socially constructed for them may differ widely and may ultimately be incapable of containing the social devastation wrought by self-regulating markets however instituted. Clearly Polanyi cannot be called upon for reassurance that markets, simply because they need governance, will ipso facto somehow attract socially benevolent governance.

While it is true, then, that markets must be governed, they may be governed in many different ways, and it is precisely this variation that social policy is all about. American capitalism differs from Japanese capitalism, and both differ from the German "social market economy" or Scandinavian Social Democracy. What gives rise to such differences is the presence of social and political resources that are resistant to erosion by market forces and are able to contain and modify the market. The future of a European social policy depends not on whether a European internal market needs institutionalization—it certainly does—but whether the European polity can muster the political resources needed to impose redistributive obligations on powerful participants in that market, in addition to, say, a common competition or research and development policy.[34] It is possible to be pessimistic about this without having

31. Leibfried, "Wohlfahrtsstaatliche Entwicklungspotentiale," p. 116.

32. Karl Polanyi, "The Economy as Instituted Process," in G. Dalton, ed., *Primitive, Archaic, and Modern Economies: Essays of Karl Polanyi* (Garden City, N.Y.: Anchor, 1968), pp. 139–74.

33. Karl Polanyi, *The Great Transformation* (New York: Farrar and Rinehart, 1957).

34. For an example of an analysis that fails to recognize this distinction, see P. G.

to assume that a completed internal market would be as self-regulating as neoclassical fiction writers would like one to believe.

Nor does the idea of spillover as the principal engine of supranational political integration help. The very image that the metaphor invokes suggests different proximities among affected policy areas. Spillovers would seem to be possible only between areas that are adjacent—that is, areas that are closely coupled functionally. Some policy areas may simply be too functionally separated for integration in one to affect integration in the other. For example, the removal of trade barriers for the purpose of completing the internal market may "require," or suggest as a way of lowering "transaction costs," extended supranational jurisdiction over product liability or over the introduction of new pharmaceuticals. It may also "require" some form of integrated European competition policy that may, more or less, "automatically" "spill over" into a common trade policy, which in turn may lead to joint Community policies on research and development subsidies for European multinationals. The spillover distance between market integration and a market-correcting social policy, however, is clearly very long, as demonstrated by a perfectly integrated market economy such as that of the United States, which continues to benefit its dominant coalition without having developed anything close to an integrated social policy.

Where social policy optimism cannot be justified by assumptions of an area-crossing automatism of supranational integration and institution building, the latter is sometimes, implicitly or explicitly, replaced with a benevolent logic of capitalist economic self-interest. However, apart from exceptional cases ("islands of excellence"), prudent behavior of employers in labor markets and organizational hierarchies typically requires insurance against imprudent behavior of other employers, affording these short-term competitive advantages. Absent reassuring institutional constraints (created, for example, by unions or governments) that apply reliably to all competitors, behaving long-term irrationally in relation to labor may be the only short-term rational thing for an employer to do. Indeed, the mere possibility that employers might defect under competitive pressures from cooperation may be enough to make workers and unions refrain from cooperation, which in turn would justify greater

Cerny, "The Limits of Deregulation: Transnational Interpenetration and Policy Change," *European Journal for Policy Research*, vol. 19 (March 1991), pp. 173–96.

vigilance on the part of employers and set in motion what Alan Fox aptly called a "spiral of low trust."[35]

In other words, social policy is less the outcome of prudent behavior of market participants than its condition. In particular, political intervention typically precedes the formation of effective business interests in stable cooperation with labor, rather than flowing from it. To the extent that such interests derive from "requirements" of quality-competitive production and business strategies, that production pattern is itself likely to become generalized, that is, typical of an economy rather than exceptional, only under appropriate institutional conditions, in other words, only if it is itself institutionalized.[36]

More generally, the argument is that rational self-interest in class cooperation can best be acted upon by employers, and in principle also by workers, in the presence of reassuring institutional safeguards and constraints, and in particular cannot be relied upon to generate these. If rational, self-interested pursuit of economic advantage was enough to bring about a market-correcting social policy, the United States would be the world's leading welfare state.[37] Rational voluntarism is an especially shaky basis for cooperation in an era of heightened competition, rapid economic change, and profound industrial restructuring, when established practices are drawn in question, strategic choices and alternatives for firms proliferate, and temptations to defect from communal understandings are rampant.

As firms struggle for advantage in an uncertain environment, it is harder than ever to see how they could write a social contract with each other and with labor out of rational self-interest. If an advanced, quality-competitive mode of production requires that firms and markets be governed by social institutions, rather than vice versa, that outcome is not likely to result from market behavior even if its absence is associated with long-term economic decline. Lacking the capacity to act together, and unable to use their autonomy for purposes other than fending off attempts to curtail that autonomy, firms will adopt alternative strategies,

---

35. Alan Fox, *Beyond Contract: Work, Power and Trust Relations* (London: Faber and Faber, 1974).

36. See Streeck, *Social Institutions and Economic Performance*.

37. One implication of this is that European employers are less unwilling than American employers to cooperate with unions and government regulations—not because they are more altruistic, more rational, or more interested in the high profits offered by quality-competitive markets but because they do not have much choice and because they know that their immediate competitors do not either.

such as cost cutting and price-competitive production, that are more compatible with economic liberty.

European Community experience conforms to this expectation. Downward restructuring of production patterns takes time; even if it had already begun, it would not yet be visible. There are also likely to be strong national economic differences related to sticky differences in national institutions. But as far as European-level institution building is concerned, the position of European business is clear: European employers have exclusively negative interests in European social policy; they participate in the social dialogue only as long as its results remain nonbinding; they reject European collective bargaining; and they concede no more than voluntary information arrangements at the European enterprise level. European employers prefer flexibility over governance, and identify governance with rigidity, and they have always been entirely unambiguous about this.[38]

Belief in the necessity for stable integration of popular identification with European citizenship was, not surprisingly, particularly widespread in West Germany before unification. Such sentiment overlooked the uniqueness and, indeed, the genius of Monnet's design, which lay exactly in its uncoupling of progress on supranational organization from progress in the formation of supranational patriotism. The European Community was conceived as a political regime that would have to, and could, survive and grow without the popular legitimacy that previous modes of state-building had required. In Monnet's pragmatic approach, European unity was to be based for the foreseeable future not on collective acceptance of a common identity but on the functional interdependence of political-administrative decisions and organized interests in an internationalized "mixed" economy. Had it been otherwise, the Community would have had even less support than it did outside West Germany and, perhaps, Italy.

One often-invoked justification for Social Europe in the 1970s was that a supranationally organized mixed economy could not forever be

---

38. The flexible specialization school expects nonobligatory, "voluntary" cooperation between capital and labor to originate from conducive regional cultures and institutional traditions, not from supranational social policy. This claim cannot be investigated here. At the very least, however, a regionalization of social policy—Charles F. Sabel, "Flexible Specialization and the Re-Emergence of Regional Economies," in Paul Hirst and Jonathan Zeitlin, eds., *Reversing Industrial Decline? Industrial Structure and Policy in Britain and her Competitors* (Oxford: Berg, 1989), pp. 17–70, even speaks of a "local welfare state"—would be bound to result in growing disparities in favor of institutionally and economically well-endowed regions.

governed on a technocratic basis and without the popular legitimacy that distributive politics generates. But while this argument might well have prevailed over Monnet and the neofunctionalists, it lost ground in the 1980s when the intergovernmental character of the Community was confirmed by the Single European Act, and integration became identified with deregulation and political disengagement from the economy. A free European market, if this is all that it is to be, does not "require" a "Europe of the citizen"; in fact, citizenship makes markets less "free." As far as the completion of the internal market is concerned, it does not matter that European citizenship, symbolized by the common color of a "European Community passport" issued by national governments, has remained limited to freedom of movement and contract within the integrated market.

The way from here to social rights is very long. To the extent that progress toward social citizenship requires as an intermediate step an extension of political rights, there is no evidence that anything like this is in the offing. Not even the most fervent European federalists predict that the European Parliament, with the Council of Ministers writing its charter, will be a focus of Europeanwide political mobilization and party identification anytime soon. That the Parliament has been directly elected for more than a decade has made no difference at all in this respect.[39] Political union in Maastricht was adopted without increased rights for the Parliament. Indeed, the post-Maastricht ratification debates reveal a widespread preference among Europeans that political rights remain vested in nation-states and that citizenship not be transferred from the national to the Community level. The Danish referendum in particular showed that, far from Community social policy advancing citizen identification with supranational union, national identification remains so strong that it stands in the way of Community social policy. This happens to mesh well with economic interests in a free-market European political economy.[40] By defending national democracy against supranational welfare state-building, European citizens in effect defend the freedom of the integrated European market from redistributive political intervention, although this may not be the outcome they have in mind.

39. The number of European citizens that are aware that the present Parliament has a slight Left majority is minuscule, and the number of those who care about this does not exceed that of the Parliament's deputies.

40. Just as rejection of monetary union in the name of protection of national sovereignty from German hegemony helps preserve the status of the Bundesbank as a German-owned de facto European central bank.

The European Community was created without citizen identification and supranational legitimacy, on the weak and indirect legitimation conferred on it by its member states. Contrary to what many believe, the completion of the internal market does not require that this be changed. In fact, transnational political institutions that offer meaningful opportunities for mass participation and enable citizens to constitute and experience a supranational political "community of fate" might well interfere with the powerful political and economic interests served by a single market without a single state.[41] It is true that a federalist European state-building project would be jeopardized by lack of citizen identification with "Europe," and would therefore require that the "democratic deficit" be closed and redistributive social policies be developed.[42] But the reigning integration project is not a federalist one. The present European accommodation between the sovereignty of nation-states and of self-regulating markets precludes supranational political development or requires that it be kept to a minimum. There are neither institutional nor economic nor political resasons for national governments promoting economic union to help European civil society build supranational political resources capable of remodeling the Community into an interventionist federal welfare state.

41. As an example of a functionalist argument that overlooks the importance of power and political resources, consider Stephan Leibfried, "Europe's Could-be Social State: Social Policy and Post-1992 European Integration," paper prepared for the conference "Europe after 1992," Ann Arbor, Mich., September 6–7, 1991, pp. 5–6, who identifies as "functional needs" leading to a European Community social policy that Europe "preserve an identifiable 'face' *vis-à-vis* Japan, the USA and the formerly socialist countries"; requires social integration for the creation of "new statehood"; and could benefit from a "link state (EC)-citizen" replacing the present "unclear and many leveled 'policy entanglement'" (p. 6). There is no reason to believe that individuals cannot get rich without these "needs" being attended to.

42. Which would be difficult enough: "By analogy with Rupert Emerson's definition of the nation as the terminal community that people are prepared to fight and die for, the social solidarity that creates the community of a welfare state can be defined as that group which, when the chips are down, people are willing to be taxed for. It is not the European Community as of today. Within Germany, France or the United Kingdom, people are prepared to pay taxes to benefit fellow citizens. But the scope of those who should be supported from a common pot of money stops at the borders of the state. Even though national economies have now been internationalized, welfare remains the responsibility of a national state." Richard Rose, "The Welfare State in an Open International Economy," University of Strathclyde (Glasgow), Centre for the Study of Public Policy, February 19, 1991, p. 23.

Analyzing European Social Policy

European Community social policy is not the same as European social policy, nor is it European social policy in waiting. Community social policy is embedded in and interacts with the social policies of the Community's member states. A realistic analysis of social policy in Europe has to take seriously the unique structure of the internal market's political system, especially the constitutionally enshrined presence of strong nation-states in an international, partly supranational, and partly intergovernmental economic order.

European social policy is made simultaneously at two interacting levels, the supranational and the national, with the latter comprising a number of sovereign nation-states.[43] Interactions within the system are complex, messy, and not well understood. National states together define supranational policies, which may in turn redefine national policies; in addition, national policies affect one another through interdependence due to common location in an integrated market. Interdependence itself is generated through international obligations to open up national boundaries and to change national policy regimes for the purpose. Interdependence may or may not be jointly managed, in the extreme case through supranational authorities harmonizing national regimes so as to contain competition among them and control their external effects on one another. Reregulation of national systems under supranational authority or international agreement may be confined to building interfaces for market making, or it may impose minimum standards of social protection on national systems that must not be undercut in search of competitive advantage. Interdependence may result in diffusion of "best practice" or in regime competition, forcing countries with high standards to cut costs. International organization may be confined to dealing with emergent transnational phenomena that defy governance by national systems, and thereby help them protect their integrity; but it may also develop into a competing federal jurisdiction or become capable of authoritative intervention in national regimes, and thereby supersede them.[44]

43. Schulte, "Role of the Court," p. 23.
44. It would appear that the same principles apply to any policy area in Europe today. Among the implications of this are that policy analysis at the level of any European nation-state requires consideration of the effects of interaction with other states and with the supranational European polity; that comparative policy analysis in Europe has to be conceptually expanded to include an analysis of two kinds of interdependence, one transmitted

There is no reason to expect relations within and between the two levels to be other than messy. European social policy is made in a multi-level political system, but analogies with other such systems—German *Politikverflechtung*, for example—make it appear more organized than it is. Not only is the institutional structure of internal market policymaking less settled, it also has to accommodate greater diversity among its constituent units and greater capacities to resist, exit, or behave unpredictably. Because European supranational regime building and market governance take place through international relations among sovereign countries, horizontal relations among lower-level units are more important than vertical relations between them and the higher level. Also, the constitutional rules of multilevel policymaking in the European Union are still being worked out and, more important, they are laid down not in a constitution proper but in international treaties. As a result, coupling between system elements is significantly looser, relations are only weakly institutionalized, and the operation of the system as a whole is more politically volatile.

Further complications arise from the fact that the political system of social policy in the internal market must respond to the interests of classes as well as of nation-states. In international social policy even more than in other fields of international relations, national states cannot be treated as monolithic. Capital and labor have different international interests: the former seeks support for increased factor mobility, and the latter wants protection of social policy standards from erosion by economic competition. At the same time, capital and labor also share some interests at the national level, and thus are to this extent jointly represented by national governments in the international arena. In addition, because they are nationally organized both capital and labor face problems in combining their class interests internationally, replicating within classes some of the complexities of multilevel decisionmaking among national states.

International social policy, then, follows a twofold, crosscutting logic of diversity, by nation and by class. In pursuit of their interests, capital and labor have a choice in principle between building cross-national alliances within classes or national alliances between classes. How group interests align themselves with each other and with national states is

horizontally among national regimes and one mediated through supranational institutions; and that the supranational policies of the European Community cannot be understood in isolation and apart from the policies of member states.

affected by the constraints and opportunities offered by national and international institutions. In the process, political resources are generated and distributed in a way that favors some interests over others, thereby conditioning the outcome of multilevel policymaking. Rather than functional "requirements," it is the political resources produced in the interplay among nation, class, and institutional structures that explain the fate of European social policy in the internal market, in particular the two-time defeat of welfare-state interventionism and federalism, the shift from harmonization to subsidiarity, and the failure of social policy during the *relance* to move the Community beyond its preconstitutional bargain of the mid-1980s.

Nation-states and the relations among them are the most important impediments to welfare-state federalism. Insofar as the Union's member states derive domestic legitimacy from social policies, they are unlikely to cede control over these to supranational agencies.[45] The very fact that the leading members are already highly developed welfare states sharply curtails the prospects of federalism, making these national governments rely on national means to deal with border-crossing externalities and delegate only as much authority to supranational governance as they must to restore national control.[46] Also, national interests in the substance of European social policy differ widely, in line with economic conditions. High common European labor standards might eliminate the only competitive advantage of countries such as Portugal and Greece in attracting investment. Indeed, there has long been suspicion that some governments that had supported a strong social dimension in the 1980s had done so knowing that the British vote would ensure that proposed policies would never pass into law.[47]

45. Jacques Pelkmans, "The Institutional Economics of European Integration," in Mauro Cappelletti, Monica Secombe, and Joseph Weiler, eds., *Integration through Law*, vol. 1, *Methods, Tools and Institutions*, bk. 1, *A Political, Legal and Economic Overview* (New York: de Gruyter, 1985), pp. 318–96.

46. As Teague and Grahl, "European Community Social Charter," point out, improved coordination at the center can loosen constraints on individual members rather than threaten them with a loss of sovereignty. An example is the directive on plant closures, which responded to a loss of control of national systems in an internationalizing economy over business decisions affecting their territorial jurisdiction. A company headquarters located outside the territory of a given country cannot be cited for failing to inform local management in time, under local law, about plans to close down a local plant. Instituting the same obligation supranationally closes a gap in the control of national authorities over events on their territory.

47. Peter Lange, "The Politics of the Social Dimension," in Sbragia, ed., *Euro-Politics*, pp. 225–56.

Not least, because it has to pass through the needle's eye of negotiations among states, European social policy has to compete for attention against other concerns that have higher priority for the maintenance of stable international relations or that may be more amenable to diplomatic treatment. International pressures on governments for harmonization of social policy are far less irresistible than, for example, those for harmonization of monetary policy: while different inflation or interest rates create international imbalances, different levels of unemployment benefits do not. Similarly, unlike trade and defense, social policies have few, if any, implications for the external relations of the Union as a whole—for example, with the United States and Japan—and are therefore not helped onto the intergovernmental agenda by demands from powerful outside interlocutors.

Nationalist reluctance of states to supranationalize European social policy coincides with a configuration of class interests and political resources that reinforces national fragmentation. As long as EU social policy is made by the Council, international class interests have no target for political mobilization, and European-level interest associations are severely disadvantaged vis-à-vis nation-states in influencing integrated policies. This places a premium on accessing EU decisionmaking nationally, by lobbying national governments. Intergovernmentalism thus prolongs nationally fragmented articulation of social group interests. Contrary to neofunctionalist theory, in which European-level interest group formation moves the international relations among states from intergovernmentalism toward supranationalism, intergovernmentalism keeps supranational interest organization weak and limits its capacity to serve as an engine of integration.[48]

National fragmentation of organized interests also reflects national differences in economic interests themselves. Economic nationalism divides not just European national states but also European interest groups. National fault lines inside European union federations were mostly invisible in the 1980s, most likely because of the foreseeably inconsequential nature of most of the unions' European social policy initiatives. This does not mean, however, that they do not exist, making societal demand and political support for integrated social policies potentially thin, uncertain, and volatile.[49]

48. Wolfgang Streeck and Philippe C. Schmitter, "From National Corporatism to Transnational Pluralism: Organized Interests in the Single European Market," *Politics and Society*, vol. 19 (June 1991), pp. 133–64.

49. Concluding the debate in the European Parliament on his programmatic speech at

Economic nationalism of organized interests is reinforced by institutional nationalism. The wide differences in national industrial relations practices and in the political traditions of national union movements in Europe have been seized upon by employers and conservative governments to argue against harmonization projects (such as EU legislation on mandatory worker participation) and in favor of decentralized governance of labor markets and employment relations, in the name of protection of cultural diversity.[50] While unions often demand harmonization to eliminate competition, they also want to protect the political resources they have accumulated in national polities. Institutional nationalism reflects both the investment of individuals and organizations in existing, inevitably national institutional structures and the uncertainty about the impact of Europeanization on them and the interests they represent. Just as national states prefer intergovernmental over supranational responses to interdependence, organized interests often eschew federal solutions that would upset national political arrangements (for example, by taking subject matter out of the hands of national interlocutors and curtailing their autonomy in dealing with one another).

Finally, the logic of class diversity reproduces in a peculiar way the fragmenting effects of the logic of national diversity. Labor's class interests demand supranational market regulation to provide protection from national regime competition, whereas capital wants to maximize mobility across national borders while minimizing market regulation by, among other things, confining it in national systems. As a result labor, acting on a class logic, fails to find an interlocutor at the international level; and capital, pursuing its class interest in international nonregulation and nondecision, refuses to play. On the other hand, forced to fall back on a national framework and acting on nationally defined interests, economic or institutional, labor is likely to be offered national cross-class alliances

---

the beginning of his second term, Jacques Delors responded to members who had complained about slow progress on social policy: "Do you realize that within the employers' organizations at European level there is no agreement, and the same goes for the trade union organizations? There is no agreement on what can be done at European level." Jacques Delors, "Statement on the Broad Lines of Community Policy," *Bulletin of the European Communities*, supplement 1/89, p. 21.

50. Jelle Visser and Bernd Ebbinghaus, "Making the Most of Diversity? European Integration and Transnational Organization of Labour," University of Amsterdam (Visser) and European University Institute (Ebbinghaus), October 1991. See also Wolfgang Streeck and Sigurt Vitols, "The European Community: Between Mandatory Consultation and Voluntary Information," in Joel Rogers and Wolfgang Streeck, eds., *Works Councils* (University of Chicago Press, forthcoming).

by capital aimed at advancing joint, nationally based economic interests (building national competitiveness for the international market, for example) and defending the autonomy of national institutions against supranational interference. Since the class interest of capital, unlike that of labor, includes regime fragmentation, national action of this kind does not compromise it; in fact, because the absence of supranational governance exposes national cross-class coalitions to international competitive pressures, capital is almost assured hegemony in such coalitions.

National governments, for their part, prosper on mediating the formation of national cross-class coalitions. One way they can reward its members, especially labor, is by protecting national institutions from supranational reregulation, thereby defending the institutional nationalism of organized interests. All governments have to do to achieve this is preserve the intergovernmental status of relations among Union member states, which is entirely in line with their own preferences. The result is tripartite national coalitions within which labor defends national economic interests as a substitute for supranational social policy, protecting national "custom and practice" from EU-initiated harmonization and in effect cementing the absence of market governance at the supranational level.

International relations and the interplay of class interests and national interests make federalism in European social policy the exception and its development dependent on special circumstances, such as weakness of national states, closeness of issues to a market-making agenda, judicial activism, or accidents of political conjunctures. Basically, horizontal interdependence among nation-states in the internal market's multilevel polity remains unmanaged, opening a wide space for economic competition among national social policy regimes. How international regime competition works in a supranational market is only poorly understood and cannot be otherwise, given the limited experience with it. Assessment of the potential impact of regime competition on European social policy was not helped by summary predictions that widespread social dumping would result from market integration; very likely, the effects of regime competition will be more diverse and subtle.

—Short of causing an instant decline in social protection and industrial citizenship rights, regime competition may *put a chill on initiatives to raise national levels of provision.*[51] For example, the long-standing demand of German unions for an increase in codetermination rights to full

---

51. Leibfried, "Wohlfahrtsstaatliche Entwicklungspotentiale," p. 117.

parity on the supervisory boards of large firms will be even more difficult to realize if non-German firms competing in the same integrated market remain subject to much lower obligations with respect to worker participation.

—Political demands to *roll back* national social policies will be supported in an integrated market by the presumed competitive advantages enjoyed by firms under less costly regimes. An extreme case is Sweden, where the imminent accession to the European Union was probably the strongest argument in the arsenal of the conservative government and revisionist social democrats for a cutback of the Swedish welfare state.

—Regime competition may *preclude* certain ways of closing gaps in social protection at the national level. For example, proposals in Germany before unification to raise minimum pensions to a subsistence level, so as to move retired people with low pensions out of the welfare system, failed because of the large number of former foreign workers drawing small German pensions from short employment spells in Germany. Under European law developed by the Court of Justice, German legislation was barred from excluding non-Germans, or people living outside Germany, from the increased minimum pension.[52] Including them, however, would have made the proposal not only excessively expensive but also electorally unviable: as international equal treatment requirements extend the circle of potential beneficiaries beyond national political communities to large numbers of "outsiders," the willingness of electorates to tax themselves is bound to decline.

—Regime competition is further likely to *result in a shift of power* inside national regimes in favor of potentially outwardly mobile production factors, above all of capital. Such a shift may be caused by the mere *threat of exit*, and indeed may make exit dispensable. For example, as market integration makes it easier for automobile manufacturers in Germany to locate part of their production in countries with less stringent labor regimes, such as Spain or Portugal, management's bargaining power in relation to German works councils increases, and settlements may gradually tilt in management's favor.

—As regime competition limits the capacity of national governments to impose obligations on potentially migrant capital, national social policy may increasingly turn into *generation of investment incentives for business* and of *production obligations for labor*. As long as capital was to some extent captive in national systems, these were under favorable

52. Ibid.

political and economic conditions able to impose on capital social obligations that firms would not have entered into on their own. Regime competition weakens that capacity. While this will not make social policy disappear, its purposes may become more subject than in the past to dictates of economic efficiency, as gauged by the response of investors. A social policy of this kind may consist, instead of decommodification of labor, in its recommodification for a mode of production determined by the market-rational behavior of highly flexible internationalized capital. For example, it may emphasize building an infrastructure of skills, productivistic industrial relations, and a cooperative work force, with the preferences of potential investors as the ultimate arbiter of its adequacy and success.

—Concerns that regime competition may *lead to regime convergence at the lowest level* are sometimes countered by pointing out the continuing differences among the social welfare provisions of individual states in the United States. In particular, it is argued that differences in entitlements for workers have not led to migration into high-provision regimes, nor have differences in taxation or social obligations for business resulted in migration of firms out of high-obligation areas. However, regimes are less different in the United States than in the European Union. Also, the overall level of provision is clearly lower in the United States, with respect to the rights of workers and unions in the workplace, as well as in terms of mandatory nonwage labor costs—which may well be an effect of regime competition chilling initiatives at the state level. Moreover, in spite of generally weak obligations for business, the 1980s have seen a vast migration of production sites from the unionized Frost Belt to the right-to-work states in the Sun Belt. It was the resulting growth of the nonunion sector of the American economy that not only undermined private-sector unionism—indeed, may have dealt it the death blow—but also enabled American business to enter its present trajectory of low productivity growth, declining real wages, rising inequality in the distribution of incomes, and expansion on the basis of an increasingly self-sustaining low-skill and low-wage equilibrium.

Regime competition in an integrated market is sometimes recommended as a virtuous way of determining the most productive system of economic governance, holding out the prospect of marketwide convergence on the most competitive institutional arrangements. But the idea of a market for regimes overlooks the differences in power that result from different degrees of attachment to territorial communities under separate and competing jurisdictions: while in principle capital has no such attachment, labor does. As a consequence, capital and labor are differently dependent on politically generated status in labor markets and on public regulation of employment contracts. Deregulation of labor markets and hierarchies—that is, the reprivatization of employment relations and the weakening of individual and collective status rights of workers—may require no more than international market integration combined with stagnating supranational institutional development: an increase in horizontal interdependence ungoverned by supranational institutions. To the extent that social policy involves the creation of market-correcting employment-related entitlements for workers, regime competition and the deregulation it entails undermines it, even if national social policies and their institutions remain unchanged for the time being.

The outcome of regime competition is biased in favor of capital. This effect need not, and probably will not, arise in one or two years, given, for example, the interest of national governments in retaining a modicum of control over their domestic political economies. But in the long run, unless national social policy regimes can somehow generate the political resources for strengthening their capacity to contain competition among them, their character will be fundamentally altered by market constraints on national initiatives to expand social protection; successful rollbacks of overextended national systems exposed to competition; the difficulty of developing innovative policies under strict international compatibility requirements; subtle power shifts inside national systems due to exit threats from mobile participants; the need to turn social policies into incentives for investors; and, not least, the response of business firms to the market incentives offered by regime competition.

Neovoluntarism: A Post–Welfare State Social Policy Regime for Europe?

If the existing social policy of the European Union is not a series of intermediary steps toward a supranational federal welfare state, then, what is it? In the final part of this chapter I argue that the developments of the late 1980s may indicate the emergence of a new type of social policy at the EU level, one that fits the political bargain underlying the internal market; conforms with the dictates of intergovernmental market making without supranational state-building; and is compatible with the fragmented polity in which it is made, with minimized supranational regulation and reregulation and high horizontal interdependence. Moreover, while emanating from the Union, the alternative social policy regime that may be in the making may in the long run have the potential to penetrate national systems by reinforcing congenial tendencies within these. The result might be a relatively stable European social policy settlement, one that would be acceptable to European business; accommodate the interests of national states and their governments in preserving their remaining sovereignty; and perhaps even give more than nothing to "realistic" European union officials.

The contours of what might become a durable settlement for European Community social policy are highlighted by the contrast between the Union's emergent social policies and the "Social Europe" initiatives of the 1970s. While the latter tried unsuccessfully to create formal, uniform supranational rights and obligations for participants in the common market, the former allow diversity of rules and regimes and choice between them, as well as the use of national machinery for dealing with international externalities; in this respect, they faithfully adhere to the spirit of the new principles of the 1980s, mutual recognition and subsidiarity.[53] Insofar as outcomes like the Charter of Fundamental Social Rights for Workers represent a new style of social policy, that style might be characterized as replacing "hard" with "soft" intervention. But it can certainly also be described as a shift of governance from the public to the private sector and as a withdrawal of state intervention before the power of market forces. The general concept I suggest for this is *neovoluntarism*.

With respect to the European Union's domestic political economy, neovoluntarism stands for a type of social policy that tries to do with a minimum of compulsory modification of both market outcomes and national policy choices, presenting itself as an alternative to hard regulation as well as to no regulation at all. In particular, neovoluntarism allows countries to exit from common standards if their polity or economy will not sustain them (*cohesion by exemption*); gives precedence to

---

53. As reflected in the Delors Commission's "realistic" shift from harmonization to coordination of national social policies, giving up the perspective of convergence. See Henningsen, "Europäisierung Europas?" Goetschy notes "the striking fact . . . that the social and political actors [at the European level] have been very careful not to jeopardize the national dynamics or national coherences at work," which she attributes to the "prudence" of European decisionmakers rather than to their impotence. Janine Goetschy, "1992 and the Social Dimension: Normative Frames, Social Actors and Content," *Economic and Industrial Democracy*, vol. 19, no. 2 (1991), p. 270. Correctly linking the Commission's reluctance to intervene in national systems to the rise of the subsidiarity formula, she notes that the latter "took its full meaning [only] when the harmonization principle was supplemented by the mutual recognition principle" (p. 269).

established national customs and practices and encourages contractual agreements between market participants (*unity by subsidiarity*); tries to enlist for purposes of governance the subtle, cajoling effects of public recommendations, expert consensus on "best practice," explication of the common elements of national regimes, and mutual information and consultation (*governance by recommendation, expertise, explication, and consultation*); offers public and private actors menus of alternatives from which to choose (*governance by choice*); and hopes to increase homogeneity among national regimes through mutual education and comparisons made by electorates of their situation and that of citizens in other countries (*governance by diffusion*).

Cohesion by Exemption

With increasing size of the Community, and with growing diversity in the economic conditions and national social policy regimes of member countries, varying the geometry of Europe may in future be even more frequently used than in the past as a means of keeping the Community together. For social policy after the British opt-out, exemption might become a routinely accepted compromise between some countries' desire for a common floor of standards and provision and others' resistance.

Unity by Subsidiarity

In recent years the concept of subsidiarity both entered the language of European integration and underwent a remarkable change of meaning. In Catholic social doctrine, where it originated, it implied a duty on the part of higher levels of governance to enable smaller units at lower levels to conduct their affairs in responsible "social autonomy." Part of this duty was to see to it that the more organic units, like parochial charities or firms, were able to resolve problems themselves that otherwise might have become problems for the community as a whole—for example, ensuring fair treatment of workers at the workplace or providing equitable social insurance to citizens. Whether or not a smaller unit was entitled to self-government under subsidiarity depended not least on the likely outcome; if this fell short of generally desirable standards, central states had to adjust a lower unit's self-governing capacities or take the matter in hand themselves.

While it seems that the Commission had this version of subsidiarity in mind when it reintroduced the term in the 1980s, the concept later was reinterpreted to mean a general presumption of precedence of lower-level over higher-level governance, and ultimately a principle of laissez-faire with respect to whatever lower units may do. In the process, subsidiarity changed from a social-Catholic concept into a liberal one, the difference being that the former requires a strong central state mandating and enabling less-encompassing social formations to govern themselves in the public interest, whereas the latter implies a weak state acting only at the request of sovereign constituencies.

Depending on the context, subsidiarity is invoked in EU usage to claim precedence for two very different kinds of lower-level self-governance: territorial and functional. Whereas territorial subsidiarity reflects the astonishing capacity of the Union's member states to preserve national sovereignty far beyond its useful historical life,[54] the space for functional subsidiarity—the devolution of public power to the social partners—is limited by both the unwillingness of employers to act positively at the European level and the much stronger role subsidiarity affords to nation-states. In fact, given the deregulatory consequences of ungoverned regime interdependence, the mobilization of subsidiarity to prohibit supranational interference with national practice amounts to giving precedence to yet another mode of lower-level self-regulation—the market—regardless of its substantive outcomes and their consequences for social cohesion or equity.[55] In this way subsidiarity becomes the same as voluntarism.

Governance by Recommendation, Expertise, Explication, and Consultation

In line with and under the constraints of a voluntaristic approach to social policymaking, European Union bodies seem to be making increasing use of nonbinding recommendations instead of binding directives.[56]

54. Application of the principle to subnational levels of government, such as regions or *Länder*, is largely rhetorical, except perhaps where subnational units have strong constitutional standing in national law that precedes EU intervention.

55. It may have been precisely because the concept does invite liberal, Protestant, Thatcherist, and "British" misunderstandings of this kind that it was introduced as a tactical peace formula by continental promoters of supranational state-building.

56. For example, the opinions passed by the social dialogue, as compared to the legislation-oriented decisions of the Economic and Social Committee. Ideologically, nonbindingness may be defended, as it is by Teague and Grahl in "European Community Social Charter," p. 231, as flowing from "a recognition of the diversity and heterogeneity of industrial relations and employment practice in the member states."

Recommendations suggest EU activity, but the actual result may be no more than a piece of paper. Nevertheless, although their adoption is entirely voluntary for both member states and market participants, recommendations may draw attention to ways of dealing with difficult problems, which may ultimately result in national legislation or voluntary adoption of "best practice." This may be the case particularly in member countries lacking a technically trained bureaucracy or developed organizations of labor and capital, such as Greece or Spain.

Similar effects may be expected from the Union's reliance on committees of experts to deal with problems that might otherwise be dealt with in political-adversarial ways. While in the past meetings of experts from member countries were convened primarily in preparation of central rule making, now the hope often seems to be that joint technical deliberations will informally bring about a convergence of standards that may render "hard," formal rules superfluous. Although the mechanisms and capacities of this kind of governance are not well known, that goal should not in principle and altogether be dismissed. German experience in health and safety and work organization and product standardization, for example, suggests that many apparently political issues may indeed be defused by turning them over to groups of experts from "all interested parties" charged with jointly establishing the technical state of the art (*Stand der Technik*). Voluntary self-regulation results to the extent that actors are averse to lagging behind publicly established standards of good practice, because of a cultural commitment to technical excellence; for reasons of image and prestige; to avoid conflict or liability suits; or in anticipation that the *Stand der Technik* will eventually become a formal norm.[57]

Third, governance by explication refers to the creation of supranational standards by making explicit the commonalities of already existing national standards. The most prominent example in the social policy field is the Charter of Fundamental Social Rights of Workers, issued in the

---

57. Daniel J. B. Mitchell and Jacques Rojot believe that "growing awareness of differences in approach to benefits across counties could have important long-term effects on benefits and social insurance within Europe. The existence of alternative routes to retirement income and health care is becoming evident"; Mitchell and Rojot, "Employee Benefits in the Single Market," in Lloyd Ulman, Barry Eichengreen, and William T. Dickens, eds., *Labor and an Integrated Europe* (Brookings, 1993). See also D. Collins, "The New Role of the European Social Fund," in Jacques Vandamme, ed., *New Dimensions in European Social Policy* (London: Croom Helm, 1985), p. 184, who points out that the role of the European Social Fund in vocational training lies mainly in the propagation of pilot projects that spread information on innovative or superior methods.

form of a nonbinding "solemn declaration." On the surface, the charter would appear to be not much more than a comparative labor law exercise extracting the common denominator from national regimes. Supranational rules that are merely a compilation of rules already in force in all member countries do not have to be made formally binding; the weak formal status of the charter therefore follows logically from its content.[58]

Nonbindingness need not mean that explication of commonalities will always be without consequence, however. Spelling out the common denominator of different legal systems is not easy, and the result may take on a life of its own. For example, an authoritative catalog of shared rules may make it more difficult for individual countries to change their rules to move below existing common standards. Moreover, there may be gaps between a country's formal rules and its actual practice that its national system of law enforcement is too weak to close. To the extent that such a country's government cannot prevent the inclusion of such rules in a joint charter-type document, citizens seeking more effective enforcement may find it easier to mobilize public pressure, or they may even try to take their national government to a supranational court.

Fourth, governance by consultation refers to the substitution of rights and obligations of mutual information and deliberation for legally mandated power sharing and joint decisionmaking. This principle has long been employed within the Community itself, where the rights of the European Parliament are basically limited to being informed and heard by other bodies. In social policy, governance by consultation has become the preferred model for labor-management relations at the European

58. It is true, however, that had the charter become law, it would have meant a major change in one EC country, the United Kingdom—which is precisely why it ultimately had to remain nonbinding. In Britain the notion of constitutionally guaranteed basic rights for workers and trade unions is unknown. Although the Parliament is free to legislate such rights as it sees fit, a new Parliament with a different majority is free to revoke them. Legal rights were therefore never high on the political agenda of British unions and, unlike in other countries, could never become an important commodity for political exchange. However, the Thatcher experience in the 1980s taught British unions that their capacity to resist a hostile government through industrial and political, as distinguished from legal, action had sharply declined. Unable to get legal protection from their national state, British unions began in the late 1980s to place their hopes on Brussels; the proposed EC Charter of Fundamental Rights of Workers, largely trivial for unions elsewhere in Europe, increasingly came to be seen as a potential substitute for a constitutionalized floor of legal protection that would be enforceable even on a Conservative parliamentary majority. This goes a long way toward explaining the change in the attitude of the British unions toward the European Community, as well as Thatcher's vigorous defense of the "sovereignty" of the British Parliament.

enterprise level, where the Union is unable or unwilling to create legally enforceable codetermination rights.

The situation is similar at the European and sectoral levels, where the Delors Commission has from the beginning promoted the nonbinding social dialogue in an effort to generate trust and cooperation through information sharing and regular discussion of interests and preferences. Even under the codecision procedure of the Maastricht treaty, it is only by specific agreement between business and labor that the results of consultations can become legally binding. To the extent that consultation is more than just symbolic, its expected effect depends on its contribution to a rational clarification of interests on both sides by forcing groups to present statements of their objectives and to explain why their position is more in the public interest than others.

Governance by Choice

EU law increasingly offers national governments or market participants a choice between alternative ways of compliance.[59] Examples are the revised drafts of the fifth directive, the European company statute, and, to an extent, the directive on the European works councils. Instead of normatively prescribing a uniform mechanism of work force participation, the drafts offer firms and countries menus of alternative models, any of which they may adopt to satisfy legal requirements. Which alternative is chosen is determined by national traditions; the preferences of management and, perhaps, workers and unions; and the relative strength of management and labor in a given institutional or economic environment.

Homogeneity by Diffusion

To the extent that neovoluntariam expects the emergence of a uniform transnational order, the mechanism for this is regime diffusion through a multinational political market.[60] A government that refuses to accept a common EU standard for, say, working hours may be attacked by the

59. This too is introduced as flowing from a need to preserve national diversity: "To make sure that the various traditions and susceptibilities in this Community of ours are respected, the Commission has proposed a choice between three forms of worker participation as a preliminary to drawing up the European Company Statute." Delors, "Statement on the Broad Lines of Community Policy," p. 7.

60. Teague and Grahl, "European Community Social Charter," p. 231.

opposition for withholding from its citizens the same rights that other Europeans enjoy. To avoid that charge, the government will fall in line with the other countries.[61] Political regime diffusion must compete, however, with economic regime competition; the former might raise national standards, but the latter will tend to lower them.

Neovoluntarism would represent a break with the practice of European national welfare states, which is to create hard, legally enforceable status rights and obligations for individual citizens and organized collectivities acting in, taking advantage of, and being disadvantaged by market relations. Reflecting the European Union's less-developed state capacities, neovoluntarism would appear much less statist than old-style social policy interventionism, in that it would entail a shift of social policymaking from the state to civil society. However, unlike neocorporatism, under which strong quasi-public organizations of social groups are charged by an affirmative public policy with controlling and correcting market outcomes, neovoluntarism would return allocative decisions to private actors in private markets, the difference being that under limited state capacities, neovoluntarism cannot rebalance the organizational and institutional resources available to actors in civil society in regulating their affairs.[62]

Neovoluntarism has the potential to be advertised and perceived as a desirable move away from etatist interference with civil society. Born out of intergovernmental constraints on the growth of supranational state capacity, nonbinding EU regulation may easily be glorified as a method of governance uniquely suited for a democratic society of high diversity and civic maturity. Presented thus, a voluntaristic social policy regime at the EU level may well radiate downward into national systems, where it may reinforce reformist pressures for "liberalization," "deregulation,"

---

61. While observing that "neither the Charter nor the action programme put important new constraints on labour markets or on national employment policies," Teague and Grahl, "European Community Social Charter," p. 209, hope that they will "increase the weight of Community comparisons and comparators both in the formation of public policy at national level and, ultimately, in employment bargaining itself." This, of course, is hardly borne out by the British experience—witness the reelection of the Major government in 1992 in spite of its opt-out from European social policy.

62. Majone, "European Community," agrees with many of the points presented here, although he regards the matter more affirmatively. Majone's notion of a "regulatory" social policy coincides with the concept of neovoluntarism, in that it shares its rejection of functionalist expectations of social policy expansion and discards the prospect of a nation-state-like social policy at the European level. According to Majone, social regulation as an alternative form of social policy is not adequately described in Marshallian terms; it is, however, compatible with the limited resources controlled by the Union, as well as with subsidiarity and preservation of national diversity.

"decentralization," "flexibility," and "individual responsibility." In this way, adding to the effects of horizontal regime competition on the one hand and the vertical imposition of compatibility requirements on the other, supranational neovoluntarism may help gradually transform national social policy regimes from social-democratic models into more liberal ones.

Soft neovoluntarist regulation is, of course, particularly acceptable to business. Potentially even contributing to a softening of "rigid" national social policy regimes, supranational voluntarism would leave large firms operating in the internal market the option of doing what they want while sparing them the hazards of either an anomic absence of all supranational rule making or a frontal attack on existing national regimes. Another feature attractive to business is that a social policy unbacked by strong state capacities cannot offer groups with limited market power recourse to legal compulsion, so as to change the power balance between them and better-endowed rivals. Under voluntarism, when all is said and done, it is those in stronger market positions who decide how much symmetry and equity between themselves and others is symmetrical and equitable, or "reasonable" and "efficient." Competing claims that fail to pass this test—that, in other words, require legitimate force for their satisfaction—are conveniently eliminated.

CHAPTER THIRTEEN

The Dynamics of
Social Policy Integration

Paul Pierson and Stephan Leibfried

T HE EMERGENCE OF THE European Union marks the remarkable transformation of sovereign, highly developed nation-states into parts of a
quite different kind of polity. Understanding this transformation and its
implications for the development of public policies poses a formidable
challenge for social scientists. The new European polity is only four
decades old; by comparative standards, it is still in its infancy. The system
itself is an unfamiliar and rapidly moving target. By both accident and
design, this new polity is also enormously complex, with multiple centers
of sometimes uncertain authority competing and cooperating while social
actors scramble to adjust to a radically altered landscape.

This essay draws on the empirical chapters in part 1 and the comparative material in part 2 to fashion some general conclusions about the
dynamics of social policy integration. Our goal is to identify the main
sources of the evolving social dimension of the European Union—both
patterns of action and inaction and focal points of political conflict over
possible reforms. In many ways our analysis plays off Wolfgang Streeck's
ambitious *tour d'horizon* of social policy in the European Union. There
are some fundamental points of agreement. Streeck's essay, like the introduction to this volume, stresses that the outcome of multilevel policymaking depends not on functional "requirements" but on the interplay
between nation, class, and institutional structures. Like Streeck, we be-

Our thanks to Elmar Rieger for helpful comments on an earlier draft of this essay and
to the participants in the Workshop on European Integration and Domestic Politics (Laguna
Beach, California, June 3–5, 1994), organized by Wayne Sandholtz and Alec Stone, for
illuminating discussions of many of the issues considered here.

lieve that the characteristics that most distinguish the European Union are a strong role for member states; a new balance of power and set of strategic options for business, labor, and other social interests; and a fragmented, territorially grounded structure of political authority with weak decisionmaking powers at the center. There is no disagreement that an analysis of the EU must begin with an appreciation of the EU's limited capacity for positive policymaking and an acknowledgment that member states and organized business will often resist centralized social policy initiatives.

Yet while effectively demolishing claims that Europe is on the road to a federal welfare state with a strong central authority, Streeck's analysis tilts too far in the other direction. Streeck exaggerates the power and cohesiveness of member states and organized business, while oversimplifying their attitudes toward EU social policy. He dismisses other dimensions of Europe's emerging multitiered system, such as the role of the European Court of Justice, that are tremendously important. As a result, Streeck understates the significance of Europe's social dimension and treats as closed a number of issues that we believe remain open.

In this chapter we return to the three distinctive features of multitiered systems identified in the introduction: the role of constituent units, the transformation of organized interests, and the dilemmas associated with institutions for shared policymaking. For each point we discuss the characteristics of social policymaking in the EU and draw some general conclusions about the state of Europe's social dimension. The European Union is not, and undoubtedly will not become, a federal welfare state like those of traditional nation-states. This scenario was never plausible, since the EU arose in a different historical context and was layered on top of already deeply institutionalized and diverse social policy structures within each member state. Hemmed in by institutional and political constraints, the European Union is incapable of the kind of positive, state-building initiatives of a Bismarck or a Beveridge. Yet the EU has become the source of considerable political authority. Social policy, broadly defined, is now profoundly influenced by activity at the EU level. European social policy does not supplant national social policy, but merges with it in an intricate process of competition, adjustment, and accommodation. What is emerging in Europe is a multileveled, highly fragmented system in which policy "develops" but is beyond the firm control of any single political authority.

Constituent Units and EU Social Policy

As noted in the introduction to this volume, the prominence of member states is exhibited in two main ways. First, the scope and diversity of member-state social policy may preempt policy space for the EU and certainly will complicate any attempt to create coherent European standards. Second, the authority and legitimacy derived from social provision gives member states strong incentives to engage in competitive state-building; at the same time the structure of EU institutions gives member states tremendous resources for protecting their interests. Streeck concludes that these conditions so constrain EU initiatives that the Union is essentially limited to "market-making" efforts.

There are two distinct issues here. First, how decisive is the influence of the constituent units of the European Union? Second, with respect to social policy, what do the member states want? The case studies and comparative evidence presented in this volume can help answer these questions.

EU policy, we have argued throughout this volume, is not simply a result of intergovernmental bargaining. What has evolved in Europe is an extraordinarily complex network of overlapping authority, in which member states play a central but far from exclusive role. It is worth returning to the four limitations on member-state power that we discussed in the introduction: (1) the autonomous activity of EU organizations; (2) the impact of previous policy commitments at the EU level; (3) the growth of issue density; and (4) the activity of nonstate actors.

The political organs of the EU are not simply the tools of the member states. Member states created the European Community, and they did so to serve their own collective purposes.[1] In order to carry out collective tasks, however, the member states felt compelled to create new institutions. As Terry Moe argues, the results are predictable: "A new public agency is literally a new actor on the political scene. It has its own interests, which may diverge from those of its creators, and it typically has resources—expertise, delegated authority—to strike out on its own should the opportunities arise. The political game is different now: there

---

1. The following discussion could be recast in the language of "principal-agent theory," which uses the analytics of microeconomics to discuss the interactions that lead to, and follow from, the delegation of authority. For a useful introduction with applications to political institutions, see Terry Moe, "The New Economics of Organization," *American Journal of Political Science*, vol. 28 (November 1984), pp. 739–77.

are more players and more interests to be accommodated."[2] In the European context, two considerations complicated the member states' problem: the need to create arrangements that would allow reasonably efficient collective decisionmaking and effective enforcement, despite the involvement of many governments with differing interests; and the need to take into account the possibility that future governments might be eager to overturn their designs. Again, the result is predictable: pressure to grant those who run EU institutions considerable authority. As Moe adds, the designers of agencies "do not want 'their' agencies to fall under the control of opponents. And given the way public authority is allocated and exercised in a democracy, they often can only shut out their opponents by shutting themselves out too. In many cases, then, they purposely create structures that even they cannot control."[3]

Over time EU organizations may use grants of authority for their own purposes, and especially to expand their autonomy. The upshot is an intricate, ongoing struggle, one that is well known to students of the European Union but would also be familiar to observers of, say, relations between congressional committees and administrative agencies in the United States. Member states generally (but not always) seek to rein in EU institutions. They recognize, however, that these crucial collective organizations cannot function without significant power, and that the requisite authority must grow as the tasks addressed at the European level expand and become more complex. For their part, European institutions such as the Commission, the European Court of Justice, and the European Parliament are always looking for opportunities to enhance their powers.

The evidence from this volume reveals a substantial accretion of authority to supranational institutions. The Council, to be sure, continues to stand watch over proposed legislation and actively protects member-state interests. Yet as Martin Rhodes and George Ross both document in detail, the Commission possesses considerable ability to advance policy initiatives. Two assets are particularly important. The first concerns the setting of agendas. Choosing which proposals to consider is a crucial (if often unappreciated) aspect of politics, and here the Commission has primacy. Ob-

2. Terry M. Moe, "The Politics of Structural Choice: Toward a Theory of Public Bureaucracy," in Oliver E. Williamson, ed., *Organization Theory: From Chester Barnard to the Present and Beyond* (Oxford University Press, 1990), pp. 116–53.

3. Moe, "Politics of Structural Choice," p. 125.

viously, this power is far from unlimited; the Commission cannot expect to pass proposals that ignore the preferences of member states. Nevertheless, an entrepreneurial Commission can frame issues, design packages, and structure the sequence of proposals in ways that maximize its room for independent initiative.[4] With the expansion of qualified majority voting comes a widening of the range of possible "winning coalitions," further increasing the Commission's influence. The Commission has effectively used its agenda-setting powers to advance aspects of the social dimension and to increase its own role in policy reform. Prominent examples include the expansion and, especially, the reorganization of the structural funds, the passage of the Social Protocol, the use of what Rhodes calls the *treaty-base game* to maximize prospects for passing directives, and the encouragement of expanded social dialogue.

The Commission's second major asset is its role as what Volker Eichener calls *process manager.*[5] Social policymaking at the EU level, as many have noted, is often a matter of "social regulation"—a type of policymaking with its own distinctive qualities.[6] The development of complex social regulations requires the assembly and coordination of dense networks of experts. This task falls to the Commission, and with it comes additional room for influence. Health and safety regulations offer the clearest evidence of this process at work. If well-developed national social policies automatically preempted EU action, there would be little European regulation in this area, because health and safety legislation has been a long-standing part of national systems.[7] Yet EU activ-

4. For a classic statement, see William H. Riker, *The Art of Political Manipulation* (Yale University Press, 1986). On the entrepreneurial role of Commission President Jacques Delors, see George Ross, *Jacques Delors and European Integration* (Oxford: Polity Press, 1994).

5. Volker Eichener, "Social Dumping or Innovative Regulation? Processes and Outcomes of European Decision-Making in the Sector of Health and Safety at Work Harmonization," Working Paper 92-28 (Florence: European University Institute, January 1993). See also B. Guy Peters, "Bureaucratic Politics and the Institutions of the European Community," in Alberta M. Sbragia, ed., *Euro-Politics: Institutions and Policymaking in the "New" European Community* (Brookings, 1992), pp. 75–122; and Peter Ludlow, "The European Commission," in Robert Keohane and Stanley Hoffmann, eds., *The New European Community: Decisionmaking and Institutional Change* (Boulder, Colo.: Westview Press, 1991), pp. 85–132.

6. On the general point, the classic statement is Theodore J. Lowi, "American Business, Public Policy Case Studies, and Political Theory," *World Politics*, vol. 16 (1964), pp. 667–715. For a discussion of this issue with respect to the EU, see Giandomenico Majone, "The European Community between Social Policy and Social Regulation," *Journal of Common Market Studies*, vol. 31 (June 1993), pp. 153–70.

7. Ostner and Lewis's chapter in this volume, revealing extensive EU initiatives on

ity has been extensive, and a very high level of standards has generally been achieved—often higher than that of any member state. To be sure, the use of qualified majority voting has been crucial, but the outcome of high harmonization is impossible to explain in terms of simple intergovernmental bargaining. Nor, to anticipate a bit, is it easy to reconcile with Streeck's view that business can and will veto anything beyond market-making initiatives. Although constructing the single market might require harmonization of health and safety standards for *products* (since national restrictions could be trade barriers in disguise), there is no obvious need for harmonized standards for production *processes*.[8] Yet here as well the European Union has been highly interventionist.

As Eichener documents, the Commission's role as process manager appears to have been critical in this low-profile regulatory environment. Much of the important decisionmaking took place in committees composed of policy experts. Some of these experts were linked to business and labor groups, but business interests could not simply refuse to participate, since regulatory action was likely to proceed without them. Representatives on these committees were often interested in innovation, having gravitated toward Brussels because it seemed to be the action arena for regulatory issues. In this technocratic context, "best practices" from many member states (and from other countries such as Sweden) were pieced together to fashion an interventionist structure of social regulation. The Commission played a central part in joining together the work of different committees and incorporating concerns of other actors (such as the European Parliament), all the while actively promoting particularly innovative proposals. Thus while the Commission, like other actors in the EU, operates under considerable constraints, it is well positioned to advance its own agenda in such a policy environment.

If the Commission's importance in this new multitiered polity is clear, so is that of the European Court of Justice (ECJ). Until quite recently political scientists paid scant attention to the role of courts in policy development.[9] For that reason it is worth being emphatic: any analy-

---

gender issues despite well-entrenched and quite diverse national policy regimes, also raises questions about the impact of member-state preemption. While national structures obviously have a considerable influence on the nature and consequences of EU interventions, there is little indication that these structures *prevent* such interventions.

8. Eichener, "Social Dumping."

9. On this point, see Joseph H. H. Weiler, "Community Member States and European Integration: Is the Law Relevant?" *Journal of Common Market Studies*, vol. 21 (September 1982), pp. 39–57; and Martin Shapiro and Alec Stone, "The New Constitutional Politics of Europe," *Comparative Political Studies*, vol. 26 (January 1994), pp. 397–420.

sis of policy evolution in the European Union must acknowledge the Court's crucial role in expanding European public authority. To quote one highly respected observer, the relationship between Community law and member-state law is now "indistinguishable from that found in the constitutional order of federal states."[10] As we documented in chapter 2, much social policymaking in Europe now occurs through the auspices of the ECJ. This activity may take the form of (usually expansive) interpretations of EU social policy initiatives (as in the case of gender issues). More often, it occurs through the Court's scrutiny of national social policy legislation. Again, much of this activity takes place in an incremental, largely unnoticed fashion. The result, however, has been an accumulation of rulings that have substantially modified the way European social policies develop.

The institutional actors that the member states created to make the European Union a reality have taken on lives of their own. These actors have hardly supplanted the member states, who continue to control the single most important center of decisionmaking, the Council. And in theory the member states, acting unanimously, could remove the powers that they have bestowed. But member states are no longer in complete control. Recapturing authority from EU institutions generally requires unanimous votes; an aggressive attempt to move in this direction would doubtless call the single-market project itself into question. Equally important, the member states *need* relatively strong EU institutions if their collective project is to remain viable. In this context institutional actors such as the Commission and ECJ are able to exert considerable influence on the development of social policy.

The second limit on member-state authority discussed in the introduction concerns the implications of previous legal commitments at the European level. Especially when all actors have adapted to the new rules of the game and made extensive commitments based on their expected continuation, these previous decisions may lock in member states to policy options that they would not now choose to pursue.[11] A central fact of life for member states is the *acquis communautaire*, the corpus of existing

10. Joseph H. H. Weiler, "A Quiet Revolution: The European Court of Justice and Its Interlocutors," *Comparative Political Studies*, vol. 26 (January 1994), pp. 512–13.

11. For good theoretical discussions, see Stephen A. Krasner, "Sovereignty: An Institutional Perspective," in James A. Caporaso, ed., *The Elusive State: International and Comparative Perspectives* (Newbury Park, Calif.: Sage Publications, 1989), pp. 69–96; and Douglass C. North, *Institutions, Institutional Effects, and Economic Performance* (Cambridge University Press, 1990).

legislation and practice. As Michael Shackleton notes, "However much Member States might deplore certain aspects of Community policy, there is no question that all find themselves locked into a system which narrows down the areas for possible change and obliges them to think of incremental revision of existing arrangements."[12] Member-state policy preferences may shift because of altered circumstances, new information, or a change in government, yet member states do not inherit a blank slate on which they can rewrite at will. The same unanimity rules that make reform difficult make previously enacted efforts hard to undo, even if such efforts begin to unexpectedly impinge on member-state sovereignty.

The extent to which member states are in fact locked in has recently been questioned. Where it was once understood that participation in the EU was an all-or-nothing proposition, Maastricht has enhanced the prospects for a Europe "à la carte" or a Europe of "variable geometries."[13] Britain and Denmark received opt-outs on monetary union; the eleven other member states circumvented the British veto by opting "up and out" with the Social Protocol. Jeffrey Anderson summarizes the new situation thus: "Threats of exclusion [from the Union] have now lost some of their power to drag members into a collective, uniform, and binding agreement."[14] Whether this change will persist in the area of social policy is open to question. As Rhodes notes, there is already considerable pressure to bring Britain back into the fold in social policy, a change that would also be likely if the Labour Party ever manages to form a government.

More important, the new flexibility refers only to *additional* treaty obligations. Member-state governments may be able to obtain opt-outs from future treaty provisions. They are not free to review and discard the commitments of previous governments, however, including those with quite different policy preferences.[15] As new policies are enacted, the

12. Michael Shackleton, "The Delors II Budget Package," in Neill Nugent, ed., *The European Community 1992: Annual Review of Activities* (Oxford: Blackwell Publishers, 1993), pp. 11–25.

13. This tendency has appeared in such areas as immigration (the Schengen group), security policy, and monetary union. It would probably accelerate if the EU were to accept members from Eastern Europe. Ulrich Fastenrath, "Variable Geometrie, konzentrische Kreise: Zukunftsmodelle für Europa," *Frankfurter Allgemeine Zeitung*, no. 207 (September 6, 1994), p. 5.

14. Jeffrey J. Anderson, "The State of the (European) Union: From the Single Market to Maastricht, from Singular Events to General Theories," *World Politics*, vol. 47 (April 1995), pp. 441–65, quote at p. 449.

15. Again, Britain's position vis-à-vis the Social Protocol is instructive. Assuming that the Conservatives continue to resist joining the protocol while Labour would reverse that

scope of the *acquis communautaire* continues to grow. Just as has always been true in domestic politics, new governments in member states now find that the deadweight of previous policy and institutional decisions at the European level seriously limits their capacity for policy maneuver.

The third limit on member-state authority relates to the consequences of *issue density*. Two distinct processes are involved here, both of which are connected to the massive expansion of EU decisionmaking that accompanied the single-market project. Each of these processes limits the ability of member states to control the pace and direction of social policy integration. First, there are growing demands on the gatekeepers of member-state sovereignty as European-level decisionmaking becomes both more frequent and more complex. Time constraints, scarcity of relevant information, and the need to delegate decisions to those with expertise may lead to more gaps in member-state control and to a propensity for unanticipated consequences.[16] As Gary Marks puts it, "A convincing analysis of institution building in the EC should go beyond the areas that are transparently dominated by member states: financial decisions, major pieces of legislation, and the Treaties. Beyond and beneath the highly visible politics of member state bargaining lies a dimly lit process of institutional formation."[17] Member-state governments, facing overloaded agendas and focused on intergovernmental bargaining over the grand decisions of treaties and budgets, are more vulnerable in this arena.[18] Several of the chapters in this volume identify this type of process. In chapter 2 we argued that the Court's role has expanded through literally hundreds of cases, most of which received no attention

---

choice, the status quo can be maintained only if it is ratified at every election. A single Labour victory would produce an institutional change that could not subsequently be reversed without provoking a constitutional crisis in Europe. The *acquis communautaire* creates a "ratchet effect."

16. This, in fact, is a central point of principal-agent theory. Agents can use their greater information about their own activities and the requirements connected to their work to achieve autonomy from principals. Asymmetrical access to information, which is ubiquitous in complex decisionmaking processes, provides the foundation for influence.

17. Gary Marks, "Structural Policy and Multilevel Governance in the European Community," in Alan W. Cafruny and Glenda G. Rosenthal, eds., *The State of the European Community* (Boulder, Colo.: Lynn Rienner, 1993), pp. 391–410. Marks's depiction of multilevel governance runs parallel to our own analysis in many respects.

18. Marks, for example, has described the Commission's ability to exploit its detailed knowledge of the policy process and its role as process manager to generate influence over the structural funds, an influence that the British government failed to anticipate. He rightly notes, however, that the exploitation of information asymmetries to produce unanticipated consequences "is tricky in the context of ongoing political relationships where learning takes place." Marks, "Structural Policy," p. 403.

or were little understood at the time. Rhodes and, especially, Ross, demonstrate how the initiation of a flurry of highly detailed proposals permitted EU actors to carve out space to pursue their own goals.

The second process triggered by issue density is one of spillover: integrating some aspects of complex modern societies is hard to do without changing other components, because the sectors to be integrated cannot be effectively isolated. Such spillovers become more prevalent as the density of EU policymaking increases. In social policy, most of these spillovers result from the single-market initiative; for example, market building in the Union is having a corrosive effect on the sovereignty of national welfare states. Some spillover effects are direct and relatively easy to identify because they stem from new regulations or ECJ rulings related to compatibility with the single market, although their implications for social policy are often difficult to predict.[19] Many of the most important effects, however, are indirect and even more uncertain; these depend on developments such as the advance of monetary union, the manner in which the ECJ chooses to adjudicate points of friction between the internal market and national social policy regimes, and the interplay of public and private social service provision in a shifting regulatory environment.

Streeck is ambivalent on the issue of spillover. On the one hand, he argues that there is "too much distance" between the single market and social policy for significant spillover to occur. But as we have shown, the distance is in fact often very short.[20] And Streeck's penetrating arguments about the "regime competition" encouraged by the single market vividly illustrate spillover processes. Streeck emphasizes that institutional arrangements can be disrupted when important actors are given significant new options. The crucial question—an extraordinarily difficult one to answer—is how stable national welfare states will be in an environment

19. On how shifting "micromotives" can give rise to sweeping changes in macrosocial structures, see Thomas C. Schelling, *Micromotives and Macrobehavior* (New York: Norton, 1978).

20. Again, the idea of "making a market" without constructing a wide range of rulings on social issues is simply untenable in advanced industrial societies. Streeck's comparison with the United States is instructive. Only by conflating social policy with the full-blown Bismarckian or Scandinavian welfare states can one say that the United States has "a perfectly integrated market economy . . . without having developed anything close to an integrated social policy." In the United States, as elsewhere, very extensive expansions of social protection accompanied the creation of an integrated and highly developed national economy. See Margaret Weir, Ann Shola Orloff, and Theda Skocpol, eds., *The Politics of Social Policy in the United States* (Princeton University Press, 1988).

that introduces many new pressures and opportunities for different actors.

One criticism of arguments about spillover is that they apply a functionalist logic, in which certain developments create "needs" to which a system is "required" to respond.[21] We agree that pressures alone do not create policies. They may, however, focus the attention of those actors who do produce policy, as well as alter the balance of influence among actors. Thus *functional* spillover can generate *political* spillover. Whether that is likely in the EU context depends on the preferences of member states and economic actors, which we discuss below. The point here is simply that increasing EU activity in areas not directly related to social policy may influence the demands placed on member states and limit the range of policies that they can autonomously pursue.

The final constraint on member-state power that we suggested concerns the role of social actors and the prospects for expanded activity through channels other than those running through the executives of member states. This is the factor most difficult to document, because the fragmented and opaque nature of decisionmaking in the EU often makes it hard to identify the key decisionmakers, let alone the sources of outside pressure on them. Because research on this issue is scarce, we have relied little on this factor in developing our analysis. Yet the issue strikes us as an important one, calling out for further scholarship. The clearest sign that social action now operates around as well as through national governments is the proliferation of interest-group activity at the European level. To take just one crude but revealing indicator, the number of officially recognized European interest groups (EIGs) increased from about 500 in 1985 to over 1,500 by 1990.[22] Assuming that groups adjust their organizational structures only when it serves their interests to do so, this development suggests that channels of influence do not run exclusively through member states.

It would be folly to suggest that the member states do not play a central part in policy development within the European Union. Rather, our point is that they do, but in a context that they do not (even collectively) fully control. Arguments about intergovernmental bargaining, even those of the more sophisticated "two-level game" variety, exagger-

21. For a devastating critique, see Jon Elster, "Marxism, Functionalism, and Game Theory," in Sharon Zukin and Paul DiMaggio, eds., *Structures of Capital: The Social Organization of the Economy* (Cambridge University Press, 1990), pp. 87–118.

22. Simon Hix, "The Study of the European Community: The Challenge to Comparative Politics," *West European Politics*, vol. 17 (January 1994), pp. 1–30.

ate the extent of member-state power.[23] In their focus on grand intergovernmental bargains, they fail to capture the various processes unleashed by a very complex, ambitious agenda of shared decisionmaking. These processes empower other actors while considerably curtailing the autonomy of member states.

Nonetheless, the member states of the European Union remain extremely powerful. A crucial issue thus concerns the circumstances under which constituent units may *want* the European Union to formulate social policy. The typical assumption is that member governments will strongly resist interference in what they perceive to be an important sphere of national sovereignty. But it is a mistake to depict policy development in the Union, or in any multitiered system, as a simple zero-sum tug-of-war between levels of government. Member states may also see the EU as a mechanism for overcoming their own incapacities. They may prefer to share authority, then, in some instances.

In democratic polities sustained power requires electoral vindication. The first concern of national governments is not with sovereignty per se but with creating the circumstances for continued domestic political success. Here the history of the Single European Act is worth recalling. Governments relinquished aspects of sovereignty not because they considered these sacrifices insignificant but because they saw them as essential to achieve important goals. Faced with the apparent bankruptcy of national strategies of economic adjustment, national autonomy was exchanged for what was hoped would be superior policy performance.[24] Paul Pierson's chapter on the gradual nationalization of income transfers in the United States reveals a similar logic. Southern politicians and business interests who stood to benefit from decentralized arrangements resisted centralization, but a competitive state-building dynamic—defending authority for authority's sake—was largely absent. Although state governments throughout the United States had established a strong role in the provision of income transfers, most did not resist nationalization—indeed, many actively sought it—as the drawbacks of decentralized policy structures became evident.[25]

---

23. For a good example, see Andrew Moravcsik, "Preferences and Power in the European Community: A Liberal Intergovernmentalist Approach," *Journal of Common Market Studies*, vol. 31 (December 1993), pp. 473–524.

24. On how member-state policy failures contributed to agreement on the SEA, see Wayne Sandholtz and John Zysman, "1992: Recasting the European Bargain," *World Politics*, vol. 42 (October 1989), pp. 95–128; and David R. Cameron, "The 1992 Initiative: Causes and Consequences," in Sbragia, ed., *Euro-Politics*, pp. 23–74.

25. The comparative evidence also suggests an important point of contrast. In the

Member-state acquiescence to an expanded EU social policy competence could result from the same hardheaded calculations, but only if national solutions fail are supranational options likely to be considered. Patrick Ireland's chapter on immigration, for instance, emphasizes this kind of policy dynamic. Governments will take steps toward supranationalization in order to respond to discontent that threatens their popularity. The empirical question for social policy is whether such challenges will be of sufficient magnitude to produce the kind of dynamic that Renaud Dehousse observed in the fields of environmental and consumer protection, where

> the increasing reach of Community law makes it evermore difficult for Member States to conduct their own regulatory policies separately. Those Member States that favour high protection levels increasingly prefer to press for a decision at Community level, rather than seeking an escape clause which might harm the interests of their own producers. Significantly, a country like Denmark, which has always shown great reluctance to delegate new powers to the Community, has been pressing for a generalization of majority voting in the areas of social and environmental protection. Thus, even for national governments, jursidictional interests can give way to regulatory concerns. Assuredly, this shift has played an important part in the further extension of Community competences enacted by the Maastricht Treaty.[26]

One cannot simply assume that member states will relentlessly cling to all social policy authority. A more reasonable assumption is that constituent units will consider relinquishing social policy authority only when pressures on them undermine their own interventions, thereby posing electoral risks. Analyzing the potential reactions of EU member states to Union-level social policy initiatives must therefore take into account the position and prospects for national welfare states.

---

federal systems of North America, the superior fiscal capacities of central authorities were often a "carrot" that made transfers of decisionmaking power attractive to constituent units. The EU emphatically lacks this capacity and would presumably have to make other carrots available.

26. Renaud Dehousse, "Integration v. Regulation? On the Dynamics of Regulation in the European Community," *Journal of Common Market Studies*, vol. 20 (December 1992), pp. 397–98.

This is a complex subject;[27] for current purposes we limit ourselves to two aspects of it: general pressures on member states resulting from the maturation of national social programs and changes in the global economy, and pressures stemming from the growing role of the European Union itself. National welfare states currently face many difficulties. Governments confront simultaneous and incompatible demands to lower taxes and maintain popular social programs. Partly, concerns about social spending are the inevitable consequence of maturing (and therefore expensive) programs operating in a context of aging populations. But added to those concerns are fears about Europe's competitive position in the world market and alarm about the causes and implications of persistently high unemployment, which have prompted calls for the reform of social programs.[28] Moreover, the European Union itself is a potentially destabilizing factor for national welfare states. Market-compatibility requirements enforced by the Commission and the ECJ constrain member-state social policies, while the development of the single market creates a series of indirect pressures to reduce spending on social programs.

There remains considerable uncertainty about these strains on national welfare states. If they worsened, the repercussions for the European Union would be significant. The welfare state remains the most popular component of the postwar social contract. As Peter Flora notes, in many countries the "welfare state constituency" of producers and beneficiaries easily approaches 50 percent of the electorate.[29] Despite mounting pres-

27. For some recent views, see Evelyne Huber and John D. Stephens, "The Future of the Social Democratic Welfare State: Options in the Face of Economic Internationalization and European Integration," paper presented at the International Sociological Association Meetings, Oxford, September 3–6, 1993; Martin Rhodes, "'Subversive Liberalism': Market Integration, Globalisation and the European Welfare State," paper presented at the twenty-second annual European Consortium for Political Research Joint Session of Workshops, Madrid, April 1994; and Paul Pierson, "The New Politics of the Welfare State," *World Politics*, vol. 48 (January 1996).

28. The view that generous social programs are a major cause of European unemployment is widespread among elites, although there is little consensus among economists. See Charles R. Beam, "European Unemployment: A Survey," *Journal of Economic Literature*, vol. 32 (June 1994), pp. 573–619; and Rebecca M. Blank, *Social Protection versus Economic Flexibility: Is There a Trade-Off?* (University of Chicago Press, 1994).

29. Peter Flora, "From Industrial to Postindustrial Welfare State?" *Annals of the Institute of Social Science*, special issue (University of Tokyo, 1989), pp. 149–62. This source of political strength, extending far beyond the traditional working class, fundamentally distinguishes the politics of social policy from that of industrial relations. Broad popular resistance to market-oriented reform is likely to be much greater in the case of social policy. On this point, see Pierson, "New Politics." For recent data on the strength of public support within the EC, see Maurizio Ferrera, *EC Citizens and Social Protection: Main Results from*

sures on national economies in the 1970s and 1980s, efforts to scale back systems of social provision met stiff political resistance. In short, the erosion of member-state standards would undoubtedly result in strong popular demands for a governmental response.

Everyone agrees that the member states are certain to be central actors in fashioning responses to the pressures on national welfare states. If governments prove unable to cope individually, however, they and a range of social actors are likely to turn their attention to Europe.[30] Two possible motivations for such a reorientation are worth mentioning. First, governments could turn to Europe in an attempt to prop up national arrangements. To date, of course, such efforts have been modest. This is not surprising, because—although concern about the future of the welfare state is widespread—immediate evidence of crisis is hard to come by.[31] As Rhodes points out, however, there are indications that many member states realize that the EU can help keep the playing field from becoming too uneven. Member states acceded to substantial upward harmonization on health and safety. They agreed to rules on maternity leave that raised standards for some member states while introducing a "ratchet" that prohibits a rollback in standards elsewhere. With the exception of Britain, the member states have chosen to accept a Social Protocol, which expands the possibilities for further initiatives. Modest steps in response to as yet modest disruption of national programs should not be read as a blanket rejection of European action.

In the current context, a second possible basis for such a transfer of authority should also be considered. If retrenchment is viewed as inevitable or desirable, member states seeking to avoid blame for cutbacks in popular social programs might find the EU an attractive vehicle for

---

a *Eurobarometer Survey* (Brussels: European Commission, Division V/E/2, November 1993).

30. Environmental policy represents an interesting point of comparison here. Initiative over environmental policymaking, a topic of great public interest, has gradually shifted to the EU level. The Union now plays a central role—in some areas it is more active than federal authorities in the United States—considerably outpacing what seems required to complete a single market. All this has come about despite the complete lack of reference to environmental issues in the Treaty of Rome. Only at Maastricht were some treaty articles on the subject added, long after the EU had obtained substantial policy competence. Alberta M. Sbragia, "EC Environmental Policy: Atypical Ambitions and Typical Problems?" in Cafruny and Rosenthal, eds., *State of the European Community*, pp. 337–52. See also Giandomenico Majone, "Regulatory Federalism in the European Community," *Environment and Planning C*, vol. 10 (1992), pp. 299–316.

31. Pierson, "New Politics."

policymaking.[32] Ironically, the European Union—a possible rescuer of national welfare states, in the recent view of social democrats—could become a vehicle for facilitating national-level retrenchment. All member-state governments are struggling with relentless cross-pressures to maintain or expand social benefits while avoiding tax increases and balancing budgets. Difficult, electorally perilous choices are inevitable, but member states may face less electoral retribution if cutbacks can be attributed to EU requirements. In this environment, shifting some decisions to the European Union may prove the least unpalatable option.

As we argued in chapter 2, member states are using some aspects of the single market initiative and European monetary union in this way. Ilona Ostner and Jane Lewis note that member states have sometimes used the EU's insistence on gender equality as a pretext for leveling down social benefits—much to the dismay of women's groups.[33] Streeck points to several ways the member states can use the EU framework to obtain some breathing room on social issues. Finally, the Commission's recent campaign for flexibility in labor markets and social provision signals a new willingness to contemplate EU regulations that would facilitate market-oriented reform of social policies.[34] During the next decade member states will probably test the possibilities for using the EU as a vehicle for blame avoidance, though the EU's own limited legitimacy is likely to constrain its capacity to take the blame for unpopular policies.

Thus there is good reason to expect that member states may on occasion be receptive to an EU role. But one more factor must be considered in evaluating the likelihood of member-state support for specific EU

32. On the logic of blame avoidance in domestic politics, see R. Kent Weaver, "The Politics of Blame Avoidance," *Journal of Public Policy*, vol. 6 (October 1986), pp. 371–98. For a discussion of how national executives of member states use the EU to insulate themselves from public opinion, see Andrew Moravcsik, "Why the European Community Strengthens the State: Domestic Politics and International Cooperation," Harvard University, Department of Government, 1994.

33. See also Catherine Hoskyns, "Women, European Law and Transnational Politics," *International Journal of the Sociology of Law*, vol. 14 (1986), pp. 299–315.

34. In addition to the discussions in this volume, see Commission of the European Communities, *Growth, Competitiveness, and Ways Forward into the 21st Century*, supplement 6/93, *Bulletin of the European Communities* (Brussels, 1993); and Martin Rhodes, "The Social Dimension after Maastricht: Setting a New Agenda for the Labour Market," *International Journal of Comparative Labour Law and Industrial Relations*, vol. 9 (Winter 1993), pp. 297–325.

initiatives: member states do not all have the same interests or policy preferences, and proposals that some favor may raise the objections of others. Again, comparative evidence concerning multitiered systems is instructive. In both Canada and the United States, territorially defined interests have often pitted some constituent units against others. In the United States, southern states have been quite effective in blocking new initiatives or forcing major concessions. In Canada, as Keith Banting notes, territorially defined interests in Atlantic Canada were able to stall efforts to scale back current commitments. Both of these examples find echoes in the European Union, where Britain has often faced off against other member states seeking to expand the EU's role, while the poorest member states have been zealous advocates of increased expenditures for the structural and cohesion funds.[35] Whether divisions among constituent units make reform more or less difficult is likely to depend on the institutional setting where differences are resolved (a point that we return to below).

The position of member states within the EU is often presented in stark terms: hegemonic in the development of policy and strongly opposed to any upward transfer of authority. The evidence, we suggest, supports a more complex picture. Member states are flanked by EU actors as well as social interests with distinct policy preferences and considerable influence, locked in by preexisting policy and procedural agreements, and subject to decisionmaking overload and the unanticipated consequences of integration. Member states are central actors, but their control over the development of policy in the Union is very far from complete. At the same time, member-state attitudes toward EU participation in policy, including social policy, are not simply obstructionist. The elected governments of member states worry about sovereignty, but they worry also about their political popularity; the evidence is that they will sometimes sacrifice the former concern to accommodate the latter in a range of fields. If EU activity can help a beleaguered government do popular things, or avoid responsibility for unpopular things, anxieties about sovereignty may take a backseat.

35. Some evidence of an often-anticipated split between the core and periphery on social policy issues can be found in recent Council decisions on the action program. Ireland, Spain, and Portugal all abstained on the directive for young workers passed in 1994, and Portugal abstained on the directive on European works councils approved under the Social Protocol.

Societal Interests and EU Social Policy

Member states do not monopolize influence in the European Union, and domestic political pressures often largely determine their policy preferences. For these reasons it is important to examine the role of social actors in Europe's emerging multitiered polity. Policy development requires the construction of coalitions with sufficent power resources to overcome political opposition. As with the preceding discussion of the member states, we need to focus here on two questions: which actors have the greatest influence over policy, and what are the policy preferences of those social groups?

Studies of national welfare state development have often stressed the contribution of social democratic forces—that is, left-of-center parties and strong union confederations.[36] As Streeck and Rhodes amply demonstrate, the representatives of social democracy are quite weak within the EU, while the Union's multitiered structure enhances the ability of their political opponents to mount aggressive challenges to social policy initiatives. The unfavorable position of social democratic forces is primarily a result of a global economic conjuncture marked by low growth, high unemployment, increased competition from newly industrialized countries, and increased capital mobility. In many countries the political influence of organized labor has declined sharply in the past twenty years. Furthermore, the EU's multitiered structure itself poses formidable challenges for the Left. Increasingly unable to exert power in national politics, unions have so far had little success in organizing transnationally.[37] Barriers to collective action on a European scale are more significant for labor than for capital. In addition, the sizable gap in economic development between South and

---

36. Michael Shalev, "The Social Democratic Model and Beyond," *Comparative Social Research*, vol. 6 (1983), pp. 315–51; and Gøsta Esping-Andersen, *The Three Worlds of Welfare Capitalism* (Princeton University Press, 1990).

37. Andrew Martin and George Ross, "Unions and the European Community: A Report to the Project on Labor in European Society," Harvard University, Center for European Studies, 1992; Jelle Visser and Bernhard Ebbinghaus, "Making the Most of Diversity: European Integration and Transnational Organisation of Labour," in Justin Greenwood, Jürgen R. Grote, and Karsten Ronit, eds., *Organized Interests and the European Community* (London: Sage Publications, 1992), pp. 206–37; Lowell Turner, "Beyond National Unionism? Cross-National Labor Collaboration in the European Community," Cornell University, School of Industrial and Labor Relations, March 1993; and Steven J. Silvia, "The Social Charter of the European Community: A Defeat for European Labor," *Industrial and Labor Relations Review*, vol. 44 (July 1991), pp. 626–43.

North in the Union causes a divergence of economic interests that intensifies conflicts within the labor movement.[38]

The same developments that have curtailed the influence of labor have generally strengthened the position of business. The loosening of labor markets has made it easier for employers to enforce changes in the work environment. The enhanced prospects for capital mobility make labor unions and national governments more compliant in negotiations with business. Indeed, the reinvigoration of European integration depended precisely on the emergence of an anti–social democratic consensus on economic policy within the major member states.[39] Moreover, the EU's multitiered policymaking environment enhances the prospects for competitive deregulation. As both Rhodes and Streeck argue, European economic integration is likely to give business even better leverage for resisting undesired regulation: business can either exit national regimes or use its more credible exit option to enhance the exercise of "voice."

It would be a mistake, however, to treat business influence over social policy development as absolute. "Business" often finds itself at cross-purposes, and internal divisions are likely to lead to political weakness. As we argued in the introduction, the existence of a multitiered institutional setting heightens the likelihood of territorially grounded conflicts that cut across class lines. Especially when territorially based disparities in social wages are wide, business and labor have incentives to form geographically based, cross-class alliances.[40] Such disparities are in fact far wider in the European Union than in traditional federal systems. One might expect, then, that social politics in the Union would be marked by arguments along territorial lines, in which debates between high-wage

38. On the particular collective action problems of labor, see Claus Offe and Helmut Wiesenthal, "Two Logics of Collective Action," in Claus Offe, ed., *Disorganized Capitalism* (MIT Press, 1984), pp. 170–220. On the size of regional differentials, see Andrea Boltho, "European and United States Regional Differentials: A Note," *Oxford Review of Economic Policy*, vol. 5 (Summer 1989), pp. 105–15. The political implications of regional disparities within the Union are examined in Peter Lange, "The Politics of the Social Dimension," in Sbragia, ed., *Euro-Politics*, pp. 225–56.

39. Andrew Moravcsik, "Negotiating the Single European Act: National Interests and Conventional Statecraft in the European Community," *International Organization*, vol. 45 (Winter 1991), pp. 19–56; and Robert O. Keohane and Stanley Hoffmann, "Institutional Change in Europe in the 1980s," in Keohane and Hoffmann, eds, *The New European Community*, pp. 1–39.

40. For an analysis of cross-class alliances in industrial relations systems, though founded on sectoral interests rather than geographical ones, see Peter Swenson, *Fair Shares: Unions, Pay, and Politics in Sweden and West Germany* (Cornell University Press, 1989).

and low-wage areas of the EU supplement or cut across divisions between capital and labor.[41]

Yet this territorial element appears weak in the most publicized disputes over social policy. The European business association, UNICE (Union of Industrial and Employers' Confederations of Europe), has generally presented a united front of opposition to corporatist-style arrangements at the European level. "UNICE," Streeck comments, has "never changed its view that social matters should be dealt with exclusively at national level."[42] Actually, as Rhodes documents, there are growing signs of division within UNICE (particularly involving the Confederation of British Industry). More important, while business may appear monolithic when it comes to public rhetoric about a corporatist or social democratic Europe, it can be expected to fragment along any of several cleavages (geography, sector, firm size, export-orientation, and so on) when less global issues are at stake.[43]

Business actors face more than internal division. They also must compete for political influence with other actors. Policymakers have a range of constituencies to whom they must respond; business, while clearly central—if not privileged—is only one.[44] As we have stressed, voters wield considerable influence over policymakers in democratic polities. Politicians are concerned about accommodating business or maintaining sovereignty, but they also need to build and sustain an electoral base. A range of interests—including organized labor—may be significant in forming the coalitions that make up that base. The popularity of social

41. This is Peter Lange's argument in "Maastricht and the Social Protocol: Why Did They Do It?" *Politics and Society*, vol. 21 (March 1993), pp. 5–36.

42. This presents an interesting and rarely discussed puzzle—not least for international relations analysts who would expect the interests of social actors to be transmitted *only* in a territorial fashion (that is, through member states). Indeed, the propensity of business and labor to discuss EU social policy as functional (class) organizations rather than territorial ones provides significant evidence that the Union is a multitiered system in which territory plays a prominent but far from exclusive role.

43. See Wolfgang Streeck, "Interest Heterogeneity and Organizing Capacity: Two Class Logics of Collective Action?" in Wolfgang Streeck, ed., *Social Institutions and Economic Performance: Studies of Industrial Relations in Advanced Capitalist Economies* (Beverley Hills: Sage, 1992), pp. 76–104; and John Bowman, "The Politics of the Market: Economic Competition and the Organization of Capitalists," *Political Power and Social Theory*, vol. 5 (1985), pp. 35–88.

44. For a study that demonstrates this point with great subtlety, see David Vogel, *Fluctuating Fortunes: The Political Power of Business in America* (New York: Basic Books, 1989).

programs makes governments reluctant to pursue policies of retrenchment that business groups would often favor.[45] At the same time, interest-
group activity has proliferated at the European level in recent years, and
many of those groups have social policy concerns.[46] Business organizations have substantial resources, which makes their support extremely
important in electoral competition, but few would argue that they hold
exclusive sway in the field of social policy. If they did, the size and
structure of systems of social provision almost certainly would be far
different in all industrial democracies.

Both internal fragmentation and competition from other political actors prevent business interests from simply dictating social policy in the
European Union. Other developments further limit business influence.
The shift to qualified majority voting has undermined a traditional source
of strength, namely, the reliable British veto. The Social Protocol has
forced UNICE to temper its positions somewhat,[47] and procedures for
social dialogue have been expanded. Business representatives can still
delay reforms, but, contrary to Streeck's claims, business no longer has
an effective veto over reform. In June 1994, for example, the failure of
the social partners to reach agreement was followed by the enactment of
the directive on the European works council, an initiative that business
groups had opposed for years.[48]

In arenas where the Council plays a less immediate role, business
influence may be even more restricted. Just as intergovernmentalist students of the EU draw a misleading picture by focusing only on intermittent, high-profile "grand bargains," students of social policy err by looking only at the prominent clashes between peak associations of "capital"
and "labor" over the development of some grand vision of corporatism.[49]
Business played a role in the reform of health and safety standards, but
did so within a technocratic context where a veto threat would have had
little credibility.[50] Business has even less control over the social policy
initiatives of the ECJ. The fight over the *Barber* protocol is instructive.

45. Pierson, "New Politics."
46. Greenwood, Grote, and Ronit, eds., *Organized Interests*; and Sonia Mazey and
Jeremy Richardson, *Lobbying in the European Community* (Oxford University Press, 1993).
47. See also Ross, *Delors*, pp. 183, 191.
48. On the employers' limited capacity to delay, see Gerda Falkner, "Die Sozialpolitik
im Maastrichter Vertragsgebäude der Europäische Gemeinschaft," *SWS-Rundschau*, vol.
33, no. 1 (1993), pp. 23–43.
49. This may be an occupational hazard for those who equate the social dimension
with industrial relations, where issues are always between employers and unions.
50. Eichener, "Social Dumping," pp. 101–04.

The Court's decision carried massive financial implications for European insurance companies. Only an unprecedented business lobbying effort averted the insurance industry's worst-case scenario. Prevention of that outcome required the unanimous support of the member states and the extraordinary vehicle of a specific protocol in the Maastricht treaty, and the outcome that did transpire was considerably less favorable than the status quo ante for insurance firms. Business groups may well approve of the Court's focus on issues of market freedom, but these actors have no direct say over decisions that they will sometimes find unsatisfactory.

The growth of business power in Europe is one of the most significant political developments of the past two decades. This development must surely be incorporated into our understandings of the contemporary European polity. Understanding is not fostered by treating business as an unstoppable monolith, however. Business power will vary from issue to issue depending on its internal cohesion, the strength of its opponents, and the institutional arena in which policy is made.

It remains true that the balance of power among economic actors is not what it was twenty years ago, and is not the same at the European level as it is within member states. The altered power position of major societal actors clearly has tremendous implications for the dynamics of European social policy integration. If social policy activity required social democratic hegemony, the barriers to development would be insurmountable. However, the importance of social democratic tendencies in social policy development is easily exaggerated—or, more accurately, misconstrued. As recent research shows, the "power resources" of the Left have more impact on *what kind* of policies are developed than on *whether* social policies are developed.[51] Arguments about the Left's power resources seem to work best in accounting for developments in certain periods (1945–75, for example) and in certain areas of social policy, such as those that impinge most directly on wage bargaining and the labor market. Neither unions nor social democrats played a key role in the earlier development of welfare states; extensive social policies emerged in many places where the Left was weak. Furthermore, welfare states have proven to be relatively durable even where the power resources of the Left have declined.[52]

51. Esping-Andersen, *Three Worlds*. Again, note that countries like the United States, with very weak labor movements, have developed elaborate systems of social expenditure and regulation, although ones that look quite different from northern European welfare states.

52. On welfare state development, see, for example, Peter Baldwin, *The Politics of*

A corporatist-style model of industrial relations and social policy at the EU level is indeed a dead letter. Yet there are other possible frameworks of social policy intervention. Since the acquiescence of business interests will usually be necessary, it is important to find out what circumstances might foster such support. This critical question is taken up especially in the chapters by Rhodes and Streeck, as well as in Pierson's comparative chapter on social policy integration in the United States. The reasons for business hostility to high levels of redistribution are evident. As Streeck notes, the antagonism of European business groups toward anything that resembles corporatist-style tripartism at the EU level suggests—not surprisingly—that business interests can be expected to resist policies that threaten the balance of class forces.[53]

That being granted, the crucial issue is how far this opposition is likely to extend to other social policy issues. Systems of social provision can benefit business in several ways: they can correct externalities, develop human capital, stabilize aggregate demand, and maintain social peace, among other things. To the extent that major European firms find advantages in a high-skill, high-productivity, high-wage development strategy, business may favor supportive policy initiatives.[54] Furthermore, businesses—especially multinational enterprises—will certainly be interested in market-making reforms of social policy, such as those that facilitate labor mobility. They may also have a stake in uniform, predictable regulations, and they might sometimes prefer one European standard of social regulation to a hodgepodge of member-state standards.[55] As

---

Social Solidarity: Class Bases of the European Welfare State, 1875–1975 (Cambridge University Press, 1990); and Theda Skocpol, *Protecting Soldiers and Mothers: The Origins of Social Policy in the United States* (Harvard University Press, 1992). On retrenchment, see Jens Alber, "Is There a Crisis of the Welfare State? Cross-National Evidence from Europe, North America and Japan," *European Sociological Review*, vol. 4, no. 3 (1988), pp. 181–207' and Paul Pierson, *Dismantling the Welfare State? Reagan, Thatcher and the Politics of Retrenchment* (Cambridge University Press, 1994).

53. See also Wolfgang Streeck and Philippe C. Schmitter, "From National Corporatism to Transnational Pluralism: Organized Interests in the Single European Market," *Politics and Society*, vol. 19 (March 1991), pp. 133–64.

54. For an analysis of this option, see David Soskice, "The Institutional Infrastructure for International Competitiveness: A Comparative Analysis of the UK and Germany," in Anthony B. Atkinson and Renato Brunetta, eds., *The Economics of the New Europe* (Macmillan, 1991), pp. 45–66.

55. According to Majone, American business has increasingly favored national rather than state environmental regulation, and he argues that this trend seems to be emerging in the Union as well. Majone, "Regulatory Federalism." For an argument that American businessmen involved in creating the Social Security Act of 1935 advocated more centralized options for the new unemployment insurance scheme, see G. John Ikenberry and Theda

Rhodes notes, recent progress on the action program to implement aspects of the Social Charter reflects in part the selective rather than absolute opposition of business to social initiatives.

What criteria might business interests use in reaching such judgments? Streeck suggests a typology of market making, market braking, and market correcting policies. *Market making* appears to refer to policies that facilitate market exchanges (for example, steps to encourage free movement of workers). *Market-braking* policies are those that correct market failures (for example, "an 'overheating' of markets that would result in destruction of productive resources"). *Market-correcting* initiatives are policies of redistribution.[56] Streeck concludes that business will move to block any market-correcting policies, although it may be willing to accept market-braking ones and will favor market-making initiatives.

This typological exercise usefully highlights aspects of social policy that generate different reactions from social and political actors. It is important to recognize that business is most likely to object to the market-correcting social policies of redistribution. Even here, however, caveats are in order. As students of the welfare state have long noted, redistributive social policy is largely an *intra*class phenomenon, redistributing over the life cycle, and therefore less threatening to business. In some instances (programs of early retirement for surplus workers, for example), businesses may in fact find redistributive policies quite useful.[57] Thus significant policies of this kind exist even in countries like Japan and the United States, where business is quite powerful and organized labor quite weak.

Two further points deserve emphasis. First, a field of play limited to the categories of market-making and market-braking interventions nonetheless allows considerable room for social policy activity. Social policy provisions frequently impinge on the free movement of goods, services, and labor. The amount of social policy decisionmaking needed for market making—even if only "negative" decisionmaking to allow markets

Skocpol, "Expanding Social Benefits: The Role of Social Security," *Political Science Quarterly*, vol. 102 (Fall 1987), pp. 389–416, and Colin Gordon, "New Deal, Old Deck: Businesss and the Origins of Social Security, 1920–1935," *Politics and Society*, vol. 19 (March 1991), pp. 165–207.

56. For complementary discussions, see Patrick Kenis, "Social Europe in the 1990s: Beyond an Adjunct to Achieving a Common Market?" *Futures*, vol. 23 (September, 1991), pp. 724–38; Lange, "Politics of the Social Dimension"; and Majone, "Between Social Policy and Social Regulation."

57. Martin Kohli and others, eds., *Time for Retirement: Comparative Studies of Early Exit from the Labor Force* (Cambridge University Press, 1991).

relatively free rein—is quite extensive. If one focuses only on positive "social dimension" regulations produced by the Commission and Council, the amount of activity may seem limited. However, the scope of ECJ actions is considerable and rapidly widening as the internal market progresses. Social policy here takes a decidedly multitiered, shared form, with the ECJ helping to establish parameters for permissible social policies while leaving it to national political systems to formulate the required adjustments.

If business groups were in fact open to the idea of market-braking initiatives, the possibilities for activity would multiply. "Market failure" is not a small, residual category justifying modest tinkering at the edges of market systems—responding to it is one of the principal rationales for social policy.[58] Braking the market economy can mean a range of efforts to cope with externalities, such as collective needs for the development and preservation of human capital and the maintenance of social peace. As Streeck acknowledges, business may find such goals desirable.[59]

Another observation about Streeck's policy typology is that it is not always easy for either policy experts or social actors to relegate social policies to one category or another. Social policies, such as pension rules, job-training programs, or unemployment protections, frequently serve multiple purposes—indeed, this is often a self-conscious technique for broadening political support. What balance of social policy activity and inactivity maximizes the prospects for business profitability is a subject of fierce theoretical and political dispute. To say that firms will support only initiatives that they believe will further their interests is both true and fairly uninformative.[60] Business associations, along with individual firms, must determine what policies best serve their interests.[61]

---

58. Nicholas Barr, *The Economics of the Welfare State*, 2d ed. (Stanford University Press, 1993). This is one reason why Majone's claim of the radical disjuncture between "social policy" and "social regulation" is overstated. Majone, "Between Social Policy and Social Regulation."

59. What is more open to question, as Streeck rightly notes, is the ability of business to organize itself—or to be organized from the outside—in ways that allow these goals to be met. We consider this question in the next section.

60. Kenis, on whom both Streeck and Lange rely in part, solves the problem by tautology: he simply distinguishes ad hoc (in truth, post hoc, after the preferences of interest groups have been revealed) between policies that help the market and those that hurt it. The policies that businesses support are by definition the helpful ones.

61. For an important argument about how the social policy preferences of business are not simply given but "constructed," see Cathie Jo Martin, "Basic Instincts: Sources of Firm Preferences for National Health Reform," *American Political Science Review*, vol. 89 (forthcoming, 1995).

As with member states, there is little reason to treat business as monolithic, all-powerful, and relentlessly hostile to social policy initiatives. Theory and available evidence suggest more nuanced conclusions. Business groups will be powerful in the EU, and their attitude toward European social policy will often be skeptical. Depending on the nature of the policy proposal and the decisionmaking rules under which the policy is developed, however, the attitudes, cohesiveness, and influence of business groups will fluctuate.

The activities of societal actors in the development of EU social policy match the general arguments that we have made about the functioning of multitiered systems. The position of business is strengthened and that of labor weakened. Both sides also become more fragmented. Struggles between areas where social wages are low and areas where they are high overlap with traditional conficts between capital and labor. The proliferation of relevant policymaking arenas leads to a sharp increase in the diversity of lobbying styles and organizational forms of interest representation. The result is likely to be, as Peter Lange says, a shift toward a "neopluralist social Europe in which temporary coalitions of interests and governments form around proposals for specific European interventions in the social area."[62] This emphasis on shifting and fragmented interest-group politics is reinforced by the EU's institutions of shared decisionmaking, the final topic of this chapter.

Fragmented Institutions and Governance Problems

We have stressed throughout this volume that the design of political institutions has crucial effects on policymaking. Multitiered institutional settings, which serve to fragment political authority, create predictable dilemmas for policymakers. In both the comparative chapters and those focusing on the EU, these dilemmas of shared policymaking appear repeatedly. Here we focus on the most crucial of these effects to explain how the preferences and power of member states and societal actors are likely to be expressed in a specific institutional setting. By now the general outline of the argument should be clear: Historically, federal institutions have been designed precisely to limit the amount of political authority concentrated at any single point in the polity. Such systems invariably exhibit a complex mixture of competition and cooperation among dif-

62. Lange, "Politics of the Social Dimension," p. 256.

ferent power centers. Concerns over substantive policy become intermingled with concerns about the distribution of public authority. The results include extensive reliance on lowest-common-denominator agreements or complex packages, an intensified search for alternative channels of decisionmaking, and a tendency toward joint-decision traps and policy stalemate.

All of these patterns are evident, usually in exaggerated form, in the development of social policies within the European Union. Multitiered systems characteristically exhibit suspicion of centralized power, and this is especially true in the case of the EU. Highly developed nation-states have attempted to build European institutions that would address collective needs while leaving as much authority as possible in the hands of the member states. This is an extraordinarily difficult balancing act. Member-state control of the EU's decisionmaking machinery is far from complete, yet the peculiar origins of the Union profoundly affect the possibilities for social policy initiatives. The narrow channels created by EU institutions produced very distinctive patterns of policymaking, which we spell out in the rest of this section.

The institutions of the European Union are designed to inhibit initiatives, except within defined areas, by giving the member states the power to veto reform. Until recently a single member state could block social policy proposals. This remains true for many issues. Even where qualified majority voting rules apply, the possibilities for obstruction are extensive. A relatively small minority of states acting together may veto reform, and even weaker coalitions can cause delay (through resort to time-consuming procedures for "consultation" or lengthy court challenges, for example). Furthermore, member-state control over implementation may present yet another formidable hurdle to effective EU policymaking.[63] All these factors foster gridlock, which creates tremendous momentum toward the lowest-common-denominator, "neovoluntarist" policy framework outlined in Streeck's essay. Indeed, all of the empirical chapters in part 1 of this volume provide examples of this dynamic.

Given the EU's institutional characteristics, the mystery is why, on occasion, initiatives have surpassed the lowest common denominator. Although it is difficult to prove what the lowest common denominator may be in any particular case, the EU's activities in some areas—for

---

63. See Francis Snyder, "The Effectiveness of European Community Law: Institutions, Processes, Tools and Techniques," *Modern Law Review*, vol. 56 (January 1993), pp. 19–54.

example, gender issues, health and safety, and redistribution to disadvantaged regions—appear to transcend that level. The essays in this volume point to three distinct answers. First, changes in decision rules (toward qualified majority voting) have clearly made a difference. It is no accident that a number of the areas in which activity has been greatest operate under qualified majority voting (QMV). A further sign of the significance of QMV is the growing prominence of Rhodes' "treaty-base game," in which the ultimate policy outcome turns on which rules of the game are applied. The importance of decision rules—and the EU's distinctive structure whereby different rules govern different policies—encourages what some have called segmented federalism, in which policy activity is far greater in some issue areas than in others.[64]

It must be emphasized that EU decisionmaking is best facilitated in the realm of what we called in chapter 2 *market-compatibility requirements*. Not only can the Council itself act on most single-market issues under QMV rules but under the Single European Act the ECJ also has considerable leeway to enforce the single-market imperative. Thus Streeck is surely right in saying that market making is at the center of EU social policy. The significance of this activity is vastly underestimated, however, if one ignores the implications of market-compatibility requirements for the sovereignty of national welfare states. Superimposed on the member states is an additional tier of decisionmakers, who have the authority to review and prohibit important features of national policy.

A second factor that pushes the EU beyond lowest-common-denominator policy outcomes is the role of institutional actors other than the member states, especially the Court and the Commission. As documented in several chapters, these institutional actors have the leverage to push the Union in a more activist direction. This point is intimately connected to the previous one. The Commission and the Court have some influence over the determination of when looser decision rules will apply. At the same time, the looser decisionmaking rules considerably enhance the influence of the Commission and Court. The Commission's agenda-setting and process-manager roles become more prominent as the range of possible outcomes expands; so does the Court's capacity to place its own stamp on EU policy.

Finally, movement beyond the lowest-common-denominator approach may occur through the successful use of linkage. Logrolling ar-

---

64. Alberta M. Sbragia, "Thinking about the European Future: The Uses of Comparison," in Sbragia, ed., *Euro-Politics*, p. 262.

rangements can persuade actors to accept policies that they dislike, or are indifferent to, in return for the acquiescence of other actors on unrelated issues. Such deals are a major part of politics, especially in political systems that call for widespread agreement as a prerequisite for action. Although explicit trades are often difficult to document, such agreements appear to have been quite relevant in the development of EU social policy. Prominent examples include the growth of the structural funds, which largely benefit the poorest members of the EU, and the passage of the Social Protocol itself.[65]

The prevalence of "package politics" has important implications for the development of social policy. First, it renders that development far less predictable, because achieving policy change is often connected to issues that are substantively unrelated to social policy itself. In the case of the European Union, this is doubly true because many of the major packages are developed in the context of the EU's intermittent grand bargains. More regularized logrolling, involving the linking of decisions that are taken at different times, requires relatively stable policymaking structures to ensure that the bargaining partners can realistically expect that each will uphold its part of the bargain.[66] With a few exceptions, such as the Common Agricultural Policy (see Elmar Rieger's discussion in chapter 6 in this volume), the EU lacks such stable structures. Because bargainers cannot be sure that their partners will be willing or able to deliver in the future, agreements usually must be simultaneous. This limits the introduction of such bargains to the EU's periodic rounds of major institutional and policy reforms, when many issues are considered together.

The second implication of package politics further complicates our ability to project the direction of EU social policy. Because social policy discussions are linked to other issues, the social policy preferences of decisionmakers do not always dictate outcomes. For example, if some subset of the European Council feels sufficiently intense about social policy issues, they may be willing to concede on other matters in order

65. Gary Marks, "Structural Policy in the European Community," in Sbragia, ed., *Euro-politics*, pp. 191–224; and Lange, "Maastricht." For a broad analysis of EU social policy that emphasizes how package deals have facilitated forward movement on social issues, see Gerda Falkner, *Supranationalität trotz Einstimmigkeit: Entscheidungsmuster der EU am Beispiel Sozialpolitik* (Bonn: Europa Union Verlag, 1994).

66. For a good discussion of this point, see John Ferejohn, "Logrolling in an Institutional Context: A Case Study of Food Stamp Legislation," in Gerald C. Wright and others, eds., *Congress and Policy Change* (New York: Agathon Press, 1986), pp. 223–53.

to get their way. On such occasions social policy outcomes may not reflect the social policy preferences of many, or even most, member states.[67] Examples include the EU's active role on gender issues—a legacy of French demands that article 119 be included in the Treaty of Rome— and Italian insistence on progress in labor mobility issues. Similarly, a small bloc of southern countries has made initiatives on other matters conditional on expansion of the structural funds. Presumably, a bloc of countries that felt strongly about some aspects of the social dimension could exert considerable influence in other areas of social policy. Again, whether such a coalition emerges will depend in part on the fate of national welfare states. Should pressures on national welfare states mount, the salience of the social dimension will undoubtedly increase.

These observations about decision rules, EU institutional actors, and package politics help to account for a striking development. In a number of realms, the European Union has moved well beyond the lowest common denominator of member-state preferences. Nonetheless, these outcomes remain sporadic. At the EU level, it remains far easier to block policies than to enact them.

This reality gives rise to an additional outcome characteristic of multi-tiered polities: the tendency to seek escape mechanisms from a highly restricted system of decisionmaking. The standard route for social policy activity within the EU—through legislation enacted under unanimity rules in the European Council—has proved highly problematic. The British veto, in particular, has prompted an extensive search for alternative institutional channels. Two such channels require particular attention: the emergence of Court-led decisionmaking and the adoption of the Social Protocol.

For reasons that are only now becoming clear, the European Court of Justice has become a major center of policymaking within the European Union. To be sure, various actors have actively sought such a development, including entrepreneurial members of the Court, allies within the court systems of member states, and Commission officials who view Court action as a useful lever for expanding the scope of their own activities.[68] But the Court also looms large because the ambitious single-market project itself creates an imperative for decisionmaking, and the

---

67. Falkner, *Supranationalität trotz Einstimmigkeit.*

68. For an excellent example of how the Commission uses Court decisions to expand its own role, see Karen Alter and Sophie Meunier-Aitsahalia, "Judicial Politics in the European Community: European Integration and the Pathbreaking *Cassis de Dijon* Decision," *Comparative Political Studies*, vol. 26 (January 1994), pp. 535–61.

sclerosis common to other EU institutions is largely absent in the ECJ. Like water running downhill, policymaking authority gravitates to the Court.

From a comparative perspective, the Court's central role is unusual. Both our own discussion of semisovereign national welfare states and Ostner and Lewis's treatment of gender issues indicate the distinctive features of Court-led processes of policy development. Substantive changes can happen relatively rapidly, because the Court does not face major impediments to decisionmaking and is in fact encouraged to act by the cases that appear before it. At the same time, significant decisions may receive little notice, because it is member-state courts and governments that must make the necessary legislative changes. Often the ECJ does not dictate a particular course of action; it simply indicates that member states must select from a smaller range of options than they had available in the past. This is a significant power, but it is not one that necessarily attracts much public attention.

But just as the Court circumscribes the policymaking authority of member states, it in turn is confined by the terms of the EU's treaties and legislation. The ECJ has certainly been innovative in expanding its room to maneuver, yet there are limits to such tactics. The structure of its own mandate constrains Court activity. Consequently, the ECJ's role in policymaking is bound to be highly uneven—extensive in areas such as gender issues and the adjudication of market compatibility requirements, and far more restrained on other matters. At the same time, as Ostner and Lewis document, the Court's ability to fashion effective interventions is modest even where it has substantial competence. Margaret Weir's comparative discussion reaches the same conclusion. Courts make policy by enforcing their understandings of legal requirements, not by designing the most effective means of achieving social goals. As issues such as the free market in services come to the fore, ECJ activity is sure to be tremendously influential in the shaping of European social policy. Nonetheless, it is likely to remain a weak base for the development of positive structures of social policy.

The enactment of the Social Protocol represents a more self-conscious attempt by European decisionmakers to increase the capacity for activist social policy at the EU level, although the protocol—a last-minute compromise—may beget many unanticipated consequences.[69] As Rhodes

---

69. Note that the compromise itself is very difficult to reconcile with a simple model of intergovernmentalist bargaining among sovereignty-conscious member states. Faced with

makes clear, the new procedures present a host of thorny problems that will take years to untangle (with heavy involvement from the ECJ helping to determine the ultimate outcome). The *possibility* of enhanced decisionmaking capacity is present—if the Court accepts the agreement and especially if Britain accedes to the protocol within a reasonable period of time.[70] The range of issues that the protocol can address through qualified majority voting is extensive: working conditions, gender equality with regard to labor market opportunities and treatment at work, and the integration of persons excluded from the labor market are among them.[71] The social-dialogue procedure may slow legislation in these areas, but it cannot prevent it.

Even if the protocol's full potential is realized, however, there is no reason to expect a flood of activity. The current public debate on flexibility is likely to prompt a pause before new initiatives are considered; action still requires a qualified majority of member states, which can be expected to move hesitantly. Moreover, a relatively small group of member states can block action altogether, and even if a minority group cannot stop an unfavorable vote in the Council, it can resort to obstructionist tactics that will either force a compromise or produce lengthy delays full of uncertainty. Barriers to decisionmaking have diminished, but even the Social Protocol's major modification of the rules leaves

---

what would have been a disastrous breakdown of the Maastricht conference because of British intransigence, the member states adopted a last-minute solution at the suggestion of Delors. The agreement that was cobbled together not only created wide room for unanticipated consequences but committed the eleven member states to a much more ambitious earlier draft on social policy, which had been designed as an opening bargaining position in the expectation that it would have to be watered down to win British acceptance. Britain's refusal to bargain appears to have had less to do with some longsighted view of sovereignty than with Major's immediate need to placate right-wing Tories by taking a tough public stance. See Ross, *Delors*, p. 191.

70. Although Streeck assumes Britain will stay out, there are several reasons to doubt this. Britain's outsider status may confer some economic benefits, but this is by no means certain because multinational firms will have to follow two sets of rules, thus incurring significant costs. Even if outsider status is economically desirable, it may be politically unattractive, as suggested by opposition parties' attacks on the Conservatives in the 1994 European elections—"Why," critics ask, "should Portuguese workers have better social protections than British ones?" Court challenges to Britain's status are inevitable (on the grounds that it promotes unfair competition, for example). Finally, despite the Conservatives' extraordinary run of electoral victories, a permanent Tory lock on the government is unlikely.

71. Streeck's view that a desire to carry out the Social Charter prompted enactment of the protocol may be correct. However, the protocol's "constitutional" mandate is abstract and authorizes entirely new directives in the extensive areas now covered by QMV.

opponents of EU social policy activism operating on favorable institutional terrain.

This tendency toward immobility profoundly affects policy content as well as the pace of policymaking. Initiatives are not only likely to be sporadic; they will often be decisively influenced by swing voters whose commitment to the policy is weak at best. Institutional protections for member-state interests, which inhibit both policy effectiveness and flexibility, will be ubiquitous. This is another clear lesson drawn from all three of the comparative chapters. Moe's comments on the design of public agencies within the fragmented institutions of the United States are equally apt for the European Union: "The American separation of powers system virtually guarantees that the losers, opposing interest groups, will have enough power to participate in some fashion as well. The losers, however, are dedicated to crippling the bureaucracy and gaining control over its decisions, and they pressure for fragmented authority, cumbersome procedures, intrusive mechanisms of political oversight, and other structures that subvert the bureaucracy's performance and open it up to attack."[72] This message is repeated in all of the empirical chapters in part 1. The Union is a long way from fashioning an effective response to the tremendous problems associated with Europe's persistently high unemployment rates. That the EU has become a force in policymaking is not to say that the policies it produces will be works of art.

The European Union is a polity in the making. A great deal is up for grabs. As the Union wrestles with issues like monetary union and further enlargements, much is likely to depend on what happens in areas far from the field of social policy. Nonetheless, some of the features of this unique multitiered system governing the development of social policy are becoming clear. Barring further institutional reforms that point the EU decisively in one direction or another, the European Union seems certain to exhibit an extraordinarily fragmented policymaking framework, one that is increasingly prone to gridlock. As Fritz Scharpf concludes, "The policy-making capacities of the Union have not been strengthened nearly as much as capabilities at the level of member states have declined."[73] It is, as one observer terms it, a "Europe of bits and pieces" where a wide range of authorities have some say over aspects of policy development,

72. Moe, "Structural Choice," p. 147.
73. Fritz W. Scharpf, "Community and Autonomy: Multi-level Policymaking in the European Union," *Journal of European Public Policy,* vol. 1 (Autumn 1994), p. 220.

but none has much grasp of the whole.[74] Activists within the Commission, along with allies on the Council, pursue initiatives wherever the Commission's role as process manager or the rules of segmented federalism creates opportunities. The ECJ makes expansive rulings, but only within the terms of its legal mandate. Member states adopt national policies, but in the face of intense popular pressures and within a broader legal and economic context that hinders their flexibility.

To be sure, the European Union does not look exactly like a traditional federal state. But it looks even less like a traditional international organization. The question is no longer whether Europe will become a multitiered polity; it already is one. Even in social policy—supposedly an area where member states still reign supreme—policymaking now occurs through the complex interplay of social actors and decisionmakers operating at multiple levels. If the experiences of other multitiered systems are any indication, the consequences will be enormous.

---

74. Dierdre Curtin, "The Constitutional Structure of the Union: A Europe of Bits and Pieces," *Common Market Law Review*, vol. 30, no. 1 (1993), pp. 17–69.

Index

Abel-Smith, Brian, 342*n*38
Abortion. *See* Women's issues; individual countries
Achterberg, 179
Ackermann, Paul, 204*n*21
Acquis communautaire. See Legal issues
ACSH. *See* Advisory Committee on Safety, Hygiene and Health Protection at Work
Addison, John T., 9*n*15, 33*n*61, 48*n*13, 244*n*37, 403*n*20, 403*n*21
Ad Hoc Committee on Women's Rights, 182
Ad Hoc Information Group, 264
Adinolfi, Adelina, 99*n*48, 117*n*81
Advisory Committee on Safety, Hygiene and Health Protection at Work (ACSH), 369
AFDC. *See* Aid to families with dependent children
Affirmative action. *See* Gender issues
African Americans. *See* Ethnic and racial issues
Agriculture: age classes in, 215–16; commodity regimes, 218, 221–23, 225, 227, 229, 230; economic issues, 223–24, 225; European Community, 214; European Economic Community, 202–04; European Union, 227; farmers and farming, 205, 212, 215*n*40, 219*n*48, 221–23, 227–29; food stamps, 320–21; modernization, 198,

200, 206–07; price supports, 204, 205, 206, 209, 223, 225; regional issues, 199, 215, 218–19, 222; social security in, 216*n*43; social structure of, 214, 215; spending on, 217. *See also* Common Agricultural Policy; Labor
Aid to families with dependent children (AFDC), 301; opposition to, 308–09, 313, 317, 326; program structure, 302, 312, 316–17
Alber, Jens, 453*n*52
Algeria, 251
Alston, Lee J., 307*n*11
Altenstetter, Christa, 65*n*63
Alter, Karen, 461*n*68
Altshuler, Alan, 339*n*27
Alvarez, Antonio Fernando, 203*n*20
Anderson, Jeffrey J., 25–26, 125*n*4, 126*n*6, 129*n*11, 135*n*19, 151*n*47, 156*n*57, 157*n*59, 194*n*1, 439
Anderson, Malcolm, 169*n*34, 176*n*58, 181*n*74, 187*n*82
Antonelli, Gilberto, 213*n*38
ARA. *See* Area Redevelopment Act of 1961
Ardy, Brian, 216*n*44
Area Redevelopment Act of 1961 (ARA), 337
Armstrong, Harvey, 126*n*6
Arnold, R. Douglas, 334, 335*n*15, 335*n*16, 339*n*25

94–95, 361, 369–72, 400; harmonization, 369–70, 371, 373, 393, 437,
446; insurance, 56, 58, 66; labor issues, 100, 166, 173, 190*n*91; mobility
issues, 62–63, 65, 100; mutual recognition, 400–401; national health care
systems, 66; pregnant women, 166–
67, 181, 375; regulatory issues, 119,
120, 436–37; Single European Act,
48, 362–63; Social Charter, 369; vot-
ing, 48, 98, 112, 166, 181, 362–63,
437. *See also* Gender issues; Labor and
employment issues
Heclo, Hugh, 19*n*38
Heering, Christiane, 180*n*71
Heidenheimer, Arnold J., 19*n*38, 21*n*41
Heidhues, Theodor, 205*n*23
Heimann, Edouard, 97*n*42
Heine, Joachim Friedrich, 221*n*50
Held, David, 74
Henningsen, Bernd, 44*n*3, 401, 397*n*9,
407*n*27, 408*n*29
Hennock, E. Peter, 20*n*39
Herden, Margaret, 194*n*1
Héritier, Pierre, 107*n*56
Hibbs, Douglas A., 72*n*81
Hill, Andrew, 115*n*75
Hirschman, Albert O., 28*n*56
Hirst, Paul, 412*n*38
Hix, Simon, 84*n*13, 442*n*22
Hobhouse, L.T., 220*n*49
Hoffmann, Stanley, 8*n*11, 84*n*16,
265*n*97, 390*n*3, 393*n*5 436*n*5,
450*n*39
Holland, Stuart, 280
Hollifield, James F., 244*n*36
Holloway, John, 80*n*7, 85*n*18
Hooghe, Liesbet, 157*n*59, 366*n*26
Hörburger, Hortense, 162*n*9, 163*n*11,
167*n*27
Horowitz, Donald L., 341*n*33, 342*n*37,
343*n*42
Hoskyns, Catherine, 159*n*1, 163*n*10,
189, 168*n*28, 168*n*29, 179*n*68,
182*n*77, 187*n*82, 188*n*85, 190*n*91,
190*n*93, 191*n*96, 191*n*97, 192*n*99,
359*n*5, 447*n*33
Housing, 351
Howard, Christopher, 322*n*56, 323*n*60,
324*n*63

Huber, Evelyne, 445*n*27
HUD. *See* Department of Housing and
Urban Development
Hungary, 157, 257
Hyman, Richard, 84*n*14

Iceland, 9*n*13
Ikenberry, G. John, 303, 310, 312*n*25,
325, 454*n*55
ILO. *See* International Labour
Organisation
Immigration. *See* Migration and
immigration
IMPs. *See* Integrated Mediterranean
Programmes
Industrial Revolution, 200
Ingrid Rinner-Kühn v. *FWW Spezial-
Gebäudereinigung GmbH Co KG,*
171/88 ECR 2757 (1989), 170, 171,
179
Integrated Mediterranean Programmes
(IMPs), 141
International Industry Committees, 89
International Labour Organisation
(ILO), 162
Insurance, 67–68, 275, 276. *See also
Barber* protocol; Health and safety;
Unemployment insurance
Interest groups: agricultural, 203, 228;
economic
issues, 418; European interest groups
(EIGs), 442; European social policies,
45; European Union, 81; gender issues, 180–81, 190; labor issues, 47;
organization of, 12–14, 88; political
issues, 457; regional interests, 129;
regulatory issues, 88; social policy issues, 452–53; structural funds, 140
International Bill of Rights, 246
International Labor Organization, 52,
246
Ireland: abortion, 79, 181, 192; citizenship, 241; economic issues, 71*n*79; European Monetary Fund, 142; gender
issues, 176–77, 180, 186, 190–93; labor and employment issues, 91, 92–
93, 98, 117, 236, 242; migration and
immigration, 236, 263; policymaking,
190–93; relations, 119; Social
Charter, 49; social welfare spending,